Readings in Accounting for Management Control

The Chapman & Hall Series in Accounting and Finance

Consulting editors
John Perrin, Emeritus Professor of the University of Warwick and Price Waterhouse Fellow in Public Sector Accounting at the University of Exeter; Richard M.S. Wilson, Professor of Management Control in the School of Finance and Information at the Queen's University of Belfast and L.C.L. Skerratt, Professor of Financial Accounting at the University of Manchester.

H.M. Coombs and D.E. Jenkins
Public Sector Financial Management

J.C. Drury
Management and Cost Accounting (2nd edn) (Also available: **Students' Manual, Teachers' Manual**)

C.R. Emmanuel, D.T. Otley and K. Merchant
Accounting for Management Control (2nd edn) (Also available: **Teachers' Guide**)

C.R. Emmanuel, D.T. Otley and K. Merchant (editors)
Readings in Accounting for Management Control

D. Henley, C. Holtham, A. Likierman and J. Perrin
Public Sector Accounting and Financial Control (3rd edn)

R.C. Laughlin and R.H. Gray
Financial Accounting; method and meaning (Also available: **Teachers' Guide**)

G.A. Lee
Modern Financial Accounting (4th edn) (Also available: **Solutions Manual**)

T.A. Lee
Income Value Measurement (3rd edn)

T.A. Lee
Company Financial Reporting (2nd edn)

T.A. Lee
Cash Flow Accounting

S.P. Lumby
Investment Appraisal and Financing Decisions (4th edn) (Also available: **Students' Manual**)

A.G. Puxty and J.C. Dodds
Financial Management: method and meaning (2nd edn) (Also available: **Teachers' Guide**)

J.M. Samuels, F.M. Wilkes and R.E. Brayshaw
Management of Company Finance (5th edn) (Also available: **Students' Manual**)

B.C. Williams and B.J. Spaul
IT and Accounting: The impact of information technology

R.M.S. Wilson and Wai Fong Chua
Managerial Accounting: method and meaning (Also available: **Teachers' Guide**)

Readings in Accounting for Management Control

Edited by

Clive Emmanuel
University of Glasgow

David Otley
University of Lancaster

and

Kenneth Merchant
University of Southern California

CHAPMAN & HALL

London · Glasgow · Weinheim · New York · Tokyo · Melbourne · Madras

Published by Chapman & Hall, 2-6 Boundary Row, London SE1 8HN

Chapman & Hall, 2-6 Boundary Row, London SE1 8HN, UK

Blackie Academic & Professional, Wester Cleddens Road, Bishopbriggs, Glasgow G64 2NZ, UK

Chapman & Hall GmbH, Pappelallee 3, 69469 Weinheim, Germany

Chapman & Hall USA, 115 Fifth Avenue, New York, NY 10003, USA

Chapman & Hall Japan, ITP - Japan, Kyowa Building, 3F, 2-2-1 Hirakawacho, Chiyoda-ku, Tokyo 102, Japan

Chapman & Hall Australia, 102 Dodds Street, South Melbourne, Victoria 3205, Australia

Chapman & Hall India, R. Seshadri, 32 Second Main Road, CIT East, Madras 600 035, India

First edition 1992
Reprinted 1992
Reprinted in new format 1995

© 1992 Chapman & Hall

Typeset in 9.5/11pt Aster by Best-set Typesetter Ltd, Hong Kong
Printed in Great Britain by the Alden Press, Oxford

ISBN   0 412 62590 3

A Catalogue record for this book is available from the British Library

Library of Congress Cataloging-in-Publication Data available

∞ Printed on acid-free text paper, manufactured in accordance with ANSI/NISO Z39.48-1992 and ANSI/NISO Z39.48-1984 (Permanence of Paper).

Contents

List of contributors

Franco Amigoni, Scuola di Direzione Aziendale, Universita 'L. Bocconi', Milan.

Chris Argyris, Harvard University Graduate School of Business Administration.

John V. Baumler, College of Business, Ohio State University.

A.J. Berry, Manchester Business School, University of Manchester.

Jacob G. Birnberg, Graduate School of Business, University of Pittsburgh.

Michael Briers, School of Accounting, University of New South Wales.

Adrian Buckley, Finance, Accounting & Economics Group, Cranfield School of Management.

Richard E. Caves, Harvard University Graduate School of Business Administration.

Jerry Dermer, Faculty of Administrative Studies, York University, Ontario.

Clive R. Emmanuel, Department of Accounting and Finance, University of Glasgow.

Kenneth P. Gee, Department of Business and Management Studies, University of Salford.

Lawrence A. Gordon, Department of Accounting, University of Maryland.

V. Govindarajan, School of Business Administration, Dartmouth College.

Severin V. Grabski, College of Business, Michigan State University.

Anil K. Gupta, School of Management, Boston University.

Susan F. Haka, College of Business, Michigan State University.

Bo Hedberg, Department of Business Administration, University of Gothenberg.

Mark Hirst, School of Accounting, University of New South Wales.

Sten Jönsson, Department of Business Administration, University of Gothenberg.

Robert S. Kaplan, Graduate School of Industrial Administration, Carnegie-Mellon University and Harvard Business School.

John L.J. Machin, School of Business, Durham University.

Norman MacIntosh, School of Business, Queens University, Ontario.

Eugene McKenna, School of Organisational Behaviour, Birmingham Polytechnic.

Jean-François Manzoni, Harvard University Graduate School of Business Administration.

Kenneth A. Merchant, School of Accounting, University of Southern California.

Danny Miller, Faculty of Management, McGill University.

David T. Otley, Department of Accounting and Finance, University of Lancaster.

William G. Ouchi, Graduate School of Management, University of California.

Lee D. Parker, School of Social Sciences, Flinders University of S. Australia.

George E. Pinches, School of Business, University of Kansas.

Robert W. Scapens, Department of Accounting and Finance, University of Manchester.

Robert Simons, Harvard University Graduate School of Business Administration.

Barry H. Spicer, College of Business, University of Oregon.

Robert J. Swieringa, Financial Accounting Standards Board, Stamford.

Lawrence Turopolec, Graduate School of Business, University of Pittsburgh.

G. Vickers

David J.H. Watson, Department of Commerce, University of Queensland.

Karl E. Weick, College of Business, University of Texas.

S. Mark Young, College of Business and Administration, University of Colorado at Boulder.

Preface

This book of readings is intended to complement our text *Accounting for Management Control* that is now entering its third edition. These readings provide some deeper insights into the fundamental issues of accounting control systems design and use that are raised in the text. It has not been easy to select the most appropriate readings from the increasing range of relevant material now available. In particular, we have often been faced with choosing between a modern summary article and an older classic piece. Generally we have opted to select the original article, partly to give some flavour for the historical development of the subject, but also because the quality and lucidity of the earlier piece was superior. In considering revising the readings to complement the third edition of the text we were faced with finding articles to omit so that we could replace them with more modern pieces. Our final decision was to leave the selection unchanged! This is not solely due to laziness on our part, but rather to the enthusiasm with which the book of readings was greeted by users who emphasized the advantage it gave in providing ready access to sources that were already becoming difficult to obtain. As recent work is more accessible, we have kept the original selections and trust this will meet with approval.

The four Parts match and follow those of *Accounting for Management Control*, a structure that has itself stood the test of time. We give our reasons for the inclusion of each reading at the commencement of each Part. Our overall aim has been to include the work that has most influenced our own thinking and which, in our opinion, has stood the test of time. Most were written in the late 1970s and the 1980s. The more recent contributions have been selected because we think they give valuable insights into worthwhile directions for future developments in the management control area.

Within each Part we have attempted to balance readings that address specific issues with those which are broader review articles; and those which rely on normative reasoning with those which seek to develop positive theories. Even so, we are conscious of omitting some interesting alternative approaches, including both critical approaches and case-based approaches that have developed extensively since the first edition. Nevertheless we hope that the wide range of perspectives included gives food for thought.

Although it was largely fortuitous, there are almost equal numbers of contributions from British and North American journals, excluding those from *Accounting, Organizations and Society*. Work published in this latter journal supplies the bulk of our selection that recognizes the growing contribution of this journal in influencing work on management control. However, the subject is of growing interest and importance, and other new journals are making a significant contribution. Of particular note are *Management Accounting Research* (UK) which is a major outlet for case-based research, the *Auditing, Accounting and Accountability Journal* which emphasizes critical approaches, and the *British Journal of Management* which had a special issue on management control systems in 1993. This contained articles given at the Second Management Control Systems Symposium run in 1992 by the UK Management Control Association. Much of the most significant recent work can be found in these sources.

The structure of the main text has remained the same since the first edition was published in 1985. The fundamental distinction between programmed and non-programmed activities and the most appropriate use of accounting information in these different circumstances is a theme that has recurred in the research literature since that time. There is also a much wider appreciation of the fact that accounting control systems operate in, and are influenced by, an organizational context; and that they are used in conjunction with other non-accounting mechanisms for achieving control. Looking back over the research literature clearly indicates to us that our thoughts on these matters were not original; our perspective is more far-reaching only due to our having stood on the shoulders of others. Yet the text has had an influence of its own, and is now used on nearly every undergraduate degree programme in the United Kingdom, and is also widely used in countries as far afield as Australia, Malaysia, Austria and Holland. It has also proved to be of interest on MBA courses.

We hope that this book of readings will enable students to gain easier access to the stream of research work on which the text was built, and also that it might inspire some of them to continue the endeavour.

Clive Emmanuel, Glasgow University
David Otley, Lancaster University

Part One

The Context of Management Accounting

In Part One of the text we try to set out some aspects of the context in which management accounting information is used in organizations. As Amigoni (1978) reminds us, Simon's (1954) research team had identified three different purposes served by accounting information in practice, namely scorecard, attention-directing and decision-making. Traditional management accounting texts strongly emphasize the last role of decision-making and consider in detail the precise accounting information that is necessary in order to take specific decisions. In so doing, they take economics as their major conceptual framework. However, they are less explicit about the attention-directing function, despite normally spending a considerable number of pages on the calculation of budgetary variances, and devote very little attention to the scorecard role of performance evaluation. Thus, the focus of traditional texts is clearly on decision-making rather than control.

Accounting for Management Control represents an attempt to counterbalance this emphasis by focusing on the role of management accounting information as a means of exercising control both within and over organizations. In part we do this because decision-making and control can be seen as complementary aspects of accounting information use. More fundamentally, we see decision-making as just one part of a larger cycle of planning and control. Thus, in order to appreciate properly the decision-making role of accounting information we need to view it in the wider context of control. Further, having adopted this point of view, we begin to understand that accounting information is just one type of information that may be used in a controlled process, and that we need to consider the wider control options that are available and the information requirements of each.

The readings presented to complement Part One of the text tend to move progressively from a fairly tight modelling of control processes, as typified by the cybernetic tradition, towards a more diffuse framework characterized by attempts to exercise control in the context of a complex and uncertainty-ridden organization. However, we break this pattern by beginning with Machin's (1983) wide-ranging definitional overview of the development of management control concepts between 1965 and the early 1980s, and by concluding with Amigoni's (1978) down to earth application of contingency ideas in a practical setting. In this way we hope to illuminate some of the many facets of control systems design and use, and to illustrate something of the complexity of the practical application of principles of control.

The readings in this section roughly parallel the chapters of the text, although several, such as Dermer (1988) and Birnberg *et al.* (1983), are difficult to categorize and are also relevant to later parts.

DEFINITIONS OF CONTROL

We cannot begin to discuss the topic of management control without mentioning Anthony's classic definition (1965) that management control is concerned with 'ensuring that organizations use their resources effectively and efficiently in achieving their objectives'. This definition neatly sidesteps two problems. First, it avoids the need to discuss the sense in which organizations have objectives and the procedures by which they establish and clarify them. That is, strategic planning is taken as given. Secondly, it saves having to delve into the complexities of exercising control in particular situations with specific characteristics and constraints. That is, operational control issues are avoided. The middle ground of management control is thus, at first sight, dominated by accounting control. However, as Machin (1983) so neatly observes, the very framework that was produced at the high point of the accounting domination of control systems theory carried within it the seeds of our present dilemma. That is, even in Anthony's own framework accounting techniques were categorized primarily into the operational control arena where the source discipline was seen to be economics. Anthony's recognition of social psychology as the source discipline for management control leads Machin to argue that it became inevitable that the mainstream of teaching and research in management control systems would swing away from accounting systems.

But such an observation only raises rather than solves the definitional problems of a discipline that seeks to be concerned with issues of control in human organizations. Machin (1983) therefore considers other disciplinary bases for such an intellectual endeavour focusing in turn upon 'management', 'systems' and 'control', and seeing in each a new facet of the issue. His own conclusion is very much at the individual level of analysis, for he approaches the problem from the point of view of a manager attempting to exercise control over any situation that may confront him (or her). But his analysis is valuable to all those who seek to understand better how the subject of management control has arrived at its present state of knowledge and development.

By contrast, Otley and Berry (1980) explore the meaning of control in an organizational context by concentrating on a cybernetic model and assessing its applicability in an organizational context. They outline four necessary conditions for control, but concentrate particularly on the need for a predictive model of any process which is being controlled. Here the gulf between cybernetics and organizational control becomes apparent, for most organizational control systems have such inadequate predictive models that the whole cybernetic concept of absolute control becomes inappropriate. Control in organizations is inevitably partial and imperfect. Machin (1983) had pointed out the oddity of the English language possessing only one term for various types of control; here this peculiarity is extended as it is realized that 'control' has very different meanings in different contexts. In particular, the concept of organizational control is problematic for several reasons. The first concerns the nature of organizational objectives; it is argued that different types of organization will have objectives that differ in nature. In general, organizations will not have agreed objectives but may have negotiated plans of action which remain valid in the short term until a further round of negotiation occurs. Secondly, the location of the predictive model necessary for control may be unclear; typically different models may reside in the minds of different managers, and all may be imperfect. Finally, the action taken in response to a mismatch signal may include the adaptation of the standard of achievement being sought; thus control becomes a dynamically changing activity, adapting to new circumstances. The paper concludes by arguing that progress may most effectively be made by the structured and intensive observation of the operation of organizational control systems in action.

ORGANIZATIONAL CONTROL

An application of this approach is supplied by Vickers' (1967) lecture entitled 'Stability, Control and Choice', given originally in 1957, for Sir Geoffrey Vickers is a rare example of a practising manager who has codified and distilled his wide experience into theoretical insights. Rooted in cybernetics and systems theory, he attempts to translate the principles of control which have been found to be applicable in the control of physical processes to the control of organizations. In passing, he remarks upon the oddity of our language not distinguishing between systems which are open to information and those which are not; still less are we able to distinguish between types of openness to information in terms of an ascending hierarchy. However, he also distinguishes between positive (goal-seeking) control and negative (threat-avoiding) control. Most discussions of accounting control are expressed in terms of goal-seeking, but it may be more realistic to think of organizational behaviour as being predominantly threat-avoiding. At the very least, such a conception avoids the need to have mutually agreed goals, for different groups may well act effectively against different types of threat with no necessity of prior agreement between them. Thus an organization may be characterized as operating in the interstices of a multitude of constraints, in a feasible region eked out by management. Vickers argues that the distinction between good and less good management may be in the size of the feasible region each develops; a poor management is characterized by being driven by circumstances beyond its control, whereas a good management keeps the initiative and preserves space in which to operate. Finally Vickers draws attention to the role of time in control; not only must an effective control response be identified, it must also be implemented and take effect within a time frame that permits reaction to its effects.

A major control in human organizations is the form of organizational structure adopted. Chapter 2 of the text outlines the development of organization theory, a theme that is later taken up in Part Three when divisional forms of organization are more extensively analysed. Organization theory provides a complement to the more abstract and impersonal systems approaches developed in the first chapter. The fundamental challenge lies in the design of control mechanisms that permit a degree of rational and ordered behaviour in human organizations. A major guiding paradigm has been that of contingency theory, the idea that the most appropriate form of organization is dependent upon external circumstances.

This approach is used by Ouchi (1979) when he draws an important distinction between behaviour controls and output controls, a distinction which is taken up in Chapter 5 of the text. He regards the ability to measure results (outputs) as a fundamental constraint upon control systems design. Where such ability is low, control has to concentrate solely on the specification and monitoring of specific behaviours. He also regards knowledge of the transformation process (an idea very similar to the predictive model in the Otley and Berry (1980) scheme) to be fundamental. Where such knowledge is imperfect control must inevitably concentrate upon outputs rather than behaviours, because senior managers do not possess the necessary knowledge to specify appropriate behaviours. Combining these two elements into a 2 × 2 matrix produces four distinct combinations, only three of which can be controlled by monitoring behaviours or outputs. Where there is low ability to measure outputs coupled with imperfect knowledge of the transformation process, neither behaviour nor output control is appropriate. Here Ouchi argues that 'clan' control, characterized by ritual and ceremony, is all that remains. However, this can perhaps be extended into the realm of all so-called 'social' controls, including personnel controls. Personnel controls involve the selection of appropriate kinds of people (i.e. those who have already been socialized into adopting particular norms and patterns of behaviour) to perform particular tasks. Thus the control of many professional activities such as accountancy work and research and development may be primarily controlled by such means when other controls become inappropriate.

It may also be argued that an emphasis on accounting-based controls tends to lead to all control situations being seen as occupying Ouchi's first box (i.e. perfect knowledge of the transformation process and high ability to measure outputs). This argument is similar to that put forward by Earl and Hopwood (1981) and outlined in Chapter 1 of the text. It needs to be recognized that not all problems are neatly analysable under conditions of assumed certainty; control systems have to operate in an imperfectly understood world of considerable ambiguity. Thus Ouchi's ideas can be seen as an early application of contingency ideas to the problem of designing information systems to help the exercise of control in conditions of uncertainty.

Contingency theories of organization developed in the 1950s and 1960s were extended into the realm of management accounting in the mid-1970s, but were treated somewhat uncritically by management accounting researchers. A brief summary of the contingency theory of management accounting is given in the text, but the article by Otley (1980) concentrates on evaluating the validity of this transfer. He argues that the field has suffered from the uncritical transfer of results; this has led to the use of an over-simple theoretical model which has given misleading results. Moreover, the concentration upon contingent variables has led to a neglect of the effects of those variables. The only writers to treat these latter seriously were Gordon and Miller (1976) and Amigoni (1978). Otley (1980) concludes that it is inappropriate to consider organizational design and accounting controls separately and in isolation. An organizational control system comprises these and other parts (as described in Chapter 5) and, in theory at least, they need to be designed conjointly. But contingency theory focuses attention on effectiveness, both as a criterion of the choice of controls and as a contingent variable in its own right. Herein lies a fundamental problem. If the effectiveness of controls influences organizational behaviour in the choice of control systems as it surely does (e.g. in the emphasis placed on short-term financial controls in organizations facing financial crisis), how can effectiveness be used as a criterion on which to base the rational selection of controls. At the very least control systems must be evaluated as integrated wholes possessing a high level of mutual interdependence. Failure to do this will lead to invalid conclusions being drawn.

Birnberg *et al.* (1983) address the same issue from the point of view of accounting controls and take up Ouchi's theme that accountants have typically sought to reduce uncertain situations into frameworks characterized by well-structured tasks and highly measurable outputs. They review the frameworks proposed by several organizational theorists, including Perrow, Thompson and Ouchi, to substantiate this contention and point out that the result of such an attitude is the encouragement of dysfunctional behaviour on the part of subordinate managers forced to work under such a control structure. They then present a valuable summary of the accounting-based literature on budgetary and organizational control. This culminates in an analysis of the methods managers may use to distort the messages conveyed by an accounting information system, categorized into smoothing, biasing, focusing, gaming, filtering and engaging in 'illegal' acts. Thus the very system designed and used by senior managers to control their subordinates can be turned upon them. Subordinate managers can take advantage of the weaknesses in the information being used for control to present the messages they wish to be received by their superiors. Practical control systems used in organizations are thus very subtle in their effects. Both superior and subordinate managers are using the information system to effect control, but each will also be using the information system to increase their own control over achieving their own personal objectives as well as achieving organizational objectives. Any organizational control system is thus attempting to exercise control over a whole set of self-controlling subsystems, and the effect of any control action is difficult to predict because it needs to take into account the responses of each of those subsystems.

A BROADER CONCEPTION OF CONTROL

Dermer (1988) takes up the point that control does not only reside at senior management levels in an organization and presents a broader conception of the control process, set within a pluralistic organizational context. He argues that conventional views of control see organizational order as the creation of management, strategy and cybernetics, but that such a view is inadequate. An alternative perspective views organizations as arenas within which a variety of stakeholders interact as they attempt to satisfy their individual needs. The resulting order, he argues, is not the creation of any one participant but rather evolves from the collectivity of interactions.

Fundamental to this analysis is the assumption that individual stakeholders engage in autonomous activity which seeks to resolve the contradictions they perceive between management's strategy and the actual conditions they face. From a managerial viewpoint, senior managers are attempting to exercise control over a situation they know less about than their subordinates. From the standpoint of the subordinates, their performance is being measured and assessed using imperfect knowledge and measurement. Under such circumstances, subversion of the official control system may be necessary in order to achieve organizational goals effectively; it may also be subverted to pursue individual goals.

The implications of this analysis are largely unexplored. In the short term, it may be that so-called dysfunctional behaviour may actually be beneficial. For example, slack may be regarded as providing the resources and discretion necessary to explore alternatives, and thus to represent an investment in creativity. Overlapping areas of authority may lead to communication which sensitizes participants to make necessary adjustments. Disconcertingly, Dermer argues, phenomena unacceptable from one point of view become desirable, if not mandatory, from another. From a longer-term perspective, the processes of control involved in maintaining a pluralistic order may be in marked contrast to those of a hierarchically managed system. In any real organization these two forces coexist somewhat uneasily; both managerial and autonomous forces exist, but only the former has legitimacy. Yet it may be the latter which most effectively guarantee the organization's long-term survival.

A more specific version of a similar general argument is developed by Hedberg and Jönsson (1978) who argue that organizations need both stabilizers and destabilizers. Current accounting and management information systems are primarily concerned with stabilizing activities. But as environments change the rigid behaviours encouraged by such systems become inappropriate, although they may persist. Thus Hedberg and Jönsson address themselves to designing information systems that will assist organizations to adapt to changing environments. Their solution lies in the design of semi-confusing information systems, and the meaning of this phrase is sketched out by means of a number of case descriptions. They fully admit that their proposals are not tested theories, but rather inductive generalizations drawn from empirical observation. Nevertheless they give insight into some possible requirements for information systems that will assist in the process of organizational learning and adaptation, as well as in controlling towards a pre-set standard. In Otley and Berry's terminology, they are concerned with updating and amending the organizational predictive model that lies at the heart of any controlled system.

Finally, Amigoni (1978) provides a much needed link between general prescriptions and practical application. He focuses on specific accounting control tools and attempts to assess their appropriateness in different conditions. In one sense, this is an application of contingency theory, for it uses very similar independent variables, but it takes the analysis one step further than most contingency work (with the exception, perhaps, of Gordon and Miller (1976)) by clearly specifying the particular accounting controls that are felt to be most appropriate in particular circumstances.

The particular conclusion Amigoni reaches is that as structural complexity increases, then additional accounting controls can be added, and they will complement those already in existence. By contrast, as the degree of environmental turbulence increases, different accounting tools are required that will replace those already in use. He also notes a shortage of accounting-based techniques that are helpful in coping with high levels of turbulence. This conclusion may or may not be valid; it is notable that it has yet to be the subject of empirical test. But its value lies in giving an indication of the type of hypothesis that can be generated from the body of theory previously outlined. Researchers appear to have experienced great difficulty in moving from the ideas and concepts presented in the literature of organization theory to their application in practical accounting and information systems design. Yet pathways do exist and need to be explored.

CONCLUSIONS

Two strands in the control literature have been identified. The first is managerial in orientation, takes cybernetics as its fundamental theoretical framework, and results in prescriptions for controls that will establish organizational order and stability. The second is pluralistic in orientation, regards control as emerging from the interaction of actors in a situation, and results in observations that are concerned to promote adaptation and learning. It could be argued that these two perspectives are conflicting, but it is probably more helpful to consider them as complementary. All organizations have problems in establishing order, and there can be little doubt that traditional control mechanisms serve a multitude of, generally useful, purposes in these processes. But the alternative view is also necessary to come to a full understanding of how control processes actually operate in practice, although a fully developed theoretical framework has yet to appear.

Both perspectives set the use of accounting information systems and controls in a wider context. Traditional approaches have taken much for granted; the purpose of this part of the text will be to open up a wider set of perspectives in which to assess the contribution that accounting controls can make. It may be true that accounting controls have usually been designed as if they operated in a world that is perfectly understood. What is now evident is that they have to be used with care and flexibility, and in conjunction with other control mechanisms, in a world that is much more complex and uncertain than their designers appreciated.

1

Management control systems: whence and whither?

John L.J. Machin

Planet-wide, the increase in knowledge each year is enormous, and the pace of generation of new knowledge seems also to be increasing. One of the challenges facing the human species is how to assimilate and then harness this new knowledge in ways which are likely to lead to the more effective use of the planet's limited resources whilst maintaining and developing an environment in which it is progressively more satisfying to live. Few would claim that anyone on the planet currently has a satisfactory way of handling that problem *in practice*. Research aimed at developing better ways of managing the use of both physical and mental resources is, therefore, both intellectually challenging and critically important for the future of the species. The potential area for research is so vast, however, that the biggest problem (rather like a child facing an enormous cream bun) is deciding where to start.

This chapter seeks to sustain the argument that:

1. the traditional definitions of the area of research interest subsumed under the title of 'management control systems' are no longer appropriate to the world we live and work in, and
2. it is possible to develop and postulate new definitions of the subject area in such a way that
3. it becomes possible to postulate a set of criteria against which to judge the effectiveness of present and future management control systems.

THE PRESENT SITUATION

'Management control systems' as a specialized subject of study at university level presents, in the 1980s, a picture of uncertainty:

1. As a subject, it has no generally accepted boundary definition.

Source: Machin, J.L.J. (1983), in Lowe, E.A. and Machin, J.L.J. (eds) *New Perspectives in Management Control* (Macmillan), pp. 22–42.
© 1983 Macmillan

2. As a topic for research, it lacks agreement on even a rudimentary paradigm.
3. The proponents of this specialism having discovered the first two facts have had the good sense to become a great deal less confident in what they do.
4. Since in any applied research, criteria of success may possibly provide guidance in the search for a paradigm, it is unfortunate that the ultimate desired results in this area can be one or more of the following:
   (a) Raising the level of managerial effectiveness, *or*
   (b) raising the justifiable level of confidence which a manager brings to his job, *or*
   (c) raising the level of organizational effectiveness.
   Especially since 'effectiveness' at either individual or organizational level is still proving a remarkably elusive concept to define, let alone measure (Machin *et al.*, 1981).

It would be reassuring to dismiss the present disarray as a period of mere semantic disagreement capable of resolution by linguistic refinement. My own view is that our current situation is sufficiently critical to merit discussion not only amongst ourselves, but also with colleagues from other specialisms who share our goal of helping managers to become more effective, but take different paths towards the achievement of that goal.

WHAT WAS THE SUBJECT AREA OF MANAGEMENT CONTROL SYSTEMS?

It is difficult to understand the present position without setting it in the dynamic of a perspective of the development of the subject over the last 15–20 years.

Taken separately, the words 'management', 'control' and 'systems' each create problems of definition. Their juxtaposition appeared to ease the problem of boundary definition only if one assumed that each of the three words described a 'set', the last two of which were progressively smaller parts of the first.

Thus:

Management was a subset of those things which went on in an organization.
Control was a subset of the total range of managerial activity (planning, motivating, coordinating, staffing, directing, controlling etc., the precise number of discrete subjects depending on the author).
Systems was the subset of organizational systems which included only formal, systematically developed, data-handling systems.

The combination of the three words, therefore, produced such a small subset of total organizational activity to study that a research focus was possible, namely:

Those formal, systematically developed, organization-wide, data-handling systems which are designed to facilitate management control which 'is the process by which managers assure that resources are obtained and used effectively and efficiently in the accomplishment of the organisation's objectives'. (Anthony, 1965)

That definition of 'management control systems' was helpful to researchers. It was clear enough so that when you were researching in an employing organization you could recognize what you were looking for and, having found it, could find where it started and finished.

The definition also has the merit that it leaves scope for academics to disagree violently whilst still perceiving themselves to be studying the same thing. In particular it does not touch on the purpose of such systems and thus gives little direction as to how better ones may be developed. Real choices have to be made of which the following are just two examples:

1. Should control be voluntary? That is, should the systems be designed to *enable* managers to control their subordinates, or should they be there to *force* them to control their subordinates?
2. How far, if at all, should top management trust their managers? That is, should systems be designed to enable/force managers to control their subordinates and other resources? – or to enable top management to check on how well their managers are controlling their subordinates and other resources?

Such questions concerning purpose are now accepted as critical in determining the design of systems for management control but fortunately they did not get in the way of early research into 'management control systems' because in the early 1960s the only 'formal, systematically developed, organization-wide, data-handling systems which were designed to enable managers etc. . . .' were accounting based, were studied by qualified accountants, and therefore were virtually immune from philosophical analysis.

Mainstream research in management control systems was accounting based and at that time, probably reasonably so. The systems in use were for the most part developed during the Second World War, brushed up during the Korean War, and were obvious candidates for computerization in the 1960s. Equally clearly, these systems are necessary for the survival and growth of large and/or complex, employing organizations, and their development was therefore a sensible and worthwhile task.

The progressive refinement of accounting-based control systems led to the recognition that whilst accounting-based control systems were necessary for the control of input costs throughout an organization, their usefulness for controlling the effective *use* of those input costs varied widely in different parts of the organization. In some areas it was clear that accounting-based systems were almost sufficient on their own to measure and to control input–output relationship; in others it was equally clear that accounting-based systems had nothing to offer in terms of input–output or process control.

The mainstream of management control systems needed further refinement and precision and Anthony provided it with his definitive framework in 1965 (Anthony, 1965).

His framework was definitive because although produced at the high point of accounting domination of management control systems it carries within it the seed of our present dilemma.

Anthony identified three types of cost, three types of activity, but only two types of formal accounting-based system. A summary of Anthony's conclusions is presented in Table 1.1.

The planning and control processes for committed and engineered costs have economics as their source discipline, and systems based on numbers such as statistical or accounting systems clearly have much to offer as suppliers of relevant managerial information. The way forward for *accounting-based* research for these two cost categories was clear.

Valuable accounting research was undertaken into financial modelling for the strategic planners, and cost/LP modelling for logistics and engineered cost control but accountants ground slowly to a halt in researching the needs of the management control process.

Anthony's framework inevitably focused attention on the need to define the purpose and nature of systems suitable to facilitate management control, and in that 'need for a definition' lie the seeds of doubt as to the future direction of research into management control systems.

Anthony himself had specified social psychology as the source discipline of management control systems, yet surprisingly continued to hope that accounting might have something to offer. He even bound together a number of cases and a sprinkling of articles in the hope that this would establish the accountants' claim to be the social psychologists of the last quarter of the twentieth century (Anthony, Dearden, Vancil, 1965).

The reality of management gave some superficial justification for such a proposal. For example:

1. Whenever an organization had a controllership function, it was invariably staffed by accountants so control must be an accounting function.
2. The budget was the principal control system in most organizations and its appropriateness in areas of committed and engineered cost significantly, and understandably, overshadowed its ineffectiveness in the area of managed cost.

From the date of the publication of Anthony's framework *it was inevitable* that the mainstream of research and teaching in management control systems would swing away from accounting systems.

What was, of course, much less clear was which of the erstwhile rivulets or tributaries of non-accounting research in 'management control' or 'systems' would prove to be the most capable of supporting mainstream focus of attention and research.

There were many strands of research to choose from.

Table 1.1 Analysis systems in terms of the costs which they are being used to control

Anthony's Classification	Cost	Example	Control Information	Techniques	Source Discipline
Strategic planning	Committed	Capital investment	Quantitative	Time value Risk Analysis	Economics Mathematics
Management control	Managed	Any 'managerial activity'	Qualitative	Judgement Persuasion	Social psychology
Operational control	Engineered	Direct product cost	Quantitative	Standard costs Variance analysis	Economics Physical sciences

SYSTEMS

'Systems' was worth considering as a serious contender. Apart from anything else, it actually had an abstract theory which claimed to relate to any group of interacting parts – which organizations either are or strive to be – and it had enjoyed successful application in the biological sciences. It had, therefore, a rigorously defined theory and a history of useful applications.

There were, however, some semantic and conceptual problems with 'systems'.

There was no clear agreement on what was meant by the word 'system' itself. Was the attributive of the word correctly expressed as 'systematic' or 'systemic'. In other words, was a 'management control system' a formal

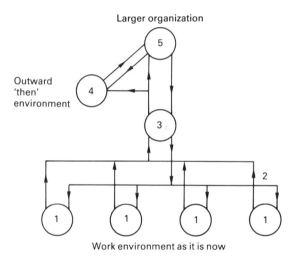

5. GENERAL MANAGEMENT
        setting aims
        making policy
        overall monitoring
        adjusting balance of resources

4. DEVELOPMENT
        looking outward and forward
        tying in subsystem 3 information (needs panic-free time)

3. CONTROLLING
        turning policy into plans
        monitoring performance short term
        feeding information upwards
        allocating resources between subsystems 1

2. LIAISING
        smoothing operations
        promoting lateral information exchange

1. DOING

Fig. 1.1 Organization systems as postulated by a leading cyberneticist, Stafford Beer.
Source: Based on Stafford Beer (1972) *Brain of the Firm* (London: Allen Lane).

data-handling system with a defined purpose which had been *systematically designed* by one or more designers to meet that purpose (i.e. a 'system' as the accountants had traditionally used the term), or was the 'management control system' the system of management control interactions which had *developed organically* over time to meet (or occasionally to defeat!) the needs of individuals and the organization, i.e. 'system' as the social psychologists had traditionally used the term.

The first approach implies a system classification by purpose, and that was capable of being provided for organizational systems by a leading cyberneticist without even mentioning the magic phrase 'management control systems' (Beer, 1972), as shown in Figure 1.1.

There is no obvious set from that figure which adds up to a – let alone, the – management control system.

Even worse, the concept of formal system might also include the organization structure as a formal system of authority and accountability which would have to be studied simultaneously if we were to understand the structure/system interface problems faced by managers.

The second approach, of course, calls for a system classification by nature or essence. A very useful one was readily to hand (Boulding, 1956), and is given in Figure 1.2.

1. Frameworks — Static structure

2. Clockworks — Simple dynamic system with predetermined necessary motion

3. Thermostat — Transmission and interpretation of information

4. Cell — Open system, self-maintaining structure

5. Genetic-societal — Plant — division of labour among cells to form a cell-society with differentiated and mutually dependent parts

6. Animal — Behaviour is response not to a specific stimulus but to an 'image' or 'knowledge structure' between stimulus and response.

7. Human — 6 + self-consciousness

8. Social organizations — Groups of 7s

9. Transcendental

Fig. 1.2 Boulding's classification of the hierarchy of systems.
Source: Based on K.E. Boulding (1956) 'General Systems Theory – The Skeleton of Science', *Management of Science*, vol. 2, no. 2.

Whatever quibbles one might have with the particular details of the classification he produced, Boulding's impact on thinking and research in management control systems was both important and clear-cut. Presently available, formally designed, systematically developed, purposeful management control systems were all around the thermostat level. Organically evolved reality was at levels 7 and 8. It seemed that the way forward lay either in conceptualizing a level 8 system which would *lead* working groups to evolve more effectively, or reverting to level 1 to produce a conceptual framework which could *help* working groups to discover more easily for themselves how to evolve more effectively.

This thinking leads inexorably to a call for either:

1. a rigorous abstract theory of purposeful interpersonal interaction – a tough task given that sociologists themselves claim to be in a pre-paradigm stage of development; *or*
2. a truly contingent system. That is also a tough intellectual task given the overwhelming recent emphasis in research and teaching on developing purposeful, specialized, evaluatable systems.

The systems route was clearly challenging and would raise fundamental questions about the purpose and nature of the systems one was seeking to develop.

The advantages of the route were the power of systems theory and the work being done by specialists in organization theory (Katz and Kahn, 1966, for example) which was throwing new light on managerial activity.

'System' is, however, only *one* of the three words in the title of the subject under study, so it was at least possible that there was an easier route mapped out by specialists in one or other of the remaining two words.

CONTROL

'Control' offered an even wider range of possibilities. Shorn of the words 'management' and 'systems', control seems to be capable of covering almost anything.

Societally, it appears (in *1066 and All That* terminology) to be a 'good thing'. Situations or people which are out of control are seen as 'bad things' and that encompasses inflation, population, epidemics, children and tightrope walkers.

Given the rich diversity of the English language, it is quite staggering that the word 'control' has not long since been discarded in favour of a plethora of words offering greater precision. Yet it remains – indeed if anything its use increases and the area it subsumes widens. It is embarrassing to have to admit that academics in the field of management control systems have even contributed to that unfortunate state of affairs.

There is, however, another side to the coin and it may in fact be much the more important side. It is important to recognize that any situation which proves durable in the face of precise and justified intellectual criticism must have a very firm basis derived from satisfying some strong needs in society. Of course, those needs may be felt by the few strong people in a community or they may be felt strongly by the majority of people in a community. 'Control' has survived or, more accurately, flourished, as a diffuse concept for so long that maybe it is supported by both sets of needs and is thus inviolate for all time!

The question we are led to ask, therefore, is not, 'How can we define better the quintessential characteristics of control?' but, 'Why has it been in apparently everyone's interests for the past three or four decades to use the word control in so diffuse a manner that misunderstanding in discussion of the subject is the rule rather than the exception?' There has to be a powerful rationale hiding somewhere in amongst a welter of ostensibly irrational behaviour. No doubt each management control systems specialist has his own pet answer because without one, research in the field would be pointless.

There certainly seems to be no currently accepted answer or even a coordinated search for one. Any quick recap of management control theory shows usually both the staggering breadth of material involved and the bias of the person doing the recapping. It would no doubt be as surprising to Giglioni and Bedeian that I see Dalton and Tannenbaum as central to what is happening currently in management control systems, as it is staggering to me that Giglioni and Bedeian in their review of management control theory (Giglioni and Bedeian, 1974) specifically excluded Tannenbaum from their consideration of control and did not even mention Dalton.

The spread of topics covered by management control can be presented as four spectra, as illustrated in Figure 1.3. The spectra can be amplified as follows:

A. The *managerial output* which has to be planned and controlled may range from 'concrete' items such as units of product to 'abstract' output such as improved teamwork or more effective coordination or job satisfaction.
B. The *information* we use to measure the successful generation of planned output will range from objective, frequently numerically-based data to subjective, usually if not invariably linguistically-based data.

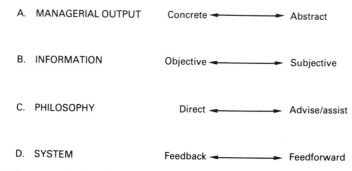

Fig. 1.3 Spectra of the elements in management control.

C. The *philosophy* underlying the control process may range from that manifested when a manager orders or directs his subordinates to carry out certain tasks to that which is manifest when a manager invites his subordinates to seek advice and assistance from him whenever they feel it would assist them to achieve their previously agreed objectives.

D. The *management control system* may be called on to operate in any mode ranging from feeding control information back to the manager who directed action to be undertaken in order to facilitate retrospective performance appraisal, to feeding changed views about the future to the subordinate so that he may decide whether advice and assistance are necessary to support the achievement of future performance objectives.

The word control is found in the literature in respect of all kinds of managerial output, using all kinds of information, with manifest philosophies of control spread across the entire spectrum and with systems which feed performance reports to the boss before the subordinate and vice versa.

To the question, 'Why, in a language so capable of precision as English, do we have one word covering such an immense range?' the author offers the answer that it is in fact necessary to have a fuzzy concept to represent fuzzy managerial reality.

The conclusion reached by the author from research into the diversity represented in the spectra in Figure 1.3 is that diversity is the reality, i.e. that managers in different organizations or in different parts of the same organization, and the same manager at different times of the day or at different points in his or her career, find it positively helpful to be able to switch their position from one stance to another without being immediately or clearly seen to be doing so.

Two of the key workers in the field of control in organizations, Tannenbaum and Dalton, offer, when their work is related, a way forward in tackling this problem of diversity and the consequential choice between contingent acceptance or rigorous analysis.

Tannenbaum's control cycle (Tannenbaum, 1968) takes the simplest of interpersonal situations and views it essentially, for discussion purposes, as a closed system (see Figure 1.4).

This cycle can be broken down into a number of elements:

(a) Intention of A.
(b) Choice by A of appropriate influence necessary to lead B to carry out the desired activity.
(c) Communication by A.
(d) Transmission of communication.
(e) Reception by B of communication.
(f) Interpretation by B of communication.
(g) Decision by B on what action if any to take.
(h) Action by B.

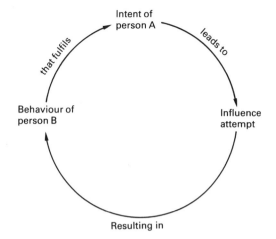

Fig. 1.4 Tannenbaum's control cycle.
Source: A.S. Tannenbaum (1968) *Control in Organisations* (New York: McGraw-Hill).

(i) Informing A of B's action (itself obviously a multistep communication and interpretation activity).
(j) Comparison by A between his intention and B's action.

If, in step (j), A discovers that B has done something quite different from A's original intention, he has a large number of variables to check to see what 'went wrong'.

Of course, Tannenbaum's cycle is a very simplified closed-system description of interpersonal control but, like all simple models, it serves to concentrate the mind on deciding which constraints should first be released.

One way of releasing constraints would be to recognize that in most organizations there will be a number of individuals trying to influence B at any point in time so there is a complex interactive network made up of Tannenbaum cycles affecting B – either protecting him or weighing him down.

Another way of releasing constraints would be to recognize the different types of control influence which can be, and almost certainly are, affecting B in an open-system view of B as a manager in an organization.

Dalton has classified control influences into three categories (Dalton and Lawrence, 1971) (see Table 1.2).

Dalton's classification highlights the fact that organizational control influences (manifest in management control systems by the formal, systematically. developed, organization-wide data-handling systems described earlier), are just one of three influences on managerial decision-making and activity; Hofstede's research indicates that the influence may not be great (Hofstede, 1968).

If 'management control systems' is the study of how managers control

Table 1.2 'Dalton's' three types of control in organization

Controls administered by	Direction for controls deriving from	Behavioural and performance measures	Signal for corrective action	Reinforcements or rewards for compliance	Sanctions or punishments for non-compliance
Organization	Organization plans, strategies, responses to competitive demands	Budgets, standard costs, sales targets	Variance	Management commendation Monetary incentives, promotions	Request for explanation Dismissal
Informal group	Mutual commitments, group ideals	Group norms	Deviance	Peer-approval, membership, leadership	Kidding Ostracism, hostility
Individual	Individual goals, aspirations	Self-expectations, intermediate targets	Perceive impending failure, missed targets	Satisfaction of 'being in control' Elation	Sense of disappointment Feeling of failure

Source: G.W. Dalton and P.R. Lawrence (1971) *Motivation and Control in Organizations* (Homewood, Ill.: Irwin).

the use of resources, it must be the case that informal group norms and informal means of influencing others form a central part of such a study (Nelson and Machin, 1976).

This in turn requires a methodology which captures situational and informal data as it is used in level 8 social interaction in working groups. Such data is communicated during the course of level 8 social interaction and the informal systems which facilitate informal group influences are communication systems. Dalton's second category, therefore, points to the importance of the communication systems as being vital for control to be exercised and informal communication of messages in language becomes a critical part of any concept of systems of control.

If 'control' in organizations has something to do with influencing human beings then a study of control in organizations after Dalton must include all the influences which affect a manager and that includes self-expectations, and must therefore include the concept of self-control.

Self-control is a very daunting concept to a management control systems specialist, because self-control affects everything which a manager does. As a result, control becomes not a subset of management, but the sum of the influences, helps or hindrances that affect the way in which each manager performs the whole of his job of managing – and management we now recognize is a very complex activity.

MANAGEMENT

Field research in management has recently been leading to the recognition by academics of what managers had known for quite a while – that managing is a complex activity and that it is getting progressively more complex. The variables involved seem to be getting larger in number and specialization seems to be increasing without a commensurate increase in our understanding of that other specialization – integration.

Human interaction based on real interpersonal understanding seems to be becoming harder with increasing job mobility. In such a situation it becomes even more difficult when things go wrong to identify which of the items in Tannenbaum's cycle was not working as well as it should – or at all!

Equally, it is becoming clear that management as an activity is not restricted solely to 'what managers do'. Indeed it is something of an American/English quirk to distinguish 'managers' from other people. Reverting to Anthony's definition, the process 'by which resources are obtained and used effectively and efficiently' is clearly influenced to a greater or lesser extent by all workers in an organization, not just by those workers we call managers. Ensuring that those who have the most to contribute beneficially to the process are given the opportunity to do so becomes a critical element in the management of an organization, and this is discussed fully by Richbell.

The need is for a better understanding of how integration, coordination, cooperation or balance can be achieved in an active manner. In particular, there needs to be some understanding of where to look for an academic rationale for approaching integration as a topic of study.

Is it an individual activity as Lawrence and Lorsch saw it (Lawrence and Lorsch, 1967a)?

Is it something to do with structure as Texas Instruments saw it (Helms, 1975)?

Is it the real subject of management control systems as Lowe and McInnes saw it (Lowe and McInnes, 1971)?

MANAGEMENT CONTROL SYSTEMS IN THE 1980s

Eighteen years after the publication of Anthony's framework, management control systems looks very different indeed. The author suggests that the subject has evolved into: 'The study of those formal and informal systems which help an individual to control what he does with himself and other resources.'

KEY DECISIONS FOR THE FUTURE

There is universal acceptance that the Holy Grail for management control systems researchers is 'effectiveness'. There is some disagreement about whether individual effectiveness will be consistent with group effectiveness and there is fundamental disagreement as to what constitutes either a theoretical definition of effectiveness or a practically useful way of measuring it. 'Effectiveness' is something like 'truth' or 'beauty' – managers can recognize it easily enough but they cannot define it!

It is the very elusiveness of the concept of 'effectiveness' which, coupled with the fuzziness of the concept of control, makes management control systems such a compulsively interesting subject to study.

The way forward in research and teaching in the subject, however, is dependent on the answers we give to a number of key questions concerning the purpose, boundaries, and methodologies of work in the newly defined field.

Purpose

Is the purpose to develop new systems which will force, lead or drag managers to be more effective? That is, systems which will normatively measure how far managers are from the level of effectiveness which they should achieve?

OR

Is the purpose to develop new systems which will help a manager to be as effective as he wishes to be? – that is, systems which will have the capacity to facilitate total effectiveness, but which will still 'work' for managers who have no intention of raising their level of effectiveness and seek only an easier way of achieving it.

This is a choice between different levels in Boulding's hierarchy.

Types of control influence

Given the acknowledged range of influence affecting a manager, should a new system support only organizational control influences or also support informal group norms? Some of the latter have been known to be antagonistic to organizational goals – should these be supported?

Is it even possible to conceive of organizational information systems supporting informal influences? Would not such an approach be doomed to failure unless the informal part were voluntary and/or individually controlled?

This is a choice between supporting only organizationally approved influences or all influences.

Variety reduction or contingent complexity?

Given the acknowledged diversity of management, should management control systems, as now defined, deal only with specific variables or accept contingent reality?

Here the choice is between a system based on the analyst's traditional approach of variety reduction, and developed to handle only certain predetermined variables, or a system whose precise content would be determined by each manager using the system, to meet his own contingently relevant complexity.

What, if any, philosophy of control should systems embody?

Given the acknowledged diffuseness of the word control, should management control systems designers choose a particular 'approved' managerial house-style for their system (as the MBO people did), or, learning from the fate of systems which are dependent on a uniform acceptance of a given control philosophy, should systems be designed to accommodate diffuseness?

This is a choice between a stated view of what an optimum control style should be or an acceptance of diffuseness of managerial style which will differ from person to person and from day to day.

The system/structure interface

Given:

(a) the fact that organizations' structures change frequently within a given form, and that new forms such as matrix and fluid structures are in current use, and
(b) the fact that structure is only a formal system of authority and accountability,

which is the key variable in the structure/system interface? Anthony had no doubts, 'Structure is a given – systems are therefore designed to meet the needs of a given structure' (Anthony, 1965). But structure is just a formal organizational influence attempt, so it could be treated as part of the new concept of management control systems.

Here we have a choice between:

1. Structure-dependent systems.
2. Structure-linked systems.
3. Systems independent of structure.

These choices are critical for the future of research, system design and development, and teaching in the field of management control systems.

The implications for research methodology

Each of the choices posed above presents a challenge to researchers in terms of both the purpose and the methodology of research. In the aggregate they highlight the need for, and present the opportunity to design, completely new research methodologies. The practical arguments for a major step function change in research methodology seem equally strong. Previous methodologies have led us to the point where integration born of effective operation of Tannenbaum's control cycle (Figure 1.4) in organizations is acknowledged to be inadequate (notably in respect of lateral and diagonal interaction). Until recently we have lacked even the most rudimentary methodology for monitoring each of the ten steps (a–j) which collectively make up that cycle, so as to be able to ascertain the cause of ineffective operation of the control process.

The increasing power of information-handling technology and the decreasing cost of information storage and retrieval provide all the practical support which researchers will need at precisely the time that theoretical considerations demand that new methodologies be found. In moving into this new and uncharted area it becomes imperative that researchers and managers jointly determine the criteria against which new research methodologies and new management control systems will be both designed and evaluated. The following set of criteria are presented only to spur others into replacing them with a better set.

A set of criteria to guide future research and system design

It is the author's belief that many of the fundamental choices which have to be made follow almost inevitably from the reasoning included earlier in this chapter.

Tannenbaum's control cycle is conceptually independent of:

1. the hierarchical relationship of B to A,
2. the managerial styles of A or B,
3. the nature of A's intention – i.e. it may be to influence B to produce anything from a concrete item to an abstract outcome.

To follow Tannenbaum means designing a system which is not dependent for its successful operation on:

1. any particular organization structure,
2. any particular philosophy of managerial interaction,
3. any particular type of managerial output.

To follow Lowe and McInnes (1971) in their concept of resolution levels, it is necessary so to design a system that it treats organizational interactions with the environment in exactly the same way as it treats an individual manager's interactions with his environment.

General systems theory indicates that any contingent system must accept the situationally-derived, complex, omnidirectional pattern of influences affecting a manager in connection with his job (Katz and Kahn, 1966). (It is worth pointing out that whilst the previous sentence poses no conceptual difficulty the practical implementation of the ideas embodied in it would have been impossible until the availability of large computers and the chip, which have made it possible to design systems which can document both the contents and direction of every interpersonal interaction in a managerial group.)

Dalton's classification can only lead to an acceptance that any system which purports to facilitate the achievement of organizational and managerial effectiveness must be capable of supporting both formal organizational influences derived from authority, responsibility and accountability, and the informal group influences derived from much more complex combinations of ostensibly the same variables.

Control theory – whether of the mechanistic, closed-loop, feedback variety or the more relevant open-looped, feed-forward variety – makes the clear demand that any management control system worthy of the name must, as a minimum, enable a manager to ascertain first, what his goals are, and secondly, whether or not he is achieving them.

Dalton's concept of self-control systems poses a real challenge to a tradition based almost exclusively on managerial and research experience of *purposeful* systems. The conflict of choice is apparent. If a management control system is to facilitate self-control then its purpose will be dependent on the motivational needs of each manager and we may reasonably assume that occasionally managers may wish to use the system to reduce both organizational effectiveness and the demands made on themselves. To people reared on a tradition of purposeful systems based on beliefs such as:

1. management control systems are there to achieve goal congruence,
OR
2. management control systems are there to prevent individuals from wasting organizational resources,

it is hard to contemplate a 'purposeless' system whose purpose would be defined by the user. Yet Dalton's classification of control influences

1. The system must permit clear links to be developed from planned organizational purpose to operational activity.
2. The system must be able to assist managers both when planning purpose and when controlling its achievement.
3. The system must be designed to help a manager deal with the actual complexity of his job.
4. The system must not be dependent for its successful operation on any particular organizational structure and, therefore, must be capable of being used successfully in matrix or even fluid structure.
5. The system must be 'open' in the sense that it will accept omnidirectional communication patterns.
6. The system must not be dependent for its successful operation on the nature of the output generated by a manager, and, therefore, must be capable of being used successfully by managers whose organizational output may range from the concrete to the abstract.
7. The system must not be dependent for its successful operation on a particular philosophy of managerial interaction, and, therefore, must be capable of being used successfully by managers whose approach may range from the completely dictatorial to completely self-effacing, group participation.
8. The system must enable a manager who so wishes to ascertain exactly what output is expected of him and by whom.
9. The system must enable a manager to obtain information on the extent to which he is generating the output which is expected of him.
10. The system must enable a manager who so wishes to explore his actual responsibility, his actual authority, and his actual accountability within the organization.
11. The system must be designed to enable each manager to develop the contents of the system to meet his own particular needs.

Fig. 1.5   Key design criteria for effective management control systems.

demands a system which can help a manager to achieve whatever he decides he will try to achieve.

In this dilemma we can turn to Boulding's hierarchy. Level 8 in the hierarchy is descriptive of self-deciding societal systems, most if not all of which are virtually purposeless in other than closed system terms.

Clearly, to service the needs of level 8 systems nothing will do between 8 and 1, so a level 1 framework, or inert contingent system, it has to be. These choices, once made, produce a set of criteria which can be postulated in a slightly fuller form. They are listed in Figure 1.5.

CONCLUSION

The criteria documented in Figure 1.5 offer both an analytical framework for research into the effectiveness of management control systems currently in use in given organizations, and a specification for the design of new and more effective management control systems. They also, of course, reflect and make public the values of the author! This is particularly appropriate at the start of a book concerned in exploring new perspectives in management control. In the past, the purposes of management control systems and the value systems of those who designed them were at worst hidden, and at best implicit, in the systems which were produced.

It is vital that those values are subject to public debate at a time when it is clearly in everyone's interest to develop more effective systems for helping us 'to control ourselves and other resources'.

REFERENCES

Anthony R.N. (1965) *Planning and Control Systems: A Framework for Analysis*, Division of Research (Boston: Harvard Graduate School of Business).

Anthony R.N., Dearden J. and Vancil, R.F. (1965) *Management Control Systems, Cases and Readings* (Homewood, Ill.: Irwin).

Beer S. (1972) *Brain of the Firm* (London: Allen Lane).

Boulding K.E. (1956) General Systems Theory – The Skeleton of Science, *Management Science*, Vol. 2 No. 2, pp. 197–208.

Dalton G.W. and Lawrence P.R. (1971) *Motivation and Control in Organizations*, (Homewood, Ill.: Irwin).

Giglioni G.B. and Bedeian A.G. (1974) A Conspectus of Management Control Theory: 1900–1972, *Academy of Management Journal*, Vol. 17 No. 2, pp. 292–305.

Helms G. (1975) Texas Instruments OST System for Management Innovation, *Management of Objectives*, Vol. 1 No. 4, pp. 11–19.

Hofstede G.H. (1968) *The Game of Budget Control* (London: Tavistock).

Katz D. and Kahn R.L. (1966) *The Social Psychology of Organisations* (New York: John Wiley).

Lawrence P.R. and Lorsch J.W. (1967a) New Management Job: The Integrator, *Harvard Business Review*, November/December, pp. 142–51.

Lowe E.A. and McInnes J.M. (1971) Control of Socio-economic Organisations: A Rationale for the Design of Management Control Systems (part 1) *Journal of Management Studies*, Vol. 8 No. 2, pp. 213–27.

Machin J.L.J., Stewart R. and Hales C.P. (1981) *Toward Managerial Effectiveness: Applied Research Perspectives on the Managerial Task and its Effective Performance* (Farnborough: Gower).

Machin L.J. and Tai C.H.S. (1983) A Communication-based Methodology for Research into, and Development of, Management Control Systems, *New Perspectives in Management Control*, Chapter 11.

Nelson E.G. and Machin J.L.J. (1976) Management Control: Systems Thinking applied to the Development of a Framework for Empirical Studies, *Journal of Management Studies*, Vol. 13 No. 3, pp. 274–87, October.

Richbell S. (1983) Management Control and Worker Participation in Management, *New Perspectives in Management Control*, Chapter 9.

Tannenbaum A.S. (1968) *Control in Organisations* (New York: McGraw-Hill).

2

Control, organization and accounting

D.T. Otley
University of Lancaster

and

A.J. Berry
Manchester Business School

ABSTRACT

Organization control is a subject of fundamental importance to the designer of accounting control systems. Yet discussions of accounting control tend to take place against a back-cloth of incomplete and outmoded theories of organization and simplistic and authoritarian concepts of control. In this paper, the applicability of a cybernetic model of control to the control of human organizations is explored, with particular reference to the role of accounting information systems. The analysis uncovers a number of issues that require resolution before the model can be applied to accounting information system design. Some directions for research on accounting controls are discussed.

Organization control is a much neglected subject. That is, the study of the ways in which organizations manage and regulate their affairs so as to remain viable and to achieve their chosen ends or objectives has received comparatively little attention. Organizational theorists have tended to emphasize the exercise of power, authority and influence within organizations, and have given little consideration to how viable patterns of behaviour are achieved; those concerned with control theory have tended to ignore the special characteristics of human organizations which distinguish them from other systems, with the consequence that inappropriate control models have been suggested. Accounting researchers have paid scant attention to either body of thought and have tended to make control recommendations in a theoretical vacuum based on incomplete and outmoded ideas of both organization and control. In this paper, cybernetic

Source: Otley, D.T. and Berry, A.J. (1980) *Accounting, Organizations and Society,*
5 (2), pp. 231–44.

concepts of control are applied in an organizational context to the design of accounting information and control systems with the aim of generating a coherent theoretical basis for future accounting research.

'Control' is a term with more different shades and nuances of meaning than almost any other in the English language, with Rathe (1960) listing '57 varieties' of its connotations. The most common idea it suggests is that of dominance; the domination of one individual or group by another through the exercise of power. However, there is a second strand of meaning that emphasizes the idea of regulation and the monitoring of activities. This latter use of 'control' is more in keeping with the original French term meaning 'inspection', and comprises the main connotation in several European languages (Hofstede, 1968). Business usage commonly incorporates both of these ideas, as is indicated by Webster's Dictionary definition:

Application of policies and procedures for directing, regulating and co-ordinating production, administration and other business activities in a way to achieve the objectives of the enterprise.

In this paper the term 'control' will be used in its full cybernetic sense of both monitoring activities and then taking action in order to ensure that desired ends are attained.

CONTROL AND ORGANIZATION

The study of organization and the study of control have been closely interrelated in the sense that control is a central and inescapable feature of all human organizations. For example, McMahon & Ivancevich (1976) state that 'there is practically universal agreement that organization implies control', a view which had received earlier support from Tannenbaum (1968) when he claimed that 'organization without some form of control is impossible'. Despite a degree of ambiguity and lack of definition in both the terms 'organization' and 'control', it is clear that control processes are a fundamental part of organizational activity. Both the exercise of power by individuals and groups and its relationship to the overall maintenance of the organization are central issues.

Indeed, organization can itself be viewed as a control process, occurring when groups of people feel the need to co-operate in order to achieve purposes which require their joint action. Following Etzioni's (1961) definition that 'organizations are social units deliberately constructed to seek specific goals' then it is vital that control over the goal achievement process is established and maintained. However, such a functional definition of organization would not be accepted by all, and, as March & Simon (1958) earlier observed, 'it is easier and probably more useful to give examples of formal organizations than to define the term'. In this way certain features of formal organizations can be made apparent, such as those outlined by Silverman (1970).

Silverman notes that organizations, unlike some other social arrangements, are perceived as *artefacts*, constructed to serve certain purposes (although such initial purposes may subsequently be displaced). As an artefact, the patterning of relationships within an organization will be less taken for granted by organizational participants than that accepted by actors in other social roles. Organizations thus possess an unusual consciousness about their own behaviour, essentially seeking to modify it to meet both internal and external situational demands. This natural concern with the processes of organizational control is an important characteristic of organizational behaviour.

The recognition that goals or purposes can be displaced emphasizes that the control process includes the adaptation of the organization to meet new situations. Control is thus importantly related to purposes, co-ordination and change, a categorization that closely parallels Parson's (1951) description of the functions of an organization as being goal-directed, integrative and adaptive. A full description of organizational control procedures must therefore include an analysis of those procedures which act to maintain viability through goal achievement, those concerned with the co-ordination and integration of differentiated parts, and those which promote adaptation to both internal and external change.

As an example it can be observed that the planning procedures of an organization can be used in ways that serve each of the three functions identified above. Much planning is concerned with goal-setting with a view to subsequent monitoring and control (e.g. budgetary planning and control); other planning activity is concerned mainly with ensuring adequate co-ordination between different departments engaged on parts of a larger task (e.g. project planning); finally, some planning is specifically oriented towards modifying the stance of the organization toward its environment (e.g. corporate strategic planning). Planning is thus an important aspect of organizational control, for as Wildavsky (1973) pithily summarizes, 'planning is future control'. It is unfortunate that everyday usage distinguishes between planning (future-oriented) and control (present-oriented), for the only meaningful distinction is perhaps that where planning uses expectations to trigger action, one type of control (feedback control) uses information on actual occurrences to trigger a reaction. We shall continue therefore to use the term control to cover both the feedback and feedforward (anticipatory) connotations and thus to include both planning and control. The extensive literature on management planning and control systems and on corporate strategy is but one indication of the perceived importance of control processes in economic organizations. However, it is notable that most of this literature pays only the most limited attention to organizational factors.

Control has been defined as the process of ensuring that the organization is adapted to its environment and is pursuing courses of action that will enable it to achieve its purposes. Thus, in order to operate such an organizational level of analysis it is necessary to consider the existence and nature of organizational purposes. Etzioni (1961) has suggested that organizations may be categorized into three main types, based on the degree of commonality that exists between individual and organizational objectives.

Type of organization	Goal alignment	Example
Normative		Religious order Charitable organization Professional bodies 'Crusade' army
Instrumental		Industrial and business organization Travel clubs Mercenary army
Coercive		Prison Slavery Conscript army

Fig. 2.1 Types of involvement in organizations.

In a *normative* organization there is a wide area of agreement on and commitment to organizational goals; in an *instrumental* organization individual goals are neutral towards organizational goals; in a *coercive* organization, many if not most individual goals are opposed by organizational goals, with the goals of a dominant group being taken as those of the organization, as illustrated in Fig. 2.1.

The idea of an objective of an organization is of most obvious use as a conceptual tool in analysing control systems in normative organizations, where overall objectives are, in some sense, an aggregation of individual objectives. In instrumental organizations the predominant pattern is one of an exchange of inducements by the organization to gain contributions from individuals (Barnard, 1938). However, certain basic objectives may still be agreed upon (often for a limited period) as being in the interests of all participants, such as the survival of the organization as a means of providing sought-after inducements. Such an approach has close parallels with a stake-holder view of the enterprise with each stake-holder's interest being maintained at a satisfactory level (Simon, 1957).

Instrumental organizations are likely to be characterized by periods of conflict during which compromise agreements are reached between stake-holder groups as to the distribution of inducements followed by periods of apparent consensus during which the agreements are implemented. Objectives thus have a different nature depending upon whether one is analysing activity during the periods of consensus or during periods of conflict. Finally, a coercive organization can exist only because of the use of power which overwhelms the ability of most of the participants to pursue their own goals. Thus the interests of a majority of the participants are irrelevant to the functioning of this type of organization, although the counter-sources of power and influence open to them should not be overlooked [see for example Mechanic (1962), Roy (1955)].

Although business organizations have been typified as being primarily instrumental in nature this over-simplifies a situation which will differ both within and between organizations. Within a single organization the type of involvement will differ from person to person, with the hierarchical level often being a major factor. For example, those at senior management levels tend to exhibit, at least publicly, a normative involvement, whereas at shop floor level an instrumental involvement is perhaps more typical with elements of a coercive involvement being apparent in certain occupations. Thus a spectrum of forms of control is defined ranging from self-regulation in pursuit of common objectives to the imposition of constraints by a dominant group acting to maintain its own self-interest.

Although organizational theorists have expressed an interest in the study of organization control, they appear to have devoted much of their effort towards studying the impact of 'controls' on organizational participants, rather than in assessing their appropriateness to organizational 'control' [to use Drucker's (1964) distinction]. Control is concerned with overall organizational effectiveness, yet it is in this area that both theoretical and empirical work is weak. Although contingency theories of organizational functioning have received widespread attention recently, it is notable that very few studies follow through their chain of logic to establish the circumstances in which one form of organization is more effective than another, rather than stopping short at observing that it exists (Otley, 1979). Again it is to be expected that those concerned with corporate strategy would have shown an interest in organization control, but the implications of the fact that the subject is concerned with the behaviour of human organizations are precisely those most neglected in this field. Thus the organizational literature, with a few notable exceptions (e.g. Vickers, 1973) has shown little concern with the idea of overall organizational control.

The neglect of control by organizational theorists has been paralleled by the neglect of organization by control theorists. Cybernetics has been defined (Weiner, 1948) as 'the science of communication and control' but relatively little work has been applied to the control of human economic organizations, although that of Beer (1959, 1966, 1973) is an important exception.

Beer (1966) notes that 'our whole concept is naïve, primitive and ridden with an almost retributive idea of causality. Control to most people is a crude process of coercion.' In contrast his analysis begins by assuming that organizational systems are complex, non-deterministic and homeostatic (that is, containing a considerable ability for self-regulation). However, although this approach allows escape from the narrow assumptions of mathematical cybernetics and mechanistic analogies, the replacement analogy is usually that of a living organism [Beer (1973), Katz & Kahn (1966)]. Even then there are considerable difficulties in the transfer of concepts and it is by no means evident that the analogies used have more than very limited validity. Cybernetics has yet to demonstrate that it can provide useful insight into the design of organizational control systems.

It is thus argued that the control literature has used over-simple or poorly validated models of organization and the organizational literature has shown only a limited concern with the idea of overall organizational control. In this paper an attempt is made to bring together these two bodies of work and to review their implications for the design of accounting control systems.

Accounting procedures are one of the few integrative devices in an organization which have an explicit model into which activities may not only be drawn together but also integrated in a quantitative manner. These procedures serve as a control system by providing both a language and a set of procedures for establishing quantitative standards of performance and in measuring actual performance in comparison with such standards. They can thus be highly effective at generating mis-match signals indicating deviations of actual performance from that which was projected, thus fulfilling Simon *et al.* (1954) attention-directing function. However, accounting procedures tend to be much less useful in providing information on which the predictions necessary for control can be made and thus fulfilling Simon's function of problem-solving. The type of variable used in predictive models of organizational performance are traditionally considered outside the scope of the accounting structure for two reasons. Firstly they often require information from sources external to the firm other than financial markets and secondly many of the variables necessary for prediction are difficult to measure in quantitative or objectively verifiable terms. Both reasons have led to the belief amongst accountants that provision of such information lies outside the scope of accounting procedures, although studies of the information requirements of managers indicate that it is often required in practice (e.g. Mintzberg, 1975).

It is becoming evident that there is a need to match accounting information and control procedures to the type of organizations in which they operate. Yet the development of accounting appears to have lagged behind developments in organization theory. The tradition of cost accounting and responsibility accounting is based on bureaucratic and scientific management models of organizations (see for example Parker's (1977) summary critique of the role of control in corporate budgeting). Meanwhile theories of organization have developed through a Human Relations phase into what has been variously described as a Systems view (Kast & Rosenzweig, 1974) or Behavioural science approach (Filley *et al.*, 1976) and currently, the Contingency Theory of organizational design. The accounting literature has lagged significantly behind, with development in this area only beginning to surface [but see Gordon & Miller (1976), Ansari (1977) and Hayes (1977)] possibly as the objections to contingency theory gain strength (Hopwood, 1978). Indeed, a survey of the literature on control systems in organizations (Lawler, 1976) concluded that very little research had been performed on why organizations end up with the control systems they have. In particular, the management control literature has neglected not only organizational factors but also the crucial role of predictive models in the control process.

There is thus a need for the construction of accounting control models appropriately related to organization theory. The value of such an approach has long been recognized, for as Horngren (1972) states:

Ideally, the organization itself and its processes must be thoroughly appraised, understood and altered, if necessary, before an (accounting control) system is constructed. That is the design of a system and the design of an organizational structure are really inseparable and interdependent.

But little attempt has been made to work through the implications of such a statement in the design of control systems for organizations. Accounting controls still appear to be designed on the basis of strictly hierarchical organizations, with well defined responsibilities at each level and where the top of the organization is the focus of all knowledge and control. Although something approximating to such an organization structure may be appropriate where an organization faces a stable technology and environment, it also represents the situation where accounting controls are of least use (Hopwood, 1974).

A body of literature which claims to have tackled the problem of the relevance of accounting to organizational control has done so under the general title of management control and the classic definition of management control is that of Anthony (1965) who defines management control as 'the process by which managers assure that resources are obtained and used effectively and efficiently in the accomplishment of the organization's goals'. Despite its initial plausibility, this definition by which management control is distinguished from strategic planning and operational control raises significant problems. Firstly the problem of defining organizational goals is explained away by relegating it to the realm of strategic planning. Secondly the issue of ensuring that desired activities occur is left to operational control. The purpose of this simplification is to define an area of study which can ignore the great differences in organization that occur due to technology and environment, so as to be able to discover a universal system of management control. Having done this leaves an emaciated concept of management control which may have been valuable as an initial strategy, but is a present embarrassment in implying an over-narrow view of the management control process. A wider view is put forward by Lowe (1971) where he defines a management control system as

a system of organisational information seeking and gathering, accountability and feedback designed to ensure that the enterprise adapts to changes in its substantive environment and that the work behavior of its employees is measured by reference to a set of operational sub-goals (which conform with overall objectives) so that the discrepancy between the two can be reconciled and corrected for.

Although accounting research is only beginning to address the issues raised by such a definition, it is now clear that such problems are a proper focus of attention and that attempts are now being made to implement Horngren's exhortation [e.g. Waterhouse & Tiessen (1978), and Hedberg & Jönsson (1978)].

The remainder of this paper is addressed to examining some of the issues that are raised when ideas of control which stem from a cybernetic approach are applied to human organizations and a consideration of their implications for the design of accounting systems.

A MODEL OF THE CONTROL PROCESS

Cybernetic approaches such as those of Ashby (1956) and Beer (1973) have a quite different focus to those of the organization theorists. The cyberneticians are primarily concerned with inner structures of variety, probability and logic which may be used to characterize organizations. They tend to accept the risk of reifying their constructs in the search for a widely applicable generality. For example the nine levels of the General Hierarchy of Systems of Bertalanffy (1956) and Boulding (1956) are derived from an implicit distinction of complexity. These nine levels are:

1. static frameworks
2. dynamic systems with pre-determined motions
3. closed loop control or cybernetic systems
4. homeostatic systems, such as biological cells
5. the living plant
6. animals
7. man
8. organizations
9. transcendental systems

The mechanistic or engineering control theory which was developed for systems of levels 2 and 3 is not simply transferable to the higher levels, not only because of the difference in complexity of the levels but also because of the shifting nature of the systems both in regard to the issue of probability and the values underlying risk preferences and choices. However, to argue that ideas are not simply transferable does not mean that they are irrelevant. The cybernetic tradition has produced a general definition of control (Tocher, 1970, 1976) which possesses some interesting and useful properties when applied to the control of organizations.

It may be deduced from Tocher's definition that at least four necessary conditions must be satisfied before a process can be said to be controlled. These state that there must exist:

1. an objective for the system being controlled
2. a means of measuring results along the dimensions defined by the objective
3. a predictive model of the system being controlled
4. a choice of relevant alternative actions available to the controller

A control system containing these elements is shown in Fig. 2.2, annotated with Vickers' (1967) terminology.

In this model the four necessary conditions for control are articulated. Firstly control can only exist when knowledge of outcomes is available; with no feedback on actual performance, improvement (and even

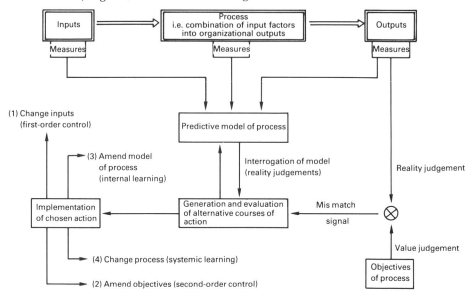

Fig. 2.2   Outline scheme of necessary conditions for a controlled process.

continued success in changing conditions) is possible only by chance. However, such knowledge of the true state of the real world is not always easy to come by and is called by Vickers the making of a 'reality judgement'. Secondly, control requires an objective; without an aim, activity can be described only as aimless. This process of deciding upon appropriate directions for activity is essentially that of making value judgements. Thirdly, having compared actual and desired outcomes and generated a mis-match signal by noting any discrepancy between the two, a control action has to be determined. This requires a predictive model of the process being controlled, that is, a means of forecasting the likely outcomes of various alternative courses of action. To the extent that such a model is non-existent or defective, then control is impossible and attempted control actions may well be counter-productive. It is noteworthy that many elementary descriptions of control processes completely omit the central position of predictive models. Finally, a selected action requires to be implemented. This may do one or more of four things. It may adjust the system inputs (first-order control); it may alter system objectives (second-order control); it may amend the predictive model on the basis of past experience (internal learning) and it may change the nature of the process itself (systemic learning).

   Such a conception of control is recursive in nature. That is, it may be applied to any level of system and therefore to any sub-system within an overall system. It may be used to analyse an individual's control of his own activities, a group of people controlling each other's behaviour (social control), an organization controlling its internal activities in response to the environment in which it operates (organizational control) or a society controlling the activities of organizations, groups and individuals within it (societal or governmental control), although the specific features of the model will obviously differ for each level of resolution. At each of the higher levels, one immediately obvious problem of control is that for each control action the response of sub-systems is often likely to be one of minimizing the effects of the control action, as each self-controlling sub-system adapts its behaviour so as to continue to achieve and modify its own objectives. There is thus no assumption of consensus in using such a control model; it may be used to examine situations of conflict.

Perhaps the most fundamental problem that is faced in transferring such a cybernetic or homeostatic model of control to an organizational level of analysis is the apparently inevitable division of labour between controllers and those who are controlled, that is the distinction between the dominator and the dominated. Even when one separates out the control exercised within organizations by managers as an interest group in their own right (and a powerful one by reason of their access to information and power over the distribution of resources and rewards), the primary function ascribed to the task of management is that of organization control. That is, their role is to ensure that the organization continues to cohere in a form that keeps all interested parties satisfied enough to continue to support the organization's activities.

In a normative organization the task of management is not primarily one of dominance, rather it is one of encouraging self-regulation; in an instrumental organization limited or partial authority is ceded to management to legitimize its control actions; in a coercive organization control rests primarily on dominance. The middle ground of the business organization is thus one where many differing styles of control might be expected to be observed.

The prior discussion has proceeded along very general lines and has viewed the organizational control process as a correlate of organization *per se*, without considering the locus and form of the control function. Much discussion of control in an organizational context has either taken the position of a particular agency or interest group (e.g. workers' control as against owners' or managers' control) or has concentrated on the effects of particular 'controls' on various groups within the organization. In business organizations authority and influence (Tannenbaum *et al.*, 1974) are a function of participants' expectations and national culture. In the typical western European and American business organization, the stereotype of which is to be found in many accountancy text books, the control function is located at the top of the hierarchy. This position is reinforced in the accounting literature with its normative assertions of profit maximization and the present legal position which establishes a bias in favour of the providers of capital (Nichols and Beynon, 1977). There is some evidence that this balance of power might be shifted with the advent of increased worker participation and of changes such as the introduction of two-tier boards. However, the mere existence of any group charged with the responsibility of organizational control seems to lead to its perceived superiority over other organizational participants (although this does not follow absolutely as, for example, hospital administrators are not usually viewed as the superiors of consultants). Such a differentiation of status is reinforced by the nature of control decisions. A control decision requires that organizational participants take actions other than those which they would have taken in the absence of the control decision (for otherwise it would not be necessary to take an explicit decision). These actions, although designed to lead to the overall good, may not be aligned with the immediate interests of those who have to implement them. On the assumption that the original actions were in their own best interests, then the control instruction is likely to reduce the benefits they receive from the organization. Control in general, and the controllers in particular are likely to be unpopular, and methods of clarifying the connection between control activities and overall organizational welfare are designed to reduce this unpopularity.

Accounting and accountants are very much caught up in the process of controlling the behaviour of others, as they constitute an agency of what Lowe & Tinker (1978) infelicitously term the 'central authority'. Indeed, many of the findings of the behavioural studies of the role of accounting and accountants in relation to managers stem from the interaction of their mutual roles. Because of these factors the integration of accounting controls into the process of overall organizational control is subject to severe limitations. We now turn to an examination of the problems posed by such an integration, through a consideration of the four necessary conditions for control derived in this section.

APPLICATION TO ORGANIZATIONAL CONTROL

In the original development of his control framework Tocher (1970) was evidently thinking in terms of the control of a system by an external agency, and it is no doubt appropriate to analyse the control of organizations from this point of view (e.g. the control of business organizations by governmental actions). However, this paper is concerned with a different level of resolution, namely the self-control exerted by organizations themselves so that they may better achieve their objectives in the face of external (and internal) circumstances. It is of interest to note that in his subsequent discussion Tocher (1976) observes that attempts were made to apply his concepts in situations where no external agency was apparent. That is, we are considering a self-regulating system where control is exercised by agencies within the system itself. Human organizations evidently exhibit features of self-regulation and this section is concerned with examining the applicability of the four necessary conditions for a controlled system in self-regulating economic organizations.

Objectives

The very idea of an objective for an organization as distinct from the objectives of the individuals involved is problematic (Simon, 1964). As Arrow (1951), following a long sociological tradition, has pointed out, even if it can be assumed that individuals have well-defined and transitive preferences there is no non-arbitrary method of deriving a group preference function from the individual preferences. A decision can, of course, be made but different decision rules give different results. Although the application of utility theory may seem appropriate, it is still necessary to combine inter-personal utilities and there is no accepted method of doing this. Thus, although use of a decision rule will give a result, such a result is essentially arbitrary, and depends for its effectiveness on its acceptance by those involved. More realistically, in such a situation, political bargaining and negotiation will occur, and a process of coalition forming and breaking takes place until the issue is resolved by the application of an accepted decision rule, be it managerial decree or democratic vote.

The consequence for the analysis of control is that considerable care has to be taken in defining objectives and assessing their status. Logically one is comparing benefits given to disparate groups of people and the satisfactions that are given by these benefits. Each group is in a different bargaining position with respect to changes and the task of the control procedures is to arrange a balance between the rewards given to competing interest groups in a changing environment. To the extent that involvement is instrumental rather than normative, control may be achieved in part by the design of reward structures which influence individuals to act in an agreed manner by pursuing their own self-interest. That is the control of the instrumental organization is achieved by means of processes within the organization which structure the distribution of valued rewards in return for compliance.

To the extent that an instrumental organization can be said to have objectives, they may be characterized as multiple, partially conflicting and subject to change in response to environmental changes. These objectives are perhaps better regarded as constraints defining a feasible region for activities (Simon, 1964). As objectives or constraints change over time so then will the feasible region change. The task of the control process is to keep actual activity within such a dynamic feasible region; that is to keep each individual and interest group satisfied enough to continue to provide their necessary support towards ensuring that appropriate activities are carried out.

Accounting systems play a significant role in both the process of objective formulation and of identifying feasible regions for organizational activity. For example, budgetary standards and targets often represent the outcome of bargaining processes where agreed expectations are negotiated. In addition, the master budget itself may be treated as an organizational model (admittedly of a very simple kind) with which the effects of alternative courses of action are evaluated. Accounting information is itself of use in the bargaining process and the provision of such information to representatives of various interest groups (e.g. trade union officials, customers on certain types of contract) is part of the negotiation activity. For example, trade unions now often use accounting information to define a company's 'ability to pay', which is their assessment of one boundary of the feasible region.

Whatever approach is adopted, it is necessary to engage with the issue of authority in organizations. As Berry (1979) has argued, accounting thrives in a culture of dependence, and that culture can be powerfully destructive. The concept of a central authority as a locus of control as developed by Lowe & Tinker (1978) is not necessarily embedded in a social hierarchy; it can be a meeting of a group of members and in this sense represent a focus of mutual responsibility. There is no doubt that the role of controller is immensely powerful, which gives all the more reason to attempt to ensure that those who fulfil such a role are held accountable to those whom they control.

Predictive models

The major purpose of the predictive model is to enable answers to questions of the form: if a certain course of action is taken, then what consequences will follow; in particular, how will the achievement of objectives or avoidance of constraints be affected? Two features of predictive models for the behaviour of organizations are immediately apparent. Firstly the available models are usually imprecise and inaccurate so that predictions made from them are likely to be at odds with actual events. Because of this, actions designed to assist control may actually turn out to hinder it because of unanticipated consequences [Forrester (1961) simulates many such systems]. When relevant reality is only imperfectly modelled it may be wise to proceed in small, incremental steps where some degree of prediction is possible, rather than by making radical changes whose effect is largely unpredictable [Lindblom (1959); Wildavsky (1973)]. Secondly within organizations there are usually multiple and partially conflicting predictive models rather than a single holistic model (e.g. separate models relating to employment of labour, production processes, marketing and finance). This situation is due to both a relatively undeveloped understanding which generates small partial models as a first step and also to the fact that organizations consist of individuals in roles, each of whom will apply his own models, insights and understandings. In addition one also finds the use of over-simple but apparently general models, often tinged with an ideological basis (e.g. the perfectly competitive economic model), in circumstances where the model's fit with reality is poor.

It is important to consider how models might be improved. If an organization remains in control by taking only those actions where reasonable prediction is possible, all is well in the short-term. However, the wider applicability of the model may need to be tested, especially as time horizons lengthen and the range of variables to be considered is extended. By taking actions whose outcomes are not as accurately predictable, the range of applicability of the model can be examined. The stimulus to learn about the model and its applicability takes place by detecting differences between expected outcomes and actual outcomes (i.e. making mistakes).

While there is clearly a role for a development activity on models the existence of environmental uncertainty must preclude an exact specification. There is again a close parallel here between the design of control processes and the design of organizations. Bureaucratic organizations can lead to efficient performance of a well specified task in a stable environment, but such organizations cope poorly with unexpected changes; organismic organizations are relatively inefficient for well specified tasks but have a greater adaptive capacity (Burns & Stalker, 1961). This insight may be extended to the models in a control process. The control model must evolve in use with due attention to the problems of immediate goal attainment (efficiency) and the attainment of future gaols (adaptation and experimentation). It is ironic that those organizations which most need to experiment and improve their adaptive capability are those where present circumstances define such necessities as luxuries. [Wildavsky (1975) gives a parallel from national planning and budgeting.]

In attaining overall organization control, the predictive model used by the control system must include a representation of the models used by individuals and groups within the organization who are attempting to control outcomes to their own advantage. For in order to predict the consequences of a given action, it is necessary to predict how relevant others will seek to affect events. In turn, the models used by the others concerned will include models of the behaviour of the organizational control system. Thus part of the difficulty in attaining overall organizational control is the interdependent nature of the models used where each attempts to include the other. (Wage bargaining negotiations provide a vivid example of this phenomenon as does the process of bias and counter-bias in the setting of budgets.)

The implications for accounting are clear enough. An accounting or financial model of an organization is only partial and contains insufficient variety for organizational control. However, the accounting model is important and necessary even though insufficient; necessary because it relates to a relevant environment, insufficient because the range of variables included is only partial and because other relevant environments are not considered. This is not to say development and improvement cannot take place; indeed, the provision of appropriate information to allow prediction of a wider range of relevant outcomes is perhaps the most important extension of an organization's accounting system that can be envisaged. In a similar vein, Lowe (1971) concludes that

accountants need not be faint of heart for they surely possess a good basis (perhaps the only one) for the development of an integrated management control (and information) system provided they extend their thinking in the application of that powerful tool – accounting method.

This implies that the accountant must be prepared to include within his remit the collection of information concerning a far wider range of variables than has traditionally been the case, and to develop the necessary skills for collecting such information.

Measures

Two distinct sets of variables require measurement. Firstly activity requires to be monitored along those dimensions defined as objectives. Thus, for example, if long-run survival requires the generation of a certain level of profitability then this requires measurement and comparison with the defined standard. Secondly, as the predictive models used contain an array of variables which are necessary to predict behaviour and performance, these predictor variables must also be measured.

Accounting procedures have traditionally been designed in response to the need for the first kind of measurement. Thus they stress the components of objective-oriented measures such as production, cost and profit. Although influenced heavily by shareholder objectives, they are compatible with measuring partial objective achievement for other groups (e.g. price for customers; wages for employees etc.). Indeed, it may be argued that certain income measures, for example, residual income, are surrogates for measures of overall enterprise viability, rather than serving the interests of any particular stakeholder group (Emmanuel & Otley, 1976). But such measures possess little predictive power. The second purpose is partially served by systems which allow causes for deviations from standard to be deduced (e.g. the calculation of cost accounting variances), but even these systems have very limited predictive ability.

One particular difficulty in providing information for predictive models is that they are concerned both with processes internal to an organization and with the interaction between an organization and its environment. Thus factors of interest will include external circumstances as well as internal responses. It would seem that most organizations are less well developed in formally monitoring their external environment than their internal state, although there is evidence that informal networks carry some information about external phenomena.[1] But even internally some variables (e.g. cost) are better dealt with than others (e.g. job satisfaction).

Thus the variables that it is necessary to measure for an effective set of processes are those defined by the objectives of the controlled process and those utilized in the predictive model. It appears that relatively little attention has been paid to the development of information systems to serve the needs of predictive models in contrast to the measurement of objective-oriented factors. This may be a further reason for the often observed lack of use of many management information systems (Mintzberg, 1975). The typical structure of accounting procedures is such as to leave aside the required measures of environment. Whether accounting should be redefined to include such measures or whether its claims should be re-assessed is a matter that will be taken up in the final section.

Choice of action

A final requirement for control is that a choice of action is available. If no relevant inputs to a system can be changed then control cannot be exer-

[1] Management Control Research Project Reports 1–4, Manchester Business School.

cised. Four different types of action can be distinguished any, or all, of which can be implemented. Firstly there are actions which change the inputs to the system being controlled and cause its behaviour to alter (i.e. first-order control). Secondly there are actions which change the objectives, or at least the level of the standards which it is deemed necessary to reach (i.e. second-order control). Thirdly there are actions which amend the predictive model of the system being controlled and the measurement and communication processes associated with it; this may be described as internal learning. Fourthly there are actions which change the system itself and hence its inputs, outputs and associated predictive models; this may be described as adaptation or systemic learning.

An organization acts only by way of the actions of the individuals who comprise it. Thus for organizational control to be effective, not only must feasible control actions be possible but individuals must also be persuaded to implement the required actions. At a minimum this requires the communication of the desired action or of other information from which an appropriate action may be deduced. Such communication alone may be sufficient in normative organizations where the goal alignment of individuals may produce sufficient motivation to act; in instrumental or coercive organizations some reward or penalty structure is likely to be required. Finally, the individual who is in a position to know what needs to be done, and who is motivated to take action, must have access to adequate resources to implement the requisite action.

The type of information that indicates control actions are necessary (i.e. attention-directing information) does not usually indicate what actions should be taken (i.e. it does not assist with problem-solving). As well as an innovative input which can suggest apt courses of action, a predictive model is necessary in order to evaluate the likely outcomes of proposed alternative actions. It is evident yet again that without prediction there is no control, and that a predictive model must contain variables outside the traditional scope of accounting systems.

CONCLUSIONS

Formal organizations continue to cohere only when the benefits they yield to each individual and group connected with them exceed the contributions to the organization required from them and when this net balance of benefits exceeds what is perceived to be available elsewhere when transition costs are taken into account. It is therefore in the interests of organizational participants to establish procedures for organizational control which are designed to help ensure that such benefits continue to be produced, notwithstanding the sectional interest of each participant to influence the distribution of benefits in his own favour. Control procedures are thus essential features of organizations.

However, it has been noted when the control process is considered at an organizational level of analysis, there are significant weaknesses in the ability of organizations to regulate their own behaviour on each of the four major dimensions identified. Firstly, organizational objectives are often vague, ambiguous and change with time. They are often set by ill-defined processes, and are multiple and partially conflicting. In addition they are congruent to only a varying extent with the objectives of various interest groups associated with the organization. Secondly, in this situation, measures of achievement are possible only in correspondingly vague and often subjective terms. Thirdly, predictive models of organizational behaviour are partial and unreliable, and furthermore different models may be held by different participants. Finally, the ability to act is highly constrained for most groups of participants, including the so-called 'controllers', by virtue of the limited range of possible actions open to them. A fundamental problem is that there is still a need for the overall regulation of the organization, although the complexity and uncertainty inherent within it may make the possibility of control very limited. In addition, the nature of control actions is such that they are perceived as undesirable in relation to the immediate interests of at least some participants. The task of the control procedures is therefore to balance the differing requirements of the various parties associated with the well-being of the enterprise, to ensure the continued satisfaction of those requirements. The strategies available for the design of control procedures should be studied in this light.

IMPLICATIONS FOR ACCOUNTING RESEARCH

The limitations shown up by this examination of the role of accounting information in organizational control are limitations caused by a lack of variety in the accounting system so that it in no way matches the complexity of the organization being controlled. However, no control system will ever be able to match the variety of an organization unless it is of an equal complexity itself (e.g. in the way that a football team may be 'controlled' by an equally skilful team of opponents). Control in a full cybernetic sense will never be achieved in the context of a human organization, although this is not to deny that existing techniques of attempting to gain control cannot be improved. However, the contrast between approaches to control in organization theory, cybernetics and accounting is such as to raise the fundamental question of the usefulness of an approach to control which has such limitations. By means of a somewhat different argument Hofstede (1975) came to the conclusion that the philosophy of management control (by which he meant the tradition following Anthony and other authors who concentrate on accounting control) was impoverished.

But we cannot leave the matter there, for in the preceding analysis it has been recognized that accounting at least provides an appropriate language for examining the relationship between an organization and its financial environment. What is at issue is whether there is an holistic approach to organizational control and, if so, whether accounting models provide an appropriate framework for their development. It is our belief that it is important to attempt to develop such an holistic approach, for the control of such important artefacts as human organizations is of vital importance to the welfare of society. Further, although accounting control procedures are admittedly inadequate for the task, they nevertheless appear to provide the best framework that is currently available. This final section therefore considers some ways forward in improving accounting systems so that they may better serve their control function.

There has been a tendency in the literature of management science and financial management, if not in practice, towards the development of elegant mathematical models for non-problems against the development of heuristics or crude models for real problems. The insistence upon an objective function to be optimized is perhaps symptomatic of this malaise. It would appear to be a logical and positive extension to the role of the academic accountant for him to be concerned with the construction of predictive models incorporating a wider range of variables than has traditionally been the case. In such a role he would concern himself with the definition and measurement of those variables which are of signficance in influencing the successful operation of an organization, and with the design of procedures to report this information to those who can take action based upon it. This is not intended to replace the financial control role of accountants, but to be additional and complementary to it.

The central issues involved in the control of organizations are of great importance and insights from a variety of academic disciplines are essential in developing improved understanding. A number of approaches are possible. Firstly following Caplan (1966) it would be possible to analyse the assumptions of modern (contingent) organization theory and to compare these with the assumptions made in accounting theory and practice, noting that the latter two may well differ. To some extent this work has begun, but it requires extension into the re-working of the design of accounting structures so that they 'fit' better the requirements of organizations. Secondly it might be appropriate to neglect the current accounting framework as being so far removed from the issue of interest as to make it inappropriate. Such a departure would require an attempt to synthesize an integrated theory of organizational control from cybernetics, general systems theory and organization theory. [Amey (1979) makes a partial start to such an endeavour.] However, even if this were to be successful in terms of providing a tidy and perceptive theoretical structure there would be considerable problems of application to particular organizational control issues. A third approach would be to leave the problem of theoretical synthesis unresolved and to concentrate on understanding how specific organizations actually go about controlling their activities. Whilst recognizing that no observation is value- or theory-free this approach might take such limited theory as has been developed and demand that the researcher develop explanations for phenomena which actually occur. This would have the advantage of not prejudging the role and relevance of accounting control procedures.

Following the argument of this paper, a sensible choice between alternative courses of action requires a predictive model of outcomes. In terms of the effectiveness of alternative research strategies to build improved theories of organizational control, we have little knowledge of the likely outcomes. The little we have suggests that the third approach, which concentrates on the structured and intensive observation of the operation of the whole range of control activities undertaken by specific organizations, offers the most hope of being fruitful in the long term.

ACKNOWLEDGEMENTS

An early version of this paper under the title 'Control and Organization' was presented at the Workshop 'Information and Control Systems' held at the European Institute for Advanced Studies in Management, Brussels, September 1977.

REFERENCES

Amey, L.R., *Budget Planning and Control Systems* (London: Pitman, 1979).

Ansari, S.L., An Integrated Approach to Control Systems Design, *Accounting, Organizations and Society* (1977), pp. 101–112.

Anthony, R.N., *Planning and Control Systems: A Framework for Analysis* (Boston, Mass.: Graduate School of Business Administration, Harvard University, 1965).

Arrow, K.J., *Social Choice and Individual Values* (New York: Wiley, 1951).

Ashby, W.R., *An Introduction to Cybernetics* (London: Chapman and Hall, 1956).

Barnard, C., *The Functions of the Executive* (Cambridge, Harvard University Press, 1938).

Beer, S., *Cybernetics and Management* (London: E.U.P., 1959).

Beer, S., *Decision and Control* (New York: Wiley, 1966).

Beer, S., *Brain of the Firm* (Harmondsworth, Middx.: Allen Lane, 1973).

Berry, A.J., Policy, Accounting and the Problem of Order, *Personnel Review* (1979).

von Bertalanffy, L., General System Theory, *General Systems, Yearbook of the Society for the Advancement of General System Theory* (1956), pp. 1–10.

Boulding, K.E., General Systems Theory: The Skeleton of Science, *General Systems Yearbook of the Society for the Advancement of General System Theory* (1956), pp. 11–17.

Burns, T. & Stalker, G.M., *The Management of Innovation* (London: Tavistock, 1961).

Caplan, E.H., Behavioural Assumptions of Management Accounting, *Accounting Review* (1966), pp. 496–509.

Drucker, P., Control, Controls and Management, in Bonini, C.P., *et al.*, *Management Controls: New Directions in Basis Research* (New York: McGraw-Hill, 1964).

Emmanuel, C.R. & Otley, D.T., The Usefulness of Residual Income, *Journal of Business Finance and Accounting* (Winter, 1976), pp. 43–51.

Etzioni, A., *A Comparative Analysis of Complex Organisations* (New York: Free Press, 1961).

Filley, A.C., House, R.J. & Kerr, S., *Managerial Process and Organizational Behavior* (2nd ed.; Glenview, Illinois: Scott, Foresman and Co., 1976).

Forrester, J.W., *Industrial Dynamics* (Cambridge, Mass.: M.I.T. Press, 1961).

Gordon, L.A. & Miller, D., A Contingency Framework for the Design of Accounting Information Systems, *Accounting, Organizations and Society* (1976), pp. 59–69.

Hayes, D.C., The Contingency Theory of Managerial Accounting, *Accounting Review* (January, 1977), pp. 22–39.

Hedberg, B. & Jönsson, S., Designing Semi-confusing Information Systems for Organisations in Changing Environments, *Accounting, Organizations and Society* (1978), pp. 47–64.

Hofstede, G., *The Game of Budget Control* (London: Tavistock, 1968).

Hofstede, G., The Poverty of Management Control Philosophy, Working Paper 75–44 of the European Institute of Advanced Studies in Management, Brussels, December 1975.

Hopwood, A.G., *Accounting and Human Behaviour* (London: Haymarket Publishing, 1974).

Hopwood, A.G., Towards an Organisational Perspective for the Study of Accounting and Information Systems, *Accounting, Organizations and Society* (1978), pp. 3–13.

Horngren, C.T., *Cost Accounting: A Managerial Emphasis* (3rd edition; Englewood Cliffs, N.J.: Prentice-Hall, 1972).

Katz, D. & Kahn, R.L., *The Social Psychology of Organisations* (New York: Wiley, 1966).

Kast, F.E. & Rosenzweig, J.E., *Organization and Management: A Systems Approach* (2nd edition; New York: McGraw-Hill, 1974).

Lawler, E.E., Control Systems in Organizations, in Dunnette, M.D. (ed.), *Handbook of Industrial and Organization* (Rand-McNally, 1976).

Lindblom, C.E., The Science of 'Muddling Through', *Public Administration Review* (Spring, 1959), pp. 79–88.

Lowe, E.A., On the Idea of a Management Control System, *Journal of Management Studies* (February, 1971), pp. 1–12.

Lowe, E.A. & Tinker, A., Some Empirical Evidence related to the case of the Superordinate Integrator, *Journal of Management Studies* (February, 1978), pp. 86–105.

McMahon, J.T. & Ivancevich, J.M., A Study of Control in a Manufacturing Organization: Managers and Nonmanagers, *Administrative Science Quarterly* (March, 1976), pp. 66–83.

March, J.G. & Simon, H., *Organizations* (New York: Wiley, 1958).

Mechanic, D., Sources of Power of Lower Participants in Complex Organisations, *Administrative Science Quarterly* (1962), pp. 349–364.

Mintzberg, H., *Impediments to the Use of Management Information* (New York: N.A.A., 1975).

Nichols, T. & Beynon, H., *Living with Capitalism* (London: Routledge and Kegan Paul, 1977).

Otley, D.T., Towards a contingency theory of management accounting: a critical assessment, Accounting Research Workshop Papers, University of Glasgow, May 1979.

Parker, L., A Reassessment of the Role of Control in Corporate Budgeting, *Accounting and Business Research* (Spring 1977), pp. 135–143.

Parsons, T., *The Social System* (New York: Free Press, 1951).

Rathe, A.W., Management Controls in Business, in Malcolm, D.G. and Rowe, A.J. (eds.), *Management Control Systems* (New York: Wiley, 1960).

Roy, D., Efficiency and the 'Fix': Informal Intergroup Relations in a Piecework Machine Shop, *American Journal of Sociology* (1955), pp. 255–266.

Silverman, D., *The Theory of Organisations* (London: Heinemann, 1970).

Simon, H. *et al.*, *Centralisation versus Decentralisation in the Controllers' Department* (New York: Controllership Foundation, 1954).

Simon, H., *Administrative Behaviour* (2nd edition; New York: Macmillan, 1957).

Simon, H., On the Concept of an Organisational Goal, *Administrative Science Quarterly* (June, 1964), pp. 1–22.

Tannenbaum, A.S., *Control in Organisations* (New York: McGraw-Hill, 1968).

Tannenbaum, A.S., Kaveic, B., Rosner, M., Vianello, M. & Weiser, G., *Hierarchy in Organisations* (San Francisco: Jossey-Bass, 1974).

Tocher, K., Control, *Operational Research Quarterly* (June, 1970), pp. 159–180.

Tocher, K., Notes for Discussion on 'Control', *Operational Research Quarterly* (1976), pp. 231–239.

Vickers, G., *Towards a Sociology of Management* (London: Chapman and Hall, 1967).

Vickers, G., *Making Institutions Work* (London: Associated Business Programmes, 1973).

Waterhouse, J.H. & Tiessen, P., A Contingency Framework for Management Accounting Systems Research, *Accounting, Organizations and Society* (1978), pp. 65–76.

Weiner, N., *Cybernetics* (Cambridge, Mass.: M.I.T. Press, 1948).

Wildavsky, A., If Planning is Everything Maybe Its Nothing, *Policy Sciences* (1973), pp. 127–153.

Wildavsky, A., *Budgeting: A Comparative Theory of the Budgetary Process* (Boston: Little, Brown and Co., 1975).

3

Stability, control and choice

G. Vickers

I am grateful to those who have done me the honour of asking me to give this address. I am also diffident, for I am conscious of being a stranger to the disciplines of the Faculty which has invited me. I approach my subject not as a scientist but as a layman, turning to science in search of the tools which he needs for his work.

These tools include abstract concepts. Faculties of applied science, such as the one to which I owe my presence here, testify to the unity of thought which links the answering of practical questions with the pursuit of abstract enquiries. So I need not apologize for giving an abstract title to an enquiry into a practical problem.

The problem is briefly this. Engineers organize physical processes; they also organize the productive activities of men. They have recently made great strides in their knowledge of how to organize physical processes so as to be self-regulating. They can build controls which will maintain the operations of a factory or the temperature of a building or the course and stability of an aircraft. The result of these arrangements is that the assembly does what the situation requires without being pushed about by some higher authority. Now this is exactly what engineers in their capacity of managers want to achieve in organizing people. So it is worth enquiring whether what they learn as engineers can help them as managers.

On the face of it, the problems are very similar. The plant manager, for example, has the familiar problem of maintaining stocks of materials at a level high enough to prevent any hold-up in production, yet not so high as to lock up capital needlessly or involve an unacceptable risk if prices drop. This is the problem of maintaining stable volume or pressure with a variable throughout, which, as an engineer, he has encountered dozens of times in the control of physical processes; and it is soluble in the same way. A fall or rise in the stock of this or that below or above appointed limits must set buyers buying or stop them buying as surely as a Watts governor opens or closes a value.

Source: Vickers, G. (1967), in *Towards a Sociology of Management* (Chapman and Hall), pp. 103–21.

As a general manager, the engineer looks outward at an environment of largely unpredictable and uncontrollable variables – customers, suppliers, competitors, prices, tariffs, freight rates; and he looks inward at his undertaking, a complex, dynamic whole, surviving only by adjustment to forces which it cannot modify; and he sees problems very like those which he had to solve when he was designing automatic pilots for aircraft. The only apparent difference here, as in the control of the inventory, is that the critical elements which open or shut, act or remain inactive, say 'yes' or 'no', are not cogs or holes in cards or electronic valves or what not but – men.

Now the sad thing is that, as our engineer progresses up the ladder of authority, reputation, salary and the other indices of success, he almost certainly becomes, as a controller, progressively less successful. As a plant manager, he will probably not be able, at least in my country, to keep the inventory down to the prescribed limits without periodically using his personal authority; though of all the processes which he controls that would seem as easy as any to make 'automatic'. There will be days when he longs to be back in the research and development department, designing electronic assemblies out of completely reliable units, endowing each with as much discretion as he wishes and no more and confident that each will do what is expected of it, not now and then or nearly always but always. On such days he will regard his fellow men as faulty circuits, unpunchable cards – or worse.

This is likely to be a mistake. In the days when our minds were dominated by mechanical analogies, industry was inclined to think of men as cogs in a machine. It is probably no less misleading to think of them as relays. Happily, science today is less prone to seek a lowest common denominator for all that it observes.

Physics nowadays is concerned with energy rather than with matter, with form rather than substance, with organization rather than with structure, with process rather than with state. The difference between the inorganic and the organic world seems to be largely the difference between relatively closed and open energy systems. The whole world of experience begins to look like a hierarchy of systems; and the main task of science to formulate the laws by which these systems maintain themselves and by which they interact. These changes seem to me to open the way to a better relationship between physics, biology, psychology and the social sciences, that is, between the concepts which we use in trying to understand the processes of matter, of life, of mind and of society. [1]

There is no reason to suppose that the laws of organization which account for the atom and the star will be sufficient to account for the cell and the elephant, let alone the human being and the Ontario Hydro-Electric Power Commission. On the contrary, there is every reason to think that these new forms have come into being through the emergence of new capacities for self-organization. So I am by no means saying that the empire of physics is on the way to absorb the sciences of life and mind. I am only expressing the belief that we are not far from developing new concepts which may be common to the natural sciences and the humanities. Should this prove true, it would simplify the education of engineers, who must somehow learn to span the whole gamut.

So I propose first to look very sketchily at the main levels of organization which we can discern, to see whether they help us to understand the organizations which we ourselves create. Then I will examine the principles which we use in the control of physical processes, to see what bearing they have on the control of organizations. Then I will roughly chart what seems to be the field where choice is not effectively governed by control.

We have been accustomed to think of things as existing, apart from what they do – as a motor car remains a motor car, whether in the garage or on the road. It seems that this is a bad habit. An atom can only be described in terms of activity; and this is equally true of an organism and an organization. Asking about any such thing, 'What is it?', we must divide the question into two to get a useful answer. We must ask, 'How does it hold together?' and 'How does it interact with its environment?' This, incidentally, seems to me to be one of those fruitful concepts which may help to provide sciences at present disparate with a common approach.

The answers will overlap and they will not be simple; for we shall find that, just as the entity we are examining is an integration of activities rather than an assembly of parts, so it is itself more or less integrated into a larger whole. Both scientists and philosophers are concerned to find a better way to represent to ourselves this hierarchy of overlapping systems, within which the things we recognize have both different kinds and different degrees of 'wholeness'. Until they succeed, we can use only a few broad distinctions.

I have not yet seen Niagara; but I understand that, when I do, I shall certainly regard it as 'something'. I shall remember it and recognize it again. This striking and enduring form, this 'steady state', is in substance as transient as a flame. If I ask a scientist, 'What is it?' he will explain it to me in terms of the shape of the river bed, itself partly the work of the river and in terms of the laws which govern the movements and interactions of molecules of water.

But if I ask him what a molecule of water is, he will describe a system of atoms in equilibrium, a closed system, held together by forces of a different order. And if I lead him to discourse on molecular organization in general, he will perplex me with crystals and viruses and arrive in no time at the cell, which organizes itself in a different way and has developed some strikingly new forms of behaviour. It is an open system, maintaining itself by constant interchange with its environment; it is excitable; it grows, reproduces itself, repairs itself, is capable of decay. It has all the characteristics of the organic world.

We have already encountered three types of organization – closed systems; systems like Niagara, which are open to the exchange of matter and energy with their surround; and systems which, even at the cellular level, are also open to information. It is strange that we still have no accepted words to distinguish the last two; still less to distinguish a hierarchy of 'dynamic-information' systems according to their progressive capacity for communication. If we regard these systems as an ascending order, we must remember that higher entities are those which are capable of higher *as well as* lower types of organization. Men in a crowd often behave like water drops; but water drops never behave like men. [2]

As we go up the scale of multi-cellular organisms we notice a very rapid growth in the scale of internal relations and a much slower growth in external relations.

External relations are rudimentary in creatures which have not yet got a central nervous system. You really need a brain to make anything of external relations – and even then the results are not always much to be proud of. But internal relations are another matter altogether. Creatures with no nervous system at all can elaborate faultlessly from a single cell a differentiated, self-maintaining structure which needs myriads of cells to complete; and in doing so they seem to follow a pattern, the nature of which is still a mystery. [3]

In external relations we can note progress in at least three dimensions. The creature becomes able to do a greater variety of things; able to do the same thing in a greater variety of ways; and able to act coherently over a greater span of time.

Compare, for example, the central heating systems of stars, dogs and men. Most stars, I understand, are believed to maintain their inner temperature at about thirty-five million degrees Fahrenheit. If we ask 'How?' and 'Why?', the answer is – 'Because that is the temperature at which the supply of energy and the loss of energy through radiation balance.' At a lower temperature, the nuclear reactions at the centre would be reduced, whereupon – I quote Von Weizsäcker [4] – '. . . the region around the centre of the star could no longer support the pressure from the outside regions. It would be compressed further and thereby its temperature would be raised. The process in the centre . . . would be accelerated by the increase of heat to such a degree that the balance of energy would be restored.'

If we ask why the warm-blooded animals also maintain a constant inner temperature at the more modest level of a little below one hundred degrees Fahrenheit, the answer is – 'Because that is the temperature required by the metabolic processes on which they depend.' But if we ask – 'How?', we receive a much more complicated answer. The creature has a whole battery of resources. Some are physiological; it erects its coat, constricts its surface blood vessels. Some are morphological; it grows a thicker coat. Some, significantly, are behavioural; it huddles together with its fellows or comes to the fire. The means to be used will be determined by something within the creature, rather than by something in the environment. They have a choice of means. But the goal is fixed; it was fixed millions of years ago, when the species took the evolutionary path which gave it this precarious enlargement of scope.

If we ask how and why men centrally heat their houses, we find that the field of choice has widened in two ways. They have immensely enlarged their behavioural responses; and they have come to direct these to goals not biologically determined but chosen from among an immense number of possibilities. Their activities have become more complex and more individual.

We can describe a simple creature wholly in terms of the activity which seems to keep it and its species alive. (At least, we think we can. I am not sure how far we are right.) But when we say of a man that he likes to spend his holidays collecting alpines or of a company that it has decided to go in for producing titanium in a big way, we are describing an activity which is not inherent in men or business corporations as such. Yet once they are committed to it, the new activity becomes characteristic of them, so that a description of them which missed it would be incomplete. They have become differentiated from their fellows by a specific pattern of activity.

It remains to notice those forms which arise from the association of living creatures with others of the same kind and with their ecological milieu. Within some limited habitat, such as a forest or a pond, life finds and holds a dynamic balance; and if disturbed (as we often disturb it by our intervention) it will find another, often after readjustments more far-reaching than we expect. Within this pattern the association of creatures of the same kind ranges from loose and transient associations, through the mutual dependence of the herd to the integration of the hive. At one extreme they are little more than crowds; at the other, little less than organisms.

Generally speaking, associations of creatures are more like crowds than like organisms; and when they approach the internal relations of an organism, as the social insects do, they pay the same price in rigidity and irreversible specialization. Humans alone manage to associate in ways which are elaborate and yet flexible and reversible. Our ability to do so falls far short of our need and we are forever oscillating between two alternatives which seem mutually exclusive – on the one hand, collective efficiency, won at the cost of individual frustration; on the other, individual freedom equally frustrated by collective anarchy. Those who believe in a middle way which is more than a compromise do so in the faith that human beings are capable or can become capable of social organization which is both individually satisfying and collectively effective. It seems fairly clear that this if true is valid only within a certain range of conditions which we cannot yet define.

When we set out to shape our institutions – even to form a company – we are not creating order out of chaos. We are intervening in a dynamic situation already regulated by its own laws. When we propose new goals and establish new organizations to pursue them, the success of our intervention depends on obedience to the same laws which determine whether other societies hold together. We cannot elude the laws of dynamic balance, in government or in management, any more than in engineering. Only so far as we understand and obey them, can we establish self-maintaining configurations of forces of our own devising.

All human institutions are hard to think about. If we personalize them, regarding a nation, a church, a trade union, as if it were a person, we are led into mistaken notions of how they work. If, on the other hand, we regard these names as mere symbols for ways in which people behave, then something essential escapes us. The fact is that we know little about them, as we soon find when we try to answer the two questions into which, as I have suggested, the question – 'What is it?' should be resolved.

How does an institution hang together? I find it convenient to regard institutions as structures of mutual expectation, attached to roles which define what each of its members shall expect from others and from himself. I distinguish them from organisms because they seem to me to hang together in a different way. The cells of an organism are subordinated to the whole by a complete and irreversible division of function which has no parallel in the relation of organisms with each other except among some of the social insects. The members of a human institution, on the other hand, are related by three main modes of interaction which we know as co-operation, conflict and competition. [6] These admit a more precise definition than they usually receive and I believe that all three are needed to maintain that dynamic balance which, in societies no less than among other forms, is the condition of survival; but we know dangerously little about what they mean and how they work.

Institutions grow, repair themselves, reproduce themselves, decay, dissolve. In their external relations they show many characteristics of organic life. Some think that in their internal relations also human institutions are destined to become increasingly organic, that human co-operation will approach ever more closely to the integration of cells in a body. I find this prospect unconvincing – not only, I hope, because I find it unpleasant – for reasons which I will not try to develop now. [7]

Thus human institutions are a distinct and confusing type of entity, built of interactions which range from the human to the mechanical. Among these, business corporations have a peculiar status. Unlike most human institutions, they are planned from the beginning and planned round their external relations, in that they exist to produce a product, to serve a purpose, to make a profit. Yet they depend on the most complex division of internal responsibility. They require of their members close co-operation and elaborate subordination; yet they are not served by a 'natural' society but by individuals who are freely recruited and are free to go, a transient society, of which the members are moved by individual motivations, probably quite foreign to those of the enterprise and have the main focus of their loyalties elsewhere. Yet these strange bodies often attain a high degree of self-regulation, both internally and externally.

I have spent some time in painting the picture of self-regulation as it exists at all levels which we can observe; for here alone we get a glimpse of the laws involved in control; and it is within the realm of these laws that management functions.

In analysing the idea of control I think we can learn from the theory and design of man-made control devices, not because their methods of working necessarily parallel those of the brain or the board-room but because they help us to understand the underlying principles.

I distinguish between two kinds of control, which I shall call positive and negative control. The distinction deserves, I think, more attention than it usually receives. Positive control is a means whereby courses are chosen and kept so as to reach goals. Negative control is a means whereby courses are changed so as to escape threats. They differ in important ways. I want first to discuss positive control.

The helmsman reads from the compass from moment to moment the actual direction of the ship's head, compares it with the course set by the navigator and turns the wheel accordingly. The wheel moves the rudder, directly or indirectly. The effect of the rudder movement, along with all the other influences which affect the ship's course, is reflected after a brief delay on the compass card and the information thus 'fed back' to the helmsman, moves him to a further adjustment of the wheel. In this familiar example of a control circuit the place of the helmsman can easily be taken by an automatic pilot and the design of such a device makes explicit what the helmsman actually does.

The automatic pilot measures both the amount of the deviation and the rate of change. It may have to measure the rate of change of the rate of change, if it is to initiate a stabilizing response. For it is concerned with a continuing process and it must derive from the past enough information to guide it in action which will take effect in the future, even though the delay be very small.

This example yields what seems to me to be the main features of control.

First, there must be a course, an 'ought-to-be', which the control can compare with the actual. If the course is not given, the control must be able to find it, either directly as the homing missile senses the target or by applying built-in rules or by experience. This course, like the actual with which it is compared, usually has a time dimension, being expressed in terms of change (or constancy) with time. The difference between the 'is' and the 'ought-to-be' is the signal for action. Such signals can occur only when the control is in a position to make the comparison. In the example given, the stream of signals is continuous but this is an ideal which is seldom attained. The control may be only intermittently aware of the actual or of the right course; and it can give the signal only when the two are present together.

Next, the assembly under control must be able from the signal to select and make an apt response. This implies, of course, that it has an apt response, which is by no means to be assumed. Here too a time element enters in; for it will take time to make the response and the response must be apt to the situation which will exist, when the response becomes effective. Thus, the A.A. gun predictor must lay off the gun to allow for the movement of the target while the shell is in flight. It must also compensate for the momentum which the gun will generate as it swings.

Finally, news of the situation as modified by the response has to get back to the control to provide the basis for further action. What I have described as 'actual' is in fact past. The helmsman reads the compass 'now' but the rate of change is derived from the recent past and has not yet taken account of rudder movements which are happening 'now'. In most control situations the delays involved are far greater.

Clearly problems of control are haunted by a complicated time factor. Each signal presents information derived from the past and initiates action which will take effect in the future. The effect of the action, more or less masked by other variables, will return for judgment at a still more remote point of time. Thus control is possible, even theoretically, only within limits; and these may present themselves as thresholds which are passed suddenly.

Psychologists have a device called the tracking test. The subject watches a window, across which there unrolls an irregularly wavering track, formed by two parallel lines. With a hand-wheel he has to keep a pointer between the two lines. He has no difficulty, so long as he can see enough of what is coming; but as the speed increases or the length of preview is cut down, he feels the strain mounting, until he passes the threshold beyond which control is lost. Thereafter, being always late, he is always wrong. His performance becomes worse than random, unless the windings of the track are sufficiently regular for memory to supply the basis of prediction. [8]

Thus the designer of control mechanisms has two main problems. First, he has to elicit what is conveniently called a mis-match signal; that is, a signal which announces the discrepancy between what is and what ought to be. This norm, which sets the control, may be a goal to be sought, a course to be held, a state or a relationship to be maintained – anything, so long as deviations from it can be noted and (preferably) measured. Secondly, the signal must set off a process which will select and initiate an apt response. Each of the two problems may raise a multitude of difficulties and either may prove insoluble. The same principles apply to the control of a business enterprise and of the processes within it; but, when we apply the analysis to the control of business, it seems that the conditions in which control is possible are exceptional.

The manger has a battery of statistics to describe periodically the situation in regard to production, costs, deliveries, stocks, orders, cash balances and so on. These refer to situations in the past, being days, weeks or months in arrear. Generally speaking, these indices deal better with money than materials, with materials than with men, with external relations than with internal relations. For some important aspects of process there are as yet no adequate indices – for example, for morale. I think it will always be easier to interpret a change in the rate of capital turnover than in the rate of labour turnover.

Again, the value of these indices depends on our being able to compare them with what should have been on the date from which they speak; and here we have to rely on estimates of varying degrees of reliability. Modern techniques of control by budget and forecast all aim at supplying reliable indices of what ought to be for comparison with what is, so that the manager may be able more regularly to check whether the undertaking is doing what it is trying to do. In practice such estimates vary greatly in value.

Furthermore, at any given moment decisions are being taken, the results of which cannot yet be known. The span between the taking of a decision and the comparison of its actual with its intended result ranges from seconds to years; and the longer it is, the more likely it becomes that no comparison will ever be possible, since so many other variables will have contributed to affect the result. An interesting recent study suggests that this time span is the index by which we measure the weight of other people's responsibilities and our own. [9]

Again, the information which is derived from the mis-match signal in business seldom contains so much guidance as the helmsman receives from his compass. The automatic pilot can derive from observing the swing of the ship's head all the information needed to correct it. The business manager may derive only the information that all is not well. When he sees that forecasts of production, orders, deliveries are not being fulfilled, he is put on enquiry but not necessarily given guidance. Still less is he guided where the frustrated expectation is in the field of human relations. His policy has not had the expected effect; should he continue it or intensify it or reverse it? The information does not tell him, until he has interpreted it by rules derived from elsewhere. It is not even a red light; for his policy may be right and his error may lie simply in his forecast of when it would show its effect.

A mere red light may be useful. There are situations in which it is sufficient that the agent shall run through its entire repertory of action, even at random, until an effective response is found. Machines have been made which work this way [10] and the process is not unknown in board-rooms, where it is signalled by the sinister phrase – 'We must do *something*'. But generally speaking, life at the higher levels of human organization moves too fast to admit of random action. The control must either contain or be capable of evolving rules which can guide it in selecting the appropriate response – if there is an appropriate response – which, of course, is not to be assumed.

It is time to supplement the idea of positive control by exploring negative control. Negative control could be illustrated by any of those devices which operate to prevent some critical limit being passed. Controls of boiler pressure and process temperature are obvious examples. The control is designed to sense when the assembly is approaching the danger point; before this is reached, it remains inactive. A simple example is supplied by a clockwork toy, which, when set to run on a table top, rushes about in all directions without falling over the edge. An antenna senses the edge when it is within reach and gives a twist to the direction. Since the goal is negative, any course which leads away from danger is as good as any other.

Negative control reminds us that every system works within limits which cannot be passed without disaster. Some conditions must be preserved if the assembly is to hold together; beyond them, the machine will break, the animal will die, the boat will capsize, the organization will break up, the business will go bankrupt. These changes are usually sudden, irreversible and complete; and when they threaten, the most cherished goals may have to be laid aside in order to escape them. Thus all positive goal-seeking, with the positive control which it involves, takes place within the framework of negative control, which ensures the continuance of the system.

When, in a tracking test, the track is narrow, it can be regarded equally well as a goal to be held or as two limits to be avoided; in other words, there is no difference between positive and negative control. But where the track is broad, the subject, whilst keeping within them, can choose a variety of courses. Having set himself a course, such as the central line, he can keep it by positive control; and only when he deviates wildly will he be conscious that limits not set by him confine his choices within a band of negative control. The analogy helps to make clear the relation between our self-chosen goals and those which the situation imposes on us.

So far I have talked as if the manager, at whatever level, were in charge of an integrated unit and were concerned only to regulate its interaction with the world outside, its *external* relations. But that is far from being the case. A business corporation is not an organism; nor at the other extreme is it a mere crowd. It is a highly structured society of a very peculiar kind. We are likely to make less serious mistakes if we regard it an as association of people than if we regard it as an imperfect entity.

At every level in a business organization we find positive and negative controls which are neither set by management nor under management's control. Each shop, each assembly line, each office has its own stabilities to guard and its own goals to pursue. It has them, it must have them and it should have them, if it is to be more than a crowd.

People sometimes liken a business corporation to an association of people with a common purpose, together achieving what all desire and none can achieve alone. This seems to me unrealistic. The forces which drive and regulate a great undertaking are legion and most diverse – individual need and ambition, the pleasures and frustrations of group activities as such, departmental habits and rivalries, professional standards and who knows what besides. The ultimate product and the ultimate profit are in a sense the by-products of thousands of diverse, individual strivings. [11]

Until recently, business management was unduly absorbed in external relations. This was natural; business corporations are formed to do business. Moreover, it is the curse of such cerebral creatures as we are to concentrate on external relations. It is a welcome development that management today should be looking inward. What it learns will not only make for efficiency in its outward relations. It will also enlighten us on what we most need to know.

The designer of control mechanisms produces machines which select the right responses in circumstances which used to require human judgment. They thus raise the question how much of the field of human choice can be explained in terms of control. What I have said already shows that there are three separate questions.

The evolution of organic forms has shown a widening in the field of choice in at least the three dimensions which I mentioned earlier. This widening of possibilities in the field of outer relationships has been largely due to the development of internal relationships. The same development is taking place in human institutions.

Whether at a given moment a particular organism is able to exercise any degree of choice is of course another matter. A man running in a race is exercising a choice, which deliberately excluded a host of alternatives. The same man with a bull after him has no choice but to run. Similarly, when a company, however large, is in the hands of its bankers, its directors have no choice but to do as the bank says – or rather, they have no choice consistent with continuing to function. When they meet to decide how to use super-abundant resources, they have a wide range of choice. What they choose will no doubt be determined by the system at the time but it will be determined by the state of the directors' heads rather than by the state of the company's bank balance.

This state of affairs is what I understand by having the initiative. It is created, preserved and lost largely by the way in which it is exercised. So long as it takes us all our time to keep alive, we have no choice of what to do with our lives. So long as it takes a company all its time to keep solvent, it has no choice of how it will develop. But as we learn to keep our systems – including ourselves – within their critical limits without undue effort, wider opportunities open within which we can set new goals and, to pursue them, build up self-maintaining activities of a higher order. The unskilled skater is wholly absorbed in keeping his balance; that is, in redressing the oscillations which his own efforts produce. The skilled skater has reduced his continuous balance-seeking to the level of unconscious adjustment; and in consequence he is free to skate as he pleases, that is to choose among an ever wider range of the things which are possible to men on skates. The analogy seems to me to hold for organisms and organizations at all levels. The range of their possible responses is limited; and within this limitation another narrower one is set by their situation, which itself is to some extent the result of their own conscious or unconscious choosing.

The question how, within these limitations, a particular choice is made is again another matter. Here, I think, the analysis of control can help us.

So far as I understand the exponents of cybernetics, there are only three theoretical limits to the ability of a control to find a response which will maintain any given state or course, if there is such a response within the assembly's repertory. These conditions are that past experience must be sufficiently regular to provide a guide for the future; [12] that the time taken to select the response and make it effective must not exceed the time within which the response is demanded; and that there must be criteria of success.

Within these limits there is room for great refinement. Thus, the simplest control mechanisms have the right responses built into them, each foreseen and set to be elicited by its appropriate signal. Such, for example, is the automatic pilot. Where this is impossible, we can build into the assembly rules for selecting the right response. Such, for example, would be a chess-playing machine. Finally, it is possible, at all events in theory, to build machines which will evolve their own rules in the light of their own experience. [13] Such, in embryo, are those automatic telephone exchanges which learn to make more quickly the connections which they have often made before.

These principles apply equally to the decisions of men and societies. Within the field which they cover, choice can be understood in terms of control and the analysis of control helps us to understand and improve our choosing. But the three limitations which I have mentioned exclude a large area within which we do in fact have to make choices. In business, as we have seen, the conditions of control are seldom fully present. We have to make assumptions about what is or what ought to be or both. Having made the assumptions, we have a choice of responses. Still more important, we can usually revise our goals and thus alter the datum from which our controls are derived; and we continually do so, partly to evade difficulties in pursuing them and partly to reconcile them with other goals which we are pursuing at the same time. This variety of choices makes up the continuous process of decision.

This process cannot, so far as I can see, be wholly explained in terms of control; but analysis in terms of control makes clearer the fields which remain to be explained. We have to explain how we set and change those positive and negative norms which control us; how we decide, when conditions of control are not present; and how we resolve the conflicts which arise, when these controls are at war. The model which I have presented so far does not help us with these problems, but I believe it has much more to teach us.

Meantime we can profit by its more obvious usefulness. It is useful to regard an organization as a tissue of feedback channels, to design it with this in mind and to interpret its achievements and failures in adaptivity in terms of the basic mechanisms of control, so far as these suffice. Most important, perhaps, it is useful to remember that the units of which it is composed are themselves highly complex organizations, possessing wide freedom of choice and governed by their own controls. Inconvenient as this may sometimes be, we should, I think, be unwise to change it, even if we could; for at the best it makes possible a combination of coherence and adaptability which would otherwise be far beyond our reach, whilst at the worst it prevents our organizations from becoming our masters and hence enables us continually to make them anew.

In this exploration I have been so rash as to speculate up to and beyond the boundary of my understanding. My only justification lies in a phrase with which I once heard a distinguished scientist end a highly technical address about the effect of drugs on the nervous system. He concluded – 'It is better to wonder than to explain.' He did not mean that we must ultimately bow before the unknowable, though that of course is true. Rather, he described perfectly the proper attitude for the scientist as he sits on the frontier of knowledge and looks out into the still unknown. We can explain only in terms of familiar concepts; but those concepts were once new and they were won by men who were not satisfied with any current explanations and who therefore wondered and went on wondering.

The engineer often becomes a manager but he should always remain a scientist. As a manager he will have little time to wonder; but as a scientist he has a duty to wonder. And if he finds a few moments to wonder now and then, he will be a better manager of men.

ACKNOWLEDGEMENT

The ninth Wallberg Lecture – given at the University of Toronto in October 1956.

NOTES AND REFERENCES

1. For a recent statement of this view I am indebted to Bertalanffy, L. von, *Problems of Life*. (1952) London: Watts and Co.
2. This point is elaborated by Ruyer, R., *Néo-Finalisme*. (1952) Paris: Presses Universitaires de France, p. 89.
3. Since these words were written, biologists believe that they have identified the structure which carries the genetic code. This astonishing achievement still falls short of breaking the code.
4. Weizsäcker, C.F. von, *The History of Nature*. (1951) London: Routledge and Kegan Paul, p. 94.
5. Cannon, W.B., *The Wisdom of the Body*. (1939) London: Routledge. Cannon and many others since have described the homeostatic processes of the body. The directiveness of organic behaviour as an observed phenomenon, irrespective of the rival theories which have been built on it, has been described by Russell, E.S., in *The Directiveness of Organic Activities* (1945. Cambridge University Press); and the justification for accepting this provisionally as an organic law which is not at present to be further resolved has been cogently stated by Dingle, H., in *The Scientific Adventure*. (1952) London: Pitman, pp. 249 and 250.
6. Space does not permit me to explore these modes of interaction adequately here. I distinguish competition from conflict, though I am aware that many regard it as merely a form of conflict. Trees in a wood mututally intensify their propensity to grow taller and mutually restrain their tendency to grow laterally. It seems to me that two forms of interaction which have such markedly different effects deserve different names. The fact that some, defeated in the race for light and air, wither and die, merely shows that the competitive situation may become conflictual. The analysis of co-operation would unduly expand the limits of a note.
7. The question is, of course, debatable. Space does not permit me to attempt a justification of the view here expressed. Much of the evidence is reviewed in the proceedings of a conference held at the University of Chicago in 1942 and edited by Dr Robert Redfield, c.f. particularly the paper on higher levels of integration by Dr R.W. Gerard, who would seem to hold a view different from that which is here expressed. (Redfield, R., editor, 'Levels of Integration in Biological and Social Systems', Vol. VIII of *Biological Symposia*. (1942) Lancaster, Pennsylvania: The Jacques Cattell Press.)

8. c.f. Poulton, E.C., 'Anticipation in Open and Closed Sensori-motor Skills'. (1950) Medical Research Council Applied Psychology Research Unit Report No. 138.

9. c.f. Jacques, E., *Measurement of Responsibility*. (1956) London: Tavistock Publications, pp. 52–60.

10. Such is the homeostat described by Ashby, Ross W., in *Design for a Brain*. (2nd ed. 1960) London: Chapman and Hall.

11. This apparent paradox is more fully treated by Simon, H.A., in *Administrative Behaviour*. (2nd ed. 1959) New York: Macmillan, pp. 17 and 18.

12. The possibility, referred to above, that a random running through of the repertory of responses will in time provide the right one is no exception to this statement; for it assumes that the situation will remain regular at least throughout the period of search and for sufficiently long thereafter to enable the response to be effectively used.

13. These possibilities are analysed in a paper to which I am indebted in many ways by Mackay, D.M., 'Towards an Information-Flow Model of Human Behaviour', *British Journal of Psychology*. (1956) p. 33.

4

A conceptual framework for the design of organizational control mechanisms

William G. Ouchi

The problem of organization is the problem of obtaining cooperation among a collection of individuals or units who share only partially congruent objectives. When a team of individuals collectively produces a single output, there develops the problem of how to distribute the rewards emanating from that output in such a manner that each team member is equitably rewarded. If equitable rewards are not forthcoming, members will, in future cooperative ventures, adjust their efforts in such a manner that all will be somewhat worse off (cf. Simon [41], Marschak [26], Alchian and Demsetz [1]).

It is the objective of this paper to describe three fundamentally different mechanisms through which organizations can seek to cope with this problem of evaluation and control. The three will be referred to as markets, bureaucracies, and clans. In a fundamental sense, markets deal with the control problem through their ability to precisely measure and reward individual contributions; bureaucracies rely instead upon a mixture of close evaluation with a socialized acceptance of common objectives; and clans rely upon a relatively complete socialization process which effectively eliminates goal incongruence between individuals. This paper explores the organizational manifestations of these three approaches to the problem of control.

The paper begins with an example from a parts distribution division of a major company which serves to give some flesh to what might otherwise be overly-abstract arguments. Through the example, each of the three mechanisms is explicated briefly and discussed in terms of two prerequisite conditions, one social and the other informational. The more concrete organization design features of the three forms are considered, along with some consideration of the unique costs accompanying each form.
(ORGANIZATIONAL DESIGN; CONTROL; ORGANIZATIONAL GOALS)

Source: Ouchi, W.G. (1979) *Management Science*, **25** (9), pp. 833–48.
© 1979

1. INTRODUCTION

Organizational control has many meanings and has been interpreted in many ways. Tannenbaum [42], whose view has dominated organizational theory, interprets control as the sum of interpersonal influence relations in an organization. In a similar vein, Etzioni [13] finds it useful to treat control in organizations as equivalent to power. Other than the power-influence approach to control, organization theorists have also treated control as a problem in information flows (Galbraith [15], Ouchi and Maguire [30]), as a problem in creating and monitoring rules through a hierarchical authority system as specified by Weber [46] and interpreted by Perrow [33], Blau and Scott [7], and many organizational sociologists, and as a cybernetic process of testing, measuring, and providing feedback (Thompson [43], Reeves and Woodward [35]).

This paper considers a more simple-minded view of organizational control stated in the following two questions: What are the mechanisms through which an organization can be managed so that it moves towards its objectives? How can the design of these mechanisms be improved, and what are the limits of each basic design?

2. AN EXAMPLE: THE PARTS SUPPLY DIVISION

For the last two years, the author has worked with the parts distribution division of a major company. From the outset, I was struck with this problem: the purchasing department buys approximately 100,000 different items each year from about 3,000 different manufacturers, and it accomplishes this huge volume of work with only 22 employees, of whom 3 are managerial-level. On the other hand, the warehousing operation, which stores these items until they are ordered by a customer and then fills the customer orders, has about 1,400 employees, of whom about 150 are managers. Why is it that it takes relatively so few people to accomplish the very complex task of evaluating the quality and price of so many items, compared to the number of people required to store and then to distribute them?

Out in a warehouse, the 'pickers' must pick out the proper items to fill an order from a customer, the 'packers' must check the items to be sure that the order is as specified and then must pack them properly for shipping, and the foreman must see to it that the work is going along properly. What we are interested in is the control process which the foreman uses to get the work out. The foreman is engaged in an elaborate task: he gathers information concerning the flow of work by watching the actions of the workers, knowing from their behavior which workers are doing their jobs well or poorly; he confirms his observations by checking a record of output for each worker at the end of each day. As he observes the pickers and packers at work, the foreman also, from time to time, will stop to inquire of a worker why he or she is doing a job in a particular manner. He may also ask someone to stop what they are doing and to do a different job instead; in some cases, he will angrily confront a 'trouble maker' and demand that they behave as he directs. In all of these actions, the supervisor is working within a well-defined set of rules which prescribe both his behavior and that of the pickers and packers; he does so within both the formal limits of authority which are given him by virtue of his rank and within the informal limits of authority granted to him by the workers as a result of their trust in and respect for him as an individual. These formal limits of authority and of power are not implicit, they are written down in black and white, and each employee, both picker and foreman, knows them by memory. The informal agreements, while equally effective, remain implicit.

In the purchasing department, each purchasing officer does his or her work by sending out a description of the item desired to three or four different manufacturers, asking each one to quote a price for it. After the prices are in, the purchaser adds in any information that he may have concerning the honesty and reliability of the supplier and the past performance that he has demonstrated, and then decides to order from one of them. The supervisor occasionally consults with each purchasing agent to see if they need help, and the supervisor strictly reminds each and every person that under no conditions are they ever to accept gifts of any sort from any supplier. Now what is the control mechanism here?

Analysis of the example

Three mechanisms have been identified: a market mechanism, which primarily characterized the purchasing function: a bureaucratic mechanism, which primarily characterized the warehousing function; and an informal social mechanism, which was mentioned in passing. This example illustrates that the mechanisms themselves overlap in organizations; although it may be helpful to treat them as conceptually distinct from one another, they in fact occur in various combinations.

Market mechanisms

The work of the purchasing agent is, largely, subject to market mechanisms. At least two important effects are evident. First, the work of each agent is greatly simplified because he is relieved of the necessity of determining, for each part purchased, whether the supplier's intended manufacturing and delivery process is the most efficient possible. Instead, he simply puts each part out for competitive bids and permits the competitive process to define a fair price. In the second place, the work of the manager who supervises these agents is also greatly simplified, because he needs only to check their decisions against the simple criterion of cost minimization rather than observing the steps through which they work and forming an assessment of their unique skills and effort (however, this is a bureaucratic mechanism). Clearly, a parts division which chose to ignore market information and relied instead upon its own internal evaluation of the particulars of each bid would be at a significant cost disadvantage due to the much greater administrative overhead that it would incur.

As a pure model, a market is a very efficient mechanism of control (cf. Arrow [4, pp. 1–29]). In a market, prices convey all of the information necessary for efficient decision-making. In a frictionless market, where prices exactly represent the value of a product or service, decision-makers need no other information. Arbitrary rules such as those found in the warehouse are unnecessary. In addition to information, prices provide a mechanism for solving the problem of goal incongruity. Given a frictionless price mechanism, the firm can simply reward each employee in direct proportion to his contribution, so that an employee who produces little is paid little, and all payments, being exactly in proportion to contribution, are fair.

Of course, in this perfect example of a frictionless market, there is little reason for a formal organization to exist at all (Coase [9]). The fact that purchasing takes place within the corporate framework in our example suggests that some major market defects must exist. At least some of the parts purchased are sufficiently unique that only one or two potential manufacturers exist, so that a more detailed evaluation of those contracts is necessary, and a more thorough bureaucratic surveillance of the purchasing agents in such cases is also called for (see Williamson, [48] for a more complete discussion). More importantly, the work of the purchasing agents themselves is controlled through a process of bureaucratic surveillance rather than through a price mechanism. That is, the director of purchasing does not simply determine a market price for purchasing agents and then occasionally audit performance. Rather, he agrees upon an employment contract with each purchasing agent at some price (cf. Simon [37, pp. 183–195]) and then resorts to hierarchical order-giving and performance evaluation to control them. It is important to distinguish between the market mechanism employed by purchasing agents and the bureaucratic mechanism to which they are subject. Thus, in reality, there is a mixture of market and bureaucratic mechanisms which provide control in the case of purchasing, although it is the market mechanisms which are most clearly evident in this example.

Bureaucratic mechanisms

In marked contrast to purchasing, warehousing in our example is subject to a variety of explicit routines of monitoring and directing which conform quite closely to the bureaucratic model described by Weber [46]. The fundamental mechanism of control involves close personal surveillance and direction of subordinates by superiors. The information necessary for task completion is contained in rules; these may be rules concerning processes to be completed or rules which specify standards of output or quality. In any case, rules differ from prices in the important sense that they are partial rather than complete bundles of information. A price implies that a comparison has taken place; a comparison between alternative buyers or sellers of the value of the object in question. A rule, however, is essentially an arbitrary standard against which a comparison is yet to be made. In order to use a rule (e.g., a budget, or cost standard), a mananger must observe some actual performance, assign some value to it, and then compare that assigned value to the rule in order to determine whether the actual performance was satisfactory or not. All of this consumes a good deal of administrative overhead. If the rule is expressed qualitatively rather than quantitatively, the cost of administration can be expected to be even higher.

Given these inadequacies of bureaucracy, one might reasonably ask why the warehouse does not emulate the purchasing office and rely instead upon a price mechanism. The answer to that question has been the subject of a good deal of recent work by institutional economists, but an organization theorist might focus on one or two dimensions of the problem. Let us approach the question by beginning with the scenario of a warehouse manager who indeed decides to manage through an internal price mechanism. His first task is to set a price for each task, a job that may be impossible since many of the tasks are at least in part unique and thus not subject to market comparisons. Supposing that he can establish reasonable prices for a number of tasks, he must then have a mode of determining when an assigned task has been completed. Unlike the purchasing manager, who can sample delivered products for the purposes of determining contractual satisfaction, the warehouse manager has no correspondingly inexpensive way to determine performance and will have to establish a set of performance standards. In order to see that these standards are applied, he will have to create a system of hierarchical superiors who will closely monitor the performance of individual workers. Furthermore, he will have to create an atmosphere in which the workers willingly permit this close surveillance, or else morale and productivity will suffer. In some cases, tasks will inherently require teamwork, and then superiors will have to apply judgment to attribute value added among the team members. In order to simplify these problems of surveillance, the manager will attempt to create sub-specialties within the warehouse to more readily permit comparison of performance between like workers. Finally, when one task becomes particularly critical, the manager will want to increase the price that he will pay for it in order to increase the supply of workers who are willing to perform it. If he is unable to exactly price the critical task, he will have either an oversupply or an undersupply of workers performing it, to the detriment of the warehouse. Given the difficulty of correctly pricing any task, he will instead invest hierarchical superiors with the right to direct the efforts of subordinates on an *ad hoc* basis; and again he will need to create an atmosphere in which such directives will be willingly followed.

Having done all of these things, our warehouse manager who set out to create an internal market will have exactly instituted a bureaucratic hierarchy instead. Both bureaucratic and market mechanisms are directed towards the same objectives. Which form is more efficient depends upon the particulars of the transactions in question. Indeed, at this point we have an answer to the original dilemma: how can the purchasing department carry out its tasks with so few people compared to the number in warehousing? Purchasing in this example participates in a market mechanism, which is a far more efficient mechanism of control in terms of the administrative overhead consumed. Prices are a far more efficient means of controlling transactions than are rules. However, the conditions necessary for frictionless prices can rarely be met, and in such conditions the bureaucratic form, despite its inadequacies, is preferred.

Clan mechanisms

The example also mentioned briefly the informal social structure which, in addition to market and bureaucratic mechanisms, also contributes to control in the warehouse. In order to illustrate the operation of these clan mechanisms, let us return briefly to the example.

Consider the foreman in the warehouse. His task is to oversee the work of pickers and packers. How is the warehouse manager to evaluate the work of the foreman? To some extent, he can rely on bureaucratic mechanisms such as output schedules, budgets, and inventory rules, but these in turn require surveillance. Given that the task of the foreman is significantly more subtle than that of the picker, the manager's task of bureaucratically supervising the foreman becomes very complex. However, if the manager is capable of selecting for promotion to foreman only that subset of workers who display a high internal commitment to the firm's objectives, and if he can maintain in them a deep commitment to these objectives, then his need for explicit surveillance and evaluation is reduced. In short, once the manager knows that they are trying to achieve the 'right' objectives, he can eliminate many costly forms of auditing and surveillance.

Consider a different example – the general hospital. In the case of many health care employees, even the most dedicated attempts at systematic performance auditing would be frustrated. Task performance is inherently ambiguous, and teamwork is common, so that precise evaluation of individual contribution is all but impossible. In such cases, we observe a highly formalized and lengthy period of socialization during which would-be doctors and nurses are subjected not only to skill training but also to value training or indoctrination. When they are certified, they are certified with respect not only to their technical skills but also with respect to their integrity or purity of values.

When these socialization processes characterize groups such as physicians or nurses who occupy different organizations but with similar values, we refer to them as professions. When the socialization process refers to all of the citizens of a political unit, we refer to it as a culture. When it refers to the properties of a unique organization, we may refer to it as a clan. The functions of socialization are similar in professions, cultures, and clans, but our present interest centers on the clan.

The discovery that an informal social system characterizes most work organizations was noted first in the Hawthorne Studies (Roethlisberger and Dickson [36]). The subtle and widespread impact of local values on behavior has been thoroughly documented (Selznick [38], Gouldner [16]) as well as theoretically treated (Blau [6], Blau and Scott [7, pp. 89–99]). In organizational studies, the socialization mechanisms have been found to be unique to a particular organization (Trist and Bamforth [44]), to an industry (Lipset, Trow, and Coleman [24], Kaufmann [19]), or they may characterize most of the firms in an economy, as in the case of Japan (Nakane [29], Dore [12], Rohlen [37]).

Until recently, however, organization theorists have regarded this informal social system as either an anomaly or an epiphenomenon, not as the subject of analysis central to the problem of organization. However, a clan may serve as the basis of control in some organizations, just as the market was the basic form in the purchasing function and bureaucracy the basic form in the warehouse.

3. THE SOCIAL AND INFORMATIONAL PREREQUISITES OF CONTROL

It is possible to arrange the three modes of control along each of two dimensions: the informational requirements necessary to operate each control type, and the social underpinnings necessary to operate each control type. These are summarized in Table 4.1.

Let us consider first the social requirements, and then we will consider the informational issues. What we mean by social requirements is that set of agreements between people which, as a bare minimum, is necessary for a form of control to be employed. Any real organization, of course, will have developed a highly elaborated set of understandings which goes far beyond this. At the moment, however, our task is to understand the bare minimum without which a control mechanism cannot function.

A market cannot exist without a norm of reciprocity, but it requires no social agreements beyond that. A norm of reciprocity assures that, should one party in a market transaction attempt to cheat another, that the cheater, if discovered, will be punished by all members of the social system, not only by the victim and his or her partners. The severity of the punishment will typically far exceed the crime, thus effectively deterring potential future opportunists (Gouldner [17]). The norm of reciprocity is critical in a market if we think, for a moment, about the costs of running a

Table 4.1   Social and informational prerequisites of control

Type of Control	Social Requirements	Informational Requirements
Market	Norm of Reciprocity	Prices
Bureaucracy	Norm of Reciprocity Legitimate Authority	Rules
Clan	Norm of Reciprocity Legitimate Authority Shared Values, Beliefs	Traditions

market mechanism as opposed to the costs of any mechanism of control. In a market mechanism, the costs of carrying out transactions between parties have mostly to do with assuring oneself that the other party is dealing honestly, since all information relevant to the substance of the decision is contained in prices and is therefore not problematic. If honesty cannot be taken for granted, however, then each party must take on the cripplingly high costs of surveillance, complete contracting, and enforcement in order not to be cheated (Williamson [48]). These costs can quickly become so high that they will cause a market to fail.

When a market fails as the mechanism of control, it is most often replaced by a bureaucratic form. A bureaucracy contains not only a norm of reciprocity, but also agreement on legitimate authority, ordinarily of the rational/legal form (see Blau and Scott [7, pp. 27–36] for a discussion). In a bureaucratic control system, the norm of reciprocity is reflected in the notion of 'an honest day's work for an honest day's pay', and it particularly contains the idea that, in exchange for pay, an employee gives up autonomy in certain areas to his organizational superiors, thus permitting them to direct his work activities and to monitor his performance. These steps are possible only if organization members accept the idea that higher office holders have the legitimate right to command and to audit or monitor lower persons, within some range (also known as the 'zone of indifference', see Barnard [5]). Given social support for a norm of reciprocity and for the idea of legitimate authority, a bureaucratic control mechanism can operate successfully.

A Clan requires not only a norm of reciprocity and the idea of legitimate authority (often of the 'traditional' rather than the 'rational/legal' form), but also social agreement on a broad range of values and beliefs. Because the clan lacks the explicit price mechanism of the market and the explicit rules of the bureaucracy, it relies for its control upon a deep level of common agreement between members on what constitutes proper behavior, and it requires a high level of commitment on the part of each individual to those socially prescribed behaviors. Clearly, a clan is more demanding than either a market or a bureaucracy in terms of the social agreements which are prerequisite to its successful operation.

The informational prerequisites of control

While a Clan is the most demanding and the Market the least demanding with respect to social underpinnings, the opposite is true when it comes to information. It has been observed (see Galbraith [15], Lawrence and Lorsch [21]) that, within large corporations, each department tends to develop its own peculiar jargon; it does so because the jargon, being suited to the particular task needs of the department, provides it with a very efficient set of symbols with which to communicate complex ideas, thus conserving on the very limited information-carrying capacity of an organization. We can also think of the accounting system in an organization as the smallest set of symbols which conveys information that is relevant to all organizational subunits. An accounting system is a relatively explicit information system compared, say, to the traditions of the U.S. Senate (see Matthews [27]). Each of these mechanisms carries information about how to behave, but the accounting system, being explicit, is easily accessed by a newcomer while the traditions of the Senate, being implicit, can be discovered by a freshman senator only over a period of years. On the other hand, the explicit system is far less complete in its ability to convey information and it has often been noted (see, for example, Vancil [45]) that there is no accounting measurement which fully captures the underlying performance of a department or corporation, since many of the dimensions of performance defy measurement (see Ouchi and Maguire [30]). Typically, an explicit information system must be created and maintained intentionally and at some cost, while an implicit information system often 'grows up' as a natural by-product of social interaction.

In a true market, prices are arrived at through a process of competitive bidding, and no administrative apparatus is necessary to produce this information. However, many economists have argued that the conditions necessary for such perfect prices are rarely if ever met in reality, with the result that inefficiencies are borne by the parties to the market. Although some would contend that markets are explicitly not organizations (Arrow [4]), we can consider as a limit case the profit – or investment – center in a business as an attempt to control an organization through a price mechanism. In some large organizations, it is possible, with great effort and a huge accounting staff, to create internal numbers which will serve the function of prices. That is, if division general managers and department heads attempt simply to maximize their profit by taking the best prices available within the firm, then the firm as a whole will benefit. These 'transfer prices' should not be confused with output, cost, or performance standards which are common in all organizations: those measures are effectively bureaucratic rules. The critical difference is that an internal price does not need a hierarchy of authority to accompany it. If the price mechanism is at work, all that is needed in addition to prices is a norm of reciprocity, accompanied by self-interest.

Only rarely is it possible for an organization to arrive at perfect transfer prices, however, because technological interdependence and uncertainty tremendously complicate the problem for most organizations, to the point where arriving at prices is simply not feasible. Under that condition, the organization can create an explicit set of rules, both rules about behavior and rules about levels of production or output. Although an organization can never create an explicit set of rules that will cover every situation that could possibly confront any of its employees, it can cut the information problem down to size by writing a relatively small set of rules that will cover 90% of all events and depending upon hierarchical authority to settle the remaining 10% of events. Thus, we see again that acceptance of legitimate authority is critical to a bureaucracy, since it is that property which enables the organization to incompletely specify the duties of an employee, instead having the employee agree that, within bounds, a superior may specify his or her duties as the need arises (Williamson [48, pp. 57–81]). In this manner, the organization deals with the future one step at a time, rather than having to anticipate it completely in advance in a set of explicit rules.

In a Clan, the information is contained in the rituals, stories, and ceremonies which convey the values and beliefs of the organization (Clark [8]). An outsider cannot quickly gain access to information concerning the decision rules used in the organization, but the information system does not require an army of accountants, computer experts, and managers: it is just there. Ivan Ligh [22] has described the Chinese-American *Hui* and the Japanese-American *Tanomoshi*, revolving-credit lending societies which provide venture capital for starting new businesses. They carry out all of the functions of any Wall Street investment bank, but, within their ethnic group, they are able to make loans which would be far too risky for any bank because they enjoy considerable advantages in obtaining, interpreting, and evaluating information about potential borrowers or members. None of their practices are explicit – even the rate of interest paid by borrowers is left unspecified and implicit. Entry into a *Hui* or *Tanomoshi* is strictly limited by birthright, a practice which guarantees that each member is a part of a social and kinship network which will support the values and beliefs upon which the control mechanism is founded. Clearly, the Clan information system cannot cope with heterogeneity nor with turnover, disadvantages which make it all but infeasible as a central mechanism of control in modern organizations, but the Clan, like the market, can operate with great efficiency if the basic conditions necessary to its operation can be met.

If the price requirements of a Market cannot be met and if the social conditions of the Clan are impossible to achieve, then the Bureaucratic mechanism becomes the preferred method of control. In a sense, the Market is like the trout and the Clan like the salmon, each a beautiful, highly-specialized species which requires uncommon conditions for its survival. In comparison, the bureaucratic method of control is the catfish – clumsy, ugly, but able to live in the widest possible range of environments and, ultimately, the dominant species. The bureaucratic mode of control can withstand high rates of turnover, a high degree of heterogeneity, and it does not have very demanding informational needs.

In reality, of course, we will never observe a pure market, a pure bureaucracy, or a pure clan. Real organizations will each contain some features of each of the modes of control. The design problem thus becomes one of assessing the social and informational characteristics of each division, department, or task and determining which of the forms of control ought to be emphasized in each case. Present organization theory, however, concentrates on the bureaucratic form to the exclusion of all else. The work of March and Simon [25] deals with decision-making in bureaucratic organizations. Parsons [32] describes problems of vertical control in bureaucracies. Perrow [33] concentrates on rules as a control mechanism in bureaucracies, and Argyris [3], Likert [23], and Tannenbaum [42] prescribe techniques for reducing some of the undesirable by-products of what remains an essentially bureaucratic mode of control.

Let us next consider some of the cost implications of each form of control. We will approach this task by looking at each of the stages at which an organization can exercise discretion over people. By doing so, we may discover some additional design variables which can influence the form of organizational control.

4. DESIGNING CONTROL MECHANISMS: COSTS AND BENEFITS

Basically, there are two ways in which an organization can achieve effective people control: either it can go to the expense of searching for and selecting people who fit its needs exactly, or else it can take people who do not exactly fit its needs and go to the expense of putting in place a managerial system to instruct, monitor, and evaluate them.

Which of these approaches is best depends on the cost to the organization of each. On the one hand, there is a cost of search and of acquisition: some skills are rare in the labor force and the organization wanting to hire people with those skills will have to search widely and pay higher wages. Once hired, however, such people will be able to perform their tasks without instruction and, if they have also been selected for values (motivation), they will be inclined to work hard without close supervision, both of which will save the organization money. On the other hand, there is the cost of training the unskilled and the indifferent to learn the organization's skills and values, and there is the cost of developing and running a supervisory system to monitor, evaluate, and correct their behavior. Once in place, however, such a system can typically take in a heterogeneous assortment of people and effectively control them; in addition, its explicit training and monitoring routines enable it to withstand high rates of turnover. High turnover is costly if search and acquisition costs are high, but turnover is relatively harmless to the organization if it hires all comers.

It has also been observed, by sociologists (Etzioni [13]), social psychologists, (Kelman [20]), and economists, (Williamson [48]), that various forms of evaluation and control will result in differing individual levels of commitment to or alienation from the organization and its objectives. In general, a control mode which relies heavily on selecting the appropriate people can expect high commitment as a result of internalized values.

At the other extreme, a control mode which depends heavily upon monitoring, evaluating, and correcting in an explicit manner is likely to offend people's sense of autonomy and of self-control and, as a result, will probably result in an unenthusiastic, purely compliant response. In this state, people require even more close supervision, having been alienated from the organizations as a result of its control mechanism. Indeed, as is always true of any form of measurement, it is not possible for an organization to measure or otherwise control its employees without somehow affecting them through the very process that it uses to measure them: there is no completely unobtrusive measurement in most organizations. In general, the more obvious and explicit the measurement, the more noxious it is to employees and thus, the greater the cost to the organization of employing such methods. However, other conditions may demand the use of these more explicit yet offensive techniques of control. We can summarize these in Table 4.2.

At one extreme, an organization could be completely unselective about its members, taking anyone (although we assume that everyone is to some extent self-interested, hedonistic, or profit-maximizing). At the other extreme, an organization could be highly selective, choosing only those individuals who already have both the skills and the values which the organization needs; this practice is most common in the 'professional bureaucracies' such as hospitals, public accounting firms, and universities. In an apparent paradox, these most and least selective kinds of organizations will both have high levels of commitment; that is, members will have internalized the underlying objectives of the organization. Of course, the paradox is resolved by noting that the completely unselective organization relies on commitment of each individual to self, since it employs a market mechanism of control in which what is desired is that each person simply maximize his or her personal well-being (profit). Since the organization's objective is thus identical to the individual's objective, we can say that internalization of objectives exists and thus no close supervision will be necessary, and enthusiasm for pursuing the organization's goals will be high (since they are also the individual's selfish goals).

Most organizations, however, cannot take on all comers (they do not have a price mechanism) and they can rely upon selection and screening only to a limited extent, that is, they can select partially for the skills and values desired but will not be able to find people who fit exactly their needs. In this case, the organization may rely on training, both in the form of formalized training programs and in the form of on-the-job or apprenticeship training, to impart the desired skills and values. Typically, training will result in the trainee identifying with either the trainer (who may

Table 4.2   Organizational control: people treatment

People Treatment	Form of Commitment*	Corresponding Control Type
Totally Unselective; take anyone, no further treatment	Internalization	Market
Selection/Screening		Clan
Training – Skill Training – Value Training	Identification	Bureaucracy
Monitoring – Monitor Behaviour – Monitor Output	Compliance	

* Taken from Kelman [20].

also be a respected superior) or with the work group or department. In this case, the employee will possess the necessary skills and will pursue the organization's objective, but only because he or she identifies with and wants to emulate the respected person or group, not because the underlying objectives have been internalized to the point where the employee believes them to be good and desirable objectives in their own right.

The link between forms of commitment and types of control is quite direct. Internalized commitment is necessary for a market, since a market possesses no hierarchical monitoring or policing capabilities. Internalization is also necessary to a clan, which has weak monitoring abilities, that is, evaluation is subtle and slow under this form of control, and thus, without high commitment, the mechanism is capable of drifting quite far off course before being corrected. A clan can also be supported with identification, however, and over time, the identification may be converted into internalization of the values of the clan.

Identification is also compatible with bureaucratic control, although it exceeds the minimum commitment that is necessary in a bureaucracy. Compliance is the minimum level of commitment necessary for bureaucratic control, but it is beneath the threshold of commitment necessary for the clan and market forms. The social agreement to suspend judgment about orders from superiors and to simply follow orders (see Blau and Scott [7, pp. 29–30]) is fundamental to bureaucratic control.

The issue of commitment and control may also pose a moral question of some significance. If organizations achieve internalized control purely through selection, then, it would seem, both the individual and the organization are unambiguously satisfied. If internalization is achieved through training of employees into the values and beliefs of the organization, however, then it is possible that some individuals may be subject to economic coercion to modify their values. Indeed, this kind of forced socialization is common in certain of our institutions (what Etzioni refers to as 'coercive' organizations) such as the U.S. Marine Corps and many mental hospitals. In some such cases, we accept the abrogation of individual rights as being secondary to a more pressing need. In the case of a company town or a middle-aged employee with few job options, however, we are less likely to approve of this kind of pressure. As long as organizations maintain an essentially democratic power structure, this danger remains remote. If the hierarchy of authority becomes relatively autocratic, however, the possibility of loss of individual freedom becomes real.

5. LOOSE COUPLING AND THE CLAN AS A FORM OF CONTROL

In the present literature on organizations, a new and somewhat revolutionary view of 'organizational rationality' is developing which has direct implications for our view of designing control mechanisms. This new view, which is coming to be known as 'loose coupling' (see Weick [47]), implies that bureaucratic forms of control are unsuitable for many contemporary organizations. Let us briefly consider the underlying 'organizational rationality' which dominates the current view of control, and then we will consider the loose coupling perspective.

The essential element which underlies any bureaucratic or market form of control is the assumption that it is feasible to measure, with reasonable precision, the performance that is desired. In order to set a production standard which effectively controls, it is essential that the industrial engineers or accountants be able to measure the desired output with some precision. In order to effectively control through the use of rules, it is essential that the personnel department know which rules to specify in order to achieve the desired performance. Indeed, the ability to measure either output or behavior which is relevant to the desired performance is critical to the 'rational' application of market and bureaucratic forms of control. Table 4.3 specifies the contingencies which determine whether or not measurement is possible.

In order to understand Table 4.3, let us agree, for the moment, that if we wanted to control an organization, we would have to monitor or measure something and that, essentially, the things which we can measure are limited to the behavior of employees or the results, the outputs of those behaviors. If we understand the technology (that is, the means-ends relationships involved in the basic production or service activities) perfectly, as is the case in a tin-can plant, then we can achieve effective control simply by having someone watch the behavior of the employees and the workings of the machines: if all behaviors and processes conform to our desired transformation steps, then we know with certainty that proper tin cans are coming out the other end, even without looking. By specifying the rules of behavior and of process, we could create an effective bureaucratic control mechanism in this case.

On the other hand, suppose that we are designing a control system for a high-fashion women's boutique. What it takes to be a successful buyer or merchandiser is beyond our understanding, so we could not possibly hope to create a set of rules which, if followed by our buyers, would assure success. We can measure with precision, however, the average markdowns

Table 4.3 Conditions determining the measurement of behavior and of output

		Knowledge of The Transformation Process	
		Perfect	*Imperfect*
Ability to Measure Outputs	*High*	Behavior or Output Measurement (Apollo Program)	Output Measurement (Women's Boutique)
	Low	Behavior Measurement (Tin Can Plant)	Ritual and Ceremony. 'Clan' Control (Research Laboratory)

which each buyer's leftover dresses must take, the average inventory turn-over for each buyer, and the sales volume and profit margin of each buyer, thus giving us the alternative of an output control mechanism. If our output control mechanism consists of this multiple set of objectives, then it is effectively a bureaucratic mechanism which will be managed by having a superior in the hierarchy who will monitor the various indicators for each buyer and, using the legitimate authority of office, will enforce not only close monitoring but also will order the necessary corrections in the buyer's decisions.

In the third case, we could be designing a control mechanism for the Apollo moon-shot program. We can completely specify each step of the transformation process which must occur in order for a manned capsule to get to the surface of the moon and back to earth, thus giving us the possibility of behavior control. However, we also have an unambiguous measure of output: either the capsule gets there and back, or it doesn't. Thus we have a choice of either behavior control or of output control. In such a case, the lower cost alternative will be preferred: clearly, since the cost of one failure is prohibitive, we will choose an elaborate behavior control mechanism, with literally hundreds of ground controllers monitoring every step of the process.

Finally, suppose that we are running a research laboratory at a multi-billion dollar corporation. We have no ability to define the rules of be-havior which, if followed, will lead to the desired scientific breakthroughs which will, in turn, lead to marketable new products for the company. We can measure the ultimate success of a scientific discovery, but it may take ten, twenty, or even fifty years for an apparently arcane discovery to be fully appreciated. Certainly, we would be wary of using a strong form of output control to encourage certain scientists in our lab while discourag-ing others. Effectively, we are unable to use either behavior or output measurement, thus leaving us with no 'rational' form of control. What happens in such circumstances is that the organization relies heavily on ritualized, ceremonial forms of control. These include the recruitment of only a selected few individuals, each of whom has been through a school-ing and professionalization process which has taught him or her to inter-nalize the desired values and to revere the appropriate ceremonies. The most important of those ceremonies, such as 'hazing' of new members in seminars, going to professional society meetings, and writing scientific articles for publication in learned journals, will continue to be encouraged within the laboratory.

Now, it is commonly supposed that such rituals, which characterize not only research laboratories but also hospitals, schools, government agencies and investment banks, constitute quaint but essentially useless and per-haps even harmful practice. But if it is not possible to measure either behavior or outputs and it is therefore not possible to 'rationally' evalu-ate the work of the organization, what alternatives is there but to carefully select workers so that you can be assured of having an able and committed set of people, and then engaging in rituals and ceremonies which serve the purpose of rewarding those who display the underlying attitudes and values which are likely to lead to organizational success, thus reminding everyone of what they are supposed to be trying to achieve, even if they can't tell whether or not they are achieving it?

Whereas output and behavior control (see also Ouchi and Maguire [30], Ouchi [31]) can be implemented through a marker or a bureaucracy, ceremonial forms of control (see Meyer and Rowan [28]) can be implemented through a clan. Because ceremonial forms of control explicitly are unable to exercise monitoring and evaluation of anything but attitudes, values, and beliefs, and because attitudes, values, and beliefs are typically acquired more slowly than are manual or cognitive abilities, ceremonial forms of control require the stability of membership which characterizes the clan.

Loose coupling

It has recently become fashionable among organization theorists to argue that relatively few real organizations possess the underlying 'rationality' which is assumed in market and bureaucratic forms of control. Parsons [32], Williamson [48], and Ouchi [31] have argued that most hierarchies fail to transmit control with any accuracy from top to bottom. Simon has made a convincing case that most organizations do not have a single or an integrated set of goals or objectives [41] and that the subunits of organizations are, as a matter of necessity, only loosely joined to each other [40]. Evan [14], Pfeffer [34], and Aldrich [2] have argued that the structure of most organizations is determined more by their environment than by any purposive, technologically-motived managerial strategy. Hannan and Freeman [18] have argued even more strongly that organizational form is isomorphic with ecological conditions, thus implying that organizations can be designed only by nature, through a process of selection; and Cohen, March, and Olsen [10] have argued that organizational decision processes are far from our view of 'rationality' and have chosen instead the metaphor of the 'garbage can' to describe them.

If there is any truth in this very considerable attack on our notions of the orderliness and rationality with which organizations function, then we must guess that the forms of control which are dominant today may be inappropriate in future organizations.

Under conditions of ambiguity, of loose coupling, and of uncertainty, measurement with reliability and with precision is not possible. A control system based on such measurements is likely to systematically reward a narrow range of maladaptive behavior, leading ultimately to organizational decline. It may be that, under such conditions, the clan form of control, which operates by stressing values and objectives as much as behavior, is preferable. An organization which evaluates people on their values, their motivation, can tolerate wide differences in styles of performance; that is exactly what is desirable under conditions of ambiguity, when means-ends relationships are only poorly understood; it encourages experimentation and variety.

6. A FEW CLOSING OBSERVATIONS

Organizations vary in the degree to which they are loosely or tightly coupled. Many organizations, particularly those in relatively stable manufacturing industries, fit the requirements for behavior control or for output control. Control mechanisms of the market or bureaucratic variety can be designed into such organizations. Organizations in the public sector, in service industries, and in fast-growing technologies may not fit these specifications and perhaps should have cultural or clan forms of control instead.

The student of organizational control should take care to understand that clans, which operate on ceremony and on ritual, have forms of control which by their nature are subtle and are ordinarily not visible to the inexperienced eye. Many is the eager young manager who has taken a quick look around, observed that no control mechanisms exist, and then begun a campaign to install a bureaucratic or market mechanism of some sort, only to trip over the elaborate ceremonial forms of control which are in place and working quite effectively.

This paper has presented the argument that the design of organizational control mechanisms must focus on the problems of achieving cooperation among individuals who hold partially divergent objectives. Basically, such a collection of people can be moved towards cooperative action through one of three devices: a market mechanism which precisely evaluates each person's contribution and permits each to pursue non-organizational goals, but at a personal loss of reward; a clan mechanism which attains cooperation by selecting and socializing individuals such that their individual objectives substantially overlap with the organization's objectives; and a bureaucratic mechanism which does a little of each: it partly evaluates performance as closely as possible, and it partly engenders feelings of commitment to the idea of legitimate authority in hierarchies.

There are two underlying issues which are of central importance in determining which form of control will be more efficient. First is the question of the clarity with which performance can be assessed. Second is the degree of goal incongruence. These two dimensions are intimately related in determining the forms of control that will emerge, but each of these dimensions is shaped by an independent set of forces.

The intimate relationship between the two dimensions is evidenced in the observation that high levels of goal incongruity can be tolerated only so long as performance can be evaluated with precision. Conversely, high ambiguity concerning performance can be tolerated only if goal incongruity is trivial. In everyday language, people must either be able to trust each other or to closely monitor each other if they are to engage in cooperative enterprises.

However, the possibility of goal compatibility is shaped by forces independent of those which determine the level of performance evaluation. It has long been argued by sociologists and organization theorists that geographical mobility, urbanization, and industrialization, which tend to occur together, all undermine the basic forms of goal compatibility on which communal trust is founded. While these arguments have been advanced to explain the increasing bureaucratization of whole societies, they apply equally to work organizations. Growth, turnover, and specialization all undermine the possibility of developing goal congruence in work organizations and thus imply the dominance of bureaucratic and market forms.

On the other hand, it has equally been argued by organization theorists that technological interdependence is inimical to clear performance assessment, and that such interdependence will increase over time among organizations generally. This argument forecloses the development of market and bureaucratic forms, which require clarity of assessment.

In the immediate sense, the problem of organization design is to discover that balance of socialization and measurement which most efficiently permits a particular organization to achieve cooperation among its members. In the longer run, the problem is to understand how, in a society that is increasingly pluralistic and thus goal-incongruent, in which interest groups become more distinct and in which a sense of community seems remote, the control of organizations can be achieved without recourse to an unthinking bureaucratization which is at odds with the increasing interdependence and ambiguity which characterize economic organizations.[1]

ACKNOWLEDGEMENT

Accepted by Arie Y. Lewin; received January 11, 1979. This paper has been with the author 3 months for 2 revisions.

REFERENCES

1. Alchian, Armen A. and Demsetz, Harold. 'Production. Information Costs, and Economic Organization,' *Amer. Econom. Rev.*, Vol. 62 (1972), pp. 777–795.
2. Aldrich, Howard, 'An Organization-Environment Perspective on Cooperation and Conflict Between Organizations in the Manpower Training System,' in Anant Negandhi, ed., *Conflict and Power in Complex Organizations*, Kent State Univ., Kent, Ohio, 1972.
3. Argyris, Chris, *Integrating the Individual and the Organization*, Wiley, New York, 1964.
4. Arrow, Kenneth J., *The Limits of Organization*, Norton, New York, 1974, pp. 1–29.
5. Barnard, Chester I., *The Functions of the Executive*, Harvard Univ. Press, Cambridge, Mass., 1938.

[1] I am indebted to Thomas R. Hofstedt, with whom I first taught a course on Organizational Control, to Thomas L. Whisler, who introduced me to this topic, and to John W. Meyer and Oliver E. Williamson, whose creative insights to the problem of control have opened up my mind. I am also indebted to Arie Lewin, Patrick Connor, Kathleen Eisenhardt, and Charles T. Horngren for their constructive criticisms.

6. Blau, Peter M., *The Dynamics of Bureaucracy*, Univ. of Chicago Press, Chicago, Ill., 1955.

7. —— and Scott, W. Richard, *Formal Organizations*, Scott, Foresman, San Francisco, Calif., 1962.

8. Clark, Burton R., *The Distinctive College: Antioch, Reed, and Swarthmore*, Aldine, Chicago, Ill., 1970.

9. Coase, R.H., 'The Nature of the Firm,' *Economica*, New Series. Vol. 4 (1937), pp. 386–405.

10. Cohen, Michael D., March, James G. and Olsen, Johan P., 'A Garbage Can Model of Organizational Choice,' *Admin. Sci. Quart.*, Vol. 17 (1972), March, pp. 1–25.

11. Davis, Stanley M. and Lawrence, Paul R., *Matrix*, Addison-Wesley, Reading, Mass., 1977.

12. Dore, Ronald, *British Factory – Japanese Factory*, Univ. of California Press, Berkeley, Calif., 1973.

13. Etzioni, Amitai, 'Organizational Control Structure,' in J.G. March, ed., *Handbook of Organizations*, Rand McNally, Chicago, Ill., 1965, pp. 650–677.

14. Evan, William M., 'The Organization-Set,' in James D. Thompson. ed., *Approaches to Organizational Design*, Univ. of Pittsburgh Press, Pittsburg, Pa., 1966.

15. Galbraith, Jay, *Designing Complex Organizations*, Organization Development Series, Addison-Wesley, Reading, Mass., 1973.

16. Gouldner, Alvin W., *Patterns of Industrial Bureaucracy*, Free Press, New York, 1954.

17. ——, 'The Norm of Reciprocity,' *Amer. Sociological Rev.*, Vol. 25 (1961), pp. 161–179.

18. Hannan, Michael T. and Freeman, John H., 'The Population Ecology of Organizations,' *Amer. J. Sociology*, Vol. 82 (1977), pp. 929–964.

19. Kaufman, Herbert, *The Forest Ranger: A Study in Administrative Behavior*, The Johns Hopkins Univ. Press, Baltimore, Md., 1967.

20. Kelman, H.C., 'Compliance, Identification, and Internalization: Three Processes of Attitude Change,' *J. Conflict Resolution*, Vol. 2 (1958), pp. 51–60.

21. Lawrence, Paul R. and Lorsch, Jay W., *Organization and Environment: Managing Differentiation and Integration*, Harvard University, Graduate School of Business Administration, Boston, Mass., 1967.

22. Light, Ivan H., *Ethnic Enterprise in America*, Univ. of California Press, Berkeley, Calif., 1972.

23. Likert, Rensis, *The Human Organization: Its Management and Value*, McGraw-Hill, New York, 1967.

24. Lipset, Seymour M., Trow, Martin A. and Coleman, James S., *Union Democracy*, Free Press, Glencoe, Ill., 1956.

25. March, James G. and Simon, Herbert A., *Organizations*, Wiley, New York, 1958.

26. Marschak, Thomas A., 'Economic Theories of Organization,' in J.G. March (ed.), *Handbook of Organizations*, Rand McNally, Chicago, Ill., 1965, pp. 423–450.

27. Matthews, Donald R., *U.S. Senators and Their World*, Univ. of North Carolina Press, Chapel Hill, N.C., 1960.

28. Meyer, John W. and Rowan, Brian, 'Institutionalized Organizations:

Formal Structure as Myth and Ceremony,' *Amer. J. Sociology*, Vol. 83, No. 2 (September 1977), pp. 340–363.

29. Nakane, Chie, *Japanese Society*, Penguin Books, Middlesex, 1973.
30. Ouchi, W.G., and Maguire, M.A., 'Organizational Contol; Two Functions,' *Admin. Sci. Quart.*, Vol. 20 (December 1975), pp. 559–569.
31. ——, 'The Transmission of Control Through Organizational Hierarchy,' *Acad. Management J.*, Vol. 21, No. 2 (1978).
32. Parson, Talcott, *Structure and Process in Modern Society*, Free Press, New York, 1960.
33. Perrow, Charles, *Complex Organizations: A Critical Essay*, Scott, Foresman, Glenview, Ill., 1972.
34. Pfeffer, Jeffrey, 'Beyond Management and the Worker: The Institutional Function of Management,' *Acad. Management Rev.*, Vol. 1 (1976), pp. 36–46.
35. Reeves, T. Kynaston and Woodward, Joan, 'The Study of Managerial Control,' in J. Woodward, ed., *Industrial Organization: Behaviour and Control*, Oxford Univ. Press., London, 1970.
36. Roethlisberger, Fritz J. and Dickson, William J., *Management and the Worker*, Harvard Univ. Press, Cambridge, Mass., 1939.
37. Rohlen, Thomas P., *For Harmony and Strength: Japanese White-Collar Organization in Anthropological Perspective.* Univ. of California Press, Berkeley, Calif., 1974.
38. Selznick, Philip, *TVA and the Grass Roots*, Univ. of California Press, Berkeley, Calif., 1949.
39. Simon, H.A., 'A Formal Theory of the Employment Relation,' in H.A. Simon, *Models of War*, Wiley, New York, 1957, pp. 183–195.
40. ——, 'The Architecture of Complexity,' *Prox. Amer. Philos. Soc.*, Vol. 106 (December 1962), pp. 467–482.
41. ——, 'On the Concept of Organizational Goal,' *Admin. Sci. Quart.*, Vol. 9, No. 1 (June 1964), pp. 1–22.
42. Tannenbaum, Arnold, *Control in Organizations*, McGraw-Hill, New York, 1968.
43. Thompson, James D., *Organizations In Action*, McGraw-Hill, New York, 1969.
44. Trist, Eric L. and Bamforth, K.W., 'Some Social and Psychological Consequences of the Longwall Method of Goal-Getting,' *Human Relations*, Vol. 4 (February 1951), pp. 3–38.
45. Vancil, Richard F., 'What Kind of Management Control Do You Need?,' in *Harvard Business Review – On Management*, Harper and Row, New York, 1975, pp. 464–481.
46. Weber, Max, *The Theory of Social and Economic Organization*, translated by A.M. Henderson and T. Parsons, Free Press, New York, 1947.
47. Weick, Karl E., 'Educational Organizations As Loosely Coupled Systems,' *Admin. Sci. Quart.*, Vol. 21 (March 1976), pp. 1–19.
48. Williamson, Oliver A., *Markets and Hierarchies: Analysis and Antitrust Implications.* Free Press, New York, 1975.

5

The contingency theory of management accounting: achievement and prognosis

David T. Otley
Department of Accounting and Finance, University of Lancaster, Lancaster, U.K.

ABSTRACT

Contingency theories of management accounting have become a current vogue but have produced few significant new results. By surveying the development and content of these theories it is argued that they have been based on an inadequate and insufficiently articulated model. An improved model, based on ideas of organizational control and effectiveness, is put forward which suggests appropriate directions for future work that will be both perceptive and cumulative.

The use of a contingency framework for the analysis of management accounting information systems is a recent vogue. Although contingency formulations were developed in the organization theory literature in the early to mid-1960s there was no reference to contingency theory in the accounting literature before the mid-1970s. However, during the past five years it has come to dominate the published work on the behavioural and organizational aspects of management accounting. This rapid rise and apparently widespread acceptance of a new theoretical framework requires examination to establish whether it represents an important advance in understanding or is merely a passing fad.

In this paper the contribution made by contingency approaches is reviewed and assessed by reference to what is considered to be a minimally necessary framework for the construction of a true contingency theory. It is argued that the contingency approach is an important development in the theory of management accounting, but that it requires both improved conceptual clarity and the use of different research methodologies to those commonly reported. Firstly, the main features of the contingency approach

Source: Otley, D.T. (1980) *Accounting, Organizations and Society*, **5** (4), pp. 413–28.

and its application to accounting control systems are examined by considering some situations where contingency theories have emerged from the interpretation of research data. Secondly, the content of current contingency theories of management accounting, both empirical and theoretical, is outlined and assessed by reference to a framework for evaluation based on an organizational control perspective. Finally, the implications of this perspective for research are discussed.

THE CONTINGENCY APPROACH

The contingency approach to management accounting is based on the premise that there is no universally appropriate accounting system which applies equally to all organizations in all circumstances. Rather, it is suggested that particular features of an appropriate accounting system will depend upon the specific circumstances in which an organization finds itself. Thus a contingency theory must identify *specific aspects* of an accounting system which are associated with certain *defined circumstances* and demonstrate an *appropriate matching*.

Although the contingency framework is new, management accounting has long recognized its inter-relationship with organizational and behavioural factors, as is exemplified by Horngren's (1972) exhortation to the effect that

the design of a (management accounting) system and the design of an organizational structure are really inseparable and interdependent.

Unfortunately he gives no practical guidelines as to how this joint design task should be undertaken. A more recent text by Dermer (1977) explicitly adopts a contingency framework emphasizing that:

the design of any planning and control system is situationally specific. The intent of this text is not to tell a system designer what should be done; rather, it is to convey the fact that there are a number of possibilities that might be done in any particular situation.... This text squarely faces the uncertain and contingent application of most of the activities and techniques which make up the planning and control system.

But although relevant contingencies are specified and some of their implications explored, few practical guidelines are given as to their impact on accounting system design. The contingency approach is invoked, so it seems, in order to cover up some of the embarrassing ambiguities that exist in the universalist approach.

Neither is the research literature of greater help. Although empirical studies exist they are vague as to the links between specified contingencies and appropriate accounting systems design, as is demonstrated later. The radical change in emphasis observed over the past five years is thus disturbing in that the insights obtained do not appear to be capable of conversion into practical design guidelines. The idea that 'it all depends' tends to be used as a means of avoiding rather than addressing design implications. The contingency approach, thus, has the appearance of being an influential but ephemeral fashion and it is particularly insidious because it occurs in a relatively immature field.

Two main lines of development can be distinguished. On the one hand, there are studies which have not explicitly attempted to use a contingency framework, but where contingent results have emerged either within the study itself or when its results have been interpreted in conjunction with those of other comparable work. On the other hand, some studies have begun with a contingency framework in mind and have explicitly attempted to assess the impact of various hypothesized contingent factors, either theoretically or by empirical testing. The first type of study will be examined in the next section, which will also serve to provide illustrations of the nature of contingency theories, whereas discussion of the second type of study will be deferred until the following section.

THE EMERGENCE OF CONTINGENCY FORMULATIONS

It might be thought that the justification for adopting a contingency theory of management accounting is that it emerged as a necessary means of interpreting the results of empirical research. This is true to a limited extent and the work reviewed in this section gives an insight into the types of hypothesis that have been put forward to explain apparently contradictory findings. However, it is also argued that this type of work does not by itself account for the rapid rise of contingency formulations; and that it is necessary to look to parallel developments in organization theory to develop an adequate explanation.

The influence of empirical results

Conflicting results which could not satisfactorily be resolved within a universal framework, have been one source of stimulus for the development of contingency formulations. Concepts such as technology, organization structure and environment have been invoked to explain why accounting systems have been found to differ from one situation to another. The studies discussed here are intended to illustrate the piecemeal way in which the need for a contingency theory has become established.

(a) The effect of technology

The simplest and longest established contingent variable used in management accounting is perhaps that of production technology. The distinction between different types of production technique [e.g. unit production, small batch, large batch, mass production and process production as defined by Woodward (1965)] is a factor that has long been recognized as influencing the design of internal accounting systems although it should be noted that it emerged in Woodward's study as a means of explaining contradictory results in what was originally intended to be an empirical confirmation of classical organization theory. The nature of the production process determines the amount of cost allocation rather than cost apportionment that takes place. In job-order costing the measure of production is well-defined and only limited allocation and averaging are required because a large proportion of total costs can be directly associated with particular jobs; in contrast, the polar extreme of process costing requires extensive allocation and averaging because the bulk of total costs are incurred jointly by a mix of final products. Thus the level of detail and accuracy that is possible in costing unit and small batch production cannot be carried over into process production, although it should be noted that 'process' type methods may be adequate and appropriate for some 'job' situations where accurate costing of individual products is of minor importance. Production technology thus has an important effect on the type of accounting information that *can* be provided and more recent work has distinguished other aspects of technology that have an effect on the information that *should* be provided for effective performance. For example, Piper (1978) demonstrates that the complexity of the task faced by an organization is relevant to defining an appropriate financial control structure and Daft & MacIntosh (1978) identify task variety and task knowledge as factors which affect the design of an appropriate management information system.

(b) The effect of organization structure

There is evidence to suggest that the structure of the organization affects the manner in which budgetary information is best used. Hopwood (1972) distinguished between a Budget-Constrained (B.C.) use of accounting information (where meeting the budget was the single most important factor in a superior's evaluation of his subordinates) and a Profit-Conscious (P.C.) style (where longer-run effectiveness was also considered). His study indicated that a rigid B.C. style was associated with high degrees of job-related tension, poor relationships with both peers and subordinates and dysfunctional behaviour such as the manipulation of accounting data, whereas the more flexible P.C. style had no such associations. He therefore concluded that the flexible style of budget use was likely to lead to more effective organizational performance (a universal result). However a subsequent study by Otley (1978), using comparable measures, yielded no such associations and appeared to suggest that the rigid style was more likely to lead to better performance than the more flexible style[1] (a contradictory universal result). But comparison of the two studies indicates an important situational difference which is suggestive of a contingent explanation.

Hopwood's study was based on responsibility (cost) centres in an integrated steel works which had extensive inter-dependence with each other. Otley's study involved responsibility (profit) centres in the coal

---

[1] It should be noted that Otley's study also suggested that style of budget use is not an independent variable, but is itself influenced by environmental and economic factors.

mining industry which were, for all practical purposes, independent of each other. As Baulmer's (1971) earlier work indicated, the rigid use of defined performance measures is inappropriate where there is extensive inter-dependence. The (contingent) explanation that an appropriate style of budget use depends upon the degree of interdependence that exists between responsibility centres may thus be put forward. Because budgetary measures of performance become less appropriate as the degree of interdependence increases, managers tend to use budgetary information in a more flexible manner. The degree of interdependence that exists is a function of both technology and the organizational structure that is adopted, the organizational structure itself being influenced but not determined by technology (Child, 1972). Organizational structure and technology may thus be seen to have an important effect upon the way in which an accounting system functions.

(c) The effect of environment

Environmental factors have also been invoked to explain differences in the use made of accounting information. Khandwalla (1972) examined the effect that the type of competition faced by a firm had on its use of management controls and concluded that the sophistication of accounting and control systems was influenced by the intensity of the competition it faced. Moreover, different types of competition, for example price, marketing or product competition, had very different impacts on the use made of accounting controls in manufacturing organizations. A similar conclusion was arrived at by Otley (1978) who studied the effect of differences in the environments faced by unit managers within a single firm. By distinguishing between a tough operating environment (in which it was difficult for a unit manager to show accounting profits) and a liberal operating environment (in which it was relatively easy to maintain profitable operations) he showed that senior managers used budgetary information to evaluate managerial performance in very different ways in the two situations. If budget accuracy is considered to be a desirable feature of an accounting system[2] different styles of budget use are necessary to achieve accurate budgets in the two operating environments.

The influence of organization theory

The three preceding examples give an indication of some of the variables that have been put forward as affecting the design and use of an accounting system. The three general contingent variables of technology, organizational structure and environment were used as illustrative examples because they have been prominent in the theoretical development of contingency theories of management accounting. This movement from a universalistic approach [perhaps best exemplified by Hofstede's (1968) study

---

[2] It is appreciated that in some circumstances other features will be of greater importance than budget accuracy, and that accuracy may well be sacrificed in order to gain other benefits.

of budgetary control] to a contingent approach in management accounting has been a feature of the 1970s, partly influenced by the necessity of explaining otherwise contradictory observations. But the recent popularity of the approach cannot be explained solely by the pressure of empirical findings in search of explanatory theories. The other major factor which influenced the development of the contingency theory of management accounting was the prior development of the contingency theory of organizations.

During the 1960s organization theory under-went a major upheaval which led to the construction of a thorough-going contingency theory. This stemmed initially from the pioneering work of Burns & Stalker (1961) and was reinforced by the work of Woodward (1965), but was perhaps most strongly influenced by the stream of work that emanated from the Aston School which is summarized in the series edited by Pugh *et al.* (1976a, 1976b, 1977). In addition work by corporate strategists such as Chandler (1962) was emphasizing the relationship between the strategy an organization selected in order to achieve its goals and the organizational structure that was most appropriate for it to adopt. By early 1970 contingency theory was firmly established as the dominant approach in organization theory (Child, 1977) although it has subsequently become subject to increasing criticism (Wood, 1979).

Simultaneously, although quite independently, the late 1960s and early 1970s saw the realization by accounting academics that the organizational context of an accounting system was of fundamental importance to its effectiveness. This had been previously recognized to a limited extent, but accounting systems had been designed on the implicit assumption that the classical theory of organizations was an adequate representation of the circumstances in which they were used. Although behavioural research had been in progress from before 1960 it had focussed upon the impact of accounting information upon individuals rather than upon the organization as a whole. It was not until around 1974 that these two movements came together. Accounting was tentatively developing contingency ideas and realizing the importance of organization structure;[3] organization theory had just developed its own contingency formulation. The result was a minor avalanche of literature including Bruns & Waterhouse (1975), Sathe (1975), Watson (1975), Gordon & Miller (1976), Ansari (1977), Hayes (1977), Daft & MacIntosh (1978), Hopwood (1978), Piper (1978), Sathe (1978) and Waterhouse & Tiessen (1978).

Both empirical necessity and the availability of a ready-made theory can thus be seen to have contributed towards the sudden popularity of contingency approaches to the design of accounting information systems. It is now necessary to examine the content of these theories in more detail so as to be able to evaluate their contribution to management accounting.

---

[3] Although this latter development can be traced back to Caplan (1966) he did not include the contingency framework in his outline of modern organizational theory.

THE CONTENT OF CONTINGENCY THEORIES OF MANAGEMENT ACCOUNTING

As has been shown in the preceding section, a substantial body of opinion holds that there is no universally 'best' design for a management accounting information system, but that 'it all depends' upon situational factors. However assent to such a general proposition does not produce consensus on what specific contingencies should result in particular configurations on accounting information. Indeed, a great variety of suggestions are available, some stemming from empirical work and others from theoretical speculation based on the results of work in organization theory. In this section the content of the main contingent formulations that have been proposed is reviewed.

Empirical studies

There are few empirical studies in the accounting area that have explicitly adopted a contingency approach prior to collecting data. Further, two of the major studies [Bruns & Waterhouse (1975) and Hayes (1977)] use a factor analytic methodology which gives rise to problems in interpretation and comparison. Interpretation is difficult because the factors derived from the original variables can be related to underlying theoretical concepts only by an intuitive leap made by the researcher. Indeed, quite small differences in random errors in measurement may result in very different factors being obtained, making comparison of different studies next to impossible. Thus, although factor analysis may be a useful method of generating underlying 'basic' dimensions [but see Armstrong's (1967) critique] it is of limited use in the accumulation of further knowledge.

Bruns & Waterhouse (1975) argue that a manager's 'budget-related behaviour is contingent upon various aspects of organizational structure such as centralization, autonomy and the degree to which activities are structured'. This leads them to conclude that different control strategies are appropriate in different kinds of organization. For example, they suggest that 'a decentralized and structured organization operating in a stable organizational environment seems particularly well suited to the use of budgetary control'. Their analysis culminates in the description of two modes of control strategy, administrative and interpersonal, which are associated with different kinds of organizational arrangements.

Hayes (1977) suggests three major contingencies which are hypothesized to affect the performance of sub-units within an organization; namely sub-unit interdependence, environmental relationships and factors internal to the sub-unit of interest. Sub-unit interdependence is examined in terms of Thompson's (1967) categorization of pooled, sequential and reciprocal interdependence; environmental relationships in terms of his stable-dynamic and homogeneous-heterogeneous dimensions; and internal factors include the nature of the tasks performed, types of people, interpersonal relationships and the ability to measure and quantify functions. Hayes concludes that his data supports the hypothesis that the effectiveness of different types of sub-unit (i.e. production, marketing and research and development) is explained by the different combinations of these contingent variables.[4]

In both the above studies a large number of potentially relevant variables were measured by interview and/or questionnaire methods and the researchers were compelled to reduce the variety of data gathered by factor analysis. Piper's (1978) study stands in stark contrast to them as it is based on intensive study of just four multiple retail organizations. By an inductive methodology he concludes that the financial control structure of an organization is affected by the complexity of the task it faces (as defined by, for example, the range of products sold, he diversity of the range, seasonal variations, and variations in type of outlet) and that task complexity affects financial control structure *via* the intervening variable of organizational structure.

Technology is specifically introduced as a major explanatory variable of an effective accounting information system by Daft & MacIntosh (1978). Following Perrow (1967), two explicit dimensions to measure work-unit technology are identified, namely the number of exceptions that arise in the conversion process and the search procedures used when exceptions arise. Together they define four categories of technology which are hypothesized to be associated with four categories of information system style. Their empirical study, based on questionnaires sent to 253 individuals in 24 different work units produced quite high correlations between technology and information system style, although it should be noted that the effectiveness of the information system is not assessed.

These empirical studies give less than clear-cut results for a number of reasons. Firstly, a wide variety of independent and dependent variables are hypothesized, with only general similarities between studies. Secondly the operationalization of the variables is problematic, with the first two studies described measuring a large number of potentially relevant variables and reducing them by statistical means. Such statistical techniques do not in general, allow cumulative research results to be generated. Finally only the association between contingent variables and accounting system type is reported; no attempt is made to measure the effectiveness of the accounting system [except by Hayes (1977) and his measure is strongly criticized by Tiessen & Waterhouse (1978)]. All that can be concluded is that there is some degree of association between some hypothesized contingent variables and the existence of certain features of an accounting system. The general case for a contingency theory is thus supported, but specific findings are sparse.

---

[4] Hayes' (1977) study has been extensively criticised by Tiessen & Waterhouse (1978) to the effect that his data does not substantiate his hypothesis. This criticism, together with Hayes' (1978) reply is worthy of close study as it indicates many of the conceptual and empirical problems which are involved in attempting to justify a contingent approach. Interestingly, the only point of agreement between the protagonists is that different methods of factor analysis would likely have produced quite different results!

Theoretical formulations

In addition to empirically based work there has also been theoretical speculation as to the nature of a contingency theory of accounting information systems. Gordon & Miller (1976) attempt to provide a comprehensive framework for the design of accounting information systems (AIS) which considers the specific needs of the organization by drawing on the literature of organization theory, management policy and accounting to identify variables which are critical to organizational performance. Environment, organizational characteristics and decision-making style are suggested to be the main classes contingent variable; each contingency identified is matched with appropriate conditions of AIS variables, although the question of AIS design when faced by environmental, organizational and decision-making style conditions that yield conflicting recommendations is avoided by noting that three 'archetypal' firms, representing typical agglomerations of contingent variables appear to exist. However two of these archetypes ('running blind' and 'stagnant bureaucracy') have undesirable characteristics which, it is suggested, can be ameliorated by utilizing an appropriate AIS. There is no explicit consideration of organizational objectives and effectiveness and the recommendations appear to be made on the basis of 'common-sense' rather than being derived from any explicit theoretical framework.

A much simpler framework is proposed by Waterhouse & Tiessen (1978) to identify control requirements of various organizational types and their management accounting system implications. Two main classes of contingent variables are suggested: environment and technology. Environment is seen as having two important dimensions, the simple–complex and the static–dynamic which may both be mapped into the single dimension of predictability. The definition of technology follows that of Perrow (1967) (i.e. number of exceptional cases and the search procedure to be followed when exceptions are found), but is also reduced to the single dimension of degree of routineness. Organizational sub-units are seen as having either predominantly operational functions [defined similarly to Anthony's (1965) operational control] or managerial functions (which includes Anthony's management control and some of his strategic planning activities). It is suggested that managerial functions can be best understood by focusing on the environmental variable whereas the structure and processes of operating units will be more directly related to the technological variable. The management accounting system is thus viewed as one type of control mechanism and will be dependent upon the control needs of an organizational sub-unit, itself dependent on organizational structure which, in turn, is contingent on technology and environment. The study concludes by noting that the evidence linking organizational and managerial variables with effectiveness is weak, definitions of important contextual variables are often unclear, and that progress may be made by the development of taxonomic schemes. The authors also concur with Hopwood's (1978) comment that 'the critical role played by accounting and information systems in organizations is now being more generally recognized and studied by scholars of organizational behaviour', by noting that 'research on management accounting system variables may be a means of conceptualizing and observing more abstract processes such as goal formation, power attempts or conflict resolution'.

Amigoni (1978) develops a different framework in which the appropriateness of various accounting control tools, ranging from financial accounting and ratio analysis to financial simulation models, responsibility accounting and strategic planning, is assessed. He identifies two major contingent variables, namely the degree of structural complexity of the enterprise in its relations with the environment and the degree of turbulence and discontinuity in the environment. He concludes that increasing structural complexity can be adapted to by adding new accounting tools to those currently in use, which still retain their function, whereas increasing environmental discontinuity will often require the replacement of old tools, which have become obsolete, by new. He also notes a shortage of techniques that are useful when high degrees of complexity are combined with high levels of environmental discontinuity and suggests that the development of new tools in this area is a research priority. Thus, although organizational structure is not directly considered, the underlying variable of structural complexity is seen as explaining both the accounting control tools used and the organizational form adopted.

A further approach is that of Dermer (1977) which is somewhat different in nature as it is written as an advanced undergraduate or graduate text on management planning and control systems. No prescriptions are given; rather an approach to systems design is recommended and various contingencies identified. It is argued that the design of any planning and control system (PCS) is situationally specific in that it depends upon:

(a) the specific objectives to be achieved by the PCS in the context of organizational objectives;
(b) the particular form of differentiation and degree of decentralization chosen (i.e. organizational structure);
(c) the nature and mix of the processes being controlled within any sub-unit, and the degree to which these are structured or unstructured (i.e. type of technology);
(d) the type of managerial style used by senior managers.

These factors are superimposed upon a three-cycle planning process closely related to Anthony's (1965) three-fold distinction of strategic planning, management control and operational control. Although not explicitly building on recent work in organization theory, Dermer's book gives the most specific guidelines for PCS design of the theoretical work reviewed, but it relies predominantly on a 'common-sense' approach rather than following from a coherent theoretical structure.

To summarize, the bulk of the empirical and theoretical work reviewed here relies heavily on a few common sources in the literature of organization theory. Environment and technology (however defined) are seen as affecting organizational structure which in turn affects the design of an

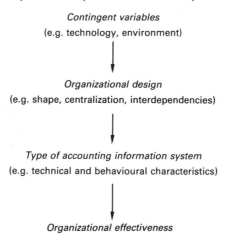

Contingent variables
(e.g. technology, environment)

Organizational design
(e.g. shape, centralization, interdependencies)

Type of accounting information system
(e.g. technical and behavioural characteristics)

Organizational effectiveness

Fig. 5.1 A simple linear framework for AIS design.

accounting information system [Sathe (1978) reviews this literature]. It is therefore not surprising that the defects of organization theory are also incorporated into this contingency theory. In particular, contingent variables are ill-defined, the dimensions of organizational structure (and process) considered differ from study to study and the link with organizational effectiveness is largely unproven.[5] The tendency of accounting researchers to take such tentative theories at face value and to extend them into the accounting area with so little apparent awareness of their defects and weaknesses is disturbing. In addition the research methodologies used are inadequate for the task demanded of them, almost invariably being arms-length questionnaire-based techniques from which reliable results are expected to emerge by statistical analysis.

A FRAMEWORK FOR THE EVALUATION OF CONTINGENCY THEORIES OF MANAGEMENT ACCOUNTING

It is now possible to examine and evaluate the underlying model on which current contingency theories of management accounting have been based. It will be argued that all the work reviewed has implicitly utilized an inappropriately simple model and a more comprehensive model is therefore put forward.

The underlying model upon which the work described in previous sections can be seen to be based is shown in Fig. 5.1. The various propositions follow from each other in a simple linear fashion: some supposedly

[5] See Karpik (1978) for a number of articles which are critical of the current status of organization theory; also Pennings (1975) for a review of the relevance of the structural contingency model in organizational effectiveness. Cooper (1980) reviews many of the criticisms and applies them to the accounting context and Burchell *et al.* (1980) expressly consider the problem of goals.

contingent variables are defined and measured; these are hypothesized to affect the structure (or perhaps the processes) of an organization; for each type of organization so defined it is possible to identify commonalities in their AIS which are associated (or are assumed to be associated) with effective performance. However it should be noted that no single study combines all four stages in the sequence, as is shown by the summary in Table 5.1. In particular, only one study (Hayes, 1977) attempts to measure effectiveness, and its methods have been seriously criticized. Yet the mere existence of particular AIS's associated with certain contingent variables is a weak basis on which to prescribe AIS design; evidently some assessment of effectiveness is highly desirable. In addition some authors (i.e. Daft & MacIntosh; Hayes; Khandwalla; Waterhouse & Tiessen) indicate direct links between contingent variables and the AIS without explicitly considering whether the intervening variable of organizational design is necessary. It is also evident that the AIS comprises only one part of the control structure of an organization. An organizational control strategy will involve organizational design considerations, the provision of other management information, and planning and control systems additional to the AIS. Indeed these may be seen as partial substitutes for each other as indicated by the often expressed sentiment of industrial managers that the particular AIS used by their company is intended to cope with known weaknesses in organizational design. The 'mix' of such components is probably not determined, but several different combinations may give equally good results, indicating that a wider perspective is necessary to yield a useful contingency theory for AIS design. Thus the AIS must be seen as part of a wider management information system, itself part of a management planning and control system, and all of which are but part of an overall organizational control package.

The folly of attempting to construct a contingency theory of the AIS outside of the context of an overall organization control package is thus apparent. Firstly, what constitutes an appropriate AIS will be influenced both by what the organization is attempting to achieve and by the other control processes that are complementary to the AIS. Secondly, there are a whole range of factors that will affect organizational performance other than its control strategy such as the entrepreneurial flair of its managers, the structure and state of its product-markets, and inter-organizational arrangements. The effect of the AIS is thus likely to be relatively small and will require carefully controlled research for it to be measured. Finally, it must be noted that what constitutes effective organizational performance must be determined, in part, by the objectives of the organization itself rather than by an externally imposed standard. There are substantial difficulties in the measurement of organizational effectiveness (Steers, 1977) and, although it is vital for such measures to be constructed in developing a true contingency theory, it may be sensible as an interim measure to be content with the measurement of intervening variables, that is, variables which are thought to pre-dispose an organization towards effective rather than ineffective operation.

These comments suggest that a rather more complex form of contingency

Table 5.1 Comparison of major studies with simple linear model

Study	Contingent variables	Organizational design	Type of accounting information system	Organizational effectiveness
Burns & Waterhouse	Organizational context (origin, size, technology, dependence)	Structuring of activities Concentration of authority	Control system complexity and perceived control leading to budget-related behaviour; interpersonal and administrative control strategies	
Daft & MacIntosh	Technology (task variety; search procedures)		I.S. style (amount, focus and use of data)	
Dermer	Organizational objectives Technology Managerial style	Decentralization Differentiation	Choice of A.I.S. or M.C.S. techniques	
Gordon & Miller	Environment (dynamism, heterogeneity and hostility)	Decentralization Bureaucralization Resource availability	Technical characteristics of accounting I.S.	
Hayes	Environmental factors Inter-dependency factors Internal factors		Appropriate performance evaluation techniques	Departmental effectiveness
Khandwalla	Type of competition faced		Sophistication of accounting controls	
Piper	Task complexity (product range and diversity variability between units)	Decentralization of decision-making	Financial control structure (e.g. use of financial planning models; frequency of reports)	
Waterhouse & Tiessen	Environmental predictability Technological routineness	Nature of sub-units – operational or managerial	Management accounting system design	

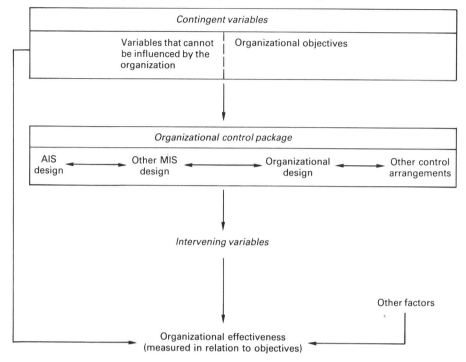

Fig. 5.2   The minimum necessary contingency framework.

framework is necessary in studying AIS design, and the minimal model required is shown in Fig. 5.2. Here the contingent variables are considered to be outside of the control of the organization, although it is recognized that organizations may try to influence some such supposedly exogenous variables (e.g. governmental regulations). Those variables believed to be controllable by the organization are not considered to be contingent variables, but rather part of the package of organizational controls selected for use. The one exception is the use of organizational objectives as a contingent variable, because of their special nature as a criterion by which organizational effectiveness will be assessed. The organization adapts to the contingencies it faces by arranging the factors it can control into an appropriate configuration that it hopes will lead to effective performance. It is, however, important to note that the level of performance potentially possible is also affected by those environmental variables that are also contingent variables for the control package. In addition, there are also a range of other factors that are likely to have an equal or more pronounced effect on effectiveness.

It is explicitly recognized that AIS design, MIS design, organizational design and the other control arrangements of the organization (such as collective agreements, personnel selection, promotion and reward systems and external lobbying) form a package which can only be evaluated as a whole. In particular, there are extensive interdependencies between AIS design and each of the other components of the package. Organizational objectives are also explicitly incorporated, for although in certain circumstances basic similarities in objectives may be assumed (e.g. when studying firms in a single industry; but even here preferences for stability versus growth, conservatism versus innovation etc. may affect comparisons), these appear to represent a fundamental contingency so far omitted from this literature (except by Dermer).

No doubt this framework is still over-simple. Part of an organization's control strategy may well be to influence its environment; little consideration has been given to the pattern of dependence of an organization on important external resources and its interdependence upon other organizations. For example, Pfeffer & Salancik (1978) argue that the key to organizational survival is the ability to acquire and maintain resources, both physical and human, and the management of boundary relationships. It has also been suggested that a likely reverse loop may operate between organizational performance and objectives [Child (1972); Cyert & March (1963)]; in addition the accounting system may affect the objectives that are being used to explain its form [Burchell *et al.* (1980)].

However, it should be noted that the proposed framework takes ends as given and is concerned with the most effective means of achieving them. It is suggested that this is an entirely appropriate task for a contingency theory,[6] but that no particular ends should be *assumed* to be of predominant importance. Thus different control arrangements may well be appropriate in organizations seeking, for example, to optimize client service than in those which are seeking to maximise returns to shareholders or to create an enriching working environment for their employees.

Although the model does not seek to give a comprehensive explanation of the development of accounting information systems [see Chandler & Daems (1979) for one such attempt] it is perhaps wide enough to stimulate the development of a broad enough perspective within which assessments of the appropriateness of an AIS can properly be made. That is, it recognizes that because accounting systems are an important part of the fabric of organizational life, they need to be evaluated in their wider managerial, organizational and environmental context.

IMPLICATIONS FOR RESEARCH

Accounting as part of a control system

The study of the effectiveness of management accounting information systems is intimately bound up with the study of all of the many kinds of control mechanisms used by organizations in attempting to influence the behaviour of their members and their relationships with the external world.[7] It is often impossible to separate the effect of an AIS from other

[6] See Otley's (1980) comments on Cooper (1980).

[7] A review of the mechanisms of organizational control from different perspectives can be found in Lawler (1976) and Salaman (1979).

controls; they act as a package and must be assessed jointly. This fact immediately widens the scope of any investigation; an indication of the range of control activities is given by Westerlund & Sjöstrand's (1979) list of formalized controls, shown in Table 5.2, although reward systems are a notable omission. In addition, different types of control can be used to achieve different purposes as Ouchi & Maguire (1975) and Ouchi (1977) have shown. The simultaneous use of a wide range of control mechanisms serving multiple purposes makes it difficult, if not impossible, to isolate the effect of any specific means of control. Perhaps an initial research strategy would be to attempt to identify those combinations of controls that appear to be particularly suited to certain circumstances.

It is evident that the same contingent variables that are relevant to organizational design are likely to be important in management accounting. Unfortunately the precise nature of such variables has as yet defied definition, for although vague classes of variable have been suggested different researchers have used such disparate definitions as to make comparison between studies virtually impossible. One way forward to greater conceptual clarification lies in the utilization of a control systems framework. Although simple mechanical models of control cannot be directly applied to organizations, Otley & Berry (1980) have identified four char-

Table 5.2 Examples of more formalized controls in an organization [from Westerlund and Sjöstrand (1979)]

Means of control for long-range activity
Laws, rules and regulations
Collective agreements
Product and Market planning and research and development
Plans for recruitment and training
Personnel selection and promotion plans
Economic planning
Investment plans
Job descriptions
Raw materials planning
Housing plans

Means of control for short-range activity
Delegation of decision
Regulations
Accounting system
Budgets
Resource allocation
Directions, instructions
'Check lists'
Standards (consumption, price etc.)
Work flow plans
Work resources
Job descriptions

acteristics of controlled processes that are necessary for effective organizational control. These are:

(a) the specification of an objective;
(b) a measure of the degree of attainment of that objective;
(c) a predictive model of the likely outcomes of control actions;
(d) the ability and motivation to act.

Use of this model helps to ensure that all stages of the control process are considered. For example, although management accounting systems have traditionally been concerned with the first two characteristics of control, they have tended to neglect the development of predictive models. Such predictive models are necessary in order to determine the reasons for inadequate performance and to evaluate the likely outcomes of proposed control actions. Effective *organizational* control is possible only with adequate *organizational-level* predictive models, for as Argyris & Schon (1978) have pointed out, organizational learning is not the same as individual learning and there are many cases in which organizations appear to know less than their individual members. It is thus important to ascertain the nature and locus of organizational predictive models if the organization is to learn how to become more effective.

It is noteworthy that, of all the contingent variables proposed, one in particular stands out, namely unpredictability (variously referred to as uncertainty, non-routineness, dynamism etc.). Even complexity and size may be important, at least in part, because of the unpredictability associated with them. Again the control framework is an aid; it is the unpredictability of those factors that are important in determining organizational success that is crucial and these factors may well differ from organization to organization. Thus a general theoretical framework must identify the major factors casually related to organizational effectiveness and use the unpredictability of such factors as major contingent variables.

Organizational effectiveness

The use of a control framework also reinforces the central role of organizational effectiveness and focuses attention on the nature of organizational objectives. Objectives are an essential part of a contingency framework not only because they are themselves one contingent variable that is likely to affect the nature of the accounting system but also, and more importantly, because they form the criterion against which the effects of different configurations of controls must be evaluated. That is, in order to progress beyond the mere association of particular contingencies and accounting systems, a judgement has to be made about the impact of the accounting system in aiding organizational performance.

However the terms 'objectives', 'performance', and 'effectiveness' tend to be used as smoke-screens to hide a lack of conceptual clarity. It is necessary to question the nature of organizational objectives and study the processes by which they are arrived at and by whom they are influenced.

The pre-eminence of a particular interest group cannot be assumed and it must be asked for what and for whom an organizational action is deemed effective. These are basically political questions concerning the relationships and relative powers of those involved in organizational functioning.

The empirical literature on effectiveness is of only limited assistance. Price's (1968) inventory of findings in the area notes that 'most of the studies (surveyed) do not demonstrate what they assert'; indeed many do not even attempt to measure effectiveness. The problem is basically at a conceptual level rather than at an empirical level as Evan (1976) points out:

One of the underlying causes of this state of affairs is the striking neglect – almost systematic – of the problem of conceptualising and measuring organizational performance or organizational effectiveness.

This issue is also noted by Steers (1977) in his unsuccessful attempt to derive agreed criteria of effectiveness from a review of previous research. Such problems indicate that different organizations will be effective in different ways and also that effectiveness will be perceived differently by various interest groups connected with them. Indeed the question of organizational ideologies and their effect on control arrangements also requires explicit attention. For example, Salaman (1979) argues that technologies and organizational structures are chosen for what are regarded as their control functions and benefits, and for their role in advancing class interests and conflicts. Developments in organizational control technology mean that considerable choice exists in control system design and use, although Banbury & Nahapiet (1979) observe that the majority of systems in use have been developed 'in support of the more bureaucratic elements of organizations, reflecting the more mechanistic models of man and of organizations'.

The evaluation of the appropriateness of particular varieties of accounting control systems must therefore take place by comparison with a range of measures of effectiveness, at both an organizational and an individual level of analysis. For example, at an organizational level of analysis, different organizations may choose to act differently because they have their own preferences regarding the distribution and timing of benefits and the levels of risk they are willing to accept. At an individual or group level of analysis an AIS may provide information that allows some groups to further their own purposes more adequately, but which is of little or no use to other groups. It is therefore important that in developing a contingency theory of accounting information systems the effect of the information on a number of dimensions of effectiveness is measured rather than an arbitrary choice of a single dimension or the issue being left implicit. A true contingency theory can only be developed as progress is made on this fundamental issue.

Research methodology

It is evident that the contingency approach is dealing with a highly interconnected structure of control devices, of which the AIS is but one, that form an organizational control package. In particular, many of the variables which are hypothesized to affect AIS design are the same as those which are believed to explain differences in organizational structure. In these circumstances it is unrealistic to expect purely statistical methods of analysis to unravel a complex pattern of interaction; the researcher must have a closer involvement and develop hypotheses as to likely relationships as he explores the organizations he is investigating. In addition, as causal relationships are of much greater interest than associations, longitudinal studies, where the interaction of variables over time may be observed, are of more value than cross-sectional studies. Longitudinal studies are also able to illuminate the processes by which an accounting system develops and is changed in response to organizational pressures.

However, being concerned with such fundamental organizational processes brings its own difficulties; power structures are notably difficult to observe reliably, particularly when the researcher is dependent upon one interest group (senior management) for access to individuals and information. It will usually require a considerable period of involvement for the researcher to be confident that his observations are representative and reliable (and, if not free from bias, at least containing a variety of biases).

These considerations suggest methodologies that are more anthropological in nature than the methods that have traditionally been used in accounting research, as Gambling (1978) has recommended. Such approaches require a close contact between the organization and the researcher and the validity of the findings will be enhanced where findings are fed back to research subjects and attempts made to introduce and monitor changes based on those findings, as suggested by Argyris (1976). A multi-disciplinary approach also seems to be highly desirable as those trained in particular fields will inevitably tend to interpret their observations according to their previous experience. However multi-disciplinary research is not a panacea and the management of such research teams raises issues about the social control processes involved that are worthy of study in their own right (Tomkins, 1980). Such research methods are intended to be illuminative rather than being concerned with the rigorous testing of pre-determined hypotheses; it is however necessary for appropriate standards for this type of work to be developed to help ensure that it produces results that are both valid and cumulative (Stenhouse, 1979). There is no universal standard against which a research methodology can be judged, rather it must be evaluated in terms of its ability to produce the type of results being sought (Mitroff & Kilman, 1978). Thus Campbell (1976) draws some object lessons from previous research on organizational effectiveness and concludes that

Firstly, it is probably counter-productive to follow the multivariate approach in the development of effectiveness measures ... Secondly, searching for so-called objective measures of organizational effectiveness is a thankless task and virtually pre-ordained to fail in the end ... Third, at this stage, it probably is a mistake to concentrate scarce research resources on attempts to develop results-oriented measures, that is, measures of the more technical outcomes of organizational functioning, such as return on investment, productivity and the like.

These comments strongly support the idea of 'case studies' in the sense used by Hägg & Hedlund (1979) which involve a small number of organizations, carefully selected so as to give a range of values on chosen contingent variables whilst controlling for other variables as far as possible, and the close involvement of the researcher with the organizations over a period of time. There is an obvious conflict between this type of intensive investigation which necessarily can include only a few cases with the development of a contingency theory which requires a large number of cases to give it validity. However the disappointing results of large-scale surveys indicate that more insight is likely to be gained from the former type of study at this, essentially exploratory, stage of research.

CONCLUSIONS

A contingency theory of management accounting has a great deal of appeal. It is in accord with practical wisdom and appears to afford a potential explanation for the bewildering variety of management accounting systems actually observed in practice. In addition, the relevance of organization theory to management accounting is being increasingly recognized and contingency formulations have been prominent in organization theory. There thus appears to be a *prima facie* case for the development of a contingency framework for management accounting.

However, despite the strong arguments for pursuing this line of research, a number of reservations need to be expressed. Firstly, the nature of appropriate contingent variables has not yet been elucidated and requires greater theoretical, as well as empirical, attention. It is suggested that a control-based approach provides a suitable theoretical starting point. The control perspective focuses attention on the unpredictability of variables crucial to organizational success as central contingent variables. Secondly, explicit consideration of organizational effectiveness is a vital part of a true contingency theory of control system design. This has been a much neglected topic from a theoretical stance and its development is urgently needed. Thirdly, the contingency theory of organizational design is weaker than some of its own literature suggests, its links with organizational effectiveness being, at best, tentative. As the same contingent variables are likely to affect both organizational structure and accounting system design, it appears unwise to use structure as the sole intervening variable between contingent variables and the choice of the accounting information system. Finally, the highly interconnected nature of the components that make up an organizational control package suggests that the management accounting information system cannot be studied in isolation from its wider context.

These considerations have implications for the selection of appropriate research methodologies. Initially an exploratory mode of research is necessary, possibly involving the careful observation of the operation of organizational control systems over a period of time, with the objective of inducing the major contingencies and mapping their interconnections with all parts of the organizational control package. For example the study by Murray (1970) is a very early example having many features of such an approach. Multivariate analysis based on brief questionnaire and interview surveys is unlikely to yield great insight. Because of the intensive nature of such research and its close relationship with many of the central internal policies of organizations, attention also needs to be paid to methods of securing the degree of co-operation with subject organizations necessary to yield valid observations.

The development of a theory of management accounting which explains how it is affected by various contingencies and how it is integrated into its wider context of organizational control mechanisms is an important research task. However, despite superficial indications that it is well under way, it has in fact yet to begin in earnest. Neither will it be quickly achieved for it requires painstaking work over considerable periods of time. It is therefore all the more important that such work that is attempted makes explicit the part of the theory that it is designed to illuminate and uses methods that allow cumulative knowledge to be built up.

ACKNOWLEDGEMENTS

An earlier version of this paper was given at the Accounting Research Workship, University of Glasgow, May 1979 and at the European Accounting Association, Amsterdam, March 1980. I am most grateful for the many helpful comments received on those occasions.

BIBLIOGRAPHY

Amigoni, F., Planning Management Control Systems, *Journal of Business Finance and Accounting* (1978), pp. 279–291.

Ansari, S.L., An Integrated Approach to Control System Design, *Accounting, Organisations and Society* (1977), pp. 101–112.

Anthony, R.N., *Planning and Control Systems: A Framework for Analysis* (Harvard U.P., 1965).

Argyris, C., Organisational Learning and Effective Management Information Systems: A Prospectus for Research, Harvard University, Program on Information Technologies and Public Policy, Working Paper 76-4 (1976).

Argyris, C. & Schon, D., *Organizational Learning: A Theory of Action Perspective* (Addison–Wesley, 1978).

Armstrong, J.C., Derivation of Theory by Means of Factor Analysis or Tom Swift and his Electric Factor Analysis Machine, *The American Statistician* (December, 1967), pp. 17–21.

Banbury, J. & Nahapiet, J.E., Towards a Framework for the Study of the Antecedents and Consequences of Information Systems in Organizations, *Accounting, Organizations and Society* (1979), pp. 163–177.

Baumler, J.V., Defined Criteria of Performance and Organisational Control, *Administrative Science Quarterly* (September, 1971), pp. 340–349.

Bruns, W.J. & Waterhouse, J.H., Budgetary Control and Organisational Structure, *Journal of Accounting Research* (Autumn, 1975), pp. 177–203.

Burchell, S., Clubb, C., Hopwood, A.G., Hughes, T. & Nahapiet, J., The Roles of Accounting in Organizations and Society, *Accounting, Organizations and Society* (1980).

Burns, T. & Stalker, G.M., *The Management of Innovation* (Tavistock, 1961).

Campbell, J.P., Contributions Research can make in Understanding Organisations Effectiveness in Spray, S.L. (ed.), *Organisational Effectiveness: Theory-Research-Utilisation* (Comparative Administration Research Institute, Graduate School of Business Administration, Kent State University, 1976).

Caplan, E.H., Behavioural Assumptions of Management Accounting, *Accounting Review* (July, 1966), pp. 496–509.

Chandler, A., *Strategy and Structure* (MIT Press, 1962).

Chandler, A. & Daems, H., Administrative Co-ordination, Allocation and Monitoring: A Comparative Analysis of the Emergence of Accounting and Organization in the U.S.A. and Europe, *Accounting, Organizations and Society* (1979), pp. 3–20.

Child, J., *Organization: A Guide to Problems and Practice* (Harper and Row, 1977).

Child, J., Organization Structure, Environment and Performance – The Role of Strategic Choice, *Sociology* (January, 1972), pp. 1–22.

Cooper, D., A Social and Organisational View of Management Accounting in M. Bromwich and A.G. Hopwood (eds), *Essays on British Accounting Research* (Pitman, 1980).

Cyert, R. & March, J.G., *A Behavioural Theory of the Firm* (Prentice–Hall, 1963).

Daft, R.L. & MacIntosh, N.B., A New Approach to Design and Use of Management Information, *California Management Review* (Fall, 1978), pp. 82–92.

Dermer, J., *Management Planning and Control Systems* (Irwin, 1977).

Evan, W.M., Organisation Theory and Organizational Effectiveness: An Exploratory Analysis in Spray, S.L. (ed.), *Organisational Effectiveness: Theory-Research-Utilisation* (Comparative Administration Research Institute, Graduate School of Business Administration, Kent State University, 1976).

Gambling, T.R., Theory Construction, Empiricism and Validation in Accounting Practice, Working Paper, Department of Accounting, University of Birmingham, May 1978.

Gordon, L.A. & Miller, D., A Contingency Framework for the Design of Accounting Information Systems, *Accounting, Organizations and Society* (1976), pp. 59–70.

Hägg, I. & Hedlund, G., Case Studies in Accounting Research, *Accounting, Organizations and Society* (1979), pp. 135–143.

Hayes, D., The Contingency Theory of Management Accounting, *Accounting Review* (January, 1977), pp. 22–39.

Hayes, D., The Contingency Theory of Management Accounting: A Reply, *Accounting Review* (April, 1978), pp. 530–533.

Hofstede, G., *The Game of Budget Control* (Tavistock, 1968).

Hopwood, A.G., An Empirical Study of the Role of Accounting Data in Performance Evaluation, *Empirical Research in Accounting, Supplement to Journal of Accounting Research* (1972), pp. 156–182.

Hopwood, A.G., Towards an Organisational Perspective for the Study of

Accounting and Information Systems, *Accounting, Organizations and Society* (1978), pp. 3–14.

Horngren, C.T., *Cost Accounting: A Managerial Emphasis* (3rd ed., Prentice-Hall, 1972).

Karpik, L. (ed.), *Organisation and Environment: Theory, Issues and Reality* (Sage, 1978).

Khandwalla, P.N., The Effect of Different Types of Competition on the Use of Management Controls, *Journal of Accounting Research* (Autumn, 1972), pp. 275–285.

Lawler, E.E. (III), Control Systems in Organizations, in Dunnette, M.D. (ed.), *Handbook of Industrial and Organizational Psychology* (Rand McNally, 1976).

Mitroff, I.I. & Kilman, R.H., *Methodological Approaches to the Social Sciences* (Jossey-Bass, 1978).

Murray, W., *Management Controls in Action* (Irish National Productivity Committee, 1970).

Otley, D.T., Budget Use and Managerial Performance, *Journal of Accounting Research* (1978), pp. 122–149.

Otley, D.T., The Role of Management Accounting in Organisational Control, in M. Bromwich and A.G. Hopwood, *Essays in British Accounting Research* (Pitman, 1980).

Otley, D.T. & Berry, A.J., Control, Organization and Accounting, *Accounting, Organizations and Society* (1980).

Ouchi, W.G., The Relationship Between Organisational Structure and Organisational Control, *Administrative Science Quarterly* (1977), pp. 95–113.

Ouchi, W.G. & Maguire, M.A., Organisational Control: Two Functions, *Administrative Science Quarterly* (1975), pp. 559–569.

Pennings, J.M., The Relevance of the Structural Contingency Model for Organisational Effectiveness, *Administrative Science Quarterly* (1975), pp. 393–410.

Perrow, C., A Framework for the Comparative Analysis of Organisations, *American Sociological Review* (1967), pp. 194–208.

Pfeffer, J. & Salancik, G.R., *The External Control of Organisations* (Harper and Row, 1978).

Piper, J., Determinants of Financial Control Systems for Multiple Retailers – Some Case Study Evidence, unpublished paper, University of Loughborough, 1978.

Price, J.L., *Organisational Effectiveness: An Inventory of Propositions* (Irwin, 1968).

Pugh, D.S. & Hickson, D.J. (eds), *Organisational Structure in its Context (The Aston Programme 1)* (Saxon House, 1976a).

Pugh, D.S. & Hinings, C.R. (eds), *Organisational Studies: Extensions and Replications (The Aston Programme 2)* (Saxon House, 1976b).

Pugh, D.S. & Payne, R.L. (eds), *Organisational Behaviour in its Context (The Aston Programme 3)* (Saxon House, 1977).

Salaman, G., *Work Organisations: Resistance and Control* (Longman, 1979).

Sathe, V., Contingency Theories of Organisational Structure, in Livingstone, J.L. (ed.), *Managerial Accounting: The Behavioural Foundations* (Grid, 1975).

Sathe, V., The Relevance of Modern Organization Theory for Managerial Accounting, *Accounting, Organizations and Society* (1978), pp. 89–92.

Steers, R.M., *Organizational Effectiveness: A Behavioural View* (Goodyear, 1977).

Stenhouse, L., The Problem of Standards in Illuminative Research, *Scottish Educational Review* (May 1979).

Thompson, J.D., *Organizations in Action* (McGraw-Hill, 1967).

Tiessen, P. & Waterhouse, J.H., The Contingency Theory of Management Accounting: A Comment, *Accounting Review* (April, 1978), pp. 523–529.

Tomkins, C., Rosenberg, D. & Colville, I., The Social Process of Research: Some Reflections on Developing a Multi-Disciplinary Accounting Project, *Accounting, Organizations and Society* (1980).

Waterhouse, J.H. & Tiessen, P., A Contingency Framework for Management Accounting Systems Research, *Accounting, Organizations and Society* (1978), pp. 65–76.

Watson, D.J.H., Contingency Formulations of Organisational Structure: Implications for Managerial Accounting, in Livingstone, J.L. (ed.), *Managerial Accounting: The Behavioural Foundations* (Grid, 1975).

Westerlund, G. & Sjöstrand, S., *Organisational Myths* (Harper and Row, 1979).

Wood, S., A Reappraisal of the Contingency Approach to Organisation, *Journal of Management Studies* (1979), pp. 334–354.

Woodward, J., *Industrial Organisation: Theory and Practice* (Oxford, U.P., 1965).

6

The organizational context
of accounting

Jacob G. Birnberg, Lawrence Turopolec and
S. Mark Young
*Graduate School of Business, University of Pittsburgh, Pittsburgh,
PA 15260, U.S.A.*

ABSTRACT

It is our contention that accountants have typically sought to reduce
uncertain situations into a framework characterized by well structured tasks and highly measureable outputs. We review the literature
on budgetary and organizational control in the light of this argument. Furthermore, we describe the many kinds of behaviors that
can result from the efforts of subordinates to distort the information
system to their desired ends when they find themselves operating
outside the structured and measureable framework.

Accounting research in the area of information and control systems has
gradually evolved from a focus on budgetary control to a broader organizational view. This evolution results primarily from a changing perspective of organizations, one that is now characterized by a richer, more
detailed understanding of the underlying organizational processes.

Within accounting research, this changing view has led to a questioning
of prior approaches taken to the study of accounting as an information
control oriented discipline. More specifically, it is now recognized that
prior accounting research has been too narrowly defined and as a result
has ignored many of the realities of organizational functioning. In this
paper, we examine the kinds of behavior that can be observed and analyzed
when a much broader view of the control problem is recognized.

After discussing the role of an accounting system in organizations, we
discuss the nature of the task facing managers. The literature is then
reviewed in the light of this broader perspective. Following this discussion,
the major thrust of the paper is presented which deals with six behavioral

Source: Birnberg, J.G., Turopolec, L. and Young, S.M. (1983) *Accounting,
Organizations and Society*, **8** (2/3), pp. 111–29.

responses to the information system. Finally, we suggest how these concepts relate to the resource allocation process.

THE ROLE OF AN ACCOUNTING SYSTEM IN ORGANIZATIONS

In attempting to relate the role of the accounting system within an organization to research problems, three questions which merit discussion arise.[1] These are:

1. How is management expected to use accounting?
2. What are the various inter- and intra-organizational relations affecting the use of accounting?
3. How do members of the organization attempt to utilize the information system to their own ends?

The first question is, in the accounting context, usually viewed as a normative one. In much of the work there appears to be agreement that Simon *et al.*'s (1954) work on the controllership function defined the three relevant activities – score-keeping, attention directing and problem solving. (For another view see Burchell *et al.*, 1980.) However, such a set of functions does not imply that each is met by a distinct set of data and reports. Rather, as their report to the Controllership Foundation noted, the organizational structure of the controllership function is important in facilitating the discharging of the three functions.

While many writers have carried the report's three uses of accounting further, only a few have used the report of Simon *et al.* as a basis for recognizing and discussing its organizational context. Noteable exceptions are Golembiewski's (1964) paper and the contingency literature in behavioral accounting research (see Otley, 1980). Typically, however, accountants have recognized the various kinds of interdependencies existing between subunits as impediments to the development of satisfactory inputs to management's decision-making function. The solution, at least in the context of the literature reviewed by Thomas (1980) in his monograph, is to enact an information system that is capable of resolving the problems and permitting the manager to behave as if the various forms of interdependencies do not exist.

Such an idealized system might be characterized in two ways. First, it suggests that accountants should develop techniques appropriate to the existing task environment. Second, it argues that if we look long and hard enough, analytic solutions to the relevant organizational interdependencies are attainable. Significantly, the adaptation that is suggested (see Thomas, 1980) is one of attempting to overcome the difficulty through the expenditure of resources leading to an analytical solution that is typical of the single actor optimization problem.

The third question suggests that people may use the accounting informa-

---

[1] The focus of this paper is on the *use* of the accounting information system rather than the design of the system or formal analyses related to the value of information.

tion system to serve their own ends. The system is not neutral or impartial. Rather, as Prakash & Rappoport (1977) argue, the information system is an integral part of the decisionmaker's environment. To the extent that it communicates to others what has happened, it is reality as far as the recipient is concerned. So far as the evaluation and rewards of the manager are dependent upon the information it provides, it becomes the manager's reality as well. Thus, in so many ways, the accounting information system and what it 'says' are critical to the perceptions of reality.

In such a situation it is not surprising that the repertoire of behaviors of managers may include (1) affecting the outputs of the information system and (2) selecting those actions that will reflect their behavior in the best possible manner. Gaming the indicator is an example of the latter, whilst selecting the accounting policy to smooth reported profits is an example of the former.

The focus of this paper is on the third question – how members of the organization can, or do, utilize the information system to their own ends. Before discussing this issue we will consider the various dimensions of the tasks performed in organizations. By contrasting the nature of real world tasks with those tasks usually discussed in the accounting literature, we can understand why the opportunity for the behavioral responses exists.

TASK CHARACTERISTICS AND CONTROL

An important issue that has a direct impact on the information and control system environment is the task and/or process that the manager is expected to perform. While the vast majority of the existing budgetary control literature is person oriented, the task characteristics have been shown to affect the manner in which the manager approaches his or her job. A variety of researchers have examined the topic. Thompson & Tuden (1959), for instance, analyzed the problem along two dimensions – 'beliefs about outcomes' and 'consensus on objectives'. These they related to the method of decisionmaking (see Fig. 6.1). Significantly, Thompson & Tuden

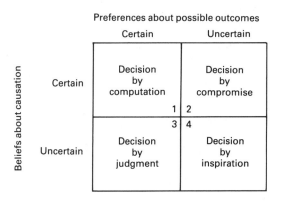

Fig. 6.1 The Thompson-Tuden model.

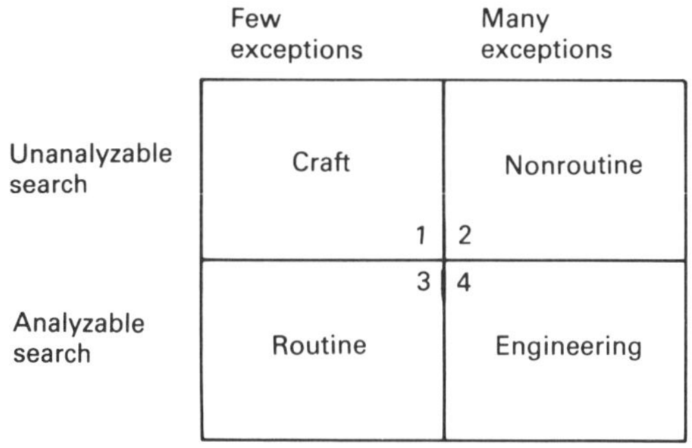

Fig. 6.2 Perrow's technology variables.

were concerned with what people (managers) *thought* they knew, not whether their beliefs were correct. Thus, a management team might *believe* they know how a job should be done, when in reality their view could be challenged by an alternative analysis. Similarly, the team may agree on what they think are the organization's goals for them (or on what they want to do quite independently of the wishes of central management). In such a case, because of their belief that they know what the task is, they can approach the problem as one that is resolvable by computation. For example, see Thomas (1980).

Managers' reliance on believing they have the answer is not unusual. In order to make problems tractable (analyzable in a more formal manner), we often make simplifying assumptions and assume something about the unknowns. These assumptions often pass from convenient tools to begin the analysis, to beliefs possessing at least an aura of reality.

From Thompson & Tuden's concern with the interconnections among our beliefs about goals, process and the approach to decisionmaking, Perrow's work (1970) turns the focus from the intersection of the elements of management to the task itself. Essentially, Perrow's framework (1970, p. 78) is concerned with the extent to which a task can be reduced to a well defined set of rules. (His discussion fits the use of a heuristic.) He argues (see Fig. 6.2) that the organization's response to the planning and control processes is related to (1) the extent to which the task is analyzable and (2) the degree to which the activities in the process are homogeneous among different performances of the task. (Perrow calls this dimension 'exceptions'.) A production line turning out Model T Fords (in black, of course) would be an example of an analyzable task with few, if any, exceptions. In contrast, an auto body repair shop would be an example of a task whose elements are analyzable, but whose heterogeneity of outputs can lead to difficulty in measuring the amount of work performed.

Viewed together, Thompson & Tuden and Perrow suggest a relationship between task and control. If the parties involved *believe* they understand the task and have (correctly or incorrectly) modeled that process, and if the goals are known, then one could expect that the control process would parallel the decision process found in Fig. 6.1 and be characterized by

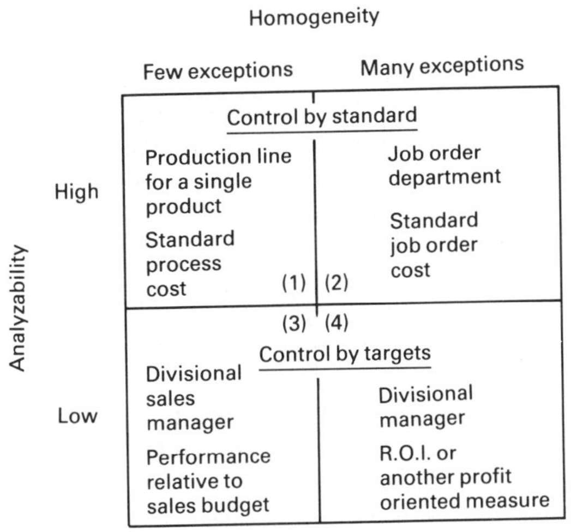

Homogeneity

	Few exceptions	Many exceptions

Fig. 6.3 Relationship between task characteristics and control.

plans based on computation and evaluation based on comparison to standard. As the task becomes more prone to exceptions, the problem of constructing a performance indicator (output measure) and controlling the process becomes more difficult. Similarly, when the task in question is not analyzable, the design of a control system becomes one of focusing solely on those aspects of the process *believed* to be important. This is in contrast to those systems based upon aspects known or stated to be important by formal analysis. The evaluator (and the decisionmaker) ought to recognize that these output data are *at best* measurable surrogates for unknown principle measures that link the performance of the subunit in question to the organization's overall performance.

Figure 6.3 shows these relationships in detail.[2] This figure reflects the relationship when it is assumed that the link between the organization's goal(s)[3] and the subunit's goal(s) (as opposed to the operationalization of that goal) is known. Should the link between the subunit's actions and the organization's goals not be able to be articulated, the control techniques and indicators adopted might be the same but we have no basis for assuming that 'good' performance by the department (meeting the standard) is, in fact, what the organization desires and should be rewarding.

The systems of control found in Fig. 6.3 can also be characterized along the dimensions of administrative, self and social control. See Hopwood (1974, pp. 21–35). Those situations characterized as analyzable, with

[2] In Fig. 6.3 the term standard is used in more or less the scientific management sense. It is based upon a technical analysis of the process. Target, in contrast, is used to denote a performance indicator reflecting a significant degree of judgment and subjectivity.

[3] In this context the term organization means both the organization as a monolith and the concept of a dominant coalition. It is used for the sake of parsimony.

relatively few exceptions and with a known link between the subunit's actions and the organization's goals, would be expected to rely heavily on administrative controls and less so on social and self controls. The social facet of control will focus on the issue of goal congruence rather than the flow of information within the organization's hierarchy.

The bottom row of situations must rely on a more tenuous set of rules and accentuate the significance of social and self control so important in Ouchi's recent work (1977, 1979). Since the task is not analyzable (or, more realistically, may be difficult to even approximate), the burden in selecting actions so as to be as close as one can to the desired (or satisfactory or 'best') outcome is not attainable through administrative controls. Rather, this issue reflects much of the earlier behavioral research. Goal congruence, work group norms, even power issues such as Mechanic's (1964) work with lower level participants becomes relevant in the second row (low analyzability) of the figure.

The work of Ouchi as depicted in Fig. 6.4 reflects his concern with control processes rather than decision processes. Implicit in his framework, is the notion that agreement on goals exists. In the high-perfect cell, cell 1, this agreement is reflected in an obvious common goal. In the low-imperfect cell, cell 4, the agreement is the result of 'clan' behavior. Ideally, in the other two cells the goals should determine which output measures and/or process measures are chosen for use in the control system.

Indeed, since two different groups can view the same activity as possessing different goals, the classification of an activity may switch from one cell to another. For example, the owner-manager of a boutique that will close at the year's end to make way for a new office building may make the decision to abandon such activities and retire. His goal is to maximize cash inflows in the next few months. In contrast, a younger manager faced with the same situation may plan to relocate and to re-open in a nearby mall (or even the office building's lobby upon its completion). In the latter case, the selection of a valid (rather than available) output measure is quite difficult. How do we measure the contribution to long term profit maximization? Thus, the goal will affect the extent of our satisfaction with the appropriateness of the approach to control.

Conditions determining the measurement of behavior and outputs

| | | Knowledge of the transformation process | |
		Perfect	Imperfect
Ability to measure outputs	High	Behavior or output measurement (Apollo program) 1	2 Output measurement (Women's boutique)
	Low	3 Behavior measurement (Tin can plant)	4 Ritual and ceremony, ''Clan'' control (Research laboratory)

Fig. 6.4   The Ouchi (1979) model.

Such studies of the complexities of organizational functioning contrast starkly with the work of accountants. However, a notable exception is seen in the paper by Burchell *et al.* (1980). Their work, too, stresses the relationship between the work of Thompson & Tuden (1959) and the utilization of accounting systems by managers. However, the vast majority of the accounting literature reflects the belief that, ideally we desire an analyzable task. It is easy to see that much of what accounting researchers have done up to now is an attempt to either examine cell 1 or to find ways to make the other cells become as tractable as, ideally, cell 1 situations ought to be. Our argument is, in essence, that researchers have directed their efforts toward uncovering models of the process or output measures that will make it possible for the decisionmaker (or subordinate or agent etc.) to behave *as if* his decision is uncoupled from those of all other managers in the organization.

The accounting literature is replete with numerous examples of this. Although it has admitted the existence of interdependencies among divisions of varying sorts, accounting researchers have repeatedly devoted inordinate amounts of time to resolving those interdependencies so that decisionmakers may behave as if the interdependencies do not exist. This would appear to be the goal of those researchers who have worked on the problem of transfer price and common and joint cost allocation.

Perhaps our inability to resolve the problem for any significant set of situations is indicative of one of the hazards present in accepting the myth (as Morgan, 1980, might view it) that all problems can be reduced to a cell 1 situation if we only look long enough and hard enough. *It should be noted that a critical assumption underlying this paper is that, in reality, a cell 1 world is not representative of those problems with which management is struggling in an uncertain world.*

BUDGETARY AND ORGANIZATIONAL CONTROL

The following section reviews the budgetary literature highlighting significant issues which accounting researchers have studied in management accounting systems. This research has been primarily micro in orientation, dealing with individuals in a management control system; it has not usually dealt with the broader, organizational aspects of the problem.

It should be noted that in this research, cell 1 characteristics are implicitly assumed. The research has centered on the issues of the appropriate level of standards, participation, and the use of standards in evaluation. It has not questioned the measurability of the output measures. Rather it has assumed them to be equal to the task. On that basis, it has been concerned with developing behavioral insights that will facilitate the implementation of the cell 1 model.

Budgetary control

While Cleveland (1912) noted the early use of budgets as an account of official stewardship, it wasn't until Argyris' (1952) pioneering study that a sustained interest developed in the behavioral aspects of using budgets in a management accounting system.

The budgetary control process was originally viewed as a simple and rational process where a superior's set of standards was communicated to a subordinate and subsequently used for performance evaluation and setting the next period's budget. A superior's task was then to set that level of standard that would maximize employee output. Yet, determining the appropriate budget level was not a simple process.

Stedry (1960) in his classic study focused on the relationship between different budget levels and performance and the aspiration levels of the subordinates. His results generally indicated that in some situations higher standards led to better performance where lower standards tended to reduce aspiration level and subsequent performance.

Stedry's study was instrumental in highlighting the effect that varying budget levels could have on motivation. Subsequent work by Stedry & Kay (1966) and Hofstede (1968) carried this line of research into the field and noted that there were limits to using budgets for affecting motivation and performance. Their findings may best be summed up by Hofstede (1968, p. 154) who noted that 'motivation at first increases up to a certain limit of standard tightness; over this limit, motivation decreases again'.

It was thus realized that employees do not blindly accept budgets. Standards that were perceived as unfair or exploitive were not internalized by the subjects and subsequently led to lower motivation and performance. As some form of internalization was viewed as necessary for budgets to have any motivating effect, participation by the subordinates in the budget setting process emerged as one means for dealing with the problem.

Participation

Initially, participation was believed to generate positive attitudes toward the job and greater acceptance of the standards by the subordinates which may result in better performance. However, the empirical evidence by both accountants and non-accountants is mixed. Many studies do support the arguments that participation produces (1) higher job related satisfaction and self actualization (Swieringa & Moncur, 1972, 1974), (2) positive attitudes toward the job and company (Milani, 1975) and (3) motivation to achieve the budget (Hofstede, 1968; Searfoss & Monczka, 1973). However, Foran & DeCoster (1974) found no difference in attitudes toward the standards when comparing open and lateral (the all channel) and hierarchical (wheel) participative models of communication. Milani (1975) noted that participation did not relate consistently to performance, thereby supporting Stedry's (1964) argument that there are weak lines (if any) between participation and productivity. Moreover, Schiff & Lewin (1970) documented some potentially dysfunctional effects, noting that participation often leads to gaming and slack. The empirical results of numerous other studies report similar conflicting results (see Becker & Green, 1962; Searfoss & Monczka, 1973; Hopwood, 1974, for reviews of the literature).

Such results are hardly surprising. Many studies have different operational definitions and attempt to deal with participation as if it were a single variable, where in reality it is a complex process which Becker & Green (1962) have viewed as an interaction of both process and content. The complexities of participation were also noted by Argyris (1952), who indicated that many participation schemes reflect 'pseudo-participation' where there is the appearance of a participative process, but in fact the output does not really result from group decisions.

Although participation has long been a popular idea and is currently finding renewed interest in the context of Ouchi's Theory Z (see Ouchi & Jaeger, 1978), its specific effects on performance and productivity are difficult to assess as other factors such as leadership styles of managers, a manager's time in a position or the company and, more recently, organizational structure (Bruns & Waterhouse, 1975) can all play a role in determining the effectiveness of participation. Nevertheless, there is still a tendency to view the potential functional consequences of participation as being greater than any dysfunctional effects which might occur.

Expectancy theory

With the shift in emphasis from a passive subordinate to one who was actively involved in the budgeting process, came the recognition that a model of the relationships between budgets and the behavior of subordinates may provide a useful too for studying the control process.

Ronen & Livingstone (1975) conceptualized such a model in the accounting literature utilizing the expectancy theory of motivation (see Lawler, 1973; Ferris, 1977, for reviews of the expectancy literature). The basic theme of the model states that subordinates will expend effort when they believe their actions will result in a certain outcome which will provide them with intrinsic and extrinsic satisfaction.

The relevance of the model is that it brings to our research on the budgeting process a recognition of the varying kinds of rewards that motivate subordinates, their relationship to the internalization of standards and the possible conflict that may occur if a subordinate perceives his rewards as being threatened by the budgeting process.

The model is generally viewed as focusing on the major behavioral variables related to the motivational effects of budgets; yet it has not shown a great deal of predictive power. Results have been conflicting. Rockness (1977) found that his subjects acted in a manner analogous to the expectancy model, while Ferris (1977) found only limited support for the expectancy theory.

Some limitations of expectancy theory lie in identifying and measuring specific parameters of the model. To the extent that a subordinate's intrinsic and extrinsic utilities associated with the task or the probabilities of achieving the budget and receiving rewards cannot be measured, the ability of the model to explain or predict performance would be limited. However, despite its limitations, the expectancy model has focused increased attention on the relationship between budgets, rewards and subordinate behavior and its use has emphasized the importance of the accounting information system as a tool for affecting organizational behavior.

Evaluation style

In the midst of all the research which centered around the subordinate and the motivational effects of budgets, a new focus which studied the behavioral consequences of different evaluation styles began to gather support. This movement was characterized by the work of Hopwood (1972) and Swieringa & Moncur (1972) and later Otley (1978) who all conducted detailed case studies of management behavior moving the research methodology into the field in contrast to the frequent use of laboratory experiments. They began to challenge some long held assumptions regarding the role of budgets in performance evaluation and seemed to continue along the lines of the early work of Argyris (1952) and Ridgway (1956) and later Hofstede (1968) who indicated the possible dysfunctional effects of the use of budgets as performance indicators.

The concern of this research was not so much *whether* budgets should be used as performance measures, but *how* they should be used. Again, however, empirical evidence produced conflicting results.

Hopwood (1972) and Swieringa & Moncur (1972) indicated that evaluation styles that placed less emphasis on standards and used them in a flexible manner produced little or no dysfunctional effect. A rigid style of budget evaluation, as characterized by Hopwood's 'budget conscious style' and Swieringa & Moncur's 'involved exponent behavior', resulted in higher tension, ambiguity and manipulation of accounting reports. It was believed that the long run consequences of the rigid evaluation styles would decrease organizational efficiency.

As these views became popular, Otley (1978) set out to investigate the issue further. Subsequently, he found that a budget oriented style of evaluation was not associated with dysfunctional effects of tension and job ambiguity and led to relatively higher budget accuracy.

While the findings of this research have been conflicting, two significant contributions to the management accounting literature have resulted. First, it has identified an additional significant variable in the control process, evaluation style, and indicated some potential dysfunctional consequences associated with a rigid evaluation style. Second, it noted that these dysfunctional consequences do not always occur, thus giving support to the contingency theories of management accounting.

Otley (1980) has recently suggested that structure may be the contingent factor that explains the conflicting results between his 1978 study and Hopwood's work. Otley's study dealt with independent responsibility (profit) centers while Hopwood's focused on interdependent cost centers. However, numerous other factors exist which could contribute to their conflicting results.

Summary of budgetary research

The literature on the behavioral aspects of budgeting began in the early 1950s by noting some potential dysfunctional effects of budgets, and has recently indicated that these effects only occur in certain situations. The research basically has taken a micro orientation dealing with the motivational and psychological aspects of budgets focusing on individuals rather than on groups and on personality rather than on process. Its major contributions have often been diluted by conflicting results.

Organizational control

While the earlier literature dealt with budgetary aspects of control, more recent work has adopted a broader characterization of control. This work has begun to move us out of a cell 1 world by implicitly indicating that it may be unsuitable in an uncertain environment. This suggests that a broader organizational view of control may be more suitable for studying complex interrelationships in organizations.

This research has utilized the work of organization theorists (see Tannenbaum, 1964; Perrow, 1970) and it appears that a richer, more detailed view of the problem is evolving as the result of the merging diverse literature such as contingency theory (Hayes, 1977; Waterhouse & Tiessen, 1978), the economics of internal organizational (Williamson, 1975; Spicer & Ballew, 1980), agency theory (Demski & Feltham, 1978; Baiman & Demski, 1980) and the changing view of organizational rationality (Weick, 1969, 1979; Cooper *et al.*, 1981).

In the view of contingency theorists, the design of accounting information and control systems is based upon specific characteristics of the organization or its environment. The characteristics that have been studied are technology (Daft & MacIntosh, 1978; and Waterhouse & Tiessen, 1978), the environment faced by the organization (Gordon & Miller, 1976; Hayes, 1977; Otley, 1978), managerial style (Dermer, 1977) and structure (Bruns & Waterhouse, 1975; Otley, 1978). In addition, Ouchi's work (1977, 1979) takes a contingency perspective by suggesting that control systems should differ according to the amount of knowledge one has about the transformation processes and the availability of output measures.

Unfortunately, research adopting a contingency orientation and explicitly building on a number of independent and dependent variables, has not been conducted in a systematic fashion. Consequently, the results of research which have been obtained using a variety of methodological techniques do not lead us to any concrete conclusions. Otley (1980), however, feels that clear results could be obtained if appropriate contingency variables were selected, more explicit consideration were to be given to the concept of organizational effectiveness and explicit consideration were to be given to the link between the accounting information system and a broader view of the control problem. In addition to these criticisms levelled by Otley, we feel that there is a need for a more explicit theory which will allow us to generate testable hypotheses.

Spicer & Ballew (1980) state that the 'essentially static method of empiricism' – cross sectional analysis of organizations – used in contingency studies offers little insight into the underlying dynamic processes occurring within organizations. They suggest that the organizational failures framework as originally developed by Williamson (1975) is much more explicit in its consideration of these processes by focusing on the dynamic nature of exchange and decision making processes.

The organizational failures framework provides a descriptive theory of economic organization which attempts to explain why economic organizations are arranged in particular ways. Spicer & Ballew (1980) feel that we cannot talk about management accounting systems in isolation, but that we must view them together with the firm's structure, its employment relations and its governance structure, with transactions costs playing a major role in choosing among alternatives.

Another approach which has provided interesting results is that of agency theory.[4] Using analytical modeling, agency theorists approach the problem of describing superior-subordinate interaction and address the problems of control and motivation. While the behavioral assumptions underlying the model are limited, results of recent work by Baiman & Demski (1981) and Evans (1981) tend to support the kinds of behavior which we observe in organizations.

An even more striking approach to the control problem is suggested by the work of Weick (1979); Cohen, March & Olson (1977); Hedberg & Jönsson (1978); and Cooper *et al.* (1981). In their views organizations must be highly adaptble, flexible and have the ability to create variety if they are to cope with a changing environment. Cooper *et al.*, in particular, argue that budgets can represent an *ex post* rationalization of actions, rather than *ex ante* statement of organizational goals. What is advocated by the 'new organizational rationality' is the need for flexibility in control systems. We would characterize the research at this stage as descriptive because its primary emphasis is in describing the world as they perceive it to be. However, it appears that field studies to validate their assertions may be possible. Such studies would require the same approach found in the work of Roy (1955); Dalton (1959) and Hopwood (1972).

Summary of organizational control

The various approaches briefly described above lead us to the same general conclusion. The control problem must be studied from a total organizational perspective and the links between the accounting information system and the wider organizational context must be ascertained and studied.

---

[4] The proper classification of the agency theory research between budgetary and organizational control was a source of some difficulty to the authors. The findings were classified under organizational control because these studies were concerned with problems in control hierarchies.

Perhaps the most important contribution of prior research is the growing realization that the accounting information system is not a neutral system, existing solely in a cell 1 world. It is often used to affect behavior and has larger organizational implications than previously believed. The potential organizational uses of accounting information opens new lines of research and provides systems' designers with additional issues which perhaps should be considered in the design of accounting information and control systems.

In the following section, we discuss behavior that can arise when a control system inappropriately assumes a cell 1 world.

DISTORTIONS OF THE INFORMATION SYSTEM

One of the methods by which managers will exploit the cell 1 model *when it is inappropriate* is through the accounting information system. They will rely on the fact that the information system is not reality, but rather an exercise in data capturing that is expected to accurately depict an essential portion of reality. If the manager can affect the operations of the accounting information system in one or more of the ways listed below, he can alter the impact of the control process on himself. Put more aggressively, the manager will use the existence of the information system to affect the behavior of his superior. He will do this by utilizing the opportunities available to him to manipulate the nature of the message received by the superior. It is assumed by the manager that certain messages will yield particular behavior by his superior. This behavior may be the result of formal prior agreements (incentive systems, standards, budgets) or be based upon some assumptions about the superior's behavior. As long as information is generated for evaluation purposes, users and producers will attempt to manipulate it to suit their own purposes. See Prakash & Rappoport (1977).

METHODS OF DISTORTING THE INFORMATION SYSTEM

Research from the sociology, political science, organizational behavior and accounting literature on information manipulation documents a number of dysfunctional behaviors.[5] What we have attempted to do is classify these into six broad categories. While some of the particular behaviors may appear to belong to several categories, we have classified them where there appears to be the best fit. Our six broad categories are:

1. Smoothing
2. Biasing
3. Focusing
4. Gaming

[5] In response to Professor Buckley's comments we note that these behaviors may not always be dysfunctional. However, in our opinion the potential for dysfunctional effects to the firm is greater than the potential for beneficial effects.

5. Filtering
6. 'Illegal' acts

Smoothing

Smoothing occurs when the manager is able to affect the natural or pre-planned flow of *data* without altering the actual activities of the organization. Smoothing behaviour could result in the information system accelerating a message and sending a message in the present period when, in reality, the event does not occur until some future period. Conversely, the manager may delay the sending of a message to a future period even though the event has occurred in the current period.

This behavior permits the manager to utilize the information system to his benefit and create a perception of reality that differs from that which the manager experienced. Given the formal and informal incentive schemes facing managers, the underlying rationale for the behavior is readily apparent. Moreover, the absence of observability of the process, lack of analyzability and heterogeneity all limit the ability of the superior to detect smoothing behaviour.

Perhaps the most common form of smoothing results from the shifting from one period to another of a revenue or expense item. Such shifts usually result from the need to hold costs down or increase revenue so as to reach a periodic performance level. In some cases, the smoothing process may operate in the opposite direction to prevent *reported* performance from appearing to be too good in the present period or to ease the work load next period.

The recent difficulties experienced by the H.J. Heinz Co. (*Wall Street Journal*, 1979) provide an excellent example of smoothing. In this case, division managers managed the flow of *billings* from suppliers at year end. This permitted the attaining of a targeted level of performance by altering the billing date for the services rather than the time when the services were performed. Since the information system was attuned to billing dates, not the job itself, the information system malfunctioned.

Biasing

In contrast to smoothing, biasing suggests those situations where the manager selects from a set of possible messages a signal that is likely to be accepted and is most favorable to him. Such situations usually exist when managers are being required to provide estimates of future events. Obviously, the budgeting and resource allocation processes are most susceptible to these.

Lowe & Shaw (1968) reported instances of this behavior by area sales managers required to make forecasts of the coming year. Since the forecast was integrated into the incentive scheme, it was in the manager's best interest to select an estimate acceptable to his superior, but one permitting slack between his true estimate of sales and that given to the superior. The difference represented the manager's insurance against the unexpected. Also see Schiff & Lewin (1968).

When the biasing behavior is applied to the reporting of past periods activities, it reflects what we often call 'creative accounting'. The manager and/or his accounting department exploit the options within the system to find the best message that can be sent subject to the events that actually occurred. The more onerous the system and the greater the implicit and explicit rewards from sending a favorable message, the greater the effort the manager and the staff are likely to put into the biasing process. Dalton (1959) found numerous examples of this behavior in his study of the manager's responses to the Milo Company's (a fictitious name) standard cost records.

Focusing

Focusing occurs when certain aspects of the information set are either enhanced (highlighted) or degraded (hidden). Kerr (1975) gives many examples of this kind of behavior. Professors applying for faculty positions will 'market' themselves at different institutions by either enhancing their teaching or research records, depending on the institution. In the President's letter to stockholders in the annual report, we find further evidence of enhancing the favorable events and degrading the unfavorable ones. See Schiff (1966). Thus evaluations based on multiple criteria are the most susceptible to enhancing and degrading.

Wilensky's study of intelligence (1967) reflects on these two aspects simultaneously when he describes the role of what he calls 'facts and figures men'. Their role, according to Wilensky, is to provide the type of evidence that is credible so as to focus the listeners toward those arguments. There is the implicit suggestion that concurrently they may be directing their attention away from other aspects of the problem. In this regard, Wilensky believes that 'facts and figures' expressed in numerical terms tend to attract the recipient's attention relative to other data. Similarly, the appeal to legal precedents and interpretation of the law, he argues, may serve to focus attention toward one alternative at the expense of others.

In the most extreme cases, focusing may take the form of highlighting aspects of a plan of action that was not considered when the course of action was selected. For example, Bower in his (1970) study of the capital budgeting decision process concluded that the capital budgeting decision reflected many considerations within the unit proposing the investment. One of these may or may not be the capital budgeting model used by the firm's investment committee. However, when such data were supportive of the proposals, the managers used the traditional models to justify their plan. Similarly, Carter (1971) studied top level corporate decision making and found numerous examples of the firm's president making a decision to undertake a project solely on the advice of colleagues, but rationalizing it through financial projections. Feldman & March (1981) provide many other examples of this behavior.

Gaming

By far the most commonly discussed form of manipulation is gaming. Smoothing, biasing and focusing are strategies intended by the sender to manipulate the recipient by affecting the set of data available to the recipient. Thus in the context of our earlier discussion, the subordinate (sender) is exploiting the superior (receiver) and the superior's lack of knowledge about the activity to send messages which are 'credible' to the recipient despite the manipulations we have already discussed. A credible message is one which does not cause the recipient to doubt its validity and desirability to the user. In all of these instances, the sender (subordinate) is exploiting some aspects of the superior–subordinate 'game' to send messages to his own advantage. It is important to note that the sender has not altered his *on the job behavior* so as to send a favorable signal to the recipient via the information system.

In contrast, gaming refers to those behaviors where the sender *through his job related acts* causes the desired message to be sent. The name quite accurately describes the superior–subordinate relationship. The superior sets the rules of the game, i.e. budget level, incentive scheme etc. The subordinate then chooses his act (or acts) so as to maximize his payoff. If the superior has set his rules properly, the subordinate will also maximize the superior's payoff. More precisely, gaming of a performance measure is said to exist when the subordinate knowingly selects his activities so as to achieve a more favorable measure on the surrogate used by the superior for evaluation at the expense of selecting an alternative course of action that would result in a more desirable level of performance as far as the superior's true goal (principle) is concerned.

Gaming exists where the superior for one reason or another (measurability, cost, analyzability etc.) uses a surrogate measure of performance rather than the principle. In doing this, the superior assumes a risk. The subordinate while attempting to maximize the surrogate measure may reject courses of action more desirable to the superior. Outside of cell 1, it is not obvious how the superior can be sure of avoiding such behavior. The subordinate will select his act with an eye to sending the superior the message the superior wants to receive and the message will be credible to the superior unless he redesigns the information system to collect other data to check on its credibility. This has been called the 'moral-hazard' issue in the agency literature.

The most common form of gaming occurs when the subordinate selects an act that is best for him subject to the need to send a report to the superior. This problem was what Ijiri (1975) had in mind when he discussed hardness. Hardness, as Ijiri defined it, means that the performance measure is verifiable, justifiable by an explicit set of rules that should be relatively few in number and uniquely defined for a given setting (p. 36). Yet, even hardness cannot avoid the problem of gaming if a surrogate cannot be found that moves very closely with its principle. It is also reflected in the phenomenon Granick (1954) described. He noted that workers would focus their efforts in a given period on the production level to the detriment of other activities, i.e. maintenance, repairs etc. Thus, the message sent was one of 'success', but future periods would bear the unreported costs of wear and tear.

In a variant of this behaviour, Berliner (1956) coined the term *storming* to describe essentially the same phenonenon but with a slight twist. In his study of soviet management practices, he found that workers essentially perceived the 'ratchet principle'. Under this principle, when production exceeds a predetermined level, the next period's quota is increased by the amount achieved above the old quota. As the managers bonus system is tied in to how much above quota he can produce, at mid-month he gets anxious to meet or exceed the quota. The dysfunctional effects of this behavior are that repairs are not made, raw materials are not ordered in time for the next period, and overtime pay is excessive leading to cost overruns.

Filtering

While many information systems designers go to great lengths to specify the information required by the system, this is the proper set of data only if the designer can indicate in advance which data are needed. Once the organization goes beyond the system design phrase, the process/person being monitored is described only by the set of data reported unless:

1. The set includes an array of attention directors, or
2. The process/person takes it upon itself to provide the attention directors.

Obviously, the person managing the process in question has a clear set of preferences in this regard. The data should be filtered (and attention focused) so that the more desirable elements of the set are communicated and the less desirable ones are not. This phenomenon is called 'filtering'. (While some instances of filtering are clearly within the realm of the manager's discretionary behavior, others may violate the organization's policies, such illegalities are discussed in the next section.) A variant of this strategy is to delay the report until it is too stale to be of use. Read (1959) found managers in firms with more upwardly mobile patterns of promotion, were more likely to withhold unfavorable results than their counterparts in less upwardly mobile situations. (Reported in Wilensky, 1967, p. 43.) Wilensky also reports other examples.

Three other interesting strategies that people use to filter information are over-collection, over-presentation, and aggregation. Over-collection involves obtaining much more information than is needed to make the decision (Feldman & March, 1981). Over-presentation occurs when one inundates receivers with vast quantities of information to confuse the recipient. This is an example of using the information overload phenomenon to one's benefit. Another strategy is to aggregate the information to a high enough level so that the critical aspects are lost. By doing this the subordinate may effectively eliminate attention directing information from the report.

Filtering and focusing are, of course, closely related ideas. The manager required to file a report he would prefer to have avoided filing, may focus attention away from the report, enhance the favorable aspects and/or degrade the unfavorable ones. Thus, the report that finally emerges may be viewed very differently from the way it might have been at the time it was requested.

'Illegal' acts

In this context an illegal act is one that violates a private law (i.e. organizational rules) *or* a public law. Examples of this behavior abound in the literature. Dalton (1959) found that managers colluded to swap 'budget lines' when it was mutually advantageous. There apparently existed the potential for a black market in budget authorizations akin to that for any commodity (or ration coupon) when administrative rules prevented the securing of a more beneficial situation. In the case which Dalton described, one manager purchased goods and/or services for another that the manager could not secure for himself because he lacked the necessary budget authorization. His cohort reciprocated and the barter transaction was completed. The result was the achievement of what the managers felt was a superior allocation of resources, but one that violated the *a priori* organization's rules (i.e. budget authorization).

Roy (1955) after posing as a machine shop worker for 11 months reported numerous examples of illegal acts on the shop floor. When quotas seemed unattainable, machine operators and others involved in the process cheated in order to attain quotas by falsifying data. He also found that workers withheld excess output to avoid an increase in the expected level of production (or a reduction in the piece rate) next period. The workers then would release the excess production in periods where they were short of their production quota or for some reason needed the extra pay. Groups also pressured deviant members who produced too much to return to group levels. They feared that continuous high levels of production would raise the expected level of production for everyone. They were deliberately altering the message to the foreman by 'illegal' acts so that he would not alter his expectations concerning their behavior. Hopwood (1972) and Flamholtz (1979) report similar findings. Flamholtz (1979) describes its relevance and discusses a toy company that was caught falsifying sales figures by manipulating accounting transactions in such a way as to increase net income. Management's concern seemed to be on the external reporting of their income figure to the stock market so that investors would be attracted to it.

Indeed, the original rationale for the Foreign Corrupt Practices Act was that subordinates were willing to take the risk inherent in violating an organization's policy and/or public laws to 'do their job'. The act was recognition that either:

1. An organization's rules are violable, or
2. That there is inadequate concern with compliance.

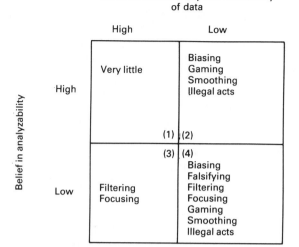

Fig. 6.5 Possible information manipulating behavior.

In either case, the falsifying of data is feasible.

RESOURCE ALLOCATION – AN EXAMPLE

To the extent that accountants are involved in the generation of data to support a given proposal, they are advocates and members of the proposing team. To the extent they fulfill a staff function to the managers who make the decision, they are aiding and therefore acting as evaluators. It is likely that there are accountants on both sides, assisting both groups.

Figure 6.5 reflects the kind of information manipulations that, *a priori*, might assist in understanding the role of information management in the resource allocation process. It assumes:

1. Some degree of goal conflict between the organization and the proposing subunit;
2. An array of expertise, size, etc. such that the authority lies with the organization's representatives; and
3. Information asymmetries which favor the subordinate(s).

It is assumed that under these conditions management will impose a model or set of criteria consonant with their interests. In the high analyzability condition, it would be some model or models akin to the capital budgeting literature. In the low analyzability condition it would more likely be consonant with the policy style considerations outlined by Carter (1971) and methods such as payback.

Under these conditions, it is reasonable to assume that management has the ability (economic resources) to analyze the proposals submitted if they so desire. Additionally, so as to make the situation non trivial, the data are also assumed to be verifiable in some cases. That is, if management is willing to expend some of those resources, there is a condition in which the ease of audit is high. Thus, in cells 1 and 3 management with a (relatively speaking) small outlay can verify the important aspects of the subunit's presentation. In contrast, in cells 2 and 4 the data are highly subjective and/or very costly to evaluate.

For the most part, it is assumed that smoothing behaviour is irrelevant to this discussion. Smoothing is, typically, a response to the evaluation of operating activities. However, it has been listed in cells 2 and 4 to make the figure more complete.

In cell 1, the intersection of the high conditions, it is assumed that gaming behavior by subunits, that is selecting projects which meet management's criteria, will exist. It will be fundamental under cell 1 conditions, as the model used to evaluate the proposals is assumed to be the appropriate behaviour and the act selected by the subordinate the one most consonant with the central management's desires.

Filtering and focusing are likely to be used where the analyzability breaks down or to add a slight advantage to one's unit's project when competition is keen. Because of the nature of the cell 1 assumptions, it cannot be used extensively. Similarly, with a clearly defined set of reporting requirements and the ability to measure and verify the relevant data economic, falsifying of data would be risky.

However, shifting from cell 1 to either cell 2 or 3 should increase the amount of manipulation present. In cell 2 (high analysis, low measureability–verifiability) biasing, gaming behavior, and illegal acts should be rampant. Within the resource allocation decision, an example of an illegal act would consist of knowingly omitting pertinent information such as the need for pollution control equipment from the proposal. When it is difficult to ascertain the quality of the data, why not put the best possible set of estimates forward? The risk is detection, *ex ante*, or the liability of discovery, *ex post*, should the project be funded. While comparing the probability and cost of detection against the enhanced likelihood and benefits from a successful proposal, the subunit will exploit any advantage to present the proposal in its best light. Clearly, more subtle behaviors such as focusing might help generate a successful submission, but it is also more difficult to be sure that they will have the desired affect.

In contrast, in cell 3 we would expect the balance to shift toward those techniques that exploit the central management's inability to be sure they are asking the right questions. (In cell 2 management knows the questions, but cannot evaluate the answers.) Thus the proposing units are likely to be truth tellers (or somewhat of that ilk), but they will carefully select the truths they elect to tell. Thus, filtering and focusing will become important in arguing the merits of the proposal.

The usefulness in cell 3 of biasing is much less than in cell 2 for potentially it is detectable with relatively little effort. Moreover, it is less beneficial than in cell 2 for, if a project has merit, why risk a potentially detectable lie when it has, objectively, merits capable of being extolled and supported.

Cell 4 is the situation where all behaviours may be exhibited. However, this cell is more akin to the evaluation of social programs and other public sector resource allocation decisions than the private sector resource allocation decision. (This does *not* mean that *all* or even the majority of the public sector evaluation/resource allocation decisions are cell 4 or that *no* private sector decisions are.) It is unlikely that the formalistic approach found in text books fits our cell 4 situation. Rather, as Ouchi *et al.* suggest in other contexts, norms, habits, and other more complex processes exert a significant effect on the decision-making process.

The range of behavior found will reflect the values emerging from the organization-subunit relationship. If it is cooperative, as an extreme interpretation of clan behaviour seems to assume, the information manipulations may disappear. If it is toward the other extreme on the clan-individualistic scale, the group may enforce a code of behavior through social pressure. For example, focusing and selective biasing may be permitted but not falsifying or filtering. If the group is to move away from decisions by inspiration or conflict it would seem likely that an implicit code of behaviour must be evolved.

CONCLUSION

While much of the laboratory oriented research has extracted the behavioral accounting research and researcher from the organizational context or dimension, the arguments in this paper have focused upon the role of the accounting information system as a link in the organization. However, because it is not only a channel through which history is communicated, but also is intricately involved in the manager's incentive system, it is argued that it is reasonable to assume that managing the information system is also part of the manager's job.

We have reviewed ways in which managers attempt to manage the system. Some are active in the sense that the manager attempts to influence the message sent without actually having his behavior affected by the information system. In other situations, the manager is more responsive to the system. He selects his actions from a set available to him trading off between how the system will represent his actions and their payoff to him. When the situation is one that is not highly analyzable, readily amenable to measurement and for which the goals are known, there is slippage between maximizing the indicator (the surrogate) and its principle. The manager attempts to exploit this slippage to his own benefit.

Within this context, it is clear that the information system may confer power to members of the organization for they are able to affect its output. This can affect the balance within the control system between superior and subordinate. It also affects the kind of behaviors we should expect to see in the resource allocation process. When the data are measurable and verifiable and the task analyzable, the traditional approach appears relevant. However, as the data become more subjective, subunits should bias their estimates and attempt to game the system. When the process is not analyzable, we would expect that managers would focus the attention toward the strengths of the project and/or away from its weaknesses. Where possible, they would filter the latter out entirely.

It would appear that the information related behavior of managers is an interesting area for accounting research. Unfortunately, the most fruitful approach – field research – has not been a popular one with accounting researchers.

ACKNOWLEDGEMENTS

The authors would like to thank participants at the UCLA/AOS Conference and Anthony Hopwood in particular for their many helpful comments on this paper.

BIBLIOGRAPHY

Argyris, C., *The Impact of Budgets on People* (Controllership Foundation, 1952).

Baiman, S. & Demski, J., Variance Analysis Procedures as Motivational Devices, *Management Science* (August, 1980), pp. 840–848.

Becker, S. & Green, D., Jr. Budgeting and Employee Behavior, *The Journal of Business* (October, 1962), pp. 392–502.

Berliner, J.S., A Problem in Soviet Business Administration, *Administrative Science Quarterly* (1956), pp. 86–101.

Bower, J., *Managing the Resource Allocation Process* (Harvard G.S.B.: Cambridge, 1970).

Bruns, W.J. & Waterhouse, J.H., Budgetary Control and Organization Structure, *Journal of Accounting Research* (Autumn, 1975), pp. 177–203.

Burchell, S., Clubb, C., Hopwood, A.G., Hughes, J. & Nahapiet, J., The Role of Accounting in Organizations and Society, *Accounting, Organizations and Society* (1980), pp. 5–27.

Carter, E.E., The Behavioral Theory of the Firm and Top-Level Corporate Decision, *Administrative Science Quarterly* (December, 1971), pp. 413–428.

Cohen, M., March, J. & Olson, J., A Garbage Can Model of Organizational Choice, *Administrative Science Quarterly* (1972), pp. 1–25.

Cooper, D.J., Hayes, D. & Wolf, F., Accounting in Organized Anarchies: Understanding and Designing Accounting Systems in Ambiguous Situations *Accounting, Organizations and Society* (1981), pp. 175–192.

Daft, R.L. & MacIntosh, N.B., A New Approach to Design and Use of Management Information, *California Management Review* (Fall, 1978), pp. 82–92.

Dalton, M., *Men Who Manage*, (New York: Wiley, 1959).

Demski, J.S. & Feltham, G.A., Economic Incentives in Budgetary Control Systems, *The Accounting Review* (April, 1978), pp. 336–358.

Dermer, J., *Management Planning and Control Systems* (Irwin, 1977).

Dopuch, N., Birnberg, J. & Demski, J., *Cost Accounting* (2nd ed.; New York: Harcourt, 1974).

Evans, H., Optimal Contracts with Costly Conditional Auditing, *Journal of Accounting Research Supplement* (1980), pp. 108–128.

Feldman, M.S. & March, J.G., Information in Organizations as Signal and Symbol, *Administrative Science Quarterly* (June, 1981), pp. 171–186.

Ferris, K.R., A Test of the Expectancy Theory of Motivation in an Accounting Environment, *The Accounting Review* (July, 1977), pp. 604–615.

Flamholtz, E., Organizational Control Systems as a Management Tool, *California Management Review* (Winter, 1979), pp. 50–59.

Foran, M.F. & DeCoster, D.T., An Experimental Study of the Effects of Participation, Authoritarianism, and Feedback on Cognitive Dissonance in a Standard Setting Situation, *The Accounting Review* (October, 1974), pp. 751–763.

Golembiewski, R., Accountancy as a Function of Organization Theory, *The Accounting Review* (1964), pp. 333–341.

Gordon, L.A. & Miller, D., A Contingency Framework for the Design of Accounting Information Systems, *Accounting, Organizations and Society* (1976), pp. 59–69.

Granick, D., *Management of the Industrial Firm in the U.S.S.R.* (New York Columbia University Press, 1954).

Hayes, D.C., The Contingency Theory of Managerial Accounting, *The Accounting Review* (January, 1977), pp. 22–39.

Hedberg, B. & Jönsson, S., Designing Semi-Confusing Information Systems for Organizations in Changing Environments, *Accounting, Organizations and Society* (1978), pp. 47–64.

Hofstede, G.H., *The Game of Budget Control* (London: Tavistock, 1968).

Holstrum, G.L., The Effect of Budget Adaptiveness and Tightness on Managerial Decision Behavior, *Journal of Accounting Research* (Autumn, 1971), pp. 268–277.

Hopwood, A.G., An Empirical Study of the Role of Accounting Data in Performance Evaluation, *Journal of Accounting Research Supplement* (1972), pp. 156–163.

Hopwood, A.G., *Accounting and Human Behavior* (Haymarket Publishing, 1974).

Ijiri, Y., *Theory of Accounting Measurement* (S.A.R. §10) (A.A.A., Sarasota, FL, 1975).

Kerr, S., On the Folly of Rewarding A While Hoping for B, *Academy of Management Journal* (Dec., 1975), pp. 769–783.

Lawler, E., *Motivation in Organizations* (Monterey, Calif.; Brooks/Cole, 1973).

Lowe, E.A. & Shaw, R.W., An Analysis of Managerial Biasing: Evidence from a Company's Budgeting Process, *Journal of Management Studies* (1968), pp. 304–315.

Mechanic, D., Sources of Lower Participants in Complex Organizations in *New Perspectives in Organization Research*, Cooper, W., Leavitt, H. & Shelley, M. (eds). (Prentice-Hall: Englewood Cliffs, N.J., 1964).

Milani, K., The Relationship of Participation in Budget Setting to Industrial Supervisor Performance and Attitudes: A Field Study, *The Accounting Review* (April, 1975), pp. 274–284.

Morgan, G., Paradigms, Metaphors and Puzzle Solving in Organization Theory, *Administrative Science Quarterly* (1980), pp. 605–622.

Otley, D.T., Budget Use and Managerial Performance, *Journal of Accounting Research* (Spring, 1978), pp. 122–149.

Otley, D.T., The Contingency Theory of Management Accounting: Achievement and Prognosis, *Accounting, Organizations and Society* (1980), pp. 413–428.

Ouchi, W.G., The Relationship Between Organizational Structure and Organizational Control, *Administrative Science Quarterly* (March, 1977), pp. 951–1113.

Ouchi, W.G., A Conceptual Framework for the Design of Organizational Control Mechanisms, *Management Science* (September, 1979), pp. 833–848.

Ouchi, W.G. & Jaeger, A.M., Type Z Organization: Stability in the Midst of Mobility, *Academy of Management Review* (1978), pp. 305–314.

Perrow, C., *Organizational Analysis: A Sociological View* (Wadsworth: Belmont, 1970).

Pondy, L. & Birnberg, J., An Experimental Study of the Allocation of Financial Resources within Small Hierarchial Task Groups, *Administrative Science Quarterly* (1969), pp. 192–201.

Prakash, P. & Rappoport, A., Information Inductance and Its Significance for Accounting, *Accounting, Organizations and Society* (1977), pp. 29–38.

Read, W., Factors Affecting Upward Communication at Middle Management Levels in Industrial Organizations, unpublished Doctoral Dissertation, Ann Arbor, University of Michigan, 1959.

Ridgway, V.F., Dysfunctional Consequences of Performance Measurement, *Administrative Science Quarterly* (September, 1956), pp. 259–268.

Rockness, H.O., Expectancy Theory in a Budgetary Setting: An Experimental Examination, *The Accounting Review* (October, 1977), pp. 893–903.

Ronen, J. & Livingstone, J.L., An Expectancy Approach to the Motivational Impacts of Budgets, *The Accounting Review* (October, 1974), pp. 671–685.

Roy, D., Efficiency and The Fix, *American Journal of Sociology* (1954), pp. 255–266.

Roy, D., Quota Restriction and Goldbricking in a Machine Shop, *American Journal of Sociology* (1955), pp. 427–442.

Schiff, M. & Lewin, A., Where Traditional Budgeting Fails, *Financial Executive* (1968), pp. 57–62.

Schiff, M. & Lewin, A.Y., The Impact of People on Budgets, *The Accounting Review* (April, 1970), pp. 259–268.

Searfoss, D.G. & Monczka, R.M., Perceived Participation in the Budget Process and Motivation to Achieve the Budget, *Academy of Management Journal* (December, 1973), pp. 541–554.

Simon, H., Guetzkow, H., Kozmetsky & Tyndall, *Centralization and Decentralization in Organizing the Controllers Department* (The Controllership Foundation, 1954).

Spicer, B. & Ballew, V., Management Accounting Systems and the Economics of Internal Organization, Working Paper (C.B.A., University of Oregon, 1980).

Stedry, A.C., *Budget Control and Cost Behavior* (Prentice-Hall, 1960).

Stedry, A.C., Budgeting and Employee Behavior: A Reply, *The Journal of Business* (April, 1964), pp. 195–202.

Stedry, A.C. & Kay, E., The Effects of Goal Difficulty on Performance: A Field Experiment, *Behavioral Science* (November, 1966), pp. 459–470.

Swieringa, R.J. & Moncur, R.H., The Relationship Between Managers' Budget Oriented Behavior and Selected Attitude, Position, Size and Performance Measures, *Empirical Research in Accounting: Selected Studies* (1972), Supplement to *Journal of Accounting Research* 10, pp. 194–209.

Swieringa, R.J. & Moncur, R.H., *Some Effects of Participative Budgeting on Managerial Behavior* (National Association of Accountants, N.Y.; 1974).

Tannenbaum, A., Control in Organizations: Individual Adjustment and Organizational Performance, in *Management Controls: New Directions in Basic Research* Bonini, C.P., Jaedicke, R.K. & Wagner, H.M. (eds.) (McGraw-Hill: New York; 1964).

Thomas, A., *A Behavioral Analysis of Joint Cost Allocation and Transfer Pricing* (Stipes Publishing Company, 1980).

Thompson, J. & Tuden, A., Strategies, Structures and Processes of Organizational Decision, in *Comparative Studies in Administration*, Thompson, J.D. *et al.*, (eds.) (University of Pittsburgh Press, 1959).

Wall Street Journal, Heinz Profit Juggling Probe is Finished by Auditors, but other Proceedings Loom, November 23, 1979, p. 8.

Waterhouse, J.H. & Tiessen, P., A Contingency Framework for Management Accounting Systems Research, *Accounting, Organizations and Society* (1978), pp. 65–76.

Weick, K., *The Social Psychology of Organizing* (1st edn.; Reading MA; 1969), Addison-Wesley.

Weick, K., *The Social Psychology of Organizing* (2nd edn.; Reading, MA; 1979), Addison-Wesley.

Wilensky, H., *Organizational Intelligence* (Basic Books: N.Y.: 1967).

Williamson, O., *Markets and Hierarchies: An Analysis and Antitrust Implications* (Free Press: Glencoe, 1975).

7

Control and organizational order

Jerry Dermer

Faculty of Administrative Studies, York University, Ontario

ABSTRACT

This paper presents a broader conception of control, exploring its role within pluralistic organization. Reconceptualization is necessary because conventional authoritative and consensual versions of the managerial control model fail to take account of autonomous activity. An alternative conception, regarding controlling as causing and attributing control to all sources of stability and change, is needed to recognize that forces other than senior management can and do shape organizational order. Control is not management's prerogative; organizations are also self-governed through the assumptions, principles and rules underlying their beliefs and behaviours. Control is, thus, a non-cybernetic system encompassing both managerial and autonomous activity. Repositioning the conventional model within a pluralistic framework provides an understanding of why conceptualizing control as the cybernetic implementation of management's intentions has often obscured rather than illuminated the concept.

Organizational order can be defined as the sustained pattern of behaviours and beliefs which characterize an organization and mould its accomplishments. Conventional thinking about order has been dominated by two concepts: strategy and cybernetics. As management's definition of what the organization is and what it should be doing, strategy articulates, shapes, and justifies the context of organizational activity for all concerned. This activity is then regulated cybernetically, that is, through goal-related feedback and adjustment.

These concepts – organizational order, strategy, and cybernetics – are based on a particular view of organizations. According to this view, management controls the organization from outside, setting the thermostat as it were, observing results, and resetting as necessary. Organizational order is thus seen as the creation of management, strategy and cybernetics as the tools it uses.

Source: Dermer, J. (1988) *Accounting, Organizations and Society*, **13** (1), pp. 25–36.

But tangential to this conventional viewpoint is an ever-increasing body of research urging the recognition of organizational order as something other than the creation of management. According to this alternative perspective, organizations are arenas wherein a variety of stakeholders (be they managers, employees, shareholders, government, etc.) interact as they attempt to satisfy their various individual wants. The resulting order is not the deliberate creation of one actor but rather evolves from the collectivity of interactions.

The literature contains a number of variously articulated models which coalesce in the notion of autonomous activity. Its authors view strategy as being what the organization actually does, not what management intends it to do (Mintzberg, 1978). They acknowledge the relevance of activities which are unknown to management, to which management is indifferent, or which management is incapable of opposing. Various labels have been used to refer to these activities: autonomous (Burgelman, 1983); emergent (Mintzberg & Waters, 1985); self-organizing (Hedberg *et al.*, 1976); self-regulating (Dunbar, 1981); anarchical (Cohen *et al.*, 1972); cultural (Weick, 1985; Ouchi & Price, 1978); and political (Pfeffer & Salancik, 1974; Pettigrew, 1977; Bower, 1979). But whatever label is used, each of these theorists concludes that because of autonomous activity, order is not shaped in the way the managerial-control model would suggest.

This paper endorses and advances this position. It rejects the argument that autonomous activity is nothing but another label for goal-incongruent behaviour best eradicated by the control system. It rejects the classification of autonomous activity as deviant, anomolous, or pathological, and challenges its relegation to the pool of unexplained and inconsequential variances. The evidence that autonomous processes are significant determinants of organizational order and outcomes is continually growing and it is persuasive.

The thesis of the discussion presented here is that forces other than senior management can and do play a role in shaping organizational order, and that appropriate reflection of this fact requires a new conception of control. Controlling, in essence, is causing to happen (Boland, 1979). It is the process of creating, sustaining and changing organizational order. Its attribution, therefore, depends on what actually happens: rather than being assigned unwaveringly to management, it belongs to whatever and/or whoever is the actual cause of belief, behaviour and outcomes. Leaving aside the assumption that control is a managerial process only and associating it instead with outcomes (Olsen, 1970) will open analysis to the true sources of organizational order.

Such causal analysis accommodates the narrow view (that organizations are only managerially-directed functional systems) but it also transcends the biases and limitations inherent in that perspective. It recognizes that organizations, as networks of interacting stakeholders pursuing individual interests, are also self-governed systems. Within this more general framework, the aim of theory is to explain the respective roles played by managed and autonomous activities in shaping order. As will be seen, this approach aids in viewing management accounting as an organizational phenomenon (Hopwood, 1978; Hayes, 1980, 1983; Otley & Berry, 1980; Birnberg *et al.*, 1983) and has the potential to provide the empirical grounding needed to yield the theory the field so sorely requires (Hofstede, 1978).

THE CONVENTIONAL MANAGERIAL CONTROL MODEL

Two variations of the managerial control model – the authoritative and the consensual – now dominate the control literature. Both presume that organizations are coherently-articulated systems oriented to functional accomplishment, and both are based on the assumptions of strategy and cybernetic adjustment. Neither fully captures the complexity of the autonomous dimensions of organizational order.

The authoritative version assumes first that control involves the exercise of authority in order to achieve compliance (Etzioni, 1961) and, secondly, that management, whether it is totally self-centered or socially responsible to stakeholder expectations (Freeman, 1984), is the dominant controlling force. The particular techniques used in controlling will vary depending on the authority-diminishing effects of ambiguity and leader–follower conflict (Lorange *et al.*, 1986). Nevertheless, the model retains its essence: strategy expresses management's expectations which in turn serve as the reference point for cybernetic control (Horovitz, 1979; Euske, 1984; Merchant, 1985; Maciariello, 1984).

In contrast with this, the consensual approach (Tannenbaum, 1968) views control more as a property inherent in interdependent social relationships than as a unidirectional imposition of authority. Since control must be accepted to be effective, it involves a two-way relationship: the person in control depends on those controlled to recognize authority. Consensus thus replaces compliance as the organizational ideal and control is seen as a multilateral negotiated process of establishing and achieving mutually acceptable expectations. In place of the authoritative (i.e. zero sum) view, conflict is now resolved by building consensus through such

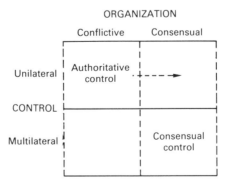

Fig. 7.1 Organizational situations and control processes.

means as participative management (Bourgeois & Brodwin, 1984) or uni-fying cultures (Ouchi & Price, 1978). This process expands control in the sense that it shares it among more participants. But while it emphasizes the sharing of control and the desirability of building a consensual organ-ization, this approach still assumes that organizations are purposive systems characterized by legitimate expectations and adaptive responses, i.e. that they are based on strategy and cybernetics. The essential dif-ference between the consensual and authoritative versions lies in the mode by which expectations are arrived at, i.e. mutually agreed upon or managerially imposed.

Using the assumptions of the managerial model, we can construct a matrix (Fig. 7.1) which depicts four possible situations. Along one dimen-sion, control is shown as either a unilateral or multilateral process, i.e. based on managerially-imposed or mutually-agreed-upon expectations. Along the other dimension, the presumed nature of organization is de-picted as either conflictive or consensual. Thus, the grid depicts four possible organizational situations.

The authoritative approach (emphasizing the unilateral control of the conflictive organization) and the consensual approach (emphasizing the multilateral control of the consensual organization) appear in diagonally opposite quadrants. But because the creation of a consensual organization is the objective of any management system, the authoritative approach also applies to the unilateral-consensual quadrant. The traditional control model thus encompasses three of the four quadrants. But as the dia-gram clearly indicates, it omits the fourth: the question of control in the multilateral conflictive situation is ignored because the strategic and cybernetic assumptions of the managerial control model are no longer applicable.

The conventional model views conflict as a temporary aberration to be ironed out by appropriate control practices. This assumption presents no problem so long as effective unilateral control exists (the top left-hand cell). But when conflict occurs in the absence of sufficient knowledge and power to exercise unilateral control, (the bottom left quadrant), the model provides no guidance. In assuming that conflict is deviant and temporary, instead of a legitimate fact of existence, it ignores a large portion of reality.

It is precisely in these situations that autonomous (i.e. independent self-governing) activity is most likely to occur. But, then, what does 'control' mean? To whom or to what should it be attributed? Is it a sequential or simultaneous process, exercised over or with (Boland, 1979)? The ever-increasing recognition of the existence of autonomous processes continually raises these questions, but managerial control theory provides no answer.

In fact, since the term 'control' tends to lead to the notion of 'controller', i.e. a single outside locus, the word itself may account for our inability or unwillingness to grant legitimate status to autonomous activity. By en-couraging a focus on the activities of one particular source, it diverts attention from activities originated elsewhere, activities that may have equal or greater effects on organizational order.

AUTONOMOUS PROCESSES

The autonomous activity engaged in by stakeholders is their solution to the contradictions which they perceive between management's strategy and actual conditions. It is made up of indepedent initiatives and self-regulating processing which produce patterns of activity and belief (Weick, 1979) unanticipated by management. In some cases such patterns are goal congruent; in others, no fit exists between them and the strategy articulated by management. Although we know relatively little about the conduct and implications of such activity, increasingly researchers are suggesting that its sanctioned or unsanctioned dimensions may involve important (albeit somewhat difficult to interpret) aspects of an organization's order (Narayanan & Fahey, 1982; MacMillan & Guth, 1985).

The literature of strategic management, organizational behaviour, management accounting and decision theory is rich in allusions to the existence of autonomous processes. The extreme position is that outcomes are completely uninfluenced and totally uncontrolled by management. An autonomous situation, i.e. one which is self-governed, implies a senior management capable only of acting as a participant in an ongoing process. Such situations are described in the organized anarchy model of Cohen *et al.* (1972), the self-designing organizations of Hedberg *et al.* (1976), Starbuck & Hedberg (1977) and Hedberg & Jonsson (1978), the emergent processes of Mintzberg & Waters (1985), the autonomous activities described by Burgelman (1983), the influences of culture by Weick (1985), the negotiated outcomes of Murray (1978), the pluralistically determined coalitions of Cyert & March (1963), the external control of Pfeffer & Salancik (1978) and the ecologically-determined fates of Hannan & Freeman (1984).

Less extreme positions, alluding to the partial deterioration of managerial control, also pervade the literature. These emphasize situations wherein management is required to make decisions with inadequate information and to implement actions with inadequate power (Landau & Stout, 1979). Activities in such situations tend to proceed incrementally (Lindblom, 1979) thereby providing opportunities for influencing choices and changing plans as they are being implemented. Limitations on management's ability to decide and act in ambiguous situations, i.e. with inadequate knowledge, are reflected in the notions of bounded rationality (Simon, 1976), enactment (Weick, 1977), action preceding rationality and justification (Weick, 1979), discontinuity and surprise (Ansoff, 1982), and incrementalism (Lindblom, 1979). Constraints on managerial control imposed by insufficient authority are reflected in the notions of logical incrementalism (Wrapp, 1967; Quinn, 1978, 1977), politically-based models (Macmillan & Jones, 1986), and behaviourally-based interventions (Bourgeois & Brodwin, 1984). Taken collectively, these models reveal many of the limitations imposed on management by an ambiguous environment and/or an insufficiency of power. They imply a management at least partially, yet significantly, incapable of controlling organizational evolution.

The conclusion to be drawn from this literature is that organizations contain both managerially and autonomously generated activity and that order is the result of some mix of the two.

Conceptual implications

Acknowledging the existence of autonomous processes leads us to reconsider two aspects of the way in which we think about control. First, as the diagram in Fig. 7.1 suggests, autonomous activities falls outside the scope of the two traditionally dominant variations of the managerial control model – authoritative and consensual – because neither addresses the situation in which autonomous processes are most likely to arise. This suggests the need for a concept of control which is decidedly broader than that associated with the conventional model. Control must therefore be redefined as that which causes activities and outcomes to happen, i.e. it must be associated with causality (Boland, 1979), order and outcomes (Olsen, 1970), not with management.

Such a causal perspective, in turn, requires a broader view of organization, a view which recognizes interdependent yet conflicting stakeholders, and which conceptualizes organization as a socio-political network (Benson, 1975, 1977; Denhardt, 1971; March, 1962) of stakeholder interrelationships reflecting mutual expectations expressed in roles (Vickers, 1956). In this more general, pluralistic framework, the character of the relationships, rather than some pre-supposed design, dictates the specific model of control which should be applied (Mason & Mitroff, 1983), with the managerial being only one possibility. Broadening the model of organization in this way explicitly recognizes that forces other than senior management can and do shape organizational evolution. New ways of viewing organizational and individual behaviour may provide a more appropriate foundation for the development of accounting theory (Dyckman, 1981; Cooper *et al.*, 1981; Wildavsky, 1978). For rather than being limited by the conventional model and its presumptions, a general theory of control must explain the effects of chance events and autonomous as well as managerial activities on the dynamic fluidity of an ever-changing social system. This requires the recognition that an organization, given its full socio-political richness, is susceptible to change in an infinity of ways because it can, theoretically, be affected to some extent by any stakeholder who chooses to do so. Union organizers, citizen advocates, and governmental interventionists, for example, are all relevant players, often excluded by traditional control models.

To reflect these potential influences organizational control theory must make use of the work of social scientists now ignored or excluded. For example, Pfeffer & Salancik (1978) emphasize the differences among organizational participants, viewing organizations as markets for power and influence. Cummings (1977) regards the organization as an arena within which participants can engage in behaviour they perceive as instrumental to their personal goals. Weick (1979) draws attention to the cognitive dimensions of organizations and emphasizes that organizational order has epistemological and preferential dimensions (i.e. that it is affected by the processes by which participants make sense out of the world and through which they form and exercise their choices) as well as cybernetic aspects (Boujon *et al.*, 1977). Such cognitive and/or political models view organizations as non goal-oriented, non-instrumental social systems, emeshed in broader socio-political contexts. They emphasize that organizational outcomes are the result of successive iterations (Hannan & Freeman, 1984; Quinn, 1981). Hence, managerial decisions are not immutable choices but are part of ongoing processes which continually change as minds are changed and events proceed (Cohen *et al.*, 1972; Hedberg & Jonsson, 1978; Burgleman, 1983). Effectiveness is no longer goal-related but can be evaluated only in terms of organizational cohesiveness, adaptability and, ultimately, survival.

A thesis of this paper, therefore, is that the inclusion of autonomous activities within the sphere of control theory requires augmenting the functional achievement model of organization with one which helps to attribute causality. If control is to have a theory capable of explaining and predicting organizational behaviour and outcomes, a pluralistic governance model or organization capable of confronting issues of differential cognition and conflict is required.

A MODEL OF PLURALISTIC ORGANIZATION

Any sustained organization of human beings, whether it be a business or a nation, will have a governance system that contains four essential elements: leadership (management), citizenship (stakeholders), institutions (formal and informal patterns of relating), and ideologies (patterns of belief). No model of control will be effective if it does not explicitly recognize these elements, grant them appropriate attention, and evaluate their respective roles in creating, sustaining and changing organizational order.

The traditional control model as we have seen has focused attention almost exclusively on only one of these elements – management. To the extent that ideologies and institutions have been considered, it has largely been from management's perspective: only management's beliefs have been granted legitimacy, only those institutions, often formal, preferred by management are stressed. That there are stakeholders has certainly been recognized but they have often been seen as peripheral problems to be dealt with rather than as active and legitimate participants. This narrow perspective has discouraged the asking of appropriate questions (e.g. who are the stakeholders, what are their characteristics, what are their various beliefs, what methods do they use, etc.), and that in turn has prevented the discovery of answers.

It is a perspective based on a view of organization as a 'tool' (Perrow, 1972), oriented to functional accomplishment, and of management as the prime causal agent. Other considerations, such as the resolution of conflicting stakeholder expectations, are viewed as constraints inhibiting functional accomplishments. Autonomous activity just messes things up!

The pluralistic governance model presented here is broad enough to encompass both managerial and autonomous activity. It views organizations not as 'tools' but as networks of inter-related, politically-motivated, conflicting groups (Bacharach & Lawler, 1980). It does not reject the validity of the managerial control model but regards it instead as one possible alternative, suspending judgement until it is proven valid. Its appropriateness will depend on the state of managerial authority which is not a given but remains as a perpetually open issue. Concern with authority is therefore broadened to include its acquisition and the political dimensions of its exercise. The model acknowledges, for example, that activities concerned with acquiring, exercising and retaining authority may be unrelated or even run counter to the ostensible purposes of the organization. In an ambiguous and politicized world, certain authority granting stakeholders may have special expectations and management, concerned with retaining authority, may engage in activities aimed at serving this stakeholder subset (Scott *et al.*, 1981).

Management's authority depends on the political role played by other stakeholders. But, because every action is evaluated as an exercise or defense of authority (Wildavsky, 1966; Cyert & March, 1963), each managerial action affects the authority granted for future activity. Authority may increase if activities and results are evaluated favourably. Stakeholders presumably are then willing to trust management by suspending judgement and postponing evaluation (Scott *et al.*, 1981). But the opposite can also be true. Unfavourable evaluations can motivate stakeholders to undermine managerial authority and, thereby, detrimentally affect future conduct and performance.

The pluralistic model acknowledges that a single, universal set of criteria may be proposed by management to shape organizational order but does not rule out the possibility that different versions of this order may exist in the minds of other organizational participants. Although senior executives may attempt to formulate and implement their vision of the future, actual activity is a composite reflection of the multiple visions held by conflicting stakeholders. The objectives and constraints of these interest groups enlarge the range and complexity of mutually-accepted solutions as well as the processes by which they are achieved. Actual outcomes reflect the resolution of a set of interdependencies over some time interval, affect the satisfaction levels of stakeholders, and provide the capability with which to address the future. By relaxing assumptions of managerial authority and unitary purpose, the necessity of a single senior management-oriented rationality gives way to the possibility of multiple rationalities whose continuing activities constitute a pluralistic system (Dermer & Lucas, 1986). Purposeful evolution, guided by shared objectives, gives way to the possibility of opportunistic thrusts executed independently as situations allow (Burgelman, 1983). Hence, the organizational order of a pluralistic organization is decidedly different from that of one which is presumed to be managerially controlled.

Relaxing assumptions of managerial authority and unitary purpose makes two other assumptions questionable, namely that managerial strategy defines organizational order and that there is a clear distinction between the processes of formulating and implementing strategies, the former task being assigned to managers and the latter to the organization. In an ambiguous and politicized world the actual efficacy of authority is often far less than presumed. Stakeholders responsible for strategy implementation, who have nominally accepted management's authority, may actually disagree with the goals chosen and/or the methods employed to achieve those goals (Halal, 1984). Involving them so as to build the original commitment necessary for beginning the process of implementation may cause management to lose some control over intentions. Moreover, stakeholders have further opportunities for changing outcomes during implementation. Recent research (Mintzberg, 1978; Hall & Saias, 1980; Burgelman, 1983) has challenged the traditional model of formulation and implementation (Chandler, 1962; Anthony, 1965) suggesting that the process is often opposite to that commonly assumed, or at least, is interactive. The term 'strategy formation' has been coined to encompass both formulation and implementation (Mintzberg & Waters 1985).

The point continually emphasized by the pluralistic governance model is that regardless of the particular type of organization, stakeholder relationships comprise a significant part of the fabric of control. In keeping with democratic ideals and the increasing advocacy inherent in our culture, and in contrast with conventional views (e.g. MacMillan & Jones, 1986; Freeman, 1984), the model regards stakeholder interests as objectives rather than constraints. Although stakeholder roles and relationships may differ by type of organization, this theme prevails. For example, in democratic societies, elected governments perceive voters as authority delegators as well as recipients of service. Cooperative organizations have a similar object but limit their milieu to designated members, differentiating these from the remainder of society. Private and independent social service and social action organizations are enfranchised by pools of shareholders or members, with management, workers, and service recipients being other stakeholders. Yet in each of these organizations, the efficacy of authority is an empirical question. Hence the issue challenging theorists is the same – to identify the locus of control of the organizational order.

THE CONTROL OF ORGANIZATIONAL ORDER

The system that controls – or shapes – organizational order is thus comprised partially of managerially-imposed regulations and partially of the self-regulatory activities referred to earlier under the rubric of autonomous activity. It is a system that provides for both functional accomplishment and the well-being of constituent stakeholders. The key point to keep in mind is that, although legal requirements necessitate codifying many activities, e.g. procedures for formulating and implementing strategy, for many if not most organizations their complete control system includes a set of regulatory activities which may or may not be documented. Such activities are the product of agreements negotiated by a variety of organizational groups, rather than of senior management alone (Strauss, 1978; Wildavsky, 1966; Cyert & March, 1963).

This system guides participants' interactions so as to yield sufficient perceived equity to maintain stability. Recognizing organization as being a pluralistically-determined order presumes that the processes of justification, negotiation and confrontation are conducted in the absence of any single overarching rationality. Cooperation sufficient to permit a commonality of action replaces goal attainment as the minimum requirement for organizational order. Fit now implies an accommodation among interest groups as well as the matching of organization to environment advocated by contingency theory. An emphasis on cohesion thus gives way to the recognition that the various parts of an organization are likely to move in independent spurts, individually disjointed, but somehow culminating in recognizable order (Weick, 1979).

The autonomous side of organizational control is most significant when external and internal forces constrain what management can and cannot do. Pressure for democratization is one such force. Many organizations, including those privately owned, are gravitating at different rates toward pluralism. The impetus is from claimants, i.e. unrecognized and illegitimate stakeholders who are increasingly pressing for recognition. Also, managerial authority is now being challenged even by the stakeholders who originally enfranchised management and delegated that authority. As stakeholders become increasingly interest-oriented, their satisfaction now becomes an equal, if not a superordinate, goal of organization along with functional accomplishment. Long guaranteed in the institutionalized arrangements of public organizations, the democratic checks and balances inherent in public arrangements are increasingly evident in the fabric of private interrelationships.

Operationally this means that analysis, which can no longer be restricted solely to managerial activity, must focus instead on issues. Hence, managerial and autonomous activities which define issue legitimacy and shape issue resolution hold the key to understanding control. In the literature of organizational decision making, this thesis has a long history. Questions of issue development, analysis and legitimacy began to be considered in the 1960s (e.g. Schattschneider, 1960), and have continued to surface since then (e.g. Bachrach & Baratz, 1970; Pfeffer, 1981; Ansoff, 1980; Dutton *et al.*, 1983). When attention is focused on issues, the notions of controller and controllee(s) are augmented by that of interest groups, interrelated and constrained by explicit (formal) and implicit (informal) rules (Diesing, 1962). An interest group can be defined as a group of individuals aware of commonalities beyond work related interdependence (Bacharach & Lawler, 1980) who coalesce around a particular issue or set of issues. Under the assumptions expressed here, an organization is seen as both a goal-oriented, consensually-unified mechanism, as well as an arena where issues are resolved by such groups, each pursuing its own vision of an ambiguous future.

The role of existing managerial control structures and processes in shaping order is ambiguous. Because rules and guidelines channel information, resources and discretion, these structures moderate the relationships which exist between responsibility units and interest groups (Dunbar,

1981). They draw attention (Cyert *et al.*, 1956) to conflicts among differing norms, values, beliefs and visions, thereby giving rise to issues. These issues are acted upon by responsibility units and interest groups in accordance with their interpretations of the world and their perceptions of equity. But, because the way an issue is initially framed significantly influences its ultimate resolution and acceptance, the relationship between issues and managerial control structures is of crucial significance. Issues may be resolved within the framework established by the existing control system or may lead to modifications in that framework. However, such changes, in turn, redirect flows of information, resources, and discretion, giving rise to new issues and new behavioural responses. This issue-stimulation-and-response process is, in part, the organization's control system.

IMPLICATIONS

Making the case for an alternative view of organizational control does not answer the question of what this view means for control theory and system design and evaluation today. In the short term, the implications are subtle and incremental; in the longer term, they may be profound.

One implication for system design and evaluation arises from the fact that different answers will be given to the same question, depending on which model of organization is used and which assumptions about organizational order are made. For example, under the functional model of organization and the managerial conception of control, slack and redundancy are usually regarded as dysfunctional and their elimination is deemed desirable. From the pluralistic perspective, however, such inefficiencies are not without benefits. Slack can be regarded as providing the resources and discretion required to explore alternatives, and hence as an investment in creativity (Slevin, 1971) strengthening pluralism. Rather than being inefficient, duplicate activities and overlapping jurisdictions may necessitate communication, thereby sensitizing participants to the manner in which they interrelate and stimulating self-organized adjustments (Landau, 1969). They make the whole more reliable than any of the individual parts by not trusting each part to work all of the time (Wildavsky, 1976). Thus, disconcertingly, phenomena unacceptable from one point of view become desirable, if not mandatory, from another. But since an awareness of the actual bases of organizational order and the true causes of organizational evolution must precede the development of more applied principles of control system design, the exploration of such apparent inconsistencies can only increase our understanding of control.

The implication for a theory of control is even more provocative. The processes involved in maintaining a pluralistic order are in decided contrast to those of a hierarchically-managed system. Assuredly, they are at the heart of control. Yet how they co-exist is now largely unknown. One possibility is that many of the managerially-based assumptions of functionalism and control are illusory (Normann, 1977; Dunbar, 1981; Salancik & Meindl, 1984) but are tolerated in order to maintain stability

(Dermer & Lucas, 1986). Such assumptions include the following: organization exists primarily for purposeful reasons; mandate legitimately entrusted to management can be exercised without challenge; management knows how and is able to conduct organizational activities; an organization has the legitimate right to expect the compliance of internal and external stakeholders. In order to preserve the illusion that these assumptions are correct, management must continually win, or at least not lose, must repress disconfirming evidence, and must save face at all costs. Challenges to these premises are undiscussable and their undiscussability is, in turn, undiscussable (Argyris, 1982).

Issues which have the potential to destroy these illusions and to destabilize coexistence between managerial and autonomous activities, are both threatening and emotional. Unless they can be framed in non-threatening, non emotional terms, they never gain legitimacy. Thus they can only be discussed within the conventional strategy/control paradigm. Questions about management's ability to effect change, for example, must be narrowly confined to specific issues so as to diffuse their potential impact. Yet within the latent subtext of organization lie the contradiction-accommodating and self-protecting activities which actually sustain order. These are among the most neglected yet essential ingredients of control theory.

Our intent has been to argue this point by reconceptualizing control and addressing its autonomous dimensions. To do so, we have approached control from a causal perspective concerned with the explanations of outcomes. We have presented a new pluralistic governance model, a model whose assumptions will permit the study of both managerial and autonomous forces. By augmenting the traditional managerial model, based on functionalism, strategy, and cybernetics, with an approach that recognizes the importance of the autonomous activity of self-interested participants, we provide ourselves with a much clearer basis from which to explore control and organizational order.

ACKNOWLEDGEMENTS

The comments of R.G. Lucas, Brenda Zinnmerman, Anthony Hopwood and an anonymous referee are gratefully acknowledged.

BIBLIOGRAPHY

Ackoff, R., *The Art of Problem Solving* (New York: John Wiley, 1979).

Allison, G.T., *Essence of Decision: Explaining the Cuban Missile Crisis* (Boston, MA: Little, Brown, 1971).

Allport, F.H., *Institutional Behavior* (Chapel Hill, NC: The University of North Carolina Press, 1933).

Ansoff, H.I., Strategic Issue Management, *Strategic Management Journal* (1980) pp. 131–148.

Ansoff, H.I., Managing Discontinuous Strategic Change, in Ansoff, H.I., Bosman, A. and Strom, P.M. (eds) *Understanding and Managing Strategic Change* pp. 1–21. (NY: Elsevier, North Holland).

Anthony, R.N., *Planning and Control Systems: A Framework for Analysis* (Boston, MA: Division of Research, Graduate School of Business Administration, Harvard University 1965).

Argyris, C., *Reasoning, Learning and Action* (San Francisco, CA: Jossey–Bass, 1982).

Ashton, R.H., Deviation – Amplifying Feedback and Unintended Consequences of Management Accounting Systems, *Accounting, Organizations and Society* (1976) pp. 397–408.

Axelrod, R., *Structure of Decision* (Princeton, NJ: Princeton University Press, 1976).

Bacharach, S. & Aiken, M., Structural and Process Constraints on Influence in Organizations: A Level-specific Analysis, *Administrative Science Quarterly* (1976) pp. 633–642.

Bacharach, S. & Lawler, E., *Power and Politics in Organizations* (San Francisco, CA: Jossey–Bass, 1980).

Barchrach, P. & Baratz, M., *Power and Poverty: Theory and Practice* (New York, NY: Oxford University Press, 1970).

Benson, J.K., The Interorganizational Network as a Political Economy, *Administrative Science Quarterly* (1975) pp. 229–249.

Benson, J.K., Organizations: A Dialectical View, *Administrative Science Quarterly* (March 1977) pp. 1–21.

Birnberg, J.C., Turopolec, L. & Found, S.M., The Organizational Context of Accounting, *Accounting, Organizations and Society* (1983) pp. 111–129.

Blau, P., *Exchange and Power in Social Life* (New York, NY: John Wiley, 1964).

Boland, R.J., Control, Causality and Information System Requirements, *Accounting, Organizations and Society* (1979) pp. 259–272.

Boujon, M., Weick, K. & Binkhorst, D., Cognition in Organization: An Analysis of the Utrecht Jazz Orchestra, *Administrative Science Quarterly* (1977) pp. 606–639.

Bourgeois, L.J. III & Brodwin, D.R., Strategic Implementation: Five Approaches to an Elusive Phenomenon, *Strategic Management Journal* (1984) pp. 241–264.

Bower, J.L., Strategy Formulation: A Social and Political Process, in Schendel, D.E. and Hofer, C.W. (eds) *Strategic Management* (Boston, MA: Little, Brown, 1979).

Braybrooke, D. & Lindblom, C.E., *A Strategy of Decision: Policy Evaluation as a Social Process* (New York, NY: Free Press, 1970).

Burgelman, R., A Model of the Interaction of Strategic Behavior, Corporate Context, and the Concept of Strategy, *Academy of Management Review* (1983) pp. 61–70.

Chandler, A., *Strategy and Structure* (Cambridge, MA: MIT Press, 1962).

Cohen, M. & March, J., *Leadership and Ambiguity* (New York, NY: McGraw–Hill, 1974).

Cohen, M., March, J. & Olsen, J., A Garbage Can Model of Organizational Choice, *Administrative Science Quarterly* (June 1972) pp. 1–25.

Cooper, D.J., Hayes, D.C. & Wolf, F., Accounting in Organized Anarchies: Understanding and Designing Accounting Systems in Ambiguous Situations, *Accounting, Organizations and Society* (1981) pp. 175–191.

Crozier, M., *The Bureaucratic Phenomenon* (Chicago, IL: University of Chicago Press, 1964).

Cummings, L., Emergence of the Instrumental Organization, in Goodman, P.S. and Pennings, J.M. (eds) *New Perspectives on Organizational Effectiveness* pp. 50–62 (Washington: Jossey–Bass, 1977).

Cyert, R.M. & March, J.G., *A Behavioural Theory of the Firm* (Englewood Cliffs, NJ: Prentice-Hall, 1963).

Davis, S., Transforming Organizations: The Key to Strategy is Context, *Organizational Dynamics* (Winter 1982).

Denhardt, R.B., The Organization as a Political System, *Western Political Quarterly* (1971) pp. 64–80.

Dermer, J. & Lucas, R., The Illusion of Managerial Control, *Accounting, Organizations, and Society* (1986) pp. 471–482.

Diesing, P., *Reason in Society* (Urbana, IL: University of Illinois Press, 1962).

Drucker, P.R., Controls, Control and Management, in Bonini *et al.* (eds) *Management Controls: New Directions in Basic Research* pp. 286–296 (New York: McGraw-Hill, 1964).

Dunbar, R., Designs for Organizational Control, in Nystrom, P. and Starbuck, W. (eds) *Handbook of Organizational Design* (New York, NY: North Holland, 1981).

Dutton, J., Fahey, L. & Narayanan, V., Toward Understanding Strategic Issue Diagnosis, *Strategic Management Journal* (1983) pp. 307–323.

Dyckman, T., The Intelligence of Ambiguity, *Accounting, Organizations and Society* (1981) pp. 291–300.

Etzioni, A., *A Comparative Analysis of Complex Organizations* (New York, NY: Free Press, 1961).

Euske, K.J., *Management Control: Planning, Control, Measurement, and Evaluation* (Reading, MA: Addison–Wesley, 1984).

Freeman, R.E., *Strategic Management: A Stakeholder Approach* (Toronto: Copp Clark Pitman, 1984).

Galbraith, J.R. & Kazanjian, R.J., *Strategy Implementation: Structure, Systems and Process* (St Paul MN: West Publishing, 1986).

Georgiou, P., The Goal Paradigm and Notes Toward a Counter Paradigm, *Administrative Science Quarterly* (1973) pp. 291–310.

Grimes, A., Authority, Power, Influence and Social Control: A Theoretical Synthesis, *Academy of Management Review* (1978) pp. 724–735.

Halal, W.E., *The New Capitalism: Democratic Free Enterprise in Post-Industrial Society* (New York: John Wiley, 1984).

Hall, D.J. & Saias, M.A., Strategy Follows Structure!, *Strategic Management Journal* (1980) pp. 149–163.

Hannan, J. & Freeman, R., Structural inertia and organizational change, *American Sociological Review* (1984) pp. 149–164.

Hayes, D.C., An Organizational Perspective on a Psycho-Technical Systems Perspective, *Accounting, Organizations and Society* (1980) pp. 43–48.

Hayes, D.C., Accounting for Accounting: A Story About Managerial Accounting, *Accounting, Organizations and Society* (1983) pp. 241–249.

Hedberg, B. & Jonsson, S., Designing Semi-Confusing Information Systems for Organizations in Changing Environments, *Accounting, Organizations and Society* (1978) pp. 47–64.

Hedberg, B., Nystrom, P.C. & Starbuck, W.H., Camping on Seesaws: Prescriptions for a Self Designing Organization, *Administrative Science Quarterly* (1976) pp. 41–65.

Hofer, C., *Strategy Formulation: Issues and Concepts* (St. Paul: West Publishing, 1986).

Hofstede, Geert, The Poverty of Management Control Philosophy, *Academy of Management Review* (July 1978) pp. 450–461.

Hopwood, A.G., Toward an Organizational Perspective for the Study of Accounting and Information Systems, *Accounting, Organizations and Society* (1978) pp. 3–13.

Horovitz, J., Strategic Control: A New Task for Top Management, *Long Range Planning* (June, 1979), pp. 2–7.

Jaeger, A.M. & Baliga, B.R., Control Systems and Strategic Adaptation: Lessons from the Japanese Experience, *Strategic Management Journal* (1985) pp. 115–134.

Landau, M., Redundancy Rationality and the Problems of Duplication and Overlap, *Public Administration Review* (1969) pp. 336–358.

Landau, M. & Stout, R., Jr., To Manage is Not to Control: Or the folly of type II errors, *Public Administration Review* (1979) pp. 148–156.

Lindblom, C.E., Still Muddling, Not Yet Through, *Public Administration Review* (1979) pp. 517–526.

Lorange, P., Scott-Morton, M.F. & Ghostal, S., *Strategic Control* (St Paul, MN: West Publishing, 1986).

Maciariello, J.A. *Management Control Systems* (Englewood Cliffs, NJ: Prentic–Hall, 1984).

MacMillan, I.C. & Guth, W.D., Strategy Implementation and Middle Management Coalitions, in Lamb, R. (ed.) *Advances in Strategic Management*, Vol. 3, (Greenwich, CT.: JAI Press, 1985).

MacMillan, I.C. & Jones, P.E., *Strategy Formulation: Power and Politics* (St Paul, MN: West Publishing, 1986).

March, J.G., The Business Firm as a Political Coalition, *Journal of Politics* (1962) pp. 662–678.

March, J.G., Ambiguity and the Engineering of Choice, *International Studies of Management and Organization* (1979) pp. 9–39.

March, J. & Simon, H., *Organizations* (New York: John Wiley, 1958).

Mason, R.O. & Mitroff, I.I., A Teleological Power-Oriented Theory of Strategy, in Lamb, R. *Advances in Strategic Management*, Vol. 2, pp 31–41 (Greenwich, CT: JAI Press, 1983).

Merchant, K.A., *Control in Business Organizations* (Pitman, 1985).

Mintzberg, H., Patterns in Strategy Formulation, *Management Science* (1978) pp. 934–948.

Mintzberg, H. & Waters, J., On Strategies Deliberate and Emergent, *Strategic Management Journal* (1985) pp. 25–37.

Morgan, G., Paradigms, Metaphors, and Puzzle Solving in Organizational Theory, *Administrative Science Quarterly* (1980) pp. 605–622.

Murray, E.A., Jr., Strategic Choice as a Negotiated Outcome, *Management Science* (May, 1978) pp. 960–972.

Narayanan, V.K. & Fahey, L., The Micro-politics of Strategy Formulation, *Academy of Management Review* (1982) pp. 25–34.

Normann, R., *Management for Growth* (New York: John Wiley, 1977).

Olsen, M., *Power in Societies* (London: Macmillan, 1970).

Otley, D.T. & Berry, A.J., Control, Organization and Accounting, *Accounting, Organizations and Society* (1980) pp. 231–299.

Ouchi, W.G. & Price, R.I., Hierarchies, Clans and Theory Z: A New Perspective on Organization and Development, *Organizational Dynamics* (1978) pp. 25–44.

Perrow, C., *Complex Organizations: A Critical Essay* (Glenview, IL: Scott Foresman, 1972).

Peters, T., Management Systems: The Language of Organizational Character and Competence, *Organizational Dynamics* (Summer 1980) pp. 3–26.

Pettigrew, A.M., Strategy Formulation as a Political Process, *International Studies of Management and Organization* (1977) pp. 78–87.

Pfeffer, J., *Power in Organizations* (Boston, MA: Pitman, 1981).

Pfeffer, J. & Salancik, G., *The External Control of Organizations* (New York: Harper and Row, 1978).

Pfeffer, J. & Salancik, G., Organizational Decision Making as a Political Process: The Case of the University Budget, *Administrative Science Quarterly* (1974) pp. 135–151.

Pondy, L., Leadership as a Language Game, in McCall, M. and Lombardo, M. (eds), *Leadership: Where else can we go?* pp. 87–99 (Durham, NC: Duke University Press, 1976).

Quinn, J.B., Strategic Goals: Process and Politics, *Sloan Management Review* (1977) pp. 19, 21–37.

Quinn, J.B., Strategies for Change: Logical Incrementalism, *Sloan Management Review* (1978) pp. 7–21.

Quinn, J.B., Formulating Strategy One Step at a Time, *Journal of Business Strategy* (1981) pp. 42–63.

Salancik, G.R. & Meindl, J.R., Corporate Attributions as Strategic Illusions of Management Control, *Administrative Science Quarterly* (June 1984) pp. 238–254.

Schattschneider, E., *The Semi-sovereign People* (New York: Holt, Rinehart and Winston, 1960).

Scott, W., Mitchell, T. & Perry, N., Organizational Governance, in Nystrom, P. and Starbuck, W. (eds) *Handbook of Organizational Design* (New York: North Holland, 1981).

Simon, H., *Administrative Behavior* 3rd Edn (New York: Free Press, 1976).

Simon, H., On the Concept of Goal, *Administrative Science Quarterly* (1964) pp. 1–22.

Simon, H., Rational Decision Making in Business Organizations, *American Economic Review* (1979) pp. 493–513.

Slevin, D., The Innovation Boundary, *Administrative Science Quarterly* (1971) pp. 515–531.

Starbuck, W. & Hedberg, B., Saving an Organization from a Stagnation Environment, in Thorelli, H. (ed.) *Strategy + Structure = Performance: The Strategic Planning Imperative* (Bloomington, IN: Indiana University Press, 1977).

Stonich, P.J. (ed.), *Implementing Strategy* (Cambridge, MA: Ballinger Press, 1984).

Strauss, A., *Negotiations* (San Francisco, CA: Jossey–Bass, 1978).

Tannenbaum, A., *Control in Organizations* (New York, NY: McGraw–Hill, 1968).

Tetlock, P., Accountability: The Neglected Social Context of Judgment and Choice, in Cummings, L. and Staw, B. (eds) *Research in Organizational Behavior* Vol. 7 (Greenwich, CT: JAI Press, 1985).

Vickers, G., The Ninth Wallberg Memorial Lecture, in Chen, G. *et al.* (eds) *The*

General Theory of Systems Applied to Management and Organization pp. 107–114 (Seaside, CA: Intersystems Publications, 1956).

Weber, M., *The Theory of Social and Economic Organization* (New York: Free Press, 1947).

Weick, K., Enactment Processes in Organizations, in Staw, B. and Salancik, G. (eds), *New Directions in Organizational Behavior* (Chicago, IL: St Clair Press, 1977).

Weick, K., *The Social Psychology of Organizing* 2nd Edn (Reading, MA: Addison–Wesley, 1979).

Weick, K., The Significance of Corporate Culture, in Frost, P.J. *et al.* (eds) *Organizational Culture* (1985) pp. 381–412.

Wildavsky, A.B., The Political Economy of Efficiency, *Public Administration Review* (1966) pp. 292–310.

Wildavsky, A., Policy Analyses Is What Information Systems Are Not, *Accounting, Organizations and Society* (1978) pp. 77–88.

Wildavsky, A., Economy and Environment/Rationality and Ritual: A Review Essay, *Accounting, Organizations and Society* (1976) pp. 117–129.

Wrapp, E., Good Managers don't make Policy Decisions, *Harvard Business Review* (1967) pp. 91–98.

8

Designing semi-confusing information systems for organizations in changing environments

Bo Hedberg and Sten Jönsson

Department of Business Administration, University of Gothenburg

ABSTRACT

Organizations have many stabilizers but quite often lack proper destabilizers. They establish fixed repertoires of behavior programs over time, and many grow too rigid and insensitive to environmental changes. Drifting into changing environments, they react with delayed and improper responses.

Current information – and accounting – systems do more to stabilize organizations than to destabilize them. They filter away conflicts, ambiguities, overlaps, uncertainty etc. and they suppress many relevant change signals and kill initiatives to act on early warnings.

Organizations in changing environments need information systems which enable them to stay alert and to detect problems, changes, and conflicts in time. Accounting information can be used to stimulate organizational curiosity, facilitate dialectical decision processes and increase organizations' ability to cope with variety in their environments. This paper formulates some principles for design of information systems that can destabilize organizations with planned confusion – in times when they ought to be confused.

Organizations have many stabilizers. Learning processes are among the most important ones. Organizations act through humans, and humans program themselves over time as they gather experience from acting. Problems that are encountered and solved repeatedly are gradually taken over by standardized responses. Success reinforces the use of such action programs and makes organizations rely increasingly upon their historical experiences. As a consequence, organizations in stable, benevolent

Source: Hedberg, B. and Jönsson, S. (1978) *Accounting, Organizations and Society*, **3** (1) pp. 47–64.

environments typically accumulate repertoires of programs and grow rather insensitive to change signals (Cyert & March, 1963).

Humans have limited information processing capacity, and so have organizations which largely rely on human brains to process information. Using standard operating procedures instead of genuine problem solving is an important way for organizations to conserve mental energy and to allocate available decision resources to problems which are new and difficult and really deserve basic problem solving. Furthermore, standard operating procedures make the behaviour of organizations more consistent over time. Enacted futures are based on experiences of the past. This is all to the good in stable environments where organizations face few discontinuities, and where the history reasonably well predicts the future. In changing environments, however, the same learning processes lead to organizational inertia that often threatens organizational survival. The more experience an organization has cast into action programs, and the more successful these programs have been, the stronger are the forces which strive to make the organization continue along its route of development. It takes a threshold amount of counter-evidence to challenge old behaviours, and it takes further efforts to unfreeze these behaviours and replace them with new ones. Unprogramming and reprogramming behaviors take time. Thus, learning and the resulting use of standard operating procedures introduce significant response delays into organizations' decision systems (Hedberg, 1975; 1978).

Information – and accounting – systems are sometimes thought of as being neutral with respect to their impacts on organizations' behaviour. The argument is that they represent potential resources which can assist and aid decision makers in many different ways, and that their impacts are determined by the way they are used. This is true, in a sense. Formalized information systems and information technologies are not good or bad, *per se*. But, there are information systems which offer less discretion to decision makers than others, and which lead to organizational rigidity; and there are information systems which stimulate organizations to experiment and innovate, and which foster organizational flexibility. Those who design information systems do indeed influence the behaviour of organizations, and the behavioural impacts of system designs are increasingly being recognized.

It appears that the majority of modern information systems, and particularly computerized ones, have made organizations more rigid rather than more flexible. Higher investment costs have lengthened payoff periods and frozen organizations into programmed behaviors and defined structures (Mowshowitz, 1976). Rigid programming techniques and ambitions to integrate administrative procedures have increased the number of interdependencies and made even minor adjustments difficult and costly. Maintenance frequently requires systems expertise, and scarcity of such expertise has forced organizations' decision makers to continue using their information systems in spite of apparent shortcomings.

All information systems imply a world view that contains assumptions about what information is relevant, which characteristics of the environment are essential, who the decision makers are, etc. These world views are usually implicit. They grow obsolete, but they do not change immediately as the world changes. Indeed, information systems often tether organizations to yesterday's perceptions. Traditional accounting systems are good illustrations of this. They reflect a historical situation when the company was considered as identical with the owner-entrepreneur who had been trusted to handle shareholders' and lenders' money and who reported his stewardship to those groups of people. Other resources, such as personnel and know-how, which certainly are important to a company's survival but which historically have lacked the backing of powerful interest groups, were not included in the information systems. These power balances are changing today: powerful trade unions and worker representatives in management have other priorities and demand other reporting. Environmental protection interests require other additions, and changing values in our society as a whole have put pressure on the development of human resources accounting, environmental exchange accounts, and social audits. The old accounting world views are clearly obsolete, but changes have been modest so far. Old information systems and their implicit world views are solidly established, and they resist change. Monetary measures are still dominant. Implicit world views in information systems frequently serve as conserving forces and delay organizations' adaptation to changing environments.

There are also indications that modern information systems tend to hamper organizational search and filter away significant amounts of relevant uncertainty, diversity, and change signals (Mowshowitz, 1976). Systems designers have dysfunctionally made information systems make sense of environments which do not make sense (Nystrom *et al.*, 1976). Certain cognitive styles (Mason & Mitroff, 1973) and learning styles (Kolb, 1974; Wolfe, 1976) have been catered for, but not others. Ambiguity, redundancy, overlap, and incongruity have been thought of as undesirable systems properties (Landau, 1969; McCall, 1975). The result has been that organizations' decision makers often have faced unrealistically homogenous and explained environments and failed to discover some real problems. Not until organizations have entered into crises have these information filters been penetrated and outside changes suddenly displayed (Starbuck & Hedberg, 1977; Jönsson, 1973). Again, information systems could well be used as – and designed to be – early warning systems, but on the whole it seems as if they currently rather conceal than reveal change signals.

It appears that many modern information systems dysfunctionally add to organizations' inertia. Access to more information and more advanced decision aids does not necessarily make decision makers better informed or more able to decide. A few examples from our own research can illustrate this point.

INFORMATION SYSTEMS AND ORGANIZATIONAL CHANGE – THREE EXAMPLES

Information systems affect organizational change. Our first example describes a case where necessary organizational changes were delayed because of the lack of proper information systems. Our second example points at profound differences in behavioural impacts when experienced and inexperienced staff were exposed to advanced information systems in a laboratory setting. Our third example illustrates the technical possibilities, but also the organizational difficulties, involved in stimulating organizations' search and curiosity.

In a study of 10 Swedish conglomerates of formerly family-owned firms Jönsson (1973) observed how formalized information systems delayed necessary reorientations. The newly created umbrella organizations employed laissez-faire strategies intially and were satisfied to provide financial support to strategic initiatives taken by the subsidiaries. Information systems were local. The head offices received infrequent aggregated reports for overall control.

Then a recession caused financial problems in many of the rapidly growing subsidiaries. The conglomerates typically reacted with considerable delays and suffered severe losses before old strategies were abandoned and replaced by new ones. The need to redesign and implement adequate corporate information systems delayed strategic reorientations significantly. As a result of these design problems many of the conglomerates came out of phase with the business cycle and failed to benefit from the consecutive economic upturn. Most of the conglomerates detected environmental changes too late. Before they realized the need to act and began redesigning their information systems to grasp the new situation, they lost slack and ended up with little room for strategic maneuvering. The information systems delayed the detection of problems, and systems redesign almost paralyzed organizational action during the upturn of the crisis.

But even when modern information systems are implemented in time there may still be little or no change in decision makers' behavior. A comparison between bank executives' and business students' decision processes in a bank management simulation game (Hedberg, 1970) illustrated the constraining impacts of human standard operating procedures on the utilization of information and decision aids in a computerized information system. Content analysis of recorded decision meetings showed that the experienced bank executives had about seven times as many standard operating procedures as the business graduates who lacked previous banking experience.

When bank executive teams and student teams in the game changed from a traditional batch-processing information system to a terminal-oriented, on-line information system which allowed the decision teams to access much more information immediately upon request, there were pronounced differences in the way the teams utilized the new possibilities.

The bank executives emulated the old information system inside the new one. The report set which they obtained was similar to the ones which they actually used in their banks. They requested the same reports, looked for the same information, and showed little interest in discovering new things in the new information environments. Students, on the other hand, expanded their information search considerably. They generated new reports and performed new types of analyses on retrieved information. There were no measureable differences in the motivation of the respective teams or in their interaction with the computer terminals. The major difference was that bank executives continued 'doing their thing' as before, not taking notice of the new opportunities. Their experience and their thought procedures appeared to act as blinkers which constrained their vision and curiosity. Their decision behavior was already stabilized, and it remained stable throughout the experiments. The student teams got many new insights in their expanded search for information, and they improved their performance somewhat as a result. But their high appreciation for new information tended to get them into other problems; they expanded their information search so much that the rest of their decision making suffered. Lacking experience-based attention rules and search constraints, they spent more than 60% of their decision sessions hunting for new data. They had less time and energy left to use these data in problem solving.

The experiments indicated that information system designs have important balances to strike. If experienced users are to make use of new potential, they need to unlearn behaviors which previous learning has accumulated. Training is one means to this end, but information systems can possibly also be designed to stimulate decision makers to scan their decision areas more frequently. Good information systems should tickle curiosity in organizations.

The other side of the balancing problem is to avoid overreactions and excessive information search. If users put high value on information, and new technologies cut the cost of search significantly, the result may well be that decision makers drown themselves in information and become unable to make decisions. Ideal designs should balance organizations' exploration of the unknown futures and their exploitation of the known pasts.

However, ideal designs are rare, and stimulating decision makers' search and curiosity can be difficult, as was illustrated in a third study.

Experiences from the second study influenced the development of an interactive marketing information system (MARKISETT) for the managers of a product group in a multinational consumer goods company (Glimell, 1975; Hedberg *et al.*, 1974). The pilot system was designed jointly by a research team and the managers and computer specialists in the firm. Deliberate attempts were made to create a good learning environment, and to develop a system that would give users fast access to large amounts of information and decision aids. A logical-tree structure enabled the system's users to direct their information search sequentially and to vary the level of detail, the mode of presentation, and the measuring dimensions from time to time.

The system worked properly after a period of initial adjustments, and appeared to be technically well designed. Unlike the old information systems of the company, it contained much environmental information – consumer data, demographical data, retail and wholesale reports, etc. – in addition to previous accounting information. Some simple routines and decision models were available to process raw data for pattern detection, forecasting, etc. Control limits, programmed scanning, exception reporting, and graphical displays were used to reduce the demands on decision makers' attention. The tree structure, the rapid access to information, and various built-in, attention-directing features were envisaged to encourage decision makers to make excursions into the data base and to maintain a high level of environmental curiosity.

But, the outcome differed from the expectations. An initial short period, when the users really began exploring the potential of the new system, was followed by a backlash during which the decision makers retreated to their previous reports and behaviors. They established a few standard paths through the search tree and began requesting the same reports over and over again. Although the users themselves had insisted that data about the environment should be included in the new data base, and even had claimed that such data were much more important to their decisions than historical accounting records, they made little use of this new information. User statistics showed that only 23 of the system's 52 search-tree nodes had been visited at all towards the end of the 9-month test period. Only 13% of about 350 reports available from the system had been used at least once. Traditional report formats had been preferred over graphical reports, summary reports, and exception reports. Accounting data from the old routines provided 65% of the utilized information, while market data and consumer data accounted for less than 15% (Glimell, 1975). The results suggested that the new information system had failed to change the decision makers' behavior, highlight developments in the market, and stimulate active search for problems and opportunities. Instead, it had lent itself to the stabilizing forces of the organization.

The related development has several possible explanations. One is that the content of the system was badly designed, so that the decision makers' reaction merely reflected that the new options were of little value. User interviews did not support this hypothesis at all. Instead it was suggested that pressure from the rest of the organization, which did not have access to the new system, played a crucial role in moving the research subjects back to their old behaviors. The pilot system approach kept the system at a relatively small and manageable scale and reduced the costs and risks involved, but it also made the decision makers included in the study, and their product group, a diverging minority within the organization. Chief executives and fellow managers continued to 'operate' in the traditional fashion, and they pressured the pilot group to conform. Furthermore, there were indications that the system itself did not trigger users' curiosity and initiate problem search actively enough. The system appeared to have the potential to facilitate organizational search, but it failed completely to make users explore this potential. What were thought to be discovery tours in the system's search tree were turned into frustrating sequences of choices to access standard reports.

Old and inefficient information systems often delay organizations' responses to environmental changes. But new and advanced information systems do not necessarily make organizations move either. The three examples illustrate that very conscious and considerable design efforts are needed, if information systems are to change organizations' behaviors and reduce their inertia. Conventional information systems are often too time consuming to redesign. They leave organizations in a chaotic state when needs for reorientations are discovered. New information systems as such do not change decision makers' behaviors. Standard operating procedures must be unlearnt if new potentials are to be utilized. But, even deliberate attempts to design for organizational curiosity and continuous learning may fail due to organizational climate, peer group pressure, and difficulties to reframe human minds. Although we know of no completely successful attempts to design information systems so that organizations adapt and respond more readily to changes, our own experiments and mistakes begin to suggest some design principles that could make organizations' life in changing environments somewhat easier.

MATCHING COGNITIVE MAPPINGS TO THE NATURE OF THE ENVIRONMENT

The problems which changing environments pose can hardly be reduced, but it might be possible to assist organizations to detect changes and to deal with environmental complexity. Viable organizations must have a reasonable fit between the complexity and changeability of their environments and the complexity and flexibility of the cognitive mappings through which they interpret situations and develop actions. Organizations in stable, benevolent environments can benefit from developing highly complex and integrated decision models and mental maps, while organizations in turbulent and rapidly changing environments must keep the complexity of their mental maps at a bare minimum. The former ones are like organizational palaces which indeed can be built when conditions are controlled and sites are on long-term lease. The latter ones should rather be like organizational tents, and their members should leave unnecessary luggage behind and travel light (Hedberg *et al.*, 1977).

Kelly (1955), Schroder *et al.* (1967) and others have shown that people's cognitive complexity can vary greatly. Streufert (1972, 1973) reported results which point at ways in which the level of cognitive complexity could be affected. Whether by control, training, or by recruitment there appears to be ways to tune organizations' mental maps to the nature of their environments.

There is no reason at all to assume that maximizing the complexity of decision makers' cognitive structures is always desireable (Miller & Gordon, 1975). While organizations in very stable and cue-rich environments may benefit from developing highly integrated cognitive structures, organizations in changing environments ought to settle for less developed structures which can efficiently handle a few key variables and which can be restructured relatively easily as outer conditions change. Decision makers with high and low integrative complexity in their cognitive structures appear to have relative advantages in these different environments. High complexity subjects show more breadth in their information search, they search more evenly over problem areas, and they differentiate more with respect to various classes of information (Karlins, 1967; Karlins & Lamm, 1967). Low complexity subjects, on the other hand, have been found to be more efficient in decision situations which offer few cues (Suefeld & Hagen, 1966). While complex cognitive structures can accommodate more contingencies and adapt to a wider range of environmental states (Schroder *et al.*, 1967), there is reason to assume that low-complexity structures can be reframed more easily (Kelly, 1955).

It is not only the complexity of people's cognitive structures that has to harmonize with the nature and changeability of the environment. Also formalized information systems and planning routines must be tuned to the various contingencies. While organizations that control or can predict their futures should refine and enrich their strategic planning systems, organizations in changing environments might do better without strategic planning, or at least with simpler and less prestigeous plans.

A study of corporate planning and financial performance in 21 British business firms (Grinyer & Norburn, 1975) raised doubts about the instrumentality of currently applied design principles for management information systems. The researchers examined relationships between several dimensions of the corporate planning ideal on one side and financial performance on the other. They concluded that few 'desirable' design features appeared to correlate strongly with financial performance, and that the results indeed suggested that ambiguity with respect to organizational roles and objectives, rather than clarity of roles and objectives could lead to better performance in many situations. Particularly, the use of many, informal information channels appeared to increase the companies' utilization of available information and result in better financial performance. Thus, while traditional design 'assets' such a clarity of roles and goals, formalization of planning procedures, and high agreement between executives' problem perceptions were not found to relate to financial performance, certain design 'liabilities' such as goal ambiguity and informal channelling of information appeared to have positive effects. While the results offer no strong indications of how better information system should be designed they do challenge the generality and instrumentality of many current design principles.

Finding balances so that learning can thrive and experience accumulate (at the same time as excessive integrative complexity and inertia in decision systems are counteracted) should be a major design concern. Organizations in changing environments should have to design information systems with built-in mechanisms which counteract the stabilizing forces which learning breeds (Hedberg *et al.*, 1976). The related findings above suggest several such counter-balances which are developed in some detail in the final section of this article.

Information system designs are important means of determining the situational factors which surround decision makers and which regulate the development of integrative complexity in cognitive structures, but they can also affect the dispositional factors, such as the long-term training conditions, under which constructs and cognitive structures are formed

(Harvey *et al.*, 1961). Information systems can be designed to encourage experimental behavior among decision makers (Box & Draper, 1969; Starbuck, 1974 and 1975), and they constitute an essential part of the learning environment in which learning and unlearning, structure building and reframing take place.

Together, the situational factors in the decision environment (such as the information load, the nature of the presented information, and the user-system interface), and the dispositional factors in the learning environment (such as the attitudes and the behavior modes which are encouraged, and the constructs and structures which are supported) provide a rich set of design variables which are crucial to good information systems performance. Designers can affect the quantity and quality of information which reaches decision makers, and they can influence the long-term training environment where learning takes place. Thus, as illustrated in Fig. 8.1, there are powerful means to tune organizations to their environments and to facilitate good fit over time between the complexity of cognitive structures and the nature of the environment.

There is a risk that our emphasis on cognitive fit between organizations and their environments leads to static interpretations, and we want to avoid that by all means. Organizations travel in changing environments, so fit is indeed a dynamic concept. The environment can be problematic all along, but there can still be different requirements on the information systems. Organizations that enter into unknown environments need to discover as soon as possible that situations are new and that old experiences must be doubted. They need destabilizers until they wake up. Then, when they have analyzed their new situation and begun to invent responses, it may well be that their information systems should filter out new problem signals and shelter emerging new routines and strategies.

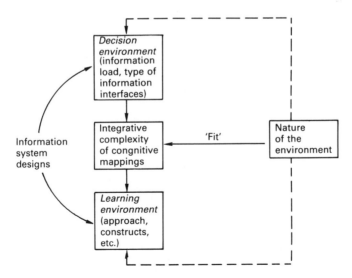

Fig. 8.1 Information systems design as a means to balance complexity.

We have found such cyclic patterns in organizations' development which appear to call for information systems that not only are contingent upon the nature of an organization's environment but also upon the state of the organization itself. Organizations change their myths – action theories – over time and in an orderly pattern. Various myth phases call for sheltering and consolidation. Others need dialectics and structural change (Hedberg & Jönsson, 1977).

ORGANIZATIONS' MYTH CYCLES

Organizations need reliable information systems that help them predict their futures and optimize their actions within foreseeable types of situations. But they also need information systems that are flexible enough to cope with unexpected developments. These different demands cause a dilemma in the design of any information system. Systems which are designed to exploit stable, predictable situations are less effective when unforeseen situations occur, and highly adaptive systems have typically less effective control mechanisms to make the most out of foreseen conditions (Boguslaw, 1965). This design dilemma will remain as long as designs are thought of as final and unique solutions to design problems. But, information systems could also be designed for different contingencies, or they could be designed to be self-designing. Designs for contingencies will require carryover mechanisms between versions of the system, so that, for example, a normal mode of rational/cybernetic operation can be temporarily replaced by a systems mode which supports vigorous action based on will, wishful thinking, and enthusiasm until a new, more analytical, system is stabilized enough to provide a forecasting model of the world. Self-designing information systems go one step further in preparing for repeated change and restructuring, rather than merely for shifts between contingent modes of operation. While there may be a good case for fully self-designing information systems in organizations in turbulent environments, we propose that a large number of organizations in changing environments develop in a cyclic pattern with two major behavior modes over time. Contingency designs, combined with efficient triggering mechanisms, could do a lot to carry organizations through changing environments. This cyclical pattern, we propose, is the result of the interaction between organizations' stabilizing and destabilizing processes and changing organizational environments.

Members of organizations interpret changes in the environment differently. They disagree on causal relations in the environment and between environments and organizations. Differences in perceptions and interpretations of the environment also lead to differences with respect to what objectives are appropriate. The result is that different members believe in different means-ends relationships and favor different actions. Organizations' decision making thus has a pronounced flavour of politics. Depending upon the degrees of agreement on means and ends there are, as illustrated in Fig. 8.2, several possible modes of joint problem solving.

We have earlier developed the theme of decision by inspiration (Hedberg

Preferences about possible outcomes (ends)

	Disagreement	Agreement
Disagreement	Inspiration	Computation
Agreement	Compromise	Judgement

Beliefs about causation (means)

Fig. 8.2 Organizational beliefs and problem solving behaviour. (See also Thompson (1967) and Ullrich (1976).)

& Jönsson, 1977). Basic to our explanation is an everyday definition of risk. When there is disagreement on means and ends, a feeling of genuine uncertainty spreads amongst organizational members. This uncertainty multiplies with the stakes (what decision makers or their organization may lose or gain from the outcome) into a risk. When there are no stakes, the multiplicative effect makes the risk zero.

Genuine uncertainty, combined with changes that are perceived as significant for the organization and therefore have high stakes (survival may be threatened), lead to subjectively high risk. Organizations' decision makers are risk avoiders. Risk must therefore be reduced before actions can be initiated to change the behavior of the organization. This can normally not be achieved through reduction of the stakes, so it will have to occur through reduction of uncertainty. This is where inspiration comes in. Inspiration and enthusiasm can eliminate uncertainty completely. Stakes are high, there is stress and a feeling of crisis, at least in some members. They search for explanations to the observed changes. When you have an explanatory model of the part of reality under discussion you can also propose meliorating actions, since such a model essentially deals with causation. A proposition of this kind in an organizational setting, where stress and search are present, will have an audience. It provides a solution-in-principle around which expectations, coloured by wishful thinking, form. These expectations support the proposition (see also Smelser's, 1963, 'generalized belief'). Hereby, the members of the organization will generate a new feeling of control over the situation. The preoccupation with a threatening environment is replaced by a we-can-do-it spirit. Action is demanded, not avoided. The new experiment is initiated with enthusiasm and has a good chance to succeed. Initial success (eucity feedback – Streufert, 1973) reduces the perceived risk and complexity further. The solution-in-principle is gradually elaborated into a domain definition which begins to serve as a forecasting model. The information system is adapted to the new world view with confidence, and organizational stabilizers dominate the development.

We have used the term myth (Hedberg & Jönsson, 1977) to refer to the theory of the world, and of action, which dominates an organization's behaviour through a cycle such as the one described in Fig. 8.3.

Thus our main proposition is that organizations develop over time through wave patterns of myths. The waves constitute cycles with spurts of enthusiasm, largely built on wishful thinking that initiate vigorous action, followed by a decline in the unifying and directing force of the leading idea, or set of ideas. The final decline – which results from the interaction between plans and real outcomes, ends in a crisis. As a consequence of the crisis, the organization often accepts a new strategy without any struggle between proponents for the old and the new strategy.

We further propose that the emergence of uncertainty together with decision makers' attitudes and behavior towards uncertainty, are the most important causal factors behind this wave pattern of myths. Behavior in the face of uncertainty depends on the interaction and relative importance of cognitive aspects on the one hand, and emotional or will-oriented aspects on the other hand in the perception of the situation at hand.

In order to demonstrate the function of myths in the strategy formulation process it is necessary to discuss some onthological aspects of the strategy concept. First; it is important to stress that strategies are action-oriented. This means that only an agent can have a strategy. It also implies that the holders of strategies usually do something, and when they act repeatedly they create habits and accumulate inertia. Second; a strategy has two parents – the myth which is the decision makers' theory for understanding the world and motivating their actions, and the situation as perceived through the filter that the myth provides. Third; strategy formulation always takes place in the presence of and in opposition to ruling myths and strategies. This means that new strategies must challenge and disprove the usefulness of the established strategies in order to take over and be successful. This is a difficult task, since the established

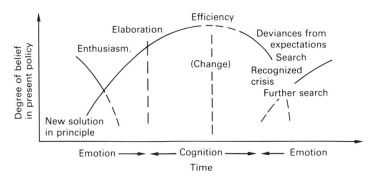

Fig. 8.3 Initiators of action in different phases of organizational belief in present policy.

strategies are consolidated through empirical evidence and have been in use for some time, while the arguments for the new strategies must be based on analogues and speculations. Applying a strategy to a situation means implicitly to test the myth on which it is based. The feedback information that results can be used as arguments against the established strategies and the ruling myths. It is thus possible to argue cognitively against established strategies, but it is much more difficult to gather empirical evidence to be used as arguments in support of new strategies.

Conceptual confusion is likely to result when myths are shifting and when competing strategies develop out of different frameworks. Arguments in favor of the employed strategies and the ruling myth are likely to lack meaning to those who believe in a new myth and advocate new strategies, and vice versa. Proponents and opponents are often unable to communicate and to problem-solve. Uncertainty increases as a result of confusion. Cognitive arguments are only effective in support of, or in opposition to, the ruling myth, since this is the only myth for which it is possible to refer to experience and empirical evidence. Arguments for the new myth will mainly have to be emotional by nature, because of the fact that a shared cognitive framework is still missing.

When new myths are established, and decision makers share the same cognitions, continuous processes of strategy elaborations can go on. But eventually other myths develop, and organizations move over to discontinuous reformulation processes. Acceptance of new myths is partly an emotional act in which individual organizational members shift their cognitive frames of reference. It is also very much a political process wherein groups of organizational members struggle for dominance and attempt to persuade a large enough majority to accept the new myth. The transition involves changes on the metalevel; and reorganizations of the metasystem appear as discontinuities to the organization (Beer, 1975). How these discontinuities occur is described in some detail below.

Our empirical observations suggest that among sociological theories of social change, conflict theories and so called rise-and-fall theories could be considered relevant for the study of strategy formulation processes. In conflict theories opposing interests of groups are seen as the source of social change (Dahrendorf, 1964). The formation of interest groups and the conflicts between them initiate changes in dominance-relations between groups. However, conflict theories tend to emphasize the differential distribution of power as the major source of change, and that is at variance with our case studies where changes in strategies seem to result from problem-solving in crisis situations more often than they result from power struggles. This points to the rise-and-fall theories (Pareto, 1966) which locate the source of change as inherent in social systems themselves.

The main features of our perception of the development and replacement of myths over time are the habit forming and filtering effects of the established strategy that create inertia which in turn results in crises, and the enthusiasm for a solution-in-principle to the crisis situation that overcomes inertia and initiates vigorous action based on a new myth. A wave pattern is the result over time.

It seems to be of great significance for the formulation of design principles for information systems to recognize the shift in attribution that occurs between the phases of emotion and cognition. In the phase of cognition, causes of success and failure are typically attributed to the environment. The mode of behavior is built on the reliability of the information system. In the phase of emotion, where enthusiasm for new solutions in principle and the formation of new cooperative relationships are driving forces, the reliance on information generated by the 'old' information system (and about the past) is minimal. Things are going to change anyhow. New trends will be created. Attention is focused on the self (we-can-do-it, it-is-up-to-us) and attribution is to the self (ego attribution: Brunsson, 1976).

We postulate that organizations can only change their mode of behavior towards the environment significantly when ego-attribution dominates. This leads to the conclusion that it is not desirable that an information system is designed and believed to be the provider-of-the-truth. A combination of an experimental attitude and a perception of the information system as a biased measuring instrument seems more appropriate, especially when organizations travel through changing environments.

ORGANIZATIONS IN DIFFERENT ENVIRONMENTS

The way in which organizations' information (and accounting) systems reflect the world depends on the designers' assumptions about important characteristics of organizations and their environments. Traditional accounting systems are small wonders of logic and consistency, much due to the fact that environments are perceived as rather simple, described by two essential variables: price and quantity. Processes in the environments, such as competition and development, are recognized, but the descriptions focus on the end products of these processes: a price and a quantity. The explanatory theory behind this assumption is that of general equilibrium. The decision problem of the firm is to calculate a mix of quantities that, given prices, makes the firm efficient. The accounting system is designed to assist such calculations. If the assumptions about the markets picture monopolies instead of perfect competition, the decision problem must include forecasting and planning but the basic thinking does not change. The same world view can be applied. It is the same kind of environmental processes that are to be matched.

Changing environments may, however, force organizations to restructure their models of the world and their ways of collecting information. Power and influence changes among critical components in organizations' task environments may call for new ways of reporting. For example, growing influence from trade unions may emphasize human resources management and devalue the importance of money management. Market dysfunctions, or structural changes in different markets, may undermine old assumptions and lead to the development of new world views. The transition periods are often filled with confusion. Decision makers disagree

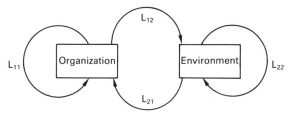

Fig. 8.4 Processes determining causal texture according to Emery & Trist (1965).

on what changes actually occurred. They have different ideas about causes, about means, and about ends. Organizations' goals are challenged, and it is difficult to decide on new directions and to redesign information systems. Abstract concepts, such as profit, costs and turnover, retain their definitions, but the important thing is how they occur – not how they are defined. They must be traced back to the causal texture of the environment in which decisions are taken. Information systems which freeze organizations assumptions about the world must be changed as environments change or as organizations' understanding of their situation changes. Different environments require different decision processes and, consequently, different information systems.

Emery & Trist (1965, p. 22) show a model illustrated in Fig. 8.4 that provides a general basis for a discussion on types of environments. If L_{22} is significantly strong, new characteristics of the environment will emerge. Spontaneous changes in the environment will thus take place. These changes are by definition difficult to forecast. They make earlier experiences from interacting with the environment obsolete. The more significant L_{22} is, the less relevant it is to design (or redesign) information systems on the basis of historical experience of information needs and the more necessary will it be to base the designs on assumptions about future characteristics. The resulting information systems should be designed as measuring instruments suited to be used to test the assumptions – the myth.

To illustrate how these assumptions could influence design, let us consider two important dimensions:

1. whether the variety of problems to be handled is high or low; and
2. whether the intelligence – design – choice sequence is analyzable, and thus possible to program, or not (see also Ullrich, 1976).

The resultant possibilities are illustrated in Fig. 8.5.

Box 1 denotes standard problems that are solved by standard operating procedures. Box 2 represents problems which are fairly easy to recognize, but where the solution process is difficult. Lacking understanding to describe and analyze how decisions are actually made, we are left with the fudge term of 'judgement'. Box 3 stands for problems that vary, but where solution processes can be divided into subprocesses and analyzed. It is

Solution process \ Problem variety	High	Low
Unanalyzable	Construct 4	Judgement 2
Analyzable	3 Program	1 Routine

Fig. 8.5   Characteristics of the decision making process.

possible to decide by contingent program in such cases. Box 4, finally, represents the case where the degree of variation in problems is high and where it is not possible to analyze the solution process. It cannot be reduced to its constituent parts in a meaningful way. In this case the type of decision making is referred to as 'construct', to indicate that it has ingredients of both synthesis and induction.

Planning is the typical behavior mode in cases where decision processes are analyzable. Coordination can then be arranged *ex ante* and the information system should be designed to evaluate the efficiency of that coordination. Where decisions cannot be programmed or routinized, on the other hand, coordination by feedback is called for. The information system should provide continuous evaluation of action. In the first case the meaning and proper interpretation of the information is laid down in the planning phase. In the second case the organization will have more need for its capacity to interpret, reinterpret, and restructure information. The design problem becomes one of building an information system and interpretative capacity to make it useful.

Management strives towards increased rationality in action. Managerial processes therefore typically attempt to close systems and to avoid uncertainty (Thompson, 1967). Whenever possible, managers will try to find ways to move problems towards Box 1 where efficiency can best be exercised. There are three main ways of doing this:

1. Increase the degree of control over the environment, so as to decrease the variation in problems encountered.
2. Increase differentiation by subdividing problems into smaller parts that can be worked on separately by specialists, with economies of scale.

3. Modelling which extends the set of analyzable problems and increases the area that is subject to planning.

Organizations can use these three ways to increase their ability to interact with the environment to their own advantage. But these managerial strategies are at the same time very powerful stabilizers. The cost, in a changing environment, may be lost capacity to see and interpret signals of change.

There are still problems that will stay in Box 4, and the turbulence loop L_{22} (Fig. 8.4) will by definition deliver new ones. However, there are interactions between construct solutions and managerial behavior over time which lead to patterns of shifting myth cycles as we described above.

We shall now proceed to discuss how these ideas can be transformed and used in designing information systems for organizations in changing environments.

DESIGNING INFORMATION SYSTEMS FOR ORGANIZATIONS IN CHANGING ENVIRONMENTS

The proposed experimental behavior – debating the validity of reported information and using information systems to test assumptions about the environment, suggests that design principles for information systems could borrow many ideas from regular research paradigms.

Strategies are organizations' theories for understanding the world. They consist of sets of hypotheses that should be tested and elaborated. The design of information systems is part of the formulation of a research program (Lakatos, 1970). A research program is a plan for the testing and elaboration of a theory. As illustrated in Fig. 8.6, the information system (I) generates the evidence (E) from the real system (R), against which the predictions of the theory (T) are evaluated. If the evidence (E) and the theory (T) are judged to be incompatible, the experimenter has to decide whether to trust the evidence and revise or reject the theory, or to distrust the evidence and redesign the measuring instrument (I). If the evidence fits the theory, more elaborated and detailed hypotheses can be tested.

If this research paradigm is applied to the situation of organizations in changing environments, it follows that the strategy of the organization is

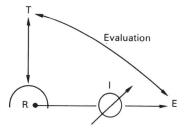

Fig. 8.6   A research paradigm.

the theory to be tested. The core of the strategy (theory) is the domain definition of the organization (Dill, 1958). The domain definition in turn defines the dimensions which the information system should measure. Evaluation of the strategy is possible only if the domain definition of the organization is stated explicitly (and is known to every member of the organization). Elaboration or falsification due to changing environments requires that strategies are stated in falsifiable forms.

The confrontation between theory and evidence envisaged above presupposes that testing the theory is the main concern. In that case the objective of the information system should be to describe reality in relevant dimensions (descriptive research). Evaluation should be left to the experimenters and the results should be subject to debate.

One problem remains; the risk of testing a theory prematurely, before it is elaborated enough to constitute a basis for evaluation at all. Here the analogy with a research paradigm falters. The theory of science very rarely deals with theory generation. We have to resort to inductive reasoning based on our own research. Strategy formulation as a rule takes place in a hostile environment – as a challenge to the existing strategy. The new strategy therefore has to build up enough emotional impetus to break through established patterns. This is typically done in crisis situations where a change in environment has been detected but where it has not been agreed what action is appropriate. This is where the self organizing forces (politics) are given room to generate hypotheses about what are the relevant problems to deal with from now on.

The analogy with the scientific enterprise should not be carried too far, but some reflexions on the analogy might give new insights into the design and implementation of information systems.

There is one aspect of the research paradigm that deserves particular emphasis: organizations in changing environments should behave experimentally. Since they will come across few lasting optima, they ought to gear themselves to impermanency and plan as if their decisions were temporary and probably imperfect solutions to changing problems. Information systems should be set up for experimenting, emphasize evaluations, and be easy to re-arrange. Decision makers should see themselves as experimenters, and they should keep challenging their findings. In short, organizations in changing environments should have inquiring systems that move towards self-evaluation and self-design (Hedberg *et al.*, 1976; Landau, 1973; Wildavsky, 1972). If they cannot predict their futures, they can at least predict that they cannot rely on their forecasts, and they can then start improving their adaptability.

There are many ways in which self-designing organizations can be brought about. Individuals' attitudes are important determinants. Evaluative man (Wildavsky, 1972), if he exists, differs quite a bit from his contemporary decision making colleagues. He takes more interest in organizations' processes than in their states. Performance matters more to him than structures and forms, and he is more inclined to observe his mode of decision making than to linger with each separate solution. No doubt, such creatures are rare. But decision makers could work towards an experimental attitude. Politicians, for example, could consider their suggested reforms as experiments, avoid committing themselves to one particular solution, and rather sell their evaluation criteria to their electorates (Campbell, 1969). More specifically, decision makers in fluid decision situations could adopt procedures for evolutionary operation, such as those suggested by Box & Draper (1969), and they could apply methodologies for optimizing unknown and changing criteria (Starbuck, 1974). They could follow experimental plans and prepare sequences of experimental actions.

Evaluation of actions and strategies could also be built into organizations and triggered by the information systems. There could be predetermined revision periods, when organizational processes are evaluated and changed (March & Simon, 1958). Since formalized information systems and advanced decision models tend to freeze organizations into certain structures and behaviors (Gershefski, 1969), one could build in obsolescence, or last-day-of-use signals, at the time of designing, so that overdue usage of decision parameters and design assumptions is counteracted. All computerized models and information systems could, for example, easily have a last-day-of-use subroutine which prohibits further use until decision makers have decided explicitly to extend the lifetime of implicit factors – such as the world view, the selection of information sources, the decision parameters, etc., of the system, or have initiated work towards systems revisions (Hedberg, 1976).

Less mechanical triggering would build upon the notion of problem-triggered search (Cyert & March, 1963) and on the related findings about cognitive reactions to noxious stimulation (Streufert, 1973) to counterbalance the growth of cognitive complexity and facilitate reframing. One way of making potential problems more visible is to increase the noxity proportion of the decision base which organizations utilize. This could in many instances be accomplished by simply avoiding to filter away inconsistencies and incompatible information as presently is done. Unfiltering and short-circuiting organizations' communication channels are relatively easy means to make decision environments more trigger rich. Dialectic techniques could be employed deliberately to amplify differences between decision makers' positions and highlight underlying assumptions and values (Mason, 1969; Mitroff & Betz, 1972).

Kolb (1974), and later Wolfe (1976), found that decision teams in organizations and in business games performed better in dynamic environments, if they were composed of individuals with different learning styles. Similarly, constructive use of the wider range of perspectives and approaches which decision makers' cognitive styles can provide might encourage organizations to challenge their behaviors and solutions. If information systems were built to cater for different cognitive types (Mason & Mitroff, 1973), there would probably be more constructive confusion, which in turn could trigger experimenting and necessary adaptation.

Semi-confusing information systems could also benefit from using multi-dimensional accounting (Haseman & Whinston, 1976), multiple evaluation criteria, and incompatible reporting dimensions. Gordon *et al.* (1974)

found, for example, that hospitals which employed performance feed-back which both measured expenses and medical performance achieved high-quality treatment at lower costs and were better able to match their internal structures to environmental requirements than hospitals which only used financial performance measures. Unclear objectives and ambiguous work roles have been suggested by Burns & Stalker (1961) as desirable properties of organismic organizations which can survive in dynamic environments. Grinyer & Norburn (1975) found no evidence that clarity in roles and objectives leads to better performance. Instead, use of multiple informal information channels and many different information processes were found to contribute to organizations' adaptiveness. Pluralism, diversity of perspectives and measuring dimensions, and modest amounts of ambiguity and uncertainty appear to be desireable properties of trigger-rich information systems for organizations in changing environments.

Differences in perspectives and perceptions do always exist between various interest groups in organizations. Instead of unifying these perspectives by mild force in formalized information systems, organizations could try to assist each group to develop their own analyses upon their own assumptions and using their own data. For example, worker representatives in participative management arrangements would often need a different cut through their company's data bases than executives do, and they need the support of powerful information technology to be able to argue their cases in competition with professional managers (Briefs, 1975). Also, company divisions and other subunits in organizations could be allowed to filter and arrange information in their own way. Organizations in changing environments should attempt to shorten their response times and to move nearer to their markets. Decentralizing and forming self-contained subunits are attempts along that line (Galbraith, 1973). Information systems could well be used to facilitate the development of organizational subcultures. The resulting differences in viewpoints and in conclusions may well be employed constructively in spotting real problems with which organizations urgently should deal.

All in all, this points towards design principles which differ considerably from current design ideals, and which turn many systems characteristics previously considered as liabilities into assets. Thus, in addition to striving for order and clarity, consistency and rationality, those who design information systems for organizations in changing environments should also be concerned with installing processes which can counteract and balance these virtues. This is where ambiguity, inconsistency, multiple perspectives, and impermanency come in. Semi-confusing information systems require learning mechanisms so that they can help organizations exploit previous experiences and detected causalities, but they need unlearning mechanisms also so that they can do away with obsolete knowledge and behaviors. Dissension can be used to counteract consensus. Dissatisfaction can help maintain long-term contentment. Scarcity can help organizations from being immobilized by affluence. Doubts make plans useful. Inconsistencies can keep organizations together and trade many evolutionary steps for traumatic revolutions. Imperfection can harness rationality so that wisdom results. Hedberg *et al.* (1976) caricatured these central organizational balances with six aphorisms:

1. cooperation requires minimal consensus,
2. satisfaction rests upon minimal contentment,
3. wealth arises from minimal affluence,
4. goals merit minimal faith,
5. improvement depends on minimal consistency,
6. wisdom demands minimal rationality.

The fulcra for each of these six balances may vary from time to time. The wave pattern of myths which we suggested as an important feature of organizations' life (Fig. 8.3), implies that the strength of destabilizing processes should be varied so that organizations in early myth phases receive relatively less change signals and are allowed to build up and consolidate their cognitive structures, while organizations which have developed mature myths and turned from ego-attribution to environment-attribution need relatively more destabilizers, so that predictions are challenged and excess cognitive complexity is counteracted. This suggests that organizations in changing environments should be able to change their filtering systems, as their strategies and myths change. Maybe they should tune their information systems for different cognitive styles over time (Mason & Mitroff, 1973; Mitroff & Kilmann, 1974) and provide for more intuition-feeling in cognitive build-up phases and relatively more sensation-thinking when the major need is to counteract complexification. Or, building on Ornstein's assertions about the different functions of the right and left brain hemispheres (Ornstein, 1975), there may be a case for a right-hand side information system that operates in a rather holistic, simultaneous and impressionistic way during the nursing phases of a myth cycle, while later on left-hand side systems, providing information for sequential, linear, analytical information processors, would be needed. Managing may require one dominant mode of decision-making behavior, and planning another (Mintzberg, 1975).

Figure 8.7 summarizes these suggested design features with respect to how they could affect organizations, individual decision makers, and the amount of signals that reach an organization.

EPILOGUE

These general directions and principles for information systems designs which are suited for organizations in changing environments are certainly easier to state than to operationalize and to implement. Our excuse for weathering them so prematurely is that we believe that they are important and that they are right. As scientific myth builders we find ourselves in a phase where we have to trust our guts, rely on an intuition-feeling mode of reasoning, and put forward a solution-in-principle. Yes, our right-hand

Components:	Needs:	Design features:
Organization (social system)	Experimental behavior	Evaluative man (Wildavsky, 1972; Campbell, 1969).
		Evolutionary operation (Box & Draper, 1969)
		Optimizing unknown criteria (Starbuck, 1974)
		Self design (Hedberg *et al.*, 1976; Landau, 1973; Wildavsky, 1972)
	Variety in Communication	Informal communication networks (Grinyer & Norburn, 1975)
		Role ambiguity (Burns & Stalker, 1961)
		Shortcircuiting levels or groups (Hedberg, 1976)
Individuals (decision makers)	Variety in perception	Mixed cognitive styles (Mason & Mitroff, 1973; Mintzberg, 1975)
		Mixed learning styles (Kolb, 1974; Wolfe, 1976)
		Multidimensional reporting (Haseman & Whinston, 1976)
		Reframing (Watzlawick *et al.*, 1974)
		Dialectics (Mason, 1969; Mitroff & Betz, 1972)
	Variety in evaluation	Ambiguous objectives (Burns & Stalker, 1961; Grinyer & Norburn, 1975)
		Multiple evaluation criteria (Gordon *et al.*, 1974)
Change signals	Counteract stability (a) Routinized triggering	Predetermined revision periods (March & Simon, 1958)
		Last-day-of-use for administrative routines (Hedberg, 1976)
	(b) Contingent triggering	Planned sequences of experiments (Starbuck, 1974) (Mature myth phases)

```
                              MUCH
                               ↑
                               |    semi-confusing  informations
                               |    systems:
                               |    — unfiltering
                               |    — inconsistency
                               |    — incompatibility
                               |    — dialectics
                               |         (Hedberg et al., 1976;
                               ↓          Hedberg & Jönsson, 1977)
                              LITTLE

                              (Infant myth phases)
```

Fig. 8.7 Summary of suggested design features.

brain hemispheres did this sketching. The work for the left-hand side hemispheres remains.

BIBLIOGRAPHY

Beer, Stafford, *Platform for Change* (London: Wiley, 1975).

Boguslaw, Robert, *The New Utopians: A Study of Systems Design and Social Change* (Englewood Cliffs, NJ: Prentice Hall, 1965).

Box, George E.P. & Draper, Norman R., *Evolutionary Operation* (New York: Wiley, 1969).

Briefs, Ulrich, Information Systems and Workers' Participation in Decision Making, in Enid Mumford and Harold Sackman, (eds.) *Human Choice and Computers* (Amsterdam: North-Holland, 1975).

Brunsson, Nils, *Propensity to change* (Gothenburg: Business Administration Studies (BAS) No. 27, 1976).

Burns, Tom & Stalker, G.M., *The Management of Innovation* (London: Tavistock, 1961).

Campbell, Donald T., Reforms as Experiments, *American Psychologist* (1969), pp. 409–429.

Cyert, Richard M. & March, James F., *A Behavioral Theory of the Firm*, (Englewood Cliffs, NJ: Prentice-Hall, 1963).

Dahrendorf, Ralf, Towards a Theory of Social Conflict, in A. and E. Etzioni, (eds.) *Social Change* (New York: Basic Books, 1964).

Dill, William R., Environment as an Influence on Managerial Autonomy, *Administrative Science Quarterly* (1958), pp. 409–443.

Emery, Fred E. & Trist, Eric L., The Causal Texture of Organizational Environments, *Human Relations* (1965), pp. 21–32.

Emery, Fred E. & Trist, Eric L., *Towards a Social Ecology* (London and New York: Plenum Press, 1973).

Galbraith, Jay R., *Designing Complex Organizations* (Reading, MA: Addison-Wesley, 1973).

Gershefski, George W., Building a Corporate Financial Model, *Harvard Business Review* (1969), pp. 61–72.

Glimell, Hans, *Designing Interactive Systems for Organizational Change* (Göteborg: Business Administration Studies, 1975).

Gordon, G., Tanon, C. & Morse, E.V., *Hospital Structure, Costs, and Innovation*, Working Paper, Cornell University, 1974.

Grinyer, Peter H. & Norburn, David, An Empirical Investigation of Some Aspects of Planning for Existing Markets; Perceptions of Executives and Financial Performance, *Journal of the Royal Statistical Society*, Series A, (1975).

Harvey, O., Hunt, D. & Schroder, Harold, *Conceptual Systems and Personality Organization* (New York: Wiley, 1961).

Haseman, William D., & Whinston, Andrew B., Design of a Multidimensional Accounting System, *The Accounting Review* (1976), pp. 65–79.

Hedberg, Bo, *On Man-Computer Interaction in Organizational Decision-Making: A Behavioral Approach* (Göteborg: Business Administration Studies, 1970).

Hedberg, Bo, Growth Stagnation as a Managerial Discontinuity, in *Proceedings of the INSEAD Seminar on Management under Discontinuity* (Brussels: European Institute for Advanced Studies in Management, 1975), pp. 34–59.

Hedberg, Bo, Mott ett manövrerbart industrisamhälle, in Birgitta Hambraeus and Emin Tengström, (eds.), *Vad kan du och jag göra åt framtiden?* (Stockholm: Bonniers, 1976), pp. 131–139.

Hedberg, Bo, How Organizations Learn and Unlearn, in Paul C. Nystrom and William H. Starbuck, (eds.), *Handbook of Organizational Design*, Vol. 1, Amsterdam: Elsevier Scientific (in press), 1978.

Hedberg, Bo, Edström, Olof & Glimell, Hans, Man-Computer Interference? The Development of a Marketing Information Systems, in Sandor Asztély, (ed.), *Budgetering och redovisning som instrument för styrning.* (Stockholm: Norstedts, 1974), pp. 107–149.

Hedberg, Bo, Nystrom, Paul, C. & Starbuck, William H., Camping on Seesaws: Prescriptions for a Self-Designing Organization, *Administrative Science Quarterly* (March 1976), pp. 41–65.

Hedberg, Bo, Nystrom, Paul C. & Starbuck, William H., Designing Organizations to Match Tomorrow, in Paul C. Nystrom and William H. Starbuck, (eds.), *Prescriptive Models of Organizations*, (North-Holland/TIMS Studies in the Management Sciences, 1977), pp. 171–181.

Hedberg, Bo & Jönsson, Sten, Strategy Formulation as a Discontinuous Process, *International Studies of Management and Organization* (1977).

Jönsson, Sten, *Decentralisering och utveckling. En fälstudie av utvecklingsbolagens planeringsproblem* (Göteborg: Business Administration Studies (BAS) No. 21, 1973).

Karlins, M., Conceptual Complexity and Remote Associative Proficiency at Creativity Variables in a Complex Problem Solving Task, *Journal of Personality and Social Psychology* (1967), pp. 264–278.

Karlins, M. & Lamm, H., Information Search as a Function of Conceptual Structure, *Journal of Personality and Social Psychology* (1967), pp. 456–459.

Kelly, George Alexander, *The Psychology of Personal Constructs*, Vol. 1 and 2, (New York: Norton, 1977).

Kolb, David A., On Management and the Learning Process, in David A. Kolb, Irwin M. Rubin, and James M. McIntyre, (eds.), *Organizational Psychology: A Book of Readings* (Englewood Cliffs, NJ: Prentice-Hall, 1974).

Lakatos, Imre, Falsification and the Methodology of Scientific Research Programs, in Imre Lakatos and Alan Musgrave, (eds.), *Criticism and the Growth of Knowledge* (Cambridge University Press, 1970).

Landau, Martin, Redundancy, Rationality and the Problem of Duplication and Overlap, *Public Administration Review* (1969), pp. 346–358.

Landau, Martin, On the Concept of a Self-Correcting Organization, *Public Administration Reveiw* (1973), pp. 533–542.

March, James G. & Simon, Herbert A., *Organizations* (New York: Wiley, 1958).

Mason, Richard O., A Dialectical Approach to Strategic Planning, *Management Science* (1969), pp. B403–B414.

Mason, Richard O. & Mitroff, Ian I., A Program for Research on Management Information Systems, *Management Science* (1973), pp. 475–487.

McCall, Jr., Morgan, A Systematic Look at Nonsense, The Congruous Side of Incongruity, Working paper, Center for Creative Leadership, Greensboro, N.C., 1975.

Miller, Danny & Gordon, Lawrence A., Conceptual Levels and the Design of Accounting Information Systems, *Decision Sciences* (1975), pp. 259–269.

Mintzberg, Henry, Planning on the Left Side and Managing on the Right,

Working paper, Institut d'Administration des Enterprises, Aix-en-Provence, 1975.

Mitroff, Ian I. & Betz, Fred, Dialectical Decision Theory, A Meta-Theory of Decision Making, *Management Science* (1972), pp. 11–24.

Mitroff, Ian I. & Kilmann Ralph H., On the Importance of Qualitative Analysis in Management Science: The Influence of Personality Variables on Organizational Decision Making, Working paper, No. 67, University of Pittsburgh, PH, 1974.

Mowshowitz, Abbe, *The Conquest of Will: Information Processing in Human Affairs* (Reading, MA: Addison–Wesley, 1976).

Nystrom, Paul C., Hedberg, Bo L.T. & Starbuck, William H., Interacting Processes as Organization Designs, in Ralph H. Kilmann, Louis R. Pondy, and Dennis P. Slevin, (eds.), *The Management of Organization Design* (New York: Elsevier, 1976), pp. 209–230.

Ornstein, R., *The Psychology of Consciousness* (New York: Jonathan Cape, 1975).

Pareto, V., *Sociological Writings*, selected and introduced by S.E. Finer, (New York: Praeger, 1966).

Schroder, Harold, Driver, Michael J. & Streufert, Siegfried, *Human Information Processing* (New York: Holt, Rinehart and Winston, 1967).

Smelser, Neil J., *Theory of Collective Behavior* (New York: Free Press, 1963).

Starbuck, William H., Systems Optimization with Unknown Criteria, *Proceedings of the 1974 International Conference on Systems, Man, and Cybernetics* (New York: Institute of Electrical and Electronics Engineers, 1974), pp. 67–76.

Starbuck, William H., Information Systems for Organizations of the Future, in E. Grochla and N. Szyperski, *Information Systems and Organizational Structure* (New York: de Gruyter, 1975), pp. 217–230.

Starbuck, William H. & Hedberg, Bo L.T., Saving an Organization from a Stagnating Environment, in Hans B. Thorelli, ed., *Strategy + Structure = Performance: The Strategic Planning Imperative* (Bloomington, Ind.: Indiana University Press, 1977).

Streufert, Susan C., Success and Response Rate in Complex Decision Making, *Journal of Experimental Social Psychology* (1972), pp. 389–403.

Streufert, Susan C., Effects of Information Relevance on Design Making in Complex Environments, *Memory and Cognition* (1973), pp. 224–228.

Suefeld, P. & Hagen, R., Measurement of Information Complexity, *Journal of Personality and Social Psychology* (1966), pp. 233–236.

Thompson, James D., *Organizations in Action* (New-York: McGraw Hill Inc., 1967).

Ullrich, Robert A., Organizational Design, Employee Motivation and the Support of Strategic Management, in H.I. Ansoff, R.P. Declerk, and R.L. Hayes, (eds.), *From Strategic Planning to Strategic Management* (New York: Wiley, 1976).

Watzlawick, Paul, Weakland, John H. & Fisch, Richard, *Change; Principles of Problem Formation and Problem Resolution* (New York: Norton, 1974).

Wildavsky, Aaron, The Self-Evaluating Organization, *Public Administration Review* (1972), pp. 509–520.

Wolfe, Joseph, Learning Styles Rewarded in a Complex Simulation with Implications for Business Policy and Organization Behavior Research, *Proceedings, 36th Annual National Meeting of the Academy of Management*, 1976.

9

Planning management control systems

Franco Amigoni

Associate Professor of Accounting and Control, Scuola di Direzione Aziendale, Università 'L. Bocconi', Milan

The Simon research team [1] found that there are three types of information needed for controlling any company, each serving a different purpose, depending on the answer to these questions:

1. Score-card questions: 'Am I doing well or badly?'
2. Attention-directing questions: 'What problems should I look into?'
3. Problem-solving questions: 'Of the several ways of doing the job, which is the best?'

From the systems theorist's viewpoint we can find a tight relationship between these questions and some control mechanisms: score-card questions can be related to the feed-back loop, and problem-solving questions to the response function, i.e. 'the function linking action variables with environmental variables' [2], while it is more difficult to find a precise cybernetics definition for the attention-directing questions.

These reference problems are a very useful starting point in designing and implementing a concrete management control system. Nevertheless the problems that controllers or consultants have to face in any specific company in order to provide managers at any level with appropriate control tools show that they need a more detailed framework. Unfortunately many of the attempts made to identify some kind of relation between company variables – i.e. dimension, turnover, number of workers, etc. – and control tools – i.e. financial and cost account responsibility accounting, budget, etc. – have failed. There are two likely explanations for this: a) the company variables identified were not the more relevant from a control point of view, and b) the description of a specific control system in terms of 'tool' is incorrect, given the fact that each tool is multipurpose, and therefore can be used in any company in a very different way.

In order to propose a conceptual framework useful in designing and implementing a management control system in any specific company, we

Source: Amigoni, F. (1978) *Journal of Business Finance & Accounting*, **5** (3), pp. 279–92.

must proceed in various directions. First of all an effort must be made in defining the appropriate independent variables, i.e. the characteristics of the company and of its environment that actually influence the control process. Secondly, we should identify some distinctive features of management control systems, because, as we said above, these systems cannot be correctly analysed in terms of tools. Thirdly, significant relations have to be found between these features of control systems and the independent variables, between control tools and system features and hence between independent variables and control tools. (See Table 9.1)

INDEPENDENT VARIABLES THAT ARE RELEVANT IN DESIGNING A MANAGEMENT CONTROL SYSTEM

The control system in any specific company must be tailored in relation to these company and environmental characteristics: a) the degree of structural complexity and b) the degree of discontinuity.

a) The degree of complexity

The structural complexity of the operations can be defined in relation to two dimensions, which, even though connected, must be considered

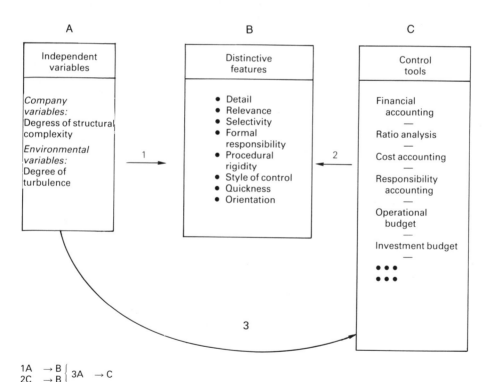

Table 9.1 Significant conditions in the design of a management control system.

separately. These are: i) number and degree of interdependence of business units and ii) number and type of organizational units.

The first dimension is related to the fact that the control process is simpler in a company, even given high turnover and a large work force, which produces and sells one or a few independent products in a single market than in another, even a small one, which operates in many different markets with joint products. Often the map of organizational units is closely linked with that of business units. However, we prefer to keep these two dimensions distinct, because their relationships are influenced by several factors, such as the size of the company, the values of the managers, business turbulence, competitive pressure, etc.

With regard to the second dimension, there is a great distinction between two main organizational settings, with reference to the differentiation already achieved by the system. Any enterprise can be considered an 'open system', when goal-directed behaviour results from the actions of its elements. In very simple systems, all the elements pursue the system's goals in an undifferentiated way, and their efforts are coordinated through the mechanism of 'dynamic interaction' [3]. In complex systems each element has a specialized function, and coordination is achieved through the process of factoring, that is through a hierarchic subdivision of the main system's goal into several coordinated sub-goals for every single organizational unit. At the unit level, the feed-back loop and response function are the mechanisms for controlling the goal-directed behaviour.

Enterprises can be considered undifferentiated systems if operations are very simple, and the few men who manage them are owners, and therefore naturally interested in the success of the business. They are complex systems, if the process of differentiation is already well ahead. In this case we have three levels of goals: the system level, the organizational unit level, and the individual level.

The distinction between these two types of system is very important because in the first one the management control system's function is mainly information. To control his company the entrepreneur, who is also the owner and the only decision taker, needs only relevant information, readily and selectively. In complex systems the functions of the control process are far more complicated and range from providing each organizational unit with relevant information to structuring a well coordinated system of sub-goals, motivating managers to achieve their own sub-goals, evaluating their performances, etc. Hence the problems to be solved in designing and implementing management control systems in enterprises already 'differentiated' are quantitatively and qualitatively far more complex than those of an 'undifferentiated' company. In the first case, more than in the second, the success of the control process cannot be guaranteed without a close fit between all the managerial tools, such as organization structure, managerial style, reward-punishment system, etc. (See Table 9.2).

b) The degree of discontinuity

The control process is simple if the company's operations are stable,

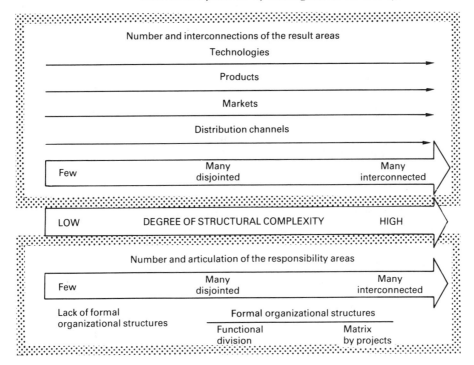

Table 9.2 Factors determining the structural complexity of the enterprise and its relations with the environment.

which implies a stable environment. It becomes difficult if the environment is dynamic, i.e. a high but predictable rate of change, and very complex if the environment is discontinuous, i.e. a high but unpredictable rate of change. The degree of discontinuity is, in our opinion, the more relevant environmental variable, because control systems are systems of order. They are, in fact, projected and implemented with reference to certain assumptions about the economic scenario. If this changes it is difficult for the control system to adapt accordingly its signals to managers.

DISTINCTIVE FEATURES OF MANAGEMENT CONTROL SYSTEMS

To describe a specific control system we can observe certain distinctive features that each system has, in differing degree. These are:

a) Degree of detail

Control systems can be more or less detailed, in relation to the number of clusters (aggregations) in which raw financial data are collected and classified. The degree of detail is less if, for instance, the only control tool employed is the company financial accounting, where data are classified with reference to type of counterpart and nature of costs of revenues. The degree of detail is greater if data are classified also with reference to products, organizational units, variables, etc., as with cost accounting for example.

b) Degree of relevance

As we know a datum is 'relevant' in a specific situation if it is related to factors that can be influenced by the decision taken. A high degree of relevance means that each manager is provided with relevant information in direct correlation to his prevailing decisional activity. Direct cost accounting, for instance, increases the system's degree of relevance with respect to full cost accounting, because the distinction between variable and fixed costs is relevant in many decisions [4].

c) Degree of selectivity

Often relevant information is confused with a lot of irrelevant information [5]. The control system has a greater degree of selectivity the higher the ratio is between relevant and irrelevant information. This means also that the key economic variables greatly influencing the profitability of operations are clearly identified and the managers are aware of them. Hence the system operates as a filter for that information not actually useful in the managerial activity.

d) Degree of formal responsibility

We have said before that in complex systems control is based on a process of the hierarchic subdivision of the main company goal into many sub-goals, one for each organizational unit. So each responsibility centre has its own financial target, such as cost, revenue, profit, etc. A control system has a high degree of formal responsibility if the system of financial targets is very well developed. This means first of all that a very in-depth analysis has been made on the economic contribution of each organizational unit to the production process. And second, that these contributions – cost, revenue, profit, etc. – have been translated into a well articulated system of sub-goals. On the other hand, the degree of formal responsibility is low if the system of financial sub-goals is not very developed with respect to the business or organizational structure.

e) Degree of procedural rigidity

As far as procedural rigidity is concerned we can distinguish two types of control systems: standard control systems and contingency control systems. The former are made using formal tools and procedures that are projected in terms of regular and continuous employment. They are based on computerized information systems, are managed with well defined

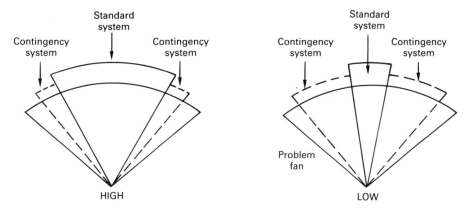

Table 9.3 Degree of procedural rigidity.

procedures and are supposed to be useful for solving the majority of problems that managers must face. Contingency control systems are 'ad hoc' systems, created for the control – i.e. decision, evaluation, etc. – of certain problems that the management considers 'unlikely' and, therefore, not worth constant attention in the control process. These systems are often managed without predefined procedures and are tailored to the specific problem to be solved at that specific moment. If we assume that any company has, in a defined period, its 'problem fan', then we can say that the manager covers this fan in two ways: with standard and with contingency systems. The relationship between the two is a matter of judgement. The degree of procedural rigidity is higher the greater the standard system's predominance over the contingency system. (See Table 9.3).

Procedural rigidity is a distinctive feature of control systems that assume a high relevance in a discontinuous environment, when the 'problem fan' is supposed to shift rapidly. Standard systems, because of their procedural rigidity, are difficult to shift accordingly. This means that the 'problem fan' can remain uncovered, or, on the contrary, that procedures are implemented to no actual purpose. (See Table 9.4).

f) Style of control

The behaviour of managers in implementing control systems has been defined as 'style of control'. This distinctive feature can be appreciated with regard to several factors. The more administrative control predominates over several and individual control, the more 'tight' is this style [6]. In the same way we can define as 'tight' a control system when participation in setting objectives is low, targets are imposed and managers must consider them firm commitments, performance evaluation is oriented to accounting measures, etc. [7]. On the other hand the style is 'loose' if managers are conscious of the social and individual side of control, if

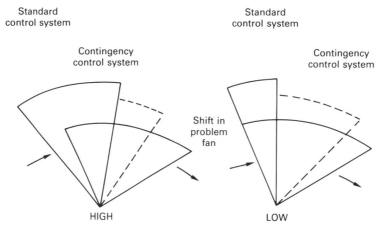

Table 9.4 Degree of procedural rigidity and environmental discontinuity.

participation is high, targets are negotiated and considered to be only reference points to be considered only in the context of actual environmental events and, finally, if managers are also evaluated on the basis of multiple, non qualitative, factors.

g) Quickness

One can evaluate the quickness of the control system by observing the period elapsing between the occurance of an environmental event and its communication in an appropriate way to managers that must in turn react. The shorter this period is, the higher the degree of quickness. This feature of control systems must, of course, be judged with regard to the decisional activity of the managers.

h) Orientation

This feature of control systems describes their tendency to favour certain types of events, information or objectives with respect to others. Systems can be 'productive factor oriented' if information is gathered mainly in accordance with production inputs, or 'product oriented' if emphasis is given to production outputs. Other types of orientation are towards managerial activities vs. legal necessities, decisional rationality vs. controllability, etc. The main distinction in this case is between systems oriented towards the past and those oriented towards the future. Management control systems are oriented to the past if they focus on past events and on hypotheses and targets defined in advance. They are future oriented if they concentrate on future events which are explicitly considered in the system and towards which the entire system is geared [8].

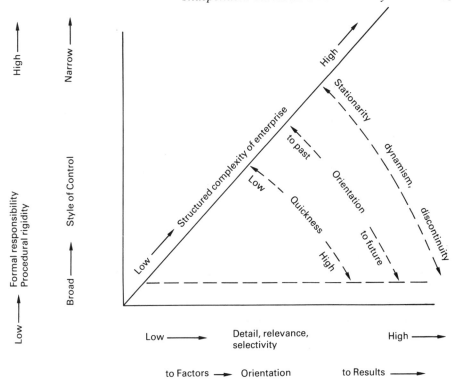

Table 9.5 The management control: a reference plan.

CONNECTIONS BETWEEN INDEPENDENT VARIABLES AND THE FEATURES OF MANAGEMENT CONTROL SYSTEMS

After having identified the independent companies and environmental variables and the distinctive features of management control systems, we can suggest some of the more important connections between the two (See Table 9.5).

1) Stable environment

(a) The more numerous are the business units and the greater is the contact between them, the more detailed the systems must be with an orientation towards outputs – i.e. products and markets.

(b) The more complex the organizational structure is, the more relevant and selective it will be with regard to the decisional activity of each organizational unit. The degree of detail must be high at the lower levels and low at the top levels.

(c) The more complex the organizational structure is the higher the degree of formal responsibility and procedural rigidity and the tighter the style of control will be.

2) Turbulent environment

The connections suggested for a stable environment are to be adjusted to the turbulence as follows:

(a) The more discontinuous the environment is, the more the system must be oriented to the future and with a high degree of quickness
(b) The less discontinuous the environment is, the more procedural rigidity should decrease and the style of control change from tight to loose.

CONNECTIONS BETWEEN CONTROL TOOLS AND THE FEATURES OF MANAGEMENT CONTROL SYSTEMS

Management control systems assume a certain set of distinctive features in relation to: i) the tools from which they are composed, and ii) the way in which these tools are employed. In this sense it is very difficult, if not impossible, to identify the connection between tools and features without making a very deep analysis of the structure of each tool and the manner in which it is employed. For example, cost accounting can make very different contributions to the relevance and the formal responsibility of the system depending on the emphasis given to the variability or controllability criterion.

The budgeting process can be oriented to decisional rationality or motivational problems, and can be used with a tight or loose style. The same can be said for every control tool. Therefore, it becomes very difficult to fulfil the 'control tool matrix' (see Table 9.6) where the connections

Control system tools \ Control system features	Detail	Relevance	Selectivity	Formal responsibility	Procedural rigidity	Style of control	Quickness	Orientation
Financial accounting								
Ratio analysis								
Financial models								
Inflation accounting								
Actual full costing								
Actual direct costing								
Standard costing								
Flexible budgeting								
Operational budgets								
Capital budgets								
Long range plans								

Table 9.6 Control system matrix.

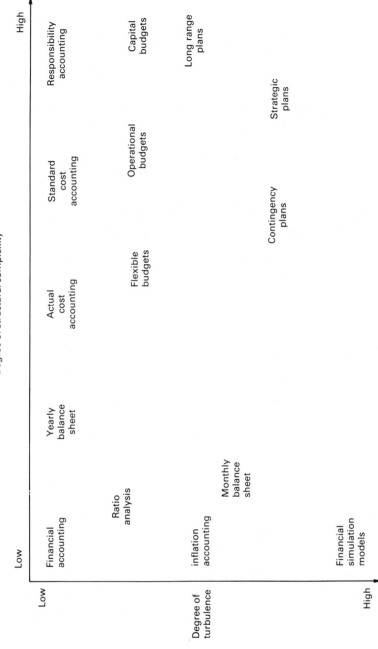

Table 9.7 Connections between independent variables and control tools.

between control tools and the features of the system are identified without reference to a specific company. Nevertheless we can try to give some guidelines. Financial accounting, the most common control tool, is oriented to the operational control of credits and debts. From a management control point of view, it contributes to the relevance and selectivity of the system mainly through Balance Sheets, where the profit and loss data constitute the main relevant information for managers. To increase the relevance of the system one must go more deeply, through ratio analysis, into the economic relations between the various items of the balance sheet. Financial models increase the future orientation, as well as the relevance, while, in our opinion, inflation accounting has a limited impact on the features of the system.

A great improvement is obtained by the use of cost accounting. This tool has a great impact on relevance, especially if it clearly shows direct costs, and on formal responsibility, if cost data are clustered according to responsibility centres and if a regular comparison between the standard and actual costs is made. Budgeting, together with responsibility accounting, contributes to all the features of the system, with special reference to formal responsibility and procedural rigidity; often it is used with tight style and has a limited orientation to the future. With capital budgeting and long range planning, formal responsibility and procedural rigidity usually remain unchanged or decrease. while orientation to the future, relevance, selectivity, etc. increase.

In conclusion we can say that each tool can contribute in varying degrees to the different features of control systems and, conversely, that each feature is obtained from an appropriate combination of tools.

CONNECTIONS BETWEEN INDEPENDENT VARIABLES AND CONTROL TOOLS

Table 9.7 presents a very general framework for identifying the main connections between independent variables and control tools. It is important to point out that with increasing structural complexity, *any tool can be added to those previously in use*, which maintain their function within the system. On the other hand, with an increase in environmental discontinuity *new tools often substitute those previously in use*, which then lose their function. This is because many control tools are projected for a stable environment and operate best under a certain set of environmental conditions. If these change rapidly, the tools lose their capacity to guide managers towards the goals of the company. An observance of Table 9.7 also reveals a shortage of tools for controlling very complex companies in a highly turbulent environment. This should probably be the main field of research on management control systems.

ACKNOWLEDGEMENT

Paper received September 1977, revised July 1978.

REFERENCES

1. Simon H.A., Guetzkow, H., Kozmetsky J. and Tyndal, J. *Centralization Vs. Decentralization in Organizing the Controller's Department*, New York Controllership Foundation, Inc. 1954.
2. Sommerhoff, J. 'The Abstract Characteristics of Living Systems' in *System Thinking*, edited by F.E. Emery, Harmondsworth 1969, pp. 147–202.
3. Von Bertalanffy, L. *General System Theory*, New York, 1968.
4. American Accounting Association, 'Report of Committee on Managerial Decision Models', *The Accounting Review*, Vol. XLIV, N. 1 (Supplement 1969), pp. 42–76.
5. Ackoff, R.L. 'Management Misinformation Systems', *Management Science* Vol. 14, n.4, December 1967.
6. Dalton, G.W., Lawrence P.R., *Motivation and Control in Organizations*, Homewood, 1971, pp. 47–63.
   Dearden, J. 'What's Wrong with your Financial Control System', *European Business*, Summer 1971.
7. Hopwood, A.G. *Accounting and Human Behaviour*, London 1974, p. 100.
8. Gilbert X.F. 'A Framework for the Analysis of Management Planning and Control Systems', INSEAD, Fontainebleau, Unpublished Working Paper.

Part Two

Accounting for Programmed Decisions

Part Two of the text is concerned with programmed decisions, that is decisions where a good predictive model of the process being controlled is available. The discussion of decision-making reviews the standard management accounting techniques used in practice and concludes that traditional management accounting techniques require far-reaching assumptions about the predictive ability of managers and their advisors to be made. In simple terms, a great deal of stability in both the external environment and in internal behaviour has to be assumed for the techniques to yield appropriate decision rules. It is convenient to focus the discussion on budgetary control for several reasons. First, budgetary control uses most of the usual management accounting techniques at some stage in its progression from planning to control. Secondly, budgetary control is used in almost every organization of any size, and this is reflected in the number of studies on the topic in the research literature. Finally, it was in this area of management accounting that the impact of human and behavioural factors on the use of accounting information was first recognized and studied.

BUDGETS IN OPERATION

The classic article by Buckley and McKenna (1972) provides an excellent summary of this early work on budgetary control which acknowledges both its technical and behavioural aspects, and clearly sets out the assumptions made in its application. Alternative behavioural assumptions are considered, and the impact of factors such as managerial participation in budget-setting are reviewed. Also apparent is the change in emphasis which has occurred over the twenty-year period reviewed. This is perhaps most neatly epitomized in the contrast between the title of Argyris's (1952) seminal contribution 'The Impact of Budgets on People' and Schiff and Lewin's (1971) article 'The Impact of People on Budgets'. The methods used by managers to subvert the rational operation of control techniques was a clear topic of study in the late 1960s and has remained as an important emphasis thereafter. Thus budgeting is being recognized as both a technical and a managerial process, and theories of the human aspects of this process are beginning to be developed. The Buckley and McKenna article can also be seen as representing the end of the universalistic road. Most of the work to this date makes an underlying assumption that there is a best way of operating a budgetary control system which remains to be discovered. The conclusions section of the article clearly reflects this, being a series of guidelines that are intended to be indicative of good budgetary practice given the implications of behavioural science. From the mid-1970s a more contingent approach was generally adopted, partly influenced by developments in organization theory during the 1960s and partly driven by research results in budgetary control itself.

The chapter selected from Macintosh's (1985) book, intriguingly entitled *The Social Software of Accounting and Information Systems*, carries on from where Buckley and McKenna left off. It reviews the early contributions of both Argyris and Hofstede, but from a perspective that is more based upon organization theory and group dynamics than individual psychology, and introduces Hopwood's famous study on the effects of reliance on accounting measures of performance (RAPM). This found that a heavy reliance on such measures could lead to a variety of dysfunctional consequences, such as high levels of stress and anxiety, poor relationships and, arguably, poor overall performance. These adverse consequences were caused by the inappropriate use of imperfect measures of performance; it appeared that a more flexible style of use was required to avoid such adverse effects. However, a subsequent study by Otley found that these results were not universal. By selecting a research site where accounting performance measures captured performance more accurately, a conflicting set of results were found. Comparison of these two studies leads to a number of conclusions. First, the impact of prevailing external circumstances appears to have more impact than was previously imagined, and individual personality and philosophy of management may be less important. Secondly, these results point toward the need to develop more contingent theories of budgetary control based on differences in organizational type, the environmental circumstances in which they operate, and the norms and values current both within the organization itself and within the society in which it is set. But as Macintosh clearly states, although the participative budgeting concept may have proved to be a myth, it has enabled us to learn a great deal about how financial controls operate in organizations and has also led to the development of new theories of information systems design and use.

The apparent conflict between Hopwood's and Otley's findings has led to a long-lasting debate in the literature, initially at a theoretical level but increasingly involving empirical work. It has thus resulted in what has been described as one of the more coherent streams of management accounting research during the 1980s. The nature and extent of the work it has spawned is well reviewed in Briers and Hirst (1990). Although steady progress has been marred by sometimes inadequate theoretical development and also by sometimes faulty operationalization of concepts, this stream of research has made substantial progress and provides a platform from which future initiatives can be launched. Figure 1 in their article lists an impressive range of relevant variables, categorized into antecedent, independent, moderating, intervening and dependent. This is a most helpful way of organizing prior studies, even though it may have to be recognized that some apparently dependent variables such as performance may also be independent variables affecting budgetary systems use. For example, increased use of financial controls is widely observed to occur when organizations are experiencing poor performance. But supervisory style still appears to be a key variable in predicting the consequences of a given system of budgetary control. However, Briers and Hirst argue that the effects of supervisory style on behaviour are not straightforward but rather that it is 'filtered' through several moderating variables. Thus their analysis provides a jumping off point for a great deal of further research.

OPERATING BUDGETS

Although behavioural factors are of central importance to the effective operation of a budgetary control system, technical factors cannot be neglected. In their article, Otley and Berry (1979) consider the consequences of aggregating budgets as they move up the organizational hierarchy. This is problematic when the budget estimates are pitched at a level that is different to the expected value of the outcome; that is, budget estimates which are either optimistic or pessimistic. They show that the result of aggregating a set of optimistic (pessimistic) budgets results in a total budget that is even more extreme. Further, commonly used methods of budget amendment, such as *pro rata* budget adjustment, designed to solve such problems result in revised budgets that have different chances of achievement for different managers. They conclude that such commonly used procedures result in unanticipated distortions and propose other methods of dealing with the problem, such as non-additive budgets. They also contend that the explanation for some observed budgetary practices, which initially may seem arbitrary and even counter-productive, may be based on such underlying features of the real world. More generally, they recommend that the budget process should be tailored to fit the requirements of the situation rather than allowing predefined technical procedures to be adopted as these may produce undesirable consequences. Budgeting in practice can thus be seen to require a unique blend of the behavioural and the technical.

These behavioural and organizational studies of the budgetary process lead naturally into Kaplan's (1983) critique of management accounting research, although he initially developed it from a different direction. In particular, he noted the need to consider both financial and non-financial indicators of performance in managing a manufacturing plant. One of the main criticisms of US industry has been the alleged concentration of senior managers on simple, aggregate, short-term financial measures of performance; Kaplan points to the need to develop indicators that are more consistent with long-term competitiveness and profitability. He also suggests that the research methods which are most common in US management accounting research (i.e. arm's length questionnaire-based studies) are inappropriate and recommends a return to more intensive, longitudinal, field-based studies designed to be more exploratory and inductive rather than hypothesis testing and deductive. However, he also recognizes that such approaches may be more risky for junior researchers, and confines his recommendation to tenured staff! Kaplan thus picks up a theme that has emerged from rather different arguments in the behavioural tradition (see, for example, Otley (1980)). It is significant that calls for a more grounded approach to the inductive generation of theory have emerged from such different traditions.

A more radical analysis of the role of management accounting information in stimulating managerial action is provided by Swieringa and Weick (1987). Traditional management accounting focuses on decision-making, but forceful managerial action does not necessarily flow from good decisions. In addition, it may be that imperfect accounting performance measures which can be viewed as misleading inputs into a decision process can still stimulate forceful, sustained and self-validating action. They thus develop an alternative rationale for the use of simple accounting performance measures, such as RoI, which Kaplan criticizes so heavily. This focus on action picks up the fourth necessary condition for control outlined in the Otley and Berry (1980) model, namely that accounting variances must lead to appropriate corrective action for effective control. However, this conclusion is now presented in a much more plausible interpersonal and social context, and the prerequisites for generating a commitment to forceful action in an organization are analysed.

10

Budgetary control and business behaviour

Adrian Buckley and Eugene McKenna

Nowadays most companies of any size employ some of the techniques of management accounting. Probably the most widely used is budgetary control.

The process of budgeting consists of planning, controlling, co-ordinating and motivating through money values, members, and departments within an organization. In a nutshell, the budget is a plan – usually for one year ahead – in quantitative terms. The control follows by means of comparing actual performance against the performance standard and taking corrective action where necessary. The key features of budgetary control are as follows:

the system is a yardstick for comparison. The planned performance is meant to be perceived by management as a target that should motivate managers towards achievement of the goal implied by the budget.
the system transfers information in quantitative terms.
it isolates problems by focusing upon variances.
The identification of variances makes the system an early warning for management action.
it should identify and highlight performance items as opposed to non-performance items (non-performance items include cause and effect outside the control of the company, e.g. a strike in a tyre supplier will affect Ford sales, but Ford cannot be said to be to blame).
it is a tool of management, not a policing mechanism.
it should be a formalized system culminating in management action.

The sinews of the budgeting process – and indeed of most other management control systems – are the influencing of management behaviour by setting agreed performance standards, the evaluation of results and feedback to management in anticipation of corrective action where necessary.

Since most management controls are conceived and operated by accountants, it is relevant to question whether accountants in general are

Source: Buckley, A. and McKenna, E. (1972) *Accounting and Business Research*, Spring, pp. 137–50.

aware of the impact upon people of these control systems. For there is a body of research findings which is highly critical of accounting control procedures. But, at least in this country, the accounting literature appears only to have given marginal coverage [1] to this most important topic and the syllabuses and examination questions of all the bodies of accountants make little reference to behavioural science. This may be because, as Tricker [2] points out 'the accountant is sometimes suspicious of the emphasis in management studies on people. People are difficult to quantify', but 'the understanding of management planning and control systems hinges on an understanding of people. Organizational theory has a place in the accountant's background knowledge.' However, the Association of Certified Accountants has recently announced a proposed new examination syllabus which includes a paper on Human Relations.

CONTROL AND COMPANY OBJECTIVES

Most management control systems are assumed to operate as part of a series of devices designed to enable the company to achieve its corporate objective. Budgetary control is in addition a monitor of actual outturns in the light of short-term estimates of performance. But given that management controls aim to help the achievement of the corporate objective, it is pertinent to ask what most meaningfully constitutes a corporate objective.

When accountants examine this problem they invariably think in terms of maximizing profit. A study by Caplan [3] showed that 75 per cent of accountants viewed this as the key business objective, whilst of a sample of non-accounting general managers only 25 per cent saw this as the primary business objective.

The traditional economic theory of the firm explains the behaviour of 'economic man' in pursuit of maximum profit. The theory views the entrepreneur as confronted with:

a demand function, in which the prices of the commodities he sells are given by the market

a cost function, in which the prices of the factors of production which he purchases are given by the market

a production function, which is essentially a statement of engineering technology.

In this situation the entrepreneur's behaviour is assumed to be predicted by his desire to maximize economic profits. This theory of business behaviour is based on the following set of assumptions:

complete knowledge of alternative courses of action
unlimited cognitive capacity
perfect knowledge of outcomes
total rationality in decision choice.

The modern theory of financial management takes a view near to economic theory in suggesting that: 'the operating objective for financial management is to maximize wealth or net present value' [4] of the owners.

But neither of these views is endorsed by research findings in this area, and it is doubtful whether the concept of profit maximization is relevant to any but the most entrepreneurial of businesses.

Indeed most economists would view the economic theory of the firm as an abstraction which hardly simulates today's business world. Ideas of rationality and perfect knowledge are inconsistent with the realities of uncertainty and limited reasoning. There is also substantial opinion which questions the profit maximizing desire of the firm. Some writers, having observed the development of the modern corporate entity, and the divorce of ownership and control, assert that managers, with minimal equity stakes in the company, are less motivated than the owner-manager. [5] Others [6] have suggested that economic survival may be the primary goal of a business. Alternatively, some firms [7] may appear to maximize sales provided that a satisfactory return on invested capital is earned.

This approach is well in line with the concept of 'satisficing' developed by Herbert Simon [8] from his observations of the workings of administrative systems. Instead of economic man, Simon talks of 'administrative man'. Whilst economic man maximizes – selecting the best course of action available – administrative man satisfies – that is, he selects a course of action which is satisfactory or good enough. In business terms, administrative man seeks adequate profit rather than maximum profit; a fair price rather than maximum price.

Another concept of the role of the company sets out somewhat ideological goals, i.e. conducting [9] 'the affairs of the corporation in such a way as to maintain an equitable and working balance amongst the claims of the various directly interested groups – stockholders, employees, customers and the public at large'. How this compromise is achieved may vary from one firm to another, but the existence of a balance presupposes a conflict with profit maximization which is solely a shareholder objective.

The interpretation of the firm's goals as the various interacting motives of the interested parties is endorsed by the research of Cyert and March, [10] who argue: 'that the goals of a business firm are a series of more or less independent constraints imposed on the organization through a process of bargaining among potential coalition members and elaborated over time in response to short-run pressures. Goals arise in such a form because the firm is, in fact, a coalition of participants with disparate demands, changing foci of attention, and limited ability to attend to all organizational problems simultaneously.' 'In the long run, studies of the goals of a business firm must reflect the adaptation of goals to changes in the coalition structure.' This concept, the behavioural theory of the firm, implies that it is meaningless to talk of a single organizational goal. It is the participants who have personal objectives, and organizational goals can only mean the goals of the dominant members of the coalition.

A similar picture has been suggested in the theory of managerial capitalism: [11] 'top management, owning little or no equity in the firm, has three main motives: growth, because growth provides job satisfaction, job expansion, higher salaries, higher bonuses and prestige; continuity of employment, which means for the management team as a whole, avoidance of involuntary takeover; and reasonable treatment of shareholders and generally good relations with the financial world.' [12]

Samuel Richardson Reid [13] has suggested that the concern of management for such factors as security, power, esteem, income and advancement within the firm may result in emphasis on growth of size rather than profit maximization.

In summary, economic theory views the firm as an entrepreneur rather than as an organization, and, assuming perfect knowledge of all market conditions, stresses profit maximization. The behavioural theory, based on observations of how modern complex business enterprises function, sees a series of goals – the goals of the key individual members of the managerial coalition – as motivating decision making. As pointed out by Caplan, [14] 'most attempts to explain, predict, or motivate human behaviour on the basis of economic factors alone are likely to be notably unsuccessful'.

THE ROOTS OF MANAGEMENT CONTROL

The underlying rationale of most business control procedures is traceable to authoritative styles of management, although this leadership pattern is gradually being superseded by a more enlightened, democratic form which is inversely opposite to its nineteenth century forerunner. But it is questionable as to whether, in general, control procedures are changing in sympathy with more participative styles of management.

In this area Rensis Likert [15] distinguishes four styles of management. System 1, the exploitive authoritative type uses fears and threats, communication is downwards, superiors and subordinates are psychologically distant and almost all decisions are taken at the apex of the organizational pyramid. System 2, the benevolent authoritative style is where management uses rewards to encourage performance, upward communication flow is limited to what the boss wants to hear, subservience to superiors is widespread and, whilst most decisions are taken at the top, some delegation of decision-making exists. System 3, the consultative type, is where management uses rewards, communication may be two-way although upward communication is cautious and limited, by and large, to what the boss wants to hear, some involvement is sought from employees and subordinates have a moderate amount of influence in some decisions – but again broad policy decisions are the preserve of top management only. System 4, the participative style, gives economic rewards and makes full use of group participation and involvement in fixing high performance goals and improving working methods. Communication flows downward, upward, with peers and is accurate; subordinates and superiors are psychologically close and decision-making is widely done throughout the firm by group processes. Various personnel in the organization chart overlap – they are members of more than one group – and thereby link members in the firm. The system 4 style of leadership is said to produce greater involvement for individuals, better labour/management relations and higher productivity.[1]

System 4 managers exercise 'general rather than detailed supervision, and are more concerned with targets than methods. They allow maximum participation in decision-making. If higher performance is to be obtained, a supervisor must not only be employee-centred' (as opposed to job-centred) 'but must also have high performance goals and be capable of exercising the decision-making processes to achieve them'. [16]

Closely associated to Likert's concepts is Douglas McGregor's postulation of Theory X and Theory Y behaviour within organizations. Theory X behaviour, as observed in the traditional concept of administration suggests that: [17]

'the average human being has an inherent dislike of work and will avoid it if he can'.
'because of this human characteristic of dislike of work, most people must be coerced, controlled, directed, threatened with punishment to get them to put forth adequate effort toward the achievement of organizational objectives'.
'the average human being prefers to be directed, wishes to avoid responsibility, has relatively little ambition, wants security above all'.

Because this philosophy of management behaviour became less prevalent in organizations which were moving towards industrial democracy, McGregor proposed alternative explanations for human behaviour in business – namely Theory Y. The assumptions behind Theory Y behaviour are: [18]

'the expenditure of physical and mental effort in work is as natural as play or rest'.
'man will exercise self-direction and self-control in the service of objectives to which he is committed'.
'the average human being learns, under proper conditions, not only to accept but to seek responsibility'.

The corollaries of Theory Y are important. They are that many more people in the firm are able to contribute constructively towards the solution of problems; second, that the main reward in the work situation is the satisfaction of the individual's self-actualization needs (see also our reference to Maslow, below); third, the potential of the average person in the organization is not being fully tapped.

McGregor makes the point that whilst staff departments exist essentially to control the line (as is postulated by Theory X), conflict will exist

---

[1] But whilst this may generally be true, Fiedler's findings (Fred E. Fiedler, *A Theory of Leadership Effectiveness*, McGraw-Hill, 1967) suggest that styles of leadership other than system 4 can be perfectly effective. According to Fiedler in any situation cognizance must be taken of the extent of job structuring, power vested in the leader, and the relationship between leader and group member.

between staff and line management. This conflict may be eliminated if the role of the staff specialist is perceived as being that of providing professional aid to all levels of management, i.e. a supportive relationship.

It should be noted that an investigation undertaken by Caplan [19] indicated that there were definite indications of cost accounting systems being based on the assumptions of the authoritative and Theory X models of behaviour. Thus, whilst management leadership styles have been evolving from System 1 through towards System 4, the management accounting system has not moved with the rest of the organization.

For budgetary control purposes, Likert's findings suggest that the more participative the process of setting budgets, the more effective they are likely to be in terms of committing personal motivation towards their achievement. This view was confirmed by Coch and French [20] in a study of the effectiveness of participative versus non-participative budgets. Similarly Hofstede [21] tested the hypothesis that higher participation leads to higher budget motivation and found a positive correlation between these factors. In support of this, Bass and Leavitt [22] found that employees participating in setting standards performed better than those who did not.

But beware budget biasing and pseudo-participation. In connection with budget biasing – which is discussed in some depth later – managers may inflate costs or reduce revenue at the budget stage, thus making the budget standard more readily achievable; this is clearly easier to do in a participatory system. However, the problems inherent in this situation may be reduced [23] by an in-depth review during the process of developing the budget. In connection with pseudo-participation there can be no better example than the following, quoted from research findings by Chris Argyris. [24] 'The typical controller's insistence on others' participation sounded good to us when we first heard it in our interviews. But after a few minutes of discussion, it began to look as if the word 'participation' had a rather strange meaning for the controller. One thing in particular happened in every interview which led us to believe that we were not thinking of the same thing. After the controller had told us that he insisted on participation he would then continue by describing his difficulty in getting the supervisors to speak freely. For example:

'We bring them in, we tell them that we want their frank opinion, but most of them just sit there and nod their heads. We know they're not coming out with exactly how they feel. I guess budgets scare them; some of them don't have too much education. . . . Then we request the line supervisor to sign the new budget, so he can't tell us he didn't accept it. We've found a signature helps an awful lot. If anything goes wrong, they can't come to us, as they often do, and complain. We just show them their signature and remind them they were shown exactly what the budget was made up of. . . .'

'Such statements seem to indicate that only "pseudo-participation" is desired by the controller. True participation means that the people can be spontaneous and free in their discussion. Participation, in the real sense of the word, also involves a group decision which leads the group to accept or reject something new. Of course, organizations need to have their supervisors accept the new goals, not reject them; however if the supervisors do not really accept the new changes but only say they do, then trouble is inevitable. Such half-hearted acceptance makes it necessary for the person who initiated the budget or induced the change, not only to request signatures of the "acceptors" so that they cannot later on deny they "accepted", but to be always on the lookout and apply pressure constantly upon the "acceptors" (through informal talks, meetings and, "educational discussions of accounting").'

BUDGET MOTIVATION

The accountant generally perceives the budget as being a commitment, in quantitative terms, of future performance. As Robert Anthony [25] says 'by agreeing to the budget estimates, the supervisor in effect says to management: "I can and will operate my department in accordance with the plan described in the budget".' Hofstede [26] summarizes this position by saying that 'budgets and cost standards act as incentives for motivating the budgetees'. However, this view is not necessarily universally accepted by authorities. Gordon Shillinglaw [27] says 'what is not commonly understood is that the budget itself is not intended to act as a motivating force'. But there is evidence that the budget can be a motivator. Is this generally true? Does motivation vary from tight budgets to loose budgets? What happens if the agreed budget becomes patently unachievable?

In examining the question of whether the budget is a stimulus or not, it is first necessary to look at some of the general concepts of motivation in business. For, as Hofstede [28] observes, 'there is no reason to assume that the basic needs of the budgeted manager will be any different from the basic needs of other people'. The theories of three of the leading writers – Maslow, Herzberg and McClelland – on the subject are therefore summarized.

MASLOW, HERZBERG AND McCLELLAND

Maslow [29] conceives of the individual as striving to satisfy a hierarchy of basic needs represented in the pyramid in Exhibit I below.

The foot of the pyramid represents the most basic need and the individual strives to move upwards through the hierarchy towards the apex of self-actualization. Maslow observes [30] that 'man is a wanting animal and rarely reaches a state of complete satisfaction except for a short time. As one desire is satisfied, another pops up to take its place'. Thus only if the lower needs are satisfied will the higher needs appear. Physiological needs include food and rest. Safety needs include job security, a modestly comfortable and predictable routine and a desire for fair treatment and justice from supervisors in the job situation. Frustration of the safety needs lies at the root of resistance to change. Higher than safety needs

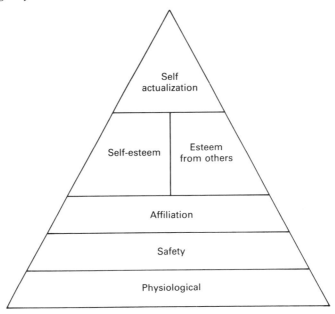

Exhibit 1   Maslow's hierarchy of basic needs.

come affiliation needs – social contacts, belonging to a group, love, etc. Maslow's next level is esteem, divided between self-esteem – the desire for achievement, competence, autonomy, strength, adequacy, mastery – and esteem from others – appreciation of performance, status, recognition. Desire for power also probably belongs in the esteem category. Self-actualization, at the apex of Maslow's pyramid, implies fulfilling one's ultimate desires, or doing what one is truly fitted for.

Maslow's concept has been tested empirically[2] and is widely accepted, for example by McGregor, [31] and in terms of explaining actions seems intuitively appealing. How it affects budget motivation is discussed below.

The second motivational theorist looked at here is Fred Herzberg. [32] His concept is empirically based – although there are dissentient views [33] to his total concept – and is built on the principle that people are

---

[2] For example D.T. Hall and K.E. Nougaim, 'An Examination of Maslow's Need Hierarchy in an Organizational Setting', *Organizational Behaviour and Human Performance*, 1968, No. 3, find support for the hierarchy in a field study based on the success of management trainees over a five-year period in the American Telephone and Telegraph Co. R. Pellegrin and C. Coates, 'Executives and Supervisors: contrasting definitions of career success', *Administrative Science Quarterly*, 1957, No. 1, observe that whilst executives tend to see success as career accomplishment, first line supervisors viewed success in terms of security and income. Similarly, L. Porter, 'Job attitudes in Management', *Journal of Applied Psychology*, 1963, No. 4, found that top executives are more concerned with esteem and self actualization than managers occupying lower levels in the organization.

motivated towards what makes them feel good and away from what makes them feel bad. Herzberg's research identifies the following factors as producing good feelings in the work situation:

achievement
recognition
the work itself
responsibility
advancement.

All of these are real motivators. By contrast Herzberg suggests that the following factors arouse bad feelings in the work situation:

company policy and administration
supervision
salary
interpersonal relations
working conditions.

These latter factors are clearly concerned with the work environment rather than the work itself. Herzberg calls these 'hygiene factors', and they differ significantly from motivators inasmuch as they 'can only prevent illness, but not bring about good health'. In other words, lack of adequate 'job hygiene' will cause dissatisfaction, but its presence will not, of itself, cause satisfaction; it is the motivators that do this. The absence of the motivators will not cause dissatisfaction, assuming the job hygiene factors are adequate, but there will be no positive motivation. Herzberg's findings are summarized in Exhibit 2 below.

As Herzberg [35] explains, referring to the above diagrams, 'the length of each box represents the frequency with which the factor appeared in the events presented. The width of the box indicates the period in which the good or bad job attitude lasted, in terms of a classification of short duration and long duration. A short duration of attitude change did not last longer than two weeks, while a long duration of attitude change may have lasted for years.' It will be noted that the length of the salary bar is such that it is both satisfier and dissatisfier. In fact, in the Herzberg experiment it was the most ambiguous of all of the factors highlighted although the negative element tended to predominate.

It is axiomatic in Herzberg's approach that job satisfaction and job dissatisfaction are not opposites. The opposite of job satisfaction is not job dissatisfaction but no job satisfaction; the opposite of job dissatisfaction is lack of job dissatisfaction. The essence of Herzberg's message to business is that employee motivation is a function of challenging work in which responsibility can be assumed. Towards this end he prescribes various methods of 'job enrichment'.

As Hofstede [36] says, in setting Herzberg's motivation, i.e. hygiene factors in the context of Maslow's hierarchy of basic needs 'although some of the hygiene factors, like salary, may be related to several basic needs

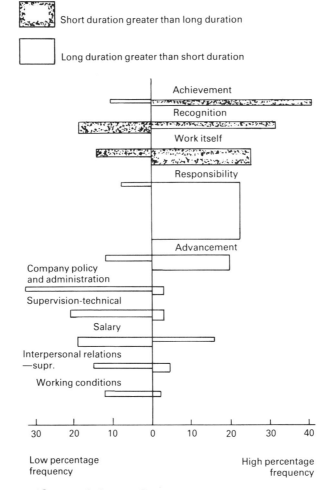

Exhibit 2 Satisfiers and dissatisfiers according to Herzberg. (See Reference 34.)

(e.g. safety, affiliation, and esteem needs), the general tendency of the above list is that the motivators are related to needs considerably higher in the pyramid...than the hygiene factors'. Hofstede goes on to point out that 'in Western countries physiological needs are almost universally satisfied; safety needs to a greater extent; on the other hand, the standard for satisfaction of, for example, achievement needs will be much higher in the case of some occupational groups, for example scientists, than for others, for example assembly line workers.' We attempt below to put the Herzberg approach into the framework of budget motivation.

The third major contributor to motivation theory considered here is D.C. McClelland. [37] He suggests that two major needs can be discerned; these are:

- the need for achievement, which should be thought of as achievement identifiable with one's own efforts. In complex working organizations this is often very difficult.
- the need for power, which is not just limited to power over others, but includes also power over one's own liberty of action. Again, in work organizations, a person's liberty of action obviously has to be constrained. Whilst constraints are necessary in the organization, unnecessary ones convert motivation to frustration.

Building in Maslow's hierarchy implies that achievement and power become dominant drives when the physiological needs are satisfield.

In developing his concept of the 'achievement motive', McClelland focuses upon the drive of people to be challenged and to be innovative and he found that the drive for achievement varies in individuals according to their personality and cultural background. Classifying people as 'high achievers' and 'low achievers', he suggests that high achievers make more successful managers than low achievers. According to McClelland, high achievers relish responsibility and seek out problems which offer challenge; he tends to set himself standards that stretch him and he derives satisfaction from their achievement. The need for positive feedback as a barometer of his performance is important to the high achiever. But with targets set too low, no challenge exists and hence no satisfaction is derived from achievement; at the other extreme, standards set too high tend not to motivate because of the high risk of failure. The high achiever is generally less directly concerned with money than the low achiever – because satisfaction flows from accomplishment – however, money reward may have significance in terms of being seen to be held in esteem. To the high achiever the opportunity for personal satisfaction from successfully accomplishing tasks is of essence. Clearly the need to identify the personal characteristics of the high achiever and the low achiever is essential, in the context of both the budget and general management, if the best is to be got out of people.

MASLOW, HERZBERG AND McCLELLAND IN THE CONTEXT OF BUDGET MOTIVATION

Having summarized each of the above experts' theses, it is necessary to place their findings within the over-all framework of budget motivation. Maslow's motivational hypothesis would suggest the need to stress those factors near the apex of the hierarchy of basic needs. Hofstede [38] interprets this theory with reference to the budget as follows. 'In the case of our budgeted managers, we can expect their . . . need fulfilment to be fairly high on the . . . pyramid. Therefore, attempts on budget motivation by building on the lower level needs for these people will be likely to have either no effect, or possibly a negative one. Positive budget motivation will only be possible by trying to fulfil the higher needs; esteem from others, self-esteem, and possibly some kind of self-actualization.'

The implications of Herzberg's findings are evidently the need to stress, in the budget system, the presence of motivating factors and an adequate level of hygiene factors.

The relevance of McClelland's approach lies in the fact that the budgeted manager should seek challenge from the setting of budget standards.

But there are additional guidelines that can be gleaned from the rules of Maslow's and Herzberg's approaches to motivation. Rewards, in terms of salary increments, promotion, etc. are often based upon performance relative to budget – although this generally operates in parallel with superiors' interpretation of the level set in the budget. However, given Herzberg's findings that salary is generally either neutral or a dissatisfier – although Maslow's and McClelland's views of salary as fulfilling esteem desires must not be overlooked – it may be logical to sever the connection of budget performance and salary review. Ross [39] has shown that separating evaluation and control improves communication. This would tend to diminish feelings of injustice relative to budget performance. If salary and promotion are based, even in part, upon performance versus budget these injustice feelings may arise because of the varying subjective standards which managers set for themselves in the budget situation. Examples of varying standards include new managers, or managers setting their first budget standards, who may desire to achieve their initial budget, and set standards accordingly; managers who have regularly achieved budget may set increasingly demanding targets; and managers who, because they have frequently failed to reach budget, set increasingly more difficult – even fantasy–budget standards. These behavioural patterns are considered further later in this paper.

In the budget situation, Maslow's affiliation needs may be met by budgetees tending to develop informal groups who will resist budget pressures exerted by the controller's department. This sort of occurrence most often happens in an authoritative management environment, or where the control system is of an authoritative type (see the discussion of Likert's work earlier in this paper). Argyris [40] observed this tendency in a study of employee behaviour in relation to budgets.

Maslow's esteem needs, and Herzberg's recognition and achievement desires are relevant to the budget because managers obviously wish to succeed and be seen to succeed. Similarly Herzberg spotlights responsibility as one of the key motivators of managers – this suggests, for budgets, the need to stress participation in setting standards.

OTHER MOTIVATIONAL THEORISTS

Many other investigators have developed formulations to explain the behaviour of people and their business motivation.

Vroom [41] is one example. His basic model is as follows:

$$\text{Motivation} = f\,(\text{Valence} \times \text{Expectancy})$$

in which the concepts are defined as follows:

Motivation: the force to perform a certain act.

Valence: the orientation (preference of attainment above non-attainment) of a person towards a certain outcome of his act.

Expectancy: the degree to which a person believes a certain outcome of his act to be probable.

In the budget context the Vroom formula becomes:

$$\text{Budget motivation} = f \, [\text{Valence of attaining budget}$$
$$\times \text{Perceived influence on results}$$
$$+ \, \varSigma \, (\text{Valences of other effects of actions}$$
$$\times \text{Expectancies of these other effects})].$$

in which the concepts mean the following:

Budget motivation: the force to take actions necessary to attain the budget.

Valence of attaining budget: the preference of attaining the budget above not attaining it.

Perceived influence on results: expectancy of the effect of one's action on budget results.

Valences of other effects of action: the preferences for these other effects.

Expectancies of other effects: the degree to which the budgetee believes these other effects to be probable.

Becker and Green [42] present precepts not dissimilar to McClelland. They accept that the level of aspiration of employees is related to their performance, and go on to show that the business firm may be highly influential in affecting levels of aspiration of employees. This, of course, would be confirmed by Herzberg.

Stedry [43] is also concerned with aspiration levels in budgeting. He set out to probe the impact of budget level on performance. He showed that aspiration level formation played a big part in actual performance, and that highest results were achieved by those with highest aspiration levels. Stedry's study affirmed the adage that budgets should be 'attainable but not too tight'. In a subsequent study with Kay [44], Stedry looked at the effect of more than one aspiration level. Goals were set either at a normal level (achievable 50 per cent of the time) or a difficult level (achievable only 25 per cent of the time). The findings of the researchers are interesting. Difficult goals appear to lead either to very good or very bad performance in comparison with performance with normal goals. In the case of the good results it appeared that the formal goal had become an aspiration level. But where very bad performance followed the difficult goal, the budgetee evidently perceived his target as being impossible, he failed to set an aspiration level and began to show withdrawal symptoms. Thus where the difficult goal was seen as a challenge (as it tended to be with the 'high achievers' and also with the younger participants), actual performance was better than target. But where the difficult goal was viewed as impossible, performance fell below even the normal goal.

With regard to aspiration levels, Child and Whiting [45] have determined that:

success generally leads to a raising of the level of aspiration, and failure to a lowering,

the stronger the success, the greater is the probability of a rise in level of aspiration; the stronger the failure, the greater is the probability of a lowering.

shifts in level of aspiration are in part a function of changes in the subject's confidence in his ability to attain goals.

effects of failure on level of aspiration are more varied than those of success.

They also found some evidence to the effect that failure is more likely than success to lead to withdrawal in the form of avoidance of setting an aspiration level. We are sure that this is in line with many accountants' experience.

Hofstede's [46] research confirms many of the above findings. Defining aspiration level as that 'level of future performance in a familiar task which an individual, knowing his level of past performance in that task explicitly undertakes to reach', he tests the effect on outturn of varying degrees of 'tightness' in the budget. His findings are summarized in Exhibit 3, which shows the level of expense on the vertical axis and the degree of 'tightness' of the budget on the horizontal axis going from very loose on the left to very tight on the right.

It can be seen that as budgets become tighter the budgetee adapts his aspiration level to the budget level. In case three the actual results coincide with the aspiration level and although the budget has not been achieved, the actual results are better than normal. The budget in case four is much tighter, and although the employee was motivated and aspires to higher levels, his actual results fail to rise. After this point his aspiration and results fall because the budgetee no longer believes it possible to reach the budget level. In case six the budgetee looks upon the budget as being utterly impossible, and this creates negative motivation and performance deteriorates in sympathy.

The key findings of Hofstede's study are that performance improves when the following features are present in the budget process:

participation in the setting of the budget
frequent communication about cost and budget variances with the boss
knowing exactly which costs one is responsible for
frequent group meetings of the boss with subordinates.

Obviously different managers and supervisors will have different aspiration levels. It may be that controllers can affect actual performance by ensuring that high achievers are set challenging targets. But there is a difference between the challenging target and the impossible. What is challenging to one manager may be impossible to another, and it is our

b – budget level
a – aspiration level
r – result

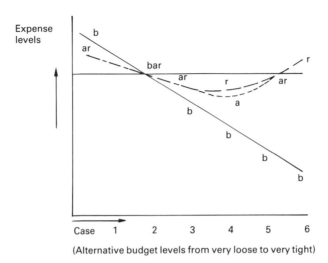

Exhibit 3 Hofstede's research findings.

contention that the controller must be sympathetic to the aspiration goals of his managers if he is to achieve full effectiveness.

BUDGET BIASING

As mentioned above, Child and Whiting showed that past budgeting performance affected aspiration levels. Lowe and Shaw [47] have also shown how past results *vis-a-vis* budget can influence the level at which future budgets are set. As would be anticipated, where budgetees 'are allowed to take part in a bargaining type process for fixing their own budget standards they tend to bias information according to the way in which they perceive themselves to secure greatest personal benefit'. Generally managers saw it in their personal interest to agree lower rather than higher budget standards. Similarly Schiff and Lewin [48] observed a tendency for managers in a participatory budget environment to bias budget costs upwards and revenues downwards. As Lowe [49] points out 'the rational economic behaviour of individual managers will be motivated by a desire to strike a balance between present security in retaining their job, and increasing future income. A manager in the budgeting process, may reason that a conservative forecast increases the likelihood of achieving a favourable budget performance in the coming budget period, and therefore his superior's approval then, but at the cost of possibly disappointing his superior now with the size of his present forecast. Where a manager has little or no goodwill left because of poor past budgeting performance he may well be tempted to make extravagantly high forecasts now in order to maintain his superior's present acceptance despite the possible dire consequences later.... In contrast the manager who has plenty of such goodwill stored up with his superior may well find it possible to temper his forecasts now with a view to obtaining more goodwill later.' Sometimes genuine over- or underestimation occurs. Here Lowe and Shaw [50] observed for level of sales budgeted that 'when sales ... are rising there is a tendency to underestimate and when falling there is a tendency to overestimate the level'.

BUDGET COMMUNICATION

The direction of flow of budgetary control information within an organization may have critical repercussions for its efficiency. The situation in which information flows from the budget controller's department upwards first to more senior management – a characteristic of the authoritative control systems referred to above – is clearly in breach of the control principles of Likert's system 4 democratic style of management in which communication is downwards, upwards, and with peers and is accurate.

In these circumstances the manager will, as McRae [51] observes, 'tend to feed up the kind of information he thinks his superior likes; and this will probably be information which causes least stress and tension.' As Argyris [52] says 'playing it safe is a way to keep the road to advancement open'.

Miles and Vergin [53] have appreciated the communications failure of traditional control systems and they have summarized their findings and precepts for a behaviourally sound control system as follows: 'The principal flaw in the traditional theory of control according to the behavioural scientists, is the assumption that control is exercised downwards in the organization – by superiors or subordinates charged with carrying out detailed organizational assignments. In the traditional control model, its critics argue, the organization is pictured as essentially machine-like. Control procedures are designed to monitor the machine's performance along a number of dimensions and to despatch various reports to upper level officials. Management, in this model, stands at the "control panel" alert to evidence of negative deviation from pre-established standards and procedures and ready to pull switches and twist dials to enforce compliance at any point at which such deviation may occur.'

'The behaviouralists grant that management may gather information on discrepancies and attempt to restore conformance. But, they argue, it is the individual organizational member who actually exercises control – who accepts or rejects standards, who does or does not exercise care in the performance of his duties, or who accepts or resists efforts to change his behaviour to achieve some objective or goal.'

'While behavioural scientists have generally not translated their criticism into detailed prescriptions for the design of control systems, it is possible to abstract from their statement some conditions which they feel must be present in the organizational environment and some requirements which they believe must be met by management control systems.

Standards must be established in such a way that they are recognized as legitimate. This requires that the method of deriving standards must be understood by those affected, and that standards must reflect the actual capabilities of the organizational process for which they are established.

The individual organization member should feel that he has some voice or influence in the establishment of his own performance goals. Participation of those affected in the establishment of performance objectives helps establish legitimacy of these standards.

Standards must be set in such a way that they convey "freedom to fail". The individual needs assurance that he will not be unfairly censured for an occasional mistake or for variations in performance which are outside his control.

Feedback, recognized as essential in traditional control designs, must be expanded. Performance data must not only flow upward for analysis by higher echelons, but they must also be summarized and fed back to those directly involved in the process.'

It has also been shown, [54] in support of the desirability of downwards communication, that knowledge of results influences favourably future performance.

On other aspects of communication, is the budget account free from criticism? In our opinion the answer is no. The marketing maxim that the seller should use the tone of voice and the words that the consumer understands applies no less in the context of a budgeting framework. The budget accountant should be aware that non-accountant managers prefer to look at management information in terms other than a matrix of figures.

As Robert Townsend says [55] 'statements comparing budget to actual should be written not in the usual terms of higher (lower) but in plain English of better (or worse) than predicted by budget. This eliminates the mental gear changes between income items (where parens are bad) and expense items (where parens are good). This way reports can be understood faster'. Becker [56] suggests that accountants should look to the coding and receiving processes of the individuals to whom information is transmitted. This view is endorsed by Bruns, [57] Dyckman [58] and Birnberg and Nath. [59] All refer to the tendency of non-accountants to look literally at the title of an accounting document – for example a profit and loss account – and perceive it as just that. But they fail to appreciate how differences may arise by virtue of accounting treatments of say stock valuation, depreciation, profit on long-term contracts, etc. Solving the questions raised by this 'functional fixation' is outside the scope of this article but all accountants must be aware of its existence if they are to provide line management with the full support that it expects from finance men.

THE BUDGET SYSTEM – PUNITIVE OR SUPPORTIVE?

Both McGregor and Likert suggest that for the modern organization to be wholly effective it is necessary that employees should see themselves as having supportive relationships to other employees. In this (perhaps Utopian) situation, the boss gives support to the employee as he wants the employee to be effective. From this it can be deduced that control systems would have the role of helping to make the manager more effective – that is, they would support him. But it has been suggested by Chris Argyris [60] (see below) that the way in which accountants operate budgetary control systems is punitive rather than supportive.

BUDGETS AND PEOPLE

The major study of the effect of budgets on people – by Chris Argyris [61] – was undertaken some 20 years ago. Nonetheless, the findings are relevant now if, as for example, Caplan [62] believes, cost accounting systems are still based on the assumptions of an authoritative model of behaviour. Argyris sets out to examine the effects of budgets on people in organizations. He observed that budget staff viewed their role as essentially one of criticism. They perceived themselves as watchdogs looking for and reporting to top management deviations from plan. The budget staff looked upon the budget as being a means of applying pressure and offering a challenge to line employees. Line supervisors objected to the method of budgetary control in the organization because:

it merely reported results without commenting on reasons for the results.
the accountants were considered inflexible.
the budget staff were always increasing pressure by increasing targets. This was resented because it implied that they (the line) lacked adequate interest in their job and would not be interested were it not for the budget.
the budgets were always set unrealistically high.

Supervisors suggested that these problems could be overcome if accountants saw the other person's point of view; and further realized that budgets were only opinions and were not final. Argyris reports an astounding degree of aggression against the budget department, which is perhaps not surprising given first that the budget system in Argyris' study appeared to be a policing mechanism, and second that 'success for the budget supervision means failure for the factory supervisor'. [63] Some of the supervisors' comments about accountants were indicative of a control system that was anything but supportive. 'Most of them are warped and they have narrow ideas.' 'They don't know how to handle people.' [64]

In the jargon of the 'managerial grid', the average budget accountant is a truly 9,1 manager. What is meant by this is explained by a brief examination of Blake and Moulton's [65] thesis. Their initial assumption is that management should aim to foster environmental attitudes conducive to efficient performance and in so doing they must stimulate creativity, innovation, experimentation and enthusiasm for the job. The managerial grid combines the two key elements of business behaviour, namely concern for production and concern for people. In this context 'concern for' is associated with the management style of the executive. 'Production' is

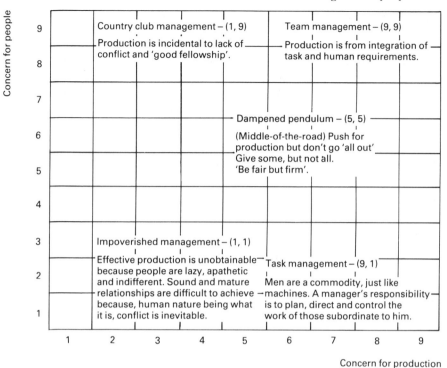

Exhibit 4 The managerial grid. (See Reference 66.)

not limited to factory manufacturing techniques, but may refer to any task of management – excluding the management of people, which falls into the other heading – for example research and development, level of sales, the logistics of depot locations, etc. Concern for people encompasses all aspects of human relations, personal motivation and inter-personal contact.

With these two concerns – for production and for people – on axes as shown in Exhibit 4, it is comparatively easy to summarize a manager's style in relation to the maximum possible of 9.

Thus 9,1 management, or 'task management', focuses wholly upon production and the manager in this category can generally be said to have acute problems in dealing with people, but to be exceptionally competent technically. The 9,1 management style is entirely geared to high level productivity – at least in the short term. Superiors make decisions, subordinates carry them out without question. But this system has inherent weaknesses because subordinates will be working in an environment where none of Herzberg's motivators are present – achievement, recognition, responsibility and advancement will probably be absent and the nature of the work will not stimulate. Such factors as company policy and administration, salary, interpersonal contacts and working conditions must therefore all be acceptable if industrial strife is to be avoided. Shop floor conditions in the motor industry are a good example of the 9,1 management style, and the fact that its record of industrial relations is punctuated with disputes is indicative of the shortcomings of the task management style. It is also possible that this style of leadership is a major contributor to the polarization of superior and subordinates, which results in the 'Them' and 'Us' thinking [67] which is at the root of so many industrial disputes.

By contrast the 1,9 style, or 'country club management', emphasizes people to the exclusion of their performance. People are encouraged and supported, but their mistakes are actually overlooked, because they are doing their best – the maxim of 'togetherness' applies. Direct disagreement or criticism of one another must be avoided at all costs and hence production problems are not followed up. This style of management can easily evolve when competition is limited, for example, the mature oligopoly.

The ideal of the managerial grid is to move towards the 9,9 style, and Blake and Moulton advocate a phased organizational development programme with this as the goal.

On the evidence presented here the budget accountant falls into the 9,1 category; it is hoped that this paper may help him to increase his concern for people and thereby move upwards in the managerial grid.

CONCLUSIONS

We now bring together our examination of available research findings into a series of guidelines which we would regard as being indicative of good budgeting practice given the implications of behavioural science. They are:

in terms of setting standards, maximum participation should be sought. As Robert Townsend [68] says 'budgets must not be prepared on high and cast as pearls before swine. They must be prepared by the operating divisions. Since a division must believe in the budget as its own plan for operations, management cannot juggle figures just because it likes to. Any changes must be sold to the division or the whole process is a sham.' But the need for an indepth review of budgets prepared on a participatory basis is paramount.

information flow should be downwards, upwards and with peers; *not* just upwards.

frequent communication about cost and budget variances with the boss

managers should know exactly which costs they are responsible for

frequent group meetings of the boss with his subordinates

performance is clearly of essence in giving salary and promotion rewards. But in making these assessments of how well managers have performed it may be wise to leave the budget outside the appraisal

budget accountants should communicate in the language of the person with whom they are dealing budget accountants should be prepared to be humble in explaining their presentations. They must remember that non-accountants may not appreciate how variations may arise through different stock valuation methods, different depreciation methods, etc. In other words the non-accountant literally believes the title of the document – for example profit and loss account – with which he is presented.

everything should be done to make the budget – and indeed any control system – supportive rather than punitive; the aim should be towards self-control rather than a policing mechanism

the budget should not be used to pressurize line management

the budget accountant must be sensitive to the reactions of management and supervisors to his control mechanisms

focus should be on efficiency variances. Variances that arise purely from accounting treatment should be omitted.

budgets which are attainable but not too tight are the best motivators.

It is also of essence that the budget accountant understands the ways in which managers play the game of budget control, for instance:

'difficult' budget goals may lead either to very good or very bad results compared with budgets set at a 'normal' level. The difficult budget may either be perceived by the high achiever, to whom it represents an aspiration level, as a challenge, or by the low achiever as impossible

managers like to achieve budget since in so doing they fulfil esteem and achievement needs

success generally leads to a raising of the level of aspiration, and failure to a lowering

the stronger the success, the greater the probability of a rise in level of aspiration; the stronger the failure, the greater is the probability of a lowering shifts in level of aspiration are in part a function of changes in the subject's confidence in his ability to meet goals

effects of failure on level of aspiration are more varied than those of success

failure may lead to withdrawal in the form of avoidance of setting a level of aspiration. This withdrawal, if failure persists, may lead to a complete breakdown in communications, and personal and industrial relations problems.

managers may bias standards conservatively in order to ensure that they achieve budget, arguing that superiors' short-term disapproval at a conservative budget will be compensated by approval when their budget is more than achieved. This tendency to play it safe more frequently occurs in an authoritative organization

when a manager has a poor track record of budget performance he may be tempted to make extravagantly high forecasts in order to gain short-term approval, despite probable dire consequences later

when sales levels are rising there is a tendency to underestimate sales outturns; when falling the tendency is towards overestimation.

What we have tried to do in this paper is to summarize some of the findings of behavioural science on the topic of the budget. Necessarily our approach has been brief and all of the theories and research work to which we have referred clearly say much more than we have reported here. However, we hope that we have made readers aware of some of the ways in which employees react to budgets. We further hope that we have shown that budgets are powerful behavioural tools and if their use is to result in consistently desirable results it is important that accounts in budget departments should be aware of their behavioural implications.

REFERENCES

1. See, for example, E.A. Lowe, 'Budgetary Control – An Evaluation in a Wider Managerial Perspective', *Accountancy*, November 1970; T.W. McRae, 'The Behavioural Critique of Accounting', *Accounting and Business Research*, No. 2, Spring 1971; I. Gibson, 'Management by Objectives', *Management Accounting*, May 1970; R.I. Tricker, *The Accountant in Management*, Bastford, 1967.
2. R.I. Tricker, ibid.
3. Edwin H. Caplan, *Management Accounting and Behavioural Science*, Addison-Wesley, 1971.
4. Ezra Solomon, *The Theory of Financial Management*, Columbia University Press, 1963.
5. For example, Thorstein Veblen, *Absentee Ownership*, Macmillan, 1923.
    Adolf A. Berle and Gardner C. Means, *The Modern Corporation and Private Property*, Macmillan, 1932.
    Robert A. Gordon, *Business Leadership in the Large Corporation*, The Brookings Institution, Washington, 1945.
    Edith T. Penrose, *The Theory of the Growth of the Firm*, Oxford University Press, 1959.
6. K.W. Rothschild, 'Price Theory and Oligopoly', *Economic Journal*, September 1947. Peter F. Drucker, 'Business Objectives and Survival Needs: Notes on a Discipline of Business Enterprise', *The Journal of Business*, April 1958.
7. William J. Baumol, *Business Behaviour, Value and Growth*, Macmillan, 1959.
8. Herbert A. Simon, *Administrative Behaviour*, Macmillan, 1960.
9. Frank Abrams quoted in E.S. Mason, 'The Apologetics of Managerialism, *Journal of Business*, January 1958.
10. Richard M. Cyert and James C. March, *A Behavioural Theory of the Firm*, Prentice-Hall, 1963.
11. Robin L. Marris, *The Economic Theory of Managerial Capitalism*, Macmillan, 1964.
12. Robin L. Marris, 'Profitability and Growth in the Individual Firm', *Business Ratios*, Spring 1967.
13. Samuel Richardson Reid, *Mergers, Managers, and the Economy*, McGraw-Hill, 1968.
14. Edwin H. Caplan, *op. cit.*

15. Rensis Likert, *New Patterns of Management*, McGraw-Hill, 1961.
16. D.S. Pugh, D.J. Hickson and C.R. Hinings, *Writers on Organisations*, Penguin, 1971.
17. Douglas McGregor, *The Human Side of Enterprise*, McGraw-Hill, 1960.
18. Douglas McGregor, ibid.
19. Edwin H. Caplan, *op. cit.*
20. L. Coch and J.R.P. French, 'Overcoming Resistance to Change', *Human Relations*, Vol. 1, 1948.
21. G.H. Hofstede, *The Game of Budget Control*, Tavistock Publications, 1968.
22. B.M. Bass and H.J.L. Leavitt, 'Some Experiments in Planning and Operating', *Management Science*, No. 4, 1963.
23. M. Schiff and A.J. Lewin, 'The Impact of Budget on People', *The Accounting Review*, April, 1970.
24. Chris Argyris, 'Human Problems with Budgets', *Harvard Business Review*, Jan.–Feb., 1953.
25. Robert N. Anthony, *Management Accounting*, Richard D. Irwin, 1964.
26. G.H. Hofstede, *op. cit.*
27. Gordon Shillinglaw, 'Divisional Performance Review: An Extension of Budgetary Control', in C.P. Bonini *et al.*, *Management Controls*, McGraw-Hill, 1964.
28. G.H. Hofstede, *op. cit.*
29. Abraham H. Maslow, *Motivation and Personality*, Harper and Row, 1954.
30. Abraham Maslow, ibid.
31. Douglas McGregor, *op. cit.*
32. F. Herzberg, *Work and the Nature of Man*, World Publishing Co, 1966.
33. See for example, J.R. Hinrichs and L.A. Mischkind, 'Empirical and Theoretical Limits to the Two-Factor Hypothesis of Job Satisfaction', *Journal of Applied Psychology*, Vol. 51, No. 2, 1957; Paul F. Wernimont, 'Intrinsic and Extrinsic Factors in Job Satisfaction', *Journal of Applied Psychology*, Vol. 50, No. 1, 1966; V.H. Vroom and N.R.F. Maier, 'Industrial School of Psychology', *Annual Review of Psychology*, No. 12, 1961.
34. F. Herzberg, B. Mausner and B. Snyderman, *The Motivation to Work*, Wiley, 1959.
35. F. Herzberg, *op. cit.*
36. G.H. Hofstede, *op. cit.*
27. D.C. McClelland, *The Achieving Society*, The Free Press, New York, 1967; D.C. McClelland, J.W. Atksinson, R.A. Clark and E.L. Lowell, *The Achievement Motive*, Appleton-Century-Crofts, 1953.
38. G.H. Hofstede, *op. cit.*
39. I.C. Ross, 'Role Specialisation in Supervision', *Doctoral Dissertation*, Columbia University, 1952.
40. Chris Argyris, *The Impact of Budgets on People*, The Controllership Foundation, 1952.
    Chris Argyris, 'Human Problems with Budgets', *Harvard Business Review*, Jan.–Feb., 1953.
41. V.H. Vroom, *Work and Motivation*, John Wiley, 1964.
42. S. Becker and D. Green, 'Budgeting and Employee Behaviour', *Journal of Business*, October, 1962.
43. A.C. Stedry, *Budget Control and Cost Behavior*, Prentice Hall, 1960.
44. A.C. Stedry and E. Kay, *The Effects of Goal Difficulty on Performance: A*

Field Experiment, Sloan School of Management, Massachusetts Institute of Technology, 1964.

45. I.L. Child and J.W.M. Whiting, 'Determinants of Level of Aspiration: Evidence from Everyday Life', in Brand (ed) *The Study of Personality*, John Wiley, 1954.
46. G.H. Hofstede, *op. cit.*
47. E.A. Lowe and R.W. Shaw, 'An Analysis of Managerial Biasing: Evidence from a Company's Budgeting Process', *Journal of Management Studies*, October 1968; E.A. Lowe and R.W. Shaw, 'The Accuracy of Short-Term Business Forecasting: An Analysis of a Firm's Sales Budgeting', *Journal of Industrial Economics*, Summer 1970.
48. M. Schiff and A.Y. Lewin, *op. cit.*
49. E.A. Lowe, *op. cit.*
50. E.A. Lowe and R.W. Shaw, *op. cit.* (1970).
51. T.W. McRae, *op. cit.*
52. Chris Argyris, *Integrating the Individual and the Organization*, John Wiley, 1964.
53. R.E. Miles and R.C. Vergin, 'Behavioural Problems of Variance Controls', *California Management Review*, Spring 1966.
54. N.R.F. Maier, *Psychology in Industry, A Psychological Approach to Industrial Problems*, George G. Harrap, 1955.
55. Robert Townsend, *Up the Organization*, Michael Joseph, 1970.
56. S.W. Becker, 'Discussion of the Effect of Frequency of Feedback on Attitudes and Performance', Empirical Research in Accounting: Selected Studies, 1967, supplement to Vol. V of *Journal of Accounting Research*, University of Chicago, 1968.
57. William J. Bruns Jr, 'Inventory Valuation and Management Decisions', *The Accounting Review*, April 1965.
58. Thomas R. Dyckman, 'The Effects of Alternative Accounting Techniques on Certain Management Decisions', *Journal of Accounting Research*, Spring 1964.
59. Jacob G. Birnberg and Raghu Nath, 'Implications of Behavioural Science for Management Accounting', *The Accounting Review*, July 1967.
60. Chris Argyris, *op. cit.* (1952).
61. Chris Argyris, ibid.
62. Edwin H. Caplan, *op. cit.*
63. Chris Argyris, *op. cit.* (1953).
64. Chris Argyris, ibid.
65. Robert R. Blake and Jane S. Moulton, *The Managerial Grid*, Gulf Publishing, 1964.
66. Robert R. Blake and Jane S. Moulton, 'The Managerial Grid', *Advanced Management Office Executive*, Vol. 1, No. 9, 1962.
67. Michael Shanks, *The Stagnant Society*, Pelican, 1961.
68. Robert Townsend, *op. cit.*

11

Human relations and budgeting systems

Norman Macintosh

Recently the organizational behavioral ramifications of management accounting and information systems have come under the scrutiny of both practitioners and academics in this field. Some evidence is surfacing to suggest that accounting systems have been creating effects within organizations we had not bargained for. Our systems, it seems, are not always embraced warmly by organizational participants; and the magnitude of the unintended negative consequences is alarming.

As a result, considerable research and theory-building has ensued over the past couple of decades; and a small number of accounting and MIS academics have devoted a lot of their time, considerably more than most accounting and information systems managers realize, to researching this problem. Early on it became something of a convenience to refer to this whole endeavor as behavioral accounting. Most of the early studies of these systems postulated that if we could somehow get the human relations aspects right, then our accounting and information systems would work as they are supposed to.

THE HUMAN RELATIONS PERSPECTIVE

The idea to involve participants in the design of organizational arrangements that affect them had its origin in the famous Hawthorne study conducted nearly fifty years ago by Mayo (1945) and Roethlisberger and Dickson (1947). This study revealed that human factors could have a profound effect on the productivity of our technical–economic organizations. From these beginnings, the human relations school of organizational behavior emerged and soon gained wide appeal.

The basic tenet of the human relations school is the belief that participation has great potential for curing many of our organizational problems. Increased productivity follows the release of an individual's creative energies. The leader's role, then, is to create a climate that allows all

Source: Macintosh, N. (1985), in *The Social Software of Accounting and Information Systems* (Wiley), pp. 9–24.

members of an organization to participate fully in the decision process. In turn, participating individuals appreciate the responsibility entrusted to them; morale is high and motivation is increased. The direction of influence, of course, is by no means clear, as Miles (1966) pointed out. Does higher morale lead to more productivity? Or does greater productivity lead to higher morale? Or are the two inextricably interwined?

Moreover, participation implies a process that is democratic, employee-centered, in which sound human relations are given priority. Few managers would deny that such a working climate has greater value than an autocratic, production-centered system, dominated by the bureaucracy. For many years participation in decision-making was thought to be a panacea for effective organizational effort.

But this school of thought was later to come under closer scrutiny. So much so that for many years participative decision-making became the most contentious and significant debate in the study of organizational behaviour. More resources and energy were devoted to this issue than to any other in the history of organizational behaviour. More recently, thoughtful and candid critiques of this approach, by notable theorists such as Perrow (1972), have helped to present a more balanced view of the human relations movement.

The outcome of the debate, unfortunately, has never been resolved. The believers have never been able to demonstrate rigorously that participative management really has a positive effect on productivity. The skeptics, for their part, have not been able to prove the opposite conclusively. So the issue remains unresolved. One cannot help but harbor the suspicion that enthusiasm for participation as a means to optimum efficiency and effectiveness outran careful research.

In any event it should be no great surprise to learn that the issue of participation found its way into the accounting and information systems field. And conventional thinking on management accounting soon embraced the concept of participation as the best means for getting managers and employees to make more effective use of accounting and information systems. Problems with imposed budgets were debated more than fifty years ago when a study by the National Industrial Conference Board (1931) indicated dissatisfaction with them and advised preparation by departments, followed by editing and revision in the central office. It was nearly twenty years later that Argyris (1952) reactivated the controversy by undertaking a study for the Controllership Foundation on the effects of budgets on people. The participation concept has troubled accountants for a long while.

NEGATIVE CONSEQUENCES OF BUDGETS

Argyris' study showed that budgets were viewed differently by budget people, factory supervisors, and front-line foremen and workers. To the budget people, who perceived themselves as the 'answer-men' of the organization, the budget served the extremely important function of being 'the eyes and ears of the plant'. As they saw it, one part of their job involved a continuous uncovering of errors and weaknesses, as well as the examination and analysis of plant operations with an eye to increased efficiency. The next stage was to report the findings to top management so that pressure could be brought to bear on the lower echelons to increase productivity and achieve greater efficiency. They also believed that budgets present a challenging goal to front-line foremen and workers. For budget people, then, budgets were a powerful lever for motivating the workforce.

Factory supervisors held a somewhat different perspective, although all those interviewed considered that the budget department affected their world to a great extent. Top factory supervisors, in particular, invoked budgets frequently and strongly to maintain their authority. Front-line factory supervisors, by contrast, hardly ever used them. Nor did they mention budgets to production people for fear of crossing them, resentment, hostility, and aggression of the workers toward the company, with a consequent reduction in production.

The research team, although they did not interview any production workers, gained the impression that budgets were viewed with suspicion by the workforce. All factory supervisors pretty much agreed on the major problems with budgets: they were geared to results only, with no discussion of the process; they emphasized past instead of future performance; they were based on rigid standards; they were used to apply pressure for increasingly higher goals; they insulted a man's integrity rather than offering him motivation; and they included unrealistic goals that were almost impossible to meet.

These observations led to speculations about the underlying behavioral dynamics of budgeting. Workers, it was posited, form cohesive groups to counteract and combat the pressure management exerts through the arbitrary imposition of budgets. This, in consequence, leaves top management in a quandary. When they relax the pressure the groups do not disintegrate; on the contrary, unreal conditions are created and existing ones are exaggerated, so that the groups continue to 'do battle' with management. Yet if further pressure is then applied, the result is head-on 'do-or-die' battles.

As a way out of this dilemma, the study recommended that supervisors participate – in a truly genuine fashion – in making or changing the budgets that affect them. Another remedy proposed was to bring all the supervisors together in small face-to-face groups where they would confront each other and their mutual problems, reveal their own feelings, attitudes, and values towards budgets and then form new ones. The report also suggested training in human relations for controllers and accountants, as well as for accounting students. And, of course, like all good academics, Argyris recommended more research. These remedies – participation, T-groups, and human relations training – would be recognized today, of course, as the standard human relations response to problems of almost any sort.

Still, for the management accountant the study makes some telling points. The first is that since foremen and workers often form cohesive groups the budget person must realize that he is dealing with groups, not individuals. The management accountant, then, should be familiar with the basics of group dynamics. The second point is that any success the budget people have in uncovering errors and weaknesses (which they then report to upper management), has the fault that it implies failure on the part of the front-line supervisors and the workforce. After all, the latter are responsible for the errors. And since the culprits can be easily singled out, they are particularly vulnerable. In short, management accountants only achieve success when they point to the failure of others. It is this dilemma that creates conflict between the management accountant and the foremen and workers. Unfortunately, this conflict is a fact of life. Once recognized, however, the management accountant may be able to find a mutually satisfactory and workable resolution to this problem.

PARTICIPATION AND GROUP DYNAMICS

Argyris' study, together with the momentum achieved by the participative management school, had a lasting influence on research into behavioural accounting. But, as it happened, participation in budgeting turned out to be more complex than Argyris anticipated. A decade later, Becker and Green (1962) wrote a thoughtful, if controversial, theoretical article on the subject. They showed how participative budgeting was not merely a simple progression from participation, through budget and performance, and finally to comparison. Rather, they argued, while budgets act as controls to limit and inform people operating under budgets, these same people determine and limit each succeeding round of budgeting. And how they affect subsequent rounds depends upon first, the cohesiveness of the work group, and, second, on the group's acceptance of the stated goal. These two factors combine in four ways as shown in Table 11.1.

The main lesson seems to be that if participation is encouraged, then the budgeting process inevitably becomes enmeshed in the group dynamics of the work force. A highly cohesive work force with a positive attitude toward the budget goal will yield maximum motivation and efficiency. But a similar highly cohesive work group with negative attitudes to the

Table 11.1

Cohesiveness	Attitudes re. goal acceptance	Outcome
1. High	Positive	Maximum motivation and efficiency
2. Low	Positive	Efficient performance
3. Low	Negative	Production depressed
4. High	Negative	Most conducive to a production slow-down

proposed goal will result in a production slow-down. Under participative budgeting, Becker and Green argue, the group process is a most important intervening determinant of final production. They also go on to show how goal aspiration levels, as suggested by Stedry (1960), complicate the process even further. Becker and Green concluded that participation can work either for or against you. It all depends upon the attitudes of the work group.

BUDGETS AND LEADERSHIP STYLE

In another effort following up the Argyris study, DeCoster and Fertakis (1968), investigated the idea that supervisors use budgets as a way of expressing their own patterns of leadership. They used the two Ohio State leadership dimensions, initiating structure and consideration. (The first refers to leadership action which establishes ways of getting the work done, clearly delineates roles, establishes channels of communication, provides detailed job instructions, and displays a definite concern for the task. The second includes respect for the ideas and feelings of subordinates, friendship, mutual trust, and communication about the process of work relationships.) Thus, they proposed that budgetary procedures encouraging supervisory consideration should be more effective than those linked with initiating structure. This proposition stemmed from the prevailing human relations belief that considerate managers achieve better performance than do those who stress output and production. The reasoning assumed that a participative approach to budget goal formulations would result in concerted effort to reach the goal, but with little felt pressure. It was also assumed, however, that when under budget pressures, supervisors would switch to structuring behavior, take greater initiative in work assignment, emphasize the need for production, make most decisions themselves, and act like a directive boss. Therefore, when supervisors felt high budget pressure, consideration efforts would be neglected or ignored. In sum, it was anticipated that budget pressure would lead to greater initiating structure behavior on the part of supervisors and to a neglect of consideration efforts.

This, however, proved not to be the case. A survey of supervisors in eight manufacturing firms indicated that *both* initiating structure and consideration were positively correlated with budget pressure. Also, the degree of pressure from immediate superiors proved to be positively correlated with both initiating structure and consideration efforts by supervisors. What might be happening, the study speculated, is that when supervisors induce budget-related pressure, supervisors increase both initiating structure and consideration efforts in order to get higher effectiveness out of the work group. They become ideal leaders. Such behavior, if applied consistently, could be constructive to the organization.

The study, then, showed that pressure from above induces leadership behavior which mirrors the ideal leadership style, rather than the detrimental effects alleged by the Argyris study. Budgets, it seems, may not be, after all, a major source of human relations problems.

BUDGET PARTICIPATION AND THE 'GAME SPIRIT'

The next milestone study of the association of human-relations variables and financial controls is Hofstede's (1967) investigation of budget-related bahaviour in six large manufacturing firms. Hofstede was puzzled by the contradiction between findings in the US and his own observations in Holland. Whereas the former reported that an emphasis on budgets was associated with pressure, aggression, conflict, inefficiency, and staff-line clashes, in Holland, in many instances, not only were such conflicts and negative human relations not noticeable, but in addition, neither managers nor employees appeared to be concerned with budgets. In fact, they seemed to motivate no-one at all. Believing these two conditions to be extremes, he set out to discover the precise conditions that lead to successful and positive attitudes to budgets. The key, he believed, would be found in participation in budget level setting.

The research plan followed a model of the effect of participation in standard setting which was much richer than the traditional model (see Fig. 11.1). Participation was thought to be the key ingredient in bringing aspiration levels in line with budget standards and ultimately lead to greater motivation and, thus, higher productivity. Participation should lead to standards which are neither impossible to achieve nor so easy as to be useless. As a result, balance and fairness are brought to the financial control system. The result is an enhancement of autonomy, affiliation, and achievement needs.

There are, however, other factors which naturally limit the positive motivation of participation. These include; personality, culture, leadership practices, machine speeds, work standards studies, and other interdependent departments. Authoritarian personalities, for example, may be quite willing to accept, even welcome, non-participative standard-setting; and machine speeds and capabilities often are the major determinant of standards. Attitudes towards the financial controls are also important, and these are shaped by people in positions of higher authority, as well as by participation.

The research sites, six plants in five large manufacturing firms, all held a reputation for being well managed and having good organizational practices. The questionnaire, administered to nearly 140 managers, supervisors, and staff officers, contained hundreds of questions about a wide range of factors including demographics, job attributes, departmental characteristics, market conditions, leadership style, attitudes, satisfaction, and morale, in addition to questions about the financial control systems. A number of major results emerged.

As anticipated, participation in the budget setting process proved to be positively associated with motivation to fulfill budget targets, but only for managers from the second level up – those who participated a great deal in setting the budget target. For first-level supervisors and employees, however, the situation was quite different. Although they did not participate in the budget process, they did participate to some extent in setting the technical production standards, thus indirectly influencing the bud-

A. The traditional view of the effect of participation in standard-setting

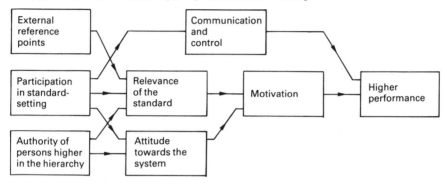

B. Improved model of the effect of participation in standard-setting

Fig. 11.1 Two views of the effect of participation in standard-setting. (*Source*: Hofstede, 1967, p. 178. Reproduced by permission of Tavistock Publications Ltd and Koninklijke Van Gorcum & Company NV, Assen, The Netherlands.)

gets. This participation by first-level supervisors in setting technical standards did not lead to greater motivation to meet them. The results regarding participation, therefore, were mixed.

Generalizations of this sort, however, can be dangerous. In one plant, for example, budget standards were based on levels used in another company-owned plant, so the managers participated little in setting them. Yet these externally set standards were seen as valid and relevant. In another plant, first-line supervisors participated in budget setting because upper management believed that foremen should be considered part of the management team. As a result, they established separate cost centers so the foremen could have their own budgets. The company was highly cost-conscious and believed that all managers are responsible for performance. Budget performance also had a large influence in overall job appraisal. Budget participation and responsibility was a key element in this company's management philosophy and practices; and the foremen in this plant held positive attitudes to budget participation. In the other plants, by contrast, the foremen had mixed reactions.

Another important finding proved to be that the budgetee's supervisor plays a key role in the motivation to meet the budget. The communication between superior and subordinate proved most crucial, particularly the frequency of person-to-person contacts about budget results and efforts related to its achievement. Positive attitudes resulted from superiors using budget results in performance appraisal, and holding meeting to discuss budget performance. The budget-related behavior of higher authorities turned out to be an important factor.

Participation in budget target setting would appear to be a necessary, but not sufficient, condition for high budget motivation. Target levels must be correct. Superordinates must hold the proper attitudes. But the key ingredient, Hofstede came to believe, was the 'game spirit' which managers relied on to 'play the budget game'. Again and again, during his interviews and investigations, he was impressed with the different ways in which managers played the budget game. Some ignored the budget, others became overly concerned with it and carefully weighed every move in terms of its effect on meeting standards, while still others treated it in a positive but not pathological manner.

The way to establish this game spirit, Hopstede believed, was to create an atmosphere where the budget process is seen as a game with the budget an end for its own sake. People play games for the game itself. Players become highly involved and enjoy the challenge of competition. Play also involves certain rules which the players accept and conscientiously follow. It is this attitude that has the potential for creating team spirit.

Similarly, planning and control, essential factors for any organization, can be seen as a game by managers. The trick, then, is to get managers to approach the budget as if it were a game – in a positive and high-spirited way. A well-played budget game means involvement, co-operation, excitement, and a positive contribution. The key to this positive game spirit, Hofstede believed, was budget participation.

Hofstede, then, had solved his puzzle. Participation by itself is not enough to get managers to live with budgets and be motivated by them. Sufficient communication, correct target levels, judicious performance appraisal, and appropriate superordinate behaviour are also necessary. But even then, only with a positive game spirit will healthy budget motivation emerge. Consequently, accountants and top management must strive to instill a game spirit into the budgeting process in their organizations.

Importantly, Hofstede also concluded that external circumstances, such as technology and markets, also explain the way organizational systems, including financial control systems, are designed and used. A good company will align its organizational and control systems to the demands of external circumstances; and, he came to believe, these external and impersonal causes are more fundamental than internal and personal ones.

LEADERSHIP BEHAVIOR AND FINANCIAL CONTROLS

The next major human-relations study with respect to the budgeting process investigated the effect of the way supervisors use budget performance information on cost-consciousness, job tension, interpersonal relations, and manipulation of accounting reports (Hopwood, 1973 and 1976). The study rested on the overriding proposition that the impact of an accounting system on job-related behaviour depends more on the style in which it is used than on its technical design.

The study identified three styles of evaluation. Some managers use a 'budget-constrained' style whereby the subordinate's performance is evaluated primarily on the basis of meeting short-term targets. These managers over-emphasize budget performance information and use it in an overly zealous and unquestioning manner. They give subordinates negative feedback for budget overruns regardless of any mitigating circumstances. Accounting information is taken at face value and used rigidly for performance evaluation.

By contrast, other managers utilize a 'non-accounting' style. They are indifferent to budgetary performance information or are unaware of its intended purposes. Accounting information plays a relatively unimportant role in evaluating the performance of their subordinates.

Still other managers follow a 'profit-conscious style'. The budget is not an end in itself, but rather a means to an end. Performance is evaluated on the ability to increase the general effectiveness of departmental operations as dictated by long-term organizational and departmental goals and programs. Accounting and budget performance information is used as part of performance evaluation, but in a careful and flexible way.

In order to test these ideas, a survey was made of 167 cost centre department heads in one large manufacturing firm. The results are shown in Table 11.2. Surprisingly, nearly half of the department heads reported a non-accounting evaluation style. As expected, involvement with costs proved lowest for this style. Budget-constrained managers were more concerned with meeting budget targets, but exhibited defensive behaviour. They reported widespread tension and job worry, and believed their superiors' evaluations of their performance to be improper and unjust. As a result, many of them responded with a host of negative and dysfunctional activities, including manipulation of accounting reports, avoidance of innovation, adoption of short-term expedients at the expense of higher long-run costs, and development of negative attitudes to accounting reports.

This last description is familiar to those who have studied enterprise managers throughout the USSR. The results, which have been documented widely, include massive underutilization of productive resources, avoidance of innovation, and preoccupation with short-run plan fulfillment at the expense of long-run improvements. The rigid plans and budgets from state central planning agencies are adhered to even in the face of blatantly obvious incongruities.

Budget-constrained cost center heads also reported a deterioration of relationships with their superiors. They felt superiors had little understanding of departmental problems. They believed the budget expectations of superiors to be unreasonable; and they reported significantly lower trust, respect and satisfaction with superiors than did the other two groups. A budget-constrained style is obviously detrimental to superordinate relationships.

The budget-constrained evaluation style also led to a deterioration of interpersonal relationships with peer managers. When superiors

Table 11.2 Style of evaluation and relations with superiors, relations with peers, and rating of evaluative criteria

	Style of evaluation		
	(a) Non-accounting (N = 73)	(b) Budget-constrained (N = 33)	(c) Profit-conscious (N = 43)
(1) *Relations with supervisor*			
(a) Trust	4.0	3.3	4.2
(b) Respect	4.3	3.7	4.6
(c) Reasonableness of expectations	3.9	3.3	4.1
(d) Satisfaction	4.4	3.3	4.6
(2) *Relations with peers*			
(a) Supportiveness	3.9	3.6	3.8
(b) Agreement	3.8	3.4	3.7
(c) Helpfulness	4.2	3.8	4.0
(d) Friendship	3.7	3.3	3.7
(3) *Rating of evaluative criteria*			
(a) Cost concern	4.1	4.3	4.8
(b) Effort	4.5	4.1	4.7
(c) Quality concern	4.5	4.5	4.7
(d) Meeting budget	3.9	4.4	4.5
(e) Attitude to work and firm	4.6	4.1	4.8
(f) Co-operation with colleagues	4.4	3.7	4.3

The above indices are based on a scale of 1 to 5.
Source: Data selected from tables in Hopwood (1973), pp. 77, 79 and 88.

continually focused on budget variances beyond the control of the department heads, they adopted a parochial stance and moved to improve their performance, regardless of any detrimental effects on other departments. They also blamed other units for budget variances. Consequently, co-operation, so vital to interdependent activities, gave way to rivalry and conflict.

Profit-conscious superiors, by contrast, proved considerably less rigid in the use of accounting information. Although they too applied budget pressure, they focused on long-run and goal-congruent cost reductions; and while they were not easy to satisfy, they applied pressure fairly, and willingly accepted reasonable explanations of variances. As a result, department heads working under a profit-conscious evaluation style had better relations with both their superiors and their peer managers, higher concern for cost and quality, and better attitudes to work and the firm. They also felt that effort was rewarded. Although this style was viewed as very demanding, it was accepted and respected. The profit-conscious style, then, very nearly mirrored Hofstede's positive game spirit of budgeting.

The profit-conscious style of evaluation also included a significantly higher degree of budget participation than did the other two styles. This finding stimulated an investigation of the impact on job-related behaviour of participation by department heads in the budgeting process. The results are noteworthy; participation appeared to have a widespread salutory effect on both the budget-constrained and the non-accounting department heads. It reduced job-related tension. It sharpened awareness of the financial aspects of performance. It improved relations both with superiors and peer managers. It increased the amount of discussions with superiors about the limitations and inadequacies of the accounting system. For the non-accounting group, it significantly boosted concern for budget attainment and cost control. In general, then, the results indicate that participation in the budgeting process has a substantial wholesome effect on department heads subjected to inappropriate use of accounting information. Importantly, though, it has little effect when accounting information is used appropriately, as is the case for the profit-conscious style, where it stimply is not necessary.

The general pattern to emerge from the above data, as summarized in Table 11.3, is both revealing and instructive. The non-accounting style is fine for superior and peer relations but, as expected, suffers in terms of concerns for, and meeting, budgets. A shift to an overconcern for meeting budgets improves attention to cost, but at the expense of attitudes, co-operation, and relations with superiors and peers. A more balanced use of accounting information, as embedded in the profit-conscious style, yields the best of all worlds – good relations with superiors and peers and high levels of concern for cost control and meeting budgets, co-operation with colleagues, and positive attitudes to work and company. Participation in the budgeting process moderates the negative effects of non-accounting and budget-constrained styles, but does not help much – indeed is not needed – under the profit-conscious style.

The study also investigated the relationship between performance

Table 11.3 Effects of different evaluation styles

	Style of evaluation		
	Budget-constrained	Profit-conscious	Non-accounting
Involvement with costs	High	High	Low
Job-related tension	High	Medium	Medium
Manipulation of the accounting reports	Extensive	Little	Little
Relations with the supervisor	Poor	Good	Good
Relations with colleagues	Poor	Good	Good

Source: Hopwood (1976), p. 113.

evaluation style and leadership behavior. Cost center heads rated their superiors on two traditional leadership characteristics – initiating structure (clearly delineated roles, clear channels of communication, well-defined patterns of organization, detailed job instructions and a definite concern for the task) and consideration (rapport, trust, communication, and respect for the ideas and feelings of others). A comparison of evaluation and leadership styles shown in Table 11.4, revealed that leadership style did influence evaluation style. Budget-concerned superiors were high on initiating structure and low on consideration, the classic 'task-oriented' boss. By contrast, non-accounting superiors were low on initiating structure and high on consideration, the classic 'country club' style. Profit-conscious superiors, by contrast, proved to be high on both dimensions. Further, some superiors, mainly the profit-conscious ones, exhibited a flexible evaluation style, depending on the past budget performance of the cost centre head and the particular circumstances such as the size of the department, the nature of the work, and the degree of skilled labor in the department. Leadership style, then, proved to have a significant effect on the manner in which accounting information was used in performance evaluation.

Table 11.4 Evaluation style and leadership characteristics

Leadership characteristics	Style of evaluation		
	Budget-constrained	Profit-conscious	Non-accounting
Initiating structure	High	High	Low
Consideration	Low	High	High

Source: adapted from Hopwood (1973), p. 178.

The study also uncovered evidence to support the notion of a 'contagion' effect in evaluation styles. This occurs when a performance-evaluation style is transferred from a superior to a subordinate at the next lower level in the hierarchy. This proved to be very strong for the budget-constrained style. It also was present for the profit-conscious managers, but they seemed to be capable of resisting it, depending on their own managerial abilities and their assessment of the situational needs. They deflected it, not by reducing the importance attached to meeting the budget, but by increasing the importance attached to other performance criteria. Non-accounting managers were successful in diverting it when they thought it unsuitable.

Hopwood's study goes well beyond previous approaches by placing the issue of participation in the budgeting process in a wider setting, including the evaluation manner of superiors, leadership styles, and situational needs. The findings are intriguing and important. The budget-constrained performance evaluation can lead to a host of negative consequences – manipulation of accounting data, short-term horizons, distrust, parochial attitudes, peer rivalry, and hostility. The non-accounting style avoids these consequences but at the expense of lower concerns for cost and budget performance. In both cases the problems are modified by participation in the budgeting process. By contrast, a leadership style concerned with both task and human relations gives rise to a profit-conscious use of accounting information which does not require participation and which avoids the problems encountered by either of the other styles.

In reviewing his findings, Hopwood calls for an expansion of the role of accounting and information systems managers. They should not merely prepare and present information to managers. Rather, they need to get involved in educating and preparing managers in the use of accounting information. A first step would be to make sure managers are informed of the assumptions and guesses that are necessary to produce accounting information. Then line managers will, in turn, recognize the inadequacies and limitations of the information and so avoid the unhappy results of attaching undue importance to it. Accountants should aso emphasize the value of information for learning and improvement and de-emphasize the practice of using accounting information for 'responsibility, accountability, past achievement and piling up a track record'. In short, accounting and information systems designers need to take an increased responsibility for the way in which line managers use accounting systems.

The important message for management accounting and information systems executives seems to be that human relations play an important role in how accounting information is used in organizations. By itself, it does not result in either negative or positive effects. Rather it is the way it is used that is critical. Use is not a straightforward matter, nor is it an inevitable consequence of mere availability.

The study also has something to say about the issue of participation in the budgeting process. Participation seems not to be a panacea. Rather, it is a complex social process that is related closely to other phenomena, including situational needs and evaluation styles. A strong concern for budget performance in evaluation styles can be moderated by a managerial style which attempts to create a friendly supportive climate conducive to trust and respect. Without this, however, accounting information can be stressful and threatening. In the final analysis, accounting information is a vehicle that assists managers to run their departments. Accounting and information system designs can play an important role by helping managers understand the best style for its appropriate use in the performance evaluation process.

ENVIRONMENTAL STRESS AND BUDGET BEHAVIOR

In a related study, Otley (1978) took a close look at the generally accepted premise that evaluations of managerial performance based primarily on budget performance lead to a variety of negative outcomes, including distrust and feelings of being treated unfairly and, consequently, practices featuring short-run action and organizational slack-ridden budgets. The research site consisted of one organization with several large production units each of which was treated as a profit centre. This particular company was selected since it had a well-developed and soundly designed accounting system, one which was highly suitable for the application of budgetary control. Several important findings emerged, not the least of which was refutation of the generally accepted premise stated above.

The data uncovered more insights into the effect of the different evaluation styles identified by Hopwood and discussed earlier in this chapter. For one thing, managers working under a budget-constrained style easily adapted to the budget system by employing a variety of covert practices. They manipulated spending, adopted 'income-smoothing' accounting customs, bargained hard for pessimistic budget levels and even resorted to 'creative' book-keeping techniques. Not surprisingly, then, their actual results consistently matched budget targets; and, contrary to Hopwood's findings, the budget-oriented evaluation style did not lead to high levels of job- and budget-related tension.

Unit managers under a profit-centered evaluation style tended to be less accurate. These managers tended to be optimistic in target setting, or they merely submitted unrealistic but acceptable budgets to a docile upper management. Moreover, when actual results fell short of targets, upper management reacted in a flexible manner. Profitable units produced accurate budgets whereas unprofitable ones tended to produce unrealistic ones which were not used later in evaluating performance. Trust in superiors was higher for the profit-conscious group but, contrary to expectations, job-related tension also was higher. Interestingly, when unit managers had either less or more than average influence on budgeted levels, both job-related and budget-related tension increased and perceived fairness of evaluation dropped. Even so, managers at all levels and under various budget evaluation styles reacted flexibly and intelligently to the budget system.

The study also indicated that the effects of participatory budget setting may not be as salutory as was previously thought, thus supporting Cherrington and Cherrington's (1973) findings during a laboratory experiment that managers operating under conditions where budget targets were either imposed or revised upward immediately after being set by the managers, outperformed those whose budgets were accepted on submittal.

Contrary to previous findings, evaluation styles did not seem to affect job-related and budget-associated tension. Nor did differences in style explain differences in performance. What seems to have happened, Otley speculates, is that senior managers adopted an evaluation style which suited the prevailing circumstances and was, therefore, appropriate for each independent operating unit. These circumstances are dependent upon factors such as the toughness of the competitive environment, the general economic conditions, the size of the operating unit (and thus the relative magnitude of the investment in the unit), the relative experience of its manager, and the degree of profitability of the unit. Senior managers seemed able to match their evaluation style to each set of circumstances; for example, they exercised closer control through a budget-constrained style, on relatively inexperienced unit managers and on the larger units. New managers were given a chance but monitored closely and replaced quickly at the first sign of incompetence. The managers generally felt that a certain degree of emphasis on meeting budget levels is helpful for technical efficiency and interpersonal relations.

This proved to be an important finding. Prevailing circumstances may have more influence on the use of accounting information than does the individual's own personality and philosophy of management.

These results point toward the need to develop a more contingent theory of budgeting control based on differences in organizational types, the environmental circumstances in which they operate, and the norms and values current both within the organization itself and within the society in which it is set (Otley, 1978, p. 146).

CONCLUSION

The idea of involving participants in the setting of targets for financial control systems as a remedy for reported negative consequences of financial controls proved to be naive. Clearly participation is not a panacea for effective budgeting systems. Nevertheless, we have learned a great deal from such studies. For example, one previously overlooked aspect is that financial people are dealing with groups and, as the groups may be protective or negative towards the company, participative target setting can have either a positive or a negative effect on motivation.

What seems to be even more important, however, is the way in which superiors use the budgets. Some use it in an overly zealous and unquestioning way to pressure subordinates continually to meet short-run budget targets. Others attribute little validity to budgetary performance, thus losing the potential positive aspects of financial controls. Still others use it in a flexible and intelligent way, treating it as a means to move their organizational units towards long-term goals. Subordinates tend to imitate their supervisors in the way they, in turn, use financial controls. The manner in which line managers use the budget proved more important than participation. Management accountants, then, should pay close attention to this aspect of budgeting, even to the extent of counselling line managers about the behavioral ramifications of budgeting systems.

The amount of environmental stress also seems to have an important impact on the way budgets are used and the amount of job-related tension. Under laboratory conditions, some line managers reacted by increasing both initiating structure and consideration efforts in their use of budgets and got constructive results. In a real-life tough competitive situation, upper line managers appeared to match their evaluative style of budget use to each set of circumstances for the various component parts of their organization.

Another critical aspect to emerge is the idea that the spirit with which managers play the budget game is important. When it is played in a high-spirited, competitive, and sportsmanlike way, it can result in involvement, co-operation, and excitement and so make a positive contribution towards the healthy functioning of the organization. The creation by financial people of a game spirit for budgeting appears to be more important than mere participation in target setting.

Finally, these studies also pointed to the important fact that the financial people are so placed that their own success is dependent on spotting and reporting the failure of others. The natural conflicts that follow is a point worth underscoring. Thus, even though the participative budgeting concept proved to be a myth, we have learned a great deal about the way financial controls work in our organizations. Even more important, it gave birth to the field of behavioral accounting and information systems.

REFERENCES

Argyris, C., *The Impact of Budgets on People*, Controllership Foundation, Inc., Cornell University, Ithaca, NY, 1952.

Becker, S., and D. Green, 'Budgeting and employee behavior', *The Journal of Business*, October 1962, pp. 392–402.

Cherrington, D.J., and J.O. Cherrington, 'Appropriate reinforcement contingencies in the budgeting process', *Journal of Accounting Research: Empirical Research in Accounting: Selected Studies*, 1973, pp. 225–253.

De Coster, D.T., and J.P. Fertakis, 'Budget induced pressure and its relationship to supervisory behaviour', *The Journal of Accounting Research*, Autumn 1968, pp. 237–246.

Hofstede, G.H., *The Game of Budget Control*, Koninklijke Van Gorcum & Comp. N.V., Assen, The Netherlands, 1968.

Hopwood, A.G., *An Accounting System and Managerial Behavior*, Saxon House, Hampshire, UK, 1973.

Hopwood, A.G., *Accounting and Human Behavior*, Prentice-Hall, Inc., Englewood Cliffs, NJ, 1976.

Mayo, I., *The Social Problems of an Industrial Civilization*, Harvard University Press, Cambridge, Mass, 1945.

Miles, R.E., 'Human relations or human resources', *Harvard Business Review*, July–August 1966, pp. 148–155.

National Industrial Conference Board, *Budgetary Control in Manufacturing Industries*, New York, 1931.

Otley, D.T., 'Budget use and managerial performance', *Journal of Accounting Research*, Spring 1978, pp. 122–149.

Perrow, C., *Complex Organizations: A Critical Essay*, Scott, Foresman and Company, 1972.

Roethlisberger, F.J., and W.J. Dickson, *Management and the Worker*, Harvard University Press, Cambridge, Mass., 1947.

Stedry, G.H., *Budget Control and Cost Behavior*, Prentice-Hall, Inc., Englewood Cliffs, NJ, 1960.

12

The role of budgetary information in performance evaluation

Michael Briers and Mark Hirst
School of Accounting, University of New South Wales

ABSTRACT

This paper provides a review of studies that focus on the use of budgetary information in performance evaluation. Our survey shows that studies have recognized that this information is used in a variety of ways. In addition, various psychological and behavioural effects of alternative uses as well as factors that give rise to a particular use have been identified. Notwithstanding this breadth of analysis, a critical review of the literature shows that in recent years theoretical development has been piecemeal, and there are instances of selective referencing and an uncritical acceptance of theory statements in related literature. More generally, theoretical development has taken a secondary role to an emphasis on statistical analysis. Further, recent empirical studies tend to be method-driven in their selection of relevant phenomena and, in addition, include several character-istics that cause an uncoupling of the connection between theory statements and empirical tests. The present review interprets these limitations as providing opportunities for future research.

For nearly four decades, accounting researchers have examined the be-havioural effects of budgetary control systems. An important area within this field focuses on supervisory style as it pertains to the use of budgetary information for performance evaluation. These studies examine the effects of supervisory style on a number of outcome variables including job re-lated tension (JRT), interpersonal relations, dysfunctional behaviour and performance.

While early studies (Argyris, 1952; Schiff & Lewin, 1968; Lowe & Shaw, 1968; Hofstede, 1968) provided case evidence relating to this issue, it was not until the work of Hopwood (1973) that a more formal (statistical) analysis was undertaken. Hopwood's concern for the generalizability of his results subsequently led researchers, beginning with Otley (1978), to adopt a contigency perspective. Such a perspective, and an interest in design issues, has also given rise to a related area of research which has investigated the determinants or antecedents of supervisory style.

Source: Briers, M. and Hirst, M. (1990) *Accounting, Organizations and Society*, **15** (4), pp. 373–98.

The aim of this paper is to critically analyse studies that have examined supervisory style. First, we provide an overview/summary of the relevant studies and then a critique of this literature. Finally, we examine possible future developments.

LITERATURE REVIEW

The studies of relevance to this review have identified a range of variables implicated in the use of budgetary information in performance evaluation. We have chosen to classify these variables as either antecedent, independent, moderator, intervening or dependent variables. 'Supervisory style' has been adopted to refer to the key independent variable of interest, the way budgetary information is used in performance evaluation. Due to the multidimensional nature of supervisory style, attention will be given to the particular definition adopted in each of the studies reviewed. Other variables were classified as: 'antecedent', if they are considered to have a causal influence on the emergence of a supervisory style; 'moderator', if the effect of supervisory style is thought to be dependent on their value (see Arnold, 1982, for a more complete definition); and 'intervening', if they are both affected by supervisory style and have a causal effect on the dependent variable of interest. Figure 12.1 shows the simple causal relations among, and examples of, these variable categories.

DEPENDENT ◄———	INTERVENING ◄———		INDEPENDENT ◄———	ANTECEDENT
		↑ MODERATOR	(Supervisory Style)	
Dysfunctional behaviour	*Tension*	*Budgetary participation*	*Needling*	*Differentiation*
	Resentment		*Raising standards*	*General leader style*
Job performance	*Pressure*	*Accounting info. accuracy*	*Uncompromising attitude*	
Budgetary performance	*Fear of failure*	*Task uncertainty*	*Reward contingent budget emphasis*	*Unit size*
Unit performance	*Budget motivation*	*Environmental uncertainty*	*Frequency of contacts*	*Contagion effect*
	Role conflict		*Focus on negative results*	*Environmental conditions*
	Role ambiguity	*Job function*	*BC, PC and NA Style*	*Realism/accurary of budget*
	Intrinsic motivation	*Business strategy*	*Evaluative/problem solving use*	*Business strategy*
		Technology	*Short/long run criteria*	*Degree of decentralization*
			Subjective formula-based criteria	
			Use of flexible/static budgets	
			General/punitive style	

Fig. 12.1 Analytical framework (including selected variables examined in this review).

Argyris: an initial exploration

Early research into the behavioural effects of budgetary control systems provide case evidence of managers engaging in dysfunctional behaviour as a response to the way supervisors used budgetary information to evaluate their performance (Argyris, 1952; Schiff & Lewin, 1968; Lowe & Shaw, 1968; Hofstede, 1968). These studies have implicitly recognized that the effects of accounting measures in performance evaluation not only depend on their technical characteristics but also on the way supervisors use them.

In his summary of the supervisory style literature, Brownell (1987b) suggested that Argyris (1952) was the first to distinguish between the technical features of accounting systems and style of use. Argyris conducted interviews with both operating and budget (accounting) personnel in four manufacturing companies to elicit their values, attitudes and feelings towards budgets and each other. He found that budgets were used as: (1) a pressure device; (2) a source of motivation; (3) a means of isolating problems; and (4) a basis for instituting improvements. These four aspects had implications for the expressed attitudes of each of the groups, budget and operating, towards each other and consequently their behaviour. In particular, the latter three styles of use had direct implications for the first, budget pressure.

In relation to Fig. 12.1, Argyris (1952) examined an extensive range of variables associated with supervisory style. The variables included three dimensions of supervisory style (needling, raising standards once they are met, and uncompromising budget attitude) and at least three antecedent variables (differentiation, economic conditions and general leader style). He also examined the impact of supervisory style on a number of intervening variables (including stress, tension and frustration) and, in turn, their effect on various dependent variables (including dysfunctional behaviour, managerial effectiveness and long-run performance). Finally, he proposed budgetary participation as a possible moderator variable.

Argyris (1952) reported that subordinate feelings of budget pressure derived from three main factors; the propensity of supervisors to emphasize the need to meet the budget (budget emphasis) by continuously 'needling' them, the raising of budgetary standards to a more difficult level once they are met, and the inflexible and uncompromising nature of the budget documents which failed to disclose the real reasons for the budget variances. Argyris also found that management pressure had dysfunctional consequences including increased tension, frustration, resentment, suspicion, fear and mistrust together with a possible deterioration in long run performance. His study indicated that where budget pressure is felt by the workers they will form groups to share and thus relieve the pressure. The formation of groups also served to reinforce their attitudes towards management. However, first line supervisors, he suggested, cannot join groups and so may respond to pressure in a number of other ways. First, they may attempt to shift the blame for their problems to their peers and superiors causing a deterioration in interpersonal relationships. Second, they may experience increased tension as a manifestation of internalizing the pressure. Increased tension, he argued, leads to frustration which reduces managerial effectiveness due to the tendency of frustrated managers to, for example, forget things, become apathetic and indifferent, make slow decisions and withdraw socially.

More generally however, Argyris (1952) alluded to the notion of differentiation (Lawrence & Lorsch, 1967) as both an outcome, via the reinforcement of group attitudes, and a determinant (antecedent) of budget pressure. Lawrence & Lorsch (1967, p. 11) define differentiation as '... the difference in cognitive and emotional orientation among managers in different functional departments'. Different orientations emerge from differences in education, training, and the specialized tasks performed in different departments. Also, as a consequence of task differences, departments will differ along several dimensions (each of which reinforce differentiation) such as the formality of their structures, their orientation toward time, their specialized use of language and their success criteria. While differentiation may be associated with effective subtask performance, they argue that as the attitudes of managers become more differentiated it becomes increasingly difficult to establish collaboration between their departments.

While not explicitly referring to this concept, Argyris' (1952) argument and evidence highlighted its existence and some of the problems associated with it. For example, the factory supervisors in his study expressed the belief that budget personnel failed to understand their problems and therefore could not appreciate their explanations. He also referred to the difference in the success criteria for each group. While finding errors, weaknesses and faults that exist in the plant are the criteria against which the success of the budget personnel is judged, such outcomes mean failure for the operating personnel. The budget personnel 'are placed in a social organization where the only way in which they can receive success is to place someone else in failure' (p. 21). Argyris argued that constant failure can have adverse effects on an individual such as loss of interest in job, loss of confidence and deterioration in interpersonal relationships.

Argyris (1952) signalled budgetary participation as a means of addressing the differentiation problem and hence as a possible moderator variable. He noted that while the need for budgetary participation was emphasized by top management, subordinates were loath to express their opinions at the budget meetings and so were not fully participating in the process. He called this 'pseudo-participation'. Training in human relations, he argued, would ensure full participation. He suggested that full budgetary participation would help top management gain subordinate acceptance of the budget and help broaden the normally 'figure conscious' budget man. Getting each group to understand the other point of view, he argued, reduces stress. Again this notion relates to what Lawrence & Lorsch (1967) later referred to as integration, an important mechanism to counteract the dysfunctional effects of differentiation without reducing subtask performance.

At least two other antecedent variables were suggested by Argyris (1952): economic conditions and general leader style. Budget personnel acknowledged that when sales and profits decreased and the economic outlook appeared gloomy, budget pressure was increased. Argyris also reported that budgetary pressure was influenced by general leader style; for example, an aggressive and domineering type leader was likely to project an aggressive and domineering style upon the use of budgets as a control mechanism.

The Argyris (1952) study provided a milestone in behavioural accounting research. It went beyond simply examining alternative uses of accounting information in performance evaluation. Importantly, it was a comprehensive study, rich in theoretical, as well as empirical, content. Argyris was not only interested in the antecedents and outcomes of supervisory style, but also suggested budget participation as a possible moderator of supervisory style. Consequently, Argyris provided a broad foundation and, indeed, motivation for future studies.

Additional case evidence

While Argyris (1952) made an important initial contribution to this area of research, further case evidence in the accounting literature was not forthcoming until the work of Hofstede (1968), Lowe & Shaw (1968) and Schiff & Lewin (1968). Hofstede's study of the budgetary process in six manufacturing plants provided further evidence concerning the effects of supervisory style and the role of budgetary participation. While his case evidence was supplemented with some statistical analysis, it was limited by the exploratory nature of the study. Nevertheless, this added a degree of analytical rigour to previous work.

Hofstede (1968) examined, *inter alia*, the effects of various aspects of superior–subordinate budgetary communication on pressure. He considered at least three dimensions of supervisory style: frequency of contacts regarding budget results, the extent to which these results were used in performance evaluation (budget emphasis) and a focus on negative results. In addition two aspects of budgetary participation were considered: the use of departmental meetings and the creation of a 'game spirit'.

Hofstede's (1968) results indicated that while frequency of contacts and budget emphasis increased budget motivation, pressure was also raised. He also found that the comments of a 'cost-conscious boss' regarding negative results are interpreted as being punitive rather than corrective. This attitude led to feelings of higher pressure and lower job satisfaction. He argued that while at least some pressure may have beneficial effects, too much pressure has adverse effects such as anxiety, stress and fear of failure (intervening variables) and results in dysfunctional behaviour such as absenteeism and interpersonal conflicts (dependent variables). This argument and evidence is entirely consistent with Argyris (1952).

Consistent again with Argyris (1952), Hofstede (1968) alluded to the moderator status of budgetary participation and its role in addressing the differentiation problem. He argued that pressure may be relieved by upward communication. He found that both department meetings and the use of budgets in a 'game spirit' had positive effects on budget motivation and satisfaction. Hofstede's general conclusion was that the creation of a 'game spirit', which in turn depends on the leadership skill of the budgetee's superior,[1] has the most beneficial overall effects.

The budgetary process was also the focus of Lowe & Shaw's (1968) case study. Their investigation of a retail chain's budgetary process over two years extended budget emphasis to include an explicit relation with financial rewards. Furthermore, their case evidence indicated an alternative dysfunctional role of budgetary participation not foreseen by Argyris (1952) and Hofstede (1968).

Lowe & Shaw (1968) found that sales managers engaged in dysfunctional behaviour as a response, *inter alia*, to the firm's budget-based reward system. They found that while involving sales managers in the budgetary process made best use of their local knowledge, it also provided them with the opportunity to bias their sales forecasts and hence build budget slack. Their evidence suggested that supervisors, although aware of the bias, were not successful in eliminating it. Thus dysfunctional behaviour, and in particular invalid data reporting (IDR), was found to be an outcome of budget emphasis combined with budgetary participation.

Consistent with Lowe & Shaw (1968), Schiff & Lewin's (1968) case evidence of three manufacturing companies facing different economic climates suggested that budgetary slack is a normal part of the traditional budgetary process where a high budget emphasis is the norm. They found that such dysfunctional behaviour occurs in both profitable and unprofitable companies whether stable or growing.

The Hopwood study

Building on Argyris' (1952) case evidence,[2] Hopwood (1972, 1973), in addition to providing a more detailed rationale for the effects of supervisory style, conducted a more formal analysis. He also extended the array of antecedent, moderator and outcome variables. In particular, Hopwood contended that accounting performance measures (APMs) may never be technically adequate because they: are an incomplete reflection of managerial performance; can only approximately represent an organizations' economic cost function; reflect aspects of performance which are not necessarily controllable; and emphasize short term evaluation of managerial performance. He argued that emphasis on such imperfect APMs will have adverse consequences.

For the purposes of his study he identified three supervisory styles: budget constrained (BC), profit conscious (PC) and non-accounting (NA). These styles varied across at least three dimensions: the range of criteria used for evaluation purposes; the flexibility with which variances from

[1] Compare this with Argyris' (1952) suggestion that supervisors may need training in human relations for effective budgetary participation.

[2] In a private communication, Hopwood indicated that 'Argyris provided a very real incentive for my study. Indeed I can remember the original question as being one of – does this always happen? Hence some notion of contingency was built into my study but one where the effects were contingent on evaluation style'.

standard are interpreted; and the manner in which short/long run concerns are handled. For example, the BC style was characterized by an uncompromising use of the budget to meet short term objectives while the PC style was characterized by a more flexible use of a wider range of performance criteria for longer term objectives.[3]

Hopwood's (1972, 1973) elaboration of Argyris' (1952) argument connecting supervisory style, stress and dysfunctional behaviour was based on role theory (Kahn *et al.*, 1964). He argued that, given the imperfect nature of APMs, a BC style will lead to role conflict and role ambiguity. Conflict and ambiguity, in turn, cause managerial stress, tension and anxiety. Dysfunctional behaviour, he argued, is a consequence of managers trying to cope with this stress and tension.

The results of Hopwood's (1972, 1973) study of cost centres in a large American manufacturing company provided support for his argument. That is, cost centre heads with BC supervisors experienced higher JRT, poorer relations with both supervisors and peers, and were more likely to engage in invalid data reporting and dysfunctional decision making than those with PC or NA supervisors.

It should be noted that Hopwood (1972, 1973) did not directly test the relation between supervisory style and managerial performance. This was at least partly because 'the available indexes of efficiency are based on the accounting data and may therefore reflect both real efficiency and successful manipulation of the data' (1972, p. 176). He did, however, provide some suggestive evidence that tension and conflict may influence long-term performance and success. He conjectured that while a PC style is likely to result in greater efficiency than the BC style, both were likely to result in greater efficiency than the NA style because 'the possibility does remain that it is still better to place at least some emphasis on the accounting data' (1972, p. 176).[4]

A further outcome variable was considered by Hopwood (1973) – the use of informal information systems. In response to the perceived inadequacies of the accounting reports, cost centre heads developed independent information systems outside of the official accounting system with the aim of providing more timely and relevant information. Holding such information, Hopwood argued, was more important for the BC departments where there was a greater need to protect themselves from evaluative pressures. Cost centre heads in these departments required the information to help them explain deviations from budget and direct their efforts to manipulate the data used for evaluation purposes. Hopwood found that such information systems were numerous and, in some cases, very extensive for

---

[3] The NA style was regarded as a residual category for the purposes of this study.
[4] Such evidence is tentative to say the least, yet subsequent researchers have relied upon Hopwood's performance result. For example, Govindarajan (1984) stated while referring to Otley's (1978) study that '[m]ore importantly, this style [Budget Constrained] was associated with higher performance, a result that is opposite to that of Hopwood' (p. 126).

budget constrained departments but were less apparent for PC and NA departments.

Three antecedent variables were also considered: cost centre size, the contagion effect and general leader style. First, Hopwood (1973) found no relationship between the absolute size of the cost centre (measured as total annual costs) and the cost centre heads' perception of the supervisory style of evaluation. In relation to the second, he argued that, due to the additive nature of accounting data, a manager who uses a BC style is more likely to be evaluated himself on the basis of a BC style. He found evidence of such a contagion effect for the BC style but not for the PC or NA styles. While Argyris (1952) provided suggestive evidence regarding the third antecedent, Hopwood operationalized this variable using the leader behaviour description questionnaire (LBDQ)[5] developed by Stogdill (1963). The LBDQ measures two dimensions of leader style: consideration and initiating structure. A leader characterized by consideration shows concern for the feelings and ideas of subordinates, while a leader characterized by initiating structure clearly defines the roles of his subordinates. Hopwood's argument and evidence indicated that BC supervisors were less considerate than either the PC or the NA supervisors; further, the BC and PC supervisors rated more highly on initiating structure than the NA supervisors.

In addition, three moderator variables were considered: budgetary participation, accuracy of accounting information and managerial aspirations. Extending the work of Argyris (1952) and Hofstede (1968) and consistent with Lowe & Shaw (1968), Hopwood (1973) recognized the ambiguous role of budgetary participation in moderating supervisory style effects. Despite this concern, he reported that budgetary participation moderated the negative psychological effects for high budget emphasis only. Hopwood argued that the effects of supervisory style will also depend on the accuracy of the APMs and the cost centre heads' needs for promotion. His results regarding these two variables were, however, non-significant.

Hopwood's (1973) conclusion that his results may not generalize to other settings, that is, from an uncertain and highly complex situation to a stable, technologically simple situation, became the impetus for the adoption of a contigency perspective by subsequent researchers. Typically these researchers have investigated the effect of various contingency variables on the relationship between budget emphasis and both intervening and dependent variables; Otley (1978) with accuracy of accounting information; Hirst (1981, 1983) and Imoisili (1985) with task uncertainty; Brownell (1982), Hirst (1987), Dunk (undated) and Bottger & Hirst (1988) with budgetary participation; Brownell & Hirst (1986) with budgetary participation and task uncertainty; Govindarajan (1984) with environmental uncertainty; Brownell (1985, 1987a) with environmental uncertainty and budgetary participation; Govindarajan & Gupta (1985)

[5] Note that De Coster & Fertakis (1968) considered LBDQ as a possible antecedent variable prior to Hopwood's study. The results of their empirical study are presented below.

and Govindarajan (undated) with business strategy; and Brownell & Merchant (1987) with technology. Implicit in some of these approaches (e.g. Govindarajan, 1984) is the assumption that a match between budget emphasis and contingency factors will have a beneficial effect. Such an approach has also led to design issues becoming more salient and, more specifically, a stronger focus on antecedent variables.

Recent studies

This new research direction began with Otley's (1978) replication and extension of Hopwood's (1972, 1973) work. Otley adopted Hopwood's definition of supervisory style but Otley's evidence indicated a continuum of style which he categorized as A, B, C, D and E, ranging from a BC style (A) to an NA style (E). A further difference was that there were fewer managers in Otley's category E than in Hopwood's equivalent NA category (3% compared to Hopwood's 44%). In addition, Otley extended Hopwood's analysis in at least two important ways. First, he suggested that Hopwood may have confounded the imperfections in the accounting sytem with supervisory style. The research site for Otley's study was an organization with independent profit centres which, he claimed, was well suited to the use of budgetary control systems. Otley claimed that this allowed him to isolate the effects of supervisory style by effectively controlling for the technical inadequacies of the accounting system. Second, he included budgetary performance as a dependent variable in the analysis despite Hopwood's comments regarding the confounding effects of accounting data manipulation. Otley also considered a number of antecedent variables: management philosophy, environmental conditions and unit size.

Otley (1978) reported that while there was some support for a positive relationship between supervisory style and poorer interpersonal relations, the relationship between supervisory style and JRT was non-significant. The latter result is therefore not supportive of Hopwood's (1973) finding. In relation to performance, Otley found that there was a significant positive relationship between supervisory style and budgetary performance but not with longer-term indicators of performance such as accident rates, wastage rates and levels of absenteeism. This result, he claims (p. 135), is contrary to Hopwood's findings. He conceded, however, that the result may be confounded by manipulations of the budget estimates (as noted by Hopwood). Furthermore, his evidence regarding the effect of certain antecedent variables (size of unit profit and the environment) led him to suggest that the relationship between supervisory style and actual performance may be spurious.

In relation to budgetary performance, Otley found a triad of relationships between supervisory style, output budget error and unit profitability (as shown in his Fig. 2, p. 139). His interpretation of this was as follows. Where senior management expected a unit to achieve an acceptable (unacceptable) level of profit, the unit's output budget was set at a relatively realistic (optimistic) level which in each case yields an acceptable profit budget. Actual performance is likely to be closer to budget when it is set realistically than when it is biased in an optimistic direction. Group managers are cognisant of these circumstances and emphasize budget standards for performance evaluation only where they perceive such standards to be realistic. Thus, both budgetary performance and budgetary emphasis may be explained by the level of realism/accuracy in the budget. Otley raised doubts, therefore, regarding the dependent variable status of budgetary performance in studies which examine supervisory style.

In relation to antecedent variables, Otley (1978) found that management philosophy, environmental conditions and unit size (in terms of profit, manpower and output) appear to influence the choice of a supervisory style. In particular, in difficult environmental and economic conditions a strong emphasis on meeting the budget (BC style) prevailed while in easy and stable conditions a less rigorous approach was adopted, thus supporting Argyris' earler case evidence. Further, larger units, particularly in terms of profit, tended to have a more budget-oriented style. However, Otley found that these latter two antecedents also affect the overall performance of the unit. This spurious effect, he argued, raises further doubts about treating supervisory style as an independent variable to explain differences in actual performance.

Thus, the results of Hopwood (1973) and Otley (1978) appear to conflict in terms of two important variables: JRT (intervening) and performance (dependent). While the first conflict is relatively unambiguous, the conflict with regard to performance is more apparent than real. Hopwood was not really concerned with the performance effects of supervisory style and Otley raised doubts about the causal direction of the relation. Much of the subsequent research has, however, sought to reconcile these apparently conflicting results believing that the models used by Hopwood and Otley were under-specified.

Hirst (1981) provided a rationale for reconciling Hopwood (1973) and Otley's (1978) results concerning JRT, interpersonal relations and dysfunctional behaviour by considering the possible moderating effects of task uncertainty. He argued that the degree of completeness of APMs used in the evaluation of subordinates by supervisors will depend on the nature of the task performed by the subordinate. Such measures are appropriate/more complete in situations of low task uncertainty but fail to capture the interdependencies in situations of high task uncertainty. The greater the incompleteness of APMs, the greater the chance of disagreement between supervisors and subordinates in performance evaluation. Further, Hirst argued that subordinates have no incentive to seek a more favourable reflection of their performance (IDR) where there is a low reliance on APMs and high task uncertainty and have no opportunity where there is low task uncertainty and a high reliance on APMs. Thus he hypothesized that a medium to high (medium to low) budget emphasis minimizes dysfunctional behaviour in situations of low (high) task uncertainty.

The above argument, Hirst (1981) suggested, may explain Hopwood (1973) and Otley's (1978) conflicting results. That is, while Hopwood examined departments which were interdependent and therefore characterized by high task uncertainty, Otley studied subunits which were independent and which therefore may be characterized by relatively low task uncertainty.

In a later study, Hirst (1983) empirically tested his hypothesis. The dimension of supervisory style adopted for the study was that of budget emphasis contingent upon extrinsic rewards. He found evidence of a linear relationship between JRT and budget emphasis which was negative (positive) for low (high) task uncertainty situations. He also found a positive relationship between social withdrawal and budget emphasis for low but not for high task uncertainty.

The moderating effects of task uncertainty were also examined by Imoisili (1985). He considered role stress as an intervening variable and a range of dependent variables including performance and dysfunctional behaviour. His results, however, were not significant due to the lack of variation in supervisory style – only a high budget emphasis was found in his study. This was, he noted, probably because the sampled organization was experiencing tight economic conditions. Such an explanation is consistent with Otley's (1978) earlier finding regarding the strong emphasis on meeting the budget in tough environmental conditions.

An alternative rationale for the moderating effects of budgetary participation was provided by Brownell (1982). Drawing from the psychological literature he developed this rationale based on operant conditioning and balance theory. He argued that a high budget emphasis is appropriate where managers have the opportunity to negotiate the criteria against which their performance is assessed. On the other hand, a low budget emphasis is appropriate in circumstances where there is a low level of participation. He suggested that such a match between budget emphasis and participation (i.e. high/high or low/low) was necessary for effective managerial performance.

Brownell's (1982) operationalization of job performance using a self-rating scale represented a further extension of both Hopwood's (1973) and Otley's (1978) work. In particular, he sought to reconcile the so-called conflicting results of Hopwood and Otley relating to performance. The results of his empirical study of a manufacturing firm tended to confirm the hypothesis that a high (low) budget emphasis results in better performance when it is coupled with high (low) participation. Hirst (1987) and Dunk (undated), however, failed to replicate this finding. Hirst, in his study of a property development firm, found no interaction effect and the results of Dunk's cross-sectional study of 26 firms showed that high (low) budgetary participation together with high (low) budgetary emphasis reduces performance, a result which is opposite to that of Brownell.

Consistent with Hopwood (1973), who earlier reported that budgetary participation moderated the negative psychological effects for high budget emphasis only, Bottger & Hirst (1988) found that participation caused a reduction in job stress where budget emphasis is high but no effect where it is low.

Brownell & Hirst (1986) attempted to link the Brownell (1982) and Hirst (1983) studies by proposing and testing a three-way interaction between budgetary participation, task uncertainty and budget emphasis. They hypothesized that compatible combinations of participation and budget emphasis (high/high and low/low) are more effective in reducing JRT and improving managerial performance in low as opposed to high task uncertainty activities. While they found that the three-way interaction affected JRT, there was no such effect on performance. Accordingly, they were unable to link the Brownell and Hirst studies,[6] nor were they able to replicate Brownell (1982). Even so, and consistent with Hopwood (1973) and the later study by Bottger & Hirst (1988), however, there was some support for an interaction between participation and budget emphasis effecting JRT. Moreover, they found that budgetary participation substantially reduced JRT independently of the other variables.

Reconciling the Hopwood (1973) and Otley (1978) results relating to performance was also the concern of Govindarajan (1984). He contended that their results were characterized by different levels of environmental uncertainty (defined as the unpredictability of the actions of customers, suppliers, competitors and regulatory groups). Accordingly, Govindarajan introduced environmental uncertainty as a possible moderator of the effects of supervisory style (characterized along a continuum from subjective (PC) to formula-based (BC) evaluation contingent upon financial rewards) on strategic business unit (SBU) effectiveness (defined in terms of unit manager ratings of unit performance relative to the supervisors expectations of performance). Three main propositions were developed by Govindarajan (1984) to support his hypotheses: realistic budget estimates subsequently used for performance assessment will only prevail when environmental uncertainty is low; knowledge of cause–effect relationships will be incomplete in high environmental uncertainty conditions; and emphasis on APMs is on outcome rather than process and managers faced with high uncertainty will have less control over such outcomes. These propositions are similar to those put forward by Otley (1978), Hirst (1981) and Hopwood (1972) respectively.

On the basis of these propositions, Govindarajan (1984) hypothesized that a moderate to low (high) budget emphasis coupled with higher (lower) environmental uncertainty will lead to increased SBU performance. His results generally confirmed this contention: a significant positive correlation was found between environmental uncertainty and the use of subjective criteria for performance appraisal in the highest performing SBUs, and no such correlation in the lowest performing SBUs.

The effects of both budgetary participation and environmental uncertainty were examined by Brownell (1985, 1987a). Both studies examined the budget emphasis dimension of supervisory style. Brownell's (1985)

---

[6] Indeed, linking the studies is an ambitious task. The studies focus on different dependent variables (i.e. job stress and job performance), use different theoretical frameworks (i.e. role theory and motivation theory) and employ different measures of budget emphasis. Moreover, an important limitation of the Brownell & Hirst (1986) study is that it does not examine, in theoretical terms, the link between job tension and job performance. Such an examination is problematic given that, as discussed more fully below, job performance is an ambiguous construct.

study of the marketing and R&D units of a multi-national electronics firm found that R&D managers perceived their environment as more complex than marketing managers. While his results indicated that participation and functional area interacted to effect managerial performance, there was no such interaction effect for budget emphasis and functional area.[7] However, after ignoring functional membership, a further statistical test provided evidence to support the proposition that a reduced budget emphasis is appropriate with a more complex environment. He did not report the interaction effects for budget emphasis and budgetary participation. Brownell (1987a) partially replicated and extended this study in the Australian subsidiary of the above multi-national firm. Confirming his previous findings, he reported that both job satisfaction and performance were enhanced in situations where there is a high budget emphasis and low environmental complexity.

The role of task uncertainty, budgetary participation, environmental uncertainty and various combinations of these, in moderating the effects of supervisory style, and budget emphasis in particular, has been the focus of much research effort. The evidence regarding task uncertainty and budgetary participation suggests that while there has been consistent support for their moderating effect on the relationship between budget emphasis and intervening (psychological) variables, the evidence has been mixed in relation to performance (dependent variable). These results seem to confirm Hopwood's (1973), and later Otley's (1978), doubts regarding the inclusion of performance in studies which examine supervisory style.

The moderating effects of business strategy were the focus of studies by Govindarajan & Gupta (1985) and Govindarajan (undated). Govindarajan & Gupta adopted Govindarajan's (1984) definition of SBU effectiveness and supervisory style (subjective/formula-based), both as previously described. They also added a further dimension of supervisory style: a reliance on short/long run criteria in the determination of managerial incentive bonuses. They classified strategies as ranging from build to harvest. A build strategy is characterized by a desire to increase market share while the objective of maximizing short term earnings and cash flow is indicative of a harvest strategy.

Govindarajan & Gupta (1985) argued that SBU effectiveness would be enhanced where there is a correct match between the incentive compensation and the strategy adopted by the unit. That is, a reliance on long run (short run) criteria in the determination of incentive bonuses should be matched with a build (harvest) strategy. Their study of profit centre managers in 20 firms found that a build (harvest) strategy, combined with a greater reliance on long run criteria, promotes (reduces) effectiveness, while the effect of a reliance on short run criteria on effectiveness was

---

[7] Consistent with Hopwood (1973), Hirst & Yetton (1984) found in their questionnaire survey of 111 managers that there was a strong relationship between budget emphasis and role ambiguity for production jobs. This strong relationship did not, however, generalize to non-production jobs, for which there was only a weak relationship. Further, this weak relationship was not independent of job structure.

independent of strategy. They also argued, and found, that greater reliance on a subjective approach to the determination of incentive bonuses will have a stronger positive impact on effectiveness under a build rather than a harvest strategy.

A further attempt to reconcile the results of Hopwood (1973) and Otley (1978) relating to performance was undertaken by Govindarajan (undated) who provided a more detailed rationale for the moderating effects of SBU strategy. He used Miles & Snow's (1978) typology in considering strategy. Miles & Snow's three categories, defender, analyser and prospector, vary according to the rate at which the organization changes its products and markets. While prospectors rate highly on this dimension, defenders tend to concentrate on existing product and market domains. Analysers fall between these two extremes.

Govindarajan (undated) argued that a supervisory style characterized by a high budget emphasis will enhance SBU effectiveness (as defined by Govindarajan, 1984) for defender SBUs but will reduce effectiveness for prospector SBUs. In relation to defender SBUs, his theory was based on the notion that defenders face relatively low environmental uncertainty, have stable products and markets and thus relatively accurate budget estimates, and emphasize efficiency which implies the need to identify performance deviations. On the other hand, prospectors face high environmental uncertainty, are unable to formulate accurate budgets, emphasize new product development which implies the need to use longer term performance measures, and require extra resources, via budgetary slack, for innovation. The results of Govindarajan's (undated) study of SBU managers of 24 Fortune 500 firms, after controlling for corporate strategy and size, strongly supported the hypothesized relationships. Thus, business strategy, however defined, seems to be an important moderator variable in supervisory style studies.

A final moderator variable has been examined by Brownell & Merchant (1987). They considered the role of technology in providing another rationale for reconciling Hopwood (1973) and Otley's (1978) results concerning performance. Two dimensions of technology were considered: the extent of product standardization (PS) and workflow integration (WI). They argued that a high PS provides a greater opportunity to reliably identify cost/volume relationships. This in turn allows for appropriate volume-based adjustments to the budget. Therefore, the use of flexible budgets for evaluation purposes is, they argued, more appropriate in this situation than the similar use of static budgets. In contrast, they argued that the extent of WI is independent of the ability to identify cost/volume relationships.

Brownell & Merchant's (1987) study of 201 production managers in the electronics industry supported their agreement. They found that the effect of using budgets as static targets on departmental performance (measured by a self-rating scale) was positive (negative) for low (high) PS. WI, on the other hand, did not moderate the effects of using budgets as static targets.

In addition to the determinants of supervisory style considered above (e.g. Argyris, 1952; Hopwood, 1973; Otley, 1978), antecedent variables have been the focus of a number of other studies. In particular, De Coster & Fertakis (1968) and Merchant (1983, 1985) examined the effect of general leader style and Merchant (1985) and Simons (1987) considered business strategy as a determinant of supervisory style.[8]

Two dimensions of general leader style, as measured by the LBDQ (Stogdill, 1963), have been examined in the supervisory style literature: consideration and initiating structure (as previously described). Consistent with Hopwood's (1973) findings as presented above, both De Coster & Fertakis (1968) and Merchant (1983) found that a leader style characterized by high initiating structure is associated with a high budget emphasis. However, there are mixed results regarding the consideration dimension. De Coster & Fertakis found that budget pressure from the immediate superior was positively related to consideration. Hopwood (as noted above) found that BC supervisors were less considerate than either the PC or NA supervisors. Merchant (1983) found no significant relationship between consideration and supervisory style of evaluation. In contrast, Merchant (1985) failed to find a significant relationship between either consideration or initiating structure and supervisory style.

The antecedent effects of business strategy were considered by Merchant (1985) and Simons (1987). Merchant's (1985) study of 62 profit centre managers in a single firm found that the decisions of units with rapid growth strategies were more highly affected by a budget emphasis style of evaluation. Simons (1987), on the other hand, used Miles & Snow's (1978) three dimensions of strategy: defender, analyser and prospector (as described above). His study of 62 defender and 46 prospector firms revealed that control system attributes differ between these two groups. In particular, dimensions of supervisory style were included among the control system attributes. He found that budget emphasis was associated with firm performance (measured as the three year mean of reported return on investment) for all firms except large defenders. He also found that the use of budgets in a problem solving/questioning way was positively related to performance for prospector firms, while for large defenders only, this relationship was negative. He also found that defenders used budget-based compensation schemes to a greater extent than prospector firms.

Thus, business strategy seems to have a dual role in its relationship with supervisory style. The evidence suggests that it both moderates the effects and influences the choice of a supervisory style.

Finally, a number of studies have examined a range of control system variables, primarily using a factor analytic methodology[9], including various dimensions of supervisory style: Onsi (1973), Kenis (1979) and Merchant (1981, 1983). The results of these studies provide some further insights.

Consistent with Schiff & Lewin's (1968) case evidence, Onsi (1973) found

---

[8] Also see Rockness & Shields (1984) and Peterson (1984) for useful summaries of the determinants of control systems.

[9] See Otley (1980, p. 417) for problems associated with interpreting and comparing the results of contingency studies which use a factor analytic methodology.

that 80% of the 32 managers interviewed in his study of five companies admitted creating slack. His results revealed that budget emphasis and budget pressure (which involved setting tight standards) were positively related to the creation of slack. Budgetary participation was found to reduce slack independently of supervisory style. Merchant's (1983) results were generally supportive of these findings. However, he reported that the correlations between the propensity to create slack and two items concerned with meeting the budget (required explanations of variance and link with extrinsic rewards) were significantly negative.

Kenis' (1979) study of 169 department heads in 19 manufacturing plants examined, *inter alia*, the effects of two supervisory styles, general and punitive, on three job related attitudes: satisfaction, involvement and tension; two budget related attitudes; attitudes towards budgets and budgetary motivation; and three performance variables; budgetary performance, cost efficiency and job performance. The items in his measures of a general and punitive style of evaluation can be interpreted as moderate and high budget emphasis respectively. He found that a general (moderate budget emphasis) evaluation style was positively related to budget motivation and budgetary performance. A punitive (high budget emphasis) evaluation style was positively related to job tension and budget motivation but was negatively related to all three measures of performance. These main effects are, however, difficult to interpret due to the possible interaction effects with his measures of participation and goal difficulty (see Hirst & Lowy, 1987).

Merchant's (1981) study of 170 managers in 19 firms in the electronics industry found a strong positive relationship between budgetary emphasis and time spent on budgeting (budgetary participation). He also reported that both size (number of employees) and degree of decentralization positively correlated strongly with budget emphasis. He also found that budget emphasis was associated with an increase in intrinsic motivation and felt usefulness of the budget. In addition he reported that while there was no effect of budget emphasis on departmental performance for the total sample, there was a positive (negative) effect for large (small) firms.

Summary

In summary, we have seen that Argyris (1952) made an important initial contribution to the supervisory style literature. This was followed predominantly by case evidence until the more thorough treatment of the issues by Hopwood (1972, 1973). Otley's (1978) seemingly conflicting evidence relating to the supervisory style effects on JRT and performance stimulated a number of attempted reconciliations by subsequent researchers. Some of these researchers adopted a contingency theory perspective. As previously discussed, such a perspective also led researchers to investigate the antecedents of supervisory style.

The previous review provides a survey of the supervisory style literature. The relevant studies are summarized in Table 12.1. One of the most conspicuous features of these studies is the breadth of analysis. Nevertheless,

Table 12.1 Summary of supervisory style studies

Study	Theory or empirical or both	Research method	Sample size	Supervisory style dimension	Relations with other variables			
					Dependent	Intervening	Moderator	Antecedent
Argyris (1952)	Empirical	Case study	4 plants	Needling Raising standards Uncompromising attitude	Dysfunctional behaviour Managerial effectiveness Long-run performance	JRT Resentment Pressure Fear of failure	Budgetary participation	Differentiation Economics conditions General leader style
Schiff & Lewin (1968)	Empirical	Case study	3 firms	Budget emphasis	Budgetary slack			
Lowe & Shaw (1968)	Empirical	Case study and document study	1 retail chain	Budget emphasis	Budgetary slack			
Hofstede (1968)	Both	Structured interviews and document study	5 firms 6 plants	Frequency of contacts Budget emphasis Focus on negative results	Dysfunctional behaviour	Budget pressure Budget motivation Job satisfaction Fear of failure Job stress	Budgetary participation	
De Coster & Fertakis (1968)	Empirical	Questionnaire survey	31 superiors 90 subordinates	Budget emphasis	Budget pressure			General leader style (LBDQ)
Hopwood (1973) Chapters 1–5	Both	Survey and case study	167 managers 20 managers	BC, PC and NA styles	IDR Interpersonal relations	JRT		

Study	Type	Method	Sample				
Hopwood (1973) Chapter 6	Empirical	Case study	20 managers	BC, PC and NA styles	Informal information systems		
Hopwood (1973) Chapter 7	Empirical	Survey and case study	167 managers 20 managers	BC, PC and NA styles	IDR Interpersonal relations	JRT	Budgetary participation APM accuracy Managerial aspirations
Hopwood (1973) Chapter 8	Empirical	Survey and case study	167 managers 20 managers	BC, PC and NA styles			General leader style (LBDQ) Unit size Contagion effect
Onsi (1973)	Empirical	Structured interviews and questionnaire survey	32 managers 107 managers	Budget emphasis	Budgetary slack	Budget pressure	
Otley (1978)	Both	Survey and case study	39 managers	Budget emphasis	Budgetary performance Long run performance Interpersonal relations IDR	JRT	Management philosophy Environmental conditions Unit size Realism/ accuracy of budget
Kenis (1979)	Empirical	Questionnaire survey	19 firms 169 managers	General/punitive style	Budgetary performance Job performance Cost efficiency	Job satisfaction Job involvement JRT Budget attitude Budget motivation	

Table 12.1 (contd.)

Study	Theory or empirical or both	Research method	Sample size	Supervisory style dimension	Relations with other variables			
					Dependent	Intervening	Moderator	Antecedent
Hirst (1981)	Theory	NA	NA	Budget emphasis	Interpersonal relations Dysfunctional behaviour	JRT	Task uncertainty	
Merchant (1981)	Both	Questionnaire survey	19 firms 170 managers	Budget emphasis	Unit performance	Instrinsic motivation Felt usefulness of budget		Unit size Degree of decentra- lization
Brownell (1982)	Both	Questionnaire survey	48 managers	Budget emphasis	Job performance Job satisfaction		Budgetary participation	
Hirst (1983)	Empirical	Questionnaire survey	11f managers	Budget emphasis	Dysfunctional behaviour JRT		Task uncertainty	
Merchant (1983)	Empirical	Questionnaire survey	19 firms 170 managers	Budget emphasis	Budgetary slack			General leader style (LBDQ)
Govindarajan (1984)	Both	Questionnaire survey	8 firms 58 managers	Subjective/ formula-based criteria	Unit effectiveness		Environmental uncertainty	
Hirst & Yetton (1984)	Empirical	Questionnaire survey	111 managers	Budget emphasis	Role ambiguity		Job function	

Govindarajan & Gupta (1985)	Both	Questionnaire survey	58 firms 46 managers	Short/long run criteria Subjective/ formula-based criteria	Unit effectiveness		Business strategy
Brownell (1985)	Both	Case study and questionnaire survey	61 managers	Budget emphasis	Job performance		Job function Environmental uncertainty
Imoisili (1985)	Both	Questionnaire survey	3 firms 102 managers	Budget emphasis	Job performance Dysfunctional behaviour	Role stress	
Merchant (1985)	Empirical	Case study and questionnaire survey	54 managers	Budget emphasis	Business decisions		General leader style (LBDQ) Business strategy
Brownell & Hirst (1986)	Empirical	Questionnaire survey	76 managers	Budget emphasis	Job performance		Task uncertainty Budgetary participation
Hirst (1987)	Empirical	Questionnaire survey	44 managers	Budget emphasis	Job performance		Budgetary participation
Brownell (1987a)	Both	Case study and questionnaire survey	50 managers	Budget emphasis	Job performance Job satisfaction		Environmental uncertainty

Table 12.1 (contd.)

Study	Theory or empirical or both	Research method	Sample size	Supervisory style dimension	Relations with other variables			
					Dependent	Intervening	Moderator	Antecedent
Brownell & Merchant (1987)	Both	Questionnaire survey	19 firms 201 managers	Use of flexible/ static budgets	Unit performance		Technology	
Simons (1987)	Empirical	Questionnaire survey	108 firms	Budget emphasis Evaluative/ problem solving use	Unit performance			Business strategy Unit size
Bottger & Hirst (1988)	Both	Questionnaire survey	44 managers	Budget emphasis	Job stress		Budgetary participation	
Dunk (undated)	Empirical	Questionnaire survey	26 firms	Budget emphasis	Job performance		Budgetary participation	
Govindarajan (undated)	Both	Questionnaire survey	24 firms	Budget emphasis	Unit effectiveness	Business strategy		

despite differences in methods and conflicting results, and overlooking differences in constructs and their measures, some general patterns emerge from the literature. In particular, supervisory style is an important predictor of behaviour. Behaviours such as invalid data reporting appear to be in response to various psychological outcomes (e.g. JRT) which are affected by supervisory style. However, these effects are moderated by various factors including task uncertainty, budgetary participation, the environment and strategy. Moreover, unit size, environmental and economic conditions, general leader style (initiating structure) and business strategy emerge as notable predictors of supervisory style.

Notwithstanding these general patterns, after nearly four decades of study, it is timely to provide a critical review of this literature with the aim of identifying potentially fruitful areas for future development. These areas emerge from an analysis of the limitations associated with the existing literature. In general, these limitations can be categorized in terms of the major sections of a typical empirical study; that is, theoretical development and empirical analysis.

CRITICAL ANALYSIS

Theoretical development

The development of rationales for the effects of supervisory style has been limited by several factors. Specifically, in recent years, theoretical development has taken a secondary role to an emphasis on statistical analysis. In addition, where development has occurred, it has tended to be piecemeal and involve selective referencing, unquestioned assumptions about the dependent variable status of overall job performance, and an inattention to the multidimensional nature of supervisory style. Moreover, rationales for the antecedents and, to a lesser extent, moderators of supervisory style have relied on contingency theory with little regard to critiques of this theory. These claims are examined below.

Initial descriptions of budgetary processes suggested the use of role theory and related stress research to explain the effects of supervisory style (Argyris, 1952). Indeed, this was the approach subsequently adopted by Hopwood (1973). A major focus of these early studies was theory development. In recent years, however, there has been a trend towards the statistical sophistication of empirical investigations. This trend was started by Hofstede (1968) and developed by others, including Hopwood (1973), Brownell (1982), Govindarajan & Gupta (1985) and Jaworski (1988). Although there are exceptions (e.g. Brownell, 1982), this trend has been at the expense of theory development. Of particular concern is the inclusion of variables in hypotheses with little supporting explanation. For example, some studies use box diagrams with arrows indicating causally related variables. Although this is a parsimonious way of communicating connections, the supporting argument in some studies is only suggestive (e.g. see Kenis, 1979).

Also of concern is the observation that some studies selectively reference, or uncritically rely on, arguments and/or evidence in related literature to support their hypotheses. For example, Brownell's (1982) hypotheses were developed using both operant analysis and balance theory. Operant analysis is a class of motivation theory that assumes behaviour is environmentally determined, whereas balance theory assumes that behaviour is the outcome of cognitive processes. Operant analysis has been at the centre of some controversy and, accordingly, it is surprising that Brownell did not refer to the relevant critiques (e.g. Locke, 1977). Moreover, he did not attempt to contrast or discuss the relation between operant analysis and balance theory. Again, this is surprising because if one believes in operant conditioning, then reference to internal cognitive events (as required in balance theory) is inappropriate for making predictions about behaviour (Mitchell, 1976, 1979). Similarly, Govindarajan (1984) relies on the contingency theory literature to support his propositions about the effectiveness of business units. In so doing, however, he does not refer to critiques of this theory (e.g. see Wood, 1979; Schoonhoven, 1981; Otley, 1980; Hopwood, 1983).

As indicated above, where underlying arguments are provided to support hypotheses, they tend to be piecemeal, with little attempt to relate new and existing rationales for the effects of supervisory style. For example, Brownell & Hirst (1986) attempted to link two prior studies, one relying on motivation theory to develop hypotheses, and the other relying on role theory and related stress research. In so doing, however, Brownell & Hirst did not provide an examination of the relation between these theories. Although piecemeal development is probably the norm in many social science disciplines, this process becomes problematic where the aim of studies (as in the case cited) is to reconcile previous research.

In addition to providing explanations for relations among variables, theory development requires the selection of outcome or dependent variables. While selection is constrained by the focal, independent variables (and in this case, supervisory style), individual researchers have some discretion. Indeed, early studies (e.g. Argyris, 1952; Hofstede, 1968; Onsi, 1973; Hopwood, 1973) focused on a variety of attitudinal, psychological and behavioural outcomes associated with budgetary control systems. More recently, studies (e.g. Kenis, 1979; Brownell, 1982; Brownell & Hirst, 1986; Hirst, 1987) have focused on overall job performance. This focus is problematic for several reasons.

First, if budgetary performance is a major component of overall job performance (see Hopwood, 1973), then there are questions about the status of job performance as a dependent variable. For example, Otley's (1978) analysis suggests that a spurious relation exists between supervisory style and budget performance, with realism/accuracy of the budget affecting both variables. In constrast, Merchant (1985) claims that budget performance is probably an independent variable for all control-related studies (see also Collins et al., 1987). Second, even if budget performance is not a major component of overall job performance, the question concerning the dependent variable status of job performance remains. For example, Brownell (1982) acknowledges that supervisory style might be a function of job performance. Third, status issues aside, overall job performance is an ambiguous construct with multiple dimensions (Otley, 1980). As these dimensions and their relations are contested (e.g. see Hopwood, 1973; Brownell, 1982; Govindarajan, 1984; Luckett & Hirst, 1989) and change over time (Hopwood, 1979; Chua & Lowe, 1984), establishing specific yet generalized relations between overall job performance and supervisory style is difficult.

Given that recent studies have not addressed issues either about the dependent variable status of overall job performance or the lack of conceptual clarity, it follows that their theoretical contribution is limited. Indeed, where budgetary performance is not a major component of overall job performance, issues about conceptual clarity bring into question the value of focusing on overall job performance in supervisory style studies.

In addition to overall job performance, there has been little concern about the multidimensional nature of supervisory style. Although Argyris (1952) examined supervisory style in terms of different *uses* of budgets, it was Hopwood (1973) who characterized supervisory style in terms of the *extent* and *manner* of budget use in performance evaluation. There was a matching of these two dimensions in Hopwood's study. In particular, a 'budget constrained' supervisory style involved a reliance on 'meeting the budget' in performance evaluation *and* the use of this criterion in an unquestioning, evaluative manner. In contrast, a profit conscious style involved a reliance on a 'concern for costs' (together with other non-budget criteria) *and* the use of this criterion in a problem solving (questioning) manner. Hopwood's (1973) theory statements assumed this matching. More importantly, this matching has remained largely unquestioned in the literature. Yet such a matching need not occur in all situations. For example, high reliance/problem solving match is possible. What are the likely effects of this supervisory style? More generally, the manner of budget use in performance evaluation may extend beyond the evaluative/problem solving dimension to include the use of budgets as 'needlers' and as a means for structuring activities and motivating performance (Argyris, 1952; De Coster & Fertakis, 1968; Hopwood, 1973). The separate effects and relations among the various supervisory styles remain uncertain.

Finally, given the potential effects of supervisory style, it is not surprising that studies have examined the circumstances which are capable of moderating the effects of various styles as well as the antecedent conditions for a given style. These studies typically adopt contingency theory as a basis for hypothesis development (e.g. Merchant, 1981, 1984; Govindarajan, 1984; Brownell, 1985; and see Jaworski, 1988, for a review). However, there is controversy surrounding contingency theory, ranging from concerns about a lack of conceptual clarity (Otley, 1980; Schoonhoven, 1981) to more fundamental concerns about the nature of change, and the role of choice, in organizational and control system design (Wood, 1979; Burrell & Morgan, 1979). With few exceptions (e.g. Brownell, 1985) accounting researchers have not acknowledged the ambiguity in underlying constructs such as 'environmental uncertainty' (Boyd, 1984). Moreover, while accounting researchers are beginning to recognize the role of strategic choice in control system design (e.g. Govindarajan & Gupta, 1985; Simons, 1987; Govindarajan, undated), the *processes* by which supervisory styles are 'chosen' has not been addressed (Dent, 1986). Without knowledge of such processes it is premature to contemplate either direct or indirect changes in supervisory style as a means of influencing organizational behaviour.

In summary, recent theoretical developments in the supervisory style literature have centred on the introduction of several moderator and antecedent variables. These developments add breadth to the literature. However, the previous analysis suggests a further broadening is possible by recognizing the multidimensional nature of several variables including supervisory style, environment, technology and so on. Moreover, the depth of understanding has progressed little since the early studies. More specifically, for example, we know little more about the *process* by which supervisory styles affect behaviour and the *process* by which supervisory styles emerge. Theoretical development is not only necessary to increase our understanding of these phenomena, but also to make more informed choices about the design of empirical studies, including choice of data collection methods, variable measures and data analysis procedures (Schoonhoven, 1981; Kidder, 1981).

Empirical analysis

The early investigations in the supervisory style literature tended to involve descriptive case studies (e.g. Argyris, 1952; Schiff & Lewin, 1968; Hofstede, 1968; Lowe & Shaw, 1968). In contrast, recent investigations tend to be cross-sectional, questionnaire surveys which involve hypothesis testing (e.g. Kenis, 1979; Merchant, 1981; Brownell, 1982; Hirst, 1983; Govindarajan, 1984; Govindarajan & Gupta, 1985; Brownell & Hirst, 1986; Jaworski, 1988). Note, however, that there are a few survey studies which also involve a case study component (e.g. Hopwood, 1973, and to a lesser extent Otley, 1978; Brownell, 1987a). This section of the paper focuses on studies that favour the use of questionnaire surveys as the main data collection method.

The advantages and limitations of questionnaire surveys are well known. In essence, they trade-off internal validity for external validity and provide data in a form that is suitable for statistical analysis (Campbell & Stanley, 1966; Kidder, 1981). Even so, there are grounds for concern about empirical studies in the supervisory style literature. These concerns centre on 'method-driven' as opposed to 'phenomenon-driven' studies and several factors that cause an uncoupling of the connection between theory statements and empirical tests. These factors include invalid measures, range restriction in variable measures, omitted variables and the use of test procedures that are only indirectly related to theory statements. As before, these claims are examined below with the aim of identifying opportunities for future research.

The persistent use of cross-sectional, questionnaire surveys limits the type of phenomena and relations that are amenable to investigation. For example, cross-sectional studies compare unfavourably with longitudinal studies when concern focuses on the *processes* involved in the design, use and effects of budgetary control systems. Note that all these processes have a temporal dimension. Moreover, questionnaire surveys are unlikely to provide valid information about confidential and sensitive variables such as those involving political, irrational and/or dysfunctional behaviours (see Moser & Kalton, 1979, for support, and Collins *et al.*, 1987, for a contrary view). As these behaviours are likely to be an important part of budgetary control systems (e.g. Birnberg *et al.*, 1983; Dent, 1986) it follows that a change in data collection method is required if information is to be gathered about the interactions and dynamics through which supervisory styles emerge and their effects are produced. The confidential, sensitive and dynamic nature of the phenomena suggests that data collection might best proceed using indepth case studies.

In addition, the value of questionnaire surveys is, in part, dependent on the validity of variable measures. In the supervisory style literature, questions arise in relation to several measures. For illustrative purposes the following will examine, in turn, measures of supervisory style and overall job performance.

The arguments supporting Hopwood's (1973) hypotheses about the effects of supervisory style critically depend on both the *extent* and *manner* of budget use in performance evaluation. As previously indicated, these two dimensions of budget use were related in his study. Accordingly it was only necessary for the measure of supervisory style to focus on one of these dimensions – the extent of budget use. Significantly, recent studies often use this measure of supervisory style without examining whether both the extent and manner of budget use are linked. Given that these two dimensions may be unrelated in the latter studies, a construct validity threat exists in relation to supervisory style. As Brownell (1985) observed, failure to capture differences in the extent and manner of budget use could explain why the hypothesized effects of supervisory style were not confirmed in his study. More generally, this construct validity threat can be added to the list of plausible explanations for conflicting results in the supervisory style literature (e.g. compare Hopwood, 1973, and Otley, 1978, or Brownell, 1982, and Hirst, 1987).

As indicated above, overall job performance is an ambiguous construct. Simply asking survey participants to rate their overall job performance is problematic because of interpretation difficulties. Respondents have discretion in judging the relevant dimensions of performance to be included in the overall judgement, the relative importance of such dimensions, the standard or benchmark level for assessing performance on each dimension, and the time period over which the rating is made. As a consequence, the comparability of responses becomes questionable, and the relation of these responses to the independent variables, such as supervisory style, becomes unclear.

Although some studies have attempted to address these issues (e.g. Govindarajan, 1984; Govindarajan & Gupta, 1985; Collins *et al.*, 1987), construct validity tests are rare in the supervisory style literature. And even though hypothesis testing jointly tests the validity of measures, care is required in assessing the extent to which empirical studies are connected with underlying theory.

Another characteristic of empirical studies that weakens hypothesis testing (and cross study comparability of results) is range restriction in variable measures. This occurs where the range of variable values is not sufficient to match the requirements of theory or, in the context of a replication, does not match the range of variable values observed in previous studies. In the supervisory style literature, many theory statements are expressed in terms of extreme values (i.e. high/low) for the focal variables (e.g. Hirst, 1981; Brownell, 1982; Govindarajan, 1984). Yet it is rare (e.g. Hirst, 1983) to find a concern for ensuring that variable measures correspond to these extreme values. If observed ranges of variable scores do not encompass high/low values, then there is an uncoupling of the link between theory and related empirical tests.[10]

Although range restriction is potentially an important problem for sensitive variables such as self-rated performance and dysfunctional behaviour, it can also be a problem for measures of supervisory style. For example, the 'non-accounting' supervisory style was the most prevalent style in Hopwood's (1973) study, and accordingly was an important style affecting his results. Yet this style was virtually non-existent in Otley's (1978) study (see also Imoisili, 1985, for a similar problem). In the absence of the full range of supervisory styles, Otley's study can provide only limited tests of hypotheses which examine the effects of supervisory styles. Moreover, Otley's study can only provide a limited replication of Hopwood's study. This is an important observation because much of the recent literature has attempted to explain, on other grounds, the apparent failure of Otley to replicate some of Hopwood's results (Brownell, 1987b).

Omitted variables may also cause an uncoupling of the link between theory statements and empirical analysis. As shown in Fig. 12.1, the effects of supervisory style are potentially dependent on several variables, including task uncertainty, budget participation, job function and so on. However, due to measurement and statistical modelling issues, as well as the cognitive limits of researchers, no study attempts to include all of the relevant variables. Again this is probably the norm for most empirical studies in the social sciences. Ultimately, however, the potential problem created here is one of internal validity. Yet it is rare for studies in the supervisory style literature to confront this problem and seriously consider alternative explanations for results. For example, Brownell (1982) found that the effects of supervisory style (called budget emphasis) on overall job performance were moderated by budget participation. These results were explained in terms of the motivational effects associated with an appropriate matching between budget emphasis and budget participation. However, these motivational effects were not empirically examined

---

[10] Brownell (1988) remains unconcerned about range restriction because he is prepared to extrapolate (typically) linear relationships outside the observed empirical ranges of scores.

in the study. More importantly, it is plausible that the pattern of results was due to an omitted variable, such as the difficulty level of budget goals.

To explain this, assume that budget performance was an important component of overall job performance in the Brownell study. Note that 69% of the managers in this study reported that budget criteria were relatively important in performance evaluation. It could be argued that high budget emphasis and high budget participation provide both the incentive and, to some extent, the opportunity for managers to secure attainable, or even slack, budgets. If so, then consistent with Brownell's findings, a positive relation would be expected between budget participation and job performance where budget emphasis is high. However, note that the explanation is now in terms of a manipulation of budget criteria and not improved motivation and actual performance. In contrast, where budget emphasis is low, there is no incentive to manipulate budget estimates. Accordingly, no relation, as reported by Brownell, is expected between budget participation and job performance where budget emphasis is low.

Although the number of alternative plausible explanations (APEs) for a given set of results might be large, some are more likely than others. In the case cited above, for example, the prior work by Hopwood (1973), and to a lesser extent Otley (1978), suggests that the dual role of budget participation (i.e. motivation versus data manipulation) might have been anticipated. Significantly, the prior illustration is not an isolated case. For example, consider the role of budget participation in providing an APE for the results provided by Hirst (1983). Lastly, the identification and analysis of APEs is important, not only because of internal validity threats, but also because they can suggest quite different design implications for a given set of results.

The final factor that can weaken the link between theoretical and statistical analyses is the choice of test procedure. Often there are alternative ways to analyse a given data set. Although the mode of analysis chosen (including test statistics) may have little effect on the conclusions of a study, some analyses provide a more powerful or direct test of the related theory. To illustrate, consider the study by Brownell (1985), which contains at least three important propositions. First, Brownell provides extensive theoretical and empirical support for the proposition that (in general terms) effective control system design depends on environmental uncertainty. Second, he proposes that organizational divisions (i.e. marketing and research and development) vary in terms of environmental uncertainty. Third, given these propositions, he proposes that effective control system design depends on the type of organizational division. The subsequent empirical analysis focuses on, and supports, propositions two and three. However, a full examination of proposition one, which provides the most immediate test of the theory underlying the study, was never attempted.[11] This is surprising because first, the data was available to test

[11] Even so, a partial examination was provided by Brownell (1985). He investigated the moderating effects of two (out of 16) items that were used to measure environmental differences.

this proposition, and second, support for propositions two and three does *not* imply support for proposition one. If proposition one could not be supported by the data, then it would be necessary to develop an alternative explanation for why the effectiveness of control system design varied across organizational divisions. Future studies might exercise some care to ensure that statistical tests are closely connected with related theory.

DIRECTIONS FOR FUTURE RESEARCH

Although several suggestions for further research have been made above, it is useful to identify some specific areas worthy of further attention. First, as indicated above, supervisory style is not a unidimensional variable. Styles differ in terms of time horizons as well as the extent and manner of budget use in performance evaluation. Moreover, differences in the manner of budget use can be distinguished. For example, Hopwood (1973) emphasized evaluative and problem oriented approaches, whereas Argyris (1952) and Kenis (1979) focused on needling/punitive uses of budgetary performance measures. Descriptions of the various supervisory styles are needed, as well as an examination of their relations.

Second, little is known about the processes by which the effects of supervisory style are obtained. These processes may well depend on the particular dimension of supervisory style in focus. For example, role theory might be important in explaining the behavioural effects of an uncompromising use of budgetary criteria in performance evaluation. In contrast motivation theory might be more important in explaining the effects of a needling supervisory style. In either case, future studies might examine the more immediate outcomes of supervisory style (such as role conflict and ambiguity, and the direction and level of effort) in order to increase our understanding of the processes associated with supervisory style.

Third, an analysis of the effects of supervisory style also requires a more detailed examination of moderator variables. In this context, for example, the ambiguous role of budget preparation has long been recognized in the literature (Hopwood, 1973), and remains unaddressed.

Fourth, although previous studies have examined a wide range of outcome variables, apart from Argyris (1952), little attention has been given to the effects of supervisory style on the formation of groups and its related role in creating and reinforcing differentiation among groups. These are important outcomes because group norms can be significant determinants of individual behaviour. Moreover, the joint study of supervisory style and group norms brings together two of the main control mechanisms in organizations. In addition, an examination of the differentiation effects brings into focus the general problems of integration and co-ordination in organizations.

Fifth, opportunities exist for further analyses of the antecedents of supervisory style. An important issue concerns the effects of multiple contingencies on supervisory style. For example, given the studies by Otley (1978), Govindarajan (1984) and Imoisili (1985), what are the likely effects of both tight economic environments and uncertain environments on the 'selection' of supervisory style? What is the role and nature of choice in this selection process? More generally, studies might investigate the effect of social/cultural factors on the emergence of supervisory style (e.g. Brownell, 1987a). Similarly, little is known about the role of government in promoting supervisory style. An interesting possibility is that new governments, for various reasons, may promote the financial accountability of public organizations. As a consequence, an opportunity (or perhaps, an imperative) is created for budgetary control systems (and associated supervisory styles) to adopt a higher profile in such organizations. Finally, studies might focus on intra-organizational factors such as organizational level (Argyris, 1952; Peterson, 1984), the contagion effect (Hopwood, 1973), task, function and the role of differentiation among groups (e.g. financial controllers and supervisors – see Argyris, 1952) in explaining the emergence of supervisory style. Note that while supervisory style is affected by factors such as differentiation and task characteristics, supervisory style, in turn, can affect these same factors. Accordingly, an examination of the causes and/or consequences of supervisory style needs to extend beyond analyses of simple bivariate relations.

Sixth, and lastly, while survey methods have their advantages, our limited knowledge about the processes involved in both the emergence of supervisory style and their associated effects, coupled with the sensitive nature of the phenomena in focus, suggests that descriptive case studies are likely to be beneficial. Such studies might focus on descriptions of the array of supervisory styles; where, in organizations (i.e. level, task, job function), are alternative styles used and how supervisory styles relate with other controls (are there patterns of controls – see for example, Rockness & Shields, 1984; Merchant, 1985); and the causes and consequences of *changes* in supervisory style (in contrast with the typical cross-sectional, questionnaire studies).

CONCLUSION

There is little doubt that supervisory style is an important predictor of different psychological and behavioural responses. Yet, as an analysis of the related literature shows, there is only a limited understanding of the processes which give rise to a particular supervisory style and the way a particular style affects behaviour. The present review indicates that the use made of accounting information in performance evaluation is neither a simple nor inevitable consequence of its availability. An attempt has been made to highlight the factors that potentially influence the 'choice' of supervisory style. Similarly, the effects of this choice on behaviour are neither a simple or inevitable consequence of a particular supervisory style. The effects of supervisory style must be filtered through several moderating variables. In addition, recall that supervisory style is only one of the means of influence and control in organizations. Accordingly, its effects must also be filtered through other administrative, social and self controls which are also operative in organizations. In attempting to understand the effects of supervisory style, our task, in part, is to explain this filtering process.

ACKNOWLEDGEMENTS

We are indebted to Peter Brownell, Anthony Hopwood and an anonymous reviewer for many helpful comments on an earlier version of this paper. Peter's particularly helpful and extended discussion of the paper has been included in the references (i.e. Brownell, 1988).

BIBLIOGRAPHY

Argyris, C., *The Impact of Budgets on People* (Ithaca: School of Business and Public Administration, Cornell University, 1952).

Arnold, J.A., Moderator Variables: A Clarification of Conceptual, Analytic, and Psychometric Issues, *Organisational Behaviour and Human Performance* (1982) pp. 143–174.

Birnberg, J.B., Turopolec, L. & Young, S.M., The Organizational Context of Accounting, *Accounting, Organizations and Society* (1983) pp. 111–129.

Bottger, P.C. & Hirst, M.K., The Interaction Effect of Budget Emphasis and Budget Participation on Experienced Job Stress, *Human Resource Management* (1988) in press.

Boyd, G.A., Management Accounting and Contingency Theory: The Problem of Borrowing the Construct of the Environment, Honours Thesis, Commerce Faculty, University of New South Wales (1984).

Brownell, P., The Role of Accounting Data in Performance Evaluation, Budgetary Participation, and Organisational Effectiveness, *Journal of Accounting Research* (Spring 1982) pp. 12–27.

Brownell, P., Budgetary Systems and the Control of Functionally Differentiated Organisational Activities, *Journal of Accounting Research* (Autumn 1985) pp. 502–512.

Brownell, P., The Role of Accounting Information, Environment and Management Control in Multi-national Organisations, *Accounting and Finance* (1987a) pp. 1–16.

Brownell, P., The Use of Accounting Information in Management Control, in Ferris, K.R. and Livingstone, J.L. (eds) *Management Planning and Control: The Behavioral Foundations* (Columbus, OH: Century Publishing Co., 1987b).

Brownell, P., A Discussion of Briers and Hirst's 'Supervisory Style: A Review of the role of Budgetary Information in Performance Evaluation', Unpublished paper, School of Economics and Financial Studies, Macquarie University (1988).

Brownell, P. & Hirst, M.K., Reliance on Accounting Information, Budgetary Participation, and Task Uncertainty: Tests of a Three Way Interaction, *Journal of Accounting Research* (Autumn 1986) pp. 241–249.

Brownell, P. & Merchant, K.A., Technology, Budget System Design, and Performance, Working Paper, Macquarie University (1987).

Burrell, G. and Morgan, G., *Sociological Paradigms and Organizational Analysis* (London: Heinemann, 1979).

Campbell, D.T. & Stanley, J.C., *Experimental and Quasi-experimental Designs for Research* (Chicago: Rand McNally College Publishing Co., 1966).

Chua, W.F. & Lowe, T., Performance Criteria in their Social Contexts: the Shifting Fortunes of Selection and Turnover in a School of Nursing, Working Paper, University of New South Wales (1984).

Collins, F., Munter, P. & Finn, D.W., The Budgeting Games People Play, *The Accounting Review* (January 1987) pp. 29–49.

De Coster, D.T. & Fertakis, J.P., Budget-induced Pressure and Its Relationship to Supervisory Behavior, *Journal of Accounting Research* (Autumn 1968) pp. 237–246.

Dent, J.F., Strategy, Organization and Control: Some Possibilities for Accounting Research, Paper Presented at American Accounting Association Conference, New York (1986).

Dunk, A.S., The Interaction of Budget Emphasis and Budgetary Participation: Implications for Managerial Performance, Working Paper, Macquarie University (undated).

Govindarajan, V., Appropriateness of Accounting Data in Performance Evaluation: An Empirical Examination of Environmental Uncertainty as an Intervening Variable, *Accounting, Organizations and Society* (1984) pp. 125–135.

Govindarajan, V., Budget Evaluation Style and Organizational Effectiveness: Strategy as an Intervening Variable, Working Paper (undated).

Govindarajan, V. & Gupta, A.K., Linking Budgetary Control Systems to Business Unit Strategy: Impact on Performance, *Accounting, Organizations and Society* (1985) pp. 51–66.

Hirst, M.K., Accounting Information and the Evaluation of Subordinate Performance: A Situational Approach, *The Accounting Review* (October 1981) pp. 771–784.

Hirst, M.K., Reliance on Accounting Performance Measures, Task Uncertainty, and Dysfunctional Behaviour: Some Extensions, *Journal of Accounting Research* (Autumn 1983) pp. 596–605.

Hirst, M.K., Some Further Evidence on the Effects of Budget Use and Budget Participation on Managerial Performance, *Australian Journal of Management* (1987) pp. 49–56.

Hirst, M.K. & Lowy, S.M., The Linear Additive and Interactive Effects of Budgetary Goal Difficulty and Feedback on Performance, Working Paper, Commerce Faculty, University of New South Wales (1987).

Hirst, M.K. & Yetton, P., Influence of Reliance on Accounting Performance Measures and Job Structure on Role Ambiguity for Production and Non-production Jobs, *Australian Journal of Management* (1984) pp. 53–62.

Hofstede, G.H., *The Game of Budget Control* (London: Tavistock, 1968).

Hopwood, A.G., An Empirical Study of the Role of Accounting Data in Performance Evaluation, *Empirical Research in Accounting, Supplement to Journal of Accounting Research* (1972) pp. 156–182.

Hopwood, A.G., *An Accounting System and Managerial Behaviour* (London: Saxon House, 1973).

Hopwood, A.G., Criteria of Corporate Effectiveness, in Brodie, M. and Bennett, R. (eds) *Perspectives on Managerial Effectiveness* pp. 81–96 (Thames Valley Regional Management Centre, 1979).

Hopwood, A.G., On Trying to Study Accounting in the Contexts in Which it Operates, *Accounting, Organizations and Society* (1983) pp. 287–305.

Imoisili, O.A., Task Complexity, Budget Style of Evaluating Performance and Managerial Stress: An Empirical Investigation, Unpublished Dissertation, Graduate School of Business, University of Pittsburgh (1985).

Jaworski, B.J., Towards a Theory of Marketing Control: Environmental Context, Control Types and Consequences, *Journal of Marketing* (July 1988) pp. 23–39.

Kahn, R.L., Wolfe, D.M., Quinn, R.P. & Rosenthal, R.A., *Organizational Stress: Studies in Role Conflict and Ambiguity* (New York: Wiley, 1964).

Kenis, I., Effects of Budgetary Goal Characteristics on Managerial Attitudes and Performance, *The Accounting Review* (October 1979) pp. 707–721.

Kidder, H.K., *Sellitz Wrightsman & Cook's Research Methods in Social Relations* (New York: Holt, Rinehart & Winston, 1981).

Lawrence, P. & Lorsch, J., *Organization and Environment* (Homewood: Irwin, 1967).

Locke, E.A., The Myths of Behavior Modification in Organizations, *Academy of Management Review* (1977) pp. 543–542.

Lowe, E.A. & Shaw, R.W., An Analysis of Managerial Biasing: Evidence of a Company's Budgeting Process, *Journal of Management Studies* (October 1968) pp. 304–315.

Luckett, P.F. & Hirst, M.K., The Impact of Feedback on Inter-rater Agreement and Self-insight in Performance Evaluation Decisions, *Accounting, Organizations and Society* (1989) in press.

Merchant, K.A., The Design of the Corporate Budgeting System: Influences on Managerial Behavior and Performance, *The Accounting Review* (1981) pp. 813–829.

Merchant, K.A., Leadership Styles and Uses of Budgeting, Working Paper no. 83–49, Harvard University Graduate School of Business Administration (1983).

Merchant, K.A., Influences on Departmental Budgeting: An Empirical Examination of a Contingency Model, *Accounting, Organizations and Society* (1984) pp. 291–307.

Merchant, K.A., Organizational Controls and Discretionary Program Decision Making: A Field Study, *Accounting, Organizations and Society* (1985) pp. 67–85.

Miles, R.E. & Snow, C.C., *Organizational Strategy, Structure and Process* (New York: McGraw–Hill, 1978).

Mitchell, T.R., Cognitions and Skinner: Some Questions About Behavioral Determinism, *Organizational and Administrative Sciences* (1976) pp. 63–72.

Mitchell, T.R., Organizational Behavior, *Annual Review of Psychology* (1979) pp. 243–281.

Moser, C.A. & Kalton, G., *Survey Methods in Social Investigation* (New York: Heinemann Educational Books, 1979).

Onsi, M., Factor Analysis of Behavioral Variables Affecting Budgetary Slack, *The Accounting Review* (1973) pp. 535–548.

Otley, D.T., Budget Use and Managerial Performance, *Journal of Accounting Research* (Spring 1978) pp. 122–149.

Otley, D.T., The Contingency Theory of Management Accounting: Achievement and Prognosis, *Accounting, Organizations and Society* (1980) pp. 413–428.

Peterson, K.D., Mechanisms of Administrative Control over Managers in Educational Organizations, *Administrative Science Quarterly* (1984) pp. 573–597.

Rockness, H.O. & Shields, M.D., Organizational Control Systems in Research and Development, *Accounting, Organizations and Society* (1984) pp. 165–177.

Schiff, M. & Lewin, A.Y., Where Traditional Budgeting Fails, *Financial Executive* (May 1968) pp. 57–62.

Schoonhoven, C.B., Problems with Contingency Theory: Testing Assumptions Hidden Within the Language of Contingency Theory, *Administrative Science Quarterly* (September 1981) pp. 349–377.

Simons, R., Accounting Control Systems and Business Strategy: An Empirical Analysis, *Accounting, Organizations and Society* (1987) pp. 357–374.

Stogdill, R.M., *Manual for the Leader Behaviour Description Questionnaire* (Columbus, OH: Bureau of Business Research, Ohio State University, 1963).

Wood, S., A Reappraisal of the Contingency Approach to Organization, *Journal of Management Studies* (1979) pp. 334–354.

13

Risk distribution in the budgetary process

David Otley and Anthony Berry

Budgeting has always been a problematic process. At the end of a budget period it is invariably found that some managers have been able to achieve their budget targets more successfully than others. But when senior managers come to evaluate their subordinates' performance they have to recognize that some apparent success is caused by certain managers having had easier budgets to attain in the first place. That is, the difficulty of budget targets is likely to vary between one manager and another. Further, it has often been recommended that budgets should be seen as targets that will be achieved only a proportion of the time. In order to motivate the best possible actual performance it is suggested[1] that a budget should be pitched at a more difficult level than the performance actually expected. Although such a target will not, on average, be attained it is nevertheless believed that it will motivate managers to achieve a better result than if the budget had been set at a lower level. It is not the purpose of this paper to argue the case for or against the use of budgets as motivational targets. Rather we take as our starting point the observation that budgets are often, in practice, set at levels other than the performance which is expected to occur, and to examine some implications of this observation.

Motivational factors are not the only reason why budgets may be set at levels other than those expected to be attained. Even budgets which managers intend to be good estimates of expected performance (which we will call Expectation Budgets) may be subject to bias by their subordinates in both upward and downward directions.[2] A number of studies have indicated that such budget bias is a common feature of the budgetary process in many types of organization and is essentially motivated by the

[1] Hofstede, G. *The Game of Budget Control* (London, Tavistock, 1968).
[2] For the sake of clarity of exposition we will consider budgets, such as output and revenue budgets, where a higher figure represents better performance and a lower figure worse performance. For other types of budget, such as cost budgets, where the reverse is true, the argument is still valid but references to up and down, higher and lower etc. should be reversed.

Source: Otley, D. and Berry, A. (1979) *Accounting and Business Research*, **9** (36), pp. 325–37.

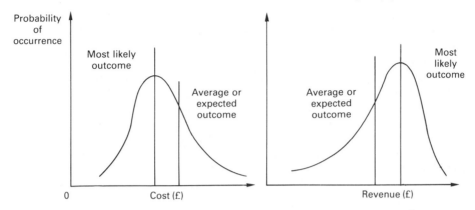

Fig. 13.1 Distributions of costs and revenues having positive and negative skewness.

desire of junior managers to be favourably evaluated by their superiors.[3] Thus junior managers currently in a strong position may bias their budgets downwards in order to give themselves an easier standard to achieve in the subsequent period. Conversely, managers currently in a weak position may bias their budget upwards so as to make it appear that, despite current problems, the future is bright.

There may be a further reason for Non-Expectation Budgets. It has been suggested that the statistical distribution of costs and revenues in many organizations is likely to be skew rather than symmetrical.[4] That is to say, errors to one side of a most likely outcome can be more extreme than on the other, as illustrated in Figure 13.1.

The argument for skewness is intuitively appealing. A certain level of cost is likely to be incurred; spending much less than this amount (at a given level of output) is increasingly improbable whereas almost any degree of overspending is possible. Similarly, a certain level of revenue may be thought likely, but it may not materialize; any great increase in revenue is rather less probable than a similar decrease. If such a situation exists then budgets set without any thought for motivational manipulation or any attempt at bias by subordinates (or superiors, for that matter!) may still not represent expectations. Typically the figure submitted as a budget will be the most likely outcome, for this represents a real event familiar to the manager in charge. But this most likely outcome differs from the long-run expectation of outcomes as shown in Figure 13.1. As an

---

[3] See for example, Lowe, E.A. and Shaw, R.W., 'An Analysis of Managerial Biasing: Evidence from a Company's Budget Process', *Journal of Management Studies*, October 1968, pp. 304–315. Other studies are reviewed in Otley, D.T., *Behavioural Aspects of Budgeting*. Accountants Digest Number 49 (London, ICAEW, 1977).

[4] Turvey, R. in Luck, G.M. *et al.*, 'The Management of Capital Investment', *Journal of the Royal Statistical Society*, Series A, 134, 4, 1971.

extreme example consider the number of children expected to be included in a family. No doubt most parents will plan on the basis of one, or two, or three (or any integer) despite the national average outcome of 2.4 children per family! Similarly a manager is much more familiar with commonly occurring outcomes, and will plan and budget on such a basis, without concerning himself about overall averages.

However, although individual managers may quite rightly be concerned with the specific details of their own particular cases, senior managers have necessarily to consider the overall performance of the aggregate of units for which they are responsible. It is suggested that in many cases, for one of the reasons discussed above, budgets will be set at levels other than those that are expected to be achieved as a long-run average. It is the aim of this paper to show that even quite mild deviations from Expectation Budgets at the unit level can produce severe distortions when the budgets are aggregated to an overall organizational level. In addition, although senior managers may attempt to adjust budgets to remove some of this distortion, it will be shown that one common method of adjustment can produce further distortions at unit level. Thus it is imperative that those concerned with the aggregation of budgetary information are fully aware of the effects demonstrated here, so that appropriate educative action can be taken.

A SIMPLE CASE

Consider the very simple case where a number of subordinate managers are each in charge of operating units producing a single product, having identical characteristics and reporting to a single superior. We shall also suppose that all managers submit output budgets having an identical chance of achievement. Although this is an idealized situation it serves to illustrate some of the most important characteristics of the budget aggregation process.

For the sake of concreteness we shall assume that the underlying distribution of output follows a Normal distribution. This assumption is not necessary for the argument, which applies to any underlying distribution (including skew distributions), but it serves to keep illustrative computation to a minimum. Thus each individual manager's budget submission can be represented by the diagram shown in Fig. 13.2.

The shaded area on the diagram represents the probability that the budget submission will be achieved (or over-achieved). We may now calculate the probability that the sum of the budgets of all the unit managers, which has been aggregated by the senior manager to form his own budget, will be achieved in a particular case.

Let us suppose that the distribution of output has an expected value of 1,000 tons and a standard deviation of 200 tons for each manager. It may readily be demonstrated, using tables of the Normal distribution, that if a unit manager submits a budget of 1,104 tons such a budget will be attained approximately 30% of the time. Further assuming that we have nine such managers who operate units which are independent of each other

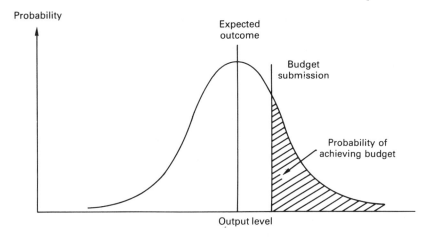

Fig. 13.2 A non-expecation budget based on a Normal distribution of output.

and who submit identical budgets, the senior manager will have an aggregate budget of (9 × 1,104) = 9,936 tons.

In order to calculate the likelihood of the senior manager achieving such an aggregate level of output it is necessary to note that the distribution of output for the senior manager is:

(a) also Normal in shape
(b) has an expected value of 9 × 1,000 = 9,000 tons
(c) has a standard deviation of $[\sqrt{(9 \times 200)^2}] = 600$ tons

A budget of 9,936 tons thus lies some [(9,936 − 9,000)/600] = 1.56 standard deviations from the mean and consequently has a probability of achievement of about 6%, as shown in Table 13.1.

The effect is thus quite startling. Each of nine managers submit budgets having the quite reasonable chance of achievement of 30%. When these are added together they result in a budget having the much reduced chance of achievement of 6%. A tight motivational budget aggregates into an impossible target. This is not a quirk of the particular figures, for, as Table 13.2 shows, the effect of aggregating budgets of varying degrees of difficulty produces similarly extreme effects.

It is evident that as the individual budget becomes attainable only slightly less than 50% of the time the aggregate budget's chance of attainment diminishes rapidly. Conversely, if the individual budget becomes attainable only slightly over 50% of the time then the attainment of the aggregate budget becomes a near certainty. To illustrate the point further, Table 13.3 gives the same information but for collections of subordinate managers varying in size from 2 to 100.

Inspection of Table 13.3 indicates that as the number of budgets aggregated increases the rate at which budgeting optimism expands is

Table 13.1 Aggregation of nine identical budget submissions

Unit	Expected Output	Standard Deviation	Submitted Budget having a 30% chance of Attainment
A	1,000	200	1,104
B	1,000	200	1,104
C	1,000	200	1,104
D	1,000	200	1,104
E	1,000	200	1,104
F	1,000	200	1,104
G	1,000	200	1,104
H	1,000	200	1,104
I	1,000	200	1,104
Aggregate	9,000	600	9,936

Aggregate budget has 6% chance of attainment as it lies $(9{,}936 - 9{,}000)/600 = 1.56$ standard deviations from its mean.

explosive. Even the mild optimism of a budget which is attainable 40% of the time becomes attainable only 10% of the time when 25 such budgets are aggregated. A target budget attainable on one occasion out of every five is attainable in aggregate on only one occasion in every hundred when as few as seven such budgets are aggregated. Thus the loss of credibility when quite mildly optimistic budgets are aggregated is a potentially serious problem.

Table 13.2 Probabilities of aggregate budget achievement when nine identical individual budgets are combined*

Probability of Individual Manager Attaining Budget (%)	Probability of Aggregate Budget being Attained (%)
90	99.994
80	99.400
70	94.200
60	77.500
50	50.000
40	22.500
30	5.800
20	0.600
10	0.006

*It should be noted that this Table is symmetrical about the 50% point. If $(100 -$ percentage) is calculated for any row, a duplicate of another row in the Table is found. This is a consequence of the Normal Distribution being symmetrical. Following Tables only consider chances of achievement less than 50% as the equivalent results for chances in excess of 50% can be calculated in a similar fashion.

Table 13.3 Probabilities of achievement of aggregate budget for varying numbers of unit budgets (%)

Number of Budgets Aggregated	*Probability of Unit Budget being Attained*								
	50%	*45%*	*40%*	*35%*	*30%*	*25%*	*20%*	*15%*	*10%*
2	50	43	36	29	23	17	12	7	4
3	50	41	33	25	18	12	7	4	1
4	50	40	31	21	15	9	5	2	0.5
5	50	39	29	19	12	7	3	1	0.2
6	50	38	27	17	10	5	2	0.6	0.1
7	50	37	25	15	8	4	1	0.3	*
8	50	36	24	14	7	3	0.9	0.2	*
9	50	35	22	12	6	2	0.6	0.1	*
10	50	34	21	11	5	2	0.4	*	*
12	50	33	19	9	4	1	0.2	*	*
14	50	32	17	8	3	0.6	0.1	*	*
16	50	31	16	6	2	0.3	*	*	*
18	50	30	14	5	1	0.2	*	*	*
20	50	29	13	4	1	0.1	*	*	*
25	50	26	10	3	0.4	*	*	*	*
30	50	25	8	2	0.2	*	*	*	*
40	50	21	5	0.7	*	*	*	*	*
50	50	19	4	0.3	*	*	*	*	*
100	50	10	0.6	*	*	*	*	*	*

* Less than 0.1%.

Table 13.4 Aggregation of budgets for units of different size but constant standard deviation

Unit	Expected Output	Standard Deviation	Submitted Budget having a 30% Chance of Attainment
A	500	200	604
B	625	200	729
C	750	200	854
D	875	200	979
E	1,000	200	1,104
F	1,250	200	1,354
G	1,500	200	1,604
H	1,750	200	1,854
I	2,000	200	2,104
Aggregate	10,250	600	11,186

Aggregate budget has a 6% chance of achievement as it lies $(11,186 - 10,250)/600 = 1.56$ standard deviations from its mean.

UNITS OF DIFFERENT SIZE

The simple example so far developed can be extended by considering non-identical operating units. A simple example of unit differences is where units are essentially similar, but differ solely in terms of their size. Perhaps a reasonable range to consider is where units range in size from one-half as large to double the size of some typical unit. Initially we will assume that the standard deviation of units' output does not vary, although this assumption will be relaxed as we proceed. The results of aggregation are shown in Table 13.4.

It can thus be seen that differences in size as such have no effect on the problems inherent in the aggregation process. However, it is likely that the standard deviation will also vary with unit size.

Table 13.5 shows the effect of aggregation where both size and standard deviation vary together in a linear fashion.

The results of aggregation are only slightly different in this case and the difference may be accounted for in the adjustment of the standard deviation for the typical unit (E) from 200 to 160 in order to keep the standard deviation of the aggregate constant from table to table.

Finally it may be argued that neither of the above examples is particularly realistic. The standard deviation of a unit's output is likely neither to remain constant regardless of size nor to vary in a strictly linear fashion. If the general argument of this paper is correct, it is perhaps most reasonable to suppose that the truth typically lies between these extremes and that the standard deviation is most likely to vary as the square root of unit size.[5] The results of aggregation under this assumption are shown in Table 13.6.

It is therefore apparent that regardless of the assumptions made about the way in which the standard deviation varies with size, a significant reduction in probability of aggregate budget achievement occurs when individually mildly optimistic budgets are aggregated.

INDEPENDENCE OF OPERATING UNITS

It has been assumed in the previous analysis that operating units are (statistically) independent of each other. That is, variations in the output of one unit are not related to variations in the output of other units. Such an assumption is undoubtedly plausible in some cases. For example, the output of coal from coal mines operated by the same concern tends to follow such a pattern, because variations in consumer demand are buffered by stockpiles and individual units attempt to maximize the output from a given set of physical resources. However, in other cases, it is likely that variations in economic conditions and other environmental factors

---

[5] The basis of this argument is that successive increments of output are independent of each other. Thus is a unit is doubled in size the standard deviation of its output will increase, but only by a factor of $\sqrt{2}$. This argument is essentially similar to that illustrated for a nine-fold aggregation in Table 13.1.

Table 13.5 Aggregation of budgets for units of different size and standard deviations

Unit	Expected Output	Standard Deviation	Submitted Budget having a 30% Chance of Attainment
A	500	80	542
B	625	100	677
C	750	120	813
D	875	140	948
E	1,000	160	1,084
F	1,250	200	1,355
G	1,500	240	1,626
H	1,750	280	1,897
I	2,000	320	2,168
Aggregate	10,250	600 *(approx)*	11,110

Aggregate budget has a 6% chance of achievement as it lies $(11,174 - 10,250)/600 = 1.53$ standard deviations from its mean.

will affect all units simultaneously and thus cause correlated changes in unit outputs. For example, the sales of different shops selling the same products in a retail chain will tend to show some correlation with each other. The result of such correlation will be to reduce the aggregation effect demonstrated above. However, even quite high levels of correlation will only reduce the effect rather than eliminating it.

Thus although the existence of interdependence between operating units reduces the effect discussed here, to remove it altogether would require

Table 13.6 Aggregation of budgets for units of different size with standard deviation proportional to the square root of size

Unit	Expected Output	Standard Deviation	Submitted Budget having a 30% Chance of Attainment
A	500	135	571
B	625	145	701
C	750	160	834
D	875	175	967
E	1,000	190	1,100
F	1,250	210	1,360
G	1,500	230	1,621
H	1,750	250	1,881
I	2,000	265	2,139
Aggregate	10,250	600	11,174

Aggregate budget has a 6% chance of achievement as it lies $(11,174 - 10,250)/600 = 1.53$ standard deviations from its mean.

perfect correlation, a condition most unlikely to occur in practice. Again, the degree of independence of operating units can be established empirically in practical applications.

THE RESULTS SO FAR

We have noted the following effects:

(a) Budget estimates which are initially submitted as mildly optimistic forecasts become grossly optimistic when aggregated. Conversely, estimates which are initially pessimistic aggregate into grossly pessimistic estimates.
(b) This effect becomes more pronounced
    (i)   the greater the degree of initial optimism (or pessimism);
    (ii) the greater the number of units that are aggregated;
    (iii) the greater the degree of independence between operating units.
(c) Quite reasonable degrees of optimism from relatively small numbers of managers give rise to marked changes in probabilities of achievement, e.g.
    (i)   9 managers submitting budgets with a 30% chance of achievement yields an aggregate budget having only a 6% chance of achievement.
    (ii) 20 managers submitting budgets with a 40% chance of achievement yields an aggregate budget having only a 13% chance of achievement.
    Although these results refer to the case of complete independence, there would still be significant differences in the likelihood with which unit and aggregated budgets would be met, even when quite high levels of interdependence exist.

A POSSIBLE SOLUTION

It is evident that the effect discussed in this paper can be very serious. It is particularly potent in that it becomes more extreme as one ascends the organizational hierarchy. Herbert Simon once pointed out that if in a five-tier organization each subordinate told his boss 90 per cent of the truth the overall superior would hear only two-thirds of the truth. If a span of control of eight subordinates at each level is assumed, it can be calculated that if each subordinate submits a budget having a 49% chance of attainment (i.e. a chance only 1% different to evens) the aggregate budget is attainable only 5% of the time. Evidently some mechanism for dealing with this escalation of optimism is required.

    Not surprisingly, organizations have developed methods of coping with this problem.[6] Most budget procedures have some mechanism to allow

[6] For two case studies illustrating different budget processes see Berry, A.J. and Otley, D.T., 'The Aggregation of Estimates in Hierarchical Organisations', *Journal of Management Studies*, May 1975, pp. 175–193.

Table 13.7   Effect of reduction of aggregate budget on size and probability of attainment of unit budgets

	Original Budget	*Amended Budget*
Unit	1,104 (30%)	1,035 (43%)
Aggregate	9,936 (6%)	9,315 (30%)

superiors to adjust the budget estimates submitted by their subordinates so as to produce better estimates at each hierarchical level. If the global estimate appears too optimistic then it is reduced. However, perhaps for the sake of arithmetic tidiness, the figures that comprise the aggregate are also reduced, often in proportion to the original submissions. That is, it is ensured that the revised budget estimates add up to the amended budget total. The remainder of this paper concerns itself with showing how this requirement of arithmetic balancing can produce some unfortunate side-effects.

THE ORIGINAL CASE

When applied to the original example, the result of budget amendment in this way is unremarkable. In Table 13.1, individual budgets having a 30% chance of attainment were aggregated into an overall budget which has shown to have a 6% chance of attainment. Let us suppose that it is desired to increase this 6% chance to a 30% chance. To do this the aggregate budget must be reduced from 9,936 to 9,315, that is a reduction of 621. If this is allocated equally between the nine units each of their budgets is reduced from 1,104 to 1,035. These amended budgets can be shown to have a 43% chance of attainment. The result of the operation is summarized in Table 13.7.

It can be seen that, although unit budgets still remain easier to achieve than the aggregate budget, the effect of reducing each unit budget *pro rata* to the aggregate reduction leaves each unit budget with an equally enhanced probability of attainment. The degree of optimism remaining in the unit budgets can be seen by making corresponding calculations for all the cases shown in Table 13.2, with results as shown in Table 13.8.

Thus, in the case of identical operating units, a simple *pro rata* operation appears to produce results which are at least equitable between individual units, although their motivational impact is likely to have been altered.

UNITS OF DIFFERENT SIZE

However, it is when the above method is applied to units of different size that problems arise. To illustrate these problems we will apply the method to the examples already given in Table 13.4, 13.5 and 13.6, which yield the results given in Tables 13.9, 13.10 and 13.11. Inspection of these Tables

Table 13.8 Probabilities of unit budget attainment when aggregate is adjusted to same probability as original unit submissions (9 units)

Probability of Original Unit Budget being Attained (%)	Probability of Original Aggregate being Attained (%)	Probability of Revised Aggregate being Attained (%)	Probability of Revised Unit Budget being Attained (%)
90	99.994	90	66.5
80	99.4	80	61.0
70	94.2	70	57.0
60	77.5	60	53.4
50	50	50	50
40	22.5	40	46.6
30	5.8	30	43.0
20	0.6	20	39.0
10	0.006	10	33.5

indicates that, in general, the *pro rata* method of budget amendment gives rise to a further problem. Although the average probability of attainment for the revised unit budget still remains around 42%, different units now have significantly different chances of attaining their budget ranging from 36% to 52% in the case of a constant standard deviation and 38% to 46% in the more realistic case of a standard deviation which varies as the square root of unit size. Only when the standard deviation is linearly proportional to the unit size does the difference disappear. Except in this

Table 13.9 Budget amendment: units of different size but constant standard deviation

Unit	Expected Output	Standard Deviation	Original Submission (30%)	Revised Submissions	Probabilities of Attainment (%)
A	500	200	604	570	36.3
B	625	200	729	688	37.6
C	750	200	854	807	38.8
D	875	200	979	925	40.1
E	1,000	200	1,104	1,043	41.5
F	1,250	200	1,354	1,279	44.2
G	1,500	200	1,604	1,515	47.0
H	1,750	200	1,854	1,751	49.8
I	2,000	200	2,104	1,987	52.2
Aggregate	10,250	600	11,186 (6%)	10,565 (30%)	

Table 13.10 Budget amendment: units of different size and standard deviation

Unit	Expected Output	Standard Deviation	Original Submission (30%)	Revised Submission	Probability of Attainment (%)
A	500	80	542	515	42.5
B	625	100	677	644	42.5
C	750	120	813	773	42.5
D	875	140	948	901	42.5
E	1,000	160	1,084	1,031	42.5
F	1,250	200	1,355	1,289	42.5
G	1,500	240	1,626	1,546	42.5
H	1,750	280	1,897	1,804	42.5
I	2,000	320	2,168	2,062	42.5
Aggregate	10,250	600 (*approx*)	11,110 (7%)	10,565 (30%)	

special case, the apparently straightforward method of budget amendment *pro rata* to the original budget submissions produces inequities between operating units. In particular it should be noted that the larger units get the better deal; smaller units get relatively unfavourable treatment.

Despite this inequity it might be argued that in realistic cases the size of the discrepancy is relatively small and can be ignored. Whereas this may be arguable in the above examples where standard deviations are small in comparison with means, this does not always hold. Most importantly it usually does not hold when profit budgets are considered.

Table 13.11 Budget amendment: units of different size with standard deviation proportional to the square root of size

Unit	Expected Output	Standard Deviation	Original Submission (30%)	Revised Submission	Probability of Attainment (%)
A	500	135	571	540	38.4
B	625	145	701	663	39.7
C	750	160	834	788	40.6
D	875	175	967	914	41.2
E	1,000	190	1,100	1,040	41.6
F	1,250	210	1,360	1,286	43.2
G	1,500	230	1,621	1,533	44.5
H	1,750	250	1,881	1,778	45.4
I	2,000	265	2,139	2,023	46.5
Aggregate	10,250	600 (*approx*)	11,174 (6%)	10,565 (30%)	

Table 13.12 Profit budgets for nine identical units

Unit	Expected Profit	Standard Deviation	Budget Submission (30%)	Revised Budget	Probability of Attainment (%)
A	100	200	205	135	43.0
B	100	200	205	135	43.0
C	100	200	205	135	43.0
D	100	200	205	135	43.0
E	100	200	205	135	43.0
F	100	200	205	135	43.0
G	100	200	205	135	43.0
H	100	200	205	135	43.0
I	100	200	205	135	43.0
Aggregate	900	600	1,845 (6%)	1,215 (30%)	

APPLICATION TO PROFIT BUDGETS

In this context the most important feature of a profit budget is that it represents a small difference between two relatively large and uncertain estimates, that is revenues and costs. In statistical terms this implies that the standard deviation of profit will be large relative to its absolute value. Thus it would be quite reasonable to expect profits of, say, £100 but having a standard deviation of £200, implying that one has 95% confidence that the final figure will lie between a profit of £500 and a loss of £300. The application of our budgetary procedures to nine identical such units is shown in Table 13.12.

So far no problems are apparent, but the situation is similar to that outlined in Table 13.7. Where all units are identical most budgetary processes produce similar and non-controversial results. However, we now turn to units expected to produce dissimilar levels of profit. We shall assume that the standard deviation of profit is the same for all units, which is perhaps reasonably realistic. If not, the effect of having different standard deviations will be to increase the variability between units above that shown in Table 13.13.

Inspection of Table 13.13 shows a similar pattern to that found in Table 13.9, but in a much more extreme form. The budget amendments used to give the revised budgets for each unit are obviously quite inappropriate. Large budgeted losses are reduced, making them even less likely to be achieved, whereas large budgeted profits are also reduced giving them much improved chances of being attained. Note also that a budget submission of zero profit would always remain as zero regardless of the underlying circumstances. Evidently the *pro rata* reduction of budget submissions gives absurd results and would almost certainly never be used in practice on profit budgets.

Table 13.13 Profit budgets for nine dissimilar units

Unit	Expected Profit	Standard Deviation	Budget Submission (30%)	Revised Budget	Probability of Attainment (%)
A	−400	200	−295	−98	6
B	−300	200	−195	−65	12
C	−200	200	−95	−32	20
D	−100	200	5	2	31
E	0	200	105	35	43
F	100	200	205	68	56
G	200	200	305	102	69
H	300	200	405	135	80
I	400	200	505	168	88
Aggregate	0	600	945 (6%)	315 (30%)	

However, it is worthwhile to ponder over the figures to consider what kind of amendment process would give more sensible results. What seems to be required is a reduction of all budget submissions by a similar amount. Perhaps the difference between the aggregate submission and the revised aggregate could be evenly spread over all budget submissions i.e. $(945 − 315)/9 = 70$. The results of this process are shown in Table 13.14.

This has obviously achieved the desired result, namely an equitable distribution of the budget reduction to each unit. And this example can give us the clue in devising a basis for a fair means of allocating budget changes in the more general case. For the method works here because the standard deviations in Table 13.14 are identical for all units.

Table 13.14 Porfit budgets amended by equal deductions

Unit	Expected Profit	Standard Deviation	Budget Submission (30%)	Revised Budget	Probability of Attainment (%)
A	−400	200	−295	−365	43
B	−300	200	−195	−265	43
C	−200	200	−95	−165	43
D	−100	200	5	−65	43
E	0	200	105	35	43
F	100	200	205	135	43
G	200	200	305	235	43
H	300	200	405	335	43
I	400	200	505	435	43
Aggregate	0	600	945 (6%)	315 (30%)	

A GENERAL METHOD

The previous result can now be generalized. The expected value of a budget submission is irrelevant to any proposed modification process designed to give equitable results. It is the variability of the output process, measured here by the standard deviation, that is of paramount importance. *Thus, to preserve equity any change in an aggregate budget estimate should be allocated to units in proportion to the standard deviation of their estimates rather than in proportion to the absolute value of the estimates themselves.*

This result indicates why we found no problem in allocating budget changes to identical units, and also why Table 13.10 somewhat unexpectedly turned out to show an equitable distribution (for in the case discussed there, standard deviations were proportional to expected values and thus to unit budget submissions).

To illustrate the point we will rework the budget amendment process according to our new model for the data originally shown in Table 13.11. That is, the difference in the aggregate budget submission and the revised aggregate will be allocated to units in proportion to their standard deviations giving the results shown in Table 13.15.

It can be seen that this method produces the desired equitable result although there will always be a difference between the units' chance of attaining their individual budgets and the chance of the aggregate budget being achieved (unless these are both 50%). To avoid this latter effect would require the sacrifice of a certain amount of arithmetic tidiness, namely that the budgets would no longer add up. However, it can now be seen that there may be strong arguments in favour of non-additive budgets. For example, to preserve equity between operating units and the aggregate corporate entity, it might be most fair to keep the original budget submissions of the units (as shown in Table 13.15) whilst reducing the aggregate budget from the arithmetic sum of the unit budgets to the figure having a 30% chance of attainment itself (10,565 tons). No doubt the difference between the two figures could be carried in an account similar to that used for planning variances[7] and perhaps be called a motivational variance!

This would also overcome a severe practical difficulty, namely that although the original *pro rata* amendment is easily implemented in practice (because all the information required is in the budget submissions themselves) the proposed amendment method requires knowledge of standard deviations which are not easily estimated. Equitable amendment may therefore pose great practical problems in implementation, regardless of the possible behavioural effects on unit managers.

One objection to the analysis that has been conducted is that it has assumed that all unit managers have biased their budget estimates in the same direction. That is, all budget estimates are either above or below

---

[7] See, for example, the discussion in Amey, L.R. and Egginton, D., *Management Accounting: A Conceptual Approach*, (London, Longmans, 1973) Chapter 15, p. 490.

Table 13.15 The general method illustrated

Unit	Expected Output	Standard Deviation	Original Budget Submission (30%)	Revised Budget	Probability of Attainment (%)
A	500	135	571	524	43
B	625	145	701	651	43
C	750	160	834	779	43
D	875	175	967	906	43
E	1,000	190	1,100	1,034	43
F	1,250	210	1,360	1,287	43
G	1,500	230	1,621	1,542	43
H	1,750	250	1,881	1,794	43
I	2,000	265	2,139	2,048	43
Aggregate	10,250	600 (*approx*)	11,174 (6%)	10,565 (30%)	

Note: The sum of the standard deviations is 1,760. The difference between the revised aggregate and the aggregate submission (i.e. 10,565 − 11,174 = −609) is divided between units *pro rata* to their standard deviation, e.g. unit A's submission of 571 is reduced by (135 × 609/1,760) = 47 units, giving a revised budget of 524.

the expected outcome by an amount that gives them identical chances of attainment. Desirable though such a state of affairs might be, it would be most unusual for subordinates to behave in identical ways. Indeed the common 'swings and roundabouts' view would suggest that there is wide variation in budget estimates with optimism and pessimism both represented.

When such budget estimates are aggregated the overall estimate may be close to its expected value (if optimism and pessimism act so as to cancel each other out), but this is largely accidental. If the aggregate budget is in need of amendment, uniform treatment of all units produces unequal results as shown in Figure 13.3.

Although the optimistic budget now becomes easier to achieve the pessimistic budget is reduced even further. Presumably what is required is an amendment which brings both figures closer to the mean value. This result is unlikely to be achieved by any budgetary technique, but requires the individual consideration of each budget submission by an experienced and well-informed superior. The essential point still holds, namely that rules of thumb can produce effects which differ from unit to unit because they ignore rather than illuminate the underlying issues.

Our conclusion is therefore that the techniques of budgetary manipulation and aggregation should be adjusted to meet the needs of the budgetary process, rather than imposing arbitrary rules of thumb which distort the underlying processes. In particular, if it is accepted that budget estimates may legitimately be set at levels that represent other than expected

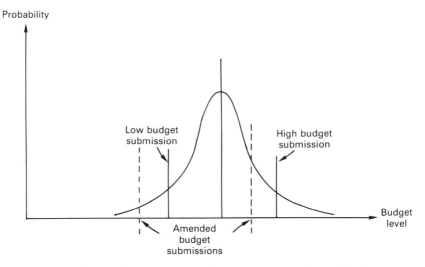

Fig. 13.3 Amendment of optimistic and pessimistic budget submissions.

outcomes, possibly because the underlying distributions are skew, then more sophisticated means of aggregation than simple addition are required. In some cases it may be that arithmetic tidiness should be sacrificed in order to preserve other features of the budgetary process, and that we need to learn to live with budgets that don't add up.

CONCLUSIONS

It has been shown that if budget estimates submitted by unit managers represent anything other than their expectation of average performance over the budget period, then the aggregation of such estimates will produce a figure having a more extreme chance of attainment than the original budget submissions. Slightly biased estimates at unit level rapidly become quite unrealistic estimates when added together in sufficient numbers.

Common methods of dealing with this effect on an intuitive basis, such as proportional changes in units' budget submissions, have two effects. Firstly, they may cause inequities between individual units. Secondly, even equitable methods of budget amendment still cause a different chance of attainment between unit and aggregate budgets. A method of dealing with the first problem is proposed, although it requires information that is unlikely to be easily available, and may also cause motivational problems. However, it does not affect the second problem which is a consequence of insisting that budget figures should add up arithmetically into an overall aggregate budget.

It is our contention that arithmetic additivity is an inappropriate requirement for budgets which represent anything other than a statistical expectation. As there are strong arguments to suggest that many budgets legitimately differ from statistical expectations, insisting on arithmetic additivity is likely to produce a variety of undesirable side-effects. The budget process should therefore be tailored to fit the characteristics of the situation in which it is to work and estimates should be adjusted to give the desired chances of attainment at each level. If the situation requires non-mean budget estimates then these should be used, but the aggregation of such estimates is a more complex process than simple addition, and requires the application of a certain amount of statistical expertise. Thus when combining budget estimates, perhaps the figures shouldn't always add up!

14

Measuring manufacturing performance: a new challenge for managerial accounting research

Robert S. Kaplan

Dean of the Graduate School of Industrial Administration, Carnegie-Mellon University

ABSTRACT

Problems with the performance of U.S. manufacturing firms have become obvious in recent years. Japanese and Western European manufacturers are able to produce higher quality goods with fewer workers and lower inventory levels than comparable U.S. firms. The ability of foreign firms to become more efficient producers has gone largely unnoticed in the education and research programs of many U.S. business schools. A much greater commitment to understanding the factors critical to the success of manufacturing firms is needed. While an understanding of the determinants for successful manufacturing performance will require contributions from many disciplines, accounting can play a critical role in this effort. Accounting researchers can attempt to develop non-financial measures of manufacturing performance, such as productivity, quality, and inventory costs. Measures of product leadership, manufacturing flexibility, and delivery performance could be developed for firms bringing new products to the marketplace. Expanded performance measures are also necessary for capital budgeting procedures and to monitor production using the new technology of flexible manufacturing systems. A particular challenge is to de-emphasize the current focus of senior managers on simple, aggregate, short-term financial measures and to develop indicators that are more consistent with long-term competitiveness and profitability.

MANUFACTURING PERFORMANCE

Problems with U.S. manufacturing performance have become painfully

Source: Kaplan, R.S. (1983) *The Accounting Review*, **LVIII** *(4), pp. 686–705.*

obvious in recent years.[1] As a vivid example, consider the following dramatic comparison:[2]

Ford Motor Company's better plants turn out an average of two engines a day per employee using 777 square feet of plant space; the plants have up to three weeks of backup inventory and use over 200 labor classifications. In contrast, a Toyota plant turns out nine engines a day per employee, or more than four times as many as Ford's; it uses only 454 square feet of plant space per engine, or less than 60 percent of Ford's. A Toyota plant has only one hour of backup inventory and only seven labor classification, less than 4 percent of Ford's.

Two basic industries, automotive and steel, are finding it increasingly difficult to compete with foreign manufacturers, and other industries, including machine tools, and many branches of electronics, are also feeling highly competitive pressures from overseas.[3]

Some believe that cultural and environmental differences are responsible for the superior manufacturing performance of Japanese firms and that these differences limit the relevance and transferability of Japanese management practices to the U.S. In comparing the U.S. and Japanese experience, one can easily observe important differences between the two countries, attempt to take comfort in such differences, and thereby believe that the adoption of various Japanese management practices would not create value in U.S. companies. But one would then have to confront the evidence presented in Hayes (1981) and Schonberger (1982) that many of the successful practices in Japan require only a management commitment to improve manufacturing performance through procedures and investments that would seem to have easy transferability to U.S. firms. For example,

- General Motors, by switching from every other day rail deliveries of a body part, at a Buick plant, to three truck deliveries per day, was able to reduce its inventory of this part by more than 80 percent.
- Ford, following a two-year effort to coordinate better its deliveries from suppliers, was able to reduce overall inventories by $750 million, reducing inventory carrying costs by about $250 million per year.[4]
- Matsushita took over a Motorola television plant in the U.S. and over an eight-year period, using essentially the same workforce, was able to

[1] Hayes and Abernathy (1980), an award-winning *and* widely read article, provides an excellent summary of problems with U.S. manufacturing performance.
[2] This quote appeared in a report, 'The U.S. Competitive Position in the 1980's ... and Some Things We Can Do About It,' published by the Center for International Business. The comparison has been verified, independently, as reported by Murrin (1982).
[3] Hayes (1981) and Hayes and Limprecht (1982) describe how Japanese and German manufacturers have been able to become effective worldwide competitors through a commitment to high-quality, efficient production.
[4] These observations were in Koten (1982).

increase production volume by 40 percent while reducing defects from 150 per 100 sets produced to three defects per 100 sets produced. In the Japanese parent company, the factory measured defect rate is 0.5 per 100 sets.

- Sony and Honda in U.S. manufacturing facilities have achieved the lowest defect rates in their respective industries. Both companies have enjoyed expanded market shares and are increasing their investment in U.S. manufacturing facilities.
- Sanyo took over a television assembly plant in Arkansas and, without any substantial change in manufacturing equipment, was able to cut the defect rate by 30 percent in two months.[5]
- A Hewlett-Packard division estimates that the ultimate result of supplanting the usual detect-and-fix methodology with a zero-defects philosophy could be a 33-percent reduction in factory workers, a 25-percent savings in manufacturing floor space, and a 66-percent decrease in inventories (Business Week, 1982; p. 66).

These examples suggest that attention to quality control and reduced inventory levels will achieve significant savings in the U.S. environment with U.S. workers. None of the management techniques is 'new' and all probably can be traced to practices started by some U.S. firms decades ago. But these practices have not been widely used by U.S. firms until very recently.

The objective of pointing out the benefits that accrue from greater attention to quality production and inventory management techniques is to illustrate the opportunities for substantial improvements in U.S. manufacturing performance that do not require major investments in sophisticated machinery. They do require, however, that we think differently about managing our manufacturing operations. Improved procedures must be developed, tested, and validated in U.S. firms, not simply transferred from a company in another nation to one in the U.S. We should learn from the experience of many Western European and Japanese firms that substantial improvements in the manufacturing performance of U.S. firms are both possible and necessary. This implies an active role for U.S. managers and academics to develop techniques that are most appropriate in the U.S. environment and that will, eventually, enable the U.S. to regain worldwide leadership in manufacturing technology and management.

ROLE FOR MANAGERIAL ACCOUNTING

The challenge of improving a firm's manufacturing performance is particularly relevant for managerial accountants. The firm's cost or managerial accounting system is supposed to provide information useful for managers' planning and control decisions. During the past 25 years, the disciplines of operations research, probability, statistics, and economics have been applied to cost accounting topics. But the cost accounting model

---

[5] See Takeuchi (1981), Tsurumi (1981), and Schonberger (1982; Chapter 3).

used, for all these developments, is based on the mass production of a mature product with known characteristics and a stable technology. The research has also accepted the production setting as given and attempted to derive optimal decisions in a well-specified and stable environment, where the cost structure (such as the existence of fixed costs or production setup costs) and the uncertainty (in demand, in actual costs, or in delivery times) are assumed exogenous to the model.

The recent experience in the organization and technology of manufacturing operations suggests that these assumptions – stable product characteristics and passive optimizing models – are inappropriate. That is, the production function assumed in all our analytic models is badly misspecified. U.S. manufacturers are learning from their overseas competitors, particularly the Japanese, that they must not accept the current production environment as a given and implement policies that are 'optimal' with respect to these existing conditions. Rather, managers must intervene actively in the production process to improve quality, reduce set-up times, increase manufacturing flexibility, overcome restrictive workforce rules, and reduce randomness caused by uncertain supply, poor quality, and erratic machine performance. Firms that wish to be world-class manufacturers must produce goods of substantially higher quality with greatly reduced inventory levels, shorter set-up times and production runs, and lower uncertainty in the overall production process than presently exists.

Traditional cost accounting systems based on an assumption of long production runs of a standard product, with unchanging characteristics and specifications, will not be relevant in this new environment. The challenge is to devise new internal accounting systems that will be supportive of the firm's new manufacturing strategy. Improved measures of quality, inventory performance, productivity, flexibility, and innovation will be required. Managerial performance measures based on achieving these manufacturing goals should be developed to replace the current emphasis on short-term financial performance measures.

This is not an easy research agenda. It will require researchers to become more familiar and more actively involved with actual manufacturing operations. It is a significant departure from the current research strategy of managerial accountants who are applying analytic tools from other disciplines to a stylized, simplified, and perhaps obsolete representation of manufacturing operations. In subsequent sections of the paper, I will describe the opportunities for new research directions to develop improved measurements of manufacturing performance.

Clearly, though, accounting is only one discipline among many that must be mobilized to improve manufacturing performance. The development of improved manufacturing processes will require the active involvement and contributions of many fields of engineering. Expertise from computer science, robotics, and statistics (especially the design of experiments for improving manufacturing processes) will also be necessary. Within business schools, the fields of operations management, management information systems, organizational behavior, industrial relations, and corporate strategy must play key roles. The study of tech-nological innovation, market structure, and supplier-customer relations will require insights from economics. For the remainder of this paper, though, I will exploit my own comparative advantage and emphasize more the opportunities for accounting research in manufacturing. In par-ticular, I will attempt to identify new areas of inquiry for management accounting research in measuring and evaluating manufacturing per-formance. While accounting can not play the key role in initiating or implementing technological innovations and organizational change, the accounting system should provide incentives for improving manufacturing performance and measurements to evaluate progress toward this goal.

MISSING MEASUREMENTS

What types of measurements are available to monitor the performance of manufacturing organizations? Let us look first at the production of a mature product, with relatively stable characteristics. In this situation, competition among firms will be on the basis of quality, cost minimiz-ation, and productivity.

1. Quality

Product quality is emerging as perhaps the most important manufacturing performance area. One of the great success stories of Japanese manufac-turing derives from a dedication to eliminating all product defects.[6] Many U.S. manufacturers have seemingly adopted a strategy of 'let's get the product out the door and if something is wrong, we'll fix it in the field.' A different version of this strategy, as part of normal manufacturing pro-cedure, has components inspected after each stage of manufacture and returned to the previous stage if a defect is found. Thus, U.S. firms typi-cally inspect quality into products. They define an Acceptable Quality Level (AQL) and accept lots when the defect rate is at or below the preset percentage.

The Japanese, in contrast, have adopted a philosophy that all defects can be eliminated. They reject the AQL approach since they do not believe that any given level of defects is acceptable. Quality is thought and planned into the product at all stages of manufacture, including engineering de-sign, supplier specifications, and training of employees (see Juran (1978)).

It is ironic that much of the original impetus to the Japanese for high quality production came from two Americans, Edward Deming and J.M. Juran. But the Japanese have now gone well beyond both in their com-mitment to quality. They no longer are content with a state of statistical control in which only one percent or 0.5 percent of the output fails to meet predetermined standards. Rather, the goal is to achieve zero defects. Defects, in many Japanese plants, are measured in parts per million. Japanese managers have the attitude that 'a defect is a treasure,' not only since defects now occur rarely but also, more importantly, because when

---

[6] See Hayes (1981), Wheelwright (1981), and Schonberger (1982).

one is found, the defect can be studied to find out how it occurred. If the circumstances that led to the incidence of the defect can be determined, then perhaps such a defect can be prevented from happening again.

Most remarkably, advocates of the zero defect approach believe that there is no trade-off between cost and quality (see, for example, Crosby (1979)). These executives claim that total long-term manufacturing costs decrease as the percentage of defects decreases. That is, a manufacturing system with one percent defects will have lower long-run operating costs than one with five percent defects, and a system with 0.1 percent defects will have lower total costs than one with one percent defects. Thus, a continuous drive to reduce defects will enhance the long-run productivity of the production process. Quality is increasingly being viewed as a key feature for improving market share and profit margins (Business Week, 1982, p. 68).

The implications of adopting the zero defect approach in a factory seem obvious. Clearly, the incidence of defects at each stage of the manufacturing process, starting from the quality of goods received from suppliers, would seem to be a valuable periodic performance measure. The Japanese have extensive and highly visible measures of quality throughout their factories. One U.S. executive, after returning from a trip to Japan, asked at one of his plants what fraction of products made it all the way through the manufacturing process without rework. This statistic was not then collected and was not, therefore, available to the executive. Not surprisingly, given that no one was evaluated by this criterion, the data, when finally collected, revealed that fewer than ten percent of the items made it through the process without rework. A program was soon initiated to improve this situation. Within one year, the fraction making it through the first time had increased to 60 percent. Also, with the higher yield, the work force devoted to this product was reduced from 400 to 300 (while still achieving the same output of finished products). Thus, a second quality-related measurement would be to document the reduction (if any) in total manufacturing cost that resulted from an increase in quality and a decrease in defects. This measurement leads to a third task: if manufacturing costs decrease as quality increases, then the financial justification for new capital equipment, including robots, should include not only the anticipated labor savings but also the savings in manufacturing cost from achieving a lower incidence of defects. Thus, measurements of quality and attempts to begin to understand the relationship between higher quality and lower costs (including testing whether this relationship does hold in practice) would seem to be new, worthwhile research areas.[7]

2. Inventory

U.S. business schools, and operations research and industrial engineering departments, have been studying and optimizing inventory models for

---

[7] See Fine (1982) for an interesting optimizing model where increasing quality reduces overall costs.

more than 25 years. By now, graduates of these schools are well versed in all manner of inventory models including those with different shaped cost functions, uncertain demand and lead times, varying demand requirements, and production smoothing models. All cost and management accounting textbooks have a section or an entire chapter devoted to a discussion of simple inventory models, with particular attention paid to estimating the actual and opportunity costs of operating an inventory management system. Surely, unlike the situation with quality measurements, the extensive research, writing, and teaching of inventory theory must make this aspect of manufacturing an area in which U.S. firms are well ahead of their foreign competitors.

Unfortunately, despite the extensive literature on optimizing inventory models, evidence is accumulating that U.S. companies do not operate the most effective inventory systems. Apparently, we adopted too narrow a focus by concentrating on optimizing with respect to a given set of parameters. Our attention was limited to estimating the costs and parameters of existing manufacturing systems and computing the optimal inventory policy with respect to these parameters.

There are several factors that cause firms to hold inventory. In the simple, deterministic EOQ inventory model, the set-up cost of initiating a new production run or switching from one model to another generates a preference for production runs longer than what is needed for immediate demand. If set-up costs could be driven toward zero, production could be matched closely with demand, thereby virtually eliminating this transaction motive for holding inventory. In more complex inventory situations, uncertainty in supply of materials or in final demand creates a demand for larger inventories. If delivery and demand uncertainties could be reduced, firms would hold less inventory of raw materials and finished goods. A third reason for holding inventory, especially work-in-process inventory, is to enable the assembly line to continue to operate even when one or more stations at the assembly line have stopped because of breakdowns or the need to rework sub-standard output. Inventory, in this setting, provides a buffer at each work station so that the entire production line is not halted when a stoppage occurs at an individual work station.

While these motives may not have been explicitly in the mind of Japanese executives, one can observe how, without the benefit of formal training and experience with mathematical inventory models, these executives were able to take actions that worked together to effect substantial reductions in inventory costs. First, rather than use the EOQ formula to compute an optimal production run size that balanced set-up and holding costs, they determined that it was cheaper to attempt to eliminate the set-up cost entirely. In cases where the set-up cost is difficult to eliminate, the Japanese opted to produce fewer versions of the basic product.

The automobile industry provides a specific example of how this policy is implemented. In the U.S. a changeover in the metal stamping of major parts (such as hoods and fenders) from one model to another can take about six hours. In the 1950s, the Japanese automobile companies had changeover times, for comparable processes, of three to four hours. By

1975, the changeover time had been reduced to 15 minutes and by 1980, the changeover time in a Toyota plant was reduced to three to five minutes.[8] The difference in inventory levels required when changeover times differ by a factor of 100 should be obvious. By going beyond a simple static analysis of a manufacturing process, the Japanese manufacturing executives have been able to change the rules of the game.

The Japanese have also reduced inventory by reducing uncertainty in deliveries from suppliers and by much tighter scheduling within the factory. Extremely close coordination with suppliers (including up to four deliveries per day) and simple but highly effective production scheduling and information systems enable many Japanese factories to run virtually without any raw material, work-in-process, or even finished goods inventory. The Kanban or 'Just-in-Time' inventory system, developed by Toyota in the 1960s and now widely used by many other large Japanese assembly companies, is a manufacturing control system that enables materials, parts, and components to be produced just before they are needed. The close coordination with suppliers also ensures that suppliers do not need to carry large quantities of inventory themselves.

The Japanese commitment to eliminate defects and machine breakdowns is an additional factor that contributes to significant reductions in work-in-process inventory. U.S. visitors to Japanese factories are frequently surprised by the virtual absence of inventory on the factory floor. The goal of zero defects, the absence of rework, the regular and preventive maintenance of machines, and the operation of these machines without overload and well within their performance specifications, all contribute to a system that can operate at minimal, if not zero, inventory levels.[9]

What are the implications of an approach that does not attempt to minimize inventory costs with respect to a fixed set of costs and parameters, but rather has as its goal to change the costs and parameters of a production process until it is not longer necessary to have any inventory? First, we should be more candid when we instruct out students that our mathematical models do not capture the large savings in inventory costs that could occur were the firm to undertake investment projects to reduce set-up costs or to schedule deliveries and production so that there was less overall uncertainty in the production system. In fact, before teaching any traditional optimizing inventory models, such as the EOQ approach, we should probably first instruct our students in inventory management systems, such as Kanban, OPT and MRP.[10]

Second, we should try to develop teaching examples where an investment in a new piece of equipment is justified not just by labor or energy savings, but because it permits more flexible or more reliable production

---

[8] These observations are taken from Hayes (1981), Monden (1981a) and Tsurumi (1982).
[9] See the discussion in Hayes (1981) Monden (1981a, b, c, d), and Schonberger (1982).
[10] See the discussion in Fox (1982) for a comparison of these three inventory control systems.

scheduling that will reduce inventory levels and, consequently, reduce total inventory costs. Third, we can attempt to devise procedures to estimate the cost savings from introducing new procedures or new equipment that will reduce overall inventory levels. Finally, we should all be reminded that any model is a simplified representation of an actual process. Elaborate optimizing procedures on overly simplified and static representations of a production setting may be less insightful than considering simple and seemingly obvious systematic changes in the parameters of the process itself. That is, instead of optimizing with respect to a given set of parameters, consider optimizing the parameters themselves to reduce overall manufacturing costs. Thus, instead of devising exotic mathematical inventory models to optimize with respect to uncertain demand and uncertain lead times, we can attempt to devise procedures and information systems to reduce uncertainty in demand and in production, and perhaps eliminate the uncertainty entirely.

3. Productivity

A productivity measure, the ratio of the outputs produced to the physical inputs consumed, is the most obvious choice for characterizing efficiency in a manufacturing setting. Productivity measurement at the firm or divisional level, though, has not received the same attention as has productivity measurement at the national, macro-economic level. Nevertheless, a number of serious and sensible studies on local productivity measures are available and could be (and have been) implemented.[11]

Productivity measurements should be useful supplements to traditional financial measures of manufacturing performance. They highlight improvements from physical operations, abstracting away from changes caused by variations in the relative prices of input factors. Traditional financial measures either concentrate on narrowly defined measures (yield and usage variances) or confound relative price effects of input factors, such as labor, material, and energy, with changes in productive efficiency. Thus, in principle, productivity measures can provide a comprehensive measure of the real efficiency gains, the ratio of outputs produced to inputs consumed, from improved production and management procedures. Productivity measurements will not replace traditional financial summary measures but should be a useful supplement enabling the analyst to separate variances due to relative price changes from those due to changes in production efficiencies.

A detailed discussion of productivity measurement is beyond the scope of this paper, but it is interesting to note that cost accounting texts do not contain even a minimal discussion of techniques, procedures, or properties of productivity measurement. Apparently, productivity measure-

[11] A list of worthwhile publications on measuring productivity at the corporate or departmental level would include Davis (1955), Kendrick and Creamer (1965), Craig and Harris (1973), Greenberg (1973), Mammone (1980a, b), Buehler and Shetty (1981), and Hayes (1982).

ment, perhaps the most basic measure of manufacturing performance over time, has not yet been considered part of the information that will assist managers in their decision-making and control activities. Also, proposed productivity measures have not yet been subjected to the scrutiny we have applied to accounting variances, one of our traditional financial-based performance measures. That is, the effects of activity volume, and of substitution among labor, capital, materials, energy and other key inputs, on proposed productivity measures, have not been the subject of any accounting research.

As a simple example of a research topic, note that productivity measures will generally increase when output expands, since greater utilization is obtained from the firm's capital resources. But this productivity gain is due to external market forces, not to improved efficiency within the organization. Clearly, some effort should be made to separate fixed and variable portions of productivity just as we separate volume from spending variances when comparing actual to budgeted overhead costs. Thus, developing improved productivity measurements would seem to be a fertile field for accounting researchers.

NEW PRODUCT TECHNOLOGIES

The preceding discussion was, by assumption, confined to measurements – quality, inventory cost, and productivity – for products with reasonably stable characteristics. In such mass production settings, competition takes place along cost minimization and productivity dimensions. But to evaluate all manufacturing performance by cost and efficiency measurements, even with the expanded set proposed in the preceding section, would be a major error. Richardson and Gordon (1980) concluded that, 'there is evidence . . . that not only is productivity a narrow indication of manufacturing performance, but in some circumstances, it may lead to corporate disaster.'

The central issue here is to recognize that the role of manufacturing differs greatly over the life cycle of a product. Skinner (1969 and 1974) was among the first to highlight the importance of manufacturing in the overall strategic mission of the firm. While recognizing that low-cost competition may be appropriate for mature products and technologies, Skinner (1974) claimed that for products in the earlier stages of their life cycles, a company's manufacturing performance may be best measured by its ability to employ technological innovation and incorporate advanced features into its new products. A low-cost plant for a new product may lead to product failure if the low cost is achieved by sacrificing flexibility, adaptability, delivery schedules, and quality. Skinner's approach was extended by Hayes and Wheelwright (1979a, 1979b), who articulated the notion of a process life cycle that parallels the sequencing of a product life cycle:

The process evolution typically begins with a 'fluid' process – one that is highly flexible, but not very cost efficient – and proceeds toward increasing standardization, mechanization, and automation. This evolution culminates in a 'systemic process' that is very efficient but much more capital intensive, interrelated, and hence less flexible than the original fluid process. (Hayes and Wheelwright, 1979a).

Richardson and Gordon (1980) summarize their beliefs about how different measures of manufacturing performance must be employed at the different stages of a product life cycle with the following propositions:[12]

1. Manufacturing performance measures for the early stages of a product's life cycle, stressing innovation and flexibility, will be more complex and require measurements over a longer time period than measures for the manufacturing of mature products. Consequently, facilities that manufacture new products are less likely to have well-defined measures of manufacturing performance than facilities with mature products.
2. Using measures appropriate for one stage of a product's life cycle for products that are in a different stage will lead to dysfunctional behavior. Most commonly, managers introducing new products, but who are evaluated on the basis of cost minimization and productivity, may not be as responsive to customer needs, will freeze the design specifications of the products prematurely in an attempt to standardize production, and may not pay sufficient attention to producing consistently high-quality products.
3. Measurement of overall manufacturing performance is especially difficult in facilities producing multiple products, at various stages of product life cycles. The most common procedure will be to use efficiency measures appropriate for mature products for the entire facility. This will have the effect of inhibiting the successful introduction of new products. This proposition was developed earlier, in somewhat different form, by Skinner (1974) who concluded, 'A factory that focuses on a narrow product mix for a particular market niche will outperform the conventional plant, which attempts a broader mission.'
4. Because of the difficulty that U.S. and Canadian firms have in competing with foreign firms on the basis of cost and productivity, many North American firms have attempted to devise product strategies emphasizing innovation, customization, and quality. Performance measures for these products, however, have been the traditional measures of cost minimization, appropriate for mature products. Manufacturing managers, responding to these performance measures, have not delivered innovative, customer-responsive, and high-quality products, thereby leading to the failure of the corporate strategy.

In a field visit study of Canadian manufacturers, Richardson and Gordon found general support for these propositions. In general, performance measures appropriate for the early stages of a product's life cycle were

---

[12] See also Williams (1983) for a discussion of the value of innovative behavior early in a product's life cycle and of efficient behavior as the product matures.

either non-existent or extremely crude. What was worse, however, is that many companies were using performance measures appropriate for mature products when evaluating the performance of facilities also producing new products. The performance measures of managers declined in plants that introduced new products since the new products could not be produced as efficiently as mature products. Also, the manufacture of these new products 'interfered' with the efficient production of the existing product line. Only firms producing exclusively new products were able to avoid the dysfunctional consequences from inappropriate performance measures. But these firms avoided these consequences by essentially having no measures of manufacturing performance at all.

Thus, at the present time, we have not succeeded in developing effective measures of the manufacturing performance of products early in their life cycle. Such measures could include the ability of a manufacturing plant to:

- Introduce new products
- Vary product characteristics quickly as customer preferences and new technological possibilities become known
- Deliver new products at high quality levels
- Deliver new products on predictable delivery schedules.

The failure of managerial accountants to devise performance measures for new products is a serious problem, since the future success of most manufacturers will depend on their ability to introduce innovative, custom-designed products, produced efficiently in small batches using automated manufacturing equipment. The advent of the new technology of Flexible Manufacturing Systems (see Bylinski (1983)), including CAD/CAM, programmable machine tools, and robots, will shift the emphasis in the U.S. from large-scale, repetitive manufacturing processes of standard products to a highly automated job shop environment, featuring the manufacture of items in small batches for specific customers.[13] I defer a discussion of the implications of this revolution in the organization and technology of manufacturing operations until the concluding section.

DISCOUNTED CASH FLOW EVALUATION

Another manifestation of a narrow focus on easily quantified, financial measures arises in the use of the discounted cash flow (DCF) approach for evaluating new investment proposals. The DCF approach has desirable properties for aggregating deterministic cash flows occurring at different points in time. But a narrow interpretation of this procedure may inhibit desirable investment projects. There is a danger from relying solely on the easily quantified savings in input factors – such as labor, energy, and materials – from new capital investments and not considering gains from improved manufacturing performance that are more difficult and

[13] See the discussion in Reich (1983) for an elaboration of this scenario.

subjective to quantify. Factors such as improved product quality, increased manufacturing flexibility, reduced inventory levels, and the capacity for increased product innovations may be ignored because we have inadequate means for quantifying their benefits. Thus, developing improved measures for these factors should promote more congruence between the firm's manufacturing strategy and the subsequent evaluation of manufacturing operations, as discussed in the preceding section. Also, considering the benefits from these factors may rationalize a higher degree of capital investment in modern production facilities than would now be undertaken when project justification is made solely on easily quantified measures of input factor savings.

In addition, the capital budgeting process should be much broader than just evaluating proposed projects. Pinches (1982) articulates a four-stage process for capital budgeting:

1. Identification Stage – to identify capital expenditure projects in response to an organizational opportunity or problem. This stage needs to be closely linked to the strategic objectives of the firm.
2. Development Stage – to develop projects and supporting cash flow information in response to the strategic opportunity or problem.
3. Selection Stage – to choose one or more projects for implementation, incorporating time value, risk, portfolio, and financing effects, and
4. Control Stage – to evaluate performance of approved projects.

Pinches concluded,

there is . . . ample evidence that financial specialists have taken a myopic or short-sighted view of the capital budgeting process. The main failure of academicians is due to focusing too much of their attention on the selection phase to the exclusion of the identification, development, and control phases. Very little attention has been given to the interface between strategic planning and capital budgeting. Likewise, academicians have tended to ignore the information requirements and the generation of cash flows – all too often they are assumed to be given. Perhaps this is why academicians have focused on developing many different techniques for dealing with risk, but none of them has much following in practice. Finally, the role of the post audit has not received much attention in academic circles (Pinches, 1982, p. 16).

In summary, massaging cash flow data is only one part of the capital budgeting process. Also, restricting analysis to readily available cash flow estimates may deprive firms from taking advantage of strategic opportunities to improve their long-term competitive position.

INCENTIVE SYSTEMS

Managerial decisions are strongly influenced by the nature of incentive systems for division and senior managers. Much contemporary research has focused on how the existence and terms of such incentive systems may influence the choice of financial reporting methods by a firm, or the firm's response to changes in proposed financial reporting rules. Less well understood is why senior managers' incentive plans should rely so heavily on financial measures of performance (e.g., earnings per share growth, return on capital in excess of a minimal rate of return) rather than operating measures more consistent with the long-term health of the firm (Rappaport, 1978). During inflationary periods, financial performance measures may vary systematically from the underlying economic health of the firm because of the use of practices that tend to increase reported income, such as the under-depreciation of long-lived assets acquired at lower price levels and the understatement of cost of goods sold.

Basing compensation on financial measures also tends to focus senior managers' attention on financial rather than manufacturing operations. Thus, firms engage in debt restructuring exercises and mergers that, in the short run, increase reported financial performance but have few demonstrable benefits for the effectiveness or efficiency of the firm. When downturns in the economy occur, many firms attempt to minimize the short-run negative impact on their reported earnings by reducing capital investment and intangible investments in areas such as research, product development, human resource development, advertising and promotion, maintenance, quality control, and customer service.[14] These practices maintain profit levels in the short run but they may prevent future gains from new products, improved processes, more skilled and loyal employees, and an expanded market share. Workers are laid off rather than reassigned to alternative activities suitable for periods of slack activity such as equipment maintenance and modernization, retraining and education, and redesign of work activities.

A few relatively small, highly innovative, and successful U.S. firms have adopted quite a different set of practices. Lincoln Electric[15] has all its production workers on piece-rate pay so that the workers capture a major share of expanded productivity. In addition, these workers receive substantial bonuses for their contribution to teamwork and reliability. Lincoln is able to achieve the cooperation of its labor force, at least in part, through a program of guaranteed employment even in a highly cyclical industry. Nucor Corporation, a relatively small steel fabricator, is an extremely effective competitor against domestic and foreign firms alike through an aggressive program of bonus payments to production workers (Manuel, 1981). Nucor believes it can produce steel cheaper than any other firm in the world through a combination of specialized and relatively low-cost capital facilities, minimal holding of inventory, and very high productivity. Bonuses that represent more than 60 percent of

[14] Banks and Wheelwright (1979); also, Tsurumi (1982) notes that U.S. memory chip manufacturers lost their production and technological lead to Japanese competitors by cutting planned R&D expenditures and capacity expansion to conserve financial resources during the 1974–75 recession.
[15] Baldwin (1982), also Lincoln Electric Company (1975).

production workers' total pay are paid weekly on the basis of the previous week's performance. Also, a number of firms have successfully adopted Scanlon Plans in which workers receive bonuses based on improvements in productivity (Moore, 1975; Moore and Ross, 1978).

These examples suggest that measurement systems to support bonus and incentive payments for productivity improvements may be highly effective when placed at the production worker level. Such payment systems will operate for employees well below the levels of senior management that customarily are paid incentive awards for financial, as opposed to operating, performance. To date, the interaction between the traditional cost accounting system and a measurement system to serve as the basis for production incentive payments in reasonably realistic manufacturing settings has not received much attention in the literature.[16]

Additional research would also seem warranted as to why senior executive compensation plans focus so narrowly on financial rather than operating performance. As Rappaport (1978) observed, corporate boards of directors could devise compensation plans that: (1) reward performance over extended time periods (this practice is growing, though still using financial performance measures only); (2) tie incentive plans to achieving strategic (not financial) goals such as market share, productivity levels, product quality and product development measures, and personnel development; and (3) use financial reporting practices (if financial measures are to be used) that do not penalize managers for making decisions that penalize short-term earnings but benefit long-term profitability. As suggested methods for implementing suggestion (3), senior managers could be evaluated on operating profits before gains from financial transactions and before deductions for approved expenditures on intangibles (R & D, quality improvements, maintenance, etc.). Also, decelerated depreciation methods could be used so that investments in long-term capital assets do not unduly penalize the income measure used to compute bonus and incentive payments. Incorporating the suggestions of an earlier section on evaluating total manufacturing performance, senior managers of companies following a strategy of product innovation (as contrasted with a strategy of efficient production of mature products) could be evaluated on non-financial measures such as the success of new products, measures of manufacturing flexibility and quality, and degree of technological innovation.

Perhaps the explanation for the popularity of financial measures is that they provide an apparent, comprehensive measure of performance. By denominating all operating and performance measures in dollars, we can aggregate across diverse operating units and divisions to get an overall

---

[16] A more general and equally interesting research question is how did U.S. manufacturers reach their current state of industrial labor relations with industry-wide (rather than company) unions, lack of bonus incentives for high-quality production and productivity in unionized plants, and lack of labor force flexibility when considering job assignments? For example, returning to our opening quote, why does the Ford plant have 200 job classifications while the Toyota plant has only seven?

performance measure. In contrast, a critical problem with real or physical measurements is that they are local measures that are difficult or impossible to aggregate into a single overall measure.

But relying on any single measure to motivate and evaluate the performance of managers in complex production and marketing settings is probably naive. Any single measurement will have myopic properties that will enable managers to increase their score on this measure without necessarily contributing to the long-run profits of the firm. That is why some firms are moving away from an over-reliance on single financial measures of managerial performance. General Electric has a flexible incentive system for the managers of its Strategic Business Units (SBUs). An SBU manager in a mature or declining business will be evaluated primarily on a mixture of current financial performance measures; factors such as sales, net income, ROI, and cash flow will be weighted to arrive at an overall performance evaluation. The incentive plans for managers of SBUs that are growing and receiving new investment from the firm, however, will have more weight placed on non-financial measures, designed to indicate longer-term benefits to the company. These include measures of increased market share, improved quality, product innovation, and leadership in efficient production.[17]

One objection to a strategy of evaluating senior managers on performance measures different from those measures used to report to external investors (such as earnings per share or return on shareholders' equity) is that the short-run financial performance of the firm will appear more erratic and unpredictable. This will occur because less attention will be paid to implementing decisions that maintain steady quarter-to-quarter or annual earnings growth. To avoid problems that senior executives or boards of directors may envision with fluctuating short-term earnings performance, an active program of investor communications could be implemented by firms committed to a long-term strategy of product and market leadership. Chief executive, operating, and financial officers could declare in shareholder newsletters, in annual reports, and in speeches before financial analysts some version of the following speech:

The goal of this firm is not to exhibit steady predictable earnings growth. Rather our goal is to become a dominant force in our product markets. This strategy will require steady investments in research, product development, process improvements, and employee training that will be made even during downturns in the economy. A strategy of stable investments will increase the operating leverage of the firm, since more expenditures will be considered fixed rather than discretionary. Also, dividend increases may be limited, since operating cash flows will be redeployed within the firm. But in the long run, we are convinced that this strategy will create

---

[17] See Landro (1982) and General Electric Company (1981). Multiple measures of performance have long been associated with General Electric incentive plans. See the discussion in Chapter VIII of Solomons (1965) for the limitations of single-dimensional performance measures and the role for multiple performance measures.

more value for the firm, its shareholders, its employees, and all the other constituents of the firm: customers, suppliers, and local communities. Therefore, the strategy must be evaluated on the firm's long-run profitability and dominant market position. For those investors for whom steady earnings and dividend growth are important, our firm is probably not a good one to hold in your investment portfolio. Only purchase and hold our shares if you are comfortable with our strategy of maximizing long-term capital gains. We will regularly provide you with operating statistics to keep you informed about our progress in becoming the most innovative or the most efficient producer in our product lines.

Do executives believe that their stock price would decline after such a speech? If not, why then do we not see more companies explicitly following such a manufacturing and investor communications strategy?

A RESEARCH STRATEGY

I have documented the gaps in our knowledge about important measurement issues related to manufacturing performance. If management accounting is to be a central discipline in the design and evaluation of information and control systems of corporations, the field will need to expand its vision beyond summary financial measures of manufacturing operations. Much time will need to be spent at factory sites to gain first-hand knowledge of the revolution in manufacturing technology that is occurring in many U.S. corporations. At present, it is difficult to define a complete and precise research agenda since the shift in thinking about manufacturing operations is relatively recent, and all the implications of this shift have not yet been revealed. Nevertheless, we can identify a number of issues that could profitably occupy the attention of management accounting researchers for the next several years.

Overseas manufacturers with lower labor costs will have a long-term manufacturing cost advantage in the mass production of standard products, products that are in the mature phase of their life cycle. Therefore, surviving U.S. manufacturers must either have a strong advantage in transportation cost (such as in cement production) or be producing items that are not standard. The non-standard nature of products can arise from continual technological change in the manufacturing process or in changing product characteristics as more knowledge of customer preferences is acquired. An additional opportunity for U.S. manufacturers to develop a comparative cost advantage is to become more involved in assembly operations. In fact, many observers forecast that U.S. manufacturers will increasingly become assemblers rather than mass producers of standard goods; that is, manufacturers will be producing for customers rather than producing for inventory. This trend toward assembly operations of custom-designed products is facilitated by the use of flexible manufacturing systems using programmable machine tools, robots, and CAD/CAM. Thus, the large-scale production of an item with unchanging specifications that is embodied in the simple standard cost model of all cost accounting textbooks, may soon become the exception rather than the rule.

New managerial accounting procedures to replace the standard cost model will probably be required when producing with flexible manufacturing systems. Can standards be kept current and relevant when product characteristics are changing, when there are short production runs tailored for each customer, or when the production method changes for each batch depending upon which machines are available when the order is processed? What form the new cost accounting systems will take is not at all clear at present. They must evolve from research to be carried out in the future. Continued use, though, of the old cost accounting model in the new environment will make it, at best, irrelevant and, more likely, counterproductive to the firm's manufacturing strategy.

Additional cost accounting issues arise when firms shift from producing large quantities of standard items to producing in the job shop environment that will be typical of flexible manufacturing operations. For example, job shop operations usually assign overhead to products through a burden rate based on direct labor hours. As the direct labor content of a product shrinks through the more effective use of fixed investment, firms are finding that their 'total cost per direct labor hour' can be in excess of $50 even though only $10 of this represents actual labor costs. Another problem which also relates to a firm's workforce strategy is whether labor should be considered a fixed or a variable cost. Thus, new procedures for cost prediction and cost control will be required for firms operating in the highly automated, flexible manufacturing settings that represent the factory of the future.

The relevant role of productivity data needs to be explored. What are the benefits of collecting partial or total factor productivity data as supplementary measures to the labor and material usage measures that are available from a standard cost approach? Some manufacturing divisions report that after investing in a successful program to increase productivity, their profitability measure has not improved. Conversely, some divisions where productivity has declined continue to show improved profitability. This suggests a conflict between physical and financial measures of performance that would be useful to understand better and explain. For any given productivity measure, it would be interesting to explore the opportunities for sub-optimizing behavior by manufacturing managers relative to this measure. Could managers take actions that are economically unsound but that cause their productivity measure to increase? Accounting researchers have conducted similar studies to demonstrate the weaknesses of aggregate financial measures, such as return on investment.

For quality measurements, researchers could attempt to validate the claim that total operating cost decreases as defects decrease. Cost savings arise from reduced inspection, rework, and scrap; fewer material handlers and less inventory if processed items do not have to be cycled back through the factory; reduced cost of warranty and field service; and the savings from the improved scheduling of the firm's human and capital resources that are possible with defect-free materials, products, and processes. An additional consideration is the increase in sales or selling price that can occur once customers are assured of receiving a high quality, dependable product. A cost allocation issue arises in the appropriate salvage value assigned to scrap or below standard-quality output. It is customary to assign to scrap at least its raw-material value were it to be purchased or sold on the open market. Perhaps, however, the scrap value should be reduced by the increased materials handling and storage costs, plus the cost of disrupting the production schedule, when defective output is produced. This places more of a premium on eliminating defective items in the production process.

The value from improved inventory management procedures can also be estimated. Investments that reduce setup times will permit shorter production runs, thereby providing benefits of reduced capital and space requirements for finished goods inventory. Better scheduling and defect-free quality of input materials produce benefits of lower raw material and work-in-process inventory, greatly reduced storage space requirements, and lower labor costs for handling this inventory. The inventory costing system should be integrated with the production planning and scheduling system needed in the factory so that production managers are rewarded for efficient utilization of bottleneck resources and the reduced inventory levels throughout the factory.

Capital budgeting procedures can be expanded to incorporate the measured benefits of improved quality, flexibility, and changeover times that can be achieved from investment in the new manufacturing technology. Documented cases where new investment yielded unanticipated benefits from new options in product development, new product introduction, manufacturing flexibility, or expanded capacity would help to provide evidence that some of the benefits from capital expenditures may not all be quantified at the time of authorization. (Of course, it would be worth noting the converse, when the savings from new investment tend to be systematically overestimated.)

On a broader set of issues, we need to examine why firms have tended to use for internal planning and control, the same accounting procedures used for external reporting purposes. Depreciation and asset valuation methods, inventory valuation rules, and procedures for capitalizing or expensing investments in intangible assets can be made to differ between internal and external reporting. The firm should select for internal reporting those practices that best promote incentives for achieving its strategy and objectives. In general, we should try to understand why there has been so little apparent innovation in firms' cost and managerial accounting systems. Is this another manifestation of U.S. firms not being very innovative in the technology and organization of manufacturing operations during the 1970s? How do Japanese, German and other foreign manufacturers, noted for their manufacturing efficiencies, measure, motivate, and evaluate the performance of their production managers? Do these foreign firms make greater use of non-financial measures of manufacturing performance than their U.S. counterparts? Are U.S. controllers collecting a narrower set of data than their foreign colleagues? Perhaps much closer coordination between operating data (mostly physical, non-financial measures prepared for production managers) and financial measures could be developed at the factory level. If we can identify U.S. firms that have been using non-financial performance measures for senior and/or plant managers, then there would be an opportunity to compare the performance of these firms (as measured say, by stock price returns, market share, or product innovation) relative to those of a comparable set of firms using mostly financial measures of performance.

Much accounting research recently has focused on explicitly incorporating the effects of uncertainty in models. Should we not also explore the value of reducing uncertainty, such as through a zero defect approach, or by closer coordination of a firm with its suppliers and customers? Thus, the value of reduced uncertainty through improved manufacturing and distribution practices is an interesting research topic.

The above list is a sketchy outline of the types of issues that can be explored when we start to study the relationship among accounting procedures, new measures of performance, and manufacturing operations. It seems most likely that this research will be best performed by visiting firms and actually learning something about contemporary manufacturing operations and practices. This new research area does not appear to be promising, initially, for arm-chair theorizing. At present, there is more knowledge about effective and efficient manufacturing operations in a select group of firms than in the research articles, textbooks, and data bases readily available to academics. Research will therefore require a greater emphasis on field studies of relatively few observation sites.

There is some precedence for this type of field study research. In the 1950s, a group of researchers at Carnegie Tech (now Carnegie-Mellon) investigated manufacturing and inventory policies at a paint company (a division of the present PPG Industries) and the inventory and distribution policies for the warehouses of the transformer division of Westinghouse. The effort resulted in a classic text in production (Holt, *et al.*, 1960) whose ideas are still influential more than twenty years after the studies were performed. This example also shows the value of collaborative research. Understanding manufacturing operations is a new field for most accounting researchers and they will certainly benefit from performing joint research with colleagues in operations management and industrial and manufacturing engineering.

The initial field study efforts should be approached without a rigid research design. The investigator will probably find it difficult to determine, in advance, those factors that will be most critical for the success of the manufacturing operation being studied. This research effort, however, should not be model-free or purely descriptive. The researcher should have in mind a large variety of models of productivity, cost reduction, quality improvement, or, in general, effective manufacturing performance that can be documented and tested at the field sites. But it will be difficult to specify in advance the exact models and tests that will be performed. These will come after the researcher gains familiarity with and the confidence of the organizations being studied. Therefore, the researcher must be flexible as well as knowledgeable when collecting data and formulating models.

Initially, this field research will likely be less elegant, less 'scientific,' and less defensible to many of our managerial and social science colleagues.[18] Also, the time frame for a recognizable unit of research in this area will be considerably longer than that required to do an empirical event study using the COMPUSTAT and CRSP tapes, or to perform a theoretical study in a newly devised, multi-person, asymmetric information setting.

Because of the newness of the research focus, change in research methods, and longer time frame required for recognizable results, this is a risky research strategy for Ph.D. students, or untenured assistant and associate professors. In part, this derives from difficulties in measuring and evaluating the quality of research done by junior researchers in a non-traditional mode of inquiry. But, for those academics who enjoy the freedom of research strategies that accrues from unlimited tenure appointments, such a strategy, although high-risk, should turn out to be a high-reward one. A commitment to understanding the basis of manufacturing operations should significantly advance the role of the managerial accounting system to support and enhance the firm's overall manufacturing strategy.

ACKNOWLEDGEMENTS

I benefited from the comments of Ilker Baybars, Chris Edwards, Dan Givoly, Jim Noel, Katherine Schipper, Pete Wilson, and especially Yuji Ijiri and Jeff Williams, on a preliminary draft of this paper. The comments of participants at the Stanford Accounting Workshop (July 1982), especially Ron Hilton, Mark Wolfson, and Jerry Zimmerman, and of participants at a University of Illinois Accounting Forum (October 1982) were also helpful in revising earlier drafts. Tom Murrin, President of Westinghouse Energy and Advanced Technology Group, and Bob Hayes of the Harvard Business School provided initial motivation for the paper as well as many valuable references.

Manuscript received November 1982.
Revision received February 1983.
Accepted February 1983.

REFERENCES

Baldwin, William, 'This is the Answer,' *Forbes* (July 5, 1982), pp. 50–52.
Banks, Robert L. and Steven C. Wheelwright, 'Operations vs. Strategy: Trading Tomorrow for Today,' *Harvard Business Review* (May–June 1979), pp. 112–120.
Buehler, Vernon M. and Y. Krishna Shetty, *Productivity Improvement: Case*

---

[18] Case studies need not be devoid of scientific content. See George (1982) and Mohr (1983) for discussions of the role of case studies in developing scientific theories.

Studies of Proven Practice (New York: AMACOM, 1981).

Business Week, 'Quality: The U.S. Drive to Catch Up' (November 1, 1982), pp. 66–80.

Bylinsky, Gene, 'The Race to the Automatic Factory,' *Fortune* (February 21, 1983), pp. 52–64.

Craig, Charles E. and R. Clark Harris, 'Total Productivity Measurement at the Firm Level,' *Sloan Management Review* (Spring 1973), pp. 13–28.

Crosby, Philip B., *Quality is Free* (New York: McGraw-Hill, 1979).

Davis, Hiram S., *Productivity Accounting* (Industrial Research Unit, The Wharton School of the University of Pennsylvania, 1955) (reprint edition, 1978).

Fine, Charles, 'Quality Control and Learning in Productive Systems,' Working Paper, Graduate School of Business, Stanford University (January 1982).

Fox, Robert E., 'MRP, Kanban, or OPT: What's Best?' *Inventories and Production Magazine* (July–August 1982).

General Electric Company, 'Background Note on Management Systems: 1981,' HBS Case 9-181-111 (Boston: Harvard Business School, 1981).

George, Alexander L., 'Case Studies and Theory Development,' Working Paper, Department of Political Science (Standford University, 1982).

Greenberg, Leon, *A Practical Guide to Productivity Measurement* (Washington, D.C.: Bureau of National Affairs, 1973).

Hayes, Robert H., 'Why Japanese Factories Work,' *Harvard Business Review* (July–August 1981), pp. 57–66.

——, 'A Note on Productivity Accounting,' HBS 0-682-084 (Boston: Harvard Business School, 1982).

——, and William J. Abernathy, 'Managing Our Way to Economic Decline,' *Harvard Business Review* July–August 1980), pp. 67–77.

—— and Joseph A. Limprecht, 'Germany's World Class Manufacturers,' *Harvard Business Review* (November–December 1982), pp. 137–145.

—— and Steven C. Wheelwright, 'Link Manufacturing Process and Product Life Cycles,' *Harvard Business Review* (January–February 1979a), pp. 133–40.

——, and Steven C. Wheelwright, 'The Dynamics of Process-Product Life Cycles,' *Harvard Business Review* (March–April 1979b), pp. 127–136.

Holt, Charles, Franco Modigliani, John Muth, and Herbert Simon, *Planning Production, Inventories, and Work Force* (Englewood Cliffs, NJ: Prentice-Hall, 1960).

Juran, J.M. 'Japanese and Western Quality – A Contrast,' *Quality Progress* (December 1978), pp. 10–18; also in *Management Review* (November 1978), pp. 27–28, 39–45.

Kendrick, John W. and Daniel Creamer, *Measuring Company Productivity: Handbook with Case Studies*, Revised Edition (New York: The Conference Board, 1965).

Koten, John, 'Auto Makers Have Trouble with "Kanban",' *Wall Street Journal* (April 7, 1982).

Landro, Laura, 'G.E.'s Wizards Turning from the Bottom Line to Share of the Market,' *Wall Street Journal* (July 12, 1982).

Lincoln Electric Company, HBS Case 9-376-028, Revision (Boston: Harvard Business School, September 1975).

Mammone, James L., 'Productivity Measurement: A Conceptual Overview,' *Management Accounting* (June 1980a), pp. 36–42.

——, 'A Practical Approach to Productivity Measurement,' *Management Accounting* (July 1980b), pp. 40–44.

Manuel, William G., 'Productivity Experiences at Nucor,' in Buehler and Shetty, *Productivity Improvement: Case Studies of Proven Practice* (New York: AMACOM, 1981), Chapter 4.

Mohr, Lawrence, B., 'The Reliability of the Case Study as a Source of Information,' in Robert Coulam and Richard Smith (Eds.), *Symposium on Information Processing in Organizations* (J.A.I. Press, 1983, forthcoming).

Monden, Yasuhiro, 'What Makes the Toyota Production System Really Tick,' *Industrial Engineering* (January 1981a), pp. 36–48.

——, 'Kanban System,' *Industrial Engineering* (May 1981b), pp. 29–46.

——, 'Production Smoothing,' *Industrial Engineering* (August 1981c), pp. 42–51.

——, 'Production Smoothing, Part II,' *Industrial Engineering* (September 1981d), pp. 22–30.

Moore, Brian. *A Plant-Wide Productivity Plan in Action: Three Years of Experience with the Scanlon Plan* (Washington, DC: National Center for Productivity and Quality of Working Life, May 1975).

——and Timothy L. Ross, *The Scanlon Way to Improved Productivity: A Practical Guide* (New York: John Wiley & Sons, 1978).

Murrin, Thomas, 'Rejecting the Traditional Ways of Doing Business' (Chicago: American Production and Inventory Control Society, October 1982).

Pinches, George E., 'Myopia, Capital Budgeting and Decision Making,' *Financial Management* (Autumn 1982), pp. 6–19.

Rappaport, Alfred, 'Executive Incentives vs. Corporate Growth,' *Harvard Business Review* (July-August 1978), pp. 81–88.

Reich, Robert, 'The Next American Frontier,' *The Atlantic Monthly* (March 1983), pp. 43–58 and (April 1983), pp. 97–108.

Richardson, Peter R. and John R.M. Gordon, 'Measuring Total Manufacturing Performance,' *Sloan Management Review* (Winter 1980), pp. 47–58.

Schonberger, Richard, *Japanese Manufacturing Techniques* (New York: Free Press, 1982).

Skinner, Wickham, 'Manufacturing – Missing Link in Corporate Strategy,' *Harvard Business Review* (May–June 1969), pp. 136–145.

——, 'The Focused Factory,' *Harvard Business Review* (May–June 1974), pp. 113–121.

Solomons, David, *Divisional Performance: Measurement and Control* (Homewood, IL: Richard D. Irwin, 1965).

Takeuchi, Hirotaka, 'Productivity: Learning from the Japanese,' *California Management Review* (Summer 1981), pp. 5–19.

Tsurumi, Yoshi, 'Productivity: The Japanese Approach,' *Pacific Basin Quarterly* (Summer 1981).

——, 'Japan's Challenge to the U.S.: Industrial Policies and Corporate Strategies,' *Columbia Journal of World Business* (Summer 1982), pp. 87–95.

Wheelwright, Steven C., 'Japan – Where Operations Really are Strategic,' *Harvard Business Review* (July–August 1981), pp. 67–74.

Williams, Jeffrey R., 'Schumpeterian Economies of Scope,' GSIA Working Paper (Carnegie-Mellon University, June 1983).

15

Management accounting and action

Robert J. Swieringa
Cornell University
and
Karl E. Weick
University of Texas at Austin

ABSTRACT

Management accounting information is intended to facilitate and enhance decision-making, but this information also may influence action. This paper explores some preliminary ideas about how and why a management accounting approach such as return on investment may initiate and sustain forceful action.

Management accounting approaches such as cost-volume-profit analysis, variance analysis, and return on investment (ROI) analysis are often treated as aids to decision-making, but less attention has been paid to their direct effects on action, motivation and commitment. However, since each approach imposes some differentiation and clarity on situations which are otherwise uncertain, these approaches are not silent in their implications for action. These imposed structures sometimes sacrifice accuracy – which may be undesirable from a purely analytic perspective, but this sacrifice may make good sense if the problem is one of producing sustained, vigorous action. Biased, incomplete analyses may mobilize strong action which, because of its strength, may often change situations so that they, in fact, eventually validate the incomplete presentation that first stimulated the action. Self-validating action stimulated by relatively crude accounting approaches may be a common though neglected pathway by which management accounting affects organizations.

Previous explanations of why management accounting systems work emphasize their ability to poke into every corner of the organization, establish cross-checks, produce multiple confirmation of mere suspicions, unmask shoddy practice and provide both goals and incentives. Vancil (1979, pp. 82–85) identifies four characteristics which he believes explain why management accounting systems are so powerful. First, these systems have inherent integrity that tends to be unquestioned by operating managers. Managers may joke about 'cooking the books', but they know that the debits must equal the credits. All cash must be accounted for

Source: Swieringa, R.J. and Weick, K.E. (1987) Accounting, Organizations and Society, 12 (3), pp. 293–308.

and the accountants have a detailed set of rules that ensure that similar transactions are recorded in a consistent manner. The accounting system provides a detailed set of rules that an organization imposes on itself.

Second, the management accounting system is comprehensive and blankets the organization. Accounting aggregates the activities of an organization and expresses them in financial terms that facilitate comparison. Aggregation can be reversed in the sense that accounting data can be decomposed to whatever level of detail a manager wants.

Third, every business organization must have an accounting system. The system is mandated reality whose data are hard to ignore. Executives ask, 'how well did we do,' which leads to 'why was our performance better or worse than expected,' which leads to 'who is responsible'.

Finally, the accounting system provides ways in which managers can obtain new insights into their business. Breaking return on investment into the components of profitability and turnover can clarify the structure of profit and loss in operations. Essentially, accounting is a way of making things visible. But, the accounting data may not always mirror economic realities and accounting reports may suggest a world that may not exist.

We argue that there may be a fifth reason why management accounting systems tend to be so powerful, namely, the better systems initiate and sustain forceful action. Traditionally, accounting systems have been thought to work because they provide trusted information which people can use to make informed decisions. What analysts miss when they focus on accounting information as a means to improve decisions is the effect this same information may have on action. Good decisions do not automatically flow into forceful action. In fact, the procedures necessary to produce high quality decisions may produce cautious, hesitant, conservative, incremental action through their effects on motivation and commitment. Alternatively, analytically imperfect, biased accounting measures which can be viewed as misleading inputs to decision-making, may sometimes stimulate forceful, sustained, self-validating action. The purpose of this paper is to explore ways in which management accounting practices may initiate and sustain action.

THE MANAGEMENT ACCOUNTING PROCESS

Management accounting systems are intended to develop and maintain records of relevant events which can be used to measure income and financial position, to assess performance in terms of established goals, and to provide management incentives consistent with those goals. These systems also are intended to provide data which managers can use to control costs, to identify problems, to assess alternative ways of solving problems, and to select and implement solutions.

Figure 15.1 provides an overview of the management accounting process. Management accounting systems are transaction-based. They record basic financial actions and events and then use the accounting model to accumulate, classify and communicate the financial effects of these actions and events. For example, the management accounting systems used in

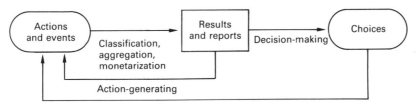

Fig. 15.1 An overview of the management accounting process.

manufacturing settings are designed to record costs associated with various production actions and events, to accumulate these costs by departments or cost centers, and then to apply these costs to units of products or services passing through the departments or centers. These systems monetarize actions and events by recording costs and then aggregate these costs by jobs, batches, processes or departments in order to apply costs to products and services.

The product of the management accounting process typically is a highly-summarized financial report. These reports are intended to summarize the financial effects of the actions taken and the events that occurred during a certain period of time. These reports provide a basis for decision-making and action.

The 'decision-making' line in Fig. 15.1 signifies processes in which individuals, groups or organizations perceive problems, generate a family of solutions, choose a solution, implement the chosen solution and observe results to see if the solution works.[1] This process is often described in normative terms – how a 'best' choice should be made, given a specific problem, specific alternatives and specific information.

Management accounting researchers have tended to emphasize a decision-making orientation. Management accounting systems are viewed as ways to collect, classify, summarize, analyze and report information that will assist managers who make decisions (decision facilitating) and control activities (decision influencing). These systems tend to be viewed as economic goods which can be acquired at various costs and which must meet the test of the economics of information – their value must exceed their cost (Feltham, 1972; Demski & Feltham, 1976; Demski, 1980). The value of information is often derived from an explicit model of the environment faced by a manager, the actions available to the manager, the possible outcomes (which are a function of the information in signaling the state of the environment and the outcome of the decision), and

---

[1] Starbuck (1982) suggests that organizations take on such a mode 'only sometimes – so infrequently that it can be considered abnormal'. Organizations do perceive problems and they do generate actions that are labeled 'solutions' to problems, but 'it is extremely rare for an organization to start by stating a problem, then to generate potential actions solely because they might solve this problem, and finally to choose a course of action solely because it appears the best solution to the problem' (Starbuck & Hedberg, 1977, p. 254).

the risk attitudes or preferences of the manager. Management accounting systems may also provide the basis for determining and enforcing contracts among managers. These employment contracts specify the resources to be controlled, the actions that are permitted, and the performance measures by which managers will be evaluated. Management accounting systems record and report the results of all transactions with the resources entrusted to managers and provide an interpretation of the consequences of these transactions.[2]

An emphasis on decision-making has, in turn, emphasized decision enhancement, the use of management accounting information to make better decisions. This orientation is reflected in a common language with economics, the management and decision sciences, and other functional areas of business (such as finance, marketing and production), a language that is grounded in rational choice. This decision-making orientation also has provided a basis for experimentation; accounting researchers have created experimental settings in which individuals who face a choice are given the same objectives but different information, and then the effects of the information on their choices are studied.[3] Yet, accounting researchers interested in decisions have tended to focus on individual choices rather than group or organizational choices and have emphasized the process of choice itself rather than other decision-making processes such as framing actions for choice or implementing the choices made (Einhorn & Hogarth, 1981).

The 'action-generating' line in Fig. 15.1 is intended to suggest processes in which individuals, groups or organizations observe the results of their decisions, appraise these results and then propose specific actions. Starbuck (1982, p. 21) suggests that results tend to be classified as good or bad after which statements are made about what the results mean and what ought to be done to change them. These statements may take the form of needs for action and discussion of 'theories' of which actions will be the most appropriate and successful.[4]

Even though we have portrayed decision-making and action-generating as separate processes in Fig. 15.1, we do not view these processes as mutually exclusive. Action-generating processes differ from decision-making processes by degree rather than in kind and can be viewed as variable simplifications of decision-making processes.[5] When people make choices (decision-making), they may express expectations that action will take place, demonstrate motivation to take action, and claim commitment to

---

[2] See Kaplan (1982, pp. 607–622) for a summary of a discussion of the nature of incentive contracts and risk sharing under conditions of uncertainty. Baiman (1982) and Demski & Kreps (1982) also provide useful reviews and discussions.

[3] See Swieringa & Weick (1982) for a review and assessment of experimental research in accounting.

[4] Starbuck (1982, 1983) provides a discussion of action-generating processes and how theories of action can develop.

[5] See Demski & Feltham (1976, pp. 42–60) and Demski (1980, pp. 44–61) for discussions of simplified decision models and analysis.

specific actions. But, going from choices to actions is not just a simple matter of intention, especially when the people who make choices are not the same people who take actions. Action-generating processes tend to simplify decision-making processes by evaluating alternatives and consequences in ways that directly intensify motivation to act.

Brunsson (1982, p. 33) suggests that an effective decision process that facilitates action-generation 'breaks nearly all of the rules for rational decision-making: few alternatives should be analyzed, only positive consequences of the chosen actions should be considered, and objectives should be analyzed, only positive consequences of the chosen actions should not be formulated in advance'. It is relatively easy to find action decision-making processes that consider few alternatives. This focused consideration is intended to reduce uncertainty and to intensify action. Considering multiple alternatives may evoke uncertainty, and this uncertainty may reduce motivation and commitment. If people do not know which action will be carried out, they may build up motivation and commitments for several alternatives at the same time, and this may diffuse the motivations and commitments supporting any single alternative.

The suggestion to consider only positive consequences of an acceptable alternative and to suppress negative consequences is also intended to reduce uncertainty and to intensify motivation and commitment for an action. Considering all relevant (positive and negative) consequences of an acceptable alternative may evoke doubt and conflict. Focusing only on the positive consequences of an acceptable alternative may reduce uncertainty and create enthusiasm. Furthermore, enthusiastic people often are able to persuade others that what they are doing is worthwhile, which may intensify both the belief in the soundness of the action and the intensity with which it is performed (e.g. Festinger *et al.*, 1956).

The suggestion that objectives should not be formulated in advance is intended to turn the objectives into instruments for motivation as well as criteria for choice. Objectives are usually viewed as criteria for choice: people are advised to state their objectives and then to assess what effects alternatives might have on them. But, people often formulate inconsistent objectives which makes it difficult to assess alternatives. To increase motivation, it may be more useful first to predict the most likely outcomes that will occur if an acceptable action is carried out, and second to formulate objectives in terms of these likely outcomes. The objectives then become arguments for action.

Cognition, motivation and commitment are aspects of all actions, but the importance of each aspect may differ in various situations. One role of management accounting information in organizations is to influence cognition. This role is reflected in a large and growing literature about how people process accounting information, how people react to accounting displays, presentations and reports, and how people react to changes in these displays, presentations and reports. Accounting information tends to influence cognition and thinking by making things visible and by framing people's concepts and choices (Einhorn & Hogarth, 1981).

Another role of management accounting information in organizations is to influence motivation and commitment. People in organizations not only wish to choose what things to do, they also wish to get things done. The literature about how management accounting information influences motivation and commitment is less well developed (Otley, 1982). Moreover, little, if any, attention has been devoted to interactions among cognition, motivation and commitment. Swieringa & Weick (1982, pp. 68–69) concluded as follows from a survey of past laboratory experiments in accounting.

. . . accounting experiments tend to view cognitive processes as very important in understanding the role and effects of accounting information. The behaviour observed in a typical accounting experiment is in the form of a response which is generated by displays, presentations, instructions, etc. But, are the effects of accounting limited to such displays, presentations, and instructions? Are the interesting and important effects of accounting information limited to cognitive processes?
Experiments may be better suited for studying cognition than for studying either sentiment or action. However, sentiment and action may dominate cognition, but this may never be discovered in conventional laboratory studies. If sentiment is not allowed to affect cognition, researchers may conclude that it will not affect cognition, in which case they will focus on an increasingly closed world in which cognition affects cognition.

The remaining sections of this paper explore some preliminary ideas about how management accounting practices and approaches may initiate and sustain action. We will use accounting return on investment (ROI) as our central illustration because of its widespread use. However, in focusing on ROI we are confronted with an interesting paradox. ROI is criticized by most academics to the point that it is difficult to find a positive discussion of its use. Discussions of the defects of ROI focus on its lack of decision rationality (Dearden, 1969; Kaplan, 1982; Solomons, 1965). For example, to maximize ROI, an organization (or division) will often reject investments that will earn below the average ROI but above its cost of capital. In other words, ROI does not encourage organizations (or divisions) to choose the 'right' investments. Discussions in the literature focus on how to increase the decision rationality of ROI by altering measures of earnings (e.g. by using cash flow measures instead of earnings measures, adjusting measures for changes in price levels, adjusting for expensing policies for intangible assets, or adjusting for leased assets) or by altering measures of investment (e.g. valuation methods, depreciation methods, capitalization policies, or treatments of leased assets).

ROI is also criticized in the financial press. In June 1977, for example, *The Wall Street Journal* noted that some businessmen, bankers and economists thought that an emphasis on return on investment was one reason why corporate capital spending was so slow to recover after the 1974–75 recession and why capital outlays would continue to be relatively conservative unless there was a change in corporate philosophy. Analysts were concerned that a whole generation of executives might develop a preoccupation with managing present assets for maximum return and become unwilling to take risks needed for growth. The ultimate result could be slower long-term economic growth, capacity shortages and more persistent unemployment (Winter, 1977).

Yet, even though ROI is criticized, it continues to be used extensively. It is a major yardstick for measuring corporate progress and executive performance. Executives are reasonably comfortable with ROI, they understand it well, and they have internalized the concepts and relationships inherent in this measure. In addition, executives are increasingly using ROI to describe their performance and their objectives to external parties.

Based on our discussions with executives in several companies, we believe that ROI remains popular, in part, because it initiates and sustains forceful action. The next sections provide a brief discussion of ROI and a speculative discussion of why and how it may influence action.

RETURN ON INVESTMENT

Return on investment (ROI) is an accounting measure of evaluation that is based on accounting data and facilitates comparisons among companies in evaluating corporate performance and among divisions within a company in evaluating divisional performance. The measure is the percentage that results from dividing a measure of earnings or operating profit (either before or after taxes) by a measure of investment (some measure of assets employed). ROI is used extensively by large companies in the United Stages (Reece & Cool, 1978).

ROI is often analyzed by means of a formula developed by Donaldson Brown at DuPont in 1915 and introduced at General Motors in the 1920s (Johnson, 1978). Brown's formula stated that ROI was the product of the ratio of earnings to sales (profitability) and the ratio of sales to total investment (turnover). The diagram in Fig. 15.2 shows the causal relationships of various operating factors to profitability and turnover.[6] Profitability (earnings as a percentage of sales) is linked to sales, earnings and cost of sales; turnover is linked to sales, permanent investment (noncurrent or fixed assets) and working capital (current assets).

The indicators and relationships in Fig. 15.2 focus on an analysis of results. Analyses of the various indicators over time and across units suggest potential problems which can be stated in terms of what actions are needed. The overall focus of the chart is on how management can increase ROI. The chart suggests that this can be done by reducing cost of sales, increasing selling prices, increasing volume of sales, or reducing the investment base. Most important, ROI focuses attention on the assets

---

[6] This diagram is from the E.I. DuPont de Nemours & Company publication *Executive Committee Control Charts*. This diagram is described in Jerome (1961) and Solomons (1965). Johnson (1975) provides a useful description of management accounting at DuPont and Johnson (1978) presents a more elaborate diagram developed by Donaldson Brown and describes its use at General Motors.

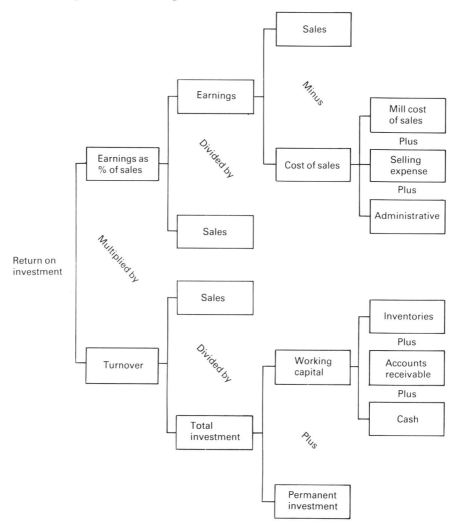

Fig. 15.2   Factors affecting return on investment.

employed (investment) and motivates investment in these assets only to the extent that an adequate return can be earned on them. If only the level of earnings was used to measure performance, there would be a temptation to increase assets employed so long as additional returns resulted. However, if ROI is used to measure performance, such expansion would lower ROI, and would not be encouraged.

The following example illustrates systematic examination of the factors in Fig. 15.2.[7] A division experienced a substantial improvement in its ROI over a period of three months:

[7] This example was described in the DuPont publication *Executive Committee Control Charts* and is also described in Solomons (1965).

Month	ROI =	Profitability ×		Turnover
January	12.6 =	17.1	×	0.736
February	13.4 =	20.2	×	0.664
March	15.4 =	22.7	×	0.679

Why did ROI increase? An analysis of profitability and turnover revealed that earnings improved (as a percentage of sales), but turnover decreased. An analysis of turnover indicated that investment rose while sales fell somewhat. Further investigation of total investment showed that it was inventory which caused the increase. An analysis of profitability revealed that earnings improved because cost of sales decreased. An investigation revealed that mill cost fell sharply, while selling expense fell somewhat. And why did mill cost decline? Because the rate of production had increased, fixed manufacturing costs were spread more thinly over units of product, thereby reducing the total mill cost of sales. Altogether, then, we have a picture of falling sales, rising production and rising inventory, even though ROI increased.

The DuPont diagram suggests how ROI can be used to present and interpret financial results within a company. Several companies, however, also use ROI (or variations thereof) to present and interpret financial results to parties outside the company. One such company is Quaker Oats Company, a major producer of grocery products, a leading toymaker, and a manufacturer and marketer of specialty products through retail outlets and mail-order catalogs. Quaker's net sales for fiscal 1983 were $2.6 billion and its net income available to common shareholders was $52.7 million.

Quaker uses ROI and return on equity (ROE) to describe and interpret its financial results in its annual reports and included the following in its 1983 annual report:

Return on Equity is an important measure of management's ability to utilize its shareholders' investment. While Return on Equity is commonly defined as net income available for common shares divided by average common shareholders' equity, actually a number of important variables determine this ratio. The table [in Table 15.1] separates out the various elements, based on results for continuing operations. The formula is as follows: Asset Turnover (sales divided by average assets employed) times

Table 15.1 Elements of return on equity: Quaker Oats Company 1983 annual report

Fiscal years	1979	1980	1981	1982	1983
Asset turnover	1.65	1.78	1.71	1.76	1.78
Return on sales	× 4.37%	× 4.14%	× 4.18%	× 4.38%	× 4.41%
Return on assets	= 7.21%	= 7.37%	= 7.15%	= 7.71%	= 7.85%
Leverage factor	× 2.20	× 2.25	× 2.33	× 2.36	× 2.31
Return on equity	= 15.9%	= 16.6%	= 16.7%	= 18.2%	= 18.1%

Return on Sales (net income divided by sales) equals Return on Assets. Return on Assets times Financial Leverage (average assets divided by average common shareholders' equity) equals Return on Equity. In fiscal 1983, Quaker improved both Asset Turnover (higher sales generated per $1.00 of assets) and Return on Sales (improved margins) for continuing operations, but a modest reduction in Financial Leverage (fewer dollars in liabilities per dollar of equity financing assets) caused a slight decline in Return on Equity, to 18.1% from 18.2% in fiscal 1982. Our first Financial Objective is still to improve Return on Equity to at least 19%, over time.

This description defines what Quaker's management considers to be the important elements of interest in interpreting the company's financial results and Quaker's results for fiscal 1983 are analyzed in terms of these elements. Table 15.1 presents the information included in the annual report for fiscal 1983. Observe that asset turnover and return on sales were up, but the leverage factor was down, resulting in a slightly reduced return on equity.

The elements used by Quaker reflect relationships which are inherent in the accounting model. The elements are calculated on the basis of financial results provided in the income statement and balance sheet. These financial results also are highly aggregated since they reflect the results for 62 plants operating in fourteen states and sixteen countries. Because of this aggregation, the overall financial results are decoupled from individual actions and events.

The elements used by Quaker can be affected in subtle ways by how events are accounted for and what measures are used in calculating each element. A careful reading of Quaker's 1983 annual report reveals some events which affected the results presented and compared in Table 15.1. In 1983, Quaker changed its actuarial assumptions for major domestic pension plans and benefited from some changes in government regulations. Changes in pension accounting increased return on sales by about 0.14%. Quaker also recorded write-offs in fiscal 1983 related to decisions to sell its chemicals business segment and to discontinue its video-game cartridge business segment. Because these write-offs were treated as special items and excluded from income from continuing operations, they did not affect

Table 15.2 Reported and adjusted numbers: elements of return on equity for 1983

	As reported	As adjusted
Asset turnover	1.78	1.67
Return on sales	×4.41%	×4.27%
Return on assets	=7.85%	=7.13%
Leverage factor	×2.31	×2.29
Return on equity	=18.13%	=16.33%

return on sales. However, because they reduced assets employed and common shareholders' equity, they increased the reported asset turnover by about 0.11% and increased the leverage factor by about 0.02%. Table 15.2 presents the reported and adjusted amounts for fiscal 1983. Without the changes in pension accounting and write-offs in fiscal 1983, Quaker's ROE would have been about 16.33% instead of the reported 18.13%. Observe that asset turnover, return on sales, and the leverage factor all would have been lower in fiscal 1983, thereby altering Quaker's interpretation of its performance for 1983.

RETURN ON INVESTMENT AND ACTION

There seem to be at least five sets of questions which can be asked in assessing the extent to which an accounting procedure or approach may initiate and sustain action. In particular, a procedure or approach such as ROI tends to influence motivation and commitment by (a) narrowing the focus to (b) specific criteria which reflect (c) presumed logical relations in ways which are (d) public, irreversible and volitional and which reflect and reinforce (e) shared beliefs.

1. Does the procedure or approach focus attention on a limited set of options?

As options increase, motivation is spread across more possibilities, the intensity of feeling for any one option decreases, and the eventual enthusiasm for the chosen alternative decreases also. Motivation tends to suffer because as more alternatives are examined, the same positive features will be found in more than one option, which diminishes the clear advantage of any one choice. Single options decrease in their power to evoke enthusiasm when parts of them are incorporated into other options. Options lose their power to motivate as they lose distinctiveness, and distinctiveness tends to disappear as more options are uncovered and as more 'new' options are created by blending portions of existing options. The epitome of motivation is embodied in the true believer, a person with a narrow, intense, singular purpose who pursues the one option that seems clearly superior to every other possibility. The energy of the true believer derives from a combination of less need to deliberate and less to deliberate about.

Reconsider the example described earlier in which a division achieved higher ROIs by increasing production in the face of falling sales. How can the division continue to increase its ROI? The diagram in Fig. 15.2 focuses attention on profitability (which has increased) and turnover (which has decreased). The division's options include some combination of increasing sales, reducing costs, or reducing investment. Since profitability has improved, attention may focus on how to improve turnover. The results achieved may, in fact, reflect the division's actions to improve profitability by cranking up production to reduce unit costs and by decreasing selling costs. But, now the division has excess inventory: 'We've got to increase sales to reduce our inventory!'

The relationships in Fig. 15.2 facilitate focusing attention on a limited set of options. If the diagram in Fig. 15.2 is turned counterclockwise 90°, it resembles a large tree with two main branches which can be selectively pruned.[8] As options are considered and rejected, attention is focused on the more limited set of options that remains. Instead of increasing sales to reduce inventory, the division could consider reducing production levels to reduce inventory. In addition, instead of increasing selling effort, the division could consider reducing prices and margins. And reducing production levels, increasing selling effort, or reducing prices or margins all impact on profitability. A delicate balancing of the effects of various alternatives on the numerator and denominator of ROI is required to achieve higher ROIs.

Similarly, the indicators in Table 15.1 focus attention on a limited set of options for increasing asset turnover, return on sales and financial leverage in increasing ROE. Focusing on a limited set of options provides strong motivation to act because focusing does three things: energize, direct and maintain. Deliberation over many options makes people hesitant rather than energized. This effect is visible in such common statements as 'we need to get more information', 'let's think about this', 'we can't rush into these things', 'let's appoint a committee to explore this', 'let's avoid precipitous action'. All such cautions, common enough when deliberations are drawn out, decrease the tendency to act.

Deliberation often generates diffuse directions rather than a single direction for subsequent action. This effect is reflected in such common assertions as 'let's keep our options open', 'we could go several ways on this', 'there is no alternative here that dominates the other ones', 'let's not decide until we have to', and 'maybe we should aim for a different goal'. In all of these cases, deliberation blurs rather than focuses direction and the effect of this is to reduce motivation.

Finally, deliberation can make it more difficult to sustain action because there is always the possibility that something else makes more sense and should be started. People are tempted to interrupt their actions frequently to assess how they are doing. And they may also interrupt their actions simply to reflect on them, since they did not seem to be obviously superior to something else they might be doing.

We believe that action is more likely when a procedure or approach such as ROI focuses attention on a limited set of options because the option chosen may be better able to energize people, provide a sense of direction, and maintain their activity.

2. Does the procedure state actions in positive terms? Does it focus on what to do rather than what to avoid? Does it define the most probable outcome as the goal of an action?

An analysis of the indicators in Fig. 15.2 reveals what is wrong: 'production and inventory have increased in the face of falling sales'. But, rather

---

[8] We are grateful to Lou Pondy for this analogy.

than focus on what is wrong – 'sales are too low', 'inventory is too high', 'production levels are too high', etc., people tend to talk about what is needed – 'we have to reduce production levels', etc. These needs for action reflect positive statements about action, and these positive statements incorporate cognitive, motivational and committal aspects.

First, these statements reflect the expectations that certain actions will take place. Organizations monitor performance variables which they expect to influence, they convert these expectations into self-fulfilling prophecies through both action and inaction, and they use these expectations to evaluate and interpret success and failure (Starbuck, 1982). The indicators in Fig. 15.2 reflect a collection of such performance variables. These indicators signify what organizations consider important, what they try to affect, and what they expect to succeed at. 'Increasing sales' and 'reducing inventories' are considered important within the context of this diagram and actions to affect sales and inventory levels are expected to be successful. Similarly, the indicators in Table 15.1 reflect what Quaker's management considers important in increasing return on equity. By increasing asset turnover, return on sales and financial leverage, management expects to be successful in increasing return on equity. Because organizations do not act where they expect to fail, they never succeed where they expect to fail. Organizations do act where they expect to succeed, and they act more forcefully where they have stronger expectations of success (Starbuck, 1982; Brunsson, 1982).

Second, positive action statements express clear commitments to specific actions. 'We need to increase selling effort to increase sales' expresses a desire to act and acceptance of responsibility for carrying out the action. The stated goal of Quaker's management to 'improve return on equity to at least 119%, over time' expresses its motivation and commitment to act. Motivation and commitment represent internal pressures for action.

Third, the cognitive, motivational and committal aspects of positive statements about action tend to be enhanced when people focus on what to do rather than what to avoid. It is easier to commit to the statement 'increase sales' than to the statement 'avoid falling sales!' Similarly, it is easier to accept 'increase selling effort' or 'reduce inventory levels' than to accept 'avoid decreased selling effort' or 'avoid increased inventory levels.' Positive statements about what to do also can be translated into performance criteria which reflect both probable outcomes from the actions and possible goals for the actions. The statement that 'we need to increase selling effort to increase sales' can be translated into goals for the selling effort in terms of increased sales and performance criteria which focus on increased sales. Feedback can then focus on whether increased selling effort resulted in increased sales. Similarly, the stated objective of Quaker's management to improve return on equity to at least 19% over time is stated in terms of probable outcomes which can be assessed by feedback about asset turnover, return on sales and financial leverage.

Altogether, making positive statements about action, focusing on what to do rather than what to avoid, defining goals in terms of the most probable outcomes, and using feedback to focus on accomplishment may provide a powerful system for initiating action. And the stronger the expectation, motivation and commitment expressed in statements about needs for action, the more power these statements are likely to exert as a basis for action.

3. How strong is the presumption of logic underlying the procedure? Is the presumption shared (do others believe it)? Is the presumption plausible (does it have face validity)?

People tend to fold attention, intention and control into their action through the mechanisms of presumptions of logic (Weick, 1983). Presumptions of logic provoke and energize action. People often have general expectations that events will be orderly. When people act on these expectations, order occurs, but not because extended prior analysis revealed it. Instead, people anticipated sufficient order that they wade into a situation, impose order among events, and then discover what they in fact have imposed. People tend to presume that a situation would make sense, act confidently, and *implant* the order that was anticipated (Snyder, 1984). The presumption of logic can lure people into situations where they act and, in acting, produce order.

It is important to realize that the content of these presumptions is less crucial than the fact that they exist in some form in the first place. Presumptions tend to be interchangeable and their accuracy may be less crucial than the fact that they tempt people to wade into a situation and act. It is the action that then determines the amount of order a situation will exhibit. And this orderliness, in turn, is the outcome that then feeds back to confirm the initial presumption of logic with which the person started. This sequence is similar to sequences associated with self-fulfilling prophecies (Snyder *et al.*, 1977).

For example, an initial presumption that the division can increase its sales may lead people to act forcefully (by increasing selling effort, reducing prices and margins, etc.) which may cause the situation to become more orderly (sales increase, inventory is reduced), which may make the situation easier to interpret, thereby confirming the original presumption that sales results are deterministic, orderly and controllable.

If people presume that there is a logic to a particular action, then this presumption may suspend doubt long enough for them to discover a specific logic within which the action might make sense. Once the action is linked with an explanation, it becomes more forceful, and the situation may be thereby transformed into something that supports the presumed underlying pattern.

For example, increasing selling effort may make sense within the context of the relationships in Fig. 15.2. People may presume that there is a logic to it. Linking this action to the explanation of 'increasing sales to reduce inventory' may give it both focus and force. Greater force, in turn, may influence the probability that increasing selling effort will modify the situation in self-confirming ways.

Presumptions of logic are likely to have large effects in managerial

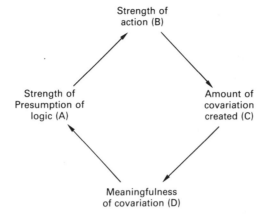

Fig. 15.3 Presumption of logic: a summary model.

activity because managers' actions are capable of a considerable range of intensity, the situations they deal with are loosely connected and capable of considerable rearrangement, and the underlying explanations managers invoke often have great potential to intensify whatever action is underway. All of these factors may combine to produce self-validating situations in which managers are sure their diagnoses were correct. What they underestimate is the extent to which their own actions have implanted the correctness they discover.

Figure 15.3 suggests that people may act with increased intention, attention and care as a result of self-reinforcing linkages between presumptions (A), action (B), consequences (C), and meanings (D). A stronger presumption may produce stronger action, stronger covariation, and greater meaningfulness, which may strengthen the original presumption. Doubt tends to weaken the strength of the presumption, which may weaken action and covariation, which may make it harder to extract meaning, which may strengthen the original doubt. In either case, the initial kick in this deviation-amplifying causal loop is crucial. An increase in any of the four variables in the loop may spread, meaning that faith may generate a world that confirms the faith; doubt may be similarly contagious.

If managers believe that turnover can be increased by increasing sales (presumption of logic), they may act forcefully to increase sales (strength of action) which may increase sales (amount of covariation created), which may confirm their original presumption (meaningfulness of covariation). If Quaker's management believes that return on equity can be increased by increasing asset turnover, return on sales, and financial leverage (presumption of logic), they may act forcefully to achieve these results (strength of action), which may increase the likelihood of these results being obtained (amount of covariation created), which may confirm their original presumption of logic (meaningfulness of covariation).

A situation of basic disorder may become more orderly when people overlook the disorder and presume orderliness, then act on this presumption, and, finally, rearrange pliant elements into a more meaningful arrangement that confirms the original presumption. A manager's preoccupation with analysis may be significant, less for its power as a decision-making heuristic, than for its power (or lack of power) to induce action that implants the rationality that was presumed.

4. Does the procedure induce public, irreversible, volitional performance?

Sustained action is encouraged by commitment and commitment tends to increase when people perform actions that are public, irreversible and volitional (Salancik, 1977; O'Reilly & Caldwell, 1981). An action that is public and irreversible is an action that cannot be denied. A public, irreversible action for which a manager also feels personal responsibility, is an undeniable action done by a specific person (being forced to do something may absolve responsibility). People who are tied to visible actions are likely to feel pressure to justify what they are doing, especially when norms of rationality are salient (Staw, 1979; Thompson, 1967).

An efficient source of justification is simply to continue acting and to identify the benefits of the action. Continuation of activity is self-justifying since, if the activity were worthless, the person persumably would stop doing it. The inference of value from observations of continued performance supplies justification to both performers and observers.

The benefits of sustained action provide an additional source of justification. The many rationales that buttress escalation (e.g. the set-back is only temporary and will disappear if we focus more resources on the problem) demonstrate the ease with which plausible, legitimate justification can be invented. The point is that the strong underpinnings for sustained action created by self-justification may be most likely to occur if the action is undertaken in a specific kind of context. And accounting procedures often create the 'ideal' context for commitment.

For example, ROI is discussed in a context that is almost ideal to produce high commitment. Managers have their past performance reviewed publicly and state, in writing, the levels they will try to achieve in the next period. Managers are held accountable for past performances, which are irreversible by definition, but they are also held to future estimates which makes these estimates also relatively irreversible. Finally, managers have a say in what they will be held to and in how they allocate resources to make those numbers, which means that volition is also introduced. When ROI targets are reviewed and set, the context within which this process occurs – high visibility, high irreversibility, high volition – virtually guarantees that managers will feel intense pressure to demonstrate that the target is reachable and worthwhile.

Jerome (1961) and Johnson (1975) describe how DuPont maintained communication between an executive committee and the general managers of various departments through such devices as monthly reports submitted by each general manager, an analysis of ROI before the entire committee once each quarter, a discussion of department forecasts each quarter, and periodic visits between the general managers and individual members of the executive committee. Department reviews were held in a specially designed room in which charts were suspended from a network of overhead tracks so that a given chart could be viewed at a moment's notice. Discussion focused on the ROI achieved and the various factors that contributed to its achievement. General managers were expected to answer detailed questions about department operations. The general managers also provided quarterly forecasts, which used in effect a rolling year; ten year forecasts about department and product lines; reports about capital projects that had not achieved the projected ROI; reports about potential trouble spots; and reports on special problems like leasing, inventory levels and purchase commitments.

Sampson (1974) and Geneen (1984) provide vivid accounts about how Harold Geneen relied heavily on public commitments and reviews at ITT. Geneen ran ITT with tight, centralized financial controls, a large head-quarters staff who monitored performance, and face-to-face meetings with the managers of ITT's profit centres. Each month all managers met with Geneen who, they knew, had gone over their monthly operating reports very carefully. In open meetings which were attended by about 120 managers in Europe or the 130 managers in the United States, Geneen would ask questions about details in the reports. He went over items which were 'red-flagged' in their reports and probed for answers in an open forum. Some executives struggled to adjust to Geneen's questioning of their decisions and actions, while others thrived on it.[9]

If people act confidently and publicly, then high commitment and escalation are possible by-products. Strong action is visible, may be irreversible, and is usually seen as volitional ('I could have done something else so this is my responsibility'), which means people may become bound more closely to their actions.

5. Is belief in the value and logic of the procedure or approach shared?

Shared beliefs tend to gain intensity more from the fact that they are shared than from the fact that they are necessarily more valid or accurate. In fact, the most intense, shared beliefs may be among the least substantiated, simply because the mere fact of being shared is treated as proof that what is shared must exist, since if it didn't exist it would not be shared. This elegant circularity, which people judiciously leave untested, intensifies action because it removes doubt. A socially constructed reality is first and foremost 'reality,' so if people agree that something is real, that agreement need not be questioned. It is easy to act forcefully if it is 'obvious' what should be done. And if people agree on the components of a situation, then they must exist. There is nothing left to deliberate about, so there is nothing left to do but act.

[9] A comparison of Sampson's (1974) and Geneen's (1984) descriptions of Geneen's management style and techniques reveals some interesting insights to life at ITT. The two descriptions are similar in content, but very different in tone.

It may be a peculiar property of ROI that it is socialized into managers earlier, longer, more frequently, and in more diverse settings than is true for other measures. Even if ROI were absurd, the fact that everyone computes it, talks about it, sees it ('believing is seeing'), draws comparisons phrased in its language, classifies novel events within its categories, and venerates it ('they sure don't make them like Donaldson Brown anymore'), may lend ROI a solidity that reduces any need to deliberate it, reflect on it, or analyze it. Believing in the value of ROI, and believing in ROI because everyone else believes in it, individual managers may act with confidence and shape events so that they conform to ROI categories and seem to prove the validity of these categories. But, people may lose sight of the fact that confident action derives from the belief that ROI premises are shared, a belief that may survive largely because it is seldom tested. ROI does reflect some real properties or organizations in the first place because there was a shared belief that they were already there. This shared belief may have led people to act in ways which then implanted what they thought had been there all along. Agreement may have intensified managerial actions, and stronger actions may have had a more decisive and long lasting effect on organizations and their environments, rearranging both so they conform more closely to the categories of ROI.

DISCUSSION

The five sets of questions described above move from the individual to the social. The first three sets focus on the number of options, how options are framed, and what people presume about actions and contexts. The first set suggests that an approach that focuses on a limited set of options may provide stronger motivation for people to act because it energizes them, provides direction and maintains activity. The second set suggests that options or 'needs for action' can have positive effects on people's cognitions, motivations and commitments if the options are stated in positive terms and tell people what to do rather than what to avoid, and if goals and performance criteria are defined in terms of the more probably outcomes of action. The third set suggests that action is likely to have more focus and force if people have general expectations about orderliness, act confidently, and thereby create the order they presumed.

The fourth and fifth sets of questions move into a social context. The fourth set builds from the third set. Actions motivated by presumptions of logic may persist if they are public, irreversible and volitional. And the fifth set suggests that shared beliefs about the value and logic of action may remove doubt and intensify action.

The preceding discussion suggests a different set of reasons for ROI's usefulness, appropriateness and durability as an accounting measure of evaluation. Companies use different definitions of profit and investment to measure ROI (Reece & Cool, 1978). Some companies use narrow, controllable measures of profit and investment, while others use broad, comprehensive measures of these concepts.

Accounting researchers tend to focus on these different definitions when they try to explain the differential effectiveness of ROI. Yet, if our speculations are correct, such assessments may miss ROI's role in providing a common language and in initiating and sustaining action. ROI may focus attention positively, provide an underlying presumption of logic and orderliness, induce public commitment, and create shared beliefs about the value and logic of action. Different definitions of ROI may influence the number and scope of the options considered, and the vigor of the resulting action once the choice is made. Since ROI may reinforce presumptions of logic and orderliness, it may operate like an idealogy [relatively coherent sets of beliefs that tend to bind some people together and may help explain their worlds in terms of cause-and-effect relations (Beyer, 1981, pp. 166–167)]. ROI may help people perceive situations similarly and share expectations and values, thereby making it easier for them to agree on what objectives to pursue, on what action alternatives hold promise, and on what outcomes are probable.

The preceding analysis also suggests a different interpretation to the recurrent observation that ROI induces short-run opportunistic behaviour (Kaplan, 1984, p. 39). Action tends to be qualitatively different from deliberation. Where action tends to be focused, concrete and to have visible, immediate effects, deliberation tends to be diffuse, abstract and to have imagined eventual effects. Where action tends to compress time (what will happen here and how), deliberation tends to stretch time (what will happen there and then). Also, action tends to induce a stronger need for feedback than does deliberation.

Procedures such as ROI may induce behaviour that incorporates some of these qualities of action such as immediacy, directness and vigor. Thus, the observation that ROI induces short-term behaviour may testify to its success as a device that creates motivation and commitment. If managers maximize in the short-run, when measured against ROI, they may tend to act rather than deliberate. They may be more concerned with action and their time perspective may become shorter. As a result, short-term maximizing may not be a flaw of ROI, but instead it may be a normal, natural accompaniement of any procedure that initiates and sustains action. Other accounting procedures such as cost–volume–profit analysis and variance analysis that also may influence action may induce a similar short-term vision.

BIBLIOGRAPHY

Anderson, P.A., Decision Making by Objection and the Cuban Missile Crisis, *Administrative Science Quarterly* (June 1983) pp. 201–222.

Baiman, S., Agency Research in Managerial Accounting: A Survey, *Journal of Accounting Literature* (Spring 1982) pp. 154–213.

Beyer, J.M., Ideologies, Values and Decision Making in Organizations, in Nystrom, P.C. and Starbuck, W.H. (eds), *Handbook of Organizational Design*, Vol. 2, pp. 166–202 (New York: Oxford University Press, 1981).

Brunsson, N., The Irrationality of Action and Action Rationality: Decisions, Ideologies and Organizational Actions, *Journal of Management Studies* (1982) pp. 29–44.

Dearden, J., The Case Against ROI Control, *Harvard Business Review* (May/June 1969) pp. 124–35.

Demski, J., *Information Analysis* (Reading: Addison-Wesley, 1980).

Demski, J. & Feltham G.A., *Cost Determination: A Conceptual Approach* (Ames: Iowa State University Press, 1976).

Demski, J. & Krebs, D., Models in Managerial Accounting, *Journal of Accounting Research* (suppl. 1982) pp. 117–148.

Einhorn, H.J., Hogarth, R.M., Behavioral Decision Theory: Processes of Judgment and Choice, *The Journal of Accounting Research* (Spring 1981) pp. 1–31.

Feltham, G.A., *Information Evaluation.* Studies in Accounting Research No. 5. (Sarasota, FL: American Accounting Association, 1972).

Festinger, L., Riecken, H.W. & Schachter, S., *When Prophecy Fails* (Minneapolis: University of Minnesota, 1956).

Geneen, H., *Managing* (Garden City, NY: Doubleday, 1984).

Jerome, W.T., III, *Executive Control – The Catalyst* (New York: John Wiley, 1961).

Johnson, H.T., Management Accounting in an Early Integrated Industrial: E.I. DuPont de Nemours Powder Company, 1903–1912, *Business History Review* (Summer 1975) pp. 184–204.

Johnson, H.T., Management Accounting in an Early Multidivisional Organization: General Motors in the 1920s, *Business History Review* (Winter 1978) pp. 490–517.

Kaplan, R.S., *Advanced Management Accounting* (Englewood Cliffs, NJ: Prentice Hall, 1982).

Kaplan, R.S., The Evolution of Management Accounting, *The Accounting Review* (July 1984) pp. 390–418.

Meyer, A.D., How Ideologies Supplant Formal Structures and Shape Responses to Environments, *Journal of Management Studies* (1982) pp. 45–61.

O'Reilly, C.A., III & Caldwell, D.F., The Commitment and Job Tenure of New Employees: Some Evidence of Postdecisional Justification, *Administrative Science Quarterly* (December 1981) pp. 597–616.

Otley, D.T., Management Accounting and Organization Theory: A Review of Their Interrelationship, Unpublished Manuscript, Department of Accounting and Financial Administration, Michigan State University and Department of Accounting and Finance, University of Lancaster, 1982.

Reece, J.S. & Cool, W.R., Measuring Investment Center Performance, *Harvard Business Review* (May/June 1978).

Salancik, G.R., Commitment and the Control of Organizational Behavior and Belief, in Staw, B. and Salancik, G. (eds), *New Directions in Organizational Behavior*, pp. 1–54 (Chicago: St. Clair, 1977).

Sampson, A., *The Sovereign State of ITT* (Greenwich: Fawcett Publications, 1974).

Snyder, M., When Belief Creates Reality, in Berkowitz, I. (ed.), *Advances in Experimental Social Psychology*, Vol. 18, pp. 247–305 (New York: Academic, 1984).

Snyder, M., Tanke, E.D. & Bersheid, E., Social Perception and Interpersonal

Behavior: On the Self Fulfilling Nature of Social Stereotypes, *Journal of Personality and Social Psychology* (1977) pp. 656–666.

Solomons, D., *Divisional Performance Measurement and Control* (Homewood: Irwin, 1965).

Starbuck, W.H., Congealing Oil: Inventing Ideologies to Justify Acting Ideologies Out, *Journal of Management Studies* (1982) pp. 3–27.

Starbuck, W., Organizations as Action Generators, American Sociological Review (February 1983) pp. 91–102.

Starbuck, W.H. & Hedberg, B.L.T., Saving an Organization from a Stagnating Environment, in Thorelli, H.B. (ed.), *Strategy + Structure = Performance*, pp. 249–58 (Bloomington: Indiana University Press, 1977).

Staw, B.M., The Escalation of Commitment to a Course of Action, *Academy of Management Review* (1981) pp. 577–587.

Swieringa, R.J., Accounting Magic, *CGSM Enterprise* (Spring 1984) pp. 21–26.

Swieringa, R.J. & Weick, K.E., An Assessment of Laboratory Experiments in Accounting, *Journal of Accounting Research* (suppl. 1982) pp. 56–99.

Thompson, J.D., *Organizations in Action* (New York: McGraw-Hill, 1967).

Vancil, R.F., *Decentralization: Managerial Ambiguity by Design* (Homewood: Dow Jones-Irwin, 1979).

Weick, K.E., *The Social Psychology of Organizing*, 2nd edn (Reading: Addison-Wesley, 1979).

Weick, K.E., Managerial Thought in the Context of Action, in Srivastra, S. (ed.), *The Executive Mind* pp. 221–242 (San Francisco: Jossey-Bass, 1983).

Winter, R.E., Avoiding Risks: Stree on Fast Profits Called A Key Deterrent to Capital Spending, *The Wall Street Journal* (Friday, 10 June, 1977) pp. 1, 27.

Part Three

Accounting for Non-Programmed Activities

Our emphasis on the distinction between programmed and non-programmed activities allows our analysis to recognize uncertainty explicitly. In *Accounting for Management Control*, the precise sources of uncertainty are not identified and this is intentional. The significance of dynamic market forces, changes in personnel, corporate strategy and internal systems of control may, individually or in combination with other sources at any point in time, render the divisional management's decision-making task more or less programmed. The important aspect to acknowledge in our view is that all decision-making under these real-life assumptions will require a degree of intuition, judgement and discretion. Whether uncertainty influences the business enterprise to adopt a different organizational structure to the unitary or functional organization, whether this consequently causes complex interrelationships to emerge in the internal operations of the organization and whether the design of the accounting information system (AIS) promotes behaviour congruence or provides an incentive for managers to emphasize short-term, quantified performance measures play a central role in the control process. The readings selected here follow this sequence.

ORGANIZATION STRUCTURE

The relationship between corporate strategy, organization structure and market performance is the focus of Caves's (1980) article which surveys the non-economic literature on this series of issues. The emergence of the multidivisional structure as a response to diversification, technological change and environmental uncertainty is traced over time. With growth in size, the need to develop and rely upon an all-embracing system to monitor diverse activities and complex interrelationships is apparent. The AIS is one such system but its imposition may itself cause managerial decision-making behaviour to change, not always in the firm's best interest. The success of corporate enterprises is therefore insufficiently explained by reference to market performance alone. The author calls for a greater interest by economists in corporate strategy and internal systems in order to explain why firms displaying different organizational designs appear to perform effectively in the same industrial markets.

Measurement of divisional performance is the focus of the Emmanuel and Otley (1976) and Scapens (1978) papers. The debate surrounding residual income may be viewed as significant when segments or divisions of the firm are treated as investment centres. Emmanuel and Otley take a managerial behaviour view which examines reactions to alternative profit performance measures. For planning and monitoring purposes, residual income can be argued to give less ambiguous signals than rate of return on investment or absolute profit measures. Despite the practical difficulty of determining which cost of capital to employ in the calculation of residual income, its successful application may be most appropriate when divisional management exercise significant influence over the capital investment decision, an issue which may reflect or influence corporate strategy itself. The effectiveness of the performance measure to obtain the correct response from managers is therefore conditioned by the strategic and organizational setting. The consistency between residual income as a short-term measure of managerial performance and the maximization of net present value (NPV) is ably demonstrated by Scapens. Economic profit, and hence residual income, can be improved by the use of an enterprise-wide decision model. This is an interesting conclusion given the differing growth, risk and profitability profiles most multidivisional firms exhibit and contradicts the view that each division should have a separate cost of capital. As in other parts of the performance measurement literature, a trade-off between the practically feasible and theoretically desirable must be made.

MANAGING COMPLEXITY

This preference for company-wide decision models has a parallel in the transfer pricing literature. With increasing size and adoption of the multi-divisional structure, the interrelationships between parts of the enterprise become more complex. Transfer pricing can be viewed as a mechanism of integrating or differentiating divisional operations. The neoclassical economic approach views this problem as finding a company-wide solution, the transfer price being the means to secure the optimal amount of inter-divisional trade. However, this approach inevitably impairs and limits the decision-making autonomy of divisional management. Watson and Baumler (1975), in their seminal paper, attempt to evaluate when transfer pricing as an integrating or differentiating mechanism could be best used. They are inevitably driven to identify not just the pricing base but also the process and objectives transfer pricing systems may serve. They recognize that whilst sub-optimization can be demonstrated by means of neoclassical economic and mathematical models, the value of decentralized decision-making can rarely, if ever, be quantified. However, this is not to say that the largely intangible benefits of decentralization are any the less important.

A transfer pricing procedure designed to balance the worst excesses of abuse of divisional autonomy and centralization is suggested by Emmanuel and Gee (1982). Uncertainty in intermediate markets is explicitly recognized and a 'fair and neutral' procedure is recommended whereby the means of calculating the transfer price is known before inter-divisional trade is undertaken, with the actual value only becoming known subsequently. Hence divisional autonomy is maintained but the choice between trading internally and externally is based on comparisons of relevant cost data for decision-making and forecasts of market prices. The possibility of sub-optimization persists but the resulting divisional profit figures are argued to reflect the decision-making responsibilities of the managers concerned.

The consideration of market imperfections is taken further by Spicer (1988) whose analysis is firmly embedded in the organizational failures and transaction costs literature. Six hypotheses are developed which for the first time offer an organizational framework in which transfer pricing can be examined. The theory of the transfer pricing process acknowledges the influence of strategy, centralization, arbitration procedures, performance related incentives and the characteristics of the item being traded. In many respects, the six hypotheses provide a structure for future research and demonstrate the ample scope that remains. If there is an apparent limitatation in Spicer's framework, it is the relatively low significance associated with divisional autonomy and the behavioural issues highlighted by Watson and Baumler. Nevertheless, Spicer has indicated a potentially fruitful way forward whilst Grabski (1985) provides an overview of current research. As his paper deftly shows there are almost as many transfer pricing techniques as there are researchers. There are also almost as many roles, especially in the international movements of goods and services, which transfer pricing may play. A comprehensive survey of empirical research reveals the variety of practice and the author concludes that a behavioural approach is likely to be the most rewarding for future research. From the plethora of options, Grabski supports negotiated transfer pricing which may reduce conflict within multidivisional firms, especially if performance of the entire firm is highlighted. Again, there is the recognition that transfer pricing must be viewed within its organizational context.

BEHAVIOUR CONGRUENCE

In our desire to establish behaviour congruent performance measures to ensure divisional management take non-programmed decisions compatible with the overall interests of the firm, we identified inaccuracy, incompleteness and non-neutrality as major obstacles. Of these, perhaps the short-term property of virtually all financial performance measures is the most pervasive in practice. Divisional management is delegated decision-making autonomy and, in return, is held strictly accountable for financial performance. When this accountability concentrates on quarterly, half-yearly or even annual evaluation, there is the distinct possibility that divisional management will perceive attainment of the financial measures as the goals themselves rather than as means to a desired end. Pressure to achieve these short-term measures may be reinforced when an incentive scheme is linked to them and this may lead divisional management to take decisions which safeguard self-interest but which result in second-best solutions for the firm as a whole. This lack of behaviour congruence is clearly seen when, for example, different accounting models are used to evaluate managerial performance as distinct from capital investment proposals. The potentially harmful effects of short-term financial performance measures being associated with incentive schemes and with capital investment proposals are addressed by the articles of Merchant and Manzoni (1989) and Haka, Gordon and Pinches (1988) respectively in this part. However, the contributions of Scapens and Emmanuel and Otley which appeared earlier are also relevant to these issues.

Although there are several surveys which indicate the use of incentive schemes in practice, there is surprisingly little evidence relating to their effectiveness, either from the viewpoint of the firm's top management or divisional management. One of the few exceptions is the article by Merchant and Manzoni. With data gathered from 54 profit centres in 12 corporations in the USA, they find that on average, eight or nine times out of ten, the annual budget target is achieved. This contrasts with the conventional claim that motivational budgets should be achieved less than 50 per cent of the time. However, the managers interviewed in this study argue that corporate reporting and resource planning, control and even motivation is improved under the incentive schemes they experience. Short-term financial performance measures may not therefore lead to incongruent behaviour if the targets set are easily achievable. Hence, the degree of difficulty of attainment may be an ameliorating variable. Defensive routines created by divisional management to provide alibis for under-performance are avoided (see Argyris (1990) in Part Four for a theoretical justification). However, the Merchant and Manzoni study does prompt the question: 'Was the incentive scheme really essential in these situations and what was it trying to achieve?' If the profit centre managers were programmed decision-makers, the findings may not be so surprising.

Another potential contradiction to the conventional wisdom is exposed by Haka, Gordon and Pinches. Firms using sophisticated capital budgeting techniques such as NPV and which account for risk should theoretically perform better than firms using naive models such as the payback period or accounting rate of return. However, for a matched pair survey of 30 sophisticated and 30 naive user firms, no evidence to support the claim can be made. One explanation which could not be controlled for concerned the individual company's incentive and reward structure. In the decentralized multidivisional firm this might result in managers submitting more or less projects for approval and these would vary in the extent to which self-interest and company interest are aligned. Both of these empirical studies indicate that our present level of understanding as to the actual use made of short-term performance measures is limited. There is a whole host of interesting issues to be researched and we are only beginning to pose the questions in a meaningful manner.

CONCLUSIONS

In total, this selection of readings provide a rich body of evidence testifying to the complexity of operating a multidivisional structure successfully. The majority of these papers explicitly recognize uncertainty, and hence the non-programmed nature of divisional management decision-making. The underlying message is that we, as accountants, advocate the use of certain techniques at our peril if we do not take into account the strategic, behavioural and organizational dimensions which are a central part of exercising effective control in today's large business enterprise.

16

Industrial organization, corporate strategy and structure

Richard E. Caves
Harvard University

Let us start with a sketch of the relationships to be surveyed in this paper. The large firm sells[1] in product markets having structural features that constrain its behaviour and define its options. 'Market structure' refers to certain stable attributes of the market that influence the firm's conduct in the marketplace. Significant elements of market structure include the number and size distribution of sellers and buyers, height of barriers to entry and exit, extent and character of product differentiation, extent and character of international competition (if the market is defined no more broadly than the nation), and certain parameters of demand (elasticity, growth rate). The firm holds tangible or intangible semi-fixed assets or skills. The top managers' perceptions of the market structure and the firm's strengths and weaknesses jointly determine their choice of *corporate strategy* (its long-run plan for profit maximization) and *organizational structure* (the internal allocation of tasks, decision rules, and procedures for appraisal and reward, selected for the best pursuit of that strategy). Both corporate strategy and organizational structure influence the economic performance of the firm and the market in which it sells.[2]

These relations between the firm and its market environment lie at the intersection between industrial organization, as a branch of economics, and the study of organizational behaviour and administration. My intention is not to survey literature familiar to economists but to synthesize and report research undertaken from other disciplinary bases. One of my objectives is to report some interesting findings about the causes

[1] The discussion in this paper will relate to the firm primarily in its capacity as a seller, although in principle the analysis should be symmetrical between the selling and buying sides of the market.
[2] By the economic performance of the firm we mean its efficiency (measured by the divergence of its input-output relation from the best attainable), its profitability relative to comparable competitors, or some other operational test of efficiency. However, our inquiry is ultimately motivated by a concern with market performance, an aggregation over the performance characteristics of firms in the market.

Source: Caves, R.E. (1980) *Journal of Economic Literature*, **XVIII**, pp. 64–92.

and consequences of market structure, arising from the firm's strategic choice and structural adaptation. The other goal is to present some promising opportunities for theoretical and empirical research flushed out by scholars in other disciplines. I shall cover a literature from business history on the evolution of the large multidivisional company as a response to changing technologies and market opportunities, studies from business policy that view the same relation in cross-section, and analyses from organizational behaviour and sociology of the influence of technology, uncertainty, and competition on organizational structure. The first two literatures are treated together in the first part of this paper because they share a common conceptual foundation. The third receives separate treatment. Economists' contributions, both theoretical and empirical, are noted where appropriate, but my emphasis is on wares imported from other disciplines.[3]

I. THE POSITIVE ECONOMICS OF CORPORATE STRATEGY

A. Corporate Strategy and Organizational Structure: Concepts and Theoretical Framework

The unifying concept of corporate strategy first emerged in the study of business decision-making to provide business managers with a simple and operational method for devising a long-term plan to assure the maximal attainment of the firm's objectives.[4] The firm rests on contractual relations that unite and coordinate various fixed assets or factors, some of them physical, others consisting of human skills, knowledge, and experience – some of them shared collectively by the managerial hierarchy. These factors are assumed to be semipermanently tied to the firm by recontracting costs and, perhaps, market imperfections.[5] An implication

---

[3] It should be stressed that the literature of business policy covers a great wealth of case studies and experience distilled by practitioners into a body of normative instruction for business students and advice for business executives. This survey makes no attempt to synthesize that material. It is concerned only with positive or explanatory models and evidence that has taken the form of systematic cross-section studies. Coverage of the case-study material would no doubt enrich the conclusions reported below.

[4] Important textbook statements are Kenneth R. Andrews (1971) and H. Igor Ansoff (1965). When we translate this process into economic terminology we shall assume that the goal is long-run profit maximization (maximum present market value of the firm). The authors surveyed in this section seldom tie their analysis to any goal that precise. They often imply that avoidance of risk (especially risk of bankruptcy) motivates the firm, and there are occasional suggestions of growth maximization. No important issues discussed below will turn on the exact ingredients in the objective function of the firm's managers or owners.

[5] Furthermore, at least some of them are simply not traded on open markets that permit capitalizing their differential qualities into their contract prices. Thus rents that the firm can earn are not entirely passed along to the unique fixed factors responsible for them. The strategy model does not itself explain why firms should

is that the firm does its long-run planning taking fixed factors as given, so that its maximization process becomes one of maximizing quasi-rents to these fixed factors. Another implication of these heterogeneous fixed assets is that a firm can succeed (i.e., forge a viable combination of fixed inputs) in a given market by possessing superior assets of any of several types. Equally successful market rivals thus may employ quite different bundles of fixed asset qualities (strengths and weaknesses).

These properties of corporate strategies and their formation hold several implications for the market environment in which strategy is to be employed. The standard model of perfect competition assumes these fixed factors away, and so the concept of corporate strategy applies to market environments that would be described as imperfectly competitive. Because the strategy model implies that competing firms earn different efficiency rents and that they can serve the same market by means of quite different input combinations, we expect that the products they offer to the market are multidimensional and heterogeneous, and that a firm's strategic strengths and weaknesses can be evaluated meaningfully only with respect to identified rivals. The strategy model hence has an affinity for a market structure of differentiated oligopoly.

Strategic choice is a general process (as defined in the business literature). However, only a few major types of strategic decisions have been studied systematically – those committing the firm to multimarket activities through diversification, vertical integration, and geographic market expansion (multiregional or multinational production).[6] Insight seems to come from less general models that explain why firms extend administrative links across activities in different markets and thereby displace arm's-length contracts, the economic use of proprietary information, etc. Although multimarket activity is clearly a central strategic choice, other strategic choices can probably be identified empirically and analyzed theoretically.[7]

The other key concept is that of organizational structure, the arrangements whereby the firm motivates, coordinates, appraises, and rewards the inputs and resources that belong to its coalition.[8] The choice of these arrangements also can be conceived as an optimizing decision, and some theoretical aspects of the allocations involved are considered in *Section*

be organized around long-term contractual coalitions. Given that they are, it explains how their shared objectives are pursued.

[6] Paul H. Rubin (1973) and Michael S. Proctor (1976) deal with the expansion of the firm holding fixed assets that cannot be costlessly divested in the short run. An important antecedent is Edith T. Penrose (1959).

[7] For an attempt, see Derek F. Abell (forth.).

[8] The term 'structure' will be employed here because it has become conventional, although it is in some ways unfortunate. It suggests – quite properly – the firm's organization chart, but it does not adequately invoke the control apparatus by which the firm keeps its records, appraises and evaluates the performance of its various inputs and activities, or motivates and rewards its employees. The breadth of the concept should be kept in mind, especially because most empirical research has addressed the organization-chart aspects of structure.

II of this survey. For now, we can view the selection of organizational structure more narrowly as a process of choosing arrangements that maximize the value of the firm's chosen strategy, given the fixed assets that warrant that strategic choice. Oliver E. Williamson (1970) has formalized Alfred D. Chandler's analysis of the properties of two key prototype structures – the functional and the multidivisional – and the relation of their respective advantages to the firm's strategic alternatives. The functionally specialized firm subdivides its activities into departments, each of which undertakes a distinctive function – production, finance, marketing, etc. Their heads report to a chief coordinator whose responsibilities must include the continuous reconciliation of the subgoals set for these departments. The multidivisional firm makes its primary organizational breakdown into divisions assigned different tasks or having responsibility for serving different markets. Each division contains an appropriate set of functional departments. The top coordinator appraises the performance of divisional profit or cost centers, characteristically using return-on-investment criteria, and concentrates chiefly on formulating long-run plans and making a consonant allocation of resources among the divisions.

A departmental organization in a functional firm can achieve economies of specialization and scale and reduce the number of communication channels needed among members of the firm. However, diversification and geographic expansion by the firm (with or without departmental proliferation) inject problems that are potentially solvable by switching to a multidivisional (henceforth MD) form. One problem arises from the mere expansion of the organization's size. Given the supervisor's span of control, enlargement of the number of primary operatives requires a predictable increase in the number of supervisory levels; more vertical levels mean greater 'control loss' as messages get garbled while passing up or down the hierarchy, and the top coordination level experiences increased problems with 'bounded rationality' – its ability to absorb and act promptly upon all relevant information (Williamson, 1970, chap. 2).

Another problem arises if the firm's growth enlarges the number of activities it undertakes. If so, each functional department may come to carry on heterogeneous activities, even if additional departments are created. Redundant communication channels are retained within functional departments, and channels between them are inefficiently used. The top coordinator's task multiplies in complexity, especially because performance criteria cannot easily be applied to the individual activities in the firm's portfolio. The MD form offers a potential solution to either or both problems.

The preceding analysis follows Williamson and others in explaining why firms may switch from the functional to the MD form as their activities grow larger and more complex. Although some writers tend to conclude that the MD firm has all the advantages, the Williamson model really implies that the rational choice between the two depends on the firm's circumstances (1975, pp. 148–50). With the firm's activity set held constant, adoption of the MD form presumptively costs the firm the resources needed to add a new top layer of coordination. It gains the efficiency of being able to use better performance criteria, and it may gain from reductions in control loss, the deletion of redundant communication channels as the functional departments undergo reorganization, and economies in the use of specialized resources as the top coordinator's elite staff is formed.

The elements of bounded rationality, control loss, and the avoidance of redundant communication channels carry many specific implications for the design of organizational structures that minimize administrative cost or maximize the expected value of a corporate strategy (James D. Thompson, 1967; Jay W. Lorsch and Stephen A. Allen, III, 1973, chap. 8). Most of these implications have emerged from empirical investigations rather than being derived from abstract premises. Consequently the next sections focus on historical evolution and cross-sectional analysis.

B. Historical Evolution

The development of the American economy in the past two centuries has brought great changes in technology, market structure, and the organization of companies, and these sweeping changes reveal starkly the power of the market environment to alter business strategy and structure. The major systematic insights stem from Alfred D. Chandler's two books *Strategy and Structure* (1962) and *The Visible Hand* (1977).[9] The former – as original conceptually as it was historically – concentrated on the changing strategies of a small group of large companies and analyzed their groping efforts to devise new organizational structures to pursue these strategies more effectively. *The Visible Hand* takes a longer perspective on the changing opportunities for business enterprise wrought by changes in technology and market organization from the late eighteenth century down to the present, but with emphasis on the nineteenth century. It stresses the connection between the market's constraints and opportunities and the frontier of companies' strategic choices – the opportunities seized by the frontrunners and later disseminated to other competitors and industries. The following analytical summary can only hint at the richness of Chandler's analysis.

Early in the nation's development the small sizes of markets, the slow pace of transportation media, and the primitive technology for transmitting information denied any reward for the productive coordination of economic activity through the large enterprise. Slow communications, whether between or within firms, forced a decentralized trading company to employ a 'trusted agent' at each trading point; it could not decentralize decision-making beyond equity participants in the firm. The restricted opportunities for hedging limited the size of the firm, as did small markets, costly transportation, and the lack of large-scale power sources. The firm had little to gain from sophisticated accounting systems (costs

[9] Chandler draws on a wide variety of historical materials, including numerous company histories. We shall not attempt to extend our survey to the level of these company histories. (See Bernard Alford, 1976.)

mattered less for trading profits than did skill in acting quickly on limited market information) or closely coordinated logistics (because of the slow pace of transportation) (Chandler, 1977, chaps. 1, 2). As a result, in 1840 there were no middle managers in the United States and, correspondingly, little scope for strategic choice and sophisticated organization.

Strategic choices leading to large-scale organization first became possible with the rise of modern modes of transportation and communication – the railroad and the telegraph. Chandler concentrates on the railroad enterprises themselves, especially the Pennsylvania (1977, chap. 3). First the consideration of safety, then the organization's sheer volume of transactions and size of its capital requirements impelled an integrated, hierarchical organization. From the railroad's efforts to deal efficiently with its complex task emerged many mainstay features of modern business organization – financial accounting, the line-staff distinction, and data flows permitting the comparative appraisal of performance. Functional, departmentalized organization evolved, as indeed did geographic divisions, and eventually the multidivisional form for managing the many properties acquired by some major railroads. Chandler contrasts this organization evolved by 'managerial' railroads such as the Pennsylvania with the very different structures of independent companies with interlocking directorates and a central financial office employed in the railroad empires dominated by financiers, such as the New York Central system. The lesser effectiveness of this later system for long-term planning and coordination was shown in the greater centralization that their managers imposed on these networks as internal reorganizations took place (1977, pp. 175–85).

Fast modes of transportation and communication gave rise to strategic options that led to national and multimarket firms in the manufacturing and distribution sectors. Successful firms could now establish branded goods, build national distribution systems, and develop multiproduct lines. Which industries seized these strategies also depended on changing technology; Chandler finds that the firms venturing to integrate forward into distribution were employing new large-scale technologies whose production outran the firm's previous distribution capacity (1977, chap. 9). He attributes the resulting large size of firms and enduring high levels of seller concentration not so much to the new capital- and energy-intensive technologies (except in primary metals) as to the resultant vertical integration into marketing and distribution systems (1977, pp. 364–67). Integrated distribution systems in turn tended to have excess capacity and hence to promote the broadening of product lines,[10] so that integration and diversification ultimately proved complementary. While some firms

---

[10] Chandler (1977, pp. 307, 326); Thomas Horst (1974, chap. 2). This analysis yields other conclusions of great interest for industrial organization. First, specific motives for displacing arm's-length distribution systems can be observed: effecting product differentiation, guaranteeing service on new and complex machinery, reducing uncertainty and delay in cash flows associated with the thinner stream of information flowing from arm's-length distributors. Second, the analysis reveals a great deal about the genesis of entry barriers, conveying the impression that

successfully chose these strategies of large-scale integration, others opted for a strategy of horizontal merger to attain monopoly profits or stem the erosion of local monopolies. Chandler argues that merger strategies failed unless the combining firms genuinely consolidated and adopted a strategy of vertical integration (1977, chap. 10). One wonders, though, whether the failures lost out through oversight or because integration in some industries failed to offer either real or pecuniary economies. This problem – whether strategic choice is determinate or involves entrepreneurial free will – turns up repeatedly in the literature surveyed in this paper.

If much of Chandler's *The Visible Hand* traces the effect of changing technology and market structures on firm's opportunity sets, his *Strategy and Structure* (1962) shows how the resulting innovations in corporate strategy subsequently induced changes in business organization. Companies whose success brought them to prominence in the national market for their principal product followed the lead of the early railroads and communication companies, employing a functional organization to minimize costs. Eventually, however, the continued expansion of companies in geographic or product space made their functional departments too heterogeneous for maximal effectiveness, and the multidivisional form was adopted. Chandler's case studies reveal that this form evolved independently in four major companies, emerging not full-blown but as a piecemeal adaptation to recurrent problems (1962, chaps. 2–5). The timing of the change, if not its ultimate fact, often depended on a perceived threat that made clear the hazards of continuing with the old organization. Although the MD organization itself serves to decentralize operating authority while centralizing the planning and coordination roles, these companies in some cases went through periods of tighter centralization when the weaknesses of previous organizational structures showed up (e.g., excessive inventory accumulation in the 1921 recession).

Foreign direct investment resembles integration and diversification in carrying the firm into multimarket activity (Peter Buckley and Mark Casson, 1976, chap. 2) and so it should receive parallel treatment. Mira Wilkins identifies the developments in market organization and public policy that brought the multinational companies into being (1970). Some companies chose a strategy of foreign production when foreign agents handling export sales failed to provide adequate servicing or to differentiate the product effectively. Others became multinational when foreign acquisitions were made to quell a price war or cement a nonaggression pact with foreign competitors. Still others were pushed into foreign production by foreign tariffs or patent laws, which made exports unprofitable. Horst's study of the food-processing firm notes the stronger propensity to foreign investment by the 'marketers' – firms skilled in the promotion of branded goods – than by the 'distributors' – firms whose domestic strategies had emphasized the low-cost distribution of undifferentiated goods through geographically integrated distribution systems (1974,

barriers we now tend to blame on advertising originally stemmed from scale economies in integrated distribution systems.

chap. 3). Clearly the former strategy would travel to distant lands more effectively than the latter. Overall, the forces that caused or facilitated multinational status correspond well to those uncovered by Chandler.

C. Cross-section Evidence

Chandler's penetrating insights were picked up by other students of business organization who applied them to cross sections of leading non-financial corporations in several industrial countries. Besides testing in cross section Chandler's hypothesis that strategic options determine organizational structures, these studies reveal the channels by which innovations in business organization spread internationally, and the social and economic forces that spur or retard them. Other systematic empirical studies have probed the association between strategy and business structure, and its implications for market performance.

John H. McArthur and Bruce R. Scott explored the reliance on strategic planning of a small cross-section of French enterprises and tested (with negative results) for a relation between major strategic moves and the choice of appropriate organization structures (1969, chap. 5). Leonard Wrigley showed that the strategies employed by large manufacturing firms can be classified systematically (1970), and that strategy and structure are aligned as Chandler's work suggested. Wrigley's classification of strategies, the basis for most subsequent work, turned on the degree of diversification of the company and the relation between its diversified activities and its basic business. Wrigley (1970) and later Richard P. Rumelt (1974, chap. 1) emphasized the subjective and company-specific character of the definition of basic business and the bonds that link it to the company's other businesses. That is, firms can make their businesses cohere in a variety of ways, and two firms' basic businesses might consist of sets of activities partly overlapping each other, integrated to equal degrees but in different ways. When he defined basic businesses in this non-mechanistic fashion, Wrigley found that large companies were not distributed continuously in their degree of diversification. He distinguished first between single-product and dominant-product firms, with non-basic businesses in the latter accounting for no more than one-fifth of sales. At that threshold he found a break in the distribution: if a company's diversified activities account for as much as 20 percent of sales, it had usually gone on to raise the diversified percentage of its sales to 40 percent or more. Companies with 40 percent or more diversified sales were classified into 'related product' and 'unrelated product' groups. An unrelated-product firm's diversifying activities carry it primarily into technologies and markets that are not shared with it basic business, whereas related-product firms exhibit one of many linkages to the basic business (similar products, processes, or markets; complementary products; jointly supplied products; common technology; common markets but new technology; or application of common research results).

Rumelt (1974, chap. 1) supplied subheadings to Wrigley's categories in order to identify the process by which basic and peripheral businesses are linked. He subdivided the 'related' and 'dominant' groups into companies whose diversification was either 'constrained' (stayed in businesses necessarily and directly related to the basic business) or 'linked' (businesses entered were initially unrelated, but the firm devised ways to tie them to its basic business). The 'dominant' category also contains a sub-category for vertically integrated dominant firms. The 'unrelated' group is subdivided into 'unrelated-passive' and 'acquisitive conglomerates' (the latter are fast-growing and thin in their top management). Rumelt's addition of these strategic linkages nicely complements Wrigley's finding that large companies were not distributed continuously in their degree of diversification.

Indeed, Wrigley's key hypothesis was that multidivisional structures would be chosen more frequently by the companies whose strategies involved greater diversification, and this pattern was strongly apparent (1970, chap. 3). None of the single-product firms in the *Fortune* 500 list were MD, while 64 percent of the dominant-product group, 95 percent of the related-product firms, and all of the unrelated-product companies were MD. This finding replicated Chandler's strategy-structure relation in cross-section and indirectly confirmed that companies' strategies could be classified on a comparable basis. Still to be answered were questions of how promptly companies adapted their structures to strategic changes, and whether the strategy-structure association could be replicated for other countries. These questions were pursued in a series of studies by Rumelt (1974) on the United States, Derek F. Channon (1973) on the United Kingdom, Gareth P. Dyas and Heinz T. Thanheiser (1976) on France and Germany, Robert J. Pavan (1972) on Italy, and Wrigley (1976) on Canada.[11] Table 16.1 summarizes their key results. The studies cover different numbers of firms, but the sample sizes are desirably correlated with the sizes of the countries and thus with their total numbers of firms; that is, roughly the same proportion of the largest nonfinancial companies is covered for each. Two principal conclusions emerge:

1. As Chandler's historical research implied, the strategies of leading companies have run toward increased diversification in all of the countries. Some companies move down the categories from single-product to unrelated-product passing through all the intermediate stages, but others make discrete jumps in classification. Moves to a less diversified strategy are uncommon although not unknown. Diversified strategies emerged first in the United States, then spread gradually to other countries. The authors suggest various factors that help to explain why diversification came no sooner to Europe. Legal access to horizontal mergers reduced the incentive to diversify in order to avert risks to the basic business, and managerial preoccupation with maintaining collusive arrangements in the basic business reduced the firm's capacity to extend its activities to other markets.[12] Similarly, operation in a regulatory and bureaucratic

[11] These studies were directed by Professor Bruce Scott. Data are also available on Japan, for 1972 only. Ken'ichi Imai reports that 2.4 percent of 124 leading firms were single-product, 22.6 percent dominant-product, 33.1 percent related-product, and 41.9 percent unrelated-product (1978, p. 51).

[12] Channon (1973, p. 90); Pavan (1972, chap. 6, pp. VII-46); Dyas and Thanheiser (1976, pp. 249–50).

Table 16.1 Strategic and structural choices of leading nonfinancial companies in five industrial countries, 1950–1970[a]

Country	Year	No. of companies		Single	Dominant	Strategic classification Related	Unrelated
United States	1949	500[b]	% dist.	34	35	27	3
			% MD	5	20	44	100
	1969	500[b]	% dist.	6	29	45	19
			% MD	24	62	90	98
United Kingdom	1950	92	% dist.	34	40	24	2
			% MD	6	11	32	0
	1970	100	% dist.	6	34	54	6
			% MD	17	73	79	50
France	1950	100	% dist.	42	21	33	4
			% MD	5	0	12	0
	1970	100	% dist.	16	32	42	10
			% MD	19	59	64	50
Germany	1950–1955	99	% dist.	34	26	32	7
			% MD	0	8	9	0
	1970	100	% dist.	22	22	38	18
			% MD	9	45	88	56
Italy	1950	84	% dist.	30	24	43	4
			% MD	0	0	14	33
	1970	100	% dist.	10	33	52	5
			% MD	0	45	58	60

Sources: Rumelt (1974, pp. 51, 71); Channon (1973, Table III-2); Dyas (1972, p. 168); Thanheiser (1972, Table V-3); Pavan (1972, Table IV-3). Figures for Canada from Wrigley (1976, p. 23) are omitted from the table because they are available only for 1961–72 and because they are not classified by organization. The percentages of Wrigley's 86 companies in the four strategic categories are respectively 31, 29, 36, and 3 for 1961; 12, 38, 44, and 6 for 1972.

[a] The line labeled '% dist.' indicates the percentage distribution of companies among the four strategic categories. The line labeled '% MD' indicates the proportion of companies in each category that are multidivisional.

[b] Rumelt's procedure is based on a sample taken from the largest 500 companies for each year (1974, Appendix A).

environment such as France tended to tie down executives to mediating with public officials on operating questions and distract their attention from questions of long-range planning (Dyas and Thanheiser, 1976, pp. 242–44). Heavier tasks of reconstruction after World War II also concentrated managerial resources on production problems in the basic business and delayed diversification.

2. A diffusion of the MD structure apparently took place during 1950–70, so that in all countries the match of structure to strategy was appreciably closer in 1970 than in 1950. The lag in structural adaptation to strategy is clear in each study, but the research designs do not focus cleanly on the average duration of the lag or on what factors explain why firms in some situations might delay longer than those otherwise situated. On this issue only a few hints appear. Channon (1973, p. 75) and Pavan (1972, p. IV-50) observe that the lag has often been long and to some degree extended by the adoption of a holding company structure that permitted diversification to continue but without central strategic control. Dyas and Thanheiser (1976, p. 115 and chap. 15) confirm this for France and Germany and put the average lag in adopting MD structure behind diversification around 15 to 20 years for the median firm (1976, pp. 73, 195). In both the United Kingdom and Italy it appears that family ownership status delayed both diversification and the subsequent adoption of the MD structure.[13]

The international spread of MD structures, like that of diversified strategies, shows a lag, which again suggests the innovative role of U.S. companies. In the European countries, foreign-controlled enterprises were in the van of local enterprises in adopting the MD structure.[14] One suspects this conclusion slightly because the structural (and strategic) classification of a company in these studies is based not on the organization chart of the subsidiary itself but on that of its foreign parent. However, the role of American consulting firms, teaching materials, and personal contacts was evident (Dyas and Thanheiser, 1976, pp. 112–13). Also, Lawrence G. Franko found that the European multinationals that were quickest to abandon an informal 'mother-daughter' control mechanism were those with the largest and most successful operations in the United States (1976, chap. 8). Pavan found a demonstration effect flowing from the two large Italian state-owned companies, I.R.I. and E.N.I. (1972, p. IV-30).

The cross-section studies document a linkage between strategy and organization, but they examine only the most aggregated traits of business organization. The vintage can be fortified somewhat by turning to research on the organization of firms' multinational activities, which complicate the choice between functional and MD organization. John M. Stopford and Louis T. Wells point out that the risk (initially, at least) and specialized knowledge associated with international operations

[13] Channon (1973, p. 76); Pavan (1972, p. IV-54).
[14] Channon (1973, p. 69); Dyas and Thanheiser (1976, pp. 65, 66, 112–13); Pavan (1972, chap. 4).

demand an internal organization different from that optimal for a strategy of diversification (1972, chaps. 2, 5). Companies manage their first foreign ventures through an international division that is viewed as highly risky and hence is cordoned off from the domestic organization (often functional, at that time). As the domestic organization gravitates to product divisions, tensions result because the domestic divisions have little incentive to share their intangibles and other assets with the international division. The larger and more diversified foreign operations become, the more likely is the firm to grope for some 'global structure' – international area divisions, global product divisions, or some combination of the two.[15]

Franko's study of the viability of multinational joint ventures also sheds light on the strategy-structure relation (1971). Broadly speaking, the multinational firms tolerant of joint ventures are the diversified MD enterprises. Conversely, a more specialized and functionally organized company frequently clings to a core technology – an intangible asset that cannot easily be shared with another enterprise on a contractual basis. The functional organization finds its access to information impaired by a joint venture and fears for the damage to its goodwill asset if its various markets around the world are interdependent.

Finally, the strategy-to-structure mapping has been checked in studies that investigate whether the locus of decision-making varies with structure as it should if structures are utilized so as to maximize the value of the strategies with which they are associated. Jesse W. Markham, following the lead of previous case studies, collected information from 202 diversified companies and from 173 firms acquired by these companies. He examined the levels at which various decisions are taken – divisional profit center or corporate headquarters (1973, chap. 4). Capital-expenditure decisions were always centralized, but the centralization of pricing, advertising, and research and development decisions declined as the acquiring company's overall diversification increased. Stephen A. Allen argues that the category of multidivisional companies can be further subdivided according to the degree of divisional self-containment, the elaborateness and complexity of interdivisional coordinating devices, and the fineness of the company's divisionalization (1978). He offered some evidence that this subdivision is operational and that firms change their subcategory membership in explicable ways. Richard F. Vancil showed that the degree to which a company decentralizes functions to its divisions varies with its strategic choices (1979); broadly, the more diversified the strategy, the more functions are decentralized.

These studies demonstrate the adaptation of business organization to

---

[15] Franko's study of European multinationals (1976, chap. 8) shows that their sequence of organizational development differed because of their heritage of less competitive domestic markets. The international division was generally skipped, and the MD organization adopted internationally and at home at about the same time. His evidence suggests that the adaptation of structure to strategy was hastened by the more competitive environment that these firms faced in their foreign operations.

strategy, but they do not explain the genesis of the whole process – the environmental forces that control the choice of corporate strategy. Because the Wrigley-Rumelt classification of strategies is obviously correlated with diversification – even if not coterminous with it – one expects the causal forces of market structure to resemble those assigned to corporate diversification. That expectation holds, but the determinants of corporate strategy and structure do reveal something more.

Chandler analyzed the association between large companies' organizational structures and the market structures of their basic businesses (1962, chap. 7) – a reduced-form relation with the intermediary choice of corporate strategy solved out. He examined the 70 largest U.S. manufacturing enterprises in 1948, adducing a generous list of environmental traits associated with the choice between functional and MD organization. Some are simply the traits that cause firms to diversify their product lines. More interesting are the factors that specifically discourage such diversification because they imply scale diseconomies in top-level managerial coordination; if the firm's main activity is monolithic and imposes a heavy task of managerial coordination, it seems to have no entrepreneurial forces 'left over' to swing into diversified activities that would lead to a MD structure. Chandler finds that the following factors discourage MD organization:

1. Customers and products that are few in number, making strategic decisions simple enough that top management needs no insulation from day-to-day concerns in order to handle them effectively. Producer-good firms hence tend to eschew MD organization unless their customers are quite numerous and/or their production facilities geographically decentralized (e.g., metal containers).

2. Vertically related production processes that require intricate temporal coordination and hence a heavy volume of top-level tactical decisions. Backward vertical integration thus is negatively related to MD organization, whereas forward integration from manufacturing into distribution or the fabrication of heterogeneous final products encourages the MD structure. The pattern is consistent with the general proposition that materials become more heterogeneous as they pass through successive stages of fabrication.

3. Large absolute scales of efficient production and high capital requirements. If a firm must be 'very large' and raise giant quantities of capital to carry out its base activity efficiently, it neither diversifies much nor becomes MD.[16] Diseconomies of scale in top-level coordination are suggested by this pattern.

4. The output of a production process can be heterogeneous without mandating a MD organization as long as the process itself remains fully integrated. Petroleum refiners, for example, have tended to retain functional organizations and to go MD through geographic rather than

---

[16] This pattern was noted among American companies by Rumelt (1974, pp. 131–35), among British companies by Channon (1973, pp. 68, 77), and among French ones by Dyas and Thanheiser (1976, pp. 207–10).

product-line divisions. The presence of a large amount of custom production promotes functional organization even though the output is heterogeneous.

MD organization, on the other hand, is encouraged by the standard causes of diversification – heavy investments in marketing and distribution systems, extensive resort to research activities or use of skilled technical personnel whose capacities can be spread to other activities, high levels of risk or cyclical instability in the base activity that promotes diversification through risk-spreading.

The subsequent country studies followed Chandler in confining themselves to an impressionistic review of the market-structure correlates of companies' organizational choices, but shifted their focus from the relation between market structure and business organization to that between market structure and corporate strategy. The patterns seem consistent with what Chandler found – both as to the specific industrial sectors associated with high and low diversification and the common structural traits attributed to these sectors. Channon argues that high concentration and the sheltering effect of entry barriers deter diversification (1973, pp. 90–91, 131), and Pavan notes that falling tariff barriers pose a competitive threat that promotes it (1972, p. VII-2). The European studies agree that family control discourages diversification because its maintenance tends to limit the firm's access to both financial and managerial resources.[17]

A statistical study of 125 Canadian companies by Caves, Michael E. Porter, and Michael Spence tested the association of strategic choice with many characteristics of the firm and its base industry, confirming statistically a number of the relations already observed (1980, chap. 12). For example, the related-product firms' base industries exhibit significantly higher levels of research outlays, labor skills, and professional and technical employment than the base industries of other firms. In addition, their analysis brings out the influence of differences in the riskiness of the firm's base industry. Single-product firms in Canada are notably free of competitive threats; compared with other strategic groups, their base industries show less exposure to international competition and penetration by multinational companies, more regional fragmentation, and more product differentiation.

We can note one recent development in the adaptation of organizational structure to market structure – the matrix organization recently surveyed by Stanley M. Davis and Paul R. Lawrence (1977) and not yet sanctified by systematic empirical study. The functional organization's main virtue is minimizing cost; the MD organization's is optimizing the firm's response to changing environmental demands (especially market conditions). The matrix organization tries for the best of both worlds by employing more than one organizational stratum, e.g., one in terms of functional departments and one in terms of product markets. The key

---

[17] Channon (1973, pp. 75–76); Dyas and Thanbeiser (1976, pp. 78–79, 202); Pavan (1972, p. IV-54, chaps. 5, 7).

The positive economics of corporate strategy 349

consequence of matrix organization is that some middle managers (e.g., plant managers) will have to answer to two bosses, and the bosses must thrash out conflicting demands or jointly supervised facilities as they appear. Although the matrix organization flies in the face of wisdom reaching back to Biblical injunction, Davis and Lawrence argue that it maximizes profits for companies that (1) must manage more than one key dimension of activity that can strongly affect the firm's performance (e.g., attaining technical efficiency and discerning the needs of particular customers) and (2) face a heavy load of information processing (because events are uncertain, the organization's task is complicated, and inter-dependencies among its parts are strong) (1977, chap. 2).[18] The matrix organization is especially promising where scale economies in produc-tion must be reconciled with fragmented and diverse product markets. This kind of organization was first identified in such sectors as aeronautics and appears to some degree in many multinational companies. Matrices can take several dimensions, and neither the incidence of the form nor its chief 'objective' structural determinants have yet been charted. Indeed, one wonders whether the matrix form can be clearly distinguished from MD organizations with interdivisional coordinating devices.

The final link in the chain of relationships runs from the firm's organ-izational structure to its market behaviour. The principal study to docu-ment this link directly is Joseph L. Bower's comparative analysis of in-vestment projects undertaken by a single large MD firm (1970a). Bower holds that a company's top management approves or rejects projects but has little direct influence on how they get defined or on which ones are pushed through the firm's lower levels of decision-making to become claimants for top-executive approval. The plans cast up at these crucial early stages depend on how problems are perceived by persons who can propose investment projects as their solutions and whether middle man-agers find their interests served by providing 'impetus' – putting their reputations on the line to support the project. Definition and impetus in turn depend on the 'situational context' of these lower-level decision-makers. Context consists of organizational structure, meaning not only the organization-chart assignment of responsibilities and powers but also the organization's system of measuring and rewarding performance; it also includes an incrustation of history and random events. Middle man-agers given responsibility for a certain portion of the firm's activities will define problems in terms of their department's assigned goals and

---

[18] This case for the matrix organization indicates a key point in the business literature on MD organization that is not stressed by economists who have written on it. If the firm possesses substantial fixed factors that cannot be costlessly divested in the short run and faces a constantly varying set of market op-portunities, it pays to allocate resources to forecasting those opportunities and optimizing the reallocation, refurbishing, expansion, or divestment of the fixed assets. The MD organization reallocates top-management resources to that purpose. The matrix organization can, among other things, diffuse that adaptation machinery downward through the organization.

formulate solutions in terms of the instruments within their experience.[19] Top management cannot keep the character and composition of the projects that rise for their approval from being colored by structural context. However, top management *can* influence that structural context by means of the organization chart it establishes (and the power relations embodied in it) and the measurement/reward system it employs. In their nature Bower's cases cannot document the effect on market competition and performance of the coloration of investment projects. But since these projects determine the long-run context of a company's behaviour in its markets, this influence seems impossible to dispute.

Bower contrasts his analysis with that of Richard M. Cyert and James G. March (1963). Although this survey cannot give recognition to the Carnegie-Mellon group's impressive body of work on organizational structure and behaviour, we must note some of its limitations pointed out by Bower in relation to the topic discussed. One is that it places great emphasis on the cognitive process of problem solving, which is supposed to proceed mechanistically from the perception of job-defined discrepancies. Bower argues that the cognitive process 'merely describes how a project gets defined' and that the surrounding contextual forces permit a mechanistic definition 'only when there is no intervention from higher levels with more aggregate viewpoints' (1970a, pp. 67–68). He also objects that the Carnegie model neglects the role of impetus and that its analysis of power relations among decision centers within a business organization loses sight of the fact that the relative weight swung by different decision-makers itself is determined by organizational choices made by the firm's top decision-makers.

Studies of the relation between a business's strategy or organization and its market behaviour have not gone beyond individual case studies. Michael S. Hunt stresses that differences in the market behaviour of firms in the major home appliance industry could be explained by differing strategic choices (1972). Indirect but compelling evidence of the importance of strategic choice for market behaviour appears in cross-industrial statistical studies, which show that industries seem typically to contain firms following diverse strategies (Porter, 1979) and that the more heterogeneous the strategic-group structure of an industry, the less fully is oligopolistic mutual dependence recognized (Howard H. Newman, 1978).

D. Normative Issues

The circuit of relations among market structure, corporate strategy and organization, and market behaviour raises several normative issues about the efficiency of firms and the performance of markets. The most central of these concerns the choice of strategy and structure. The development of diversified strategies and MD structures was evidently an innovative

---

[19] This much of the analysis is anticipated by Yair Aharoni's study of the foreign investment decision process (1966, esp. chap. 6).

response to changes in market opportunities. Although the strategies facilitated by the MD corporation may have their drawbacks in that they raise entry barriers to new competitors – an issue not dealt with in this paper – this invention clearly substituted organizational for market allocation of resources in many settings where society's resources could thereby be used more effectively. Given the distribution of corporate strategies and structures that we now observe in modern industrial countries, has this boundary between administration and the market been optimally located?

Business administration specialists have approached this question obliquely via the proposition that some one strategy or structure might be intrinsically better than any other. Bruce R. Scott, in particular, argues that MD structures are intrinsically more efficient than functional ones (1973) and that the normative problems of John Kenneth Galbraith's *New Industrial State* (1967) – information impacted in the technostructure, non-profit maximizing motivation, etc. – are strictly those of the functionally organized company. Does this mean that any group of activities that the firm can encompass are better organized in MD than functional form? That merging five functionally organized companies into a five-division MD enterprise will automatically reform allocations among the subtended functional departments? Scott seems to offer an unsupported affirmative answer. Rumelt clearly recognized that strategy should be matched to the opportunities inherent in the firm's environment (1974). His first attempt to control for the firm's opportunities was not successful (1974); subsequently he developed a procedure of comparing each firm's actual profit rate to a synthetic profit rate that is a weighted average of aggregate profits for the industries in which this firm operates, using its own distribution of activities for weights (1977). The best-performing firms, on this test, are the single-business firms, and the poorest performers the unrelated-product group. *Without* controlling for industry mix, the best-performing firms would be those related-product firms that link all their activities around a common core skill; but they do not significantly outperform their competitors, on average. Rumelt's findings suggest the hypothesis that a firm doing very well in its base activity carries on with more of the same, whereas less successful enterprises seek their fortunes elsewhere (with results depending on the transferability of their talents).

Caves, Porter, and Spence employ a different approach designed to test the effect of *optimal* strategic choice on performance (1980, chap. 12). Using many characteristics of firms' base industries, they develop a model that yields an estimate of the probability that a given firm should be in each of the four strategic categories (set out in Table 16.1). They then regress a measure of each firm's profits on numerous control variables and on the probability that it should have chosen the strategy that it in fact employs. They indeed find a significant positive influence of the probability of correct choice for dominant-product and related-product firms (unrelated-product firms were too few and had to be dropped). The positive regression coefficient for the single-product group is not significant, however, suggesting that the single-product group includes both 'mature' single-product firms and adolescents that will grow into other strategies.

Just as correct strategic choice should improve economic performance, so should an organizational structure that is correct given the strategy that the firm has chosen to follow. Two recent studies test this hypothesis. In both cases the control for strategy is an indirect one, provided by restricting the sample and/or including controls for differences in the firm's opportunities. Both classify organizational structures not just as functional or multidivisional, but in a more elaborate classification derived from Williamson and Narottam Bhargava that includes holding companies, firms in transition to MD organization, and 'corrupt' MD forms, in which top management is still preoccupied with operating problems (1972).[20] Peter S. Steer and John R. Cable conclude that the functional organizations perform best when the firm is based in a process industry or an uncertain environment, but otherwise an MD form is preferred (1978). Henry Ogden Armour and David J. Teece structured their analysis of oil companies to emphasize the diffusion of the MD innovation throughout the industry (1978). They find that during the 1955–58 period MD firms were significantly more profitable, but by 1969 MD had been adopted wherever appropriate, and the difference in profits had disappeared.

Other studies using different approaches have found that firms' profits are impaired – and the social allocation of resources worsened – if organizational structure is improperly matched to strategy or if the elements of the structure are improperly combined. Joan Woodward (1965), discussed below, seems to have innovated the systematic empirical testing of the hypothesis that a firm performs better if its structure matches the requisites of its environment. Stopford and Wells found evidence that firms whose overseas operations are organizationally mismatched to their domestic structures earn lower profits abroad than those with consistent structures (1972, pp. 79–80). An elaborate study by Jay W. Lorsch and Stephen A. Allen turns on the proposition that the firm that has rationally chosen a multidivisional or a functional (vertically integrated) structure must then optimize the inputs needed to coordinate and integrate its divisions (1973). They find that the less successful diversified companies in their small sample undertook too much coordination; the less successful vertically integrated companies too little; but they recognize that the errors could just as easily have gone the other direction. Finally, K.R. Srinivasa Murthy finds that the incentive structure of the firm's executive compensation must accord with its strategic choice (1974). He investigates how tightly the top executive's compensation is keyed to the firm's short-run performance (return to book equity, growth in earnings per share). If most disturbances faced by the firm are exogenous, as for a vertically integrated dominant-product firm, there is little point in inflicting

---

[20] This classification itself incorporates performance judgments directly, and so a test of profitability in relation to these organization structures must take this potential circularity into account. Both studies mentioned in the text deal adequately with the problem.

risk on the president by tying his salary to swings in the firm's fate. On the other hand, the incentive value of profit-leveraged compensation can be realized in a related-product or unrelated-product firm where the top executive's primary role is long-range planning. The 53 companies sampled by Murthy generally match the hypothesized pattern, but the match is clearly better for the more profitable ones. Interestingly, the overall level of top-executive compensation does not vary with strategy.

Doubts have been voiced about the vaunted effectiveness of the MD organization, echoing the more general concerns heard from economists about the efficiency of the large, highly diversified company.[21] Dennis C. Mueller argues that the large MD firm becomes ripe for growth-maximizing managerial behaviour (1972), and Henry G. Grabowski and Mueller found suggestive statistical evidence that the mature company (judged by age of the company and of its principal products) experienced a lower incremental return on its investments than did younger companies (1975). Also, Bower (1970b) and the European studies stress that a holding company is a poor approximation to an MD structure and unlikely to impose rational allocation of resources upon its controlled firms as would a MD company on its component divisions.

These studies of strategy, structure, and performance nearly all agree on two propositions: (1) correctly matching strategy to opportunities and structure to strategy increases a firm's profits and presumably increases the efficiency with which society's resources are used; (2) certain strategies and structures have diffused as innovations, with large firms progressively moving toward choices that make the best of their opportunities.

II. TECHNOLOGY AND ORGANIZATIONAL DESIGN

Running parallel to the analysis of corporate strategy and structure is an independent line of inquiry, carried out by students of industrial sociology and organizational behaviour, into the relation between the technology of a production unit and certain detailed features of its organization chart. Corporate strategy is invisible in this literature, as indeed are the broad organizational divisions of the enterprise. The hypotheses developed and tested deal with the relation between market structure and organizational structure. But the spotlight now shines on details farther down the organization chart – how the span of control of each supervisor, the number of supervisory hierarchies, and the flexibility of these hierarchical arrangements respond to differing tasks of the organization. This literature hence addresses the production function of organizational design: how the organization's structure is best adapted to performing

---

[21] We note the considerable number of papers by economists who sought to determine whether corporations that have engaged in extensive conglomerate expansion are more or less profitable as a result; for a survey, see Peter O. Steiner (1975, chap. 8). Many of these papers pay little attention to the opportunity set of the diversifying firm and the very subtle problem of finding an appropriate control group for comparison.

a given task in a given market environment. It complements the strategy-structure literature described above while sharing a common form of hypothesis: market structure determines organizational structure, which in turn affects market behaviour and performance.

A. Economic Theory

This organizational production function has received some attention in economic theory. Although the theoretical contributions are empirically more tantalizing than informative, they should be juxtaposed with the evidence if only to promote future integrative efforts. A staple of the literature of public administration is a model that relates the span of control (s, number of employees supervised by each supervisor) and the number of hierarchical levels (k) to an organization's total number of employees (n). Thus, $n = (s^k - 1)/(s - 1)$. If s is taken as given, the formula explains how k must vary with n. Certain questions naturally occur to an economist who contemplates this model:

1. Why should the span of control not be considered a policy variable, to be optimized for the technical and market environment of each organization? Not much economic theory addresses optimal spans of control directly, but a good deal is indirectly relevant. Harvey Leibenstein has elaborately investigated the behaviour of employees performing under incomplete (output cannot be specified) employment contracts (1976, chaps. 6–10). Armen A. Alchian and Harold Demsetz emphasize the productivity of supervision for monitoring contracts and curbing the opportunism that would otherwise limit human participation in efficient cooperative endeavors (1972). It is also pointed out by Williamson, Michael L. Wachter, and Jeffrey E. Harris that many jobs are idiosyncratic (1975); their content cannot be determined in advance through a complete contract, nor are spot contracts viable, and so a supervisory relationship becomes the efficient choice. These considerations are closely related to the optimal structuring of the employment contract, e.g., the combination of piece-work and straight-time rates to be offered (Joseph E. Stiglitz, 1975). The interrelation between organizational structure and compensation has been developed by James A. Mirrlees on the assumption that risk-averse individuals behave to maximize individual utility and not some goal of the firm (1976). Spans of control turn out to depend on supervisors' levels of risk aversion (constant, increasing, or decreasing) and to be determined jointly with the structure of compensation. The model is extended to multiple levels of hierarchy.

2. How does the optimal span of control relate to the flow of information within the organization? The theory of teams investigates the case in which members of a coalition share common preferences but have access to diverse information (see Jakob Marschak and Roy Radner [1972]). Certain conclusions follow about the optimal amount of information to be shared and about efficient coordinating devices for sharing information or decentralizing decisions.

3. How does the multiplication of hierarchical levels, as an organiza-

tion grows, affect the organization's efficient overall size? Williamson shows formally how control loss and bounded rationality within a hierarchical organization can limit its efficient size (1967). Without any limitation placed on the firm's size by factor supplies, technology, or market demand, size is nonetheless limited by the inefficiency of expanding levels of hierarchy because (by assumption) those farther up in the hierarchy are paid more, and the control loss occurring at each hierarchical level is cumulative (that is, not offset by adding higher levels). Mirrlees's model similarly implies a limitation on firm size (1976). Guillermo A. Calvo and Stanislaw Wellisz (1978) drop Williamson's assumption about the relation between pay and hierarchical position and instead allow employees at each level to optimize effort (and thus determine their pay) contingent on the process by which they are supervised. Whether or not the optimal size of the firm is bounded depends on the nature of that process.

B. Technology and Organization: Empirical Evidence

These theoretical contributions are striking and insightful, but they do not easily yield testable hypotheses about the structures of actual organizations. Therefore we pick up the inductive empirical literature that started two decades ago from the insight that optimal organization is not a constant, but rather a set of parameters that depend on the organization's tasks, the stability of its environment, etc. Tom Burns and G.M. Stalker dramatized the issue by contrasting firms in a highly dynamic industry (electronics) with those in a stable environment (textile machinery) (1961). The latter firms chose a 'mechanistic' system of management, with well-defined responsibilities and specialist functions laid down from the top. Electronics firms employed an 'organic' approach with ill-defined hierarchies and responsibilities and little stable content to any individual's job. In an organic firm, changes coming from any direction generally modify (and are expected to modify) everybody's responsibilities. When something disturbs a mechanistic firm, it characteristically creates a new group to deal with the problem and leaves other responsibilities unchanged. Similarly, William R. Dill argued in an influential case study that the delegation of authority in a managerial hierarchy depends on the structure of the firm's environment, access to information about that environment, and managerial perceptions about the meaning of the information (1958).

These insights came together into a systematic line of research with the publication of Joan Woodward's *Industrial Organization: Behaviour and Control* (1965) (see also, 1970). Woodward's study of one hundred firms and plants in the southeast-Essex area began from the hypothesis that successful firms (successful relative to their competitors) share common organizational traits that will reveal the vaunted universal best organization. But she found that the best-performing firms were quite diverse organizationally, as were the worst-performing. Then began the search for a correlation between the unit's organization and its technology or task. The initial hypothesis was transformed: the best-performing units are those using organizational structures most appropriate to their tasks.

Woodward's procedure for detecting links between technology and organization was largely ad hoc but contains threads of a model. She eventually arrived at a taxonomy of production systems dichotomized between assembly and process technology; the former is divided into small-batch or custom production, large batch, and mass production; the latter is divided into batch and continuous-flow production. As we move from customized assembly to continuous-flow processes, the decision-making autonomy best delegated to the primary operatives diminishes and the optimal span of control changes at various levels of the organization. The span for top management widens as the pacing of production becomes more built into the technology, but the span of control of middle management shrinks as technology grows more complex. On balance, Woodward concludes that the ratio of managerial to total personnel increases along her scale, with the size of the organization held constant (1965, chap. 4).

The mechanistic-organic distinction of Burns and Stalker does not change monotonically along Woodward's typology, however. The largest spans of control for first-line supervisors come in the large-batch and mass-assembly firms, where relationships with operatives are least informal and intimate. The line/staff distinction is most fully developed here, and these firms find it easiest to produce an organization chart. Fluid, organic management systems appear at the ends of Woodward's spectrum, where either the heterogeneity of the output or the complexity of the technology is great (Woodward, 1965, pp. 60–65; Tom Kynaston Reeves and Barry A. Turner, 1972).

Woodward tests her hypothesis about performance by cross-classifying firms by technology and degree of success (1965, pp. 68–72). The highly successful tend to cluster tightly around the organizational characteristics best suited to their technologies; the poor performers are more dispersed.[22] Thus, technology appears to determine the optimal structure of an organization.

Woodward's insights have generated a large literature that refines and retests her propositions and seeks to place some of them alongside competing hypotheses. This body of material makes somewhat frustrating reading for an economist. On the one hand, the authors deserve great credit for attempting to explain features of economic organization that have suffered almost total neglect from professional economists. On the other hand, the authors are addressing problems of optimizing behaviour by the firm, although they are largely unfamiliar with the methods devised by economic theory for dealing with the firm's decisions. As a result, parameters determined outside the firm are treated as decision variables and vice versa, and many asserted results become unacceptable. Empirically, some bizarre samples are drawn that mix branch plants with

---

[22] Woodward supports this proposition only with charts for selected organizational traits, so the robustness of the finding is hard to judge.

independent firms, service establishments with manufacturing companies, and government departments with profit-seeking enterprises.[23] I shall report what conclusions seem sound from these studies and forego criticism except in a few strategic cases.

Some studies replicate Woodward's analysis or propose direct extensions or modifications of it. William L. Zwerman (1970) repeated Woodward's procedure using a sample of 55 firms in the Minneapolis-St. Paul area, drawn once again from a wide range of manufacturing industries. Like many subsequent studies, Zwerman shrinks Woodward's typology of production structures somewhat – in this case to small batch, large batch or mass production, and process technologies. He confirms most of her results while employing somewhat improved controls for other variables that might affect them. Her association of mechanistic management with large-batch and mass-production technologies is confirmed and shown to survive after control for the size of the organization and any divorce of ownership from management of the enterprise. There is no relation between the mechanistic/organic management distinction and company size except for some suggestion of a mechanistic tilt for firms employing more than one thousand. Owner-controlled firms lean toward organic management, but there is no tendency for management-controlled firms to choose a mechanistic style.[24] Zwerman confirmed Woodward's finding that top-management spans of control enlarge as we proceed from unit or small-batch to process technologies, but her nonmonotonic relation for first-line supervisors (broader spans for mass assembly technologies) was not confirmed. Zwerman found (1970, chap. 4), as did Woodward, that the proportion of supervisory personnel and the number of levels of management hierarchy both rise as we move along the technology scale. Zwerman finds some support for the hypothesis that successful firms have chosen better suited organizational arrangements than have other firms; it is not clear, though, that he follows Woodward in defining success relative to competitors in the firm's chief industry.

Woodward's model leaves little room for a nation's cultural and legal institutions to affect the firm's organization, and Zwerman's replication on U.S. firms of her findings for a U.K. population supports this negative implication. Charles J. McMillan *et al.* addressed this issue directly by drawing two transitional samples (U.K.–Canada, U.K.–U.S.) of firms or plants matched by base industry and size (1973). They found no difference in the extent of functional specialization, formalization of role definitions

---

[23] A particularly unfortunate victim is the ambitious series of studies by the University of Aston group; for a critique, see Howard E. Aldrich (1972).

[24] Zwerman (1970, chap. 3). Zwerman hypothesized that the controlling owner would choose a narrower span of control at the top in order to maximize his knowledge and control of his subordinates, and confirmed this in his sample (1970, chap. 5). Because owner-control tends to diminish along the technology scale, however, the respective influence on control spans of technology and owner-management is not clear (either for Zwerman or Woodward, who did not address the implications of an ownership–control split).

in the managerial hierarchy, or the autonomy of decision-making at various levels. The only difference was more formal documentation – more things get written down – in North American firms J.H.K. Inkson *et al.* undertook a similar study that reached the same conclusion (1970).

Woodward's election of technology types as key determinants of organization has met general acceptance, but not all have agreed with her specific predictions. Edward Harvey argues that technology types should run from the specific (unitary, turning out a fixed menu of product) to the diffuse (heterogeneous, producing a variable and/or changing mix of products) (1968). Specific and unitary technologies should require more levels of authority, a higher ratio of managers and supervisors to total personnel (Woodward would agree with these propositions), more specialization of subunits, and more formal definition of roles and procedures (Woodward would disagree with the last, for process industries). Cross-tabulations of the organizational traits of the 43 firms sampled by Harvey seem to conform to his amended technology scale, although no formal tests of significance are used. A composite score on the four aspects of organization mentioned above is strongly related to the technology scale but unrelated to the sizes of the sampled firms. Harvey's technology scale is somewhat unsatisfying because it assumes that the static variability of a firm's output mix is highly correlated with the dynamic turnover of new products – an assumption one expects to hold for the industries Harvey chose but not necessarily for all samples. Robert T. Keller, John W. Slocum, and Gerald I. Susman (1974) sought to resolve the key empirical difference between Woodward and Harvey on whether continuous-process firms run to organic or mechanistic management. Among a sample of continuous-process firms, they found organic management to be associated with successful firms, but no association between the turnover of products and factors indicating organic management (lack of impersonal hierarchy, presence of group decision-making, lack of formal rules for decision-making). Thus, they support Woodward against Harvey. Ample room remains for further work because all these studies are less than rigorous in their hypotheses and open to some criticism on their controls for the size and industry mix of the sampled firms.

An example of the microtheoretical structure needed in this literature is supplied by William G. Ouchi, who proposes that the alignment of organizational structures to the technological situation depends on how managers meter their employees' activities (1977). Methods of control vary, depending on whether or not the activity's output is measurable and whether management has specific knowledge of the transformation process. With management informed on the transformation process but unable to measure the output, control rests on monitoring the behaviour of the primary operators. In the opposite situation output norms can be set. Where management lacks both kinds of information, it rationally buys high-quality inputs and hopes for the best.[25] Ouchi tested these pro-

---

[25] Ouchi's research comes closer than most of this literature to addressing issues raised in the economic theory of agency and hierarchy (1977). Also see Ouchi's extension of this analysis to multiple levels of hierarchy (1978).

positions on data for a sample of department stores. A store with more horizontal subdivision of departments or more vertical levels of hierarchy should resort more to output-related controls because direct observation of behaviour (i.e., the transformation process) becomes more costly. This prediction is not fully supported, but among groups of employees Ouchi does find that output measures are used where the transformation process is less well known and that training of employees (as a form of behaviour control) and managers' access to output measures are inversely related.

An issue discussed more extensively than fruitfully in this literature is the relative influence of size and technology on business organization. The trouble is immediately apparent to an economist: Given input prices, any technology has its own well-defined scale-economy characteristics, which will surely influence the sizes of establishments using it (if not determine them entirely). Because size and technology are collinear, the researcher must either go after their joint influence or use a fine hand in sampling to hold one constant while letting the other vary. Before Woodward, analysts of organizations had presumed a relation between the size of a functional organization and the height and breadth of its best managerial hierarchy, and many empirical studies of the relation had been carried out.[26] Post-Woodward researchers have found that her relation between technology and organization tends to weaken or disappear in any heterogeneous sample of establishments (or whatever) that vary widely in size of unit, and the authors of the Aston studies (e.g., D.S. Pugh *et al.* [1969]) generally conclude that Woodward's findings hold for only small establishments or enterprises. This conclusion was not supported by one of the better size-*vs.*-technology studies, Peter M. Blau *et al.* (1976), who observe correctly that Woodward's technology scale is really a list of categories and not a monotonic ordering. Organizational variables – horizontal subdivision of the organization, number of vertical hierarchies, extent of functional specialization, width of spans of control, etc. – are all correlated with size (for a sample of 110 New Jersey manufacturing plants), but none shows any relation to a linearized score based on Woodward's technology scale except for the smaller plants. With the nonmonotonic character of her scale recognized, however, most of her conclusions come through.[27] It is regrettable that the authors of these studies have tended to see technology and scale as competitive rather than additive explanations of organizational structure. No samples have been drawn to isolate size variations for a given technology (or industry) or technology differences for a given size of unit.

[26] See John R. Kimberly's critical survey, which concludes rhetorically, 'Does size determine structure? Does structure determine size? Or, perhaps more fundamentally, are these even the right questions to ask?' (1976).

[27] An interesting incidental result of Blau *et al.* is that the introduction of computers affects organization in a way similar to the use of process technology, raising average skill levels and narrowing the spans of first-level supervisors (1976); but it does not have the effect sometimes predicted of reducing the horizontal subdivision and number of vertical hierarchies in the organization.

A more fruitful line of research has tested Max Weber's proposition that organizations can pursue coherent purposes either by centralizing authority (controlling the substance of decisions as they get made) or by structuring the activities of persons within the hierarchy (prescribing decision rules through specialization, standardization, formalization, or high vertical spans of control). The prediction translates comfortably into economic analysis of the organization of firms; the proportion of these control techniques should evidently depend on the nature and frequency of events requiring decisions. The Aston study had not confirmed a trade-off between centralization and formalization; however, that study's scoring system, when applied to a sample of units varying widely in their independence of higher authority, could not be expected to produce satisfactory results. John Child (1972) replicated the Aston procedures on a carefully selected sample of companies in Britain and tended to support Weber's hypothesis.

C. Effect of Competition

The studies reported so far deal mainly with the 'production set' for organizing a firm or division – how to find the most effective organization, given the technology of the unit's activity. Its organizational structure can also be affected by the market processes surrounding the unit, and the influence of competition and uncertainty have both received a good deal of attention.

The central hypothesis in Jeffrey Pfeffer and Huseyin Leblebici (1973) flow from the economic argument that a competitive environment requires tighter coordination and more shipshape use of the firm's resources, while in its absence the additional profits can be taken partly in the utility derived from organizational slack. Thus, a competitive firm should choose less horizontal separation into departments and more hierarchical layers of supervisors. It should demand more frequent reporting and specify decision-making procedures more fully in advance. It should restrict the resources under discretionary control of department heads and depend more on oral communication (writing it down takes too long). Pfeffer and Leblebici (1973) recognize that these hypotheses interact with Woodward's; diverse and changing technologies are a countervailing force for decentralization and horizontal differentiation, so some parts of her technology-structure relation should be more evident in less competitive environments. For a sample of small manufacturing firms (for which size is uncorrelated with the extent of competition), they find competition (measured from the chief executive's perception – a worrisome practice) indeed to be positively related to advance specification of decision procedures, proportion of oral communication, and review of performance. The interaction with Woodward's hypotheses also emerges clearly. For example, department heads' ceilings on discretionary spending are positively and significantly correlated with the number of product and process changes only in non-competitive environments; the same holds for the horizontal decentralization of the company and the absence of advance specification of decision procedures.[28]

Pfeffer's and Leblebici's finding that competition is inimical to written communication and performance review accords with a study by Pradip N. Khandwalla, which posits that sophisticated formal management controls may not pay their way where quick competitive response is necessary (1973a). The intensity of competition (price, product, marketing) rated subjectively by executives is correlated with measures of the delegation of authority and the use of sophisticated controls in nine decision areas, and with a measure of the selectivity of delegation and control usage. The use of controls actually shows a significant positive relation to competition overall, but this turns out to ride on product competition alone (their relation to the intensity of price competition is negative and insignificant), and product competition similarly encourages the delegation of authority (which has an insignificant negative relation to price competition). The selectivity with which controls are used is positively and significantly related to the intensity of competition (all dimensions) and positively but not significantly related to the selectivity of delegation. Thus, the speedy and selective response necessary to compete in product dimensions turns out to qualify Khandwalla's hypothesis, but generally it gains strong support. Broadly similar results emerge from a paper by Jack L. Simonetti and F. Glenn Boseman, who conclude from a study of Italian and Mexican companies that firms in competitive markets perform better if they employ more decentralized decision-making structures, whereas this trait is unrelated to the performance of firms in noncompetitive markets (1975).[29]

Another arresting analysis of competition and organization emerges from Michael A. DuBick's study of 72 newspapers (1978). The differentiation of their organizational structures (number of departments, unevenness of department sizes) is positively related to the intensity of competition (a two-firm concentration ratio), after account is taken of their sizes and various aspects of the differentiation of their urban environments. Competition induces a significant increase in the number of departments; also, the organizations of newspapers in competitive markets respond more sensitively to the degrees of differentiation found in their environments than do those of noncompetitive papers.

The firm's autonomy or competitive vulnerability should influence a very different aspect of its organization – the composition of its board of

---

[28] Contrary to Pfeffer and Lablebici, Johannes M. Pennings treats competition as an incentive for relatively loose control (1975; 1976). His sample of branch brokerage offices of a single company seems to confirm this. However, one wonders whether, within a company, the causation might not be reversed; the better performing offices are given a longer leash by top management.

[29] Simonetti and Boseman compile not only an index of economic performance (profits, growth of sales) but also one of behavioural performance that chiefly registers employees' contentment. Contentment always increases with decentralization, but economic performance does not. For a similar but less satisfactory study see Anant R. Negandhi and Bernard C. Riemann (1973).

directors. Pfeffer argues a co-optation hypothesis: when the firm is be-holden to an external power center which it can neither absorb nor be absorbed by, it awards a 'say' on the board of directors (1972). Firms with larger capital requirements should have more outside directors and more representatives of financial institutions. Firms based in regional industries should appoint more outside directors affiliated with local power centers. The total number of directors should increase with needs for external funds and the presence of regulation as well as with the firm's size (because the bigger and more diversified firm has a wider range of impacts on the community). A sample of 80 large nonfinancial companies provides confirmation for essentially all of these hypotheses (not every-thing is quite significant statistically), and firms using the 'wrong' pro-portion of inside directors (i.e., deviants from the regression plane) tend to be less profitable.[30]

D. Effect of Environmental Uncertainty

Although the effect of uncertainty on organization had been recognized in the organic-mechanistic distinction of Tom Burns and G.M. Stalker (1961), Paul R. Lawrence and Jay W. Lorsch advanced the analysis greatly with their specific and subtle treatment of uncertainty's effects on an organization's differentiation and integration (1967). Whereas Woodward emphasized uncertainty in the production department (1965), Lawrence and Lorsch are concerned with uncertainties facing all departments (production, sales, research, etc.) and in particular the problems of inte-grating these departments when uncertainty levels differ considerably among them. Empirically, they compare better-performing with worse-performing firms in a given industry as well as the organization of better-performing firms in different industries. The more that uncertainty levels faced by a firm's departments differ, the more differentiated those de-partments' organizational traits should be (formality of organization, goal orientation, time horizons, style of personal interaction, etc.). Lawrence and Lorsch find that the better-performing firms have matched the organ-izational traits of each department more effectively to the demands of its environment[31] and also attuned the relative importance of their depart-ments better to the importance (for the firm's objectives) of uncertainty stemming from various environmental corners (1967, chap. 2).[32] The more

---

[30] Michael Patrick Allen suggests (and confirms) that directoral interlocks grew less localized over a 35-year period in which the average large company surely found itself subject to more national than localized disturbances and threats (1974). Otherwise, Allen's empirical conclusions diverge somewhat from Pfeffer's.

[31] The same conclusion seems to emerge from Khandwalla (1937b), although the conceptual basis of his study is rather murky.

[32] Kawrence's and Lorsch's measure of environmental uncertainty (subjectively, from top-managers' responses to a questionnaire) has been criticized by W. Kirk Downey, Don Hellriegel, and John W. Slocum for its low correlation with objective measures of short-term uncertainty (e.g., number of competitors, volatility of price

differentiated are departments, however, the more resources must be devoted to integrating their efforts to the performance of their joint task; the better performing organizations also distinguished themselves in seeming to allocate the right amount of resources to the integrating function.[33]

The research design developed by Lawrence and Lorsch (1967) for the functionally organized firm was applied by Lorsch and Allen (1973) to the multidivisional firm. Once more, they find that the companies performing better have suited the structures of their division more aptly to the uncertainties of their environments. Given the differentiation (defined as before) of the divisions of the MD firm, the conclusion again emerges that the commitment of resources to integrative effort must be optimized. The conclusions of the two studies parallel each other quite extensively and lead the authors to a rich 'contingency theory of complex organizations' (1973, chap. 8), i.e., that optimal organization depends in a complex but predictable way on the firm's market environment. Nonetheless, I am not convinced that the problem of differentiation *vs.* integration translates from the functional to the MD organization as simply as Lorsch and Allen imply. In the MD organization, the fineness with which activities are divided among divisions is itself a policy variable – one that should be optimized jointly with the differentiation of those divisions and the integrating effort applied in coordinating them, in order to maximize the value of the firm's strategy. The findings of Lorsch and Allen imply that integrative effort should be optimized for any given degree of differentiation of divisions, but the joint decision variable – degree of subdivision – does not receive parallel attention.

Lawrence and Lorsch show that uncertainty affects not only the differentiation of the organization's departments but also the structure of those departments and the character of the devices used to integrate them (1967). Pennings drew a blank in his attempt to associate external uncertainty with the absence of bureaucracy in brokerage-house offices (1975). He explains that failure (1977) on lines consistent with Lawrence and Lorsch – that the firm may respond to uncertainty not by adopting a more flexible organization (as Burns and Stalker [1961] had suggested) but by creating organizational buffers to fend it off.

III. CONCLUSIONS

The goals of this paper, mainly positive and methodological, are best stated in terms of the structuralist paradigm of industrial organization.

___

or sales) (1975). It is not clear which group is closer to the ideal concept of the *ex ante* probability distribution of outcomes.

[33] Lawrence and Lorsch give some evidence of the resources committed to integration, but their measure of 'integration' is *ex post* contentment of managers with the achieved state of coordination. Integration in this sense does not vary among better performing companies in different industries, although differentiation differs substantially. For a study that identifies a specific resource commitment to integration, see Anders Edström and Jay R. Galbraith (1977).

We have been concerned with the way in which the firm's rational selection of a corporate strategy and an internal organizational structure responds to the market structure surrounding it and with the effect of those choices on the firm's behaviour, and hence on the structure and performance of markets. Although economists have made important contributions to our knowledge of these relations, this survey has concentrated on evidence from other fields – business history, business policy, and organizational behaviour.

Two symmetrical types of conclusions result. First, economists have something to learn from this literature. For example, there is strong evidence to support the following propositions: The structures of markets have been affected by the organizational options open to firms. The productivity with which resources are used depends on whether or not firms make the best choices of strategy and business organization, given the market and technological environments in which they operate. Innovations in business organization have arisen in the United States and diffused through the industrial world. They have enlarged the feasible scope of the corporation but have not liberated it from diseconomies in the top-level coordination of diffuse activities. Diversification is not, in the long run, a continuous process because organizational choices are discrete. Economists' vague suspicion that competition is the enemy of sloth can be specifically documented in the effect of competition (and environmental uncertainty) on the decision-making structures and control devices used by firms.

The second conclusion is that economists have something to offer in this line of research. I shall not let professional modesty blur an important conclusion: well-trained professional economists could have carried out many of the research projects cited in this paper more proficiently than did their authors, who were less effectively equipped by their own disciplines.[34] If one accepts the weak postulate that the firm is a purposive organization maximizing some objective function, it follows that its strategic and structural choice represents a constrained optimization problem. My reading is that students of business organization with disciplinary bases outside of economics would accept that proposition but have lacked the tools to follow its blueprint. Constrained-maximization problems are mother's milk to the well-trained economist. However, economists' preconceptions have steered them away from business strategy and organization as an area of research. Business organization involves

---

[34] The shortcomings include both errors and omissions. In business administration, the field of business policy has downplayed the influence of market environment on the firm's strategic choices and has sometimes fostered the delusive notion that a 'best strategy' does not depend sensitively on the firm's market opportunity set. Students of organizational behaviour have recognized the dependence of optimal organization on the environment ('contingency' in their parlance). But they have dealt too casually with the theoretical complexities of optimizing organizational structures, have treated the firm's objectives unclearly, and have embraced research designs that lack controls for differing opportunity sets and objectives.

in essence selecting the right point on a production function, but 'production function' for the economist evokes only the harmonies of labor, capital, and land. Business organization is concerned with assigning responsibilities to persons and evaluating and rewarding their performance – matters that turn on individuals' optimizing behaviour. The ingenuity lavished on individual optimizing behaviour in marriage, procreation, and church attendance has not been matched by attention to persons' adaptation to an organizational hierarchy.

There are many opportunities for the logical extension of economic research into the questions covered in this survey, and they range widely from pure theory to empirical and statistical research. Here are a few tentative suggestions:

1. The standard taxonomy of corporate strategies has proved fruitful, but is certainly incomplete. For instance, the alternative strategies available to firms directly competing in a given market often seem to differ in many ways other than the extent of their diversification and vertical integration. We must determine what other families of strategic choices are widely represented in industrial markets, what conditions lead firms to select them, and what consequences they hold for firms' organization and market behaviour.

2. Industrial organization economists have only begun to incorporate strategic choice into their analyses of market structure, conduct, and performance. The central hypothesis considered to date is that the more heterogeneous are the strategies chosen by an industry's oligopolistic members, the less effectively monopolistic will be the bargain they reach. The quality of performance associated with particular strategies could be investigated more effectively, and the performance dimensions should reach beyond allocative efficiency, the sole one addressed so far.

3. Even more incomplete is the taxonomy of organizational structures. The prototypes of personal, functional, and multidivisional organization do not necessarily exhaust the possible alternatives. And the structural options for organizing and transmitting information, or appraising and rewarding performance have hardly been identified as prototypes, let alone tested for their optimal selection. Economic theorists have recently made some arresting contributions in this area; can theory and evidence be brought closer together?

4. There lurks in the literature on organizational behaviour an unfamiliar but fundamentally economic notion of an organizational production function. The 'output' is the ability to reallocate the firm's complement of fixed factors (especially its personnel, contractually committed and with fixed endowments of skills) in response to unexpected disturbances. 'More output' means faster adjustment to a new optimal configuration of activities, following an unexpected change. The inputs are resources devoted to collecting and analyzing information, coordinating agents to whom different tasks are assigned, etc. Can theorists clarify this concept of resources committed to a capacity to adapt to disturbances and indicate the specific kinds of optimization that it implies?

ACKNOWLEDGEMENTS

The author is indebted for comments and suggestions to Alfred D. Chandler, Jr.; Herman Daems; Sharon Oster; Michael E. Porter; and Oliver E. Williamson.

REFERENCES

Abell, Derek F. *Defining the business: The starting point of strategic planning.* Englewood Cliffs, N.J.: Prentice-Hall, forthcoming.

Aharoni, Yair. *The foreign investment decision process.* Boston: Division of Research, Graduate School of Business Administration, Harvard University, 1966.

Alchian, Armen A. and Demsetz, Harold. 'Production, Information Costs, and Economic Organization,' *Amer. Econ. Rev.*, Dec. 1972, *62*(5), pp. 777–95.

Aldrich, Howard E. 'Technology and Organizational Structure: A Reexamination of the Findings of the Aston Group,' *Admin. Science Q.*, March 1972, *17*(1), pp. 26–43.

Alford, Bernard W.E. 'The Chandler Thesis – Some General Observations,' in Hannah, Leslie, ed. (1976), pp. 52–70.

Allen, Michael Patrick. 'The Structure of Interorganizational Elite Cooptation: Interlocking Corporate Directorates,' *Amer. Soc. Rev.*, June 1974, *39*(3), pp. 393–406.

Allen, Stephen A. 'Organizational Choices and General Management Influence Networks in Divisionalized Companies,' *Acad. Management J.*, Sept. 1978, *21*(3), pp. 341–65.

Andrews, Kenneth R. *The concept of corporate strategy.* Homewood, Ill.: Dow Jones–Irwin, 1971.

Ansoff, H. Igor. *Corporate strategy: An analytic approach to business policy for growth and expansion.* New York: McGraw-Hill, 1965.

Armour, Henry Ogden and Teece, David J. 'Organizational Structure and Economic Performance: A Test of the Multidivisional Hypothesis,' *Bell J. Econ.*, Spring 1978, *9*(1), pp. 106–22.

Blau, Peter M., *et al.* 'Technology and Organization in Manufacturing,' *Admin. Science Quart.*, March 1976, *21*(1), pp. 20–40.

Bower, Joseph L. *Managing the resource allocation process: A study of corporate planning and investment.* Boston: Division of Research, Graduate School of Business Administration, Harvard University, 1970[a].

——. 'Planning within the Firm,' *Amer. Econ. Rev.*, May 1970[b], *60*(2), pp. 186–94.

Buckley, Peter J. and Casson, Mark. *The future of the multinational enterprise.* New York: Holmes and Meier, 1976.

Burns, Tom and Stalker, G.M. *The management of innovation.* London: Tavistock, 1961.

Calvo, Guillermo A. and Wellisz, Stanislaw. 'Supervision, Loss of Control, and the Optimum Size of the Firm', *J. Polit. Econ.*, Oct. 1978, *86*(5), pp. 943–52.

Caves, Richard E.; Porter, Michael E. and Spence, Michael. *Competition in the open economy: A model applied to Canada.* Cambridge: Harvard University Press, 1980.

Chandler, Alfred D., Jr. *Strategy and structure: Chapters in the history of the industrial enterprise.* Cambridge: M.I.T. Press, 1962.

——.*The visible hand: The managerial revolution in American business.* Cambridge: Harvard University Press, Belknap Press, 1977.

Channon, Derek F. *The strategy and structure of British enterprise.* Boston: Division of Research, Graduate School of Business Administration, Harvard University, 1973.

Child, John. 'Organization Structure and Strategies of Control: A Replication of the Aston Study,' *Admin. Science Quart.*, June 1972, *72*(2), pp. 163–77.

Cyert, Richard M. and March, James G. *A behavioural theory of the firm. Englewood Cliffs, N.J.: Prentice-Hall, 1963.*

Davis, Stanley M. and Lawrence, Paul R. *Matrix.* Reading, Mass.: Addison-Wesley, 1977.

Dill, William R. 'Environment as an Influence on Managerial Autonomy,' *Admin. Science Quart.*, 1958, *2*, pp. 409–43.

Downey, W. Kirk; Hellriegel, Don and Slocum, John W., Jr. 'Environmental Uncertainty: The Construct and Its Applications,' *Admin. Science Quart.*, Dec. 1975, *20*(4), pp. 613–29.

DuBick, Michael A. 'The Organizational Structure of Newspapers in Relation to Their Metropolitan Environments,' *Admin. Sciencxe Quart.*, Sept. 1978, *23*(3), pp. 418–33.

Dyas, Gareth P. *The strategy and structure of French industrial enterprise.* Unpublished D.B.A. thesis, Graduate School of Business Administration, Harvard University, 1972.

—— and Thanheiser, Heinz T. *The emerging European enterprise: Strategy and structure in French and German industry.* London: Macmillan, 1976.

Edström, Anders and Galbraith, Jay R. 'Transfer of Managers as a Coordination and Control Strategy in Multinational Organizations,' *Admin. Science Quart.*, June 1977, *22*(2), pp. 248–63.

Franko, Lawrence G. *Joint venture survival in multinational corporations.* New York: Praeger, 1971.

——.*The European multinationals: A renewed challenge to American and British big business.* Stamford, Conn.: Greylock, 1976.

Galbraith, John Kenneth. *The new industrial state.* Second edition. Boston: Houghton Mifflin, [1967] 1971.

Grabowski, Henry G. and Mueller, Dennis C. 'Life-Cycle Effects on Corporate Returns on Retentions,' *Rev. Econ. Statist.*, Nov. 1975, *57*(4), pp. 400–409.

Hannah, Leslie, ed. *Management strategy and business development: An historical and comparative study.* London: Macmillan, 1976.

Harvey, Edward. 'Technology and the Structure of Organizations,' *Amer. Soc. Rev.*, April 1968, *33*(2), pp. 247–59.

Horst, Thomas. *At home abroad: A study of the domestic and foreign operations of the American food-processing industry.* Cambridge, Mass: Ballinger, 1974.

Hunt, Michael S. *Competition in the major home appliance industry, 1960–1970.* Unpublished Ph.D. dissertation, Harvard University, 1972.

Imai, Ken'ichi. 'Japan's Industrial Organization,' *Japanese Econ. Studies*, Spring–Summer 1978, *6*(3–4), pp. 3–67.

Inkson, J.H.K., *et al.* 'A Comparison of Organization Structure and Managerial Roles: Ohio, U.S.A., and the Midlands, England,' *J. Management Stud.*, Oct. 1970, *7*(3), pp. 347–63.

Keller, Robert T.; Slocum, John W., Jr. and Susman, Gerald I. 'Uncertainty and Type of Management System in Continuous Process Organizations,' *Acad. Management J.*, March 1974, *17*(1), pp. 56–68.

Khandwalla, Pradip N. 'Effect of Competition on the Structure of Top Management Control,' *Acad. Management J.*, June 1973[a], *16*(2), pp. 285–95.

——.'Viable and Effective Organizational Designs of Firms,' *Acad. Management J.*, Sept. 1973[b], *16*(3), pp. 481–95.

Kimberly, John R. 'Organizational Size and the Structuralist Perspective: A Review, Critique and Proposal,' *Admin. Science Quart.*, Dec. 1976, *21*(4), pp. 571–97.

Kynaston Reeves, Tom and Turner, Barry A. 'A Theory of Organization and Behavior in Batch Production Factories,' *Admin. Science Quart.*, March 1972, *17*(1), pp. 81–98.

Lawrence, Paul R. and Lorsch, Jay W. *Organization and environment: Managing differentiation and integration.* Boston: Division of Research, Graduate School of Business Administration, Harvard University, 1967.

Leibenstein, Harvey. *Beyond economic man: A new foundation for microeconomics.* Cambridge: Harvard University Press, 1976.

Lorsch, Jay W. and Allen, Stephen A., III. *Managing diversity and interdependence: An organizational study of multidivisional firms.* Boston: Division of Research, Graduate School of Business Administration, Harvard University, 1973.

Markham, Jesse W. *Conglomerate enterprise and public policy.* Boston: Division of Research, Graduate School of Business Administration. Harvard University, 1973.

Marschak, Jakob and Radner, Roy. *Economic theory of teams.* Cowles Foundation Monograph No. 22. New Haven: Yale University Press, 1972.

McArthur, John H. and Scott, Bruce R. *Industrial planning in France.* Boston: Division of Research, Graduate School of Business Administration, Harvard University, 1969.

McMillan, Charles J., *et al.* 'The Structure of Work Organization across Societies,' *Acad Management J.*, Dec. 1973, *16*(4), pp. 555–69.

Mirrlees, James A. 'The Optimal Structure of Incentives and Authority within an Organization,' *Bell J. Econ.*, Spring 1976, 7(1), pp. 105–31.

Mueller, Dennis C. 'A Life Cycle Theory of the Firm,' *J. Ind. Econ.*, July 1972, *20*(3), pp. 199–219.

Murthy, K.R. Srinivasa. *Corporate strategy and top executive compensation.* Boston: Division of Research, Graduate School of Business Administration, Harvard University, 1974.

Negandhi, Anant R. and Reimann, Bernard C. 'Correlates of Decentralization: Closed and Open Systems Perspective,' *Acad. Management J.*, Dec. 1973, *16*(4), pp. 570–82.

Newman, Howard H. 'Strategic Groups and the Structure-Performance Relationship,' *Rev. Econ. Statist.*, August 1978, *60*(3), pp. 417–27.

Ouchi, William G. 'The Relationship between Organizational Structure and Organizational Control,' *Admin. Science Quart.*, March 1977, *22*(1), pp. 95–113.

——.'The Transmission of Control through Organizational Hierarchy,' *Acad. Management J.*, June 1978, *21*(2), pp. 173–92.

Pavan, Robert J. *The strategy and structure of Italian enterprise.* Unpublished D.B.A. thesis, Graduate School of Business Administration, Harvard University, 1972.

Pennings, Johannes M. 'The Relevance of the Structural-Contingency Model for Organizational Effectiveness,' *Admin. Science Quart.*, Sept. 1975, *20*(3), pp. 393–410.

——.'Dimensions of Organizational Influence and Their Effectiveness Correlates.' *Admin. Science Quart.*, Dec. 1976, *21*(4), pp. 688–99.

——.'Structural Correlates of the Environment,' in *Strategy + structure = performance: The strategic planning imperative.* Edited by Hans B. Thorelli. Bloomington: University of Indiana Press, 1977, pp. 260–76.

Penrose, Edith T. *The theory of the growth of the firm.* Oxford: Basil Blackwell, 1959.

Pfeffer, Jeffrey. 'Size and Composition of Corporate Boards of Directors: The Organization and Its Environment,' *Admin. Science Quart.*, June 1972, *17*(2), pp. 218–28.

——and Leblebici, Huseyin. 'The Effect of Competition on Some Dimensions of Organizational Structure,' *Social Forces*, Dec. 1973, *52*(2), pp. 268–79.

——and Salancik, Gerald R. *The external control of organizations: A resource dependence perspective.* New York: Harper & Row, 1978.

Porter, Michael E. 'The Structure within Industries and Companies' Performance,' *Rev. Econ. Statist.*, May 1979, *61*(2), pp. 214–27.

Proctor, Michael S. 'Production, Investment, and Idle Capacity,' *Southern Econ. J.*, July 1976, *43*(1), pp. 855–63.

Pugh, D.S., *et al.* 'The Context of Organization Structures,' *Admin. Science Quart.*, March 1969, *14*(1), pp. 91–114.

Rubin, Paul H. 'The Expansion of Firms,' *J. Polit. Econ.*, July–August 1973, *81*(4), pp. 936–49.

Rumelt, Richard P. *Strategy, structure, and economic performance.* Boston: Division of Research, Graduate School of Business Administration, Harvard University, 1974.

——.'Diversity and Profitability,' Paper MGL-51, Managerial Studies Center, Graduate School of Management, University of California, Los Angeles, 1977.

Scott, Bruce R. 'The Industrial State: Old Myths and New Realities,' *Harvard Bus. Rev.*, March–April 1973, *51*(2), pp. 133–48.

Simonetti, Jack L. and Boseman, F. Glenn. 'The Impact of Market Competition on Organization Structure and Effectiveness: A Cross-Cultural Study,' *Acad. Management J.*, Sept. 1975, *18*(3), pp. 631–638.

Steer, Peter S. and Cable, John R. 'Internal Organization and Profit: An Empirical Analysis of Large U.K. Companies,' *J. Ind. Econ.*, Sept. 1978, *27*(1), pp. 13–30.

Steiner, Peter O. *Mergers: Motives, effects, policies.* Ann Arbor: University of Michigan Press, 1975.

Stiglitz, Joseph E. 'Incentives, Risk, and Information: Notes Towards a Theory of Hierarchy,' *Bell J. Econ.*, Autumn 1975, *6*(2), pp. 552–79.

Stopford, John M. and Wells, Louis T., Jr. *Managing the multinational enterprise: Organization of the firm and ownership of the subsidiaries.* New York: Basic Books, 1972.

Thanheiser, Heinz T. *Strategy and structure of German industrial enterprise.* Unpublished D.B.A. thesis, Graduate School of Business Administration, Harvard University, 1972.

Thompson, James D. *Organizations in action: Social science bases of administrative theory.* New York: McGraw-Hill, 1967.

Vancil, Richard F. *Decentralization: Managerial ambiguity by design.* New York: Dow Jones–Irwin, 1979.

Wilkins, Mira. *The emergence of multinational enterprise: American business abroad from the colonial era to 1914.* Cambridge: Harvard University Press, 1970.

Williamson, Oliver E. 'Hierarchical Control and Optimum Firm Size,' *J. Polit. Econ.*, April 1967, 75(2), pp. 123–38.

——. *Corporate control and business behavior.* Englewood Cliffs, N.J.: Prentice-Hall, 1970.

——. *Markets and hierarchies.* New York: Free Press, 1975.

—— and Bhargava, Narottam. 'Assessing and Classifying the Internal Structure and Control Apparatus of the Modern Corporation' in *Market structure and corporate behaviour.* Edited by Keith Cowling. London: Gray-Mills, 1972, pp. 125–49.

——; Wachter, Michael L. and Harris, Jeffrey E. 'Understanding the Employment Relation: The Analysis of Idiosyncratic Exchange,' *Bell J. Econ.*, Spring 1975, 6(1), pp. 250–78.

Woodward, Joan. *Industrial organization: Theory and practice.* London: Oxford University Press, 1965.

——, ed. *Industrial organization: Behaviour and control.* London: Oxford University Press, 1970.

Wrigley, Leonard. *Divisional autonomy and diversification.* Unpublished D.B.A. thesis, Harvard Business School, 1970.

——. 'Conglomerate Growth in Canada,' brief prepared for Royal Commission on Corporate Concentration. Mimeographed. London, Ontario: School of Business Administration, University of Western Ontario, 1976.

Zwerman, William L. *New perspectives on organization theory.* Contributions in Sociology, No. 1. Westport, Conn.: Greenwood, 1970.

17

The usefulness of residual income

C.R. Emmanuel and D.T. Otley
Department of Accounting and Finance, University of Lancaster

There is still a controversy over the use of residual income as a tool for
the measurement of the performance of units and managers in divisionalized organizations. This has been highlighted by the recent debate in
this journal between Cyril Tomkins [1, 2] and Lloyd Amey [3]. Tomkins
advocates the use of residual income for profit centres where control
over working capital is vested with the division, although he dismisses
it as redundant for full investment centres. Amey specifically denies the
appropriateness of residual income in either case. David Solomons [4]
originally proposed residual income as a measure capable of separately
appraising the performance of both an investment centre and its manager.
There is thus wide disagreement as to the validity and usefulness of residual income. The objective of this note is to outline the practical and
theoretical benefits and limitations of the residual income concept as a
means of appraising performance in divisionalized organizations.

THE AREAS OF AGREEMENT

Despite their disagreement on the issues mentioned above, the authors
quoted (and all the other literature on the topic of which we are aware)
do agree upon certain fundamental points. On the basis of certain assumptions, namely:

(i)   an *ex post* measure of performance is required.
(ii) the objective of the company is to maximize its net present value
      (NPV), which is equivalent to maximizing economic income as Amey
      [5] has shown.
(iii) certainty is assumed (at least initially),

it is possible to obtain agreement in the following areas.
   Firstly, if the capital base of a division is fixed outside the division and
is held approximately constant over the planning period, then residual
income is irrelevant. Profit will do equally well as a measure of divisional
performance. Secondly, if the divisional capital base varies owing to decisions taken at the corporate or divisional management level, optimal

Source: Emmanuel, C.R. and Otley, D.T. (1976) *Journal of Business Finance and
Accounting*, **3** (4), pp. 43–51.
© 1976

performance will be achieved if each investment decision is taken on the basis of NPV. Also, it is essential that each operating decision should be taken on the basis of costs which do not include an imputed interest charge on capital employed. This is the position taken by Amey. However, Tomkins has shown that the use of residual income as a means of appraising investment is consistent with NPV as long as the capital base, on which interest charges are imputed, is measured in terms of economic (NPV) value. Thus residual income (RI) is a conceptually valid, although unnecessarily complicated, means of investment appraisal. Finally, it should be noted that in evaluating divisional performance over a period, residual income for the period, with an interest charge levied on total investment valued at NPV, is exactly equal to the difference between actual and expected cash flows for the period. Thus the computation of residual income yields no more information than a comparison of actual and expected cash flows, yet is considerably more involved. It is on these grounds that Tomkins rejects the use of residual income for investment centres. It should be observed that these areas of agreement are based on economic reasoning, where valuation is achieved by taking the NPV of expected future cash flows. The results outlined above follow directly from this premise.

THE CONTROVERSY

The observed differences of opinion revolve essentially around an organizational issue. Are divisional managers in a position to take investment decisions? If they are, should a charge upon capital employed be imputed? The various protagonists give widely differing answers to these questions.

Amey holds the view that 'in the interests of achieving the firm's overall objective, divisions should not . . . have the power to determine their own capital investment' [6]. His preferred approach is to distinguish clearly between investment decisions, which should be taken by corporate management, and operating decisions which may be taken by divisional management. If this distinction is made then corporate management should take investment decisions on the basis of their NPV being greater than zero and divisional managers should not include imputed interest charges as a factor in making operating decisions as such charges are relevant only to the investment decision. However, the rationale under-pinning divisionalization is that due to time, size and informational constraints, corporate management may be unable to react effectively to dynamic changes in the business environment as they affect each part of the firm hence delegation of authority is necessitated. In practice, Tomkins believes that this delegation extends to operating decisions and their direct consequences. Thus working capital management falls into the decision making scope of the divisional manager.[1] However, the *a priori* relation-

---

[1] However with regard to raw material stock valuation Tomkins [7] suggests that realizable value should be used when increases occur in response to expected future sales, and that replacement cost should be used when the future costs of

ship between the output level decision and working capital changes which Tomkins suggests, ignores the counter-effect which credit terms and discounts can have upon the output demanded by potential customers. Nevertheless, Amey would agree that the cash outlay relating to working capital is a cost to be included in the appraisal of the division. Neither author equates working capital management at the divisional level with the creation of investment centres, even though it may involve a permanent commitment. This may be a result of the accountant's method of categorization of assets as current or fixed. When the focus of attention is the decision maker this distinction can become difficult to apply. For instance, the decision to increase sales levels may require the purchase of additional vehicles for distribution and the construction of further storage facilities. Such expenditures, although a direct consequence of an operating decision, do not easily fit into a 'current' category. Perhaps the type of capital expenditure that can typically be authorized at divisional level is characterized by being relatively small in amount, non-specific in use or directly contingent on operating decisions.

There is some evidence from the U.S.A. [8] and the U.K. [9] that divisional managers are free to authorize capital expenditures up to an agreed limit. Also, managers may 'invest' in relatively quick-returning assets or policies [10]. Perhaps of greatest importance in deciding who makes the capital expenditure decision is an acknowledgement of limited human information processing capacity which forms the rationale of setting up divisionalized companies. The ultimate decision to accept or reject a capital project rests with corporate management, but their awareness of the possible multitude of sub-decisions which have taken place and from which the final data is derived is limited. In practice, one would suspect that investment decisions may be effectively taken at a level close to where the project originates, which is typically within the division [11]. Finally, it should be noted that if the delegation of decision making to the divisional manager extends to control over the capital base, it must equally apply to the dis-investment decision. To pre-empt the discussion on our second question, if a division 'is charged for the capital it uses, it will have every incentive to liquidate, or to transfer to other divisions, assets which it can no longer profitably use' [12].

Given the empirical evidence available, it seems that there are cases where investment decisions are taken or substantially influenced by divisional managers. For such situations a measure of overall performance is required which includes both investment and operating performance. The defects of both profit and return on capital employed in this respect are well known [13] whereas residual income appears to be a *prima facie*

---

production are expected to rise. Unless the firm is planning on discontinuing business, replacement costs will always give a higher value than realizable value and it would be extremely unlikely that a divisional manager would allow replacement cost to form the basis of an imputed capital charge. This view may be explained by Tomkins' unconcern with evaluating the performance of the divisional manager, as distinct from the unit for which he is responsible.

candidate for such a measure. The value of such a composite performance measure obviously depends on the type of organizational control system that is operated, and particularly on the way in which information on performance is used by senior managers in evaluating their subordinates' performance [14]. It is assumed here that the performance measures constructed will be used in a way which have a significant impact on the behaviour of divisional managers.

To turn to the second question, Amey [15] argues that it would be incorrect to impute a charge for capital employed even where the capital is controllable by a divisional manager. In the context of Tomkin's example his argument runs as follows. Interest on debt capital is already included in the total cost curve (TC_1) and to impute an additional charge would lead to a sub-optimal decision. This is more than simple double counting for the interest cost included will be for the interest on a particular loan whereas the imputed interest charge in a residual income calculation will be generally at a quite different rate.

Amey's first point is quite correct, although it should be noted that it assumes that working capital is debt financed and that individual loans can be identified with separate divisions. But, even on the theoretical plane, the economic costs TC_1 would normally include the costs of all capital, both debt and equity [16]. Thus, the difference between the two costs arises solely because it has been assumed, quite contrary to the usual practice in the theory of business finance, that working capital is debt financed by a specific loan. If it is assumed to be financed by the usual capital mix, and the imputed interest charge is the company's overall cost of capital, then the problem reverts to one of simple double counting. It is, of course, quite immaterial whether debt interest is included as a cash cost, in which case both NPV and RI calculations will proceed with an interest rate representing the cost of equity capital, or excluded, when the average weighted cost of capital is appropriate.

In conclusion, it is quite clear that there is no economic objection to interest charges on capital, both cash and imputed, being included in a performance measure for a division which, *inter alia* is being evaluated on its investment performance. Such an approach is consistent with economic income maximization and thus NPV maximization. The rationale of an imputed interest charge is that divisional managers are made aware of the cost of using capital and, as a matter of routine, can clearly see the impact this makes upon their operating performance. The justification for making a charge on existing assets is that there is always a potential disinvestment decision. If the capital base is held constant over the planning and reporting period, then the capital charge is irrelevant although not liable to lead to sub-optimal decisions.

IMPLICATIONS FOR PRACTICE

Although the use of residual income has been shown to be consistent with economic theory there are a number of considerations which may constrain its usefulness in practice.

1. It is conceptually impossible to evaluate an investment decision on *ex post* figures until all returns have occurred. Residual income may do no more than compare actual cash flows with those expected for the single accounting period being considered. It is for this reason that Tomkins rejects RI for investment centres. But it is then inconsistent of him to advocate its use for those 'profit' centres where working capital is controllable.

2. The above analysis has been conducted in terms of economic valuation (i.e. taking the NPV of expected future net cash flows which have to be estimated subjectively). If an accounting valuation is substituted for the economic valuation then various manipulations are possible which will improve the current performance measure but at the expense of long-run performance (e.g. accepting projects with relatively high initial cash inflows but with an NPV less than zero). There is a need for research to discover accounting methods which will minimize this distortion along the lines of that carried out by Flower [17] and Henderson and Dearden [18]. If residual income is computed on a conventional accrual accounting basis the result will differ from a comparison of actual and budgeted cash flows. The realization principle affects the point in time at which certain types of change in asset value will be recognized so that there is no exact relationship between residual income and cash flows. Residual income, computed on a conventional accounting basis, appears to be an improvement on unadjusted accounting profit, even if it is conceptually inferior to economic profit (which has itself suffered a deduction for all capital costs), although it must be appreciated that a danger exists in reading information into figures which differ solely because of accounting practice.

3. It has previously been argued that the interest rate that ought to be used in residual income calculations is the cost of equity capital (if debt charges are included in cash flows) or the average weighted cost of capital to the company (if they are excluded). However, the discussion has been conducted in terms of certainty whereas the major reason for the higher cost of equity capital is that it bears risk. It has been argued elsewhere that the use of an inflated interest rate to take account of risk and uncertainty is at best crude and at worst misleading [19]. It may also lead to further double counting [20].

The authors' preference is that it is the cash flows themselves that should be adjusted for uncertainty either by calculating certainty equivalents or, better still, by combining probability distributions [21] rather than modifying the discount rate. If this is accepted then the interest rate used in NPV calculations should be something akin to a default free interest rate. This would apply equally to RI and it seems regrettable that Shwayder's [22] proposals for the use of interest adjusted income have not been considered more fully. Such an approach would also avoid the problematic calculation of risk adjusted rates for individual divisions required by the premise that the risk structure of the division will differ from that of the divisionalized company as a whole.

4. An advantage of RI is that it also allows a measure of managerial performance to be constructed by deducting a charge for capital which

relates solely to the investment controllable by the manager concerned. This Solomons calls controllable residual income as distinct from net residual income which is the performance measure for the division. An equivalent measure to controllable RI may be given by monitoring the cash flows on controllable investment only. In practice, this latter approach is likely to be heavily subjective and liable to manipulation because cash flows may not be readily identifiable with specific investments. The advantages and and disadvantages of presenting RI rather than cash flow reports are exactly those of monitoring profits rather than cash flows with perhaps two notable exceptions. RI overcomes the opportunitst manager's incentive to undertake investments which yield a sub-standard return but which give large positive cash flows initially. Secondly, the divisional manager cannot improve his performance by substituting so-called uncontrollable investments for controllable investments, for if controllable profit is used as the performance measure, the alert manager may substitute capital equipment for labour, and thereby effect an improvement in his performance measure where no real improvement has occurred.

5. Finally, the cost of capital employed in calculating RI must approximate to the opportunity cost of capital for the period concerned. Amey [23] has stated elsewhere that 'once investment has taken place opportunity cost is only relevant when the firm has to take further decisions concerning the use to which the asset is put, not in evaluating performance'. But this is the responsibility of the manager of an investment centre, that is, to decide whether to continue using the asset, to replace or abandon it. The alternative use of already installed capital goods and the alternative use of investible funds merge when the possibility of disinvestment of individual assets by the divisional manager is allowed.

CONCLUSIONS

Residual income, measured according to accounting conventions, is superior to accounting profit as a measure of divisional performance where some capital investment is authorized by the division. As long as double counting is avoided there can be no objection to its use on economic grounds as it is more nearly equivalent to economic income than is accounting profit. Any objection to residual income would apply equally to accounting profit.

However, the residual income for a period calculated on the basis of economic valuation is exactly equal to the difference between actual and expected cash flows for that period. Residual income therefore has no apparent advantage over cash budgeting. Indeed if residual income is calculated according to accounting conventions there is a danger of management believing the result to contain more information than is in fact there. But, in our opinion, this does not dismiss residual income out of hand, for there has been a long standing demand for income figures in addition to cash flow figures. If such income figures are useful, we would maintain that residual income figures would serve the same purpose with fewer disadvantages. Residual income also commends itself by providing separate measures of the performance of both the division and the division management.

This argument points towards the use of an array of performance measures rather than any single overall measure. We have proposed residual income as one of these measures, but as it is based on accounting valuations, additional information about the expected future cash flows of investment projects requires to be presented to corporate management, perhaps following the approach of Henderson *et al.* [24].

Finally the issue of what interest rate to use in both NPV and RI calculations requires to be faced. There appear to be formidable objections to the use of an overall company cost of capital which includes an element to take account of risk, if only because the risk structure of the division is most unlikely to be the same as the risk structure of the company as a whole. Moreover, we would argue that it is inappropriate to take account of risk via the discount rate, preferring an adjustment to be made to cash flows. If this is done then a default free interest rate is appropriate and residual income calculations would also use this rate.

In order to determine the comparative usefulness of residual income in evaluating the decisions which a company takes relating to capital investment, managerial promotion and the allocation of resources more empirical research is required.

ACKNOWLEDGEMENT

Paper received July 1975, revised March 1976.

REFERENCES

1. Tomkins C.R. 'Another Look at Residual Income', *Journal of Business Finance and Accounting*, Spring 1975, pp. 39–53.
2. Tomkins C.R. 'Residual Income – A Rebuttal of Professor Amey's Arguments', *Journal of Business Finance and Accounting*, Summer 1975, pp. 161–168.
3. Amey L.R. 'Tomkins on "Residual Income"', *Journal of Business Finance and Accounting*, Spring 1975, pp. 55–68.
4. Solomons D., *Divisional Performance: Measurement and Control*, Irwin, 1968.
5. Amey L.R., op. cit., p. 58.
6. Amey L.R., *The Efficiency of Business Enterprises*, George Allen and Unwin, 1969, p. 145.
7. Tomkins C.R., *Financial Planning in Divisionalized Companies*, Accountancy Age, 1973, pp. 23–24.
8. Mauriel J.J. & Anthony R.N., 'Misevaluation of Investment Centre Performance', *Harvard Business Review*, March–April, 1966, pp. 98–105.
9. Tomkins C.R., op. cit., pp. 172–175.
10. 'Who makes the Profit Decision?', *Dun's Review and Modern Industry*, Vol. 80 No. 3, September 1962, (quoted in Solomons [4]).
11. Morgan J. & Luck M., *Managing capital investment*, Mantec, 1973.

12. Solomons D., op. cit., p. 155.
13. Bromwich M., 'Measurement of Divisional Performance: A Comment and an Extension', *Accounting and Business Research*, Spring 1973, pp. 123–132.
14. Hopwood A.G., *An Accounting System and Managerial Behaviour*, Saxon House, 1973.
15. Amey L.R., op. cit., pp. 61–65.
16. Lipsey R.G., *An Introduction to Positive Economics*, Weidenfeld and Nicholson, 1963, p. 482.
    Baumol W.J., *Economic Theory and Operations Analysis*, Prentice-Hall, 1965, p. 315.
    Samuelson P.A., *Economics*, McGraw-Hill, 1967, p. 443.
17. Flower J.F., 'Measurement of Divisional Performance', *Accounting and Business Research*, No. 3 Summer 1971, pp. 205–214.
18. Henderson B.D. & Dearden J., 'New System for Divisional Control', *Harvard Business Review*, September–October, 1966, pp. 144–160.
19. Robichek A.A. & Myers, S.C., *Optimal Financing Decisions*, Prentice-Hall, 1965.
20. Fawthrop R.A., 'Underlying Problems in Discounted Cash Flow Appraisal', *Accounting and Business Research*, Summer 1971, pp. 187–198.
21. Hertz D.B., 'Risk Analysis in Capital Investment', *Harvard Business Review*, January–February, 1964, pp. 95–106.
22. Shwayder K., 'A Proposed Modification to Residual Income – Interest Adjusted Income', *The Accounting Review*, April 1970, pp. 299–307.
23. Amey L.R., op. cit., p. 144.
24. Henderson B.D. & Dearden J., op. cit.

18

Profit measurement in divisionalized companies

Robert W. Scapens
Senior Lecturer in Accounting, University of Manchester

The recent debate on the role of residual income in the measurement of divisional performance seems to be far from settled. There has been much discussion about the validity of including an interest element in the income calculation. It has been suggested that divisional income measurement should include interest on capital employed (or at least, some part thereof) to ensure that divisional managers are encouraged to operate with the optimal capital resources [21, 24]. However, Amey [2] argued that it is theoretically erroneous to deduct interest in the appraisal of operating decisions. Some attempts have been made to reconcile the arguments of both sides to the debate [8, 22, 23], but without much success [1].

The objective of this paper is to explore the characteristics of a profit measure which could be used to appraise the performance of divisional managers. This will inevitably lead into the residual income debate. However, reconciliation of prior debate is not the primary objective of this paper, although it will be possible to make some observations about previously published arguments. A mathematical model will be used to demonstrate a relationship between income measurement and divisional objectives expressed in terms of NPV maximization. As the model is taken from the economic theory of the firm in which profit maximization plays a central role, the term profit measurement will be used rather than income measurement.

The economic profit measure which will be obtained from the mathematical model is not the same as economic income, except in certain special cases. 'Economic profit' can be defined as the excess of benefits over costs of productive activities in each period measured in terms of their shadow prices (or opportunity costs). It will be demonstrated that a policy of maximizing economic profit in each period will lead managers to take the NPV maximizing decisions. Before presenting the mathematical model it will be appropriate to consider the potential usefulness of a profit concept for the appraisal of a divisional performance.

Source: Scapens, R.W. (1979) *Journal of Business Finance and Accounting*, **6** (3), pp. 281–305.

APPRAISING DIVISIONAL PERFORMANCE

A division has been defined as 'a company unit headed by a man fully responsible for the profitability of its operations, including planning, production, financial and accounting activities...'. [7]. The senior (or corporate) management delegate to the divisional manager the authority to take decisions relating to such activities. The corporate management, however, remain responsible for the entire operations of the business and must exercise some control over delegated activities.

This control function could be implemented by setting divisional objectives (criteria which define the required or desirable performance for the division), reinforced by periodic reports of actual divisional performance. Such *ex post* reports provide the element of feedback in the control system by reporting data about actual performance to both the controller and the controlled. Such data enables the corporate management to monitor divisional activities and acts as a motivating device for the divisional management. These two aspects of feedback, monitoring and motivating are interrelated. The corporate management can review the performance of their divisional managers and encourage good performance or discourage poor performance. Poor managers could be removed from their position or warned that sanctions may be taken against them if their performance does not improve. Good managers could receive rewards related to their performance. However, it should be stressed that there is unlikely to be a clear distinction between good and bad performance, particularly when certain divisions are inherently more profitable than others. High profits could be earned in a particular division despite a poor manager, whilst a very good manager may only be able to break even in another, less profitable, division. If divisional objectives are expressed in terms of maximizing profits, the corporate management must take such situational factors into consideration in their appraisal of divisional managers. This might be achieved by comparing each division's actual profits against the corporate management's *ex ante* expectations.[1]

The rewards given to divisional managers need not be financial, although monetary rewards may be important in some cases. Managers should receive the rewards which will effectively motivate them as individuals. This brings the discussion to the other aspect of feedback, i.e., motivation. In recent years there has been much research designed to identify effective motivators. Researchers have examined the motivational effects of financial rewards, such as salary increments, bonus payments, profit sharing, etc., and also social and esteem factors, such as promotion, recognition of ability by superiors and peers, etc. (for a review see 13, ch. 3). Furthermore, it has been suggested that the feedback itself can be an important element of motivation [6]. Managers, it is argued, desire self-actualization (i.e., the satisfying feeling of a job well done) and perform-

---

[1] Tomkins suggested that it might be appropriate 'to compare actual (residual) income earned with the maximum which could have been earned given hindsight'. [24, p. 36].

ance reports (even without an associated reward structure) may motivate them to achieve the acknowledged 'good performance'. For the purposes of this paper, the particular rewards which motivate divisional managers are unimportant, provided the appropriate motivating factors can be identified by the corporate management. However, it should be recognized that unless there is effective motivation (for instance, through a system of rewards) periodic performance reports are unlikely to contribute to the control of divisional activities.

When effectively motivated the divisional managers may be expected to seek to achieve the level of performance which will appear as the best attainable in their periodic performance reports. However, if divisionalized operations are to be controlled in this way, it is essential that the performance reports are expressed in terms of the criteria which were used by the corporate management to define the performance required of the divisions. For example, if a division's objective is expressed in terms of maximizing the NPV of its projects, its actual performance should be measured in terms of NPV. The control function would probably be ineffective if divisional performance were measured in different terms, such as the accounting profit or accounting return on capital employed. Such differences can introduce a bias into the control system.

In general, control could be accomplished by a comparison of budgeted and actual cash flows for the division [11]. However, as most operating decisions must be anticipated in the preparation of a cash flow budget, the specification of required performance in terms of such a budget may destroy divisional autonomy. For maximum delegation of authority the performance required of divisions should be expressed in very general terms, such as: 'earn as much profit as possible', 'maximize the NPV of divisional projects', 'obtain the largest possible market share', and so on. But at the same time, for effective control the periodic performance reports must measure the extent to which the required performance has been achieved.

In the residual income literature it has generally been assumed that the corporate objective of a divisionalized company is to maximize its NPV [8, p. 43]. This objective may, under certain conditions, also be expressed as maximizing shareholder wealth or economic income [1]. In addition, it is generally assumed that the corporate objective can be broken down into divisional objectives, each expressed in terms of NPV maximization. This implies minimal inter-divisional relations and an absence of corporate resources, or a 'perfect' system of transfer pricing. These conditions may not exist in the real world, but they provide a reasonable set of working assumptions which will be taken as the starting point for this paper. Accordingly, it will be assumed that divisions are required to maximize the NPV of their operations. Under conditions of certainty such a divisional objective raises no serious problems. In each period the NPV of divisional projects will be computed and performance evaluated. If a periodic income measure is required, economic income could be used.

When the certainty assumption is relaxed a NPV maximizing divisional objective can give rise to difficulties. A performance measure expressed in terms of NPV (or economic income) requires an estimate of future cash flows. Divisional managers are generally in the best position to estimate the future cash flows of their divisions, but the use of such estimates may defeat the control function, as divisional managers could bias their estimates in order to improve their apparent performance. It may be argued that the effects of any bias will be transitory as the division must ultimately generate the cash flows and any over-estimates will be identified. However, as divisional managers may spend only a relatively short period of time in a particular division, the existence of over-optimistic cash flow estimates may not be discovered until after the manager concerned has left the division. Some writers avoid this problem by suggesting that performance appraisal should be based on *ex post* cash flows, together with any other evidence available to the corporate management [9, 11]. Such proposals provide only a tenuous link between the required performance expressed in terms of maximizing NPV and actual performance measured in ex post cash flows. The linkage will be strong only when all divisional projects have been completed. It is usually impracticable to wait until such a time, as individual managers will retire, quit or be promoted in the meanwhile. Furthermore, because of the importance attached to profit measures in the past [18, 24] there is likely to be considerable resistance to performance measures which do not include a profit concept.

The above discussion suggests that an ideal measure of divisional performance will be a profit concept which is consistent with the objective of maximizing NPV. If managers are effectively motivated to maximize this profit they will take decisions which lead to the maximum NPV. Tomkins attempted to demonstrate that residual income provides such a concept [22, 24]. However, his principal concern was with the interest element of residual income and he intentionally assumed away many other interesting problems. In a reply to Tomkins, Amey pointed to some of the problems which may arise when other aspects of residual income are considered and he suggested that it is necessary to examine a constrained maximization problem [1, p. 58]. The residual income literature has become so totally immersed in the controversy surrounding the interest adjustment that other issues relating to the use of an income (or profit) concept for the measurement of divisional performance have not been fully discussed. In this paper some initial steps are taken in the exploration of Amey's constrained maximization problem and some observations are made about the nature of profit measurement for divisionalized companies.

It can be shown that an economic concept of profit will satisfy the above requirements for a measure of divisional performance, and under certain conditions will be similar to some accounting profit concepts [20]. In Tomkin's diagram [24, p. 19], shown in Figure 18.1, economic income represents a periodic measure of the NPV objective, which will be maximized at an output of Q^*. If there are two surrogate performance measures available, surrogate A should be preferred as it also is maximized at Q^*. Thus a divisional manager motivated to maximize surrogate A will operate

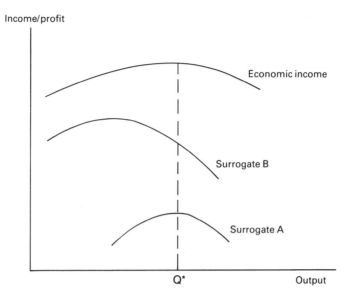

Fig. 18.1

at the NPV maximizing output. This is a characteristic of the economic concept of profit which is used extensively in the theory of the firm. As Amey [2, p. 139] pointed out, under conditions of certainty economic profit will be zero if perfect competition exists in all markets. This is because the normal return (i.e. interest on invested capital) will be included in the average (total) cost. However, if the assumptions of certainty and market perfection are relaxed, non-zero valued profits could be earned.

In the next section of this paper a simple neoclassical model of the firm will be presented to demonstrate the characteristics of economic profit. This simple model will allow some comments to be made about the interest element of residual income. In later sections the model will be extended and the validity of economic profit as a divisional performance measure will be discussed.

THE NEOCLASSICAL MODEL

Jorgenson used the neoclassical theory of the firm in his development of a theory of investment behaviour [15, 16, 17] and he demonstrated that, on certain assumptions wealth maximization could be achieved by maximizing profits at each point of time. Wealth maximization is restated in terms of maximizing NPV [12] and profit is defined in such a way that profit maximizing decisions are consistent with wealth maximization. To avoid confusion profit defined in this way will be referred to as economic profit.

In developing his theory, Jorgenson defined the present value of an enterprise (or in our case, a division) as follows:

$$W = \int_0^\infty e^{-rt} R(t) \, dt, \tag{1}$$

where r is the rate of time discount and R(t) the net receipts at time t. For simplicity, the analysis is limited to a production process with a single output, a single variable input (labour) and a single capital input. Thus, if Q, L and I represent output, variable input and additional investment in the capital input and p, w and q represent the corresponding prices, the flow of net receipts in each period can be expressed as follows (time scripts omitted):

$$R = pQ - wL - qI$$

The objective of the firm (or division) is to maximize its NPV as expressed by equation 1. But this maximization is subject to two constraints. First, the level of output and the required inputs are constrained by the production function, which is assumed to be convex and twice differentiable with positive marginal rates of substitution and non-increasing returns to scale. If the capital input is represented by K, an implied production function can be expressed as:[2]

$$F(Q, L, K) = 0 \tag{2}$$

The second constraint relates to the capital input. The rate of change in the flow of capital services used in production is assumed to be proportional to the flow of additional investment. This proportionality may be interpreted as the flow of capital services from each unit of capital stock. It is assumed that the capital stock is fully utilized and the constant of proportionality is unity. Net additional investment is equal to total additional investment less replacement, thus:

$$\dot{K} = I - \delta K, \tag{3}$$

where $\dot{K}$ is the time rate of change in the flow of capital services and δ is the rate of usage of existing capital stock. This constraint holds at all points of time so that $\dot{K}$, K and I are all functions of time.

To maximize NPV as specified in equation 1, subject to the constraints of equations 2 and 3, consider the Lagrangian expression:

---

[2] An implied production function is a rearranged version of the function Q = F(L, K).

Table 18.1 First order conditions for maximization

$$\frac{\partial f}{\partial Q} = e^{-rt} p - \lambda_0 (t) \frac{\partial F}{\partial Q} = 0,$$

$$\frac{\partial f}{\partial L} = -e^{-rt} w + \lambda_0 (t) \frac{\partial F}{\partial L} = 0,$$

$$\frac{\partial f}{\partial I} = -e^{-rt} q - \lambda_1 (t) = 0$$

$$\frac{\partial f}{\partial K} - \frac{d}{dt} \left[\frac{\partial f}{\partial K} \right] = \lambda_0 (t) \frac{\partial F}{\partial K} + \delta \lambda_1 (t) - \frac{d}{dt} (\lambda_1 (t)) = 0$$

$$\frac{\partial f}{\partial \lambda_0} = F(Q, L, K) = 0$$

$$\frac{\partial f}{\partial \lambda_1} = \dot{K} - I + \delta K = 0$$

$$\mathcal{L} = \int_0^\infty [e^{-rt} R(t) + \lambda_0(t) F(Q, L, K) + \lambda_1(t) (\dot{K} - I + \delta K)] \, dt$$

$$= \int_0^\infty f(t) \, dt$$

The first order conditions for the maximization of this expression, set out in Table 1, can be resolved in terms of the marginal productivity conditions for labour and capital, as follows:

$$\frac{\partial Q}{\partial L} = \frac{w}{p} \tag{4}$$

and

$$\frac{\partial Q}{\partial K} = \frac{c}{p}, \quad \text{where } c = q\left(r + \delta - \frac{\dot{q}}{q}\right) \tag{5}$$

This c term may be interpreted as the implicit rental value of the capital services used by the division. In other words, it is the shadow price of capital services.[3] This may be illustrated by taking the value of the marginal product in the optimum plan; i.e., the income derived from the last unit of the variable input (= shadow price). Equations 4 and 5 may be rearranged to show the values of the marginal products of labour and capital input:

[3] As $\dot{q}$ represents the time rate of change in the price of new investment in capital input, the term $\dot{q}/q$ is the proportional change in that price.

$$p\frac{\partial Q}{\partial L} = w, \qquad (6)$$

$$p\frac{\partial Q}{\partial K} = c. \qquad (7)$$

A measure of profit can be defined with inputs valued at their shadow prices. Thus, the economic profit, P, for each period (time scripts omitted) can be expressed as follows:

$$P = pQ - wL - cK \qquad (8)$$

A firm (or division) which maximizes these profits in the short run will also maximize its NPV in the long run. This can be demonstrated by considering the first order conditions for the maximization of P in any period. This maximization is constrained by the production function. Thus, consider the Lagrangian expression:

$$\mathscr{L} = pQ - wL - cK + \lambda_2 F(Q, L, K) \qquad (9)$$

The first order conditions for the maximization of this expression can be resolved in terms of marginal productivity conditions for labour and capital which are identical to equations 4 and 5 above. Accordingly, a division which maximizes economic profit will take decisions which satisfy the wealth (NPV) maximizing conditions.

To examine the nature of economic profit equation 8 can be rewritten using the definition of c in equation 5.

$$P = pQ - wL - \delta qK - rqK + \dot{q}K \qquad (10)$$

This measure of profit comprises sales revenue (pQ) less labour costs (wL), depreciation (δqK) and interest on capital employed (rqK), and plus an adjustment for price changes ($\dot{q}K$). The deduction of interest on capital employed suggests a similarity between economic profit and residual income. It may be observed that capital employed is valued at the market price of capital assets (q) and not explicitly at NPV. However, with perfect markets in a certainty model the market value of an asset will be identical to its NPV. The model will have to be extended before any meaningful comments can be made about the valuation of capital employed. It may also be noted that there is an adjustment for price changes in the profit measure. Such an adjustment is not normally included in residual income.

In the model used to derive the measure of economic profit set out in equation 10, it is assumed that the division selects the optimal capital input each period. Accordingly, capital assets are a decision variable which must be considered in solving the maximization problem. This will not be the case, however, when the stock of capital assets is fixed or is exogenously determined as, for instance, when such assets are provided by corporate management. If K and I are not decision variables, labour will be the only input to generate a marginal productivity condition and a shadow price. Hence, economic profit need not contain any terms in K. The revised profit measure can be expressed as follows:

$$P = pQ - wL \qquad (8')$$

The maximization of this version of economic profit will lead to the necessary marginal productivity condition for labour.

Thus, where capital assets of a division are completely outside the control of divisional management, that division should be required to maximize expression 8'. This conclusion is to some extent consistent with the residual income literature. Emmanuel and Otley [8] found general agreement in the literature that when a division's capital base is fixed outside the division, then the interest element is irrelevant. However, the present conclusion goes further and suggests that all costs associated with capital assets are irrelevant when the division's capital base is fixed. In such cases divisional managers should be encouraged to maximize contribution – i.e., sales revenue less variable costs.

If certain capital assets are fixed outside the division, while the decisions taken by divisional management influence the investment in some other capital assets (for instance, working capital) then economic profit would include an interest element and, if appropriate, a depreciation charge and price adjustment in respect of these controllable assets. This is consistent with the view taken by Tomkins [22, pp. 41–42] who includes interest on working capital in residual income.

To conclude this discussion of the simple model it may be said that the inclusion of interest (and, also depreciation charges and price adjustments) in a division's profit depends on the extent to which the capital assets are decision variables at the divisional level. This conclusion is consistent with much of the residual income literature. To take the discussion further requires an extension of the model.

THE MODEL EXTENDED

The assumptions of Jorgenson's neoclassical model have been the subject of some criticism. In particular, it assumes that the firm (or division) can invest or disinvest without restriction or delay at the prevailing market price for capital assets. This enables the firm to move instantaneously and costlessly to the optimal production plan in each and every period. Accordingly, the market values of capital assets divide the (infinite) planning horizon into a series of independant decision periods and hence, multiperiod effects are avoided. Amey [1, p. 59] criticized Tomkins for failing to include multiperiod effects in his discussion of residual income. In this section, some simple multiperiod dependencies will be added to the model. Furthermore, as the primary objective of this paper is to examine profit measures for reporting divisional performance during an accounting (or control) period, the continuous time frame of the neoclassical model is not particularly convenient. Thus, the extended model will be framed in discrete time.

The multiperiod effects will be introduced into the model through the device of an adjustment cost which must be paid each time the gross investment in capital assets is changed. Such costs may be external (e.g., a commission paid to an agent for buying or selling capital assets) or internal (such as foregone opportunities). This paper will examine external adjustments costs. These costs add an interesting dynamic element to the model. They also provide a simple device for analysing situations where capital assets are bought and sold at different prices. In such a case, the adjustment cost will measure the difference between the buying and selling prices.

It is intuitively plausible that the existence of adjustment costs will cause a lag in the response of investment in capital assets to changes in other variables. For instance, a division may spread an increase in its capital assets over several years. Brechling [3] in his examination of investment and employment decisions examined the nature of different adjustment cost functions.[4] He concluded that lagged response occurs only when the marginal cost of adjustment increases with the absolute size of the adjustment. However, this is probably typical of most capital assets. Costs will increase at the margin because of the need to place special orders, find new suppliers, etc., when larger quantities are required. Furthermore, a limit on the amount that can be acquired implies that the marginal acquisition cost increases to an infinite amount.

The procedure adopted earlier to derive a measure of economic profit will be used again. The shadow prices obtained from a NPV maximization model will be used to define profit. However, it will not be necessary to retain the assumptions of neoclassical economic theory. The assumption of perfect markets will be relaxed, although the firm is assumed (without loss of generality) to be a price-taker in all markets.

For the present, it will be assumed that each division is required to maximize the NPV of its operations using a risk adjusted discount rate computed at the corporate management level by means of an appropriately constructed portfolio model. In order to generate such a discount rate it must be further assumed that the risks associated with divisional returns, period by period, are serially independent and that the covariance of the division's returns with a market portfolio are independent of its scale of operations. These assumptions are quite restrictive, but are necessary to retain the simplicity of the NPV model and to maintain a link with the residual income literature which generally takes the existence of a divisional discount rate for granted. The appropriate discount rate for a division, and its cost of capital are still areas for research [10, 14], but they will not be explored in this paper.

---

[4] Brechling defined his adjustment costs as a function of *net* investment in capital assets, $\phi(K_j - K_{j-1})$. In this paper adjustment costs are expressed in terms of *gross* investment, $\phi(K_j - K_{j-1}) + \delta K_{j-1}$. However, this difference of expression does not affect the generality of the discussion.

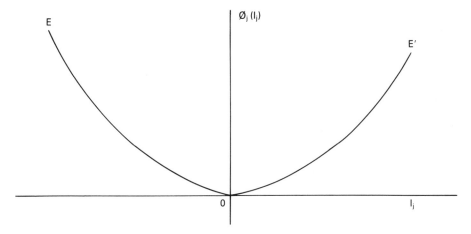

Fig. 18.2

Once again a simple production process will be considered, with a single output Q and two inputs, labour L, and capital K. The divisional cash flow equation for period j will be written (with the subscripts indicating time periods) as follows:

$$R_j = p_j Q_j - w_j L_j - q_j I_j - \phi_j(I_j), \tag{11}$$

where $\phi_j(I_j)$ represents the external cost of adjusting capital stock during period j. This cost is a function of the level of purchases or sales of capital assets (i.e., gross investment) and is payable in addition to the market price of assets acquired or, out of the market proceeds from assets sold. According to Brechling, for a lagged response these adjustment costs must be positive for both negative and positive I_j and increasing at the margin. Moreover, it seems plausible to suppose that the cost will be zero when $I_j = 0.$[5] The characteristics of such an adjustment cost function are illustrated by the curve EE' in Figure 18.2.

The divisional NPV maximization objective can be expressed in discrete terms as follows:

$$\text{Max W} = \max \sum_{j=0}^{\infty} \frac{R_j}{(1 + r)^j} \tag{12}$$

Where R_j represents the expected cash flow for period j, and r the appropriate risk adjusted discount rate for the division.

[5] Formally, these characteristics can be stated as:

$$\delta_j'(I_j) \gtreqless 0 \text{ as } I_j \gtreqless 0, \phi_j''(I_j) > 0, \phi_j'(0) = 0$$

and by implication, $\phi_j''(0) = 0$.

If the production function and change in the stock of capital assets are expressed as follows:

$$Q_j = F(L_j, K_j)$$

$$K_{j+1} - K_j = I_j - \delta K_j$$

the objective function (equation 12) may be expanded and multiplied through by $(1 + r)^j$ to give the following expression in which only periods $j - 1$ and j of the infinite series are shown:

$$
\begin{aligned}
\text{Max } W(1 + r)^j = \max \ldots + (1 + r) \{ & p_{j-1} F(L_{j-1}, K_{j-1}) - w_{j-1} L_{j-1} \\
& - q_{j-1}(K_j - K_{j-1} + \delta K_{j-1}) - \phi_{j-1}(K_j - K_{j-1} + \delta K_{j-1}) \} \\
+ \{ & p_j F(L_j, K_j) - w_j L_j - q_j(K_{j+1} - K_j + \delta K_j) \\
& - \phi_j(K_{j+1} - K_j + \delta K_j) \} + \ldots
\end{aligned}
$$

For the firm (or division) to maximize the NPV of its operations it will choose all future L's and K's so as to maximize this expression. The optimal conditions for period j can be found by taking partial derivatives with respect to L_j and K_j, and equating to zero. Only that part of the expansion which is shown above will contain the choice variables, L_j and K_j.

$$\frac{\partial W(1 + r)^j}{\partial L_j} = p_j \frac{\partial F}{\partial L_j} - w_j = 0$$

and

$$\frac{\partial W(1 + r)^j}{\partial K_j} = -(1 + r) \{ q_{j-1} + \phi'_{j-1}(I^*_{j-1}) \} + p_j \frac{\partial F}{\partial K_j} + q_j(1 - \delta)$$

$$+ (1 - \delta) \phi'_j(I^*_j) = 0$$

where $\phi'_j(I^*_j)$ represents the marginal cost of adjusting capital assets in the optimal investment plan. These expressions can be rearranged to determine the values of the marginal products.

$$p_j \frac{\partial F}{\partial L_j} = w_j \tag{13}$$

$$p_j \frac{\partial F}{\partial K_j} = (1 + r) \{ q_{j-1} + \phi'_{j-1}(I^*_{j-1}) \} - (1 - \delta) \{ q_j + \phi'_j(I^*_j) \} \tag{14}$$

Equation 13 is identical to the value of the marginal product of labour derived earlier (equation 6). However, the value of the marginal product of capital (equation 14) is somewhat different to the expression derived from the continuous time model. The discrete equivalent of equation 7 is:

$$p_j \frac{\partial F}{\partial K_j} = (1 + r)q_{j-1} - (1 - \delta)q_j \qquad (7')$$

In addition, equation 14 contains the marginal adjustment cost for the optimal investment policy. Brechling has demonstrated that an expression for the marginal product of capital (similar to equation 14) is consistent with the well known condition of price theory that marginal cost must equal marginal revenue at the optimum output [3, p. 45]. Appendix 1 adapts Brechling's proof to the definition of adjustment cost used in this paper.

An important point to note is that equation 14 has a dynamic element which captures the multiperiod effects of the model. Because of increasing marginal adjustment costs, a division may not fully adjust its capital stock in a single period in response to changes in other variables. The appropriate response may be spread over a number of periods. As a result, the value of the marginal product of capital in each period will be dependent upon the time path of the optimal investment decision, I_{j-1}^* and I_j^*. By contrast, equations 6 and 7 do not contain any interperiod dependence. It may be observed that equation 14 reduces to equation 7' when the marginal adjustment costs are zero.

The effect on economic profit of this dynamic element can be seen by using the values of the marginal products in equations 13 and 14 to define economic profit, P_j.

$$P_j = p_j Q_j - w_j L_j - [(1 + r)\{q_{j-1} + \phi'_{j-1}(I_{j-1}^*)\} - (1 - \delta)q_j + \phi'_j(I_j^*)]\,K_j$$

Rearranging this expression provides a revised measure of economic profit:

$$P_j = p_j Q_j - w_j L_j - \delta \alpha_j^* K_j - r\alpha_{j-1}^* K_j + (\alpha_j^* - \alpha_{j-1}^*)\,K_j \qquad (15)$$
$$\text{where} \quad \alpha_j^* = q_j + \phi'_j(I_j^*)$$

This measure is not fundamentally different to the economic profit measure derived from Jorgenson's neoclassical model – see equation 10. It comprises sales revenue ($p_j Q_j$) less labour cost ($w_j L_j$), depreciation ($\delta \alpha_j^* K_j$) and interest on capital ($r\alpha_{j-1}^* K_j$) and plus an adjustment for price changes ($(\alpha_j^* - \alpha_{j-1}^*)\,K_j$). The only difference is the price used to value capital assets. In this case, such assets are valued at their market price plus the marginal adjustment cost in the optimum investment plan. If the Brechling conditions for lagged response apply (namely $\phi'_j(I_j) \gtrless 0$ as $I_j \gtrless 0$ and $\phi'_j(0) = 0$), then $\alpha_j^* \gtrless q_j$, as $I_j^* \gtrless 0$. Accordingly, if the optimal investment plan calls for the sale of capital assets, such assets will be valued at below market price in the measurement of economic profit.

The maximization of economic profit, as defined in equation 15, will generate marginal productivity conditions identical to the corresponding conditions derived from the NPV maximization model. Now, consider a divisional manager who holds a set of expectations concerning the future returns for his division. If he wishes to maximize the net present value of his division's operations there are two approaches he can adopt:

(i) He can derive the optimal conditions for each future period from the NPV model. Solving the set of these conditions he can determine the optimal production plans and the optimal investment strategy, or
(ii) He can maximize economic profit in each period, provided he is already following the optimal investment plan.

Both these approaches ensure that the division undertakes the optimal productive activities for the given set of expectations. But expectations will be revised as time passes and it may be necessary to revise production plans at some future time. However, so far as the next period is concerned, decisions must be based on the existing set of expectations.

The interesting point to note about the profit maximizing alternative is that the optimal investment plan is a necessary prerequisite. Thus, the divisional manager must adopt the NPV maximizing approach, at least for his investment decisions. Furthermore, once such decisions are taken the associated production decisions may be implied. However, this does not necessarily rule out the use of economic profit for *ex post* reporting of divisional performance, as will be discussed later.

The adjustment cost function may be very simple in some divisions and the optimal investment plan easy to identify; while in other divisions the multiperiod effects may be very complex. In the following section a special case of the adjustment cost function will be considered because its implications are of topical interest.

A SPECIAL CASE

In the neoclassical model the division was able to buy and sell unlimited quantities of capital assets at the ruling market price. But in practice, most firms can dispose of capital assets only at a price which is substantially lower than the current buying price. A special case of the adjustment cost function can be used to incorporate separate buying and selling prices into the model.

It will be assumed that there are no limits on the number of capital assets that can be bought or sold at the appropriate buying price, q_j^b, and selling price, q_j^s.[6] The adjustment cost function will be used to reflect the difference between the two prices. The market price, q_j, will be set at the current selling price, q_j^s, and the adjustment cost will represent the excess of the buying price over the selling price. If q_j^b and q_j^s are fixed for all possible quantities bought or sold,[7] then the total adjustment cost payable on the acquisition of new investment will be a linear function, thus:

---

[6] In general, $q_j^b > q_j^s$.
[7] This assumption does not affect the general applicability of the conclusions, but it does simplify the analysis.

$$\phi_j(I_j) = \beta_j I_j \text{ for } I_j > 0$$

where β_j represents the difference between the buying and selling prices. It follows that $\phi'_j(I_j) = \beta_j$, for $I_j > 0$. These relationships can be expressed as follows:

$$q^s_j = q_j$$

and

$$q^b_j = q_j + \beta_j \tag{16}$$

Furthermore,

$$\phi_j(I_j) = \beta_j I_j \text{ for } I_j > 0$$
$$\phi_j(I_j) = 0 \quad \text{for } I_j < 0 \tag{17}$$

This adjustment cost function is illustrated in Figure 18.3. The function has two separate linear sections, but is not strictly linear. It follows the line AOA', with a point of inflection at 0.

The relationship described by equations 16 and 17 can be used in the definition of economic profit with equation 15 re-written in the following form:

If $I^*_j > 0$

$$P_j = p_j Q_j - w_j L_j - \delta q^b_j K_j - r q^b_j K_j + (q^b_j - q^b_{j-1}) K_j$$

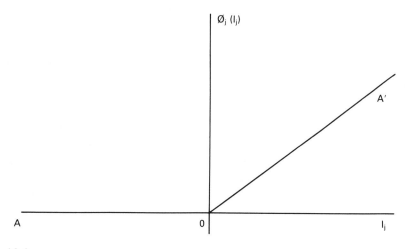

Fig. 18.3

and if $I_j^* < 0$

$$P_j = p_jQ_j - w_jL_j - \delta q_j^s K_j - rq_j^s K_j + (q_j^s - q_{j-1}^s)K_j$$

These equations indicate that the buying price should be used to value stocks of capital assets in a period when the division is acquiring new investment and the selling price used when assets are being sold. It may be noted that I_j will be positive for any purchase of new capital assets, including the replacement of assets used up in production. If there is no replacement, nor any sales of capital assets, i.e., $I_j = 0$, then neither buying nor selling prices are appropriate. This is the point of inflection in the adjustment cost function and the valuation of capital assets is not immediately clear. It was stated earlier (and demonstrated in Appendix 1) that the value of the marginal product of capital used to define economic profit can be shown to be consistent with the condition of price theory that marginal cost will equal marginal revenue in the optimum plan. Appendix 2 uses this condition to demonstrate that when $I_j = 0$ the capital assets should be valued at their NPV.

The above discussion suggests a set of rules which are similar to the valuation rules favoured by the Sandilands Committee [19]. Capital assets which are worth replacing should be valued at current buying prices, while assets not worth keeping should be valued at current selling prices. Assets which are worth keeping, but not replacing, should be valued at their NPV. Thus, current cost profit and economic profit are to some extent comparable. However, the assumptions of the present model should be kept in mind.

It was assumed that capital assets can be bought or sold without restriction at the current buying and selling prices. The assumption that prices are not affected by the quantity bought or sold is not central to the analysis. For instance, an imperfect market for new capital does not substantially change the measurement of economic profit. Furthermore, the market for secondhand assets does not need to be well developed. In fact, the selling price could represent the asset's scrap value. The crucial assumption for the present analysis is that there are no restrictions on the quantity of capital assets which can be bought or sold. The existence of such restrictions will complicate the adjustment cost function and may impair the usefulness of buying and selling prices for asset valuation. However, it is possible that some divisions will be able to acquire or sell all reasonable quantities of their capital assets without restriction. In this case, economic profit could be derived from a current cost accounting system. But it must be stressed that the profit measure will be valid only if the division is following a previously determined optimal investment policy. In view of this restriction, measures of economic profit (and also residual income) are probably of limited usefulness, as will now be discussed.

IMPLICATIONS OF THE MODEL

The model presented in this paper has demonstrated a connection between a short-run profit (or income) measure and the long-run objective of

NPV maximization. The term economic profit was used to refer to the short-run measure, but certain similarities with residual income were noted. Accordingly, the implications of the model will apply also to residual income.

Where there are no multiperiod effects, as in the simple neoclassical model, economic profit provides a useful surrogate for NPV in the evaluation of divisional performance. If managers are motivated to maximize economic profit, for instance by evaluating their performance in terms of such a measure, then the NPV maximizing operating and investment decisions will be taken. The amount of new investment in each period will depend entirely on the planned productive activities for the following period. However, such a simple situation is unlikely to be typical of the real world. Tomkins also showed that when multiperiod effects are ignored 'the residual income concept . . . is consistent with the maximization of NPV' [22, p. 42]. Amey argued that when multiperiod effects are considered it is invalid to consider any one year in isolation; '*the future may interact with the present and the present with the future*' [1, p. 59]. The extended model set out above suggests that Amey is correct so far as investment decisions are concerned.

The adjustment cost function gave the model an element of interperiod dependency. The revised measure of economic profit represents a short-run surrogate for NPV maximization only when the optimal investment decisions have been taken. Appendix 3 demonstrates that a policy of maximizing economic profit in each period will not generate the optimal investment plan unless the adjustment cost function is strictly linear. It may be concluded that economic profit is not generally valid for investment decisions. However, there may still be a role for economic profit in the appraisal of operating decisions.

A performance measure in terms of economic profit may be a useful device for motivating managers to take the NPV maximizing operating decisions when it is possible to separate such decisions from the investment decisions. For instance, marginal replacement costs can be used in the profit measure of a division which should be expanding (or at least replacing) its capital assets. Furthermore, when there is a fixed buying price, a fixed selling price and no constraints, profit may be measured by a current cost accounting system – with an interest charge.

Although Bromwich was against using residual income for operating decisions, he did not completely reject the concept. He claimed that 'residual income, if correctly defined, can help by monitoring whether correct investment decisions have been made in the past' [4, p. 129]. This proposition is not inconsistent with the conclusions of this paper. As discussed, a policy of maximizing economic profit will not necessarily generate the NPV maximizing investment plan. However, divisional managers will be aware, when taking investment decisions, that their subsequent operating performance will be charged with interest on capital assets employed. Thus, managers should not ignore the long-term implications of their investment decisions. Nevertheless, this may not be sufficient to encourage managers to accept an optimal investment plan which would involve low profits in the early years. Managers in general do not stay in the same job for the 'long-run' – they may change employers, get promoted, etc. Accordingly, their personal planning horizons may be shorter than the firm's planning horizon. It follows, therefore, that investment decisions themselves must be monitored and evaluated separately. As already discussed, measuring performance in terms of economic profit will not necessarily promote the optimal investment plan. Perhaps a capital budget derived from the NPV evaluation of investment projects, as suggested by Henderson and Dearden [11] will provide a suitable device for evaluating investment decisions.

It has been argued in the literature that an interest charge should not be included in a divisional performance measure; for instance, because it is already included in marginal costs [1] or, because it is irrelevant to operating decisions [4]. These objections have arisen principally because advocates of residual income have related the interest charge to the book value of capital assets. Bromwich argues that 'such interest charges are unlikely to reflect accurately the incremental investment cost of expanding output' [4, p. 128]. The models presented in this paper suggest that the interest charge should reflect the marginal cost of investment – a conclusion which reinforces Bromwich's argument. In addition, Bromwich and Amey were concerned about the measurement of the incremental investment cost of expanding output. This concern appears justified in view of the complex nature of the economic profit measure when adjustment costs were added to the model. However, if capital investment decisions are taken at the divisional level some measure of the marginal cost of investment is required.

Amey has argued that divisions should not have power to determine their own capital investment [1], and the empirical evidence indicates that investment decisions are frequently centralized [24, p. 174]. As was demonstrated above, if a division has no control over the quantity of its capital output, then all capital elements can be removed from the profit calculation and the division instructed to maximize 'contribution'. However, centralized control over capital assets restricts the autonomy of divisional management. Furthermore, Tomkins argues that operating decisions taken at the divisional level must inevitably affect the investment in certain capital assets – namely, working capital. Accordingly, it may not be desirable or possible to centralize all capital investment decisions.

The models described in this paper indicate that where divisional managers have control over their own investment in capital assets the short-run profit measure should include a charge for the use of such assets evaluated at the marginal cost of the optimal investment plan. As suggested above, it may be possible in some circumstances to identify this marginal cost without real difficulty. But in other circumstances, it may be extremely difficult to do so. When the marginal cost of the optimal investment plan is not obvious, a theoretical solution might be to use the shadow prices for capital inputs derived from a company-wide multi-period decision model of the type which has been suggested in the asset valuation literature [5]. This proposal is very tentative as such models may be extremely complex. Nevertheless, research in this direction may suggest a means of making progress with economic profit (or residual income).

Amey has argued that a company-wide decision model should be used for setting transfer prices within divisionalized companies [2]. This approach is similar to the above tentative proposal, although Amey uses single-period models in his analysis. The criticism in the transfer pricing literature that company-wide models impair the autonomy of divisional managers will also apply to the multiperiod model suggested above. Thus, the practical value of these models may be questionable. But their use to generate shadow prices which are then used in the measurement of economic profit may be preferable to the complete centralization of all investment decisions.

CONCLUDING REMARKS

This paper has examined the relationship between NPV maximization and profit measurement in divisionalized companies. It was demonstrated that a policy of maximizing economic profit will generate NPV maximizing decisions and it was noted that economic profit has the characteristics of residual income. A distinction between operating and investment decisions was shown to be important and it was concluded that economic profit and residual income have only a limited role in the evaluation of operating performance in divisionalized organizations. Finally, it was suggested that the usefulness of these measures might be enhanced by the use of a company-wide decision model for divisional investment plans.

APPENDIX 1

The Value of the Marginal Product of Capital

To explore the significance of the identity of price theory that marginal cost equals marginal revenue it will be necessary to determine the marginal cost and marginal revenue of capital assets. For the present model, the marginal cost of adding one unit to the capital stock and maintaining it until period T (i.e., the planning horizon which in theory could be at infinity) consists of three elements:

(a) the current price of the capital good, q_j
(b) the current marginal adjustment costs, $\phi_j'(I_j^*)$ and
(c) the sum of the discounted future replacement costs, namely:

$$\frac{\delta\{q_{j+1} + \phi_{j+1}'(I_{j+1}^*)\}}{(1 + r)} + \frac{\delta\{q_{j+2} + \phi_{j+2}'(I_{j+2}^*)\}}{(1 + r)^2} + \cdots + \frac{\delta\{q_T + \phi_T'(I_T^*)\}}{(1 + r)^{T-j}} \quad (A.1)$$

The first two elements of marginal costs are self-explanatory and the third arises because the additional unit of capital depreciates at a rate of δ per period. As the market price and adjustment cost must both be paid, the replacement cost amounts to $\delta\{q_{j+1} + \phi'_{j+1}(I^*_{j+1})\}$ in period $(j + 1)$.

The marginal revenue to be derived from the additional unit of capital stock is the sum of the discounted future values of the marginal products of that unit and its replacements. As a unit of capital stock acquired in period j is not available for use until period $j + 1$, the marginal revenue can be expressed thus:

$$\frac{p_{j+1}\dfrac{\partial F}{\partial K_{j+1}}}{1 + r} + \frac{p_{j+2}\dfrac{\partial F}{\partial K_{j+2}}}{(1 + r)^2} + \ldots + \frac{p_T\dfrac{\partial F}{\partial K_T}}{(1 + r)^{T-j}} \qquad (A.2)$$

It should be noted that the marginal adjustment cost and the marginal products of capital are calculated at the margin of the optimal plan in each period.

Equating marginal costs and marginal revenues for two periods, $j - 1$ and j, implies the following two equations (amongst others):

for period $j - 1$

$$q_{j-1} + \phi'_{j-1}(I^*_{j-1}) + \frac{\{\delta q_j + \phi'_j(I^*_j)\}}{(1 + r)} + \frac{\delta\{q_{j+1} + \phi'_{j+1}(I^*_{j+1})\}}{(1 + r)^2}$$

$$+ \ldots + \frac{\delta\{q_T + \phi'_T(I^*_T)\}}{(1 + r)^{T-j+1}}$$

$$= \frac{p_j\dfrac{\partial F}{\partial K_j}}{(1 + r)} + \frac{p_{j+1}\dfrac{\partial F}{\partial K_{j+1}}}{(1 + r)^2} + \ldots + \frac{p_T\dfrac{\partial F}{\partial K_T}}{(1 + r)^{T-j+1}} \qquad (A.3)$$

for period j

$$q_j + \phi'_j(I^*_j) + \frac{\delta\{q_{j+1} + \phi'_{j+1}(I^*_{j+1})\}}{(1 + r)} + \ldots + \frac{\delta\{q_T + \phi'_T(I^*_T)\}}{(1 + r)^{T-j}}$$

$$= \frac{p_{j+1}\dfrac{\partial F}{\partial K_{j+1}}}{(1 + r)} + \ldots + \frac{p_T\dfrac{\partial F}{\partial K_T}}{(1 + r)^{T-j}} \qquad (A.4)$$

Now, multiply equation A.3 through by $(1 + r)$ and then deduct equation A.4:

$$(1 + r)\{q_{j-1} + \phi'_{j-1}(I^*_{j-1})\} + \delta\{q_j + \phi'_j(I^*_j)\} - \{q_j + \phi'_j(I^*_j)\} = p_j\frac{\partial F}{\partial K_j}$$

Rearranging this equation yields the value of the marginal product of capital derived in equation 14 of the paper, i.e.,

$$p_j \frac{\partial F}{\partial K_j} = (1 + r) \{q_{j-1} + \phi'_{j-1}(I^*_{j-1})\} - (1 - \delta) \{q_j + \phi'_j(I^*_j)\} \qquad (14)$$

Thus this expression is consistent with the identity of price theory that marginal cost equals marginal revenue.

APPENDIX 2

Value of Capital Assets When $I_j = 0$

It was demonstrated in Appendix 1 that the value of the marginal product of capital (used in the text of this paper to derive economic profit) is consistent with the price theory condition that marginal cost must equal marginal revenue. If equation A.4 is rearranged a well known proposition can be derived:

$$q_j + \phi'_j(I^*_j) = \frac{p_{j+1} \dfrac{\partial F}{\partial K_{j+1}} - \delta \{q_{j+1} + \phi'_{j+1}(I^*_{j+1})\}}{(1 + r)} + \ldots$$

$$+ \frac{p_T \dfrac{\partial F}{\partial K_T} - \delta\{q_T + \phi'_T(I^*_T)\}}{(1 + r)^{T-j}} \qquad (A.5)$$

This equation implies that the marginal cost of investment must equal the net present value of the future benefits that will be generated, less the periodic replacement needed to maintain the increment through to period T.

In the measurement of economic profit the term $q_j + \phi'_j(I^*_j)$ is used to value capital assets and this valuation implies the right hand side of equation A.5. If the special case of the adjustment cost function (as summarized in equations 16 and 17) is introduced, equation A.5 can be rewritten as follows:

If $I^*_j > 0$

$$q^b_j = \frac{p_{j+1} \dfrac{\partial F}{\partial K_{j+1}} - \delta q^b_{j+1}}{(1 + r)} + \ldots + \frac{p_T \dfrac{\partial F}{\partial K_T} - \delta q^b_T}{(1 + r)^{T-j}}$$

If $I^*_j < 0$

$$q^s_j = \frac{p_{j+1} \dfrac{\partial F}{\partial K_{j+1}} - \delta q^s_{j+1}}{(1 + r)} + \ldots + \frac{p_T \dfrac{\partial F}{\partial K_T} - \delta q^s_T}{(1 + r)^{T-j}}$$

The case of $I_j^* > 0$ was described above – the price of the marginal unit added to the capital stock should equal the NPV of the marginal benefits (less replacement). When $I_j^* < 0$ the interpretation is quite similar. Consider the marginal unit of capital input. At the margin the benefit derived from its use in production should equal the sale proceeds, q_j^s. If this marginal unit is retained for production and maintained until period T, it will be used up at the rate of δ per period and replaced by restricting future sales of capital assets. Accordingly, the replacement is priced a q^s in each period. For instance, in order to maintain the marginal unit in production a sale of δq_{j+1}^s will be foregone in period $j + 1$.

It may be concluded from the above that when q_j^b and q_j^s are used in the measurement of economic profit the capital assets are valued at the NPV of the marginal units (which equals their buying/selling price). Now, turning to the case of $I_j^* = 0$, as neither q_j^b nor q_j^s are applicable it will be appropriate to measure NPV directly. Accordingly, when $I_j^* = 0$ equation A.5 can be used to substitute for $q_j + \phi_j(I_j^*)$ in equation 15. This indicates that capital assets should be valued at the NPV of their future benefits for the measurement of economic profit when the division is neither buying nor selling such assets.

APPENDIX 3

Maximizing Economic Profit

If the investment plan is to be determined by a policy of maximizing profit in each period the marginal adjustment cost function must replace the optimal marginal adjustment cost in the profit calculation, as the optimal position cannot be determined until the investment plan has been derived. Accordingly, equation 15 must be revised:

$$P_j = p_jQ_j - w_jL_j - [(1 + r)\{q_{j-1} + \phi'_{j-1}(I_{j-1})\} - (1 - \delta)\{q_j + \phi'_j(I_j)\}]K_j$$
$$(A.6)$$

Maximizing this expression for each period j, $j + 1$, ... ∞, subject to the production function, will provide a sequence of the marginal productivity conditions for labour and capital assets. The time path of the marginal capital conditions will general the investment plan. This policy will lead to a maximum NPV only if these marginal conditions are consistent with the corresponding conditions for NPV maximization. Consider,

$$\frac{\partial P_j}{\partial K_j} = \frac{p_j\partial Q_j}{\partial K_j} - [(1 + r)\{q_{j-1} + \phi'_{j-1}(I_{j-1}^*)\} - (1 - \delta)\{q_j + \phi'_j(I_j^*)\}]$$
$$- [(1 + r)\phi''_{j-1}(I_{j-1}^*) + (1 - \delta)(1 - \delta)\phi''_j(I_j^*)]K_j = 0 \qquad (A.7)$$

This expression will lead to the NPV maximizing marginal productivity condition for capital assets (see equation 14 in paper) only when $\phi''_{j-1} =$

$\phi_j'' = 0$. In other words, when the adjustment cost function is strictly linear. A linear adjustment cost suggests that the division should make an instantaneous adjustment to the optimal capital stock and, hence, does not induce multiperiod effects in the model. Such adjustment costs are analytically identical to a perfect market price for capital assets – a constant is added to the prevailing market price and paid on acquisitions or received on disposals.

ACKNOWLEDGEMENTS

This paper was presented at the Annual Conference of the Association of University Teachers of Accounting at the University of Exeter in March 1978. The author gratefully acknowledges the many valuable comments which were received from AUTA members.

Paper received October 1978, revised February 1979.

REFERENCES

1. Amey, L.R., 'Tomkins on "Residual Income"', *Journal of Business Finance and Accounting* (Spring, 1975), pp. 55–68.
2. Amey, L.R., *The Efficiency of Business Enterprises*, George Allen and Unwin (1969).
3. Brechling, F., *Investment and Employment Decisions*, University of Manchester Press (1975).
4. Bromwich, M., 'Measurement of Divisional Performance: A Comment and an Extension', *Accounting and Business Research* (Spring, 1973), pp. 123–132.
5. Carsberg, B.V., 'On the Linear Programming Approach to Asset Valuation', *Journal of Accounting Research* (Autumn, 1969), pp. 165–182.
6. Cook, Doris M., 'The Effect of Frequency of Feedback on Attitudes and Performance', *Journal of Accounting Research*, Supplement to Vol. 5 (1967), pp. 213–224.
7. Division Financial Executives, *Studies in Business Policy*, No. 101, New York National Industrial Conference Board (1961).
8. Emmanuel, C.R. and D.T. Otley, 'The Usefulness of Residual Income', *Journal of Business Finance and Accounting* (Winter, 1976), pp. 43–51.
9. Flower, J.F., 'Measurement of Divisional Performance', *Accounting and Business Research* (Summer, 1971), pp. 205–214.
10. Gordon, M.J. and P.J. Halpern, 'Cost of Capital for a Division of a Firm', *Journal of Finance* (September, 1974), pp. 1153–1164.
11. Henderson, Bruce D. and John Dearden, 'New System for Divisional Control', *Harvard Business Review* (September–October, 1966), pp. 144–160.
12. Hirchleifer, J., 'On the Theory of Optimal Investment Decision', *Journal of Political Economy*, Vol. 66 (August, 1958), pp. 329–352.
13. Hofstede, G.H., *The Game of Budget Control*, Tavistock (1969).
14. Jarrett, J.E., 'Estimating the Cost of Capital for a Division of a Firm, and the Allocation Problem in Accounting', *Journal of Business Finance and Accounting* (Spring, 1978), pp. 39–47.

15. Jorgenson, D.W., 'Theory of Investment Behaviour', *Determinants of Investment Behaviour*, Universities National Bureau Conference Series No. 18 (1967), pp. 129–155.
16. Jorgenson, D.W., 'Anticipations and Investment Behaviour', *The Brookings Quarter Econometric Model of the United States*, eds. J.S. Duesenbury, *et al.* (1965), pp. 35–92.
17. Jorgenson, D.W., 'Capital Theory and Investment Behaviour', *American Economic Review*, Vol. 53, Papers and Proceedings (May, 1963), pp. 247–257.
18. Mauriel, J. and R.N. Anthony, 'Misevaluation of Investment Centre Performance', *Harvard Business Review* (March–April, 1966), pp. 98–105.
19. Sandilands Committee, *Report of the Inflation Accounting Committee*, Cmnd. 6225, HMSO (1975).
20. Scapens, Robert W., 'A Neoclassical Measure of Profit', *Accounting Review* (April, 1978), pp. 448–469.
21. Solomons, David, *Divisional Performance: Measurement and Control*, Irwin (1965).
22. Tomkins, C.R., 'Another Look at Residual Income', *Journal of Business Finance and Accounting* (Spring, 1975), pp. 39–53.
23. Tomkins, C.R., 'Residual Income – A Rebuttal of Professor Amey's Arguments', *Journal of Business Finance and Accounting* (Summer, 1975), pp. 161–168.
24. Tomkins, C.R., *Financial Planning in Divisionalised Companies*, Haymarket (1973).

19

Transfer pricing: a behavioural context

David J.H. Watson
Assistant Professor of Accountancy, University of Illinois at
Urbana-Champaign
and
John V. Baumler
Associate Professor of Accounting, Ohio State University

The accounting, management science, and economics literature contains numerous models addressing the resource allocation and transfer pricing problems. Some of the earliest statements on the transfer pricing problem are recorded by Hirshleifer (1956 and 1957), Dean (1955), and Cook (1955). These authors suggest solutions to the transfer pricing problem which reflect the analogy of the internal price problem to the determination of the (Competitive) market price of traditional economics. The advent of mathematical programming produced another stream of articles addressing the transfer price problem, especially after the relation between a decentralized firm and the Dantzig and Wolfe (1960) decomposition principle was stated by Whinston (1964) and Baumol and Fabian (1964).[1]

This paper represents an attempt to place the solutions proposed by the mathematical programming models as well as other traditional solutions in an appropriate context. Since the transfer pricing problem only arises within a recognizable social system (be it an organization or a socialist economy) the paper considers the solutions in a social system context.[2] The paradigm developed can then be used to evaluate the usefulness and limitations of the various proposed solutions.

DECENTRALIZATION AND DIFFERENTIATION

Decentralization is one approach to organizational design. Implicit in this approach is the segmentation of the organization into various specialities. Numerous reasons are provided in the transfer price literature for decentralization. For example, Dean (1955) suggests, '... the modern

---

[1] As examples of this see the articles by Dopuch and Drake (1964); Godfrey (1971); Gordon (1970); Hass (1968); Ruefli (1971 a and b).
[2] In this paper we only consider an organizational context, but there seems to be a direct analogy to a planned (or socialist) economy.

Source: Watson, D.J.H. and Baumler, J.V. (1975) *The Accounting Review*, July, pp. 466–74.
© 1975

integrated multiple product firm functions best if it is made into a miniature of the competitive free enterprise system.' Dopuch and Drake (1964) suggest that the division managers are in a better position to process information concerning resource allocation. Along a similar vein Ronen and McKinney (1970) argue that the division manager's nearness to the market place provides relevant information regarding changes in prices of inputs and outputs and that more effective coordination of production factors should be obtained at the divisional level. Reasons such as size and diversity of modern corporations and the promotion of morale (because of the decision-making autonomy of managers) are also offered in support of decentralization (Godfrey, 1971). While each of these reasons may be true, none of the authors has offered a coherent theory of decentralization. Consequently, the implications that the authors see of decentralization for transfer pricing are fairly restricted and pragmatic.

We consider the central problem facing complex organizations is one of coping with uncertainty. This is the view many current organizational theorists propose. Similarly, we identify the two major sources of uncertainty for a complex organization as its technology and its environment. An organization's design, then, represents a response to these sources of uncertainty.[3] Specifically, an organization may create parts to deal with the uncertainty and thereby leave other parts to operate under conditions of near certainty, i.e., the organization will departmentalize and decentralize.[4] Decentralization is a response to uncertainty.

Decentralization, however, does not quite explain the process involved. A consequence of the segmentation of the organization into parts (departments, divisions, etc.) is that the behaviour of organizational members will be influenced by the segmentation. Because of the differences in the nature of the task and in the environmental uncertainty facing various segments, the organizational members will develop different mental processes and working styles, adopt different decision criteria, and may have varying perceptions of reality. A well-known example of this differentiation at the perceptual level is the research report of Dearborn and Simon (1958) which demonstrated that different executives can interpret differently the same organizational problem. The differences in interpretation reflect the departmental identification of the executives.

Therefore, we use the term *differentiation* to include not only the segmentation of the organization into specialized parts, but also to include the consequent differences in attitudes and behaviour of organizational members. Requisite differentiation is a requirement for organizational success. That is, each organizational unit must be designed so as to cope effectively with the demands of its technology and environment. Later we

---

[3] The exact roles technology and environment play in determining organizational design is still the subject of research: see Burns and Stalker (1961); Lawrence and Lorsch (1967); Mohr (1971); Thompson (1967); Woodward (1965).
[4] Even in the most dynamic industries manufacturing operations are often sufficiently buffered to allow the effective use of standard cost systems to control manufacturing processes.

will discuss the role of management accounting and transfer pricing in achieving the requisite degree of differentiation between organizational units.

ORGANIZATIONAL INTEGRATION

The Concept

Differentiation is only one design problem facing the organization. The other side of the same coin, and another design problem, is integration: the process of insuring that efforts of the several organizational units, now appropriately differentiated, do collectively attain the goals of the total organization.

Lawrence and Lorsch (1967) in their research demonstrated that the most successful firms (in terms of the traditional measures of profitability) in the various industries studied were the firms that achieved the required differentiation and were then able to integrate the diverse units. Further, the research indicates that only firms that achieve these dual requirements can be successful. However, a basic organizational dilemma is that the more successful an organization is in achieving the requisite differentiation (especially those organizations requiring significant differentiation) the more difficulty the organization has in achieving the necessary integration. But, of course, the difficulties in achieving the required degree of differentiation and then integrating the total organizational effort is not uniformly distributed over all firms and industries. Rather, the more diverse and dynamic (uncertain) the subenvironments faced by organizational units, the more differentiated they must be. The greater the degree of differentiation, the more difficult is integration.

We stated, originally, that the central problem facing organizational designers is one of coping with uncertainty. This problem has now been restated in terms of achieving requisite differentiation of organizational components while simultaneously coordinating (or integrating) their collective efforts. The magnitude of the differentiation problem is basically determined by uncertainty in technological and environmental factors. However, the magnitude of the integration problem is partly determined by uncertainty factors and partly by the state of interdependence between organizational components.[5] To summarize, the most challenging problems to those seeking integration arise when organizational components

[5] (i) We are considering interdependence basically from a technological (the actual technical processes employed) and resource allocation viewpoints, although interdependence may also arise through the environment (e.g., from operating in common input and output markets). Environmental interdependence is not excluded, although we believe the most important aspect of the environment is the uncertainty dimension.

(ii) We are using the term 'interdependence' in the Thompson (1967) sense. He identifies pooled, sequential, and reciprocal interdependence. Pooled interdependence is a situation in which each part of the organization renders a discrete

are strongly differentiated and highly interdependent. At the opposite extreme, mildly differentiated subunits which exhibit only minimal inter-dependencies do not pose significant integration problems.

Integrating Mechanisms

Integration is achieved by the use of integrating mechanisms of which there are obviously many. One list of such mechanisms is indicated below. This list is adapted from an article by Galbraith (1972).[6]

Rules, Routines, Standardization
Organization Hierarchy
Planning
Direct Contact
Liaison Roles
Temporary Committees (task forces or teams)
Integrators (personnel specializing in the role of coordinating inter-subunit activities)
Integrating Departments (departments of integrators)
Matrix Organization (an organization that is completely committed to joint problem solving and *shared* responsibility)

The list is ordered from the least elaborate to the most sophisticated integrative mechanisms. All organizations employ the first several mech-anisms on the list. These mechanisms are sufficient for integrating many organizational functions and are probably all that is needed by organ-izations facing minimal environmental and technological demands. However, when environmental and technological demands become more complex, organizations become more differentiated and this increases the problem of integration. Consequently, more sophisticated integrating mechanisms (the latter ones listed), in addition to the simpler mechan-isms, are required.

contribution to the whole and each is supported by the whole. The parts do not interact directly with one another. This is basically the situation where the only major common organizational link among subunits is some scarce organizational resource, e.g., capital. Sequential interdependence is a situation in which, in addition to the pooled aspect, direct interaction between the units can be pinpointed and the order of that interdependence specified. Reciprocal interdependence refers to the situation in which the outputs of two units become inputs for each other. The three types of interdependence are, in the order indicated, increasingly difficult to coordinate.
[6] (i) Galbraith actually expands this list somewhat especially with regard to organizational planning.
   (ii) Thompson (1967) has provided a somewhat different list. He suggests three mechanisms for achieving integration, coordination by standardization, coordina-tion by planning, and coordination by mutual adjustment. The first two mech-anisms we present correspond to Thompson's No. 1, while mechanisms 4 to 9 (lateral mechanisms in Galbraith's terminology) correspond to Thompson's No. 3.

DIFFERENTIATION, INTEGRATION, AND MANAGEMENT ACCOUNTING

The amount of differentiation required is determined primarily by technological and environmental demands, and an organization's adaptation to these demands is reflected in the first instance by the organizational design. The accountant, in designing the management accounting system, needs to consider the requisite degree of differentiation as a constraint. That is, the accountant cannot create or demand differentiation when behavioural factors dictate otherwise.

This is not to say that the management accounting system has no part to play in organizational design. In fact, the accounting system can be designed to facilitate or enhance the differentiation achieved. For example, each of the concepts – expense center, profit center, and investment center – may be employed, depending upon the differentiation required by the technological and environmental demands. When the appropriate accounting techniques are used in conjunction with required organizational design we expect the claimed benefits of decentralization to be realized.[7]

We are now in the position to consider the role of the accounting system in integration. An accounting system is a well-defined, formal information system within an organization. Basically, it is a set of rules and standard procedures. The accounting system can thus be classified as an integrating mechanism primarily of the first type listed above.[8] In more complicated integrating situations, although the accounting system (or, more precisely, the costs and prices generating by the accounting system) may be helpful in obtaining integration, this will only be *one* input to the integrating process.

DIFFERENTIATION, INTEGRATION, AND TRANSFER PRICING

Essentially we have argued that the requisite differentiation has to be taken as given by the accountant when he designs an organization's formal control and reporting subsystems. In some cases there will be a one-to-one mapping between the differentiated units and the accountant's responsibility centers, i.e., the expense, profit, and investment centers. However, when there is not this convenient mapping we would argue that the behavioural factors dominate, and that the accountant should not try to impose differentiation through the creation of artificial responsibility centers. Organizational design is a complete task. Numerous variables

---

[7] For one listing of these claimed benefits 'automatically' arising from decentralization see Horngren (1972), p. 693.
[8] Budgeting and planning are also usually considered part of the management accounting system. Notice, however, that planning has also been classed as a fairly simple or routine integrating mechanism.

must be simultaneously considered. The accountant must accept the organizational structure as given. Restructuring the organization merely to facilitate the management accounting system is not recommended.

What then is the role of transfer pricing? Obviously, once responsibility centers are established, goods and services transferred among these units need to be priced. This helps separate and pinpoint responsibility for different aspects of the firms functioning. In other words, to some extent, the transfer pricing mechanism *enhances* differentiation. But, we have also demonstrated above that differentiation is only one part of the problem. Integration is another facet of this problem. Can the transfer pricing mechanism be used to help achieve the required integration? Again the answer is obviously 'yes.' In many cases the pricing mechanism is a routine or standardized process, a formula like, for example, standard cost, cost plus, marginal cost, a fixed price, etc. This type of transfer pricing is at least applicable in simple integrating situations, although in more complicated integrating situations it may be only one input to the integrating process.

MATHEMATICAL PROGRAMMING SOLUTIONS TO THE TRANSFER PRICING PROBLEM

As stated in the introduction to this paper many of the papers proposing programming solutions to the transfer price problem rely on the interpretation of the decomposition principle as a model of decision making in a decentralized firm. While the analogy is undoubtedly useful for analyzing some situations, the methodology appears to have some limitations.

The first limitation of these approaches is that they maintain only the facade of decentralized decision making. The last phase of the process is usually dictated by central management. For example, in the Baumol and Fabian (1964) model, although the optimal divisional plan will be a weighted average of the plans submitted by the division, the weights are entirely determined by central management. Godfrey (1971, pp. 289–90) in evaluating the Baumol and Fabian article and the more recent refinements to their model says:

Despite the appeal of the decomposition technique, in our opinion, it is still a highly centralized decision making procedure. The divisions are at the mercy of central headquarters and would probably not agree that they enjoy the autonomy of decision making that is intended.[9]

There seems to be two explanations for this problem. The first is that many authors of the programming solutions are primarily interested in the mathematical properties (or elegance) of their solutions and only secondarily in the model's organizational implications. The second is that most authors in the transfer price literature are asking the question, 'What transfer price will result in the decentralized firm maximizing joint (or

[9] Godfrey also uses the decomposition approach in his short-run planning model but freely admits it is a centralized decision making model.

corporate) profits?' Since the emphasis is on the maximization of joint profits whenever conflict arises between this goal and the decentralization philosophy, the latter tends to be sacrificed. The solution is always centralized decision making whether this is through some stated price rule, a wishful appeal to competitive market prices and their surrogates, or to mathematical programming solutions. The result is predictable since none of these authors has offered a coherent theory for decentralization. On the other hand, we have offered a theory for explaining decentralization, and under this theory it is not clear that decentralization should be sacrificed or that sacrificing decentralization will optimize decision making.

A second limitation of this approach is that they concentrate on the behaviourally simple integration problems.[10] The environments are stable and the interdependencies are of the simplest kinds. This is true even of recent articles in the area. Ruefli (1971a), for example, develops a decomposition model which can be interpreted as a representation of decision making in a three-level hierarchial organization. Ruelfi greatly restricts the degree and incidence of interdependent relationships within his tri-level hierarchy.[11]

THE CASE AGAINST NEGOTIATED PRICES

The use of negotiated prices has rarely been seriously entertained by those writing in the transfer price literature. Joel Dean (1955) pressed for negotiated prices, but in such a way that they simulated a competitive market. The foundation for his recommendations really lay in the availability of markets outside the decentralized firm. Cook (1955) also discussed the use of 'free negotiation' but proceeds to point out two disadvantages: (1) the amount of executive time it is likely to take, and (2) negotiated prices may distort the profit center's financial reports.[12] However, Cook

---

[10](i) We are using mathematical programming models as the example. However, the same argument could be made against the economic solutions and against the traditional accounting solutions.

(ii) We are not arguing against the future development of programming models. Even the development of more efficient algorithms for handling solved problems is undoubtedly important.

[11](i) Ruefli's model, as he notes, is easily generalized to an *n*-level hierarchial model.

(ii) In a second article Ruefli (1971b) does mention, with regard to behavioural externalities, the question of bidirectional effects (reciprocal interdependence) for operational units within a management unit. However, he does not propose any solution. Ruefli even proposes an integrating mechanism (a behavioural center) which he says could be a liaison arrangement, a joint planning committee, etc. However, this behavioural center seems to act very similarly to the central management unit and consequently be subject to the same 'centralization' criticism.

[12]One, often mentioned, example of this is when one division occupies a monopoly position.

(1955, p. 93) does suggest, '... if managers are sophisticated and equipped with good accounting data on their operations, such a free negotiation system could satisfy the basic criteria outline above; that is, a transfer price that will not lead to transfers which will reduce the company's profit but will permit and encourage any transfer which increases the company's profit.'[13] Dopuch and Drake (1964, p. 13) also seem to be concerned about Cook's second point above when they state:

In evaluating the resulting performance of the divisional managers, however, the central management may be evaluating their ability to negotiate rather than their ability to control economic variables. Accordingly, the information economies of decentralization may be more apparent than real.

Later, in their paper, when discussing the decomposition procedure solutions Dopuch and Drake (1964, p. 18) suggest:

The relevant point is that, if this method can be applied in practice, it will provide a basis for negotiation between the departmental and central management levels. In this respect it would not be necessary for the divisional managers to negotiate with each other. This in itself may be an advantage since situations of negotiation between divisional managers may degenerate into personal conflicts.

Although there is undoubtedly some truth to each of these observations, that is, at times negotiated transfer prices may have these dysfunctional effects, we believe a very strong case can be made for the use of negotiated transfer prices. In presenting this case we will also be suggesting a way for obtaining suitable transfer prices for the complicated integrating situations.

TRANSFER PRICES AND CONFLICT RESOLUTION

Lawrence and Lorsch (1967) in their research were able to isolate three conflict resolution mechanisms in the firms they studied. One of their most interesting results was that the successful firms facing uncertain environments were able to resolve effectively interdepartmental conflict, and the most important means of resolving this conflict was confrontation, i.e., negotiation.[14] This effective resolution of interdepartmental conflict seemed to be an important reason why these successful firms could

---

[13] Unfortunately, (technically) sophisticated managers and good accounting data are probably not sufficient conditions for insuring proper integration. Dean (1955) also suggests the position of 'price mediator' for a company when *initially* installing his system. These ideas are similar to the concepts of an integrator which we will discuss later.

[14] Forcing was also an important back-up means. Smoothing was the third method and generally was the least effective.

achieve a high degree of integration as well as the high degree of differentiation demanded by their uncertain environment.

A second point worth noting is that within a complex organization conflict is going to be multidimensional. In a highly differentiated organization this will at times involve the transfer and pricing of goods and services within the organization. But it may also include design and engineering changes, production and delivery schedules, and quality control. Seen in this light, the transfer pricing question becomes one facet of a multidimensional conflict resolution process.[15] If the appropriate conflict resolution process is negotiation, then it appears the transfer price should be one arrived at through negotiation.[16] Specifically, determination of transfer prices could be part of the integrative process. Note that this is not a wholesale endorsement of negotiated transfer prices in all cases. There are undoubtedly instances in which unalterable formulas could be employed (e.g., the least difficult integration situations). Such formulas may be necessary to guard against obvious diseconomies or, more importantly, to enhance requisite differentiation. But if the requisite degree of differentiation is achievable and the problem is to obtain adequate integration, one of the integrative tools available might well be negotiating intra-firm prices. If organizational subunits seek to resolve conflict by confrontation – possibly with the aid of an integrator – and negotiate their differences, negotiated transfer prices might well be the desired result.

IMPLICATIONS FOR RESEARCH ON TRANSFER PRICING

The obvious implication is that we need to know something about the conflict resolution processes. In particular, we would like to know how accounting data are, or can be, used in a conflict situation. It may be, for example, that accounting data are completely irrelevant or unimportant in the more difficult integrating situations. Alternatively we may find some accounting data useful and other accounting data less useful. It may even be that we need to develop new kinds of data for these tougher areas.

---

[15] Hence, it makes little sense to be concerned about a possible monopoly position by one department. It is unlikely, if at all possible, in uncertain environments or reciprocally interdependent situations (or both) that one department will have a monopoly position on all dimensions of the conflict.

[16] This general argument for negotiated prices could probably be extended into the simpler integrating situations. Resolving conflict in part depends upon how close the protagonists' expectations of a suitable solution point are (see Schelling for a clearly stated exposition of this point). The similarity of expectations is also a function of the complexity of the situation. Thus, it could be argued that, when environmental demands or organizational interdependencies or their interaction are least complex, expectations of a mutually agreeable solution point are closest and so the conflict is easily resolved. This seems to be, for example, the conditions when a competitive market transfer price can be established. In other words, the market-based transfer price is a limiting (or simple) case of negotiated prices. See Schelling (1960).

Let us for the moment consider a difficult integrating situation – one that requires a formal integrator to integrate successfully the differentiated units. What can we say about this situation? First, although the protagonists may have somewhat different working styles, time horizons, decision criteria, and perceptions of reality (because they are part of a differentiated firm facing different subparts of the organizational environment), they are still members of the one organization and consequently have some attributes in common. There is some basis therefore for believing agreement can always be attained. Second, successful integration will depend largely on the skill of the integrator and how the personnel in the differentiated units perceive him.[17] Third, from a strict accounting viewpoint, instead of giving point estimates to all the parties on the 'correct' transfer price (as, for example, the output of a mathematical program) we may wish to provide guides to simply bound the solution area.[18] These bounds could then reflect other accounting restraints on the transfer price (e.g., the fact that the transfer price may be used in the evaluation of the economic performance of the units). However, within the guides set, the final transfer price is a result of the confrontation process.

If we move to a more complicated integrating situation requiring an integrating department, some members of this department may need to be experts in internal financial matters. The implications of this and the wider implications of a matrix organization, for management accounting practice, are still very open questions. We are saying that at times the management accounting process must perform more than a mere score-keeping or attention-directing function. The integrator has one of the most crucial roles within the organization. Certain aspects of the managerial accounting system – specifically, resolving transfer price disputes – must perhaps be merged within the integrator's total activities.

Further, little empirical evidence has been gathered on how transfer prices are established in various organizations. In gathering such evidence in the future, it is suggested that assessments of the states of differentiation and integration between buyer and seller subunits, the degree of interdependence between them, and the mode of conflict resolution utilized be made. This will allow the transfer pricing techniques to be viewed in terms of the relevant organizational and behavioural variances. Finally, it might be worth while to investigate the relative trade-offs

---

[17] Again notice Dean (1955) argues along a similar line when discussing his successful price mediator. He suggests the prime role of the mediator is not to dictate a price but to keep the negotiations flowing until that is a settlement.
[18] (i) For example, the variable costs of the input units may represent a lower bound, and the selling price less the variable costs of the output units may represent an upper bound. We may also give the integrator various other combinations of cost data to facilitate his integrating role (e.g., full costs (plus a markup), the mathematical programming solutions, etc.)
(ii) These behavioural questions obviously require future empirical verification or falsification.

between nonoptimal transfer prices and the dysfunctional consequences of removing this subject from the integrator's purview.

CONCLUSION

We have attempted to place the transfer pricing question in a relevant behavioural setting. Briefly, we have suggested the management accountant needs to consider organizational differentiation a constraint in designing the management accounting system. Working within this constraint we suggested the management accounting system can be designed to enhance the organization differentiation achieved or to facilitate organizational integration. The transfer pricing mechanism, being part of the management accounting system, can be used to enhance organizational differentiation and to facilitate organizational integration. The transfer pricing mechanisms will probably play the role of enhancing differentiation in those instances in which integration is easily attained. This may well be achieved by the use of formula pricing mechanisms. In other cases, integration will be a major organizational problem. Consequently, the transfer pricing mechanism could be utilized to facilitate integration. An appropriate transfer price mechanism in this case seems to be negotiated pricing. Further areas of research suggested by this conclusion were discussed.

REFERENCES

Baumol, W.J. and Fabian, T., 'Decomposition, Pricing for Decentralization and External Economics,' *Management Science* (September 1964), pp. 1–32.

Burns, T. and Stalker, G.M., *The Management of Innovation* (London: Tavistock Institute, 1961).

Cook, P.W., 'Decentralization and the Transfer Price Problem,' *Journal of Business* (April 1955), pp. 87–94.

Dantzig, G.B. and Wolfe P., 'Decomposition Principles for Linear Programs,' *Operations Research* (February 1960), pp. 101–11.

Dean, J., 'Decentralization and Intracompany Pricing,' *Harvard Business Review* (July–August 1955), pp. 65–74.

Dopuch, N. and Drake, D.F., 'Accounting Implications of a Mathematical Programming Approach to the Transfer Pricing Problem,' *Journal of Accounting Research* (Spring 1964), pp. 10–24.

Galbraith, J.R., 'Organization Design: An Information Processing View', in J.W. Lorsch and P.R. Lawrence, eds., *Organizational Planning: Cases and Concepts* (Georgetown, Ontario: Irwin-Dorsey Limited, 1972).

Godfrey, J.T., 'Short-Run Planning in a Decentralized Firm,' *The Accounting Review* (April 1971), pp. 282–97.

Gordon, M.J., 'A Method of Pricing for a Socialist Economy,' *The Accounting Review* (July 1970), pp. 427–43.

Hass, J.E. 'Transfer Pricing in a Decentralized Firm,' *Management Science* (February 1968), pp. B-310–B-331.

Hirshleifer, J., 'On the Economics of Transfer Pricing,' *Journal of Business* (July 1956), pp. 172–84.

——,'Economics of the Divisionalized Firm,' *Journal of Business* (April 1957), pp. 96–108.

Lawrence, P.R. and Lorsch, J.W., *Organization and Environment* (Irwin, 1967).

Mohr, L.B., 'Organizational Technology and Organizational Structure,' *Administrative Science Quarterly* (December 1971), pp. 444–59.

Ronen, J. and McKinney, G., 'Transfer Pricing for Divisional Autonomy,' *Journal of Accounting Research* (Spring 1970), pp. 99–112.

Ruefli, T.W., 'A Generalized Goal Decomposition Model,' *Management Science* (April 1971), pp. B-505–B-518.

——,'Behavioral Externalities in Decentralized Organizations,' *Management Science* (June 1971), pp. B-649–B-657

Schelling, T.C., *The Strategy of Conflict* (Oxford University Press, 1963).

Thompson, J.D., *Organizations in Action* (McGraw-Hill, 1967).

Whinston, 'Pricing Guides in Decentralized Organization,' in W.W. Cooper *et al.*, eds., *New Perspectives in Organizational Research* (Wiley, 1964).

Woodward, J., *Industrial Organizations: Theory and Practice* (Oxford University Press, 1965).

20

Transfer pricing: a fair and neutral procedure

Clive R. Emmanuel and Kenneth P. Gee

This paper presents a fair and neutral transfer pricing procedure for a divisionalized company. 'Fairness' is said to be present where there is a minimum of discrimination against the transferor (selling division) or the transferee (buying division). It requires that divisional managers should agree upon how to price internally traded goods, and that any manager should be able to verify that any transfer price charged has been computed consistently with the agreed procedure. 'Neutrality' is present where there is the minimum inducement for the profit-seeking managers of either the buying or the selling division to arrive at decisions inconsistent with profit-seeking by the divisionalized company as a whole.

The concern of this paper is solely with market-based transfer prices, because they are not derived from financial allocations which can neither be verified nor refuted [Thomas, 1980]. Further, market-based transfer prices are considered to be compatible with the philosophy underlying divisionalization [Dean, 1955; Haidinger, 1970]. Unlike the transfer pricing procedures discussed by Gould [1964] and Manes [1970], they incorporate directly information available to divisional managers, and do not rely upon the divisional managers submitting information without bias to optimization exercises conducted centrally, from which transfer prices emerge as mere 'by-products'. Market-based transfer prices are commonly used by British and North American companies [N.I.C.B., 1967; Tomkins, 1973] and have recently received some support on behavioural grounds [Arvidsson, 1973; Watson and Baumler, 1975]. They can, however, offend against the canons of fairness and neutrality for the following three reasons:

(i) The markets for intermediate commodities tend to be characterized by imperfect competition [Stigler and Kindahl, 1970; Hague, 1971; Atkin and Skinner, 1975] in which buyers face a range of prices at a moment in time for basically similar goods. Sellers' discount terms and amounts are not uniform, and without considering quality, delivery date and other dimensions of non-price competition, 'the market price' is rendered indeterminate. The price range facing the selling division may overlap only

Source: Emmanuel, C.R. and Gee, K.P. (1982) *Accounting and Business Research*, Autumn, pp. 273–8.

in part with that facing the buying division. In such conditions, the derivation of a 'fair' transfer price, discriminating against neither the selling nor the buying division, becomes problematical [Solomons, 1965, pp. 177–178].

(ii) It is normal practice to agree that a transfer price should remain applicable for a period, incorporating the price in that period's operating budget. Movements of market price inconsistent with the expectations upon which the budgeted transfer price was predicated can give rise to time-consuming transfer price renegotiations, in which divisional managers seek to maintain their profit performance as against one another. Mediators from corporate management, if called in, are likely to find themselves in no better a position to reset the transfer price than the divisional managers concerned, and any compromise solution is likely to be seen by at least one of these managers as being inconsistent with fairness.

(iii) A problem regarding neutrality arises where the selling division is working below capacity. This problem is exemplified in the Birch Paper Company case [Anthony and Dearden, 1980, pp. 251–253] and may be explained by reference to symbols as follows. At a moment in time, let:

m_s represent the transfer price per unit offered by the selling division;

m_b represent the lowest external price per unit available to the buying division;

c_s represent current variable cost per unit in the selling division;

c_b represent current variable cost per unit in the buying division; and

m_e represent selling price per unit of finished product.

Then for the alternatives of interdivisional or external trading, contribution figures per incremental unit of product will be as follows:

Interdivisional Trading
Selling division earns $m_s - c_s$.
Buying division earns $m_e - (m_s + c_b)$.
Company as a whole earns $m_e - (c_s + c_b)$.

External Trading
Selling division earns zero.
Buying division earns $m_e - (m_b + c_b)$.
Company as a whole earns $m_e - (m_b + c_b)$.

So long as $m_b > c_s$, the company as a whole will earn more profit from an interdivisional transaction. An interdivisional transaction will be more profitable for the selling division so long as $m_s > c_s$, but for the buying division an interdivisional transaction will only be more profitable if $m_b > m_s$. A 'compromise price' for interdivisional trading m_g, such that $m_b > m_g$ but $m_g > c_s$, would increase the profit of the selling division, of the buying division and of the company as a whole relative to that obtainable through external trading. The difficulty lies in the negotiation of m_g, in that the magnitude of m_g represents the outcome of a zero-sum game between the buying and selling divisions. A larger m_g benefits the selling division at the expense of the buying division, and vice versa. Negotiations over the magnitude of m_g may therefore end in deadlock, either because the buying division, from its market perspective, sees the selling division's price concessions as inadequate or because the selling division, from its perspective, sees itself as being required to offer an exaggerated discount. This latter cause of breakdown is especially likely if the selling division has no guarantee that the buying division will not resell the transferred commodity, with minimal further processing, in the selling division's market. Whatever the cause of breakdown, its consequence is likely to be that the buying division will purchase externally to the detriment of corporate profitability. This problem can be dealt with through the mechanism of a lost contribution charge to be levied on the selling division by corporate headquarters, coupled with an internal trading discount allowed by the selling to the buying division, as in the procedure outlined below.

THE PROCEDURE: FAIRNESS

Some notation required to present the procedure is as follows. Let:

S_t represent the standard variable cost per unit in year t for the selling division;

M_s represent the weighted average market price per unit obtained on external sales by the selling division in year t, as computed at the year-end (note that where the selling division produces only for internal sale M_s will be absent, thus making a market-based transfer pricing system unfeasible);

d_{tj} represent a discount on internal trading determined by the selling division *ex ante* and allowed to the buying division in respect of the jth quarter of the year t, this discount being expressed as a proportion of M_s (the choice of a quarterly revision period for this discount is arbitrary, but consistent with the practice of quarterly rolling budgets [Judelson, 1977]);

Q_s represent the year t production capacity in units of the selling division;

M_b represent the weighted average market price per unit paid by the buying division for outside purchases in year t, as computed at the year-end; and

Q_{tj} represent the number of units purchased in quarter j of year t by the buying division from the selling division.

Under this 'fair and neutral' procedure, the charge made to the buying division for internal purchases is in two instalments as follows:

(a) A product cost of $£Q_f S_t$ is charged when (say) Q_f units are bought.
(b) At the end of year t, a period cost of

$$£\sum_{j=1}^{4}(1 - d_{tj})Q_{tj}M_s - \sum_{j=1}^{4}Q_{tj}S_t \text{ is charged.}$$

The effect of this is to bring up the charge for Q_f units bought (say) in the rth quarter of year t to $£(1 - d_{tr})Q_fM_s$, applying to the quantity purchased year t's weighted average market price on external sales, less any internal trading discount for quarter r. Where discounts are offered, these arise because the selling division's expectations about their external market have led them to the view that discounts are necessary to stimulate internal trade – thus increasing their capacity utilization and so constraining the amount of any lost contribution charge levied upon them (see below). By contrast, the period cost is not based upon expectations but it wholly objective. The period cost is not related to the lost contribution charge; both are calculated *ex post* but the period cost is calculated by reference to external market prices obtained by the selling division while the lost contribution charge is calculated by reference to external market prices paid by the buying division.

Because the period cost is calculated *ex post*, the fairness problems associated with market-based transfer prices and represented by (i) and (ii) above, cease to be of significance. The period cost is charged only when the prices actually obtained by the selling division are known, and internal auditors may supply documentation to satisfy the buying division that the computation of the weighted average market price relates solely to *bona fide* external sales. *Annual* weighted average prices are used to render impractical the possibility that the selling division might attempt to obtain an unduly favourable transfer price by selling only a relatively small quantity externally at an inflated price – this tactic would be unduly costly to the selling division over so long a period as a year.

Two important advantages are claimed for the above procedure in the context of fairness. First, it does not require inspection of the market at any particular instant in order to establish what the market price currently 'is' for a specific size and type of transaction. Thus it avoids the problem outlined in (i) above as arising where non-price competition in imperfect markets gives rise to a complex, ill-publicized price structure. Second, the procedure does not involve divisional management in a zero-sum game of bilateral transfer price negotiation, thus saving time and avoiding the possibility outlined in (ii) above that corporate management may be placed in the stressful and unsatisfactory role of mediator.

This second claim is probably more controversial than the first. Is not the negotiation of the discount on internal trading d_{tj} just as much a zero-sum game as was the negotiation of the compromise transfer price m_g, and therefore just as likely to break down and require mediation? What in fact keeps the negotiation of d_{tj} from being a zero-sum game is the potential levying of a lost contribution charge. This is a charge imposed by corporate management as a deduction from the selling division's profitability measure under the following circumstances:

(a) Suppose that during year t the selling division manages only to sell Q_a units, where $Q_a < Q_s$, while the buying division purchases externally Q_b units, such that $Q_a + Q_b < Q_s$. Then the lost contribution charge to the selling division will represent the contribution the selling divisions would have earned had it supplied the buying division's entire needs at the annual average price negotiated by that division with outside suppliers, i.e. £$(M_b - S_t)Q_b$.

(b) Suppose that $Q_a < Q_s$ but $Q_a + Q_b < Q_s$. Then the lost contribution charge will consist of the contribution the selling division would have earned had it used its remaining capacity in the partial fulfilment of the buying division's needs at the annual average price negotiated by that division with outside suppliers, i.e. £$(M_b - S_t)(Q_s - Q_a)$.

Where there are lost contribution charges, the effect of negotiating d_{tj} downward towards zero is to present the selling division with both a benefit and a potential hazard. The benefit consists of a higher internal selling price for the product, and the hazard is that at this higher price the volume of internal sales may be such as to leave some of the selling division's capacity unused, thus attracting a lost contribution charge. Hence a lower value of d_{tj} is unlike a higher value of m_g in that it does not confer an *unambiguous* benefit upon the selling division. Conversely, a higher value of d_{tj} is beneficial to the buying division in that it offers them a lower unit price, but it may also be beneficial to the selling division if it averts or diminishes a lost contribution charge. In negotiating d_{tj} the buying and the selling division are not playing a zero-sum game against one another but are playing against 'nature' in the form of the *external* market. Negotiating stances on d_{tj} are derived from the forecasts which both the buying and the selling division must make about the prices and quantities involved in their divisions' external transactions, these forecasts being made in the knowledge that errors will automatically be penalized without the need for corporate management's intervention. Internal trade is conducted by reference to *external* criteria and not by reference to bargaining ploys focused upon an 'opponent' within the company.

It has now been shown that the procedure advocated in this paper meets objections (i) and (ii) advanced at the beginning against market-based transfer prices in the context of fairness. The next task is to consider the context of neutrality.

THE PROCEDURE: NEUTRALITY

In essence, the neutrality problem outlined in (iii) above arises because of the lack of sufficient organizational inducement to the selling division to set its transfer price below market price when it has (or expects to have) spare production capacity. This problem is dealt with by the lost contribution charge, which represents the budgeted profit and net cash flow lost to the company as a whole as a result of the external purchase of units that could have been made internally. Any such loss is charged to the division responsible for it. For example, in case (a) above external purchase has given rise to a cash outflow of £Q_bM_b, while averting a budgeted cash outflow of £S_tQ_b as a result of the production by the selling division of Q_b fewer units than would have been produced had the

buying division bought internally. Standard variable costs are to be preferred to actual variable costs in the computation of the lost contribution
charge. If actual variable costs were to be used, the charge in respect of
the external purchase of a given number of units would be *larger* to the
extent that standard variable cost exceeded actual variable cost, thus
penalizing good cost control in the selling divison. If $M_b < S_t$ there will
be no contribution charge, but this will act as a signal to investigate the
curtailment of the selling division's activities.

The magnitude of S_t is known centrally since it must be agreed with
corporate management as part of the process by which the selling division's budget is ratified. Consequently, information about S_t passed
from the selling to the buying division can be checked by consultation
between the buying division and corporate management; the buying
division is not dependent upon the selling division's cooperation in providing an accurate figure for S_t. When the buying division's manager
has to decide whether or not to purchase internally, he will know S_t and
must act by reference to his *estimate* of the value M_s will take. Let us
call this estimate M_{se}. In evaluating an externally-supplied quote of £M_q
per unit, his decision rule for the jth quarter of year t will be to accept
if $M_q < (1 - d_{tj})M_{se}$, and to reject if otherwise. Thus in deciding *ex ante*
how large an internal trading discount d_{tj} to offer for quarter j, the selling division has to balance the loss of revenue resulting from a lower
discount-adjusted transfer price against the fact that a transfer price so
lowered may generate a larger volume of internal sales and hence reduce
or eliminate the selling division's lost contribution charge. The size of the
internal trading discount offered will consequently depend on the selling
division's expectation regarding the likelihood that they will be operating
below capacity during the coming quarter. If they expect $Q_a = Q_s$ during
this quarter, they will have no incentive to offer a discount in order to
avoid a lost contribution charge, though a small discount may still be
offered if cost savings on internal trade in respect (e.g.) of transport, administration and debt collection give rise to the prospect of favourable
budget variances against standard variable cost on such trade.

A further influence on the size of the internal trading discount will be
the presence of inflation during a year. If there were no discount, the
buying division would always be charged £M_s per unit irrespective of
the time of year at which it purchased. This weighted average price M_s
would tend to exceed externally-quoted prices during the first half of an
inflationary year, and to fall below them during the second half. Consequently, if the selling division expected to be working at a constant
proportion of its capacity throughout the year, it would be likely to set
$d_{t1} > d_{t2} > d_{t3} > d_{t4}$ so as to keep its quarter j internal price of £$(1 - d_{tj})M_s$
per unit in a fixed relationship with external quotes and to counter-
balance the tendency of the buying division to purchase externally in the
first two quarters and internally in the second two quarters. If the selling
division expected to be operating at capacity during the third and fourth
quarters it would be free to set d_{t3} and d_{t4} negative, i.e. to impose a sur-
charge on internal trading to bring up the internal price to a level in ex-

cess of M_s and in line with external quotes on a market characterized by supply shortages. In a very volatile market, the magnitude of the internal trading discount could be set on a monthly or even a weekly basis, rather than being set quarterly as previously specified.

SOME OBJECTIONS AND SHORTCOMINGS

The following are some objections which may be raised against the proposed transfer pricing procedure. There is no doubt that the procedure has genuine shortcomings, though none are considered to constitute conclusive counter-arguments:

(i) If M_s were to be derived by reference to transactions of quite different size from those carried out by the buying division, then the presence of quantity discounts would cause it to diverge from external market prices obtainable by the buying division. Thus, if M_s arose from transactions by the selling division each of which were of considerable size while the buying division habitually purchased only relatively small quantities, M_s would tend to be pulled down by comparatively large quantity discounts to a level beneath the external market prices available to the buying division. Conversely, if the buying division bought in bulk while the selling division's external sales involved relatively small quantities per transaction, M_s in reflecting comparatively small quantity discounts would tend to lie above the external market prices available to the buying division. Here, the role of the internal trading discount would be to bring the unit price on internal transactions back into line with the external market opportunities available to the buying division, giving rise, *ceteris paribus*, to a negative figure for d_{tj} in the first case above and a positive figure for d_{tj} in the second. The selling division would be motivated to make d_{tj} responsive in this way by a desire both to earn contribution on internal sales and to avoid the possible levying of a lost contribution charge.

(ii) The proposed procedure places the buying division's manager in the position of comparing a *certain* external price of (say) £M_q against his *estimate* of the internal price £$(1 - d_{tj})M_{se}$. If the manager is risk-averse he will require his estimate of the internal price to be below the external price by an amount greater than or equal to his risk premium if he is to trade internally. The size of the required risk premium could be substantially reduced, however, if M_s were calculated every quarter over the preceding four quarters instead of being calculated once a year at the year end. A period cost would then be charged to the buying division every quarter instead of every year, this period cost being obtained by applying, to the quantity traded internally in a quarter, the weighted average market price obtained by the selling division over the 12 months preceding the quarter's-end. (This price would be adjusted for any internal trading discount offered during the quarter.) Thus the weighted average market price would be computed on a quarterly rolling basis, the oldest quarter's figures being dropped and the newest added into the averaging process every time the period cost was computed. During any quarter, the buying division could estimate M_s by reference to its knowledge of the weighted average market price obtained by the selling division over nine of the twelve months which made up the year over which M_s would be computed at the quarter's end. This would reduce the uncertainty associated with M_s, and with it the size of the risk premium required for internal trading. At the same time, M_s would still be computed over a complete year, a period sufficiently long to deter the selling division from deliberately inflating its external prices and accepting minimal external sales volume in order to distort M_s and hence the transfer price charged.

(iii) Problems may be encountered in defining Q_s (the production capacity of the selling division) where Q_s relates to capacity in units for a single product within a multi-product division. All other things being equal, the size of any lost contribution charge will increase as Q_s increases, giving the selling division an incentive to provide misleading information biasing Q_s downwards. The most practical expedient here would be to take Q_s as representing *budgeted* sales volume for each product, so that biasing Q_s downwards would automatically depress budgeted profit, thus damaging the organizational standing of the division concerned. But this would not provide a complete solution to the problem, in that the lost contribution charge would then understate the costs of below-capacity working to the extent that budgeted sales volume fell below volume at full-capacity working. Problems of equity to the selling division could also arise where actual sales mix diverged very greatly from budgeted mix even though the selling division was working to capacity overall. Lost contribution charges might then be levied for individual products forming a smaller proportion of the actual than the budgeted mix, creating perhaps a perception of unfair treatment within the selling division. The potential for unfairness here could be eliminated by a central management rule waiving any lost contribution charges where *both* the sales mix and pure sales volume variances of the selling division were favourable.

(iv) The transfer pricing procedure advocated in this paper may penalize a division selling a finished product externally at a price which only just covers the variable cost of that product to the company as a whole. While such a division could obtain information on the standard variable cost of processing a unit of product within each of the divisions through which the product had previously passed, the sum of these standard variable processing costs must be less than the transfer price charged to the division selling the final product if each preceding division is to comply with its budget in earning a contribution on internal trade. Hence a price for the finished product which covered the standard variable cost of processing and provided a contribution toward budgeted fixed costs for the company as a whole might fail to cover the final selling division's standard variable cost, composed in part of the transfer price it had paid. However, where the final market is depressed, interdivisional transfers may well take place at prices not far exceeding variable costs of processing, as divisions selling intermediate products respond to the threat of lost contribution charges.

(v) Internal and external transactions give rise under the proposed transfer pricing procedure to different cash flow patterns. Since for internal transactions the period cost is paid by the buying division only at the end of a year, the present value of the cost of internal transactions will, *ceteris paribus*, be less to it than the present value of the cost of external transactions. The dysfunctional incentive to internal sales arising from this can, however, be dealt with by the selling division in so reducing d_{tj} as to compensate for the differing time patterns of receipts from its internal and external sales. Such adjustments to d_{tj} would become less necessary if period cost payments were made quarterly instead of annually, as advocated in (ii) above.

(vi) The buying division may insist upon a policy of dual-sourcing, preserving access to an alternative source of supply by purchasing some of its requirements from outside, irrespective of the size of the discount offered on internal trading. If this is the case, then, when $Q_a + Q_b < Q_s$, the selling division will bear a lost contribution charge of $£(M_b - S_t)Q_b$ which no internal pricing policy on its part could have avoided. However, dual-sourcing is less likely to be insisted upon where there is an internal source of supply than where all sources are external to the company, on the grounds that while an *external* supplier may cease trading abruptly and thus dislocate material procurement, *intra-company* communication can usually be relied upon for reasonable notice of impending cessation of supply, enabling alternative arrangements to be made. The extra costs imposed by dual-sourcing relative to reliance upon the cheapest single source will also tend to be greater where the cheapest source is an internal one, offering trading discounts under threat of a lost contribution charge, than where the cheapest source is an external one facing similar costs to its competitors and consequently quoting broadly comparable prices.

CONCLUSION

The proposed transfer pricing procedure is consistent with the philosophy of divisionalization in that internal operations are subject to the influence of market forces. It facilitates the production of a profit figure for a division that reflects both its economic viability as a quasi-autonomous unit and its function within the company as a whole. The procedure is not a panacea for all transfer pricing problems; in particular it has little relevance where the product transferred is subject to so much technical change that its character changes during the year. In such a case it would be meaningless to compute an average market price over a year, for this average would be made up of the prices of essentially different commodities.

The great strength of the procedure, though, is that it requires divisional managers to focus on external market developments, diminishing the emphasis placed upon internal negotiations and considerably reducing the need for central management intervention in the process of transfer price determination. Divisional managers thus have their autonomy reinforced, and are encouraged to see transfer pricing as a game of 'company vs. environment' rather than one of 'manager vs. manager'. Another important feature of the procedure is that it is explicitly designed to cope with the commonly encountered situation in which imperfect competition gives rise to a range of market prices. The *ex post* calculation of period cost, taken in conjunction with a lost contribution charge/internal trading discount mechanism, would seem to give rise to a transfer price which is to a substantial extent both fair and neutral.

REFERENCES

Anthony, R.N. and Dearden, J. (1980) *Management Control Systems: Text and Cases*, (4th ed.), R.D. Irwin.

Arvidsson, G. (1973) *Internal Transfer Negotiations – Eight Experiments*, The Economic Research Institute, Stockholm.

Atkin, B. and Skinner, R. (1975) *How British Industry Prices*, Industrial Market Research Ltd.

Dean, J. (1955) 'Decentralization and Intra-Company Pricing', *Harvard Business Review*, July–August, pp. 65–74.

Gould, J.R. (1964) 'Internal Pricing in Firms When There Are Costs of Using an Outside Market', *Journal of Business*, January, pp. 61–67.

Hague, D.C. (1971) *Pricing in Business*, George Allen and Unwin.

Haidinger, T.P. (1970) 'Negotiate for Profits', *Management Accounting* (NAA), December, pp. 23, 24, 52.

Judelson, D.N. (1977) 'Financial Controls that Work', *Financial Executive*, January, pp. 22–25.

Manes, R. (1970) 'Birch Paper Company Revisited: An Exercise in Transfer Pricing', *Accounting Review*, July, pp. 565–572.

National Industrial Conference Board (1967) *Inter-Divisional Transfer Pricing: Studies in Business Policy No. 122*, NICB.

Solomons, D. (1965) *Divisional Performance: Measurement and Control*, R.D. Irwin, Inc.

Stigler, G.J. and Kindahl, J.K. (1970) *Behavior of Industrial Prices*, Columbia Press.

Thomas, A.L. (1980) *A Behavioral Analysis of Joint-Cost Allocation and Transfer Pricing*, Stipes Publishing Company.

Tomkins, C.R. (1973) *Financial Planning in Divisionalized Companies*, Haymarket Publishing Ltd.

Watson, S.J.H. and Baumler, J.V. (1975) 'Transfer Pricing: A Behavioural Context', *Accounting Review*, July, pp. 466–474.

21

Towards an organizational theory of the transfer pricing process

Barry H. Spicer
University of Oregon

ABSTRACT

Understanding the transfer pricing issue as it arises in large decentralized firms is important, because it represents a pervasive problem in the design of managerial accounting and control systems in complex organizations. This paper draws on the growing literature on the economics of internal organization to develop an understanding of the strategic, organizational and transactional conditions under which transfer pricing (and related control) issues arise, and the organizational processes used to implement intra-firm transfers of products and to determine transfer prices. The objective of the paper is to develop a theory of the transfer pricing process and to deduce hypotheses from the theory.

The objective of this paper is to build a theory of the transfer pricing process within firms and to develop testable hypotheses about transfer pricing mechanisms and policies given variations in firms' strategic, organizational and transactional conditions. The paper responds in a general way to recent cells by Hopwood (1983), Kaplan (1983, 1984, 1986a, 1986b), Jensen (1983) Covaleski & Aiken (1986), and Johnson & Kaplan (1987) to study accounting, not in simplified, abstract settings, but rather richly imbedded in organizational context. More specifically, the paper fits into that set of research which is aimed at the eventual development of a positive theory of management accounting. Preliminary efforts in this direction are to be found in recent papers by Spicer & Ballew (1983) and Waterhouse & Tiessen (1983).

There are two points of departure for the paper. The first is the growing body of work on the economics of internal organization which is aimed at improving our understanding of alternative ways of organizing economic activities in markets and hierarchies. Of particular importance for this paper is the work of Williamson (1970, 1975, 1979, 1985) which develops a theory of economic organization that tries to explain why economic

Source: Spicer, B.H. (1988) *Accounting, Organizations and Society*, **13** (3), pp. 303–22.

activities have been organized in particular ways and the key factors involved in these choices. The second point of departure is an important theoretical paper by Watson & Baumler (1975) which attempts to place transfer pricing into a behavioural context by introducing a theory of decentralization into the transfer pricing literature. This paper accepts Watson & Baumler's work as the state of the art in terms of theoretical understanding of the transfer pricing process, and draws on the developing literature on the economics of internal organization to address issues not answered or insufficiently developed by Watson & Baumler.[1]

The paper is structured as follows: the first section provides a perspective for the rest of the paper based on a brief review of the classical transfer pricing literature and recent calls for the introduction of organizational context into the study of management accounting issues. The second section draws on the literature on the economics of internal organization to address a number of theoretical issues either not answered, or insufficiently developed, by Watson & Baumler in their article. The objective is to construct a theoretical framework of the transfer pricing process and to present a number of hypotheses relating to the internal transfer of intermediate products. The third section presents a series of hypotheses based on the theoretical framework developed in the second section of the paper. The final section of the paper presents a summary and conclusions and suggestions for follow-on empirical research.

CLASSICAL VS AN ORGANIZATIONAL APPROACH TO THE TRANSFER PRICING PROBLEM

Internal transfers of intermediate products between subunits of firms take place under a wide range of organizational conditions. Understanding how internal transfers are governed clearly involves a consideration of the organizational setting in which the transfers take place. However, classical academic treatments of transfer pricing generally start by specifying a restrictive set of assumptions on organizational conditions under which the analysis will be conducted: interest is centered on '. . . presenting a set of transfer pricing rules that integrate the complex elements of the organization in order to allow for divisional autonomy while recognizing global organizational goals' (Abdel-khalik & Lusk, 1974, p. 9). Using this global profit maximizing approach it is common to attribute conflicts between the subgoals of divisions, and the global goal of the firm itself, to inadequacies in the transfer pricing model. Development of an optimum transfer pricing model (using analytical, mathematical or simulation techniques) that does not result in some form of subopti-

---

[1] The Watson & Baumler (1975) paper is not the only paper in the literature that has taken, or has alluded to, an 'organizational behaviour' approach to transfer pricing. However, it does represent the most complete, integrated organizational behaviour approach to transfer pricing that currently exists. As such it is convenient and useful to accept it as 'state of the art' and proceed from there.

mization is not an easy task; as can be seen from the current state of the transfer pricing literature.[2]

This classical approach has both advantages and limitations. One advantage of the use of restrictive assumptions on organizational conditions is that it allows the researcher to define the problem to be studied as a transfer pricing problem without explicit reference to the wider process of management control. This allows the researcher to investigate the properties of new or alternative ways to set transfer prices, and to study incentive and risk-sharing attributes of reward systems based in whole, or part, on performance measures making use of transfer prices. What this approach does not do, is lend itself to a deeper understanding of the dimensions of the entire transfer pricing process, in the wide variety of organizational contexts within firms in which transfer pricing systems operate.

An organizational theory of the transfer pricing process requires a wider consideration of relationships among a firm's diversification strategy, its intra-firm transactions, its organization structure and its management accounting and control systems. The resulting theory should help to explain observed transfer pricing practices and provide a context for intrepreting research aimed at investigating the properties of new or alternative ways of setting transfer prices under restrictive assumptions about underlying organizational conditions.

There is growing support for such an approach to the transfer pricing problem. Both Swieringa & Waterhouse (1982) and Eccles (1983), for example, insist that the objectives that can be accomplished with a particular transfer pricing method are dependent on a firm's organization structure – a position that stands in sharp contrast to the classical approach. Based on his recent extensive review of the transfer pricing literature, Grabski (1986, p. 61) concludes that one of the things that is now needed '... is further examination of the impact of the organization of the firm on transfer pricing.' This conclusion is best viewed as a reflection of the growing support among accounting researchers for developing theory and studying accounting issues in their organizational contexts. Commenting on the presentations at a conference at UCLA on 'Accounting in Its Organizational Context' Hopwood (1983, p. 303) notes that to date '... we have few insights into factors which influence accounting systems in the contexts in which they operate.' In his view 'What is needed are more substantive investigations oriented towards providing bases for understanding or explaining the workings of accounting in action'. Other academics have also written about the need for the development of insight, understanding, and the eventual development of positive theory by observing management accounting practice in its organizational context. Kaplan (1986b, pp. 445–446), a prolific writer on this theme,[3] writes:

---

[2] See Grabski (1986) for a useful, up to date review of the transfer pricing literature.
[3] Kaplan makes similar points in Kaplan (1983, 1984, 1986a) and in Johnson & Kaplan (1987).

Cost accounting and management control procedures function in complex organizational settings. Therefore, our initial effort to observe and describe management accounting practice must capture the richness of the organizational context.... it is hard to imagine how to test theories in management accounting if the testing is not performed in actual organizational contexts.

The approach adopted in this paper is to draw on existing theoretical work to deduce a theory of the transfer pricing process to guide later empirical investigation in the field. Maher (1983, p. 25) provides support for this approach when he writes about the general state of research in management accounting:

The lack of theory and testable hypotheses [in management accounting] limits our opportunities for systematic empirical work. Of course much can be learned from purely descriptive studies – inductive reasoning can play an important role in developing theory and testable hypotheses. But I believe that the next major breakthroughs will come from empirical work that follows theory.

TOWARDS A THEORY OF THE TRANSFER PRICING PROCESS: POINTS OF DEPARTURE

The economics of internal organization

Recent work on the economics of internal organization can assist understanding of alternative ways of organizing economic activities in markets or hierarchies (firms). Seminal works in the field include Coase (1937), Alchian & Demsetz (1972), Williamson (1970, 1975, 1979 and 1985) and Jensen & Meckling (1976).[4] Recent papers in the accounting literature by Spicer & Ballew (1983), Waterhouse & Tiessen (1983) and Swieringa & Waterhouse (1982) have drawn on the theoretical work of Williamson, in particular, to understand firms' choices of internal accounting and control mechanisms.

The markets and hierarchies approach, or organizational failures framework (OFF), regards transactions and contracts as the basis of all economic exchange. The fundamental unit of analysis is the transaction, which can vary from simple to complex. The analysis of transactions focuses on the differential costs of completing transactions under alternative institutional arrangements that govern the contracting relationships. Transaction costs are recognized as nonzero, nontrivial, and generally

---

[4] Jensen (1983, p. 324) also notes that 'The last decade has been marked by a growing interest in organizations in the economics profession' and that while the science of organizations is still in its infancy, the foundations of a powerful theory of organizations is being put into place. Jensen (1983, p. 324, footnote 9) provides a more extensive list of references to scholars who have made contributions in this area.

increasing with the complexity of the transaction. Thus different types of transactions may require different types of governance structures to organize them. 'Organization failure' is said to occur when transaction costs (or difficulties) can be reduced by shifting those transactions to an alternative organizational arrangement.

For any like set of transactions there are two basic levels of choice: a choice between markets and hierarchies; and for those transactions organized within hierarchies, joint choices of strategy (with respect to the firm's market and technological opportunities) and internal organizational structures and processes to achieve these chosen strategies. The efficiency with which a firm pursues its chosen strategy will depend on the manner in which the firm subdivides its economic activities, forms the employment relation and structures its management accounting and control systems (Spicer & Ballew, 1983, p. 82).

In the markets and hierarchies framework, the level of transactional difficulties associated with exchanges (in both markets and hierarchies), are linked to the interaction of a core set of human and environmental factors with the dimensions of the transaction itself. Bounded rationality and opportunism are key human factors. Bounded rationality refers to individuals' limited abilities to avoid error and behave in a rational manner when faced with complex problems and decisions. Opportunism extends the usual economic assumption of self interest to allow for strategic behaviour by individuals. Because opportunistic behaviour can involve strategic distortions and misrepresentations of intentions and outcomes, adverse selection and moral hazard problems are introduced into exchange relationships. It is the possibility of opportunistic behaviour where there is uncertainty, and only a small number of buyers and sellers, that information impactedness (information asymmetry that cannot be overcome at low cost) can occur. It is the potential opportunistic use of impacted information that subjects transactions to hazard and raises the question of appropriate organizational arrangements.

It is important to note that the degree to which the above factors are present is linked to the dimensions of the transactions involved in the exchange. Williamson (1979) identifies three critical dimensions of transactions: (1) the investment characteristic (the degree to which suppliers need to make investments in human and physical capital to realize production cost economies); (2) the extent of buyer activity (frequency and volume); and (3) the degree of uncertainty and/or complexity that surrounds the transaction. Williamson argues that variations in these critical dimensions of transactions can affect both the relative economies of scale for internal production vs external purchase; and the level of transactions costs encountered under these alternative modes of organizing the transaction. In this context, a firm's decision to 'make-or-buy' will be made so as to economize on the sum of production and transactions costs (Williamson, 1979, p. 254).

The effects of variations in the dimensions of transactions on economies of scale in internal production vs external purchase, and on contracting hazards associated with buying, will be discussed later in the paper. The point to be made here is that because intra-firm transfers of intermediate product represent transactions between subunits, the theoretical framework developed in the economics of internal organization can be used to consider contracting issues involved with these internal transfers and the transfer pricing process.

Theoretical development by Watson & Baumler (1975)

Watson & Baumler make two main contributions to the development of a theory of transfer pricing. Their first contribution comes from proposing that explicit attention be given to underlying organizational conditions (uncertainty, differentiation and integration) if we are to understand how the transfer pricing question arises and the process used in setting prices. Watson & Baumler (1975, pp. 466–467) point out that most authors provide reasons for decentralization when addressing the transfer pricing question; but

> ...none...has offered a coherent theory of decentralization. Consequently, the implications that the authors see of decentralization for transfer pricing are fairly restricted and pragmatic.

The theory of organizational decentralization which Watson & Baumler introduce was drawn from the contingency literature and, in particular, from the work of Lawrence & Lorsch (1967). Watson & Baumler consider the degree of uncertainty, which is defined as contingent on technology and environment, as fundamental to the design of the firm's organizational structure and management accounting and control systems. Decentralization is viewed as a response to uncertainty which will, in turn, influence the attitudes and behaviour of the members of the resulting segments of the firm. This process is referred to as differentiation. Following Lawrence & Lorsch, Watson & Baumler hypothesize that organizational success is dependent on two things: (1) requisite differentiation – i.e. each organizational subunit must be designed so as to cope effectively with the demands of its technology and environment; and (2) integration – i.e. the process of insuring that efforts of appropriately differentiated subunits are motivated to maximize overall firm goals. Integration is achieved through the use of a multidimensional process of conflict resolution.

Watson & Baumler's second contribution lies in their proposition that transfer prices play a dual role in the differentiation and integration of the decentralized firm. Transfer prices enhance differentiation by helping separate and pinpoint responsibility in different segments of a firm. Transfer prices also can help achieve the required integration when organizational components are strongly differentiated, yet highly interdependent. In these complex organizational situations, Watson & Baumler argue that transfer prices will be only one of a number of inputs to a multidimensional process of conflict resolution. In this process they believe that negotiation will play a central role – covering not only transfer prices, but also related items such as design and engineering changes, production and delivery schedules, and quality control.

Issues for elaboration and extension drawing on the economics of internal organization

The economics of internal organization addresses a number of issues that are either not answered, or are insufficiently addressed, by Watson & Baumler.

First, the markets and hierarchies framework views uncertainty as only one of several interrelated factors which create the transaction costs that cause firms to differentiate and integrate. By considering other factors the OFF can provide a richer and more insightful explanation of the process of differentiation and integration and the role that transfer prices play in this process. The crucial role of process also has been emphasized by others. For example, based on the perspectives gained from four alternative, but complementary, organizational models, Swieringa & Waterhouse (1982, pp. 159–160) conclude that '... the process of devising pricing rules, procedures, and prices may be as important in achieving some degree of organizational control as the rules, procedures and prices themselves'.[5] More recently, Eccles (1985) and Grabski (1986) have both commented on the importance of a consideration of process when studying transfer pricing.

Second, Watson & Baumler do not explicitly consider the possible relationship among strategy, structure, management control systems and the dimensions of intra-firm transactions between differentiated subunits. A firm's diversification strategy is of particular importance when trying to explain a firm's organization structure and its management accounting and control system choices[6] because it can affect not only the types of transactions organized in a particular firm, but also the extent to which a firm chooses to decentralize its operations using profit centers.[7]

Some evidence that the extent of intra-firm transactions are associated

[5] The markets and hierarchies approach is only one of four organizational perspectives used by Swieringa & Waterhouse (1982) to examine the transfer pricing question in the context of the Birch Paper Company case. The other models used were the behavioural model of Cyert & March (1963); the garbage can model of organizations (Cohen, March & Olsen, 1972; Cohen & March 1974); and the organizing model (Weick, 1969, 1979).

[6] Caves (1980) summarizes studies of the association between diversification strategy and organizational structure in the U.S.A., U.K., France and Italy over the ten-year time period 1950–1970. His collected data show that as the degree of diversification increases across firms, so too does the proportion of firms that have adopted a divisionalized organization structure.

[7] Caves (1980, p. 87) writes: 'In the MD [multi-divisional] organization, the fineness with which activities are divided among divisions is itself a policy variable – one that should be optimized jointly with the differentiation of those divisions and the integrating effort applied to coordinating, in order to maximize the value of a firm's strategy.'

with diversification strategy is reported by Umapathy in Vancil (1979). Using categories of diversification developed by Rumelt (single product, dominant product, diversified-related products and diversified-unrelated products), Umapathy found that less diversified firms have more transfers of goods between profit centers than firms with higher levels of diversification.[8] This is not a surprising finding: profit centers in firms diversified into unrelated businesses are more likely to be independent with few intra-firm transfers taking place. If such a firm structures itself along divisional lines, with a separate profit center for each product grouping, there will be few control problems arising from the need to coordinate intra-firm transactions. Performance measurement and evaluation will be straight-forward and will focus on the independent contributions of each profit center to firm profits.

This is not the case in a vertically integrated single or dominant product firm (or even a related products firm) that adopts the increasingly common business strategy[9] of decentralizing its operations in a way that gives technologically separable processes profit center standing.[10] In these cases the organization and control issues (arising from OFF factors within the firm) are very different because of the different dimensions of transactions between profit centers. Typically, because of the interdependence between profit centers, intra-firm transactions in these firms will be frequent and at a material volume level, and will involve the supplying division in investments of human and/or physical capital directly related to the internal transfer. Whenever this involves the acquisition of special purpose assets, or labor skills that cannot be readily shifted to the production of other products with a ready external market, profit center managers who are evaluated solely on divisional profit performance, will have opportunities to behave opportunistically.

In summary, control problems of intra-firm transfers are hypothesized to be a function of the dimensions of intra-firm transactions which are, in turn, dependent on both the diversification strategy of the firm and its decentralization strategy, the latter being reflected in the firms' organizational design. Watson & Baumler do acknowledge that a firm's needs for differentiation and integration will vary with the degree of diversity and uncertainty faced by organizational subunits, but they do not relate this explicitly to the types of transactions handled by subunits. While a subunit is defined by its transactions, the reason to have the analysis focus on transactions – rather than the subunit – is because the transactional

---

[8] Umapathy (in Vancil, 1979, p. 170) reports that among highly diversified firms it is unusual to find transfers of goods between profit centers accounting for more than 10% of the value of the profit centers' finished goods, yet among less diversified firms it is common.

[9] Vancil (1979, p. 20) refers to a firm's choice of how to compete within the lines of business that it chooses to enter as its business strategy. Business strategy is reflected in the firm's organizational design.

[10] The studies reviewed by Caves (1980, p. 72) also show a clear trend over time towards the use of decentralized, divisionalized organizational structures in all diversification categories – including single and dominant product firms.

focus allows the analysis to clearly and explicitly consider the dimensions of the transactions between subunits; and their interrelationships with strategy, organizational structure, the nature of the firm's control problems, and the resulting demands placed on the firm's management accounting systems.

Finally, Watson & Baumler argue that transfer prices will most likely be negotiated as an aid to integration when profit centers are strongly differentiated and highly interdependent. But they do not discuss the nature of these negotiations or, as Grabski (1986, p. 44) points out, potential covariates: the process of evaluation of managers and organization structure. One of the advantages of viewing the negotiating process from the contracting perspective of the OFF is that it allows questions to be asked about those aspects of internal transfers that subect the exchange to hazard. It also allows questions to be asked about: the role of corporate level managers in the arbitration of disputes; and the role of performance evaluation, promotion and other incentive mechanisms (within the context of the organizational structure of the firm) to control conflict and promote cooperation among subunits.

The remainder of the paper builds on Watson & Baumler's work by drawing on the economics of internal organization to develop a more comprehensive theory of the transfer pricing process. Figure 21.1 provides a visual representation of some of the relationships discussed above and provides a basis for the ensuing discussion.

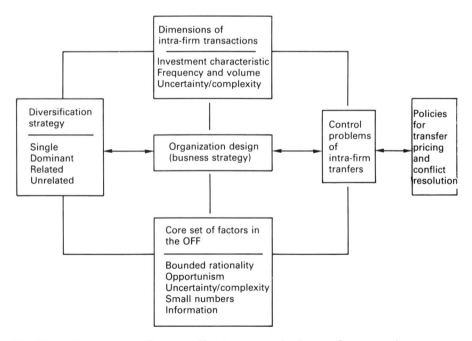

Fig. 21.1 Some major factors affecting control of inter-firm transfers.

THE CONTROL OF INTRA-FIRM TRANSFERS: THEORETICAL DEVELOPMENT

Firms have two decisions to make about intermediate products:

(1) A decision about the design features or specifications of the product. The chosen design will be a function of the firm's perceived market opportunities, competitive strategy and desire to differentiate its end products in the market. Intermediate products, therefore, may range from completely standardized components to highly specialized components with many unique design features.

(2) A decision to either 'make-or-buy' the intermediate component. As noted in an earlier section, the decision to make-or-buy will be made so as to economize on the sum of production and transaction costs: the choice involves not only a consideration of the cost of making internally vs the cost of buying externally, but also the degree to which exchange hazards are associated with external procurement.

Table 21.1 provides an overview of the relation between the dimensions of intermediate product transactions, and the production economies and exchange hazards associated with the make-or-buy decision.

The first three columns of Table 21.1 specify the dimensions of the intermediate product transactions using the categories identified by Williamson (1979). This is followed by two columns which characterize respectively: (1) the relative economies of scale from making the intermediate product internally, and (2) the contracting hazards that may be associated with buying. Some explanations, in terms of the dimensions of the transactions, are in order:

(1) *The investment characteristic.* This is defined as the degree to which transaction-specific investments in human or physical capital are required to realize production cost economies. The greater the need for special-purpose (as compared to general-purpose) plant and equipment, or labor with special skills, to produce the product which is the subject of the transaction, the more likely it is that economies of scale can be captured by making internally. At the same time, exchange hazards associated with buying increase because the difficulties of shifting special-purpose, transaction-specific assets to other uses can create opportunities for opportunistic behaviour. As can be seen from Table 21.1, the categories of product that are associated with the different levels of special-purpose, transaction-specific investment are referred to respectively as standardized, customized and idiosyncratic.

(2) *The extent (or frequency and volume) of buyer activity.* The greater the frequency and volume of the transaction involving the intermediate product, the greater is the likelihood that economies of scale can be captured by making internally, and the greater the possibility of being able to support a more elaborate organization structure and control system. When a transaction takes place only occasionally, it is not likely that economies of scale will accrue to manufacture within the firm. Even in those circumstances where occasional transactions require highly specific investments in human or physical capital, the occasional nature of the

Table 21.1 Dimensions of transactions and effects on production economies and transaction costs

| Investment characteristic | Dimensions of transactions | | Make | Buy Contracting hazards |
	Frequency and volume	Level of uncertainty/complexity	Relative economies of scale	(transaction costs assoc. with buying)
Non-specific (standardized product)	Occasional to recurring	Low to high	Strongly favour buying externally	Negligible
Semi-specific (customized product)	Occasional	Low to high	Strongly favour buying externally	Low to moderate
	Recurring	Low to intermediate	Moderately favour buying externally	Moderate to high
		High	Inherently difficult to organize. (Products either standardized and acquired in markets or made more idiosyncratic and made internally)	
Highly specific (idiosyncratic product)	Occasional	Low to high	Buying externally favoured	Moderate
	Recurring	Low to intermediate	Economies of scale may be captured by making	High
		High	High probability of capturing economies of scale by making	Extremely high

Source: Adapted from Williamson (1979) and Williamson & Ouchi (1980).

transaction generally will not support an elaborate governance structure. Means other than internalization of the transaction may be used to deal with the increased level of exchange hazard involved.

(3) *Uncertainty and complexity*. The effect of an increase in the uncertainty or complexity surrounding a transaction is to increase the probability that adaptions will be needed as the future is revealed. The result is that at low levels of uncertainty there are few contracting problems because contingent claims contracts are easy to write. As uncertainty increases (along with the degree of special-purpose, transaction-specific investment and the extent of buyer activity), the cost of writing contingent claim contract rises and rapidly becomes infeasible. For this reason, other (non-market) forms of organizing that allow the transaction to be readily adapted to changing circumstances by sequential decisions making will be favoured.

Table 21.2 can be viewed as an extension of Table 21.1 and assumes that the intermediate product is made within the firm and transferred between profit centers with separate profit streams. Its purpose is to provide an overview of the relationships among: (1) the dimensions of intra-firm transactions, (2) the extent to which internal contracting hazards can arise (and the resulting need for arbitration of disputes), and (3) the need for adaptation and cooperation between profit centers if overall firm interests in corporate profits are to be protected.

The following discussion provides a detailed look at the relationships (and their implications) in Table 21.1 and, in particular, Table 21.2. From this discussion nine propositions (hypotheses) are developed and then summarized in the final section of the paper: The first hypothesis deals with the relationship between diversification strategy, organization design and the dimensions of intra-firm transfers. Three hypotheses deal with the relationship between dimensions of intra-firm transfers and respectively: (1) the centralization of control over the make-or-buy decision, (2) the existence of well specified arbitration procedures, and (3) the choice of performance measures and incentives. Two further hypotheses deal with conditions for conflict over internal transfers and the areas of conflict between divisional managers. And finally, three hypotheses deal with the relationship between the dimensions of intra-firm transfers and the setting of transfer prices.

Transactions involving standardized components

The make-or-buy decision with standardized components (Table 21.1). Buyers and sellers face few contracting hazards in markets where standardized intermediate products are exchanged. The buyer is protected against possible opportunistic behaviour of the supplier by the ease of turning to alternative sources of supply. The seller is similarly protected against possible opportunistic behaviour of the buyer by the ease of selling to other buyers. Because hazards associated with buying a standardized component are minimal, there will be normally be few, if any, transaction cost economies associated with making the component. Economies of

Table 21.2 Dimensions of intra-firm transactions, internal contracting hazards and the need for cooperation and adaption

Investment characteristic	Dimensions of intra-firm transactions		Need for adaptability and cooperation between profit centers	Internal contracting hazards and need for arbitration of disputes
	Frequency and volume	Level of uncertainty/complexity		
Non-specific (standardized product)	Occasional to recurring	Low to high	Low	Negligible
Semi-specific (customized product)	Occasional	Low to high	Low to moderate	Low to moderate
	Recurring	Low to intermediate High	Moderate to high Moderate to very high	Moderate to high Moderate to very high
Highly specific (idiosyncratic product)	Occasional	Low to high	Moderate to high	Moderate
	Recurring	Low to intermediate High	High High to very high	High High to very high

scale in production will accrue to those suppliers who aggregate buyer's demands to reach optimal capacity. Under these conditions, buying the component externally will usually be favoured and there will typically be no economic incentive for the firm to make the component.[11]

Internal transfers of standardized components (Table 21.2). A firm that supplies a standardized intermediate product may also make internal transfers of components between subunits. If no transaction-specific investments in human or physical capital are associated with the internal transfer, then the need for adaptation and cooperation between the buying and selling units will be low. Internal transfers will be controlled by external market forces and will take place at market prices. The internal supplier is protected against the opportunistic behaviour of the internal buyer by being able to sell externally; and the internal buyer is similarly protected by being able to turn to other sources of supply with relative ease. Top managers will not need to constrain the buy and sell decisions of subunit managers to protect the firm's overall economic interests.

An exception occurs when the economies of scale of the supplying division are critically dependent upon the volume of internal demand and there is uncertainty about the capacity of the external market to absorb the expected volume of internal transfers. In this case, the supplying division and the firm as a whole have a strong interest in continuing internal transfers of the standardized component.[12] The supplying division will seek a long-term internal contract to protect itself against potential opportunistic switching by the buying division, and the firm will have an incentive to ensure that the firm's overall economic interests in the continuing make-or-buy decision are considered. The use of arbitration mechanisms for resolving internal contractural disputes are discussed in the following subsection.

Transactions involving components with specialized design or performance specifications

The make-or-buy decision for specially designed components (Table 21.1). The firm has incentives to make rather than buy intermediate products which require substantial transaction-specific investment in specialized productive assets. Because of this needed investment there may be few production economies available to external producers that are not also available to the firm through internal manufacture. And the greater the frequency and

---

[11] The exception is where the volume of the firm's internal demand is sufficiently high for the firm itself to capture economies of scale, or by aggregating internal and external demands. The decision is one that is based solely on economies of scale in production and does not involve transaction costs associated with exchange hazards.

[12] What needs emphasis here is that this assumes that the investment involved is specialized to the production of the standardized components in question and cannot be easily shifted to the production of other products. This is in contrast to general-purpose productive assets which can be readily shifted to other uses.

volume of the internal demand for these components, the more likely it is that making will be preferred to buying. However, where the intermediate product is merely customized, and the needed transaction-specific investment in specialized assets is less, buying may still be favoured on production cost grounds.

Investment by one of the firm's divisions in transaction-specific specialized assets also provides a transactional incentive for the firm to make (or continue to make) an idiosyncratic intermediate product. This is best seen by considering the situation where a firm enters into an arrangement with an external supplier for the regular supply of a component with unique specifications, the production of which requires investment by the supplier in assets specialized to its production. Under these conditions, the buyer and seller will typically negotiate a long-term contract. The seller, with few if any alternative uses for the transaction-specific, specialized assets, will seek to recover his investment plus some return; the buyer will want to be assured of a regular supply of components. In this setting, the contracting problem is how to adapt the relationship over time as future contingencies are revealed.

This is a problem that becomes more acute the greater the degree of uncertainty associated with the ongoing exchange. Where future uncertainties can be foreseen they can be negotiated into the contract. Generally, however, there will be a need for future adaptations of the original agreement to deal with unforeseen contingencies. And, because each party to the agreement appropriates a separate profit stream, there is always the possibility that *ex-post* adaptations proposed by one of the contracting parties may be at the expense of the other's profits. Therefore, when there is considerable uncertainty about future technologies and market conditions, and speedy and efficient adaptations to future contingencies are critical, making may be preferred to buying on transactional grounds. However, even when a decision is made to continue to buy the intermediate components because the level of uncertainty is less, the contracting parties will still seek means to make changes to the agreement over time in ways that do not disrupt the long-term relationship. On this Williamson (1979, p. 251) writes:

What is needed . . . is some way for declaring admissible dimensions for adjustment, such that flexibility is provided under terms in which both parties have confidence. This can be accomplished partly by (1) recognizing that the hazards of opportunism vary with the type of adaptations proposed and (2) restricting adjustments to those where hazards are least. But the spirit within which adaptations are affected is equally important.

In markets, *ex-post* adaptations to contracts can only be made by mutual agreement of the parties to the contract. Proposed adaptations can be of two types: (1) quantity adjustments which involve proposals to adjust quantities or delivery times; and (2) price adjustments. Of the two types, proposed quantity adjustments are the least likely to involve opportunistic behaviour because in these cases there is generally '. . . a presumption that the exogenous events, rather than strategic purposes, are responsible for quantity adjustments' Williamson (p. 251). The buyer is protected from the seller withholding supply and pursuing other opportunities because of the specialized investment that the seller has devoted to the recurring transaction. The seller is also protected to some extent against the buyer by the cost to the buyer of negotiating a new contract with another supplier.

Proposed price adjustments will not be as routinely accepted as quantity adjustments because, in Williamson's words, they can '...involve the risk that one's opposite is contriving to alter the terms of the bilateral trading gap to his advantage.' However, different types of price adjustments vary in their degree of hazard and may still be agreed to by the parties. Generally speaking, only proposed adjustments that can be closely tied to exogeneous, germane and easily verified events, involving quantifiable cost consequences, are likely to have a chance of mutual acceptance. For example, verifiable increases in direct material prices due to exogeneous events may be readily agreed to or passed through according to some formula. Similarly, those involving the operation of crude escalator clauses tied to general economic conditions and negotiated as part of the initial contract may be permitted; crises which jeopardize the continuing relationship also may result in *ad hoc* price relief. On the other hand, price adjustments which involve adjustments to changes in local conditions are likely to involve contracting hazards and are, therefore, likely to be rejected. Similarly, changes in overhead or other expenses that do not relate to readily verifiable events, or have clear-cut cost consequences, will not be passed through as readily because they involve the risk that one's trading partner is behaving in an opportunistic manner.

Internal transfers of components with specialized designs (Table 21.2). Where a firm is so organized that divisions can, or do, engage in internal transfers of customized or unique (idiosyncratic) components, the firm has a clear economic interest in subunit decisions to make-or-buy. The control question is: how to structure the relationship between self-interested (opportunistic), profit-seeking divisional managers in a way that protects the firm's economic interests? Treated as a contracting problem there are three main possibilities:

(1) Allow divisional managers full autonomy to negotiate their own arrangements to buy inside or outside the firm.

(2) Allow divisional managers to negotiate their own arrangements; but provide for intervention, as needed, by corporate managers to protect the firm's economic interests in the overall make-or-buy decision.

(3) Reorganize the firm in such a way that control over independent activities are placed, to the greatest possible extent, within the boundaries of a single division, under the control of a single manager.

Each of these possibilities is discussed in turn below and related to the dimensions of intra-firm transactions (i.e. degree of transaction-specific investment, frequency and volume, and uncertainty and/or complexity associated with the transaction).

Allow full divisional autonomy

To the extent that the measure of a divisional manager's performance is closely tied to divisional profits; and managers have differential access to local information about production technologies, manufacturing costs, or outside market conditions which are not fully shared between them, then the same contracting hazards that arise in markets will arise with respect to internal transfers of components. As is the case in markets, after the initial agreement is reached, proposed quantity adjustments are not likely to lead to serious conflicts provided these adjustments do not seriously disrupt production schedules. (This possibility becomes more likely if the firm adopts 'just-in-time' inventory systems.) Similarly, proposals for price adjustments resulting from external, verifiable events are not likely to cause major conflicts because there is a high probability that the external supply prices will also be affected. Other proposed price adjustments will not be so readily accepted and conflict is likely. Where these conflicts threaten the overall economic interests of the firm, it is unlikely that divisional managers will be totally free to buy or sell inside or outside the firm.

Constrain divisional autonomy

One way to protect the overall economic interests of the firm, yet retain a profit center structure and a measure of divisional autonomy, is through the introduction of a provision for arbitration into the negotiating process. Such a provision has a number of functions:

(1) *It provides an economical way to deal with the bounded rationality of corporate managers and for safeguarding internal transfers from opportunism.* Because corporate managers are boundly rational, they have limited ability to become involved in the operating decisions of the divisions. However, where functional interdependence exists between profit centers (as will be the case when there are recurring transfers of intermediate products) corporate managers must guard against opportunistic behaviour on the part of the division managers which is inimical to joint profits and, hence, the firm's interests. Provision for the arbitration of conflict between division managers, who are otherwise free to negotiate with each other, provides a means of freeing corporate managers from over-involvement in day to day operations, yet provides for their involvement at critical times when the firm's economic interests are at stake.

(2) *It provides an economical way of overcoming information asymmetries in a firm decentralized into profit centers.* Contrary to the impression given in much of the literature on transfer pricing, conflicts over internal transfers or transfer prices can have a control purpose and are not necessarily dysfunctional. If properly managed, disputes can provide a means whereby corporate managers acquire critical, local information about internal transfers and their alternatives. Where arbitration of a dispute takes place, the arbitrator will receive information and analyses from both division managers in support of their positions. Eccles (1983, p. 158),

for example, in his study of the transfer pricing process concludes that when conflict occurs:

... unit managers are likely to present information on roughly comparable external transactions or bids, differences in the cost of products sold externally, lack of cooperation in the relationship (poor R & D and service support or short lead times and canceled orders) inadequate and inflated gross margins and so forth.

In short, extensive local information will be presented to the arbitrator who, presumably, will have incentives to adjudicate the dispute with the overall interests of the firm in mind. The transfer pricing and arbitration process then are means of generating information necessary for the control of interdependent activities in a way that can achieve corporate objectives. The arbitration process itself, however, is subject to hazard as divisional managers have an incentive to systematically bias information presented to arbitration in their own self interests. However, relative to external arbitrators who may be called upon to arbitrate external contractual disputes, internal arbitrators will typically have a good working knowledge of internal operations, the performance histories of operating managers and, perhaps most important, strong powers of internal audit. Combined with a corporate manager's powers to terminate or revise contracts and adjust rewards, these powers will, in most cases, be sufficient to detect and control the biased reporting of information. In addition, each division manager in presenting his case to the arbitrator, will have incentives to reveal biased representations of other divisional managers in the arbitration process.

(3) *It ensures that the firm's overall economic interests in the make-or-buy decision are taken into account.* When internal transfers of intermediate products involve investments by the supplying division in transaction-specific assets, conflicts are most likely to arise when: (a) the buying division wishes to switch to an external source of supply, or (b) changes in transfer prices are proposed which cannot be directly tied to exogenous, germane and easily verified events with quantifiable cost consequences. In both cases, the proposed change can affect the profitability and self-interest of one of the divisions. Arbitration of the conflict can be used to protect the firm's interest in the outcome. Consider a dispute involving a buying division wishing to switch from internal to external purchase of a frequently used component because of a proposed change in a transfer price that is not tied directly to an exogenous event. One obvious alternative is for the internal arbitrator to require that the buying division continue to purchase inside, but at outside market prices. While this solution is only really feasible where the intermediate component is not so unique that it is impossible to obtain a realistic market price or outside bid, it does have the following advantages: (a) the outside price protects the buying division from the opportunistic behaviour of an inside supplier with a captive buyer: (b) the requirement on the buying division to buy internally allows the supplying division (and hence the firm) to recover its

investment in specialized productive assets which have few, if any, other uses; and (c) the outside price forces the supplying division to operate efficiently because it is subjected to the outside pressure of the market place transmitted through a market-based transfer price. The other option is for the arbitrator to allow the buying division to purchase the component externally. As this will involve the supplying division (and the firm) in opportunity losses associated with shifting specialized investments to purposes other than those for which they were originally intended, it is important that the economics of the decision be monitored from the firm's perspective.[13]

Reorganize the firm

Conflict and disputes over internal transfers and transfer prices can also be a signal that the present organization structure is not conducive to organizational efficiency. Consider the situation where frequently recurring, inter-divisional transfers involve significant transaction-specific investment in human or physical capital and involve a high degree of uncertainty and/or complexity. Under these conditions, the need for co-operation and adaptation between division managers with respect to these internal transactions is critical. Egregious conflicts arising from the process of internal transfers may be a strong indication that the decentralization of interdependent activities within profit centers should be reexamined. The choices open are either to realign the organization structure in a way that eliminates, or at least reduces, the volume of these types of transfers between divisions (for example, by placing the control of the interdependent activity under the control of a single division), or to treat the supplying division as a cost center subject to strong centralized control through budgets.

HYPOTHESES ABOUT INTRA-FIRM TRANSFERS, CONFLICT RESOLUTION AND THE TRANSFER PRICING PROCESS

This third section of the paper pulls together the prior theoretical discussion by presenting nine interrelated propositions (hypotheses) together with a brief review of the reasoning supporting each hypothesis. Hypothesis 1 is a general hypothesis relating to the relationship between diversification strategy, organization design and the dimensions of intra-firm transfers. Hypotheses 2, 3 and 4 relate to various aspects of the process of control of intra-firm transfers; Hypotheses 5a and 5b deal with conflict over internal transfers; and Hypotheses 6a, 6b and 6c deal with the setting of transfer prices.

The dimensions of transactions referred to in the following hypotheses can be seen in Table 21.2 they are: the degree of transaction-specific

---

[13] Important elements of a firm's vertical integration strategy can be involved in this decision. For an excellent strategic analysis of vertical integration see Porter (1980).

investment, the frequency and volume with which the transaction (transfer) takes place, and the uncertainty and/or complexity which surrounds the transaction.

Hypothesis 1. Strategy, structure and the dimensions of intra-firm transfers

The dimensions of intra-firm transfers of intermediate product are jointly related to a firm's diversification strategy, its product design and its organization structure.

Diversification strategy and product design determine the types of transactions entered into by firms. Organization structure determines how the firm will divide these transactions or activities among operating subunits. Holding other things constant, firms with higher levels of diversification are likely to have lower volumes of intra-firm transfers than are firms with lower levels of diversification. Similarly, how a firm arranges its organization structure to decentralize its activities will affect the dimensions of transactions taking place across subunit boundaries.

Hypothesis 2. Centralized control of the make-or-buy decision

The greater: (1) the degree of transaction-specific investment, (2) the frequency and volume, and (3) the degree of uncertainty and/or complexity associated with intra-firm transactions, the stronger will be the firm's interests in centrally controlling the make-or-buy decision.

Where close coordination and rapid adaptation of intermediate product transactions are critical to overall firm profitability, corporate managers will centralize the decision to buy or sell inside or outside the firm either: (1) by making the decision themselves, or (2) by placing intermediate product transaction completely within the boundaries of one division. Where the frequency and volume, degree of transaction-specific investment, and uncertainty and/or complexity are less extreme, other options are possible.

Hypothesis 3. Existence of arbitration procedures

The greater: (1) the degree of transaction-specific investment, (2) the frequency and volume, and (3) the degree of uncertainty and/or complexity associated with intra-firm transactions, the more likely it is that the firm will have well specified arbitration procedures to safeguard the firm's interest in the make-or-buy decision.

When an intra-firm transfer takes place only occasionally, it is unlikely that the firm will have well developed arbitration procedures. Disputes between divisional managers which cannot be settled by managers themselves will be dealt with on an *ad hoc* basis by more senior corporate managers. However, when intra-firm transfers are recurrent and material in volume, the need for divisions to work things out in a way that is not inimical to the firm's economic interests becomes important. As the degree of transaction-specific investment and uncertainty also increases, there will be increasing pressure for a well specified arbitration procedure to overcome information asymmetries and to promote coordination and adaptation between divisions in a way that does not damage the economic interests of the firm.

Hypothesis 4. Performance measurement and incentives

The greater: (1) the degree of transaction-specific investment, (2) the frequency and volume, and (3) the degree of uncertainty and/or complexity associated with intra-firm transactions, the more likely it is that the firm will deemphasize performance measurement and incentive mechanisms that focus entirely on divisional profitability, in favour of broader measures and incentives that recognize the need for cooperation and adaptation.

When intra-firm transfers of intermediate product do not require transaction-specific investment in productive assets, when they are infrequent and do not involve a high level of uncertainty and/or complexity, then performance measurement based on divisional profitability will be emphasized. In these cases, there is little need for close coordination or rapid adaptation to changing circumstances so divisional managers can be evaluated and rewarded as if their divisions are independent entities. On the other hand, when divisions are highly interdependent due to frequent transfers of intermediate products, extensive transaction-specific investment, and/or a high degree of uncertainty and/or complexity, performance evaluations will tend to deemphasize measurements that focus entirely on divisional profitability, in favour of broader measures that recognize the need for broad-scale cooperation and adaptation between divisions.

To the extent that rewards of divisional managers are tied to joint (firm) profits, the greater will be the incentive for division managers to cooperate and adapt their separate operations to changing market conditions, and technologies. Also, to the extent that performance measurement, evaluation and incentive mechanisms can be used to motivate cooperative, adaptive behaviour on the part of divisional managers, the pressure on centralized control mechanisms (such as arbitration procedures) will be reduced.

Hypothesis 5. Conflict

There are two hypotheses regarding conflict: the first specifies the general conditions under which conflict is most likely to occur; the second specifies which proposed adaptations are likely to cause the greatest conflict.

Hypothesis 5a. The greater: (1) the degree of transaction-specific investment, (2) the frequency and volume, and (3) the degree of uncertainty and/or complexity associated with intra-firm transactions, the more likely is conflict between divisional managers involved in internal transfers of intermediate products.

This hypothesis is a collorary of Hypothesis 4 on performance measures and incentives. If performance measures and incentive mechanisms focus entirely on divisional profitability, then conflict is most likely under the conditions specified in Hypothesis 5a. To the extent that this likelihood for conflict is recognized and divisional manager's rewards are tied to performance measures that promote cooperation and adaptation (for example, measures of corporate profits), conflict will be mitigated.

Hypothesis 5b. Conflict between divisions involved in intra-firm transfers of intermediate product is more likely for *ex-post* proposals for transfer price adjustments than it is for *ex-post* proposals for quantity adjustments.

These two types of proposed adaptations pose different degrees of hazards of opportunistic behaviour: *ex-post* proposals for transfer price adjustments, because of their zero-sum quality will not be as readily accepted as *ex-post* proposals for quantity adjustments. However, not all ex-post proposals for transfer price adjustments will necessarily result in conflict. Where proposed transfer price adjustments involve quantifiable cost consequences which are closely tied to exogenous, relevant and easily verifiable events, they may be accepted without conflict. On the other hand, if the proposed price adjustments cannot be directly attributed to exogeneous events, or these events do not have readily quantifiable and verifiable cost consequences, they will not be as readily accepted and conflict over the adjustment is a likely outcome.

Hypothesis 6. Transfer pricing policies

Transfers pricing policies may vary throughout the firm because they are related to the dimensions of intra-firm transactions between specific subunits.

From the limited number of empirical studies that have been made of actual transfer pricing policies, it is known that a range of transfer pricing rules are used by firms; but explanations of why variations exist have been lacking.[14] The general hypothesis given above can be broken down into three, more detailed, subsidiary hypotheses.

[14] Commenting on the results of his extensive study of the management processes of 296 decentralized companies, Vancil (1979, p. 142) notes that he was disappointed when he was unable to arrive at any definitive conclusions on transfer pricing. He writes: 'To my knowledge, our data are the only empirical data ever gathered on the topic, and we had plenty of other data to help explain the variations in practice that we found. But no pay dirt, only a dry hole. The issue remains as a perennial puzzle to academicians, while practitioners continue to cope. I wish the best of good fortune to the next researcher to tackle the problem.'

Hypothesis 6a. Where standardized intermediate products are the subject of the transfer, or the transfer involves products for which the degree of customization is minor, market prices will be the primary basis for setting internal transfer prices and for profit center managers choosing between internal and external suppliers and customers.

From a contracting perspective, there is no transfer pricing problem associated with intra-firm transfers of a standardized intermediate product. Transfers will usually be negotiated by profit center managers at market prices, with adjustments confined to such things as volume discounts and differences in terms of sale and delivery. The decision to buy or sell components inside or outside the firm will be left to the subunit managers allowing the firm's interests to be safeguarded by market forces.

Where the degree of customization of the intermediate product is minor, and the extent of transaction-specific investment in human or physical capital is small, market prices of similar products will still act as an initial basis for establishing a transfer price. It is expected that adjustments to market prices for the costs of customization will typically be negotiated by divisional managers. While there is some potential for haggling, firm interests are still well protected by market forces, so that any intervention by corporate managers will be minor; perhaps taking the form of a simple policy requiring that internal suppliers be given the opportunity to meet external bids.[15]

Hypothesis 6b. Where the internally transferred intermediate product involves a moderate degree of customization and a material transaction-specific investment, internal manufacturing costs will play a greater role in the initial negotiations to set transfer prices and in *ex-post* proposals to adjust them.

Where a more extensive investment in transaction-specific assets is involved, the firm has a greater need to protect its economic interests in the decision making process and to ensure that adaptations to uncertain market and technological opportunities and constraints are made as efficiently as possible.[16] With profit center managers having differential access to local information about manufacturing costs and markets, a bargaining process that makes use of cost-plus pricing and competitive bids or other market information to bound transfer prices can be expected. Because of the firm's heightened economic interests in the outcome of the make-or-buy decision, an arbitration mechanism is likely to be introduced into the

---

[15] An exception can arise when the economies of scale of the supplying division are critically dependent on the frequency and volume of internal demand, and there is uncertainty about whether the external market is sufficiently large to absorb the current volume of transfers between profit center at the prevailing market price.

[16] If proprietary processes, technology or other trade secrets are involved in the manufacture of a component, and these must be shared with the supplier, the hazards of outside purchase are clearly increased.

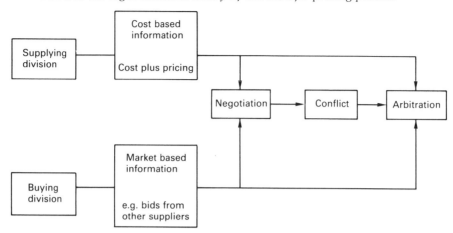

Fig. 21.2 Process of negotiation, conflict and arbitration.

process. An important function of such an arbitration mechanism is to overcome information asymmetries between profit centers. Negotiations, conflict and arbitration, therefore, provide, within limits, a cost-effective way of dealing with information impacted-ness within the firm.[17] The process is diagrammed in Fig. 21.2.

Hypothesis 6c. Where the internally transferred intermediate product is idiosyncratic, and involves a large investment in transaction-specific human and/or physical capital, internal manufacturing costs will be the primary basis for setting transfer prices; and there will be strong central control over the make-or-buy decision. Whether internal transfers are made at simulated market prices (cost-plus), or simply at some measure of cost, is a function of the degree of uncertainty associated with the intermediate product and the control strategy adopted by the firm.

Because of the specialized nature of production process, it is unlikely that idiosyncratic intermediate products made internally will have external market prices. Where uncertainty and/or complexity is not great, and the need for adaptations over time only moderate, the firm may continue to use a decentralized, profit center structure, combined with a negotiation-arbitration process, to set cost-plus transfer prices and control the flow of intermediate product between profit centers.

Where uncertainty is greater and the need for rapid adaptation to uncertainty more critical, conflicts between profit center managers are more likely. In these circumstances, corporate managers can be expected to

---

[17] There are a number of possible outcomes of arbitration under these conditions. One is to require internal purchase of the needed component but allow the buying division to buy at cost, yet credit the selling division at market price (either simulated as a cost-plus price or on the basis of actual bids received).

decentralize the decision making process in two ways: (1) by placing the control of the interdependent activity under the control of a single division, or (2) by simply designating the supplying division as a cost center and mandating internal transfers of the intermediate product.[18]

SUMMARY, CONCLUSIONS AND SUGGESTIONS FOR FUTURE RESEARCH

While the literature on transfer pricing is replete with economic and mathematical programming models for setting transfer prices to meet some objective of the model, there have been few attempts, apart from Watson & Baumler (1975), to develop a theory of the transfer pricing process which could be used to help explain observed transfer pricing policies and practices. Drawing on the growing literature on the economics of internal organization, this paper develops a theory of the transfer pricing process and presents a number of hypotheses based on the theory relating to internal transfers of intermediate products. The basic premise of this theory is that it is variations in a firm's strategic, organizational and transactional circumstances that explain a firm's choices of transfer pricing mechanisms and policies.

Some evidence bearing in the hypotheses presented above has been recently provided by Eccles (1985) based on extensive interviews with managers involved in transfer pricing in thirteen firms in three industries: chemicals, electronics and heavy machinery. Based on inductive reasoning from his observations, Eccles develops a series of conclusions and inferences that he refers to as a theory for practice. These conclusions and inferences can reasonably be viewed as a source of potential support for, or contradiction of, the propositions presented above. For the most part, Eccles' observations and the conclusions he draws from them, support the hypotheses developed here from theory.

What must be done now is to empirically investigate the setting of transfer pricing policies in practice in a way that allows for the testing of hypotheses developed in this paper. This empirical work should include: (1) an investigation of the link between diversification strategy, organizational design and the dimensions of intra-firm transactions; and (2) an investigation into the relations between the dimensions of transfers between specific selling and buying centers within a firm, and observed transfer pricing processes and practices. That is, the investigation should start by looking at how the firm's various strategies affect the dimensions of transfers between specific buying and selling centers throughout the organization; and then, having done this, investigate how control problems and transfer prices differ among them. On *a priori* grounds it seems useful to distinguish between these two parts of the investigation because,

---

[18] In this case, variable cost may be used as the transfer price if production volume is determined by the subunit managers. Full cost might be used if the production volume is determined centrally. In the latter case, conflict is more likely if inefficiencies can be passed along in the cost price.

in large companies, different strategies may apply to different parts of the firm. For example, a firm may be vertically integrated within divisional groupings but diversified between groups. Focusing on the dimensions of transactions between specific buying and selling units (whether these units are at, or below the group level) allows the investigation to focus on different control issues in different parts of the firm.

The objective of this empirical work in the field should be to determine if practice is consistent with the hypotheses advanced in this paper and to lead, eventually, with additional theoretical work, to a genuine organizational theory of transfer pricing.

ACKNOWLEDGEMENTS

The author wishes to thank Frank Selto, Gary Sundem, Rudolph Schattke, Gwen Totterdale, David Watson and an anonymous reviewer for their helpful comments on this paper. The research was supported by the Accounting Fund of the University of Oregon. The paper was revised while the author was a Visiting Fellow at the University of Manchester in 1987.

BIBLIOGRAPHY

Abdel-khalik, A. & Lusk, E., Transfer Pricing – A Synthesis, *Accounting Review* (January 1987) pp. 8–23.

Alchian, A.A. & Demsetz, H., Production, Information Costs, and Economic Information, *American Economic Review* (December 1972) pp. 777–795.

Caves, R.E., Industrial Organization, Corporate Strategy and Structure, *Journal of Economic Literature* (March 1980) pp. 64–92.

Coase, R.H., The Nature of the Firm, *Economica* (November 1937) pp. 386–405.

Cohen, M.D. & March J.G., *Leadership and Ambiguity: The American College President* (New York: McGraw-Hill, 1974).

Cohen, M.D., March, J.G. & Olsen, J.P., A Garbage Can Model of Organization Choice, *Administrative Science Quarterly* (March 1972) pp. 1–25.

Covalski, M. & Aiken, M., Accounting and Theories of Organizations: Some Preliminary Considerations, *Accounting, Organizations and Society* (1986) pp. 297–319.

Cyert, R.M. & March, J.G., *A Behavioral Theory of the Firm* (Englewood Cliffs, NJ: Prentice–Hall, 1963).

Eccles, R.G., Control with Fairness in Transfer Pricing, *Harvard Business Review* (November–December 1983) pp. 149–161.

Eccles, R.G., *The Transfer Pricing Problem* (Lexington: Lexington Books, 1985).

Grabski, S.V., Transfer Pricing in Complex Organizations: A Review and Integration of Recent Empirical and Analytical Research, *Journal of Accounting Literature* (1985) pp. 31–33.

Hopwood, A.G., On Trying to Study Accounting in the Contexts in Which it Operates, *Accounting, Organizations and Society* (1983) pp. 287–305.

Jensen, M.C., Organization Theory and Methodology, *Accounting Review* (April 1983) pp. 319–339.

Jensen, M.C. & Meckling, W.H., Theory of the Firm: Managerial Behavior, Agency Costs and Ownership Structure, *Journal of Financial Economics* (October 1976) pp. 306–360.

Johnson, H.T., Markets, Hierarchies and the History of Management Accounting, Paper prepared for the Third International Congress of Accounting Historians, London Business School, London (16–18 August, 1980).

Johnson, H.T. & Kaplan, R.S., The Rise and Fall of Management Accounting, *Management Accounting* (January 1987) pp. 22–30.

Kaplan, R.S., Measuring Manufacturing Performance: A New Challenge for Managerial Accounting Research, *Accounting Review* (October 1983) pp. 686–705.

Kaplan, R.S., The Evolution of Management Accounting, *Accounting Review* (July 1984) pp. 390–418.

Kaplan, R.S., Accounting Lag: The Obsolesence of Cost Accounting Systems, *California Management Review* (Winter 1986a) pp. 174–199.

Kaplan, R.S., The Role for Empirical Research in Management Accounting Research, *Accounting, Organizations and Society* (1986b) pp. 429–452.

Lawrence, P.R. & Lorsch, J.W., *Organization and Environment* (Homewood, IL: Irwin, 1967).

Maher, M.W., Management Accounting Literature: Past, Present and Future, Paper presented at the American Accounting Association Meeting, San Diego, CA, 1982.

Porter, M.E., *Competitive Strategy: Techniques for Analyzing Industries and Competitors* (New York: Free Press, 1980).

Rumelt, R.P., Strategy, Structure and Economic Performance (Boston: Division of Research, Graduate School of Business Administration, Harvard University, 1974).

Spicer, B.H. & Ballew, V., Management Accounting Systems and the Economics of Internal Organization, *Accounting Organizations and Society* (1983) pp. 73–96.

Swieringa, R.J. & Waterhouse, J.H., Organizational Views of Transfer Pricing, *Accounting, Organizations and Society* (1982), pp. 149–165.

Umapathy, S., Transfers Between Profit Centers, in Vancil R.F. *Decentralization: Managerial Ambiguity by Design*, (Homewood, IL: Dow Jones-Irwin, 1979) pp. 167–193.

Vancil, R.F., *Decentralization: Managerial Ambiguity by Design* (Homewood, IL: Dow Jones-Irwin, 1979) pp. 167–193.

Waterhouse, J.H. & Tiessen, P., Towards a Descriptive Theory of Management Accounting, *Accounting, Organizations and Society* (1983) pp. 251–267.

Watson, D.J.H. & Baumler, J.V., Transfer Pricing: A Behavioral Context *Accounting Review* (July 1975) pp. 466–474.

Weick, K.E., *The Social Psychology of Organizing* (Reading, MA: Addison-Wesley, 1969).

Weick, K.E., *The Social Psychology of Organizing*, 2nd ed. (Reading MA: Addison-Wesley, 1979).

Williamson, O.E., *Corporate Control and Business Behavior* (Englewood Cliffs, NJ: Prentice-Hall, 1970).

Williamson, O.E., *Markets and Hierarchies: Analysis and Antitrust Implications* (New York: Free Press, 1975).

Williamson, O.E., Transaction-Cost Economics: The Governance of contractural Relations, *The Journal of Law and Economics* (October 1979) pp. 233–261.

Williamson, O.E., *The Economic Institutions of Capitalism* (New York: Free Press, 1985).

Williamson, O.E. & Ouchi, W.G., The Markets and Hierarchies Program of Research: Origins, Implications Prospects. Discussion Paper No. 64, Center for the Study of Organizational Innovation, University of Pennsylvania, January 1980.

22

Transfer pricing in complex organizations: a review and integration of recent empirical and analytical research

Severin V. Grabski
Assistant Professor of Accounting
Michigan State University

INTRODUCTION

Transfer pricing literature can be categorized according to the type of model employed and whether it is analytical or empirical. The major models are economic [based on Hirshleifer, 1956]; mathematical programming [Dopuch and Drake, 1964]; and behavioural [Watson and Baumler, 1975]. The objective of this paper is to review the recent literature (1974–1983) on transfer pricing and to try to discern future directions and possibilities for research. In particular, research relating to the major theoretical models (economic, mathematical programming, and behavioural) and other more *ad hoc* approaches is integrated with the empirical research on transfer pricing practices. In addition, the behavioural and organizational implications of transfer pricing are addressed with respect to the issues of organizational optimization, and integration and differentiation.

Prior to an examination of the various transfer pricing methods, the rationale of why transfer prices exist is briefly addressed along with the properties commonly associated with them. An understanding and appreciation of the underlying causes of transfer pricing is required before any discussion of the goals of the transfer pricing system can occur. Transfer prices arise in response to decentralization in which responsibility centers trade among themselves and an evaluation of the responsibility centers is desired at the level of 'profit.' Decentralization is at least a necessary condition for a transfer pricing system to develop. Consequently, a review of decentralization is warranted.

Decentralization is generally thought to provide several benefits [see Flavell, 1977; Thomas, 1980]. These include advantages related to the

Source: Grabski, S.V. (1985) *Journal of Accounting Literature*, **4**, pp. 33–75.
© 1985

managerial span of control, management development, and management motivation. Individuals have been shown to have limited information processing capabilities [see Miller, 1956; Simon, 1978]. This limited processing capability implies that there is a limit to the number of individuals that a given manager can effectively and efficiently supervise and to the number and types of problems that the manager can address. Consequently, there are benefits associated with limiting the span of control of any manager. One way that decentralized firms overcome the limited processing capabilities of individuals is to encourage certain decisions to be made on lower managerial levels in order to help economize on the transmission of information.

The second benefit that decentralization is thought to provide is management development. Managing a large division can be at least as complex as managing an independent company (as the divisional manager must not only control the subordinates but must also respond to the desires of central management and, possibly, the board of directors). The experience gained is perceived to be beneficial to the manager who desires to advance. Caution is advised in evaluating this benefit, as the advantages associated with the management development concept may not be generalized on a global basis. Differing national career patterns emerge and must be considered [see Granick, 1975, especially the French managerial career pattern].

A final advantage of decentralization is managerial motivation. Given the responsibility and authority (autonomy) to run a division as an entrepreneur, a manager should be motivated to perform in a more efficient, effective manner. Thomas [1980] provides an excellent review of the literature surrounding the psychological theories and empirical evidence as it relates to divisional autonomy and motivation. He concludes that although the literature seems to support the contention of the dysfunctional nature of a violation of divisional autonomy, it is not conclusive.

All of the transfer pricing literature implicitly assumes the existence of benefits that divisional autonomy and motivation are thought to provide.[1] However, this is where the basic conflict in decentralization arises. In decentralization, a lack of coordination between the divisions and central management may occur if the division managers are given full autonomy. Division managers might engage in actions that would benefit their divisions to the detriment of the entire firm. This behaviour is counter to central management's objective of maximizing the well-being of the entire firm (regardless of how it is measured), and they would want the decentralized divisions to behave as if the firm was centralized. As Thomas [1980] noted, central management would want 'to obtain the information economics and divisional elan of decentralization without sacrificing the coordination associated with centralization.'[2]

---

[1] This paper will examine the literature based on this assumption.
[2] Thomas, A.L. *A Behavioral Analysis of Joint Cost Allocation and Transfer Pricing.* Arthur Andersen & Co. Lecture Series 1977. Stipes Publishing Company, 1980, p. 125.

Central management desires a method of 'decentralized-centralization.' This is why transfer pricing is employed. Unfortunately, central management has, in general, tried to do too much with a one-dimensional tool. The transfer price is an excellent mechanism to use to coordinate the activities of autonomous divisions. It can also be used to achieve the goals of central management if the transfer price is imposed. Unfortunately, problems develop when central management uses imposed transfer prices in the evaluation of the 'autonomous' divisions. This violates one of the basic tenets of performance evaluation, the evaluation of individuals on items beyond their control.

Objectives of transfer pricing systems

Several authors have identified various objectives of transfer pricing systems [see Flavell, 1977; Thomas, 1980]. In general, three main objectives are noted: preserve or maintain divisional autonomy; encourage divisions to achieve central management optimal results; and allow or provide a measure of divisional (product) performance that would lead to long-run optimal decisions on the part of central management. These objectives, while desirable, do not seem to be internally consistent but rather contradictory. How could autonomy be maintained while ensuring (encouraging) optimal results for central management? How could one evaluate a division or product based on a price that ensures central management optimal results because the price was dictated by central management?

Two empirical studies highlight this dilemma. Tang [1980] asked respondents to name the dominant objective of their transfer pricing system. Almost half said it was performance evaluation, and a little over a third said it was profit maximization of the consolidated firm (i.e., achieving central management optimal results). Preservation of divisional autonomy was not mentioned. Wu and Sharp [1979] found that the major criteria for domestic transfers were firm profit maximization and divisional performance evaluation. Preservation of divisional autonomy was ranked less important than compliance with GAAP and tax regulations. It appears that divisional autonomy in fact is not important. Rather, it seems that autonomy in appearance is more important.

OVERVIEW OF CURRENT RESEARCH

In the following sections, the literature on transfer pricing is presented according to the type of model employed. A sizable portion of the work related to transfer pricing is based either on the economic model as postulated by Hirshleifer [1956], on the mathematical programming model, which was developed as a response to some of the limitations in the economic model, or the behavioural model, which addressed how individuals would react to various transfer pricing schemes. In addition, there have been attempts at integrating these alternative models. A large portion of the transfer pricing literature exists that cannot be directly classified in any of the above 'pure' catagories. Articles of this type are categorized in this work as '*ad hoc* approaches.' Transfer pricing articles dealing with tax aspects are ignored as they are an artifact (albeit an important one) caused by various taxing authorities attempting to obtain their share of the profits or value associated with the transferred goods. In addition, articles that address the impact of transfer prices on multinational enterprises are not considered because multinational transfer pricing stratagies are generally the result of both the regulations enforced by the various taxing authorities in the countries in which the multinational corporation produces goods and the foreign exchange rates. In summary, any article that does not focus on the issues of decentralization and organizational optimization is ignored. Table 22.1 provides a summary by year and major emphasis of the articles reviewed in this work. The Appendix provides a listing by year, author, and topical area.

Examination of Table 22.1 gives a clear picture of transfer pricing research. *Ad hoc* theory articles account for almost 60% of the current research (these are detailed in a later table), while only six integrative articles have been published. (The most recent state of the art research is by Thomas [1980] and is highly recommended.) A limited number of works has been published that is of an economic genre, and the interest in the mathematical programming approaches seems to have tapered off since the mid-1970s (the last five works have been published in *Management Science*, the *Journal of the Operational Research Society* and *Review of Business and Economic Research*). It is disappointing that only six articles have specifically dealt with the behavioural issues of transfer pricing. (This count excludes the integrative works that are concerned with and even deal heavily with the behavioural problems.) The first four behavioural works published addressed the impact of transfer prices on the individual, and the latter two examined the impact of transfer pricing schemes on the firm's organizational structure. It appears that the *ad hoc* theory articles have proliferated, while the integrative and behavioural issues have been neglected. The latter area appears especially fruitful for future research.

When the literature is examined on an analytical – versus – empirical basis, a surge of empirical articles is noticed in 1979. However, the real increase in knowledge of current methods was appreciably less than indicated. Two articles [Mednick, 1979; Schiff, 1979] only reviewed annual reports. While providing additional information, the value of this information must be questioned because of the lack of meaningful detail available in annual reports. Two relatively comprehensive articles, [Tang, 1979; Tang et al., 1979] were based on the same data. The work by Choudhury [1979] was based on 1971 data. Ackelsberg and Yukl [1979] reported on a lab experiment (not actual current transfer pricing methods). The data reported by Wu and Sharp [1979] were ordinal. Lambert [1979] presented a study of interdivisional conflict as perceived by chief financial officers. The most comprehensive study was reported by Vancil [1979], who provided a wealth of information relating to methods employed, firm demographics and extent of transfers between profit centers.

Table 22.1 Summary of recent transfer pricing literature by major topical intent and year[1]

	1974	1975	1976	1977	1978	1979	1980	1981	1982	1983	Total
Analytical	7	8	10	7	4	7	6	6	8	3	66
Empirical	1	1	0	0	1	9	2	0	0	1	15
	8	9	10	7	5	16	8	6	8	4	81
Economic	0	1	1	1	1	1	0	0	0	0	5
Mathematical Programming	4	3	2	1	0	1	2	0	2	0	15
Behavioural	0	2	0	0	0	2	0	0	1	1	6
Integrative	1	0	1	2	0	1	1	0	0	0	6
Ad hoc Approaches	3	3	6	3	4	11	5	6	5	3	49
	8	9	10	7	5	16	8	6	8	4	81

[1] The works are classified according to the major objective of the author(s). 'Comments' are not included, nor are textbooks.

Upon examination of the above research, it seems fair to assert that only two new, in-depth sets of data that report percentage usage of the various transfer pricing methods employed were published in 1979 [Tang and Vancil], and one in-depth study that reported ordinal data [Wu and Sharp.] Consequently, although a number of articles were published in 1979, the real gain in knowledge of current practice was not as large as the table indicates.

With the exception of 1979, there have been relatively few empirical works. The vast majority of works reported on here (over 80%) are analytical in nature. This does not mean that all knowledge of what methods are being used, why these methods are used, and what the objectives of transfer pricing are is known with certainty. More empirical research on these issues is needed to determine why some methods are used, while other, possibly more theoretically correct methods are ignored (or possibly point out flaws in the theory).

The remainder of this paper is presented in six sections. Three of these sections deal with the three major models of transfer pricing. The other three discuss the *ad hoc* approach, empirical research and conclusions and directions for future research.

Economic models

Most of the literature dealing with transfer pricing from an economic view-point is based on the analysis of Hirshleifer [1956]. The assumptions characterizing the structure of the economic modeling approach have been addressed in detail previously and will only be summarized here [see Abdel-khalik and Lusk, 1974; Enzer, 1975; Blois, 1978; Kanodia, 1979; Thomas, 1980]. The objective here is to assess advances and to help determine directions for future research.

The basic Hirshleifer model assumed a firm with two profit centers, a manufacturing division and a distribution division, a competitive external market for the final product, and no market for the intermediate product. The optimal solution for the firm was to equalize the quantity of output of both the manufacturing division and the distribution division. The quantity supplied was given when the combined marginal costs of the manufacturing division and the distribution division were equal to the external market price. This was accomplished by having the manufacturing division supply the distribution division with a schedule giving the quantity produced at any given transfer price. The schedule was the manufacturing division's marginal cost curve. The distribution division used this information to determine the optimum level of output, which occurred when the marginal distribution costs were equal to the difference between the market price and the price that the distribution division paid for the transferred goods. Relaxing the assumption of no external market for the intermediate product, and examining the intermediate product market in both perfect and imperfect competition (also when the manufacturing division acts as a discriminating monopolist), did not change the basic conclusion of pricing along the marginal cost curve of the distribution division. Other restrictions of the model included assuming temporal stability, independence of demand, and a linear production function with constant proportions.

Abdel-khalik and Lusk [1974] noted that dysfunctional division manager behaviour could be induced (e.g., misstatement of the marginal cost and revenue curves) and that inefficiencies could be passed along. The authors also noted that the necessary cost-benefit analysis of installing the system was missing and that only a limited, two-division model had been developed.

The Hirshleifer analysis was extended by Kanodia [1979] to incorporate uncertainty and to allow risk-sharing between divisional managers and central management. The model developed, while very elegant, still has all of the defects associated with the simple Hirshleifer model. The author stated that the 'paper characterizes and analyze several transfer price systems, in terms of such issues (uncertainty, risk-sharing and Pareto optimality), but does not formulate mechanisms for achieving them. The latter problems would require a solution to the unresolved issue of incentive compatibility in the presence of risk. In fact, one would expect that the transfer price systems characterized here are not incentive compatible.[3]

Hirshleifer's analysis was also expanded by Blois [1978] to account for the pricing of purchases by large customers. He showed that although the firms are independent, a large customer might be able to impose the transfer price rule of marginal cost upon its suppliers. The implication was that evaluations were still able to be made since this was a competitively determined price and not one administered by central management.

Enzer [1975] claimed that Hirshleifer's conclusion of setting the transfer price at the marginal cost of the producing division under static conditions and certainty was incorrect. Enzer argued that the transfer price was not independent of the amount acquired. Rather, the generally correct transfer price was shown to be a form of average cost. Hirshleifer's result (i.e., the setting of the transfer price at marginal cost) was obtained when the production function is homogeneous of degree one. Enzer's work is therefore an extension of Hirshleifer's and a relaxation of the constraint of a linear homogeneous production function (the assumption made in linear programming techniques). An important ramification of Enzer's research is the theoretical vindication of firms that set their transfer prices at some form of average cost. Enzer also examined the following cases with solutions: when market prices exist for the intermediate product (price at the market price); transfer pricing in the presence of constraints (price at average cost plus or minus the average opportunity profit); and transfer pricing when an alternative objective besides profit maximization exists (price at an adjusted average cost).

The model proposed by Enzer is not without faults. Jennergren [1977]

[3] Kanodia, C. 'Risk Sharing and Transfer Price Systems Under Uncertainty' *Journal of Accounting Research* Vol. 17 (Spring 1979), pp. 74–75.

pointed out that while Enzer's solution will end the exploitation of the production division by the selling division, the production division must now be totd at which production level to operate. This situation unfortunately eliminates the concept of a decentralized firm and centralizes decision making for the production division. The production division can no longer be considered a profit center. This result may really be the best alternative, since some authors [e.g., Thomas, 1980; Dearden, 1973; Henderson and Dearden, 1966] note that serious transfer pricing problems arise from or are symptoms of an illogical organization structure.

In general, the economic models are limited in scope, i.e., are able to deal with only the conceptually simple cases. In addition divisional autonomy is not preserved because divisions are required to price at marginal cost (average cost), which defines the level of production and consequently profits. Since profits are administered, it is impossible to evaluate division managers based on profits and it is impossible (in the long run) to use this to motivate managers to perform in order to attain optimum results for central management. The economic models also encourage dysfunctional effects as noted, such as gaming. However, they theoretically allow the maximization of central management's total profits.

Mathematical programming models

The mathematical programming literature is a response to the inability of the simpler demand-supply economic models to deal with the complexities of multiple products, divisions, and goals. In this literature, the transfer price is based on the opportunity cost of producing the product rather than its marginal cost (which equals the opportunity cost only at equilibrium). The mathematical programming methods explicitly consider externalities. They require the enumeration of the goals and/or objectives of central management (or divisions), and the enumeration of the constraints faced by the economic entities.

Baumol and Fabian [1964] introduced the application of the Linear Programming Decomposition Principle to a decentralized firm and Hass [1968] suggested the applicability of quadratic programming.

Abdel-khalik and Lusk [1974] summarized the mathematical programming literature. The majority of work since then has been to refine or expand the model into other areas.

The objective of most programming approaches is to determine a transfer price that optimizes central management's objective. The decomposition model was embraced since it enhanced computational efficiency and also reflected the decentralized operations of an enterprise. Two different decomposition algorithms have been developed. One, a price-driven model, allocates corporate resources on the basis of transfer prices. The other model employs a resource (quantity)-driven algorithm. Resources are allocated to each division and the divisions are evaluated on their measures of economic efficiency based on the allocations [Burton *et al.*, 1974]. Both algorithms are iterative in nature and require central management to specify its objective (e.g., profit maximization) or goals (in the goal programming situations). The divisions must also specify their own objectives or goals. They then solve their mathematical program based on inputs specified from central management (e.g., transfer prices or resource allocations) and other endogenous and exogenous variables. Results are communicated to central management to be used as input for its mathematical program. If the objectives (goals) are not maximized (or, in the case of resource-driven algorithms, satisficed), incentives (transfer price or resource allocation changes) are employed so that the divisions will develop a plan that is harmonious with maximizing (satisficing) the firm's resources.

The efficiency of the decomposition algorithm was found to be influenced by the *a priori* information used to initialize it in a simulation by Burton and Obel [1980]. The price-driven algorithm generally performed the best under the five *a priori* information modes considered: (i) no *a priori* information; (ii) high initial transfer price and equal resource sharing; (iii) market-based transfer price; (iv) equal resource sharing and production capacity constraints; and (v) historical prices and budgets. The mixed approach (which incorporated the logic of the price and resource approaches) generally performed next best, and the resource approach generally performed the worst.

In general, the simulation indicated that more *a priori* information led to better results. Historic information was found to be superior only to the no *a priori* information condition. One anomaly was reported: The mixed approach yielded an average performance of over 82% of optimality after only one iteration when the *a priori* information included market price, equal resource sharing, and capacity constraints. This result seems to indicate that firms that desire to employ mathematical programming approaches should use the price-driven algorithm if *a priori* information is poor or if they plan several iterations. Alternatively, if the information set is rich and only one iteration is desired (due to time, budget constraints, etc.), the mixed approach should be employed.

Advances and extensions of the basic formulation were reported primarily in non-accounting publications. Stochastic processes were introduced in a resource – directed algorithm by Hurwicz *et al.* [1975]. The approach employed a bidding procedure that continues until the divisions make central management acceptable bids. Kydland [1975] presented a decomposition model based on a hierarchical ordering and claimed that the divisions were given more autonomy in their decision-making. Kornbluth [1974] presented a goal-programming algorithm that was price-driven. The model, a 'multiple objective linear program,' did not require central management to weight or rank objectives nor did it require a specific central management utility function. However, optimal results for central management were not obtained on the basis of transfer prices along. Preemptive goals, central management preferences, etc., were required to be imposed on the divisions in order to obtain optimality. Hayhurst [1976] proposed a model in which central management would develop an optimized plan and supply the divisions with the appropriate directives (e.g., production and supply requirements, transfer prices). The division managers could opt to follow the directives or to negotiate with other divisions for a different transfer price. The imposed plan would be considered the norm, and the division managers would be evaluated against it. Harris *et al.* [1982] considered the problems of asymmetric information properties (the information available to the division manager is not available to central management) and the divergent interests of the managers from the firm (managers might overstate divisional resource requirements to the extent that resources could be converted into the reduction of managerial effort.) The problem was formulated on a cost minimization basis, which was considered necessary for profit maximization. In the scheme developed, central management would announce a schedule of transfer prices, and each division would choose the price it was willing to pay. Ismail [1982] expanded the model to recognize external demand uncertainty for the selling-division products, particularly the intermediate product. Linearity was assumed for all other parameters. A decision rule was developed that would be perceived to reduce the information flow between the divisions and central management rather than employing the decomposition principle. This rule was to maximize the product of the amount of goods transferred multiplied by the difference between the bid and asked transfer prices. The rule was formulated under the assumption that the price that the purchasing division is willing to pay is a decreasing function of the quantity demanded and that the price that the selling division is willing to accept is an increasing function of the quantity demanded.

Baily and Boe [1976] attempted to give a behavioural orientation to the mathematical programming literature. A satisficing, decomposed, goal-programming model was presented. The algorithm is elegant and applicable to an n-level organization. In this approach, the division managers have more autonomy than in other programming approaches. However, it also has serious shortcomings. Gaming could occur and is a critical issue. But more destructive is the possibility that central management may have to specify the transfer prices or allocations and thereby negate the autonomy issue. The firm in that case would be operated in a centralized manner, and divisional managers would be evaluated on items over which they had no control, e.g., book profits.

Outside of the accounting applications, Love [1980] developed a transfer pricing system for determining optimal equipment transfers in multiple-location and period-server systems. A price-driven decomposition algorithm was employed. The approach was claimed to allow a firm to operate its service facilities in a profit-center approach. This approach, however, like all the rest, has a common shortcoming.

In general, the mathematical programming techniques seek to maximize (satisfice) total firm profits on the basis of inputs from divisional managers (on an iterative basis). This method may lead to a dissipation of divisional autonomy (e.g., division managers are free to do whatever they want as long as it coincides with central management's wants). In addition, the divisional profit on the transferred goods is controlled by central management's setting of the transfer price that maximizes total firm objectives. The profit earned by a division in this case may be less than it would be if the division did not follow central management's directives. This result leads to dysfunctionalism and the realization by the manager of the division that the decentralization is only a farce and that the firm is really operating in a centralized manner.

Other shortcomings have been noted by various authors. Large changes in the transfer price occur as divisions operate at or near capacity. Also, small changes in the firm's opportunity set could lead to a material re-allocation of the various divisions' profits [see Abdel-khalik and Lusk, 1974; Kaplan, 1977; Thomas, 1980].

The most critical problem in Kaplan's [1977] opinion was obtaining viable information from subordinates for model input, when the subordinates know that they will be evaluated on that input. He doubted whether the mathematical programming approaches would have much influence on the transfer pricing issue.

Similarly, Thomas [1980] commented about the problems associated with the mathematical programming approaches. The various approaches (linear programming, goal programming, and decomposition algorithms) were examined with respect to 'behaviour-congruence' (the approach taken will result in desirable actions). The approaches were found to be congruent with respect to the division manager's input/output decisions (or they could be made congruent). However, none was found to be congruent relative to the division manager's performance evaluations; all were perverse with respect to possible 'elan' decisions (decisions based on other motivational factors, not profits); and all were threatened with self-destruction (divisional profits administered on transfer products do not reflect the division manager's performance and, in the long run, will not be taken seriously and will be rendered ineffective for motivating central management optimal decisions). Thomas's final conclusion for the mathematical programming approaches is bleak: that 'these opportunity-cost approaches are intellectual dead ends' (italicized in original).[4]

In order to try to determine the value of the mathematical programming approaches, the original purpose of the methodology should be considered. Weitzman [1970] explained that the approach was a learning process for central management. On each iteration central management learned more about the relevant parts of the production possibilities set, even though no division was required to communicate the entire set. It was a learning process that allowed central management some information economics inherent in decentralization. The purpose was not evaluation but the determination of (in central management's view) the optimal level of output. Attempting to use this tool for performance evaluation is a *non sequitur*. Its use as an input should be limited to helping determine production levels. Divisional managers, however, should be allowed to negotiate and take advantage of changes that occur between the time that production levels are set and implemented. Hayhurst [1976] astutely recognized that by the time the planning period is somewhat advanced,

---

[4] Thomas, op. cit., p. 194.

central management's plan is outdated. Otherwise, if central management insists on using the programming approaches for evaluation, the worst case (a complete breakdown), as identified by Thomas [1980], Abdel-khalik and Lusk [1974], and others, will be realized.

Behavioural models

It seems strange that there is such a small amount of research dealing with the behavioural aspects of transfer pricing. There are probably several reasons for this lack of research. One reason that behavioural research might be lagging is that researchers believe that the technical aspects of this issue need to be addressed prior to investigating the behavioural aspects. That is, the transfer pricing technique is needed before the impact of the method on an individual and an organization can be addressed. Another reason is that researchers might not see this as an area that is fruitful for research or that they see other areas to be more promising. Most authors only provide the mandatory acknowledgements of behavioural influences, i.e., that one method is beneficial in some aspects but dysfunctional for others, but relatively little empirical research has been conducted. Research that has been conducted has focused on two areas, the behavioural influences exerted by various transfer pricing methods on individual managers and, more recently, the impact of various transfer pricing systems on the organizational structure of a firm.

On a purely conceptual basis, Watson and Baumler [1975] provided a behavioural analysis of transfer pricing. They examined the impact of decentralization (an organizational response to uncertainty); differentiation (the segmentation of the organization and the attitudinal and behavioural changes caused by segmentation); and integration (the process of insuring that the differentiated units attain the total organizational goals). Transfer pricing was viewed as a tool that enhanced differentiation and at the same time served to integrate the organization.

The basic premise that Watson and Baumler relied on was supplied by Lawrence and Lorsch [1967], who demonstrated that the most successful firms (in terms of profitability) were the ones that achieved the necessary differentiation and integration. The most successful firms in uncertain environments resolved interdepartmental conflict through confrontation (negotiation). Consequently, a negotiated transfer pricing method can be viewed as promising.

The negotiated approach was also mentioned in Abdel-khalik and Lusk [1974], who based much of their discussion on Cyert and March's [1963] coalition theory. The often mentioned dysfunctionalism of using negotiated transfer prices was noted. These included the time-consuming nature of the negotiation process, the possible distortion of profit centers results, and the potential evaluation of negotiation ability rather than divisional performance.

An experiment conducted by Ackelsberg and Yukl [1979] examined conflict related to negotiated transfer prices. A multiperiod business game employing students as subjects was used to simulate the negotiation process between organizational divisions. The results indicated that a smoothing and integrative problem-solving process occurred through the use of negotiation when the evaluation process was based on corporate profits rather than divisional profits. Less aggressive and less competitive behaviour was observed along with better relations and more cooperation among divisions in decisions unrelated to transfer pricing. In addition, corporate profits from the transfer product tended to be larger. The importance of the transfer product amplified the results.

The Ackelsberg and Yukl [1979] study, since it used students as the respondent group, contains external validity limitations. In addition, there was not any reward that would be meaningful to a student who was associated with the manner in which the simulation profits were allocated. In addition, the participants were required to take part in face-to-face bargaining. Such may not be realistic in a large firm, and it may have introduced a confounding variable that could have increased the integration and helping effects noted. These same effects may also have resulted from the fact that the participants were acquainted with each other outside of the simulation environment and desired to aid their friends.

Nevertheless, this study provided some evidence that negotiated transfer prices can have integrative properties. It also pointed out an important co-variate that was neglected by Watson and Baumler [1975], the evaluation process. It appears that for transfer pricing to perform the integration process, the evaluation of managers must be based on *corporate profits* rather than division profits. In addition to the evaluation process, the organization type may also be an important co-variate. Eccles [1983] reported that in highly integrated firms where bonuses were based on corporate performance and on individual performance appraisal, a 'shared fate' mentality existed. A manager whose decision reduced divisional profits but increased corporate performance would not be adversely affected. Given this fact, a determination must be made whether the integrating factor is the negotiation process, the evaluation process, or the organizational structure, or whether all are necessary but not sufficient reasons independent of one another but are necessary and sufficient taken together.

In another investigation of conflict and transfer pricing, Lambert [1979] surveyed chief financial officers from a random sample of Fortune 500 companies. This selection may contain a severe limitation, as perceptions of conflict were requested from a party not directly involved in a possible conflict. Three major transfer pricing approaches were considered: cost based, market price, and negotiated. The results indicated a higher level of perceived conflict with negotiated transfer prices than a cost- or market-price-based transfer price. This result reinforces the results obtained by Ackelsberg and Yukl [1979], since it is implicit in Lambert's study that the divisions were being evaluated on divisional results rather than on corporate results. (See Figure 22.1 for an integrated model of the Ackelsberg and Yukl and Lambert results). Conflict was also found to be higher when the customer division could not purchase from suppliers outside the firm

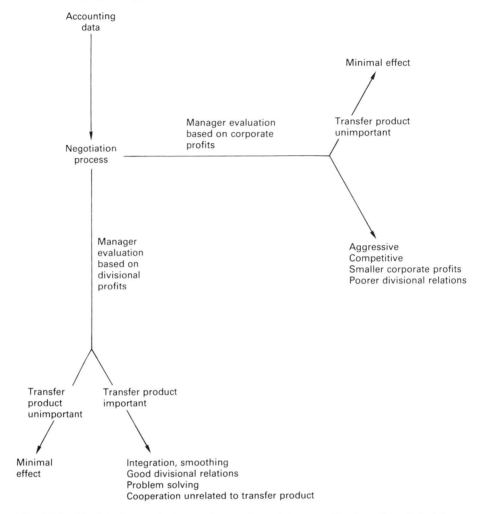

Fig. 22.1   Model of negotiation and transfer pricing conflict based on Ackelsberg & Yukl (1979) and Lambert (1977).

and when there was an impact on the division's profits. Conflict decreased when corporate profits were viewed as increasing from transfer pricing. There was also a strong negative association between the respondent's perceptions of benefits to the firm and conflict (i.e., a higher degree of conflict would not be beneficial).

Expectancy theory was also associated with transfer pricing as a behavioural model by Earnest [1979]. Three possible transfer pricing methods were considered: incremental cost, opportunity cost, and market price. A serious limitation of the study was that only a trivial case was considered, when external market prices existed. It was argued that based on the expectancy model the use of market-price-based transfers will result in a higher level of work motivation by divisional managers, an intriguing argument when the contradictory results of Lambert [1979] are considered. Lambert indicated that there was about the same amount of conflict present when either a market price or full cost transfer price was employed.

An 'organizational behaviour' approach to the transfer pricing issue is a fairly recent avenue of research, which has been followed by several authors. Swieringa and Waterhouse [1982] and Eccles [1983] both insisted that the objectives that can be accomplished with a particular transfer pricing method are dependent upon the firm's organizational structure. This position is in marked contrast to the previously discussed analytic approaches to determine a transfer pricing scheme which accept 'the existence of a well-defined pre-existent organizational objective, the drive for behavioural and attitudinal consistency, and the dominance of economic rationality in organizational decision making.'[5] Swieringa and Waterhouse examined the implications of various organizational models on the transfer pricing decision whereas Eccles recommended various transfer pricing schemes which were dependent upon a firm's level of integration and diversification.

The major contribution of Swieringa and Waterhouse [1982] is that they made salient the impact of the perceptual frame. Four alternative organizational models were utilized as conceptual lenses to view the transfer pricing issue and to interpret a series of hypothetical events based on the Birch Paper Company case [1976]. The models were used to produce different explanations of the events in order to provide insight as to the events' occurrence. The focus was on problem definition, goals to be accomplished, perceived options, consequences associated with the options, and option choice. The various alternative models led to different problem definitions, different series of diagnostic questions, and different answers to the questions. The models employed included the behavioural theory of the firm [Cyert and March, 1963], the garbage can model of organizations [Cohen *et al.*, 1972], the organizing model [Weick, 1969, 1979] and the markets and hierarchies model of organizations [Williamson, 1975]. The explanation of events based on these models was contrasted with the traditional view of pre-existent purpose, consistency, and economic rationality.

Swieringa and Waterhouse [1982] provided a brief summary of the major precepts of each of the organizational models. The alternative organizational models were generally viewed as being complementary and requiring more information than the traditional view. The alternative models focused on the factors that determined an outcome rather than the traditional focus, which seeks to determine what goals account for a particular action. In addition, the alternative models suggested that the *process* of generating transfer rules, procedures, and prices may be at least as important in obtaining some organizational control as the procedures, rules, or prices themselves. This finding is in contrast to the traditional

---

[5] Swieringa, R.J. and J.H. Waterhouse, 'Organizational Views of Transfer Pricing,' *Accounting, Organizations and Society* Vol. 7, No. 2 (1982) p. 150.

view, which generally focused on the search for the appropriate transfer pricing scheme that would provide motivation to managers to make firm-optimal decisions. Implementation issues are rarely addressed under the traditional view, and when they are, the issue is generally a means of inducing managers to accept the externally devised (imposed) prices. The alternative models also emphasized the importance of learning, adaptability, and flexibility, while noting the pervasiveness of stabilizing elements within the organization. A transfer pricing scheme is often associated with the stabilizing elements.

The research reported by Eccles [1983] related the firm's organizational structure with particular transfer pricing methods. The research was based in part on interviews with nearly 150 executives of thirteen companies. A firm could be located anywhere on a grid depending on its level of integration and diversification. Four pure organizational types were identified; collective (low integration and low diversification), cooperative (high integration and low diversification), collaborative (high integration and high diversification), and competitive (low integration and high diversification). For a competitive firm, a market-based transfer price with free sourcing (the buyer is not obligated to purchase from within) was recommended. This technique was also viewed as most fair. If the firm desires to increase interdependence among the divisions, a dual pricing method was endorsed, with the warning that the dual pricing method be employed for only a short period of time because of problems inherent in that technique. A transfer price based on actual full cost, standard full cost, or cost plus return on investment was recommended for firms located in the cooperative continuum. A strong note of caution was issued – that the performance evaluation and measurement scheme must be consistent with the transfer pricing method chosen; i.e., when a transfer price is based on actual full cost, contribution to corporate profit should be emphasized. A collaborative firm was seen to have the most complex transfer pricing problems of the four organizational types and to find it impossible to find a transfer pricing policy that would both satisfy central management's need for control and be perceived as fair. A collaborative firm was recommended to require internal sourcing with market-based transfer prices or mandated prices. It was recommended that high vertical integration requires mandated transfer prices whereas low integration does not, that low diversification requires cost-based transfer prices, and that high diversification requires market-based transfer prices. Dual pricing and constrained sourcing were recommended for firms located midway on the integration continuum.

A different examination of the behavioural aspects of transfer pricing was performed by Granick [1975]. The study compared how differences in national backgrounds and societal differences impact the transfer pricing method employed. The research, based on in-depth interviews involving major corporations in England, France, and the United States, concluded that a transfer pricing system should not be viewed only as an information transmission device. It must also consider incentive and organizational effects, which will differ depending on the pattern of managerial expectations involved for a particular country, even for the same firm. This study reported on a survey of upper management in large British industrial firms during the 1950s and 1960s which showed that only one-fourth to one-third were graduates of any university (a low proportion by international standards) and one-fourth to one-third did not complete secondary education. In general, a managerial career in industry was not considered to be a proper type of employment for upper to middle-class individuals who had viable alternatives, and individuals from the lower classes who succeeded in receiving prestigious types of higher education also tended to avoid industry. Promotion was based on job performance; managers typically moved upward through a single, narrow job function and did not receive broad experience.

The opposite career pattern existed in France, where the top management positions were considered to be prestigious. Education was shown to be a criterion for promotion in the managerial ranks. A reported analysis of the chief executives of the 100 largest private firms (excluding food, textiles, and paper) in the mid-1960s disclosed that over 80 percent of the chief executives had higher education degrees, as opposed to only 2.5 percent of the French male population over age twenty-five. In addition, there was considerable stratification of middle and upper management by the higher educational institution from which the manager originally graduated (62 percent of the chief executives graduated from one of three elite educational institutions whereas only 7.3 percent of the total male population earned degrees from these institutions). The career advancement of lower and middle managers was shown to be relatively independent of their performance after entering the firm.

The research reported by Granick [1975] is based on somewhat dated material from the mid-1960s, and hence must be viewed with caution. What was indicative twenty years ago might not be true today. However, the message presented is still valid regardless of whether these conditions exist today. The multinational firm must consider not only taxes and the foreign exchange rate, but it must be aware of and take into consideration the national managerial career patterns and the societal implications of the countries in which they are located, the fact that a motivational approach that works in one country might not work in another because of these differences.

Thomas [1980] and Flavell [1977] reviewed various transfer pricing methods with respect to their behaviour congruence. Thomas's work is the most complete in its review. The general conclusions reached by Thomas are that 'An allocation method that is behaviour-congruent with respect to one decision and set of circumstances need not be with respect to others'[6] and that 'Transfer-price allocations happen to be universally *perverse* with respect to decisions involving the evaluation of division managers' performance.'[7]

In summary, almost all authors acknowledge the behavioural impact

---

[6] Thomas, op. cit., p. 211.
[7] Ibid., p. 212.

of the various transfer pricing models, and various authors realize that a particular transfer pricing method will not lead to optimal firm and behavioural decisions all the time. The implication is that a firm should decide what it wants its transfer pricing policy to accomplish, whether it be motivation, profit maximization, performance evaluation or risk-sharing. It should then institute a transfer pricing policy that is harmonious with its current or desired organization structure to accomplish this goal and not use it for any other purpose. If a transfer pricing method is used for performance evaluation, the basic responsibility-accounting tenets of evaluating a manager for what he has responsibility and authority for must be followed. If profit maximization is desired, then a centrally administered transfer price should be used. If risk-sharing is a goal, then the evaluation based on responsibility and control is not valid. Rather, in order to maximize the expected utility of both the agent and the principal, the evaluation should be based on a scheme that includes a sharing of the non-controllable, risky factor(s), i.e., actual profits [Demski, 1976; Kaplan, 1982]. This latter statement is an information economics (principal-agent contracts) result.

Ad hoc approaches

This section reviews a fairly diverse and wide range of topics. Consequently, some of the works are reviewed in depth and some are contained only in Table 22.2. (The interested reader is encouraged to pursue the other works). Table 22.2 presents these recent analytical works and details the transfer pricing method advocated and the transfer pricing methods examined.

An examination of Table 22.2 indicates that various authors consider conflicting transfer pricing methods to be superior. The models most often recommended include the setting of the transfer price at the standard variable cost plus any lost contribution margin, the use of negotiated transfer prices, the use of market based transfer prices, or some form of dual pricing. A discussion of some of the recent works follows.

Emmanuel and Gee [1982] proposed a 'fair and neutral' transfer price. They defined fair as a minimum of discrimination against either the transferor or the transferee and claimed that neutrality was present when there was a minimal inducement for managers to behave in a suboptimal manner from the company's view. They limited themselves to market-based transfer prices, acknowledging that any other transfer price was derived from financial allocations that could not be supported or refuted. The authors cited several instances when market-based transfers were not fair or neutral: (1) in imperfect competition; (2) under price fluctuations in the market which were inconsistent with the budgeted transfer price; and (3) when the selling division was operating at less than capacity. The last situation evolves into a zero sum game in the determination of a price less than the market and greater than the standard variable costs of production.

The transfer price proposed by Emmanuel and Gee was calculated and 'paid' in two installments. The first occurred at the time of transfer of goods. It was composed of the actual quantity transferred at the standard variable cost. The second occurred at year end when the difference between the weighted average market price adjusted for quarterly discounts on the amount purchased in the quarter and the amount paid in installment one was charged. They claimed that since the period cost was charged at the end of the year when the prices were known, the fairness problem became insignificant. Price fluctuations were accounted for by employing a one-year weighted average, and documentation could be supplied by the internal auditors as to the computation of the transfer price. They also allowed a lost contribution charge to be imposed by corporate managemet on the transferor. The penalty would be imposed when the selling division had excess capacity but did not supply the purchasing division's needs. The penalty would be equal to the contribution that would have resulted to the selling division had the internal sales been made. The effect would be to cause both divisions to compete against the market in negotiating the discount rather than the zero sum game that would result otherwise.

A problem with Emmanuel and Gee's approach is that the onus is on the selling division to make the discount attractive to the purchasing division. The purchasing division is not affected by any penalty regardless of its decision, i.e., it is not assigned a portion of the penalty of the costs that could have been saved had the manager correctly estimated that external prices would be greater than any price he could have received in-house. Yet the selling division is penalized by this amount even though all estimates generated in that division were correct. The argument could be made that since excess capacity exists, the selling division should have made the price more attractive to generate internal sales, but, as pointed out above, all responsibility falls on the selling division for any decision made, whether it was correct or not. The approach is otherwise reasonable and well thought out. It is limited to the case when an external market exists. The authors have succeeded in addressing some of the problems of 'fairness' in imperfect competition. They have also eliminated some of the gaming that would usually occur in the imperfect market condition and would cause the managers to act in a dysfunctional manner rather than for the good of the firm.

A novel approach for the determination of transfer prices was suggested by Manes and Verrecchia [1982]. They proposed the use of the 'Massachusetts Formula' (MF) or a Shapley-adjusted MF. The MF is a concept from public finance and is utilized by states in the determination of state corporate income and franchise taxes. It is computed as follows: Total Tax = [Total corporate income] × [Tax rate] [Apportionment ratio] where the apportionment ratio = $\frac{1}{3}$ ([In state capital/total capital] + [In state payroll/total payroll] + [In state sales/total sales]). The authors operationalized the MF in a corporate transfer pricing setting as total assets associated with the transferred good, total payroll associated with the transferred goods, and total external sales of the transferred goods.

The MF approach, while providing insight, is not without problems. Of the three factors in the apportionment ratio, only the external sales figure

Table 22.2 Recent *ad hoc* transfer pricing research examining or recommending particular models

Author	Year	*Transfer Pricing Model*																	
		Market	Adjusted Market	Marginal Cost	Negotiated	Contribution Margin	Cost Plus	Variable Cost	Variable Cost Plus	Standard Cost	Full Cost	Manufacturing Cost	Dual Pricing	Opportunity Cost	Input/Output Analysis	SVC	SVC + LCM	Massachusetts Formula	Mandated
Benke & Caster	1983															R			
Lococo	1983					R@							R						
Wraith	1983												E						
Benke et al.	1982															R			
Emmanual & Gee	1982	R$																	
Manes & Verrecchia	1982																	R	
Owens	1982			R															
Benke & Caster	1981																R		
Benke & Edwards	1981	E	E		E	E			E		E								
Ferguson	1981	E			E	E	E		E		E					R			
Gunn	1981					E	E		E		E								R

Author	Year	1	2	3	4	5	6	7	8
Benke & Edwards	1980	E	E	E	E	E	E	E	R
Harding & Houlden	1980	E	E			E		R	
Hilton	1980	E	E	E	E	E			
Madison	1979	E	E		E	E	R		
Clinton	1978	E		E		E	E		
Davies	1978	R	R	E		E	E		
Shaub	1978	R	R	E	E	E	E		
Dagher	1977	R	R	E	E	E			
Emmanuel	1977(a)	E		E					R*
Emmanuel	1977(b)	E	E						R*
Edwards & Roemmich	1976	E	E			E	E		
Ferrara	1976	E	E	E		E	R		
Young	1976(a)	R	R	E			R		
Mailandt	1975		R						
Schwab	1975	R	E	R					
Fantl	1974	E	E	E					
Sharav	1974	E	E	E	E	E			

@ Recommends a combination system incorporating a proration of contribution margin and dual pricing.

$ The transfer price is the weighted average market price over the current year and is paid to the selling division 2 installments, at the time of transfer at the standard variable cost and the remainder at year end.

* Expressed as SVC + amount equal to net contribution from outside sales.

' Also introduces an index.

Key: R = Recommended Model   E = Examined Model
      LCM = Lost Contribution Margin   SVC = Standard Variable Cost

can be verified. The total asset figure is subject to gaming, especially about what percentage of a fixed asset to allocate to a particular product. A division could increase its share of the allocated profits by increasing the amount of assets that are utilized (or claimed to be utilized) for a product. The determination of payroll is less of a problem, but an allocation problem could exist for supervisory payroll costs. The method seems to encourage the divisions to incur excess costs by allocating the profits from the sale of the transferred goods on the costs incurred. This method could generate misleading signals to corporate management in the sense of showing a small profit margin on the transferred good and a large profit margin on some other product that is not involved in any transfers, when in fact the opposite is true. This problem could be reduced through the use of standards, but gaming would seem to be encouraged.

In addition to the problem of gaming, the authors presented their example as a centrally determined product mix that may or may not be beneficial to each division, yet they insisted that a return on investment figure could be utilized for evaluation purposes. Their approach appears to be deficient for all the reasons listed in the mathematical programming section. The MF or the Shapley-adjusted MF approaches are still allocations of profit and, as such, are subject to gaming and are useless as a means of evaluating the performance of managers (unless one wanted to evaluate their ability at gaming).

Mays [1982] examined two of the pitfalls of most transfer price systems, central-management-controlled transfer prices employed for performance evaluation and negotiated transfer prices that could cause suboptimization. Several divisional performance measures were discussed. The most intriguing was an 'index of negotiation.' It was claimed that the index would allow managers to be evaluated on their negotiation ability without confounding this evaluation with an evaluation of their ability to administer a division.

The work by Benke *et al.* [1982] is based on the work reported by Benke and Edwards [1980]. Consequently, only the latter work will be discussed. Benke and Edwards examined various transfer pricing models and developed a generalized rule. The study was based on interviews with corporate controllers of nineteen firms. Transfer pricing was viewed as a part of the management-control process, which had as its objectives goal congruence and performance evaluation. The objectives of transfer pricing were therefore to 'promote goal congruence and enhance performance evaluation.'[8]

Upon examination of all current transfer pricing practices, Benke and Edwards judged them all to be inadequate or dysfunctional. They developed a general rule of how to set the transfer price: the transfer price should equal the standard variable cost (SVC) plus the lost contribution margin (LCM). They demonstrated the rule in seven different economic situations that a firm might find itself in, ranging from a perfectly competitive market for the transferred good to no external markets.

---

[8] Benke, R.L. and J.D. Edwards, Transfer Pricing: Techniques and Uses, National Association of Accountants, New York, 1980, pp. 18–19.

From a practical view, the suggested model is as good as or better than any other models currently in use. But, it too has weaknesses. It is an opportunity-cost-based transfer price method, and it is difficult to determine the appropriate opportunity cost. Gaming could be introduced, both in the development of the standard variable costs and, more easily, in reporting different 'opportunity costs.' The possibility exists that the transfer price may change whenever the producing division has a different opportunity. The purchasing division would then see their costs changing and more profits being allocated to the producing division even though there was no change in production costs or in the market-place. The changes in costs would be due solely to the new opportunity set faced by the producing division. It may be argued that this situation represents the same forces that are present in the open market, the 'invisible hand', but as Thomas [1980] argues, this is really a visible hand which is administering and manipulating prices, not the impersonal market. This view would inevitably conflict with some managerial goals (e.g., of maximizing divisional income), and the internal accounting reports would not be taken seriously since they would appear to be arbitrary. Dysfunctionalism would result.

Benke and Caster [1983] take a slightly different course. They advocated different costs for different needs. Absorption costing should be used for inventory valuation, and any fixed-cost allocation scheme could be employed as long as the resultant unit cost would not be used for pricing or profitability analysis. They recommended both setting the transfer price at the standard variable cost to enhance performance evaluation and direct costing for pricing decisions. They also advocated central control of the allocation of resources, coordination of the production, and sale of products. This approach certainly will generate central management optimum results. But, it is centrally administered, and the responsibility centers are thereby converted into cost centers.

Owens [1982] recommended using an incremental cost approach in the setting of transfer prices since the best corporate decisions would result. He stated that managerial performance should be evaluated only on controllable revenue and cost items. The role of the internal auditors in the evaluation and setting of transfer prices was also addressed.

Wraith [1983] did not recommend any particular transfer pricing method. Rather, he observed that since no one transfer pricing system can accomplish all the objectives of management, two transfer pricing systems be employed, one for performance evaluation and internal control and the other for maximizing corporate goal congruence and public reporting. A limitation to this approach was noted by the author, that it tended to convey a sense of dishonesty.

Other *ad hoc* research approaches

A mixture of topics was included in this section that could not be classified in any of the previously discussed topical areas. Among them was a demonstration of the use of input/output analysis [Martin, 1981]. Another dealt with elimination of intercompany profits on inventory transfer [Stern, 1980]. Benke and Edwards [1981] examined the problems associated with using pseudo profit centers. They concluded that since profits were administered, the only meaningful evaluation device was based on cost control. Schiff [1980, 1979] looked at the regulatory impact on transfer prices and concluded that regulations have influenced transfer pricing practices, making the market-based approach more appealing.

Several authors have examined the transfer price problem in relation to banking and the pricing of funds (Lucien, 1979; Tewes, 1976; Tyler and Fridholm, 1975]. Their general conclusion was that a marginal cost approach should be used but that different marginal transfer prices should exist based upon differing maturities.

Owens [1981] examined transfer pricing of services in a governmental context. Four methods were examined: full allocation; incremental cost allocation; allocating estimated committed costs by user department and incremental costs; and allocating estimated committed cost by funding source and incremental cost. While cautioning that all the methods have drawbacks, it was recommended that some method other than full allocation be used.

Metcalf [1979] examined the changes that have taken place in governmental transfer pricing regulations in the United States and Great Britain. He argued for self-policing and development of a disclosure standard of transfer pricing methods for Great Britain.

No clear-cut conclusions can be drawn from these other analytical approaches surveyed. There is no consensus on a general transfer pricing model (although the 'trivial' solution of pricing at the market price in a purely competitive market when operating at capacity comes close). In addition, various specific concerns were discussed. The next section will review the empirical research and relate it to both the *ad hoc* approaches as well as the more analytical transfer pricing models that were discussed in the previous sections.

Empirical research on transfer pricing practices

In the previous sections the theoretical basis for various transfer pricing methods was emphasized. The objective in this section is to assess the impact of the theoretical works on practice; that is, are any of the conceptually preferred methods employed, and, if not, what methods are employed? A limited number of empirical works have been published (See Table 22.3).

Prior to reviewing any of these works in detail, a discussion of the data presented in Table 22.3 is necessary. Only two of the works surveyed over a hundred U.S. corporations [Tang, 1979; Vancil, 1979]. The other research reported on transfer pricing practices in Canada or Great Britain was more limited in scope or was based on a survey of annual reports. Nonetheless, when the two U.S. based surveys are examined along with the Canadian-based survey [Tang 1980], some inferences can be drawn as the overall results are similar. Approximately 30% of the firms used

Table 22.3 Recent empirical studies and percentage of respondents employing a particular transfer price method

Author	Year	Market	Adj. Market	Contribution Margin	Negotiated	Dual Pricing	Cost Plus	Actual Full Cost	Standard Full Cost	Actual Variable Cost	Standard Variable Cost	Actual Variable Cost Plus	Centrally Established	Other
Eccles[1]	1983	X	X		X		X	X	X					
Benke & Edwards[2]	1980	17	26	13	13		13	4	13					
Tang[3]	1980	26	8		19		15	9	12	3	1	1		5
Choudhury[4]	1979	22	16		16		27	17						2
Mednick[5]	1979	75	X		X		X	X	X	X	X			
Tang[6]	1979	22	8		18		19	9	17		3	1		3
Vancil[7]	1979	31			22		17	13	12	2	3			
Finnie[8]	1978				28		28						44	
Larson[9]	1974	X							X				100	

X = Percentage not reported, but technique mentioned

[1] Based on interviews with nearly 150 executives involved in transfer pricing in 13 firms.

[2] Based on a survey of 19 firms. Percentages were derived from the primary transfer pricing techniques employed by the respondents. A total of 23 responses were presented.

[3] Based on a survey of 192 of the 400 largest Canadian companies. Percentages represent transfer pricing methods used for domestic (Canadian) transfers.

[4] Based on 1971 survey data from 193 British corporations. The author did not disclose whether full cost was at actual or standard. In addition, the cost plus includes 7% who negotiated the additions.

[5] Based on a review of 250 annual reports, in which approximately 100 firms reported relatively significant transfers. The author reported that 25% of the transfer pricing policies were described as either cost, cost plus a percentage markup, market less a discount, or negotiated rates.

[6] Based on a survey of 133 U.S. corporations. The percentages represent the transfer pricing methods used for domestic (U.S.) transfers.

[7] Based on a survey of 239 firms that reported the transfer pricing policy employed. Data did not disclose if any adjusted market price method occurred, and if so, if it was included as a market price or negotiated method.

[8] Based on a survey in Great Britain in which 33 firms completed questionnaires and 36 methods were employed. The data were classified as only negotiation, standard cost plus mark-up, and centrally administered.

[9] Based on in depth interviews with representatives of 8 firms. The author stated that the transfer price ranged from market based to cost and were established by top management action.

either a market- or adjusted market-based transfer price while about 20% utilized a negotiated price. The remaining firms employed some type of cost-based transfer pricing system. About 10% used actual full cost, slightly more than 12% used standard full cost, and about 17% used cost plus. Less than 5% reported using any type of variable-cost-based transfer price (either at standard or actual). None of the firms used a marginal cost approach nor did any use an opportunity cost method (including the mathematical programming techniques).

It is interesting to compare these empirical results with the recommendations presented in the *ad hoc* research reviewed in the previous sections. Market-based transfers and negotiated transfer prices are employed by approximately half of the firms (based on the results reported by Tang [1979, 1980] and Vancil [1979]). Only a minimal number of firms utilized a transfer price based on the standard variable cost, and only in the survey performed by Benke and Edwards [1980] did any firm acknowledge using a contribution margin-based transfer price. Consequently, there appears to be some agreement between the methods employed in practice and the methods most often recommended in the *ad hoc* literature, but diverse opinions still exist on the best transfer pricing method.

All of the transfer pricing approaches employed were based on accounting data or on data determined exogenously in the marketplace. None was based on any complex mathematical approach, which would seem to imply that a premium is placed on simplicity, understandability, and cost minimization. Perhaps managers and top management realize the limitations inherent in the transfer pricing system and are willing to make subjective corrections for these defects as long as other critical corporate and divisional performance data are disclosed (i.e., a chief executive officer is willing to use a standard full-cost transfer pricing system because the entire firm performance can be evaluated through a few key ratios even though a market-based approach would show the relative contribution to profits of the products in one document, or managers are evaluated not only on profit but to a greater extent on quality of effort [see Eccles, 1983]).

This view indicates that methods that are claimed to be more theoretically correct are ignored. It would be useful to know why the present methods are employed. Is it because there is little awareness of the more advanced methods? Is it because the cost to implement other methods exceeds the incremental benefits? Is it because the other methods apply only to conceptually simple situations that are unrealistic? These data would provide an impetus for future accounting research. Perhaps there is a critical reason why certain transfer pricing methods are not employed i.e., the desire for simplicity and understandability discussed above. This desire raises questions about the fruitfulness of certain avenues of research.

The final conclusion that can be inferred from the empirical studies is that there is no 'best' method. A variety of methods was employed and was probably based on the primary objective the firm was attempting to accomplish through the transfer pricing process. A discussion of some of these empirical works is presented next.

The research reported by Eccles [1983] has been previously reviewed in the behavioural research section and that by Benke and Edwards [1980] has been reviewed in the *ad hoc* research section. These are not reviewed again; the interested reader is referred back to the appropriate sections.

Vancil [1979] studied the management of decentralized firms under the auspices of the Financial Executives Research Foundation. The reported data are based on a mail survey of the senior members of the Financial Executives Institute located in the corporate offices of 684 manufacturing firms. A total of 313 questionnaires were returned, in which 239 firms specified transfer pricing policies. It was determined that the primary factors in decentralization were authority and autonomy, and, although not primary, the measurement system was important.

The financial measurement system (of which the transfer pricing method is a part) was viewed as an important managerial tool. The uses of the financial measurement system included coordination, motivation, operational guidance, and monitoring organizational effectiveness. It was believed that motivation was one of the most important tasks of financial measurement systems and that the measurement system (i.e., transfer price) should not be perverse in performance evaluation.

The study disclosed that about 85% of the profit centers transferred goods and the amount of transfers varied up to 65% of the total value of goods sold (or manufactured, depending upon whether a profit- or cost-based transfer price was used) by the profit center. Relationships between the extent of transfers and various demographic variables were investigated. The data indicated that less diversified firms were more involved with inter-profit center transfers than highly diversified firms. Sales revenues and two measures of profitability, profit margin and return on investment, were positively correlated with the amount of goods transferred. It was thought that although some intervening variable could exist (possibly diversification strategy), these relationships could be explained. Profit centers in large firms produce finished goods that contain large amounts of transferred-in goods and services, whereas, in smaller firms, goods transferred in from other profit centers would be less important. (In firms with sales exceeding \$1 billion, more than 30% of the firms transferred over 15% of their goods while this occurred in only about 8% of the firms with sales less than \$200 million).

This study also investigated whether there was a difference in the transfer pricing method used depending upon whether the goods were transferred out from a cost or a profit center. It was found that if a corporate manufacturing function shipped the goods, a cost-based method was used over 80% of the time. If goods were shipped from one profit center to another profit center, a cost-based method was used less than half the time. When profit centers traded with each other, a market-based method was used over 30% of the time, and negotiation occurred more than 20% of the time. These results are intuitively appealing. A profit center would transfer goods out above cost so as to generate some contribution to profit. However, a corporate manufacturing function that generally served several profit centers would not be required to show a profit. There was no uniformity in the way all firms set transfer prices (i.e., each of the methods was used regardless of supplier by some of the firms).

Tang [1979] (and Tang *et al.* [1979], which was based on the same data) reported on domestic transfer pricing methods employed in the United States and Japan. A questionnaire was sent to 300 U.S. firms and to 369 Japanese firms, which yielded 145 and 102 usable responses, respectively. The firms selected were from the 1,000 largest American and the 1,121 largest Japanese mining and manufacturing firms. It was reported that for domestic transfer of goods, a market-based approach was employed by about 30 percent of the U.S. firms, while negotiation was employed by about 20 percent, and some form of a cost-based transfer price was utilized by almost 50 percent. The results for the Japanese firms were not significantly different.

Tang [1980] surveyed the 400 largest Canadian-based companies, getting 192 usable responses. This study investigated the objectives of the transfer performance method in addition to the methods employed. The dominant objective was performance evaluation (46%) followed by profit maximization (38%) with the remainder being some other consideration. These findings seems to reinforce what academicians have said about the purposes of transfer prices.

Wu and Sharp [1979] reported on the dominant transfer pricing policies when the market price was not available, the motivational criteria that account for the dominance of some transfer pricing schemes, and the dominant arbitration methods employed in settling transfer pricing disputes. They also contrasted the difference between domestic and international transfer pricing policies. Two questionnaire surveys were conducted, the first for identification of transfer pricing criteria, the available transfer prices, and the arbitration methods employed, and the second to obtain the rating of various items on a six-point scale (e.g., motivation for transfer pricing). A total of 61 firms (from a reported eleven different industries) from the 1976 Fortune 500 participated in the second survey. Data analysis included tests of differences for ranked data. Profit maximization and performance evaluation were ranked as the two most dominant objectives of the domestic transfer pricing policy from a list of fourteen possible objectives, whereas complying with foreign tax and tariff regulations and overall firm profit maximization were the dominant objectives of international transfer pricing policies. Wu and Sharp also reported a consistency in the ranking of preferred transfer pricing systems across the industries they examined. When market prices were not available, the top three transfer pricing methods for both domestic and international transfers were full cost plus profit margin, negotiation, and full cost. The arbitration methods employed by firms in both domestic and international transfers were also found to be statistically similar. The two methods ranked as most preferred in both domestic and international transfers were a two-level approach with reconciliation attempted at the local level first, followed by top management involvement only if the disagreement could not be settled at the local level; and disputes reconciled at the local level through consultation with top management. The benefit of this research is the identification of the issues that firms seek to address in their development of transfer pricing systems and the impact that domestic and international transfers makes on these objectives. It is also the only study that provided statistical tests for differences and similarities between the domestic and international transfer pricing policies. Wu and Sharp also explicitly addressed the issue of determining the dominant practices when a market for the transferred good does not exist, and the arbitration methods. The major findings of these last two issues point to potential benefit for future behavioural research on the transfer pricing issue. A negotiated price was the second most highly ranked method for determining transfer prices when a market price did not exist. Future research should extend and integrate this work with the work of Eccles [1983].

Emmanuel [1977b] also examined the principal uses of division performance measures in Great Britain. The prevalent use of the manager's performance measure was for career development/dismissal (42%). It was also used for control over the manager (24%), bonus and remuneration (16%), motivation (9%), and other purposes (9%). Again, performance evaluation was the most important, and the transfer price may have a major impact if the effect is material. However, the results must be viewed in light of the national differences in managerial career paths [Granick, 1975], and the findings may not be generalizable in the United States. Emmanuel also argued that the market price could be dysfunctional in nature, and a dual pricing approach was advocated.

Finnie [1978] reported on an open-ended questionnaire provided to British companies. Thirty-three usable responses were obtained. This study concluded that the most important aspects of transfer pricing were for control (measure performance and identifying contribution to corporate profit) and motivation (profit consciousness). Central influence was found about 70% of the time.

Larson [1974] contacted eighteen firms, of which eight agreed to in-depth interviews. The interviews covered the degree of autonomy of divisions, performance evaluation, and transfer price administration. The transfer prices employed ranged from market-based to cost and were established by top management action. It was reported that less than 25% of all input decisions were divisional decisions and that performance evaluation was generally based on the budget that was partially determined by the prior years' performance (and would have been affected by the transfer price).

Choudhury [1979] reported on a 1971 survey conducted by the British Institute of Management in which 193 firms participated. The survey disclosed that 54% of the participating firms used some form of market-based transfer prices, while the remainder used cost-based approaches (negotiation was classified under both approaches and was employed by a total of 23% of the firms). It was concluded that the method employed was dependent on top management's view of the benefits of profit centers *vis-à-vis* cost centers. The approach taken, therefore, was dependent on the attitude of the importance of division autonomy for manager motivation.

In summary, there has been a limited amount of in-depth, broadly based empirical research on transfer pricing. Only two of the works reported on here surveyed over a hundred U.S. corporations [Tang, 1979; Vancil, 1979]. Only the work by Eccles [1983] involved a series of in-depth discussions with individuals who administered the transfer pricing scheme, who were evaluated under the transfer pricing scheme, and who provided the evaluations of the various managers (on the average, over ten executives were interviewed in each firm). Consequently, a need exists for more research of this type. The focus of this research should not be on just what transfer pricing methods are employed; rather the focus should be on why a particular transfer pricing scheme is employed, and, if that scheme is not the theoretically correct approach, why a theoretically inferior method is being utilized. This type of research would provide evidence about the fruitfulness of certain avenues of research. A final conclusion to be inferred from the empirical studies presented here is that no one best transfer pricing method exists. About on-third of the firms employ market-based methods, about half used a cost-based scheme, and about one-fifth employed negotiation. Obviously the method employed depends upon whether a cost or profit center is transferring out the goods. The method employed by the firms probably reflected this and other goals and objectives that the firms were attempting to accomplish.

CONCLUSIONS AND DIRECTIONS FOR FUTURE RESEARCH

The transfer pricing problem will remain as long as (and to the extent) top management seeks to decentralize operations and use a single tool to communicate, motivate, direct, and evaluate. Regardless of top management's objectives, foremost in mind should be the behavioural implications of the transfer pricing method employed. This area is also the one most fruitful for future research.

In order to alleviate the potential conflicts of transfer pricing, management may seek to reorganize the structure of its profit centers, possibly converting some into cost centers or combining several to form one larger profit center. Conflict might be a symptom of an inadequate organizational structure.

Top management should also decide what the transfer pricing mechanism should accomplish and use the method that best fills its needs. However, the transfer pricing mechanism cannot be used effectively for more than one objective. In fact, the transfer price should not be the sole, or even a major, determinant in performance evaluation since so many other factors (i.e., cost efficiency, total product performance, and other subjective measures) are important in determining managerial effectiveness and efficiency.

The economic models and methods appear to be of limited value for the future since they are limited to conceptually simple cases. The same conclusion holds for the mathematical programming methods. All result in central management specifying the optimum amounts or minimum acceptable actions (in the case of satisficing). Work is needed in the area of negotiated transfer pricing. Although readily dismissed by many authors, it seems to hold promise. A negotiated transfer price could act as an integrator in a decentralized organization, and if managers are evaluated on the entire firm (rather than on a small section) even further integration and helping may occur.

Another research area that appears to be fruitful is further examination of the impact of the organization of the firm on transfer pricing systems. The foundation for this research has already been laid. Now is the time to build on the foundation that has been developed by Swieringa and Waterhouse [1982] and Eccles [1983]. Research of this nature should try to integrate those works and others that have dealt with organizational design, such as Mintzberg [1979, 1983].

Mintzberg identified five basic or pure organizational structures. The first was the 'simple structure,' characterized as a centralized organization with little or no technostructure, some support staff, and a small managerial hierarchy. It makes minimal use of planning, training, and liaison devices. This stage is the one in which small entrepreneurial firms are found. It is unlikely that any transfer pricing system would be found in this type of organizational structure. The second type of structure was the 'machine bureaucracy,' characterized as an integrated, regulated machine. It can have vertical and horizontal job specialization (generally by functional areas), vertical centralization, and limited horizontal decentralization. The standardization of work processes is normally viewed as the prime coordinating mechanism. A control mentality pervades a machine bureaucracy. Consequently, it can be postulated that any transfer pricing systems employed in this type of organization would have control as its prime objective and could well be mandated by central management. Managerial motivation and development would be expected to be subordinate to the goal of control (performance evaluation). The third organizational structure discussed was the 'professional bureaucracy.' This structure relies on the skills and knowledge of its operating professionals to function. It produces a standard product or service and relies on the standardization of skills, training, and indoctrination for coordination (examples of professional bureaucracies include school systems and public accounting firms). A professional bureaucracy differs from a machine bureaucracy because, in the latter, authority of hierarchical nature (the power of the office) is relied upon, whereas in the former, the authority of a professional nature (the power of expertise) is important. If a transfer pricing system were employed in a professional bureaucracy, it would not be used primarily for control; rather it would probably be employed to help standardize the environment.

The fourth organizational structure discussed by Mintzberg was the 'divisionalized form.' This structure can be characterized as a set of semi-autonomous entities (divisions) held together by a central administrative group (central management). The flow of power in this organizational structure is top-down. This type is probably the most common organizational structure employed by the major firms in the United States at this time. A divisionalized structure does not imply a decentralization;

rather the opposite can be true, that a divisionalized structure can be very centralized. The form of control or coordination employed is the review of standardized outputs (e.g., return on investment), and a vital design parameter is the performance control system. The transfer pricing system is employed as a part of the performance control system. In general, the divisionalized form works best when the divisions are structured as machine bureaucracies, and this structure will cause other divisional structures (e.g., professional bureaucracy) to become more like machine bureaucracies. This occurs because the only way central management can retain control over (and yet protect) divisional autonomy is by *post hoc* monitoring of divisional performance. It requires an integrated structure that has operational or quantifiable goals, and only the machine bureaucracy meets these criteria. A transfer pricing system within a divisionalized structure would therefore be dependent on the degree of autonomy allowed the divisions and also the underlying structure of the divisons.

The last structure identified by Mintzberg was the 'adhocracy.' A matrix type organization (i.e., specialists are grouped by functional areas for 'house-keeping' purposes but are used to form teams comprised of members from various functional areas for projects) that employs liaison devices to encourage mutual adjustments within and between teams. In this organization structure, the transfer price would be used as a liaison device rather than a control device. Consequently, a negotiated transfer price would probably be best suited.

These organizational structures specified by Mintzberg [1979, 1983] can be related to the four organizational types identified by Eccles [1983]. These included the collective, competitive, collaborative, and cooperative organizations. A collective organization has little or no diversification and little or no integration. It would be similar to a simple structure and would not require the use of transfer prices. The competitive type organization is viewed as having little vertical integration between business units. This type would be similar to a divisionalized machine bureaucracy with decentralized decision-making. In this situation, it is expected that a market-based transfer price would be preferred so that divisional managers could be evaluated on their areas of responsibility and decision-making. A collaborative organization exhibits both the interdependence of vertical integration and the independent contributions of the diversified business units. This characteristic could apply to at least two variations on the five 'pure' organization structures identified. It could be a variation on a divisionalized machine bureaucracy where there is a limited amount of decentralization or a divisionalized form of adhocracy. However, the scenario presented by Eccles leads to the conclusion of the former. In this situation market-based transfer prices could be used, as could negotiation or cost-based transfer prices. The method employed would depend upon whether central management wanted a certain type of information or wanted to somehow mold the organization (i.e., for capital budgeting purposes a cost plus investment approach could be employed, or negotiation for more integration, or a market-based one in order to find out how efficient the divisions are performing relative to the 'outside world').

A cooperative organization is one in which there is a high degree of vertical integration. However, one item makes Eccles' cooperative organization unique: that bonuses, salary increases, and promotions for the individual managers are based primarily on corporate performance. A cooperative organization could be either a machine bureaucracy or a divisionalized form of it in which some critical functions are centralized. However, the managerial evaluation procedure would differ from the norm and be based on corporate performance. Eccles is correct in noting that in a pure cooperative organization transfer pricing systems would not exist, and that if a transfer pricing system was employed it would be mandated by central management as a direct result of the high level of vertical integration.

The organizational structure paradigm suggested by Mintzberg [1979, 1983] appears to encompass more basic and differentiating types of structures than the approach taken by Eccles. In fact, the four organizational types that Eccles identifies can be classified under Mintzberg's scheme, and three of the four organization types identified by Eccles could be classified as a type of a divisionalized form of machine bureaucracy. Additional research, going beyond the work of Eccles, that examines the impact of the transfer pricing system on these different organization structures is required. In particular, emphasis should be on the objectives of the transfer pricing system, given the particular organization structure. The research should also classify the transfer pricing system employed and type of organization structure in order to determine whether there is one best or a set of best transfer pricing schemes that are or could be employed by firms.

Research should also address the integration process. Factors that need to be considered include the organization structure, the evaluation procedures, and the transfer pricing system. In particular, negotiated transfer prices should be examined in different organizational structures. The objective would be to determine what are the encessary and sufficient factors for integration. This research could build on the work of Eccles [1983], Mintzberg [1979, 1983], Swieringa and Waterhouse [1982], Ackelsberg and Yukl [1979], and Lawrence and Lorsch [1967]. In general, Mintzberg postulated that the prime coordinating mechanism (which would be considered an integrating factor) is direct supervision in the simple structure, a type of standardization in the bureaucracies (standardization of work processes in a machine bureaucracy and standardization of skills in a professional bureaucracy), standardization of outputs in a divisionalized form, and mutual adjustment in an adhocracy. This research would relate to the research conducted under the organizational structure paradigm.

Empirical research should also focus on why firms utilize certain transfer pricing methods (and possibly ignore more theoretically correct methods), and relates the methods employed to the stated objectives of transfer pricing system, and determines whether the objectives are consistent with the system employed given the firm's organizational structure. With this information, advances could be made in adapting the theoretically correct methods to meet the needs of businesses so that more informed and reliable decisions could be made. Alternatively, this system may point out flaws in the current theory or current practice.

Other research could be of a behavioural nature, with the individual rather than the firm as the focal point. This research could address the individual manager's perception of fairness of various transfer pricing schemes. The research could examine cost- and market-based schemes and also examine the impact of the evaluation method employed (e.g., does corporate or divisional evaluation have an impact on the perceived fairness of a transfer pricing scheme?). Equity theory [Walster *et al.*, 1978; Leventhal, 1976; Adams, 1965] could serve as a theoretical basis for this type of research. Other research could employ attribution theory [Jones and Nisbett, 1971; Kelly, 1971; Jones and Davis, 1965] and investigate the central management-divisional manager evaluation process to determine if different transfer pricing systems lead to different attributions for failure and success, given a certain organizational setting. Other research could relate the transfer pricing scheme to the motivational factors that impact a manager. In other words, which transfer pricing schemes motivate a manager in a given organizational structure? This research could draw on expectancy theory [Porter and Lawler, 1968; Vroom, 1964] and on goal-setting theory [Hamner and Organ, 1978]. Research that has utilized expectancy theory as it relates to transfer pricing systems has only examined a conceptually simple case [Earnest, 1979].

In closing, the transfer pricing problem exists as a symptom of the desire for decentralization and the concomitant need for congruence with a common goal. There is no best transfer price for all situations. Top management should be aware of the behavioural impact of any transfer pricing policy.

ACKNOWLEDGEMENTS

The author wishes to thank S. Haka, R. Marshall, P. McKenzie and an anonymous reviewer for their comments and suggestions.

BIBLIOGRAPHY

Abdel-khalik, A.R. and E.J. Lusk, 'Transfer Pricing – A Synthesis,' *The Accounting Review* (January 1974), pp. 8–23.

——, 'Transfer Pricing – A Synthesis: A Reply,' *The Accounting Review* (April 1975), pp. 355–58.

Ackelsberg, R. and G. Yukl, 'Negotiated Transfer Pricing and Conflict Resolution in Organizations,' *Decision Sciences* (July 1979), pp. 387–98.

Adams, J.S., 'Inequity in Social Exchange,' in L. Berkowitz (Ed.), *Advances in Experimental Social Psychology*, Vol. 2 (New York: Academic Press, 1965).

Baily, A.D. and W.J. Boe, 'Goal and Resource Transfers in the Multigoal Organization,' *The Accounting Review* (July 1976), pp. 559–73.

Baumol, W.J. and T. Fabian, 'Decomposition, Pricing For Decentralization and External Economies,' *Management Science* (September, 1964), pp. 1–13.

Benke, R.L. and A.B. Caster, 'Information Systems and Fixed Costs in Multi-divisional Companies,' *Cost and Management* (March-April 1983), pp. 21–25.

——, 'An Application of the General Rule for Transfer Pricing: The Birch Paper Company Case,' *The Accountant's Magazine* (August 1981), pp. 259–62.

Benke, R.L. and J.D. Edwards, 'Should You Use Transfer Pricing to Create Pseudo-Profit Centers?,' *Management Accounting* (NAA) (February 1981), pp. 36–39, 43.

——, *Transfer Pricing: Techniques and Uses* (New York: National Association of Accountants, 1980.

——, 'Transfer Pricing: Techniques and Uses,' *Management Accounting* (NAA) (June 1980), pp. 44–46.

Benke, R.L., J.D. Edwards, and A.R. Wheelock, 'Applying and Opportunity Cost General Rule for Transfer Pricing,' *Management Accounting* (NAA) (June 1982), pp. 43–51.

Blois, K.J. 'Pricing of Supplies by Large Customers,' *Journal of Business Finance & Accounting* (Autumn 1978), pp. 367–79.

Buckhout, W.E., 'Transfer Pricing Identifies Source of Profits and Loss,' *Chemical Marketing Reporter* (March 8, 1976), pp. 16, 18, 23, 24.

Burton, R.M., W.W. Damon, and D.W. Loughridge., 'Economics of Decomposition: Resource Allocation vs. Transfer Pricing,' *Decision Sciences* (July 1974), pp. 297–310.

Burton, R.M. and B. Obel, 'Efficiency of the Price, Budget, and Mixed Approaches Under Varying A Priori Information Levels for Decentralized Planning,' *Management Science* (April 1980), pp. 401–17.

Carleton, W.T., G. Kendall, and S. Tandon, 'Application of the Decomposition Principle to the Capital Budgeting Problem in a Decentralized Firm,' *Journal of Finance* (June 1974), pp. 815–27.

Choudhury, N., 'Transfer Pricing Practices: Room for Debate,' *Accountancy* (Eng.) (August 1979), pp. 105–6.

Clinton, G.S., 'Ditton Corvedale Company,' *Management Accounting* (Eng.) (February 1978), pp. 69–70, 73.

Cohen, M.D., J.G. March and J.P. Olsen, 'A Garbage Can Model of Organizational Change,' *Administrative Science Quarterly* (March 1972), pp. 1–25.

Cyert, R.M. and J.G. March, A Behavioral Theory of the Firm (Englewood Cliffs, NJ: Prentice-Hall, 1963).

Dagher, S.P., 'What's the Price When a Company Buys From Itself?,' *Administrative Management* (May 1977), pp. 32, 33, 36, 48, 51, 53, 55, 57.

Davies, J.R., 'How to Determine Transfer Prices,' *Management Accounting* (Eng.) (October 1978), pp. 392–93.

Dearden, J., *Cost Accounting and Financial Control Systems* (Reading, MA: Addison Wesley, 1973).

Demski, J., 'Uncertainty and Evaluation Based on Controllable Performance,' *Journal of Accounting Research* (Autumn 1976), pp. 230–45.

Dopuch, N. and D.H.F. Drake, 'Accounting Implications of a Mathematical Programming Approach to the Transfer Price Problem,' *Journal of Accounting Research* (Spring 1964), pp. 10–24.

Earnest, K.R., 'Applying Motivational Theory in Management Accounting,' *Management Accounting* (NAA), (December 1979), pp. 41–44.

Eccles, R.G., 'Control with Fairness in Transfer Pricing,' *Harvard Business Review* (November-December 1983), pp. 149–61.

Edwards, J.D. and R.A. Roemmich, 'Transfer pricing: The Wrong Tool for Performance Evaluation,' *Cost and Management* (Can.) (January-February 1976), pp. 35–37.

Emmanuel, C.R., 'Birch Paper Company: A Possible Solution to the Interdivisional Pricing Problem,' *The Accountant's Magazine* (Scot.) (May 1977a), pp. 196–98.

——, 'Transfer Pricing: A Diagnosis and Possible Solution to Dysfunctional Decision-Making in the Divisionalized Company,' *Management International Review* Vol. 17, No. 4 (1977b), pp. 45–49.

Emmanuel, C.R. and K.P. Gee, 'Transfer Pricing: A Fair and Neutral Procedure,' *Accounting and Business Research* (Autumn 1982), pp. 273–78.

Enzer, H., 'Static Theory of Transfer Pricing,' *Naval Research Logistics Quarterly*, Vol. 22, No. 2 (1975), pp. 375–89.

Fantl, L., 'Transfer Pricing – Tread Carefully,' *CPA Journal* (December 1974), pp. 42–46.

Ferguson, R., 'Transfer Pricing: Selecting Suitable Methods,' (Accounting Principles and Practices), *Cost and Management* (Can.), (March-April 1981), pp. 53–57.

Ferrara, L., 'Accounting for Performance Evaluation and Decision-Making,' *Management Accounting* (NAA) (December 1976), pp. 13–19.

Finnie, J., 'Transfer Pricing Practices,' *Management Accounting* (Eng.) (December 1978), pp. 494–97.

Flavell, R.B., 'Divisionalization and Transfer Pricing: A Review,' *Omega*, Vol. 5, no. 5 (1977), pp. 543–56.

Granick, D., 'National Differences in the Use of Internal Transfer Prices,' *California Management Review* (Summer 1975), pp. 28–40.

Groves, T. and M. Loeb, 'Reflections on Social Costs and Benefits and the Transfer Pricing Problem,' *Journal of Public Economics*, Vol. 5, 1976, pp. 353–359.

Gunn, B., 'Profit Maximization Versus Profit Optimization,' *Journal of Contemporary Business* (August 1981), pp. 113–23.

Hamner, W.C., and D.W. Organ, *Organizational Behavior: An Applied Psychological Approach*, (Dallas, TX: Business Publications, Inc., 1978).

Harding, B. and B. Houlden, 'Using Input-Output Models for Planning in Groups with Considerable Intercompany Trading,' *Long Range planning* (June 1980), pp. 35–39.

Harris, M., C.H. Kriebel, and A. Raviv, 'Asymmetric Information, Incentives and Intrafirm Resource Allocation,' *Management Science* (June 1982), pp. 604–20.

Hass, J., 'Transfer Pricing in a Decentralized Firm,' *Management Science* (February 1968), pp. B310–B333.

Hayhurst, G., 'A Proposal for a Corporate Control System,' *Management International Review* Vol. 16, No. 2 (1976), pp. 93–103.

Henderson, B.D., and J. Dearden, 'New System for Divisional Control,' *Harvard Business Review* (October 1966), pp. 144–146.

Hilton, I.H., 'Transfer Pricing', (Students' section), *Australian Accountant* (June 1980), pp. 336–38.

Hirshleifer, J., 'On the Economics of Transfer Pricing,' *Journal of Business* (July 1956), pp. 172–84.

Hurwicz, L., R. Radner, and S. Reiter, 'A Stochastic Decentralized Resource

Allocation Process,' *Econometrica* (March 1975), pp. 187–221, (May 1975), pp. 363–93.

Ismail, G.E., 'Transfer Pricing Under Demand Uncertainty,' *Review of Business and Economic Research* (Fall 1982), pp. 1–14.

Jennergren, L.P., 'Divisionalized Firm Revisited – Comment on Enzer's "The Static Theory of Transfer Pricing,"' *Naval Research Logistics Quarterly*, Vol. 24(2), (1977), pp. 373–76.

Jones, E.E., and K.E. Davis, 'From Acts to Dispositions: The Attribution Process in Person Perception,' in L. Berkowitz (Ed.), *Advances in Experimental Social Psychology* Vol. 2 (New York: Academic Press, 1965).

Jones, E.E., and R.E. Nisbett, *The Actor and the Observer: Divergent Perceptions of the Causes of Behavior* (Morristown, NJ: General Learning Press, 1971).

Kanodia, C., 'Risk Sharing and Transfer Price Systems Under Uncertainty,' *Journal of Accounting Research* (Spring 1979), pp. 74–98.

Kaplan, R.S., *Advanced Management Accounting* (Englewood Cliffs, NJ: Prentice-Hall, Inc., 1982).

——, 'Application of Quantitative Models in Managerial Accounting: A State of the Art Survey,' in *Management Accounting – State of the Art* (Madison, WI, 1977), pp. 29–71.

Kelly, E.E., *Attribution in Social Interaction* (Morristown, NJ: General Learning Press, 1971).

Kornbluth, J.S.H., 'Accounting in Multiple Objective Linear Programming,' *The Accounting Review* (April 1974), pp. 284–95.

Kydland, F., 'Hierarchical Decomposition in Linear Economic Models,' *Management Science* (May 1975), pp. 1029–39.

Lambert, D.R., 'Transfer Pricing and Interdivisional Conflict,' *California Management Review* (Summer 1979), pp. 70–75.

Larson, R.L., 'Decentralization in Real Life,' *Management Accounting* (NAA) (March 1974), pp. 28–32.

Lawrence, P.R. and J.W. Lorsch, *Organization and Environment* (Homewood, IL: Richard D. Irwin, 1967).

Leventhal, G.S., 'Fairness in Social Relationships,' in L. Thibaut, J.T. Spence, and R.C. Carson (Eds.), *Contemporary Topics in Social Psychology* (Morristown, NJ: General Learning Press, 1976).

Littrell, E.K., 'Taking a Dim View of Profits,' *Management Accounting* (NAA) (March 1980), p. 60.

Lococo, L.J., 'Selecting the Right Transfer Pricing Model,' *Management Accounting* (NAA), (March 1983), pp. 42–5.

Love, C.E., 'Optimal Equipment Transfer Pricing in Service Systems,' *Journal of the Operational Research Society* (July 1980), pp. 657–66.

Lucien, K., 'Transfer Pricing for the Cost of Funds in a Commercial Bank,' *Management Accounting* (NAA), (January 1979), pp. 23–4, 36.

Madison, R. L., 'Responsibility Accounting and Transfer Pricing: Approach with Caution,' *Management Accounting* (NAA), (January 1979), pp. 25–9.

Maier, S.F. and J.H. Vander Weide, 'Capital Budgeting in the Decentralized Firm,' *Management Science*, (December 1976), pp. 433–43.

Mailandt, P., 'Alternative to Transfer Pricing,' *Business Horizons* (October 1975), pp. 81–6.

Manes, R. and R. Verrecchia, 'A New Proposal for Setting Intra-Company

Transfer Prices,' *Accounting and Business Research* (Spring 1982), pp. 97–104.

Martin, J.R., 'Segment Planning and Reporting for Firms with Reciprocal Intersegment Transfers,' *Business Economics* (May 1981), pp. 25–9.

Mays, R.L., Jr., 'Divisional Performance Measurement and Transfer Prices,' *Management Accounting* (NAA) (April 1982), pp. 20–4.

Mednick, R., 'Companies Slice and Serve Up Their Financial Results Under FASB 14,' *Financial Executive* (March 1979), pp. 45–56, *passim.*

Metcalf, M., 'Related Party Transfactions – Why a Standard is Needed,' *Accountancy* (May 1979), pp. 99–100.

Miller, G.A., 'The Magical Number Seven, Plus or Minus Two: Some Limits on Our Capability for Processing Information,' *The Psychological Review* Vol. LXIII, No. 2 (March 1956).

Mintzberg, H., *Structure in Fives*, (Englewood Cliffs, NJ: Prentice-Hall, Inc., 1983).

——, *The Structuring of Organizations*, (Englewood Cliffs, NJ: Prentice-Hall, Inc., 1979).

Morris, J.R., 'Application of the Decomposition Principle to Financial Decision Models,' *Journal of Financial and Quantitative Analysis* (March 1975), pp. 37–65.

Obel, B. and J.H. Van der Weide, 'On the Decentralized Capital Budgeting Problem Under Uncertainty,' *Management Science* (September 1979), pp. 873–83.

Owens, R.W., 'Pricing Internal Transfers,' *Internal Auditor* (August 1982), pp. 14–17.

——, 'Pricing Goods and Services of an Internal Service Department,' *Government Accountants Journal* (Spring 1981), pp. 43–46.

Porter, L.W., and E.E. Lawler, *Managerial Attitudes and Performances*, (Homewood, IL: Irwin-Dorsey, 1968).

Ronen, J., 'Social Costs and Benefits and The Transfer Pricing Problem,' *Journal of Public Economics*, Vol. 3, 1974, pp. 71–82.

Ronen, J., 'Transfer Pricing – A Synthesis: A Comment' (Correspondence), *The Accounting Review* (April 1975), pp. 351–54.

——and Schiff, M., 'Transfer Pricing for Public Reporting: A Case Study,' *Accounting and Business Research* (Eng.) (Autumn 1980), pp. 440–43.

——, 'Note on Transfer Pricing and Industry Segment Reporting,' *Journal of Accounting, Auditing & Finance* (Spring 1979), pp. 224–31.

Schwab, R.J., 'Contribution Approach to Transfer Pricing,' *Management Accounting* (NAA) (February 1975), pp. 46–48.

Sharav, I., 'Transfer Pricing – Diversity of Goals and Practices,' *Journal of Accountancy* (April 1974), pp. 56–62.

Shaub, H.J., 'Transfer Pricing in a Decentralized Organization,' *Management Accounting* (NAA) (April 1978), pp. 33–36.

Simon, H.A., 'Rationality as Process and as Product of Thought,' *The American Economic Review Proceedings* (May 1978), pp. 1–16.

Stern, R.D., 'Accounting for Intracompany Inventory Transfers,' *Management Accounting* (NAA) (September 1980), pp. 41–44.

Swieringa, R.J. and J.H. Waterhouse, 'Organizational Views of Transfer Pricing,' *Accounting, Organizations and Society* (1982), pp. 149–65.

Tang, R.Y.W., 'Canadian Transfer Pricing Practices,' *CA Magazine* (Can.) (March 1980), pp. 32–38.

——, *Transfer Pricing Practices in the United States and Japan* (New York: Praeger, 1979).

Tang, R.Y.W., C.K. Walter and R.H. Raymond, 'Transfer Pricing – Japanese vs. American Style,' *Management Accounting* (NAA) (January 1979), pp. 12–16.

Tewes, J.A., 'Valuing Bank Funds for Allocation and Pricing Decisions,' *Management Accounting* (NAA) (November 1976), pp. 27–33.

Thomas, A.L., *A Behavioral Analysis of Joint-Cost Allocation and Transfer Pricing*, Arthur Andersen & Co. Lecture Series – 1977, (Champaign, IL: Stipes Publishing Company, 1980).

Tyler, W.H. and R. Fridholm, 'Internal Transfer Price of Bank Funds,' *Burroughs Clearing House* (March 1975), pp. 18–19, 56, 58–59.

Vancil, R.F. *Decentralization: Management Ambiguity by Design*, (Homewood, IL: Dow Jones-Irwin, 1979).

Vroom, V.H., *Work and Motivation*, (New York: John Wiley and Sons, Inc., 1964).

Walster, E., G.W. Walster, and E. Berscheid, *Equity: Theory and Research* (Boston, MA: Allyn and Bacon, Inc., 1978).

Watson, D.J.H. and J.V. Baumler, 'Transfer Pricing: A Behavioral Context,' *The Accounting Review* (July 1975), pp. 466–74.

Weick, K.E., *The Social Psychology of Organizing* 2d ed. (Reading, MA: Addison-Wesley 1979).

——, *The Social Psychology of Organizing*, (Reading, MA: Addison-Wesley, 1969).

Weitzman, M., 'Iterative Multilevel Planning with Production Targets,' *Econometrica, Vol. 38, No. 1*, (January 1970), pp. 50–65.

Williamson, O. E., *Markets and Hierarchies: Analysis and Antitrust Implications: A Study in the Economics of Internal Organization* (New York: The Free Press, 1975).

Wraith, P., 'Taking a Bitter Medicine,' *Accountant* (January 6, 1983), pp. 16–17.

Wu, F.H. and D. Sharp, 'An Empirical Study of Transfer Pricing,' *The International Journal of Accounting Education and Research* (Spring 1979), pp. 71–99.

Young, A., 'Birch Paper Company: A Transfer Pricing Case Study' (Students' Section), *Accountant's Magazine* (Scot.) (August 1976a), pp. 308–11.

——, 'Interdivisional Transfer Pricing' (Students' Section), *Accountant's Magazine* (Scot.) (March 1976b), pp. 103–6.

ANNOTATED BIBLIOGRAPHY

1. Abdel-khalik, A. and E.J. Lusk, 'Transfer Pricing-A Synthesis,' *The Accounting Review* (January 1974), pp. 8–23.

   This is the seminal work of its time. The authors provide a thorough examination of the literature and address the behavioural economic and mathematical programming developments and limitations.

2. Ackelsberg R. and G. Yukl, 'Negotiated Transfer Pricing and Conflict Resolution in Organizations.' *Decision Sciences*, Vol. 10 (July 1979), pp. 387–398.

   The authors investigated the presence of conflict and helping induced by a negotiated transfer pricing system in a business simulation using students. The major variable investigated was whether the individuals were evaluated on divisional profit or on corporate profit. Evaluation based on corporate profit was found to generate a helping, integrative effect.

3. Bailey, R.L. and W.J. Boe, 'Goal and Resource Transfers in the Multigoal Organization.' *The Accounting Review* (July 1976), pp. 559–573.

   A brief review of the transfer pricing literature is presented. More importantly, the authors incorporated the behavioural and mathematical programming approaches in the development of a generalized goal decomposition programming methodology.

4. Benke, R.L., and J.D. Edwards, *Transfer Pricing: Techniques and Uses*. New York, NY: National Association of Accountants, 1980).

   This study was commissioned by the National Association of Accountants. The authors presented the results of interviews with personnel from 19 companies in 10 different industries as to the primary and secondary transfer pricing method employed. Both profit- and cost-based responsibility centers were examined. A general rule of setting the transfer price equal to the standard variable cost plus the lost contribution margin was developed.

5. Eccles, R.G., 'Control with Fairness in Transfer Pricing.' *Harvard Business Review* (November-December 1983), pp. 149–161.

   This research examined the impact of the firm's organizational structure on the transfer pricing method employed. Nearly 150 executives from 13 firms were interviewed. A firm was expected to belong at some point on a two-by-two matrix depending on their levels of integration and diversification. The author then postulated the appropriate transfer pricing policy that should be implemented based on a firm's relative location on the matrix.

6. Granick, D., 'National Differences in the Use of Internal Transfer Prices.' *California Management Review* (Summer 1975), pp. 28–40.

   The author reported on a series of interviews conducted with French, British, and American firms during the mid-1960s. It was determined that a difference existed in the societal expectations associated with the managerial career patterns. The author concluded that systems of transfer pricing differed within companies among industrial nations and that no single system was best under all managerial environments.

7. Swieringa, R.J. and J.H. Waterhouse, 'Organizational Views of Transfer Pricing', *Accounting, Organizations and Society* (1982), pp. 149–165.

   The implications of various models of the organization on the transfer pricing system was investigated by the authors. The importance of the perceptual frame of reference on the transfer pricing method was made salient. The authors also provided a brief review of four models of the organization.

8. Tang, Y.W., *Transfer Pricing Practices in the United States and Japan* (New York: Praeger, 1979).

   The author presents the results of a comprehensive survey that addressed the differences and similarities of transfer pricing practices in the United States and Japan. Over 130 domestic corporations took part in this survey.

9. Thomas, A.L., *A Behavioral Analysis of Joint Cost Allocation and Transfer Pricing*. Arthur Andersen & Co. Lecture Series 1977 (Champaign, IL: Stipes Publishing Company, 1980).

   This work contains two distinct parts, the first dealing with joint-cost allocations and the second with transfer pricing. The approach taken is to review the various techniques with respect to a variety of 'behaviour congruence properties.' A comparison of the various transfer pricing methods with respect to their behaviour congruence properties was also presented.

10. Vancil, R.F., *Decentralization: Management Ambiguity by Design* (Homewood, IL: Dow Jones-Irwin, 1979).

This study was commissioned by the Financial Executives Research Foundation. A total of 313 questionnaires out of 684 were returned in which 239 firms specified the transfer pricing policy employed. A wealth of information regarding the current uses of transfer prices was presented. In addition to reporting the methods employed, the author investigated the relationships between the transfer pricing method and various demographic variables.

11. Watson, D.J.H. and J.V. Baumler, 'Transfer Pricing: A Behavioral Context,' *The Accounting Review* (July 1975), pp. 466–474.

This was one of the first articles that was primarily concerned with the behavioural implications of a transfer pricing policy. The authors suggested that firms evaluate the impact of the transfer pricing system on the firm in order to enhance organizational differentiation and facilitate integration.

Appendix Listing of recent transfer pricing literature by author, topic and year

Author	Year	Analytical	Empirical	Economic	Mathematical Programming	Behavioural	Integrative	Ad Hoc
Abdel-Khalik & Lusk	1974	x		x	x	x	x	
Acklesbert & Yukl	1979		x			x		
Bailey & Boe	1976	x			x	x	x	
Benke & Caster	1983	x						x
Benke *et al.*	1982	x						x
Benke & Caster	1981	x						x
Benke & Edwards	1981	x						x
Benke & Edwards	1980		x	x		x	x	x
Blois	1978	x		x				
Buckhout	1976	x						x
Burton *et al.*	1974	x			x			
Burton & Obel	1980	x			x			
Carleton *et al.*	1974	x			x			
Choudhury	1979		x					x
Clinton	1978	x						x
Dagher	1977	x						x
Davies	1978	x		x				x

Appendix   (contd.)

Author	Year	Analytical	Empirical	Economic	Mathematical Programming	Behavioural	Integrative	Ad Hoc
Earnest	1979	x				x		x
Eccles	1983		x			x		
Edwards & Roemmich	1976	x						x
Emmanual & Gee	1982	x						x
Emmanuel	1977(a)	x						x
Emmanuel	1977(b)	x						x
Enzer	1975	x		x				
Fantl	1974	x						x
Ferguson	1981	x						x
Ferrara	1976	x						x
Finnie	1978		x					x
Flavell	1977	x		x	x	x	x	
Granick	1975		x	x		x		
Groves and Loeb	1976	x		x				
Gunn	1981	x						x
Harding & Houlden	1980	x						x
Harris et al.	1982	x			x			
Hayhurst	1976	x			x			
Hilton	1980	x						x
Hurwicz *et al.*	1975	x			x			
Ismail	1982	x			x			
Jennergren	1977	x		x				
Kanodia	1979	x		x				
Kaplan	1977	x			x			
Kornbluth	1974	x			x			
Kydland	1975	x			x			
Lambert	1979		x			x		
Larson	1974		x					x
Littrell	1980	x						x
Lococo	1983	x						x
Love	1980	x			x			x
Lucien	1979	x						x
Madison	1979	x						x
Maier & Vander Weide	1976	x			x			
Mailandt	1975	x						x
Manes & Verrecchia	1982	x						x
Martin	1981	x						x
Mayes	1982	x						x
Mednick	1979		x					x
Mctcalf	1979	x						x
Morris	1975	x			x			

Appendix (contd.)

Author	Year	Analytical	Empirical	Economic	Mathematical Programming	Behavioural	Integrative	Ad Hoc
Obel & Vander Weide	1979	x			x			
Owens	1982	x						x
Owens	1981	x						x
Ronen	1974 & 75	x		x				
Schiff	1980	x						x
Schiff	1979		x					x
Schwab	1975	x						x
Sharav	1974	x						x
Shaub	1978	x						x
Stern	1980	x						x
Swieringa & Waterhouse	1982	x				x		
Tang	1980		x					x
Tang	1979		x					x
Tang *et al.*	1979		x					x
Tewes	1976	x						x
Thomas	1980	x		x	x	x	x	
Tyler & Fridholm	1975	x						x
Vancil	1979		x			x		x
Watson & Baumler	1975	x				x		
Wraith	1983	x						x
Wu & Sharp	1979		x				x	
Young	1976(a)	x						x
	1976(b)	x						x

23

The achievability of budget targets in profit centers: a field study

Kenneth A. Merchant
Associate Professor, Harvard University Graduate School of Business Administration
and
Jean-François Manzoni
Doctoral Candidate, Harvard University Graduate School of Business Administration

ABSTRACT

This paper reports the findings of a field study aimed at providing a better understanding of how and why managers of corporations with multiple divisions set the levels of achievability of annual profit center budget targets. The data, gathered from 54 profit centers in 12 corporations, show that most budget targets are set to be achievable an average of eight or nine years out to ten. This finding contrasts with the prescription made in most management accounting textbooks suggesting that for optimum motivation budget targets should be achievable less than 50 percent of the time. Managers maintain, however, that these highly achievable targets provide considerable challenge, and the high achievability actually provides many advantages, including improved corporate reporting, resource planning, control, and, combined with other control system elements, even motivation.

Most textbooks and articles on budgeting suggest that for maximum motivation budget targets should be 'tight, but achievable.' Although agreement as to how to operationalize this phrase does not exist, most authors (e.g., Horngren and Foster [1987], Horngren and Sundem [1987], Otley [1987], Hopwood [1974], Shillinglaw [1982], and Dunbar [1971]) describe the probability of achievement of tight but achievable goals as less than 50 percent.[1] For example, Dunbar [1971] concluded that budget targets

---

[1] Anthony *et al.* [1985] and Welsch *et al.* [1988] are in the minority in recommending the probability of achievement as 50 percent or even higher.

Source: Merchant, K.A. and Manzoni, J.-F. (1989) *The Accounting Review*, **LXIV** (3), pp. 539–58.

should be set so that they are achievable between 25 percent and 40 percent of the time, and Otley [1987, pp. 44–45] notes that, 'The budget level which motivates the best performance is one that is somewhat more demanding than the level of performance that will actually be achieved.'

In the early stages of a field study focused broadly on control of profit centers (PCs) in corporations with multiple divisions, we observed that the typical level of profit center budget achievability was considerably higher than 50 percent. We found that corporate managers espouse a 'tight but achievable' budgeting philosophy, but they implement it so that profit center managers *expect to* and *actually do* achieve their budget targets almost every year. This apparent conflict with predominant textbook theory suggested the need for further exploration of the issue.

This paper describes the study, reports data on the achievability of budget targets in 54 PCs in 12 corporations, and examines the rationales underlying managers' budget target choices. It describes the differences between theory and practice and discusses the causes of these differences.

BACKGROUND

Textbook prescriptions to set budget targets with less than a 50 percent chance of achievement are supported by evidence provided in the psychology literature showing a negative relation between target achievability and performance. That is, less achievable (more challenging) performance targets lead to higher motivation and performance.[2] For example, in a review of more than 100 laboratory and field experiments in the psychology literature, Locke *et al.* [1981, p. 131] conclude that the consistent finding is that 'specific hard goals [induce] better performance than do-your-best or no goals.' They also conclude that 'the beneficial effect of goal setting on task performance is one of the most robust and replicable findings in the psychological literature' [p. 145]. Similarly, Latham and Lee [1986, p. 105] concur that 'the results are overwhelming in both laboratory and field settings.'

Most experimental studies published in the accounting literature also show that less achievable targets lead to higher performance [Stedry, 1960; Stedry and Kay, 1966; Rockness, 1977; and Chow, 1983]. In Stedry and Kay's [1966] field experiment, for example, less achievable goals (previously attained only 25 percent of the time) led to good performance when the subjects perceived the goals as challenging and raised their 'level of aspiration' to try to achieve them. Their findings, however, also

---

[2] In this paper, we refer to the achievability of budget targets, whereas most prior research refers to the difficulty of budget targets or goals. In laboratory or field experiments, the notion of difficulty is usually operationalized by using an objective probability of achievement (e.g., how often a particular objective is achieved in a trial run). Given this operationalization of difficulty, the concepts of achievability and difficulty are exact opposites. The term 'achievability' is used here because it best expresses the preoccupations of the managers (corporate as well as profit center) interviewed.

point to one of the limits to the generalizability of the achievability/
performance relationship: Less achievable goals led to poor performance
when the subjects were not committed to achieve the goals because they
perceived them as unattainable. This commitment constraint has been
repeatedly replicated (see Locke *et al.* [1988] for a review). Evidence also
exists, however, that other contextual factors (e.g., incentives) can correct or compensate for a lack of commitment, but to date 'not enough is
known about the relative importance of the various determinants of goal
commitment to permit meaningful predictions of their effects on commitment when there are conflicting elements' [Locke *et al.*, 1988, p. 34].

Other contextual limits on the achievability/performance relation have
also been shown or suggested. Garland [1984] concluded that the relation is more likely to hold in experimental settings characterized by tasks
of relatively short duration, where ability does not account for most of
the performance variance, and where feedback is immediate but no external rewards are provided. Huber [1985] found that the achievability/
performance relation reversed in a setting characterized by uncertainty
and complexity. Hollenbeck and Klein [1987] suggested that goal commitment is low under conditions where exogenous factors exert a high
influence on the outcome because failure to achieve the goal can be easily
attributed to those factors. Finally, Chow [1983] and Mowen *et al.* [1981]
suggest that the relation between achievability and performance is contingent on the financial incentives associated with performance; they
report a negative relation under a piece-rate pay plan but not under an
all-or-nothing bonus system.

These findings are significant because PC managers typically operate
under conditions of high uncertainty and high complexity, and their performance measures *are* affected by many exogenous factors.[3] They also
face reward systems with both piece-rate and all-or-nothing characteristics. Thus, it must be concluded that the research literature does not
support any clear prescription for budget target-setting in profit centers
except to avoid targets that lose their motivational appeal because the
managers perceive them as unattainable.

No specific evidence exists about the actual levels of budget target
achievability at PC levels within corporations. Most field-based studies
of budget targets (e.g., Otley [1985], Cress and Pettijohn [1985], Kenis
[1979], and Hofstede [1968]) have focused on cost center managers and
measured achievability using ambiguous verbal scales.[4] For example,
Umapathy [1987] reported the following distribution of budget targets

---

[3] Hirst [1987] developed a theoretical argument suggesting that budget achievability should be high (low) where budget targets are important and task uncertainty is high (low).
[4] PC budgets may be quite different from cost center budgets for any of the following reasons. (1) PC managers are not as buffered from the external environment as
are cost center managers (particularly those in production areas). The resulting
higher uncertainty in planning may lead them, for example, to incorporate more
slack in their budgets. (2) PC managers can make more tradeoffs (e.g., reducing

from a survey of 402 firms in a variety of manufacturing and service industries:[5]

Descriptor	n	(%)
Almost impossible	28	(7)
Challenging	201	(52)
Slightly beyond our reach	72	(19)
Just right	64	(16)
Relatively easy	24	(6)

These data appear to show that budget targets are on the challenging side of a 'best guess,' but the achievability levels are not specific and the ordering of the verbal scale may be unreliable as it implies that 'challenging' is less achievable than 'slightly beyond our reach.' These meanings differ from those attached to the terms by the managers we interviewed, many of whom described their budgets as challenging even though they were confident they would achieve them.

Verbal-scale, field-based studies have consistently shown that considerable variation exists in the levels of budget-target achievability, but only a small amount of evidence exists to explain this variation. Simons [1988] found budget tightness to be positively associated with the use of monitoring and reporting controls and formula-based remuneration. He also reported a relation between strategy and budget-target achievability: budget targets of 'defenders' were on average more achievable than those of 'prospectors.' Several studies [Lukka, 1988; Merchant, 1985a; and Onsi, 1973] found uncertainty, information asymmetry, and profitability to be positively associated with the creation of budgetary slack which, in turn, was related to budget-target achievability.

Several theoretical papers add still another complication that may occur. These papers [Barrett and Fraser, 1977; Hopwood, 1974; and Stedry, 1960] point out that no one single target can serve all budget purposes (e.g., planning, motivating, evaluating) optimally. The authors suggest that for motivational purposes the target should be challenging, whereas for planning purposes, budgets are most useful if they 'reflect management's best estimates of revenues and expenses . . . what is most probable' [Barrett and Fraser, 1977, p. 141].

As one possible solution to the conflicts among budget purposes, Hopwood notes the possibility of a 'bottom drawer phenomenon' in which

---

price to make a sale, cutting advertising to boost current period income) to achieve their budget targets. This additional flexibility may mean that profit targets are achievable even if some portions of the budget forecast (e.g., revenue) are inaccurate. (3) PC managers are more likely to experience a direct link between reaching budget targets and receiving significant rewards linked directly to budget accomplishment. For these managers, therefore, the stakes are higher. Risk aversion may lead them toward defensive routines, such as the creation of budgetary slack.

[5] Only 389 firms responded to this question.

upper-level managers use budgets for motivational purposes while keeping another, realistic set of numbers for planning and decision making purposes in the bottom drawer of their desks. Otley [1982] speculated that most firms use one form or another of this method. But Umapathy's [1987] survey found that only seven percent of corporations actually use more than one budget. This finding suggests that firms make compromises in the uses of their budgets, that they have other ways of solving the conflict between motivation and planning, or that the survey respondents were not aware of the alternate budgets some managers may have had in their desk drawers.

RESEARCH METHOD

Three research questions were used to guide the exploration of budget-achievability issues. The first is suggested by the theoretical writings describing the advantages of having multiple budget targets to serve multiple budget purposes:

Research Question 1:
Do PCs have multiple budget targets?

The second question asks whether the finding showing budget targets as slightly more challenging than a best guess, on average, can be generalized to PC organization levels.

Research Question 2:
How achievable are PC budget targets?

The third motivates an exploration of managers' rationales for choosing their level(s) of budget-target achievability.

Research Question 3:
Why are PC budget targets set at the level(s) they are?

Sample selection

The study was conducted in a diverse set of 12 corporations to increase possible generalizability of findings. The firms were in different industries and ranged in size from $40 million to $8 billion in annual sales (median = $2.6 billion). They exhibited wide variations on a number of characteristics, including the following: service versus manufacturing industries, rapid growth versus stability, capital-versus labor-intensive production processes, high- versus low-technology products, customer base (government versus commercial, consumer versus industrial marketing), and degree of diversification.

In each firm, initial interviews were conducted with corporate-level managers, including the chief financial officer and/or controller, top-level general managers (chairman, president, chief executive officer, chief operating officer), staff officers (vice president, administration; vice president, planning; treasurer), and other financial staff (assistant controller, director of internal audit). These interviews were used to gather information on the firm's businesses, its organization, its current business situation, and its control systems, including planning, budgeting, measurement, and incentive compensation, as applied to PCs within the firm.

Interviews were then conducted within a small number (from two to six) of PCs in each firm and at the organization level of the PC managers' immediate superiors. The PCs were selected (in discussions between the authors and corporate managers) to provide a cross-section of those in the corporation. The only constraint imposed was that the interviews be conducted within North America. In each of the 54 PCs selected for study, the PC manager was interviewed and, where possible, his or her immediate superior and the controllers reporting both to the PC manager and the superior were also interviewed. Typically, the PC manager interviews were two hours in length and the other interviews were one hour.

In sum, 203 individuals were interviewed for a total of 312 meeting hours. Two interviewers were present at most of the meetings. To enhance the consistency of the investigations, the principal author participated in all but three of the interviews.

Measures

Budget-target achievability was measured from both an *ex ante* and *ex post* standpoint. The *ex ante* measure was a subjective probability estimate of achievability gathered from multiple respondents including the PC managers and, where possible, immediate superiors and controllers at both organization levels.[6] Each manager was asked the following question:

At the time your profit budget for this year was approved, what did you feel the probability was that it would at least be achieved?

To improve the reliability of these responses, we asked the question in several ways using Chesley's [1975] suggestions for eliciting subjective probabilities.[7]

The *ex post* measure of budget achievability was in the form of information on the PCs' past- and current-year performances as compared with budget targets. These data were not available for the whole sample,

[6] Inclusion in the sample of the incumbents of identical positions in each profit center increases the representativeness and standardization of the data. Use of multiple informants in semistructured interviews increases the validity of the data [Seidler, 1974, pp. 816–820].

[7] For example, if the interviewee responded that the subjective probability of achieving the budget was 90 percent, we sometimes asked if this figure meant that the budget was relatively easy to make, or if it meant that there was a 10 percent probability of something going wrong. These questions often made the interviewees think more deeply about their responses. On no occasion, however, did it cause any of the respondents to alter their initial estimates.

but the existing data provide some validation of the managers' estimates and comments.[8]

Finally, to test whether the data were consistent with the corporations' budget-target philosophies, a questionnaire was sent to the most senior financial executive (generally the CFO) with whom we had contact in each firm. One of the questionnaire items asked respondents to rate their extent of agreement, on a scale from one (strongly disagree) to five (strongly agree), with the following statement:

Annual profit budgets are commitments from our general managers to the corporation. They are expected to make their targets.

CFOs (or their equivalent) in 11 of the 12 corporations responded.

FINDINGS

Number of budget targets

Research question 1 motivated the exploration of whether PCs have more than one budget target. In each of the 12 corporations, a single detailed budget is prepared, although one corporation does a small amount of contingency budgeting, one uses a form of flexible budgeting to supplement its static budgets, and one uses tacit corporate-level reserves to protect against possible optimism in the PC budgets ('bottom-drawer phenomenon'). Most of the corporations, however, do identify more than one financial target within the framework of an annual bonus plan. Nine identify a threshold level of performance; if actual profit performance falls below this level, PC managers are paid no bonuses and in some cases they are warned that their jobs are in jeopardy.

Nine of the corporations (not the same nine) identify a maximum performance level that is associated with the maximum bonus. In only one corporation is the maximum performance level equal to the budget level (and in this corporation, the condition exists for only about half of its PCs). Thus, in 11 of the 12 firms, PC managers are paid extra bonuses for exceeding budget levels of performance.

Distribution of budget-target achievability

The budget-target achievability finding contrasts sharply with the findings of the existing descriptive surveys. A large majority of the PC managers interviewed estimated high probabilities of achieving their budget

---

[8] The historical data set is incomplete for two basic reasons. First, in the corporations studied early, we neglected to ask for the data because we had not yet identified their value. Second, in some situations we judged that the data were not indicative of the current situation because the organization structure or the PC manager had changed.

targets, and they reported that, historically, they have achieved their targets much more often than not.

Table 23.1 shows the *ex ante* subjective probabilities of budget-target achievement. Of the 45 PC managers responding to the subjective probability question, 39 (87 percent) reported a probability greater than or equal to 75 percent.[9] Even more striking, 24 (53 percent) reported a probability of 90 percent or greater, while only 3 (7 percent) felt they had less than a 50 percent chance of achieving their target. The median response was 90 percent; the mean was 83 percent.

The historical data support the managers' subjective estimates of success. Data were collected on the budget-target achievement of 39 of the 54 PCs for the year completed before the interview. Of these, 29 (74 percent) achieved or exceeded their budget targets. In addition, 21 PC managers gave their latest estimates of budget achievement in the current fiscal year (on average half completed); 18 (86 percent) reported they were confident they would achieve their budget targets.[10]

The high probabilities of achievement are probably not specific to the interview year. Many managers spoke proudly of their ongoing streak of achieving their budget targets, including one who reported never missing a budget in his 33 years as a manager. Also, the controller of one firm provided five-year histories of the budget performance of three of the PCs included in the sample.[11] He reported that these PCs achieved their profit targets in 12 of the 15 profit-center-years. Furthermore, because the over-achievements were considerably larger than the misses, the average actual profit performance for those years exceeded the budget targets by 39.5 percent. Finally, the questionnaire responses show a corporate budget philosophy consistent with high budget achievability. All 11 respondents agreed with the statement that profit budgets are commitments from the PC managers to the corporation; of these 11, three agreed 'strongly.'

Thus, the available evidence suggests that a large majority of PC budget targets are highly achievable. It is tempting to call these budgets 'easy,' but almost all the PC managers interviewed objected to this term. As one manager put it:

[9] This data set is also incomplete for two basic reasons. First, some interviews were not possible because the role did not exist (particularly PC controller), the role was not filled, the person in the role was too new or otherwise not knowledgeable about the relevant questions (not part of the management team), or scheduling could not be arranged. Second, some individuals did not answer the question about budget-target achievability either because they were not asked (they were interviewed before achievability had been identified as a focal issue) or because they were unable or unwilling to put a probabilistic estimate on the likelihood of achievement.

[10] This data set is incomplete for the same reasons as for Table 23.1. In addition, data on the current, revised estimates of budget-target achievement were not collected when the interviews occurred early in the fiscal year.

[11] The fourth (PC 3) was part of a division that was being divested (for lack of strategic fit, not poor performance), and historical records were not easily accessible.

Table 23.1 Subjective probability of budget-target achievement at time of budget approval

Entity		Probability Estimates			
Corporation	Profit Center	Profit Center Level		Level of Immediate Superior	
		General Manager	Controller	General Manager	Controller
A	1	90%	85%	b¹	b
(Diversified luxury goods)	2	0	40	b	b
	3	80	95	90%	100%
	4	75	–	78	–
	5	80	–	b	–
B	1	88	a	50	a
(Electronic equipment)	2	90	70	a	50
	3	23	a	30	a
C	1	100	100	a	a
(Distribution)	2	90	b	a	a
	3	90	90	a	a
	4	90	a	75	70
	5	75	–	75	b
	6	60	–	75	b
D	1	100	b	78	a
(Diversified industrial products)	2	90	b	55	a
	3	b	80	a	a
	4	99	b	a	a

E	(Diversified chemicals)				
	1	30	38	10	a
	2	75	50	50	a
	3	b	a	a	a
	4	85	–	a	50
	5	73	50	a	–
	6	b	a	a	a
F	(Hospitality)				
	1	b	–	95	–
	2	90	–	90	–
	3	95	–	95	–
	4	b	–	80	–
	5	100	–	100	–
	6	b	–	a	–
G	(Electrical connectors)				
	1	90	a	100	100
	2	80	a	100	70
	3	97	b	100	100
	4	63	a	100	90
H	(High technology)				
	1	b	b	b	–
	2	100	–	b	a
	3	b	–	b	a
	4	90	a	a	–
	5	99	b	a	–
J	(Consumer products)				
	1	93	b	a	b
	2	95	b	b	b
	3	100	99	b	b
	4	95	a	99	70
	5	80	80	a	80

Table 23.1 (contd.)

Entity		Probability Estimates			
		Profit Center Level		Level of Immediate Superior	
Corporation	Profit Center	General Manager	Controller	General Manager	Controller
K	1	83%	90%	a	80%
(Electronic systems)	2	75	–	a	80
	3	b	–	b	75
L	1	90	78	b	a
(Specialty chemicals)	2	85	>50	b	a
	3	100	80	b	a
	4	100	–	100	b
	5	80	–	a	a
M	1	80	80	80	b
(Consumer durables)	2	80	b	a	a

[1] Symbols:
– position does not exist
a. was not interviewed
b. did not answer question

We have to work very hard to make it happen. . . . Each day is a struggle for us. . . . It's not like we're coasting.

After hearing the managers talk about the highly achievable budget targets, we conclude that these targets can best be described as *challenging, but very likely to be achieved by the PC management team if they exert a consistently high level of effort.* This meaning is attached to the expression 'highly achievable budget target' throughout the remainder of the paper.

In other terms, highly achievable budget targets assume that managers will work as hard as they can but *protect them to some extent against possible negative exogenous influences.* This interpretation is consistent with a 'tight, but attainable' budgeting philosophy, which is espoused by both PC and corporate managers. A key difference between the managers' philosophy and textbook writings, however, is that the managers' budgets are not missed more than, or anywhere near 50 percent of the time, nor do 'many managers . . . fail to meet [them] by a small margin,' as Otley [1982, p. 39] suggested. The reasons for this key difference are described in the following sections.

Factors affecting budget-target achievability

Highly achievable budget targets are consistent with the theory that PC managers create high amounts of budgetary slack that go undetected by top management. Our findings suggest, however, that the PC managers' superiors are generally aware of the high achievability of the PC budget targets. The Table 23.1 data show that the superiors' budget achievability estimates are not systematically different from those of the PC managers. For the 21 PCs for which both estimates are available, the mean probability is 80 percent for the PC managers and 78 percent for their superiors.

These data and the understanding obtained during the interviews led to the conclusion that the primary parties involved in the target-setting processes – PC managers and top management – typically have incentives to establish highly achievable PC budget targets. Budget-target setting is best described as a bargaining process between parties whose incentives are, in the vast majority of cases, well aligned.

INCENTIVES TO NEGOTIATE FOR HIGHLY ACHIEVABLE BUDGET TARGETS

PC managers' incentives

1. *Increase expected bonuses.* Nine of the corporations' bonus contracts (or plans) explicitly state that PC managers start earning bonuses at a lower bound that is either equal to or a function of the budget target. Furthermore, in these and two other firms, the size of the bonus is influenced by whether budget targets are met. Thus, other things equal, managers in 11 of the 12 corporations can increase the expected values of their bonuses by negotiating a lower budget target.

2. *Protect management credibility and antonomy.* Managers in all 12 corporations are subjected to top-down pressure to meet the budget target. Managers who miss targets suffer credibility losses that harm promotion possibilities, chances for good salary increases, and ability to sell their ideas and to have resources allocated to their PCs. Furthermore, top management is more likely to intervene in the management of PCs that are under their budget targets. Thus, the PC managers risk losing some of their operating autonomy if they fail to meet their targets.[12]

3. *Increase chances of 'winning.'* Most PC managers have strong desires to make their budget targets because they equate achieving budget targets with 'winning.' 'If I were to miss my budget,' said one manager, 'I would feel like a failure. When I exceed my budget, I feel proud.' The general feeling that managers want to feel like winners and 'winners are people who make their targets' provides a strong incentive for PC managers to negotiate budget targets that are likely to be achieved.[13]

4. *Increase operating flexibility.* Many of the PC managers admitted that they biased their budget profit submissions downward not only to increase the likelihood of achieving budget targets, but also to build in some slack resources to increase their operating flexibility. This flexibility reduces the need to react to every short-term contingency with sometimes extreme and costly actions such as layoffs, and it allows them to make some discretionary investments without having to request either corporate approval or budget renegotiation.

5. *Protect against inducements to overconsume resources.* Almost all PC managers face the four preceding incentives to negotiate lower, more achievable budget targets. Some mentioned a fifth incentive, a desire to avoid optimistic budgets with high forecasts of sales and profits that they consider dangerous for resource planning purposes. They felt that budgets with optimistic profit forecasts provide a sense that extra expense can be afforded. For example, managers may staff for expected high activity levels that may not be forthcoming and it is costly to eliminate unneeded resources.

Top management's incentives

One might expect that top management, knowing that PC managers have incentives to negotiate highly achievable targets, would try to exert an upward pressure on the targets. We found, however, that top-level managers also have significant incentives to allow highly achievable budget

---

[12] Thus, while bonus plans are bounded piece-rate plans, the organizational penalties associated with missing budget confer to the reward system some all-or-nothing properties.

[13] This finding is consistent with that of Maccoby [1976] who found that many modern managers, whom he called 'gamesmen,' are interested in proving themselves as 'winners.' But they also tend to be worriers, 'constantly on the lookout for something that might go wrong' [p. 49]. Both traits would lead the managers to negotiate for achievable (even conservative) budget targets.

targets in the PCs for which they are responsible. They reported a tendency to accept PC manager's conservative budget submissions with, perhaps, minor upward modifications, and sometimes they actually lower targets that they feel are optimistic. They reported any of seven incentives for doing so:

1. *Increase predictability of corporate earnings.* Some corporate managers treat budget targets as PC managers' commitments to the corporation to increase the predictability of corporate earnings. The philosophy that the budget is a commitment provides top management with some peace of mind. The consolidated PC budgets represent a highly probable lower bound of the annual corporate profit.

2. *Protect against overconsumption of resources.* Corporate managers share PC managers' concern about the tendency of optimistic plans to induce overconsumption of resources. In the words of one corporate president:

I think we ought to have a semiaggressive plan, but one that is achievable. We want to make it every year. It's too hard to adjust on the downside, to slough off commitments of expenses, or not launch something you have a psychological commitment to.

3. *Reduce risk of lack of goal commitment.* Most corporate managers recognize the importance of PC managers being committed to their budget targets throughout the year. Lack of commitment leads to reduced motivation and an inclination to position their PC for the following accounting periods by loading expenses into the current period.

Loss of target commitment during the year is most likely where PCs are affected by large, unforeseen influences that adversely affect their earnings (e.g., recession, price war). As the vice president–finance of one corporation expressed it:

You want [a budget target] that is achievable but that does not require a superhuman effort to make it. . . . The probability of success when the budget is approved should be between 75 percent and 90 percent. A 50 percent probability is inadequate because the first negative incident can make people give up.

Corporate managers can protect against the loss of commitment by agreeing to adjust the budget targets (or actual performance) *ex post* for the effects of these influences. Managers in the vast majority of the firms are reluctant to make these adjustments, however, because:

1. Such adjustments almost invariably require subjectivity evaluations. Most PC managers do not like subjectivity in performance evaluations because they fear biases and favoritism.
2. PC managers can spend considerable time trying to influence their bosses' decisions as to what needs to be adjusted, at the expense of effectively managing their units.

Highly achievable budget targets essentially incorporate an *ex ante* allowance for the unforeseen, negative influences and thus decrease the risk that PC managers must bear. Even though the targets do not require maximum effort to be achieved, most corporate executives and PC managers interviewed expressed more concern about PC personnel giving up than about their 'coasting.'

4. *Reduce need for control analyses/interventions.* In most corporations, budgets are used to implement a management-by-exception philosophy; negative variances from budget signal the need for intervention, or at least investigation. Highly achievable budget targets make negative variances relatively rare and top management attention is directed to the few situations in which problems are most likely and most acute.

5. *Allocate discretion to effective managers.* Highly achievable budget targets are consistent with the theory that PC managers create large budgetary slack. The interview data suggest that budgetary slack is indeed common. Top management allows slack both to reward good performance and to allow the PCs increased operating discretion, hoping to stimulate creative thinking. The PC managers in this study enjoying the largest amounts of budgetary flexibility are long-time employees of their firms who have demonstrated their effectiveness over an extended period. Top management apparently trusts these managers to make good judgments about consuming the slack and relies on them to continue working hard.[14]

6. *Reduce incentives to engage in harmful earnings management practices.* Short-term 'earnings management' is one means available to most PC managers for achieving their budget targets. It includes taking potentially risky operating actions (e.g., delaying preventive maintenance) and engaging in deceptive accounting practices (e.g., manipulating reserves). A large majority of the managers interviewed described ways that they could manage earnings if the need arose. Moreover, most of them believed that should they do so, they could conceal their actions (up to a point) from their superiors, the corporate finance organization, and auditors.

The danger of earnings management varies across corporations and across PCs within corporations. Some PC managers have greater abilities to manage earnings because, for example, they can move sales and discretionary expenses between accounting periods. In addition, some corporations have a greater ability than others to control these actions because they have a strong internal audit function or solid line reporting of PC controllers into the finance organization. Among top-level managers, however, the concern that too much earnings pressure could trigger these manipulative short-term behaviours is pervasive.

7. *Ensure a competitive compensation package.* In two of the corpora-

---

[14] This is consistent with Holmstrom's [1979] conclusion that long-term employment relations contribute to alleviating the moral hazard problem. It is also consistent with the possibility that these managers have accumulated more power in the organization and use this power to enhance their bargaining position. For a

tions, top management allowed all or some PC managers to have highly achievable budget targets to ensure that some performance-dependent bonuses would be earned in order to provide the managers with a competitive compensation package. The need for almost-guaranteed bonuses arose because in both cases top management had frozen salaries during difficult operating times. When the freeze was removed, salaries were below competitive levels, but top management was reluctant to increase the corporation's fixed costs sharply through an immediate boost of salaries. Instead, both corporations began using variable compensation (bonuses) to make the managers' total compensation packages competitive with industry and local averages.

The influence of compensation practices on budget-target achievability may be greater when compensation consultants are involved. Members of two major compensation consulting firms told us that consultants generally design compensation packages assuming payment of a 'target bonus' which most firms choose to calibrate based on achievement of budget targets. This method of calibration creates organizational pressures to set budget targets that will be achieved most of the time because achievement is necessary for compensation to reach competitive levels.

BUDGET ACHIEVABILITY AS A PART OF THE CONTROL SYSTEM

The preceding discussion described one purpose of highly achievable budget targets as protecting PC managers against some of the downside risk of exogenous factors. Baiman [1982] suggested that when rewards are contingent on performance, tradeoffs have to be made between the motivational properties of the reward structure and the risk that managers have to bear and highly achievable budget targets may be the outcome of such a tradeoff.

This tradeoff view, however, implies that some motivation is lost when highly achievable budget targets are set. This conclusion may not be correct. Allowing hard working managers to 'win' nearly every year seems to have positive motivational effects by preserving an upbeat emotional spirit and, thereby, inducing managers to raise their aspirations level for the following year.[15] Managers who feel good about themselves and their organizations seem to be more likely to be highly energized and willing to take prudent risks.

It remains possible that highly achievable budget targets can lose most of their motivational properties if, *during a year*, the exogenous factors unfold to make achievement of the budget nearly certain. However, virtually

discussion of how managers accumulate and use organizational power, see Kanter [1977].

[15] There is a large body of evidence on the level of aspiration and how aspiration increases following feelings of success (see Lewin *et al.* [1944] and Bandura and Cervone [1983]). Also, Hollenbeck and Williams [1987] and Locke *et al.* [1984] provide evidence that past performance is a major determinant of the goal level chosen.

all the managers interviewed stated the belief that their corporation's management systems have been structured to give PC managers reasons to strive for (and produce) earnings in excess of their budget targets. Almost all PC managers are promised substantial extra bonuses for performance exceeding budget. They are also given other incentives, including the recognition associated with high performers, credibility leading to increased command over resources, and increased prospects for advancement. Furthermore, some PC managers are given little choice but to produce earnings in excess of their budget targets because it is not uncommon for top management to call PC managers during the year and ask them to 'turn in more' profit than originally budgeted. These requests are apparently often made to offset below-budget performances of other PCs, but they also serve to provide challenge for PCs that have enjoyed some good fortune.[16]

LESS ACHIEVABLE BUDGET TARGETS

Despite incentives inducing both PC managers and top management to establish highly achievable budget targets, for a few situations managers described the probability of achievement of their budget targets as low (0–30 percent). PC managers facing these less achievable budget targets reported that the targets did not induce them to work more hours (they were already working hard), but they said the targets did change their attitudes toward costs and, thereby, led to increased reported profits in the short term. These managers took painful actions, such as reducing discretionary expenditures and effecting layoffs. They were not sure whether these actions would have irreparable, long-term consequences.[17] These managers reported a personal commitment to try to achieve these targets and expressed no despair or discouragement. None of these managers, however, had missed budget targets for more than two years in a row.

The forces behind less achievable budget targets can come from either corporate management or PC management and are described below.

Corporate managers' motives for requiring less achievable budget targets

1. *Corporate desire for immediate profit.* When corporate managers perceive an urgent need for short-term earnings, they may feel that the ben-

[16] When top management issues such an order, it modifies the structure of the rewards associated with budget-target achievement by increasing the value of the dollars delivered today. The PC managers can enhance their reputations of reliability and competence by delivering what is required, thus building some organizational power [Kanter, 1977]. The sword is double-edged, however, as they can also create or enhance their reputations as sand-baggers.

[17] Several managers explained that decisions based on *quarterly* budgets often had detrimental effects. For example, for one corporation K group, repeated end-of-quarter discounting had led to a situation in which 85 percent of the quarterly sales were recorded in the quarter's last month. This group was having difficulty breaking this costly pattern.

efits of less achievable budget targets outweigh the associated costs and risks. The perceived urgency may occur for any number of reasons, such as the desire to signal stability to customers or creditors or the desire to boost stock price to dissuade a takeover. In these situations, top-level managers tend to rely most heavily on relatively large PCs for the additional profits. Small PCs often escape unscathed because even a sharp increase in their budget targets will not greatly increase corporate profit.

2. *Desire to signal that short-term profit is the PC's priority.* Even when corporate profit is not an immediate concern, top management may require aggressive budget targets to signal to PC managers that short-term profit is a now priority (e.g., to reflect transition from development to an emphasis on profitability). A less achievable budget target provides a signal that the PC's mission has changed, thus reinforcing strategy discussions, and limits the PC managers' discretion. Harmful myopic actions (e.g., cutting of crucial developmental expenditures) are not a problem because cost-cutting is the mandated corporate objective.

3. *Dissatisfaction with a PC's performance.* When top-level managers feel that the performance of particular PC managers (or management teams) has been weak, or when they suspect 'organizational fat,' they sometimes impose a budget target to which the profit center managers attach a low probability of achievement. This action has three purposes. First, it provides a signal to the managers that performance improvements are expected. Signalling through the budget is powerful because the many rewards and punishments that are linked with achieving budget targets ensure that the message will be received. Second, it reduces the discretion of managers whose performances are judged unsatisfactory. Third, it sets up a clear rationale for relieving the managers of their jobs. In these situations the risk of harming the long-term health of the business through cost-cutting is small; the managers will first respond by eliminating or reducing inefficiencies, before they cut useful investments. Furthermore, hurting the feelings of poor performing PC managers is not a major top management concern.

4. *Desire to make interyear adjustments for managers' good luck in prior year(s).* As discussed earlier, most managers are reluctant to adjust budgets *ex post.* They also have difficulty equalizing budget achievability across divisions *ex ante.* Although most corporate and group managers agreed that they would like to equalize budget difficulty, the pervasive feeling was that doing so was impossible. In an attempt to be fair to PC managers, some corporate and group executives make interyear adjustments by requiring less achievable budget targets (or by accepting easily achievable targets) depending on whether the managers have been lucky (or unlucky) in the past year(s).

PC managers' motives for submitting less achievable budget targets

PC managers can also provide the impetus for less achievable budget targets because they sometimes have incentives to submit optimistic (less achievable) budgets. This planning bias, which Lowe and Shaw [1968] term 'negative slack,' was observed in several corporations where it was caused by any of four different motivations.

1. *Improve ability to compete for organizational resources*. Budgets are part of the bargaining process in which managers compete for organizational resources [Hopwood, 1974, p. 42]. To obtain funds, requests must be supported by acceptable and credible returns on the proposed investments.

2. *Signal managerial ability*. Negotiating budget targets almost always involves a series of meetings with managers from multiple organizational levels. These meetings provide PC managers opportunities to signal to higher-level managers their initiative, energy, creativity, and qualification for higher duties. These signals are often undercut when the managers attempt to negotiate for conservative budgets.

3. *Survive*. PCs that are performing well can secure organizational resources and signal managerial competence by *delivering results* (i.e., exceeding budget) instead of by *promising* those results. Bad performers, however, do not have track records that generate confidence. Accordingly, they submit optimistic budgets on their own, knowing that if they fail to achieve the higher, less achievable level of performance, they will probably lose their jobs anyway.[18]

4. *Enhance personal challenge*. Most PC managers have risen through the management ranks because they are high achievers with strong internal drives. Such individuals have a tendency to budget optimistically because, as one manager expressed it, 'Achievers set difficult goals for themselves.' Without challenging goals to strive for, their sense of arousal and competition is reduced.[19]

The strength of this desire for a challenge varies significantly across individuals. Most of the top executives felt that managers with sales or marketing backgrounds are more likely, on average, than those with other functional backgrounds to submit budgets with aggressive (less achievable) targets.

Since top management generally has incentives to establish highly achievable PC budget targets, the question is raised as to why top-level managers would accept optimistic budgets from PC managers. Three answers are conceivable: (1) top-level managers are unable to detect the optimism, (2) they are reluctant to remove it, or (3) they value it. We found no significant examples of an inability (or, at least, the perception of an inability) to detect optimism in budget plans. Most corporate managers avowed that they could detect optimism (or lack of realism) and that they generally chose to remove such biases from the budgets. We found a few situations where PC managers, in their role as superiors, were reluctant to remove the optimistic budget-target biases for reasons that included either 'not wanting to destroy the manager's enthusiasm'

---

[18] This is a form of bonding expenditure (see Jensen and Meckling [1976]).
[19] This is consistent with experimental evidence showing that individuals with a high need for achievement set higher goals for themselves [Matsui *et al.* 1982].

or the desire to 'hang them with their own numbers to teach them a lesson.' And, as was described earlier, we found a few situations where top-level managers value optimism. Where they exist, PC managers' optimistic biases give superiors the option of accepting budget targets that are not likely to be achieved, but we found few examples where executives chose to exercise that option.

CONCLUSION

In this study, we found evidence that the vast majority of PC budgets investigated are challenging, but through the management team's consistent effort, very likely to be achieved. This finding was surprising insofar as it seemed inconsistent with conventional wisdom that suggests that for optimum motivation budget targets should be missed more often than they are achieved.

The finding was explored through indepth interviews and the incentives of the primary negotiating parties – top management and PC management – were analyzed. Our explanations highlight the somewhat surprising finding that these parties' incentives are fairly well aligned, except in a few specific circumstances, and that they lead to the setting of highly achievable PC budget targets.

To summarize our explanations, PC managers want to be sure they will make their budget targets to build their management credibility, to enhance their bonuses, to give themselves some operating flexibility, and to give themselves and those in their organizations the motivational boost provided by a winning feeling. PC managers are ready to accept goals that require their working hard, but they want to be protected somewhat from the adverse impacts of exogenous factors. Corporate managers allow the PC managers to have achievable budget targets because these targets increase the predictability of corporate earnings, reduce the time spent on control analyses and interventions, and reduce the risk that the PC managers will either lose goal commitment or engage in earnings management. Some top-level managers also use highly achievable budget targets to allocate discretion to effective managers and to ensure a competitive compensation package. And both PC managers and their superiors see a need for achievable, slightly conservative budget targets to protect against inducements to over consume resources. These explanations provide the start of a predictive theory of budget achievability at PC levels in firms with multiple divisions.

The discrepancy between textbook theory and practice as we observed seems to stem from the fact that budgeting is not a system in itself, but rather is a *part of* the control system [Flamholtz, 1983]. Goal achievability *cannot* be separated from issues of compensation, design of the reward function, role of accounting measures in performance evaluation and reward, and organizational structure. Although textbooks do not argue that budgeting stands on its own, they often present only one possible design alternative and fail to highlight the complementary and compensating relationships among the various control system elements.[20]

Corporate conditions at PC organization levels are often quite different from those described in textbooks in two critically important ways. First, PC managers are held accountable for many factors over which they have little, or even no, control because it is often extremely difficult to separate the endogenous and exogenous performance factors. Corporations are generally unable to implement flexible budgets or explicit forms of variance analyses related to specific factors (e.g., see Merchant [1987]). Thus, any adjustments for uncontrollable factors are bound to involve subjectivity, and most managers interviewed (subordinates as well as superiors) expressed a strong dislike for allowing significant amounts of subjectivity to enter into performance evaluations.[21]

And second, highly achievable budget targets often have practical advantages that can more than offset whatever motivational deterioration they may cause. The achievable targets can improve corporate financial reporting, resource planning, control, and in some situations, compensation.

LIMITATIONS

The findings presented in this paper must be described as tentative. This study did not build on the findings of prior studies because very little prior evidence existed either about managers' choices of levels of profit center budget achievability or about the factors that influence those choices. The study also has several significant limitations.

The corporate sample is one limitation. The 12 corporations studied obviously do not span all industries, and it is likely that other influences on budget achievability exist in other settings.

A second limitation is on the number of PCs studied in each corporation. The PCs chosen were intended to represent a cross-section of PCs in the firm. In several (but not all) of the companies, corporate managers appeared to steer us away from talking to managers in troubled PCs for reasons such as 'they're too busy,' or 'the manager is too new.' In some instances, we were able to gather secondhand information on the poor

---

[20] There are some notable exceptions. For example, Dopuch *et al.* [1982] and Magee [1986] follow arguments made in Demski and Feltham [1978] and outline the close interdependence between goal setting and design of the reward function.

[21] This finding is consistent with the large amount of evidence indicating that subjectivity in performance evaluation and reward poses significant practical problems. For example, individuals tend to overrate their performance (see Baker *et al.* [1988]). Individuals tend to attribute success to internal factors but failure to external uncontrollable factors [Lewin *et al.*, 1944; Reinfenberg, 1986; and Russell and McAuley, 1986]. And superiors avoid subjectivity because they lack specific information about subordinates' performances and fear interpersonal conflict, while subordinates do not trust superiors to evaluate their performance accurately [Longenecker and Gioia, 1988].

performing PCs, but it remains likely that PCs in difficulty are under-represented in the sample of 54 PCs.

Third, the interviews were conducted during a relatively good economic period. Since budgets tend to become tighter when economic conditions worsen (e.g., Merchant, [1985b]), researchers conducting a similar study during a recessionary period would probably find budget targets that were less achievable, on average.

Fourth, the managers' subjective estimates of the probability of budget achievement were the primary evidence of budget-target achievability. These data were often collected in the middle of the fiscal year, so their accuracy depends on managers' recollections of their feelings at the time the budget was approved. Ideally, the PC data would have been collected shortly after budget approval and would have included a full set of data on historical budget accomplishment. While we acknowledge these limitations to the data, we have confidence that the estimates we received are reasonably accurate. We have evidence that the managers were able to distinguish their estimates from knowledge of subsequent events, and the partial set of historical data collected is quite similar to the subjective data.

Finally, some would criticize the use of interviews for data collection with the assertion that managers' responses are likely to be biased. We acknowledge that possibility. However, we were able to follow up the responses in some depth if the interviewees' logic was not internally consistent, and we posed the questions to multiple respondents to cross-check the answers for reliability. The number of contradictions we discovered in facts or perceptions was minimal.

Subjective estimates of the probability of budget achievement are superior to the verbal scales used in some prior research because their quantitative nature makes them more comparable across settings. The managers' estimates may not reflect difficulty of budget achievement, however. Measuring difficulty would involve assessing the size of the gap between current performance and planned performance; in other words, how far out the target is pushed. Managers' subjective estimates of achievability are affected by difficulty, but they are also affected by other confounding factors – managers' abilities to manipulate short-term earnings reports, managerial (and organizational) talents and expected levels of effort, and a potentially large number of uncontrollable factors that affect earnings both favorably and unfavorably. Because in-depth interviews allowed us to develop a good understanding of the meaning each manager associated with his or her estimate, each of these factors appears either directly or indirectly in our explanations of the observed levels of budget achievability. Admittedly, though, our adjustments lack the precision of quantitative measures.

Subject to these limitations, our findings suggest that budget achievability is an important organizational control-system variable, as managerial choices about it can have significant effects on individuals and organizations. Furthermore, textbook prescriptions do not seem to describe the practices that appear to dominate at the PC-organization level in most firms.

ACKNOWLEDGEMENTS

We are grateful for the assistance of Lourdes Ferreira, who participated in many of the interviews and discussion sessions that helped shape this paper; for helpful comments from Chris Argyris, Peter Brownell, William Bruns, Robin Cooper, Robert Eccles, Julie Hertenstein, Morris McInnes, C.J. McNair, Krishna Palepu, Robert Simons, Kiran Verma, Lawrence Weiss, Karen Wruck, M. Edgar Barrett (editor), and two anonymous reviewers; and for financial assistance from the Division of Research, Harvard Business School.

Manuscript received June 1988.
Revisions received December 1988 and January 1989.
Accepted January 1989.

REFERENCES

Anthony, R.N., G.A. Welsch, and J.S. Reece, *Fundamentals of Management Accounting*, Fourth Edition (Richard D. Irwin, 1985).

Baiman, S., 'Agency Research in Managerial Accounting: A Survey,' *Journal of Accounting Literature* (Spring 1982), pp. 154–213.

Baker, G.P., M.C. Jensen, and K.J. Murphy, 'Compensation and Incentives: Practice vs. Theory,' *Journal of Finance* (July 1988), pp. 593–616.

Bandura, A., and D. Cervone, 'Self-Evaluative and Self-Efficacy Mechanisms Governing the Motivational Effects of Goal Systems,' *Journal of Personality and Social Psychology* (1983), pp. 1012–1028.

Barrett, M.E., and L.B. Fraser, III, 'Conflicting Roles in Budgeting for Operations,' *Harvard Business Review* (July–August 1977), pp. 137–146.

Chesley, G.R., 'Elicitation of Subjective Probabilities: A Review,' *The Accounting Review* (April 1975), pp. 325–337.

Chow, C.W., 'The Effects of Job Standard Tightness and Compensation Scheme on Performance: An Exploration of Linkages,' *The Accounting Review* (October 1983), pp. 667–685.

Cress, W., and J. Pettijohn, 'A Survey of Budget-Related Planning and Control Policies and Procedures,' *Journal of Accounting Education* (Fall 1985), pp. 61–78.

Demski, J.S., and G.A. Feltham, 'Economic Incentives in Budgetary Control Systems,' *The Accounting Review* (April 1978), pp. 336–359.

Dopuch, N., J.G. Birnberg, and J.S. Demski, *Cost Accounting: Accounting Data for Management's Decisions*, Third Edition (Harcourt Brace Jovanovich, 1982).

Dunbar, R.L.M., 'Budgeting for Control,' *Administrative Science Quarterly* (March 1971), pp. 88–96.

Flamholtz, E.G., 'Accounting, Budgeting, and Control Systems in Their Organizational Context: Theoretical and Empirical Perspectives,' *Accounting, Organizations and Society* (No. 2/3 1983), pp. 153–169.

Garland, H., 'Relation of Effort-Performance Expectancy to Performance in Goal-Setting Experiments,' *Journal of Applied Psychology* (February 1984), pp. 79–84.

Hirst, M.K., 'The Effects of Setting Budget Goals and Task Uncertainty on Performance: A Theoretical Analysis,' *The Accounting Review* (October 1987), pp. 774–784.

Hofstede, G.H., *The Game of Budget Control* (Van Gorcum, 1967).

Hollenbeck, J.R., and H.J. Klein, 'Goal Commitment and the Goal-Setting Process: Problems, Prospects, and Proposals for Future Research,' *Journal of Applied Psychology* (May 1987), pp. 212–220.

——, and C.R. Williams, 'Goal Importance, Self-Focus, and the Goal-Setting Process,' *Journal of Applied Psychology* 72 (May 1987), pp. 204–211.

Holmstrom, B., 'Moral Hazard and Observability,' *Bell Journal of Economics* (Spring 1979), pp. 74–91.

Hopwood, A., *Accounting and Human Behavior* (Prentice-Hall, 1974).

Horngren, C.H., and G. Foster, *Cost Accounting: A Managerial Emphasis*, Seventh Edition (Prentice-Hall, 1987).

——, and G.L. Sundem, *Introduction to Management Accounting*, Seventh Edition (Prentice-Hall, 1987).

Huber, V.L., 'Effects on Task Difficulty, Goal Setting, and Strategy on Performance of a Heuristic Task,' *Journal of Applied Psychology* (August 1985), pp. 492–504.

Jensen, M.C., and W.H. Meckling, 'Theory of the Firm: Managerial Behavior, Agency Costs, and Ownership Structure,' *Journal of Financial Economics* (October 1976), pp. 305–360.

Kanter, R.M., *Men and Women of the Corporation* (Basic Books, 1977).

Kenis, I., 'Effects of Budgetary Goal Characteristics on Managerial Attitudes and Performances,' *The Accounting Review* (October 1979), pp. 707–721.

Latham, G.P., and T.W. Lee, 'Goal Setting,' in E.A. Locke, Ed., *Generalizing from Laboratory to Field Settings* (Lexington Books, 1986), pp. 101–117.

Lewin, K., T. Dembo, L. Festinger, and P.S. Sears, 'Level of Aspiration,' in J.M.V. Hunt, Ed., *Personality and the Behavior Disorders* (The Ronald Press Company, 1944), pp. 333–378.

Locke, E.A., G.P. Latham, and M. Erez, 'The Determinants of Goal Commitment,' *Academy of Management Review* (1988), pp. 23–39.

——, E. Frederick, C. Lee, and P. Bobko, 'Effect of Self-Efficacy, Goals, and Task Strategies on Task Performance,' *Journal of Applied Psychology* (May 1984), pp. 241–251.

——, K.N. Shaw, L.M. Saari, and G.P. Latham, 'Goal Setting and Task Performance: 1969–1980,' *Psychological Bulletin* (July 1981), pp. 125–152.

Longenecker, C.O., and D.A. Gioia, 'Neglected at the Top – Executives Talk About Executive Appraisal,' *Sloan Management Review* (Winter 1988), pp. 41–47.

Lowe, E.A., and R.W. Shaw, 'An Analysis of Managerial Biasing: Evidence from a Company's Budgeting Process,' *The Journal of Management Studies* (October 1968), pp. 304–315.

Lukka, K., 'Budgetary Biasing in Organizations: Theoretical Framework and Empirical Evidence,' *Accounting, Organizations and Society* (No. 3, 1988), pp. 281–301.

Maccoby, M., *The Gamesman: The New Corporate Leaders* (Simon & Schuster, 1976).

Magee, R.P., *Advanced Managerial Accounting* (Harper & Row, 1986).

Matsui, T., A. Okada, and T. Kakuyama, 'Influence of Achievement Need on

Goal Setting, Performance, and Feedback Effectiveness,' *Journal of Applied Psychology* (October 1982), pp. 645–648.

Merchant, K.A., 'Budgeting and the Propensity to Create Budgetary Slack,' *Accounting, Organizations and Society* (No. 2, 1985a), pp. 201–210.

——, 'Organizational Controls and Discretionary Program Decision Making: A Field Study,' *Accounting, Organizations and Society* (No. 1, 1985b), pp. 67–85.

——, 'How and Why Firms Disregard the Controllability Principle,' in W.J. Bruns, Jr., and R.S. Kaplan, Eds., *Accounting and Management: Field Study Perspectives* (Boston: Harvard Bus. School Press, 1987), pp. 316–338.

Mowen, J.C., R.D. Middlemist, and D. Luther, 'Joint Effects of Assigned Goal Level and Incentive Structure on Task Performance: A Laboratory Study,' *Journal of Applied Psychology* (October 1981), pp. 538–603.

Onsi, M., 'Factor Analysis of Behavioral Variables Affecting Budgetary Slack,' *The Accounting Review* (July 1973), pp. 535–548.

Otley, D.T., *Accounting Control and Organizational Behavior* (William Heinemann Ltd., 1987).

——, 'The Accuracy of Budgetary Estimates: Some Statistical Evidence,' *Journal of Business Finance & Accounting* (Autumn 1985), pp. 415–428.

——, 'Budgets and Managerial Motivation,' *Journal of General Management* (Autumn 1982), pp. 26–42.

Reifenberg, R.J., 'The Self-Serving Bias and the Use of Objective and Subjective Methods for Measuring Success and Failure,' *Journal of Social Psychology* (October 1986), pp. 627–631.

Rockness, H.O., 'Expectancy Theory in a Budgetary Setting: An Experimental Examination,' *The Accounting Review* (October 1977), pp. 893–903.

Russell, D., and E. McAuley, 'Causal Attributions, Causal Dimensions, and Affective Reactions to Success and Failure,' *Journal of Personality and Social Psychology* (June 1986), pp. 1174–1185.

Seidler, J., 'On Using Informants: A Technique for Collecting Quantitative Data and Controlling Measurement Error in Organization Analysis,' *American Sociological Review* (December 1974), pp. 816–831.

Shillinglaw, G., *Managerial Cost Accounting*, Fifth Edition (Irwin, 1982).

Simons, R., 'Analysis of the Organizational Characteristics Related to Tight Budget Goals,' *Contemporary Accounting Research* (1988), forthcoming.

Stedry, A.C., *Budget Control and Cost Behavior* (Prentice-Hall, 1960).

——, and E. Kay, 'The Effects of Goal Difficulty on Performance: A Field Experiment,' *Behavioral Science* (November 1966), pp. 459–470.

Umapathy, S., *Current Budgeting Practices in U.S. Industry: The State of the Art* (Quorum, 1987).

Welsch, G.A., R.W. Hilton, and P.N. Gordon, *Budgeting: Profit Planning and Control*, Fifth Edition (Prentice-Hall, 1988).

24

Sophisticated capital budgeting selection techniques and firm performance

Susan F. Haka,
Assistant Professor of Accounting, Michigan State University
Lawrence A. Gordon
Ernst & Whinney Alumni Professor of Accounting, University of Maryland
and
George E. Pinches
Professor of Business, University of Kansas

ABSTRACT

Firms using sophisticated capital budgeting techniques (i.e., those that employ present value analysis and account for risk) should theoretically perform better than firms using naive models such as the payback period or accounting rate of return. However, previous empirical work examining this question has produced mixed results. To correct for limitations in these studies, several tests were conducted on firms that adopted sophisticated selection techniques versus a control group of firms that employed naive techniques. After controlling for differences in systematic risk, industry effects, and size, interrupted time-series tests of relative market returns were performed. Based on the results of this study we conclude that the adoption of sophisticated capital budgeting selection techniques will not, *per se*, result in superior firm performance. It is possible that the adoption of sophisticated selection techniques is one of many policies the firm pursues in the face of economic stress, and this, in combination with other policies, may help to bring about economic recovery for the firm.

I. INTRODUCTION

Corporate managers continually allocate resources among competing investment alternatives during the capital budgeting process. Numerous methods of financial analysis can be employed to make the decision

Source: Haka, S.F., Gordon, L.A. and Pinches, G.E. (1985) *The Accounting Review*, **LX** (4), pp. 651–69.

whether to accept or reject proposed capital expenditures. The financial methods can be grouped into two basic classes – sophisticated and naive selection techniques. *Sophisticated* techniques are those that consider the risk-adjusted discounted net cash flows expected from a project. Thus, risk, cash flows, and the time value of money are considered. The net present value, internal rate of return, and profitability index are three widely used sophisticated selection criteria.[1] In contrast, *naive* methods generally do not use cash flows, consider present values, or incorporate risk in any systematic manner. Two commonly used naive selection techniques are the accounting rate of return and the payback period.

The purpose of this study is to determine the effect on a firm's market performance of switching from naive to sophisticated capital budgeting selection procedures. Theoretically, a firm should perform better if it employs sophisticated techniques than if it uses naive techniques. However, previous research [Christy, 1966; Kim, 1975, 1982; and Klammer, 1973] has produced mixed results. The results have also suffered from a variety of theoretical and methodological limitations. Accordingly, they do not provide reliable evidence of the effect of capital budgeting selection techniques on firm performance.

II. PREVIOUS RESEARCH

The trend toward greater use of sophisticated capital budgeting selection techniques has been well documented [Klammer, 1972; Moore and Reichert, 1983; Scapens and Sale, 1981; and Schall, Sundem and Geijsbeek, 1978]. At the same time, a number of studies have attempted to determine whether there is any relationship between the type of capital budgeting selection procedure employed and firm performance. These studies, by Christy [1966], Kim [1975, 1982], Klammer [1973] and Sundem [1974, 1975], are summarized in Table 24.1.

Prior research has provided some insight into the relationship between firm performance and the use of sophisticated versus naive capital budgeting selection techniques. However, three issues stand out in attempting to evaluate the results of previous empirical work. First, they have depended on mailed questionnaires – which have several limitations. For example, Schall and Sundem [1980, p. 10] note:

Terminology is not precise enough for a questionnaire to discover exactly what kind of capital budgeting environment a firm operates in and what kind of methods it uses. Only detailed analysis of capital budgeting methods will generate the needed data.

Another problem with the use of questionnaires is that an individual may fill out the questionnaire without actually possessing the information

---

[1] Our view is the way most have distinguished between sophisticated and naive selection techniques. However, it might be argued that truly sophisticated methods require something beyond the straight-forward application of the net present value or internal rate of return models.

Table 24.1 Previous research on the relationship of firm performance and capital budgeting selection techniques

Author	Performance Measure	Research Method	Results
Christy [1966]	Earnings per share trend	Cross-classified four groups of firms based on earnings per share trend with capital budgeting techniques.	No relationship between earnings per share trend and the use of sophisticated capital budgeting techniques.
Klammer [1973]	Operating rate of return	Multiple regression: Independent variables—capital budgeting technique, size, risk, and capital intensity.	No significant relationship between profit performance and the use of sophisticated capital budgeting techniques, but size and risk were positively related to performance.
Sundem [1974, 1975]	Value given up by not using time-state preference model	Simulation with a time-state preference model.	Net present value models with two or three risk classes are cost/benefit efficient. In highly uncertain environments the use of a payback period is rational.
Kim [1975]	Average earnings per share	Multiple regression: Independent variables—degree of sophistication of the capital budgeting process, size, risk, and capital intensity.	Positive relationship between degree of sophistication of the capital budgeting process and firm performance.
Kim [1982]	Operating rate of return	Multiple regression: Independent variables—degree of sophistication of the capital budgeting process, size, risk, and capital intensity.	Positive relationship between degree of sophistication of the budgeting process, firm performance, size and risk.

desired by the investigator. In addition, without an indication of the percent of the total capital budget that is evaluated via the sophisticated technique, the results become suspect [Gordon, Larcker and Tuggle, 1979]. Other potential problems with mailed questionnaires include nonresponse bias and low response rates.

The second issue in evaluating previous empirical research concerns the experimental design used. These studies relied primarily on cross-sectional designs. However, a pure cross-sectional design cannot control for many firm-specific factors. As Kim [1975] and Klammer [1973] have pointed out, other factors such as marketing, product development, executive recruitment and training, labor relations, and so forth may have confounding effects on any measure of performance.

A third issue concerns the correct measure of firm performance. Financial economic theory indicates that the use of sophisticated capital budgeting techniques helps management maintain or increase shareholders' wealth [Fama, 1977; Gordon and Pinches, 1984; and Myers and Turnbull, 1977]. Both Kim [1982] and Klammer [1973] acknowledge the theoretical superiority of a performance measure based on the firm's common stock. However, each rejected this approach on the grounds that shareholders know little about corporate capital budgeting practices. Consequently, previous empirical research has gauged firm performance based on measures derived from accounting data which are not necessarily consistent with the goal of shareholder wealth maximization. In fact, the argument for using sophisticated capital budgeting techniques is in part an argument against the use of traditional (i.e., naive) accounting-based selection techniques.

In sum, earlier empirical studies assessing the effect of using sophisticated versus naive capital budgeting selection techniques have suffered from theoretical, statistical, and data collection problems.[2] The method employed in this study overcomes many of these problems.

III. HYPOTHESIS

A fundamental issue is when market participants learn about the policy change. If the use of sophisticated capital budgeting techniques provides benefits to shareholders, a firm's market value should increase when market participants learn that sophisticated techniques are being used. However, it is not clear when the market becomes informed about the use of sophisticated capital budgeting techniques. One line of reasoning is that information on the policy change is disseminated gradually over time. The market participants will learn about the policy change by observing the capital expenditures made by the firm. If firm A adopts sophisticated techniques and firm B does not, we would expect the gradual dissemination of information to result in the average returns of firm A, $\bar{R}_A$, over the time period which it takes for the market participants to observe the

---

[2] This is not the case with Sundem's [1974, 1975] work. However, his work did not include an empirical study but rather was based on a simulation derived from a time-state preference model.

actual application of the policy change, to be greater than the average returns of firm B, $\bar{R}_B$ (i.e., $\bar{R}_A \geqslant \bar{R}_B$).

Alternatively, it could be argued that market participants learn of the policy change at the time of its initiation. This scenario suggests that the market returns of firm A would impound the policy change information at a given point in time (e.g., in a given week, month, or year) rather than across several time periods. To accept this scenario, however, market participants must assume the firm will properly use and regularly apply sophisticated capital budgeting techniques. Even though many of the firms we initially contacted said they were using sophisticated capital budgeting techniques, upon further questioning it was apparent that such techniques were improperly used and/or used for less than 25 percent of their capital projects. (These firms were not used in our empirical study, as discussed in the next section.) Further, this immediate dissemination and recognition scenario requires that the market participants are either notified of, or are able to derive information on, the actual timing of the policy change. No evidence suggests that a discrete notification of such a policy change occurs, nor is it a trivial task for market participants to acquire this information. On the contrary, finding out about a capital selection policy change requires extensive investigation.

Given the above, we expect, other things being equal, firms adopting sophisticated capital budgeting selection techniques to outperform matching firms employing naive techniques over the time period it takes for the information on the policy change to be gradually disseminated to the market participants. The null hypothesis of interest is:

H_0: A firm's average relative performance after the adoption of sophisticated selection techniques is *not* better than its average relative performance before the adoption of these techniques.

The alternative hypothesis is:

H_1: A firm's average relative performance after the adoption of sophisticated selection techniques is better than its average relative performance before the adoption of these techniques.

The ideal test would be to compare a firm's average market returns over a time period when it uses sophisticated techniques with its average market returns over the same time period while it uses naive techniques. Unfortunately, this approach is not possible. The next best alternative, and the one used in this study, is to match a firm which switched from a naive to a sophisticated technique (i.e., an experimental firm) with one using a naive technique (i.e., a control firm) over the same time period. A comparison of the average relative market returns both before and after the experimental firm adopted the sophisticated technique can then be conducted. In the above hypothesis, the words 'relative performance' refer to the performance of experimental firms using sophisticated capital budgeting techniques compared to the performance of matched control firms using naive selection techniques.

The use of a matched pairs approach has been employed in several studies which have attempted to assess the economic consequences of a change in management policy [Biddle, 1980; Dukes, Dyckman and Elliott, 1980]. Harrison, Tomassini and Dietrich [1983] argued, contrary to Brown and Warner's [1980] conclusion, that complicated methods (based on various types of control groups) may be more appropriate in actual settings than simpler methods. Further, Harrison, Tomassini and Dietrich [1983] found that empirical results were sensitive to the control group choice, as well as the impact period. Recognizing this problem, we employ a series of tests to examine the effect of switching from naive to sophisticated capital budgeting selection techniques on firm performance.

IV. SAMPLE SELECTION

Experimental group of firms

To obtain a set of firms that switched from naive to sophisticated selection techniques, we used personal interviews for two main reasons. First, it was crucial to determine that the firm had indeed adopted sophisticated capital budgeting techniques for evaluating a large part of their capital budget and that such techniques were properly employed. Second, it was important to ascertain, as precisely as possible, when the adoption took place.

Based on preliminary analysis, 50 firms that were believed to have adopted and consistently applied sophisticated capital budgeting techniques between 1956 and 1976 were initially selected. Forty-one agreed to allow an interview at their corporate headquarters. Six of these firms were used for a pilot study, a match could not be obtained for four of the remaining firms, and one firm did not have enough market return data to be included in the final study. Thus, the final sample of experimental firms was 30.[3]

---

[3] Additional demographic data (from 1981) on the 30 experimental firms is given below:

Number of Employees

0–1,000	1,000–10,000	10,000–50,000	over 50,000
4	10	10	6

Total Assets ($)

0–100 million	100–500 million	500 million– 1 billion	1–5 billion	over 5 billion
3	8	7	9	3

The interviews were generally conducted with either the vice-president of finance, financial planning manager, corporate controller, or treasurer. Approximately two-thirds of the firms provided their capital budgeting forms or manuals, and 18 of the interviews were tape-recorded. In addition to determining when the adoption of sophisticated capital budgeting techniques took place, the interviews provided an overview of the degree to which sophisticated methods of capital budgeting were used in these firms. Over 90 percent of the firms employed sophisticated capital budgeting selection techniques for evaluating more than half of their capital expenditures.

Control group of firms

To obtain control firms, all firms with the same Standard Industrial Code (SIC) on the COMPUSTAT tapes in the year the experimental firm adopted sophisticated capital budgeting techniques were obtained from the tapes. These firms provided pools from which the matching control firm was chosen [Harrison, Tomassini and Dietrich, 1983; Klammer, 1973; Larcker, 1983]. Second, the three firms in each pool which had the closest match on asset size and risk to the experimental firm's asset size and risk were selected as potential matches. Third, a letter was sent to the controller of each potential matching firm, followed a week later by a phone call soliciting information about the types of capital budgeting techniques employed by the firm and if and when changes in those techniques had occurred. The firm using naive techniques over the entire time frame under study with the closest matches on size and beta was selected as the matching firm. For two firms, the pool of potential matches had to be expanded beyond the initial pool of three before a match could be found.

Table 24.2 provides an indication of the quality of the matches. Columns three, four, and five consist of ratios of the matching criterion. These ratios were constructed by dividing the experimental firm's variable by the control firm's variable (i.e., the beta or asset size of the experimental firm was divided by the beta or asset size of the control firm). The closer the ratio is to one, the better matched the two firms are on the variable in question. The average betas for the experimental and control portfolios were calculated using the value-weighted market index from the CRSP tapes. These betas were 1.126 for the experimental group and 1.153 for the control group. The difference between the portfolios' betas is small, 0.027, indicating the sample was well matched on beta.[4] With regard to asset size, we again appear to have a good match. Further, any individual matching disparities should be offset when the firms are considered as portfolios of experimental and control firms. Additional evidence on the quality of the matched portfolios is provided later in the paper (see

---

[4] Using the equally weighted market index from the CRSP tapes provides substantially the same results. The difference in the experimental and control portfolios' betas using the equally weighted index is 0.047.

Table 24.2 Adoption dates, relative betas, and relative asset sizes

Matched Pair Number	(1) Industrial Code	(2) Year of Adoption for the Experimental Firms	(3) Beta Ratio	(4) Asset Ratio At Adoption Date	(5) Asset Ratio 1981
1	2000	1968	1.328	0.986	1.078
2	2065	1975	0.895	3.904	3.699
3	2830	1975	0.585	0.576	1.621
4	2400	1976	0.945	2.202	1.641
5	2830	1968	0.720	1.034	1.232
6	2870	1971	0.688	0.771	0.764
7	2911	1956	0.689	0.802	0.746
8	2911	1962	1.034	0.517	0.701
9	3270	1967	1.714	0.638	0.733
10	3310	1959	0.869	0.929	0.862
11	3310	1967	0.636	1.160	1.032
12	3449	1958	1.434	0.893	0.857
13	3510	1965	0.895	1.979	1.930
14	3520	1961	1.739	1.255	1.522
15	3531	1975	1.733	0.810	0.758
16	3630	1965	0.505	1.141	1.161
17	3651	1976	0.512	0.292	0.187
18	3662	1974	0.682	2.732	3.123
19	3711	1965	1.088	3.971	4.671
20	3721	1969	1.063	0.566	1.091
21	3721	1972	0.424	0.638	0.720
22	3841	1975	0.921	1.059	0.988
23	3861	1971	0.863	2.981	3.676
24	3940	1962	1.484	2.681	0.852
25	4210	1973	0.857	1.700	1.726
26	5311	1965	0.841	6.828	3.235
27	5311	1972	1.441	1.008	1.541
28	5411	1965	0.911	1.534	1.184
29	5411	1973	1.893	4.931	4.587
30	5912	1971	1.943	1.662	1.335

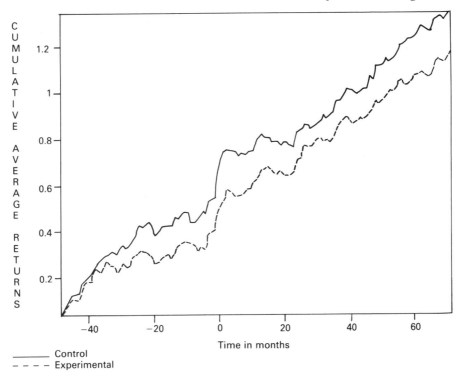

Fig. 24.1 Cumulative average returns: experimental and control.

Figure 24.1) where the cumulative average returns of the two portfolios are plotted on the same graph.[5]

V. EXPERIMENTAL DESIGN

To test for a relative shift in firm performance, an interrupted time-series design was constructed. The primary procedure for testing our hypothesis was in accordance with the general argument that the market participants learn of the experimental firms' capital budgeting policy change (i.e., the switch from naive to sophisticated methods) over time as actual application provides the information. We compared the differences in market returns of the experimental and control firms for 48 months prior to the first month of the year in which the experimental firm switched to sophisticated capital budgeting techniques with 48 months of differences after the switch. However, since the impact of sophisticated capital budgeting

[5] The Brown and Warner [1980] mean adjusted return method was also employed, as described subsequently. Since the mean adjusted return approach (which does not rely on control firms) provides the same conclusions, this provides further evidence of the validity of the matches employed.

methods may take time to begin to filter into the marketplace, we followed this basic approach under three alternatives. The first assumed that the market begins learning of the experimental firms' policy switch one year after the switch. Thus, the 'after' period was for 48 months beginning after a one-year holdout time frame. The second alternative assumed that the market begins learning of the switch two years after the switch. Thus, the 'after' period for this alternative was for 48 months beginning two years after the switch. The time periods for alternatives one and two were selected based on findings by Pettit and Miller [1980] and observations conveyed to us by executives with the experimental firms. The third alternative did not hold out any time period, thereby assuming that market participants begin learning of the policy switch right after it occurs. Thus, the third alternative used as the 'after' time period the 48 months from the first month of the year of the switch. Under all three alternatives it is assumed that the market participants are gradually learning of the policy change over time as actual applications of sophisticated capital budgeting techniques are made, but they differ as to when such learning begins – immediately, or one or two years after the switch.[6] A total of 120 months of data was ultimately collected (i.e., four years prior to the switch, plus as much as a two-year holdout period and four years after the holdout period).

The adoption of sophisticated techniques could have an effect on the risk and/or return of the firm's stock. Therefore, before examining market returns it was necessary to examine whether risk changes occurred for either the experimental or control firms. If such a change occurred, any analysis of the difference in market returns between the experimental and control firms would be confounded. Accordingly, tests for shifts in beta were conducted before any analysis of the shifts in returns.

Tests for shifts in risk

To test for a shift in beta, an analysis of covariance (ANCOVA) procedure was employed. This procedure involved dividing the overall time period under investigation into two nonoverlapping subperiods. The subperiods were differentiated by the adoption of sophisticated techniques. The sum of squared residuals from a regression with a single independent variable covering both subperiods (the reduced model) was compared with the sum of squared residuals from a regression with two independent vari-

---

[6] To examine the differences for a more immediate market reaction (i.e., during one month) we performed t-tests on the portfolio differences for each of the 120 months where H_0 is

$$\sum_{j=1}^{30} (R^e_{tj} - R^c_{tj}) = 0; \text{ for each } t = -48, \ldots 71.$$

The results, which provide no significant patterns, are available from the authors on request.

ables, one for each of the subperiods (the full model).[7] The ANCOVA test was run on each firm individually and then an additional procedure was used to examine the significance of the results. Since the test statistic for the individual firm ANCOVA comes from an $F(1, n - 3)$ distribution, the approach used was to examine the experimental and control portfolios' Fs with a X^2 goodness-of-fit test. If a significantly larger number than expected of the observed F-statistics falls in the right tail of the $F(1, n - 3)$ distribution, that provides evidence of a shift in beta for the total sample of experimental or control firms.

Tests for shifts in return

The tests for a shift in average returns were performed on 30 difference series of 120 observations each, one constructed for each matching pair of firms. Let j represent a matched pair, R^e_{tj} be the return in month t on the experimental firm in pair j, and R^c_{tj} be the return on the control firm. The difference, d_{tj}, is:

$$d_{tj} = R^e_{tj} - R^c_{tj}, \text{ where}$$
$$t = -48, \ldots, 71, \text{ and } j = 1, \ldots, 30. \tag{1}$$

Then, the average difference before the switch, d_{bj}, and the average difference after the switch, d_{aj}, were constructed for each matched pair by finding the mean of the 48 monthly differences before the switch and the 48 monthly differences after the holdout period, respectively (where $h = 0$, $h = 12$ months or $h = 24$ months, depending on the holdout period). With $t = 0$ as the first month of the year in which the experimental firm adopted sophisticated capital budgeting techniques, the average differences for the before and after periods were computed as follows:

$$\bar{d}_{b_j} = \sum_{t=-48}^{-1} \frac{d_{tj}}{48} \tag{2}$$

and

$$\bar{d}_{a_j} = \sum_{t=0+h}^{47+h} \frac{d_{tj}}{48}, \text{ where } h = 0, 12 \text{ or } 24. \tag{3}$$

The result was one sample of 30 average differences before the switch and three such samples for the periods after the switch for each pair of matched firms.

To test for significant change in the average relative performance as

---

[7] Toyoda [1974] investigated the effect on the distribution of the F-statistic when the assumption of equal subperiod variances is violated. The results indicate that the test is well-behaved even under substantial heteroscedasticity for subperiods of the size used in this study.

a result of the adoption of sophisticated techniques, the following null hypotheses were constructed. The first examines individual pairs before and after the adoption while the second examines the matched portfolios:

H_{0_1}: $\bar{d}_{b_j} \geq \bar{d}_{a_j}$ for each matched pair j, and H_{0_2}: $\mu_b \geq \mu_a$ for matched portfolios where

$$\mu_a = \frac{1}{30}\sum_{j=1}^{30}\bar{d}_{a_j}, \text{ and} \tag{4}$$

$$\mu_b = \frac{1}{30}\sum_{j=1}^{30}\bar{d}_{b_j}. \tag{5}$$

The first hypothesis, H_{0_1}, was tested using a matched pairs *t*-test. The second hypothesis, H_{0_2}, was examined employing both the *t*-test, which assumes normality, and the Mann-Whitney, which only assumes a continuous distribution.

VI. EMPIRICAL RESULTS

Risk shift

The results of the individual ANCOVA tests for the experimental and control firms are presented in Table 24.3. As these results indicate, for 15 firms the null hypothesis – H_0: $\beta_b = \beta_a$, where β_b = beta for the time frame before the adoption by the experimental firms and β_a = beta after the adoption – was rejected at the 0.05 level for at least one of the three time periods. That is, these firms (six from the experimental group and nine from the control group) experienced a significant shift in beta (at the 0.05 level) in one, two, or three of the before and after time periods examined.

The next step was to determine if the change in beta evidenced by some of the firms in Table 24.3 was a non-random occurrence. Three of the matched pairs show significant changes for both the experimental and control firms over the time frame. If the change in beta was a result of adopting sophisticated selection techniques, the beta shift should appear only for the experimental firm. Since the change in beta was significant for both firms, the implication is that an industry-wide factor was the cause of the shift. However, the critical question is whether six firms from the experimental group, or nine firms from the control group, out of a sample of 30 pairs of firms, is a significantly large enough number to conclude that there has been a shift in beta for the portfolio as a whole.

The goodness-of-fit tests based on a χ^2 statistic using expected versus observed frequencies in partitions of the F distribution are reported in Table 24.4. The χ^2 statistic tests the null hypothesis: H_0: $P_A = P_B = P_C = P_D = 25$ percent of the sample. P_A, P_B, P_C, and P_D denote the true proportions of the sample which are expected to occur in the A, B, C, and D partitions of the $F(1,93)$ distribution. The A, B, C, and D partitions were

Table 24.3 Tests for shifts in systematic risk

Matched Pair Number	βb	ANCOVA Results: Experimental Firms						βb	ANCOVA Results: Control Firms					
		h = 0 months		h = 12 months		h = 24 months			h = 0 months		h = 12 months		h = 24 months	
		βa	F	βa	F	βa	F		βa	F	βa	F	βa	F
1	0.85	0.90	0.250	0.91	0.006	0.98	0.010	0.64	0.71	0.130	0.69	0.051	0.68	0.185
2	0.77	0.99	2.689	0.99	3.098	0.98	4.537*	0.86	0.98	1.877	0.98	0.774	0.98	0.194
3	1.21	1.44	2.894	1.45	1.849	1.45	0.360	2.07	1.74	4.796*	1.74	1.392	1.74	0.097
4	1.04	0.91	1.464	0.90	1.040	0.90	1.001	1.10	0.93	1.588	0.94	2.657	0.94	2.657
5	0.85	0.84	0.002	0.84	0.001	0.85	0.436	1.18	1.34	0.578	1.34	0.436	1.36	0.123
6	0.53	0.34	2.190	0.37	0.490	0.42	1.232	0.77	0.33	6.201*	0.28	3.240	0.25	1.489
7	0.84	1.21	0.005	1.23	1.932	1.24	3.062	1.22	1.77	0.533	1.79	5.153*	1.80	6.554*
8	1.23	1.37	0.307	1.37	1.416	1.31	1.369	1.19	1.22	0.036	1.20	0.002	1.23	0.006
9	1.56	0.74	10.240*	0.79	5.924*	0.85	5.290*	0.91	0.67	4.368*	0.67	1.210	0.73	0.723
10	1.26	1.27	0.160	1.26	0.000	1.27	0.130	1.45	1.33	0.068	1.33	0.578	1.34	1.040
11	0.42	0.27	0.109	0.29	1.188	0.30	0.941	0.66	0.74	0.410	0.74	0.292	0.74	0.078
12	1.33	0.97	6.400*	0.97	2.465	0.97	5.523*	0.93	1.24	5.108*	1.25	5.018*	1.24	6.078*
13	1.02	1.02	0.001	0.99	0.232	0.97	0.230	1.14	1.34	0.960	1.32	0.706	1.36	0.152
14	1.60	1.67	0.608	1.68	0.410	1.67	4.537*	0.92	0.72	1.020	0.72	1.166	0.72	0.384
15	1.49	1.47	0.325	1.47	0.008	1.47	0.004	0.86	1.22	2.789	1.22	3.920	1.22	2.372
16	1.39	1.67	1.742	1.68	2.723	1.67	1.988	2.75	2.53	0.706	2.54	0.846	2.56	0.941
17	0.64	0.62	0.063	0.66	0.036	0.63	0.001	1.25	1.04	0.022	1.02	0.723	1.04	0.922
18	1.46	1.29	0.203	1.34	0.432	1.28	0.000	2.14	1.84	0.130	1.92	0.336	1.88	0.250
19	1.49	1.80	2.590	1.81	5.569*	1.81	7.509*	1.37	1.58	4.537*	1.58	3.648	1.58	11.088*
20	1.69	1.45	1.877	1.14	1.188	1.45	1.440	1.59	1.61	0.250	1.61	0.014	1.61	0.000

Table 24.3 (contd.)

Matched Pair Number	ANCOVA Results: Experimental Firms								ANCOVA Results: Control Firms					
	βb	$h = 0$ months		$h = 12$ months		$h = 24$ months		βb	$h = 0$ months		$h = 12$ months		$h = 24$ months	
		βa	F	βa	F	βa	F		βa	F	βa	F	βa	F
21	0.61	0.34	5.523*	0.14	3.459	0.20	2.789	1.44	1.42	0.078	1.33	0.109	1.18	1.392
22	0.93	1.31	1.124	1.33	2.098	1.35	1.796	1.01	1.12	0.017	1.13	0.203	1.14	0.068
23	0.88	1.03	1.299	1.01	1.145	0.98	0.003	1.02	0.61	7.896*	0.58	9.986*	0.56	6.452*
24	1.11	1.06	0.091	1.05	0.090	1.02	0.029	0.75	1.04	4.750*	1.03	3.610	1.01	3.764
25	1.02	1.14	0.001	1.14	0.533	1.12	0.397	1.19	1.06	0.129	1.05	0.689	1.04	2.132
26	0.90	0.81	0.026	0.84	0.144	0.86	0.012	1.07	1.22	4.244*	1.26	2.102	1.26	2.465
27	1.34	1.37	0.012	1.36	0.008	1.34	0.048	0.93	0.70	1.563	0.71	1.742	0.71	3.133
28	1.64	1.62	0.036	1.62	0.008	1.60	0.212	1.80	1.62	0.109	1.62	0.260	1.57	0.006
29	1.06	1.17	0.078	1.17	0.281	1.16	1.188	0.56	0.73	0.002	0.72	0.846	0.73	0.846
30	1.22	1.18	0.410	1.19	0.044	1.20	0.044	1.17	1.02	3.133	1.02	0.884	1.02	0.137
Averages	1.113	1.109		1.100		1.111		1.198	1.181		1.177		1.174	
σ^2	0.118	0.157		0.166		0.159		0.219	0.212		0.208		0.208	

* Significant at $\alpha \leq 0.05$

Table 24.4 χ^2 goodness-of-fit test results for shifts in systematic risk sample size: $N = 30$

Partitions	0.000–0.102	0.103–0.460	0.47–1.320	1.330–a	χ^2
Expected	7.5	7.5	7.5	7.5	$\chi^2 = 0.05 = 7.81$
Actual					
I. Experimental Firms					
A. $h = 0$	10	7	3	10	5.00
B. $h = 12$	10	4	6	10	3.60
C. $h = 24$	10	5	4	11	4.94
II. Control Firms					
A. $h = 0$	6	6	5	13	5.47
B. $h = 12$	3	6	10	11	5.47
C. $h = 24$	6	8	4	12	4.67

calculated by dividing the area under the F-curve into four equal parts (e.g., $A = 0.0$ to 0.102 contains 25 percent of the F distribution). The expected or true frequency in each partition is 7.5 (25 percent of 30 matched firms). The actual frequency in each partition is reported in Table 24.4.

The results of the χ_2 tests reported in the last column of Table 24.4 indicate that the null hypothesis cannot be rejected at the 0.05 level for either the experimental or the control portfolios in any of the three comparison periods. That is, the observed frequencies were not significantly different from the expected frequencies for an $F(1,93)$ distribution and thus there was not a larger number of F-statistics falling in the right tail than would be expected. These statistics support the conclusion that the adoption of sophisticated capital budgeting selection techniques does not cause a shift in risk. Therefore, the tests for a shift in average returns will not be confounded by a change in beta over the time period of the tests.

Return shifts

Table 24.5 provides results of individual t-tests on each matched pair of firms for holdout periods of $h = 0$, $h = 12$, and $h = 24$ months. The hypothesis examined by the tests in Table 24.5 is $H_{0_1}: \bar{d}_{b_j} \geq \bar{d}_{a_j}$. Three matched pairs in the $h = 0$ and $h = 12$ groups and one matched pair in the $h = 24$ group show a significant difference in their average relative performance between the before and after periods. The only matched pair to show a sustained significant improvement over the entire time period tested was number seven. These results do not support the theoretical argument of greater firm performance for firms adopting sophisticated capital budgeting techniques. However, further tests over the entire portfolio of matched firms are necessary.

Figure 24.1 is a plot of the cumulative average returns for the experimental and control portfolios over the 120-month test period. The plot indicates that the performance of the two portfolios was similar over months -48 to about -30, but during the two-and-a-half years prior to the adoption of sophisticated techniques by the experimental firms, months -30 to 0, the performance of the experimental portfolio began to decline relative to the performance of the control portfolio. That is, the vertical distance between the two curves, $\bar{d}_t$, increased. After the first month of the adoption year, month $t = 0$, the experimental firms were able to halt the relative decline in their performance, but they were not able, at least in months 0 to 71, to make up the distance they lost during the two-and-a-half previours years. The tests on $\bar{d}_t$ for shifts in market returns for the entire portfolio of matched firms reported in Table 24.6 confirm the visual analysis of Figure 24.1. For the $h = 0$, $h = 12$, and $h = 24$ month holdout periods, the differential mean returns $(\mu_a - \mu_b)$ decreased slightly. This is illustrated by noting that μ_a is 0.00323 larger at $h = 0$, 0.00173 larger when 12 months were omitted, and 0.00131 larger when 24 months were omitted. While in each case the average relative performance of the portfolio of experimental firms improved slightly after adopting sophisticated capital budgeting techniques, the numbers are small relative to the

Table 24.5 Individual matched pair t-tests for $H_{01}: \bar{d}_{b_i} \geq \bar{d}_{a_i}$

Matched Pair Number	$\bar{d}_{b_i}$	$h = 0$ $\bar{d}_{a_i}$	p-value	$h = 12$ $\bar{d}_{a_i}$	p-value	$h = 24$ $\bar{d}_{a_i}$	p-value
1	0.00616	0.00779	0.4590	0.00265		−0.01106	
2	0.01050	−0.00365		0.00052		−0.00237	
3	0.04536	−0.04202		−0.01235		−0.00311	
4	−0.02918	−0.00742	0.1122	−0.00479	0.1642	0.00453	0.0633
5	−0.00490	−0.00319	0.4408	−0.00329	0.8893	−0.00048	0.7003
6	0.00468	−0.00418		−0.02039		−0.03225	
7	−0.04112	0.01580	0.0203*	0.02048	0.0217*	0.01639	0.0292*
8	−0.00923	−0.01073		−0.14141		−0.00424	0.6089
9	0.00035	0.01216	0.2066	0.00257	0.8810	0.00106	0.9618
10	0.01061	−0.00520		−0.00288		−0.00535	0.2315
11	0.00147	0.00767	0.3333	0.00418	0.8525	0.00187	0.9780
12	−0.01684	0.01159	0.0732	0.00448	0.2968	0.00866	0.2315
13	0.00261	−0.00771		−0.00490		0.00738	0.7651
14	−0.02521	0.02951	0.0066*	0.02831	0.0163*	0.01588	0.0748
15	−0.01638	−0.01213	0.8554	−0.01101	0.8341	−0.01882	0.9236
16	0.01201	−0.04181		−0.05412		−0.01584	
17	0.01325	−0.00203		−0.01429		−0.00391	
18	0.00324	0.00406	0.4833	0.01269	0.6708	0.01711	0.5022
19	−0.00988	−0.00113	0.2644	−0.00134	0.4874	0.00521	0.2693
20	0.00945	−0.00244		0.00525		−0.00158	

Table 24.5 (contd.)

Matched Pair Number	$\bar{d}_{b_j}$	h = 0		h = 12		h = 24	
		$\bar{d}_{a_j}$	p-value	$\bar{d}_{a_j}$	p-value	$\bar{d}_{a_j}$	p-value
21	-0.06279	0.03834	0.0002*	0.01652	0.0044*	-0.01383	0.0652
22	0.01572	0.00607		-0.00101		0.01372	
23	0.00661	-0.00907		-0.00978		0.00498	
24	-0.00525	0.00846	0.1883	0.00576	0.4883	0.01112	0.2907
25	-0.00041	0.00318	0.4174	-0.00411	0.8283	-0.00083	
26	-0.01063	0.00385	0.1203	0.00536	0.1860	0.00251	0.2892
27	0.01033	0.01211	0.4619	0.01589	0.7572	0.01908	0.6161
28	0.00451	0.01325	0.3824	0.00997	0.8458	-0.01001	
29	-0.02338	-0.00280	0.1280	-0.00250	0.2531	0.00452	0.1233
30	0.01007	-0.00945		-0.01012		-0.02190	

* Significant @ $p \leq 0.05$

Note: Blanks for p-values indicate that $\bar{d}_{b_j} > \bar{d}_{a_j}$.

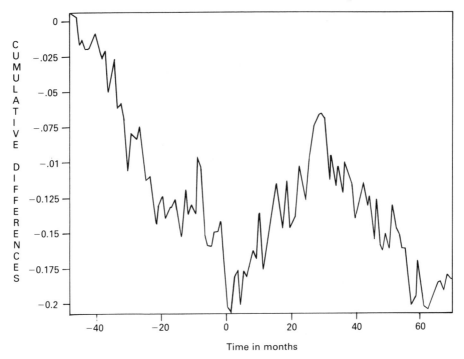

Fig. 24.2 Cumulative average differences.

standard deviation and the tests were not statistically significant. Further, it is worth emphasizing that the smaller the holdout period, the greater the improvement in the performance of the experimental firms relative to the control firms. Although it has been argued that a capital budgeting policy change is recognized by the market participants over time, it would appear that the dissemination of information begins around the beginning of the year of the switch.

The results reported in Table 24.6 indicate that the difference in returns between the experimental and control firms was reduced in the time period after the capital budgeting policy switch. However, statistically speaking, the reduction was not significant. Although the control firms outperformed the experimental firms over both the 'before' and 'after' time periods, the difference was reduced after the switch. Accordingly, we decided to examine further the average differences between experimental and control firms for the entire 120-month period. A plot of the cumulative average differences in returns for the portfolio of firms over the 120 months is shown in Figure 24.2. This graph confirms that the cumulative negative difference between the returns of the experimental and control firms grew to be large before the adoption date, but began to narrow by the second month of the year the experimental firms adopted sophisticated capital budgeting methods. It appears that the time periods

Table 24.6 Test of shifts in average relative performance for the portfolio of matching firms H_{0_2}: $\mu_b \geqslant \mu_a$

	$h = 0$	$h = 12$	$h = 24$
μ_b	−0.00294	−0.00294	−0.00294
μ_a	0.00029	−0.00121	−0.00163
σ_b	0.020	0.020	0.020
σ_a	0.016	0.015	0.012
t-statistic	−0.689	−0.380	−0.307
p-value	0.247	0.353	0.380
U-statistic	888.5	917.5	927.5
p-value	0.356	0.456	0.492
Improvement in relative performance $\dfrac{\mu_a - \mu_b}{\mu_b}$	110.0%	58.6%	44.6%

where the greatest changes took place were somewhere between the −28th and second months (when relative return differences increased), and the third and 33rd months (when return differences decreased). Accordingly, using the same method discussed earlier, the 30 months up to and including $t = 2$ and the 30 months after $t = 2$ (the second month of the adoption year) were examined for shifts in risk and returns.

Not surprisingly, in light of Figure 24.2, we found that the difference in average returns had a significant p-value of 0.03 for the portfolio of firms when comparing the two 30-month time periods. That is, the returns of the experimental firms had moved significantly closer to the control firms in the 'after' time period compared to the 'before' period, thereby statistically confirming the plot in Figure 24.2. This change in the distribution of average returns was not accompanied by a statistically significant change in risk (beta) for the experimental or control firms over the two time periods.[8] Therefore, it would appear that some shift in the experimental firm's returns relative to the control firm's returns did take place beginning a few months after the capital budgeting policy change.

To examine our findings in a manner that does not depend on the matching process, we also employed the mean adjusted returns procedure [Brown and Warner, 1980] which uses a firm as its own control. This procedure computes the abnormal performance measure for a given security in a particular month by taking the difference between the security's estimated average (mean) return over a specified period and its realized return for the month in question. This difference, which is stan-

---

[8] The p-value for the two-sample t-test for a change in means between months −28 to 2 and 3 to 30 is 0.0393. The two x^2 values to test for a shift in beta over the same time period are 4.40 for the experimental portfolio and 5.47 for the control portfolio.

dardized by the estimated standard deviation of the security's return, is averaged over the number of months being examined on a security by security basis.

In our study, the estimated average return for each security was estimated over months -48 through -7. The approach can be algebraically expressed as follows:

$$\text{Estimated Average (mean) Return} = \hat{K}_j = \sum_{t=-48}^{-7} \frac{R_{tj}}{42}, \tag{6}$$

where R_{tj} is the return of the jth experimental firm in the tth month,

$$\text{Estimated Standard Deviation of Security's Return} = \hat{\sigma}(R_j) = \frac{1}{41} \sum_{t=-48}^{-7} (R_{tj} - \hat{K}_j)^2 \tag{7}$$

$$\text{Mean Adjusted Return in Month } t \text{ for Firm } j = A_{tj} = \frac{R_{tj} - \hat{K}_j}{\hat{\sigma}(R_j)}, \text{ for each } t \text{ from } -6 \text{ to } 71. \tag{8}$$

Similar to our earlier tests to determine if significant returns were evident around and after the adoption of sophisticated selection techniques, the portfolio monthly mean adjusted returns for both the control and experimental firms were averaged over months -6 to 29 and tested to see if they were significantly different from zero. The null hypothesis for the portfolio t-tests over this 36-month period is as follows:

$$\text{H}_{0_3}: \bar{A} < 0, \text{ where } \bar{A} = \frac{1}{36} \sum_{t=-6}^{29} A_t.$$

For the experimental firms the t-statistic to test for a significant difference in the period $t = -6$ to $t = 29$ compared to the base time period ($t = -48$ to $t = -7$) was 1.096 (p-value of 0.14). For the control firms the t-statistic was 0.171 (p-value of 0.43). Thus, using the mean adjusted return method, there is an indication of higher returns for the switching firms around and in the two-and-a-half years after $t = 0$, but it is not statistically significant. For the control firms there is little evidence of increased mean adjusted returns during the same time period.

Figure 24.3 (which is a plot of the cumulative mean adjusted returns) provides additional evidence for the analysis presented earlier on the experimental firms.[9] Note that before the adoption of sophisticated capital budgeting techniques, the standardized excess returns are negative, while they become positive in the first four months of the year of the switch to sophisticated techniques. These results indicate, as did the earlier analysis, that the adoption of sophisticated selection techniques had a short-run

---

[9] We also performed t-tests on the mean adjusted returns for each of the months from $t = -6$ to $t = 71$. These results provided no significant patterns and are available from the authors on request.

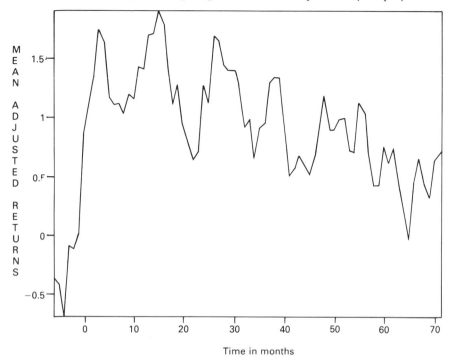

Fig. 24.3 Cumulative mean adjusted returns for experimental firms.

impact on the adopting firm's returns. However, over the longer run we see that the cumulative mean adjusted returns drifted downward. When this information is coupled with the known inferior performances of the experimental firms relative to the control firms (discussed earlier), the similarity of the results from the two approaches becomes even more striking. Using either method leads to the conclusion that the adoption of sophisticated capital budgeting techniques, contrary to financial economic theory, did not lead to superior returns.

VII. CONCLUDING DISCUSSION

Klammer [1973] concluded that the mere adoption of various analytical tools for capital budgeting was not sufficient to bring about superior operating performance. Christy [1966] showed that the earnings per share trends were not significantly different for companies using different kinds of standards for selecting capital projects. In contrast, Kim [1975, 1982] found that firms which used more sophisticated methods for selecting capital projects tended to have higher operating rates of return and higher earnings per share. The results of this study provide a more definitive conclusion. An examination of the 48 months before the switch with three different 48-month periods after the switch indicates no significant improvements in the relative market performance of the firms adopting sophisticated selection techniques. However, it is obvious from Figures 24.1, 24.2, and 24.3 and the statistical tests conducted around and in the two-and-a-half years subsequent to the policy switch that the relative return was changing for the experimental firms near the point of the policy switch. Thus, while we found no long-run effects on relative market returns for adopting firms, our results do suggest, contrary to the gradual dissemination hypothesis, that there is a short-run positive effect when firms adopt sophisticated capital budgeting selection procedures.

Although our study controlled for risk, size, and industry effects, there are several other factors which may vitiate the improvement of firm performance after a switch from naive to sophisticated capital budgeting selection techniques. These factors may have affected the analyses and as such represent limitations to our work. The first of these factors is what we term an *economic stress hypothesis*. Implementation of sophisticated capital budgeting methods may be one of many means for coping with acute resource scarcity (i.e., economic stress). In times of economic stress, firms do some 'belt tightening' by instituting cost reduction procedures, tighter and more careful budgeting, and so forth. The adoption of new criteria for capital budgeting could be one of these belt tightening procedures. Our analysis indicated a decline in the returns of the experimental firms compared to the control firms before they revised their capital budgeting policy. Additional support for this position is provided by the fact that approximately 60 percent of the experimental firms implemented sophisticated capital budgeting techniques in a period when there was a reduction in the gross level of investment for capital expenditures. Future studies might control for this economic stress phenomenon by dividing firms into resource-abundant and resource-scarce groups [Pfeffer & Salancik, 1974; and Pike, 1983].

A second factor which may affect the results is the degree of environmental uncertainty, beyond that related to industry effects, facing a firm. The results of the Christy [1966] and Schall and Sundem [1980] studies point toward the hypothesis that firms will experience more benefits from using risk-adjusted discounted cash flow techniques for capital budgeting the more stable (i.e., less uncertain) their environment. For example, Schall and Sundem [1980] found that the use of sophisticated techniques declined with increases in environmental undertainty, where beta measured uncertainty. Future work in this area might control for the environmental dynamism facing a firm in trying to evaluate the effects of a policy switch related to capital budgeting techniques. There may also be an interactive effect between this variable and the resource scarcity/abundance variable.

A third factor that may affect the improvement in firm performance is the company's reward structure. Companies that reward their employees on the basis of long-term incentive plans may experience more benefits from sophisticated selection techniques than companies that reward using a short-term reward plan. Addressing a different but related issue, Larcker [1983] found that firms employing long-term incentive plans were more prone toward capital expenditures than those firms not employing such plans.

Another limitation to our study concerns the sample of firms. The sample size of only 30 pairs of firms limits the power of our statistical tests. Nevertheless, research on many managerial accounting and finance issues (such as this one) requires careful analysis of individual firms even at the expense of sample size and reduced power in statistical tests [Kaplan, 1983, 1984].

Finally, our sample was chosen in a nonrandom fashion, especially in terms of geographical location of the firms' headquarters. Although we know of no reason to assume the results were biased due to this fact, our conclusions should be interpreted with care in reference to firms outside the study.

The above points notwithstanding, our results present a clearly discernible pattern. We conclude that the adoption of sophisticated capital budgeting selection techniques, in and of itself, does not result in superior market performance. However, we did find some suggestion of short-run improvement in the returns of adopting firms around and during the two-and-a-half years beginning with the year firms adopt sophisticated capital budgeting selection techniques. Finally, it appears that the adoption of sophisticated selection techniques may be one of many policies firms pursue in the face of economic stress. This switch in capital budgeting selection procedures may, in combination with other policies, bring about economic recovery.

ACKNOWLEDGEMENTS

The authors would like to thank Sharon Fettus for her helpful comments regarding this manuscript.

Manuscript received October 1983.
Revisions received November 1984 and March 1985.
Accepted April 1985.

REFERENCES

Biddle, G.C., 'Accounting Methods and Management Decisions: The Case of Inventory Costing and Inventory Policy,' *Journal of Accounting Research* (Supplement, 1980), pp. 235–280.

Brown, S.J. and J.B. Warner, 'Measuring Security Price Performance,' *Journal of Financial Economics* (September 1980), pp. 205–258.

Christy, G.A., *Capital Budgeting – Current Practices and Their Efficiency* (Bureau of Business and Economic Research, University of Oregon, 1966).

Dukes, R.E., T.R. Dyckman and J.A. Elliott, 'Accounting for Research and Development Costs: The Impact on Research and Development Expenditures,' *Journal of Accounting Research* (Supplement 1980), pp. 1–26.

Fama, E.R., 'Risk-Adjusted Discount Rates and Capital Budgeting under Uncertainty,' *Journal of Financial Economics* (August 1977), pp. 3–24.

Gordon, L.A., D. Larcker and F.D. Tuggle, 'Informational Impediments to the Use of Capital Budgeting Models,' *Omega* (No. 1, 1979), pp. 67–74.

——and G.E. Pinches, *Improving Capital Budgeting: A Decision Support System Approach* (Addison-Wesley, Inc., 1984).

Harrison, W.T., L.A. Tomassini and J.R. Dietrich, 'The Use of Control Groups in Capital Market Research,' *Journal of Accounting Research* (Spring 1983), pp. 65–77.

Kaplan, R.S., 'Measuring Manufacturing Performance: A New Challenge for Managerial Accounting Research,' *The Accounting Review* (October 1983), pp. 686–705.

——, 'The Evolution of Management Accounting,' *The Accounting Review* (July 1984), pp. 390–418.

Kim, S.H., *Capital Budgeting by the Machinery Industry and Its Impact on Overall Profitability*, Unpublished dissertation (St. Louis University, 1975).

——, 'An Empirical Study on the Relationship Between Capital Budgeting Practices and Earnings Performance,' *Engineering Economist* (Spring 1982), pp. 185–196.

Klammer, T.P., 'Empirical Evidence of the Adoption of Sophisticated Capital Budgeting Techniques,' *Journal of Business* (July 1972), pp. 387–397.

——, 'The Association of Capital Budgeting Techniques with Firm Performance,' *The Accounting Review* (April 1973), pp. 353–364.

Larcker, D.L., 'The Association Between Performance Plan Adoption and Corporate Capital Investment,' *Journal of Accounting Economics* (April 1983), pp. 3–30.

Moore, J.S. and A.K. Reichert, 'An analysis of the Financial Management Techniques Currently Employed by Large U.S. Corporations,' *Journal of Business, Finance and Accounting* (Winter 1983), pp. 623–645.

Myers, S.C. and S.M. Turnbull, 'Capital Budgeting and the Capital Asset Pricing Model: Good News and Bad News,' *Journal of Finance* (May 1977), pp. 321–333.

Pettit, R.R. and J.U. Miller, 'Capital Investment, Returns to Investments, and Security Price Performance,' Working Paper #62 (College of Business Administration, University of Houston, 1980).

Pfeffer, J. and G.R. Salancik, 'Organizational Decision Making as a Political Process: The Case of a University Budget,' *Administrative Science Quarterly* (June 1974), pp. 135–151.

Pike, R.H., 'The Capital Budgeting Behavior and Corporate Characteristics of Capital-Constrained Firms,' *Journal of Business, Finance and Accounting* (Winter 1983), pp. 663–671.

Scapens, R.W. and J.T. Sale, 'Performance Measurement and Formal Capital Expenditure Controls in Divisionalized Companies,' *Journal of Business, Finance and Accounting* (Fall 1981), pp. 389–419.

Schall, L.D. and G.L. Sundem, 'Capital Budgeting Methods and Risk: A Further Analysis,' *Financial Management* (Spring 1980), pp. 7–11.

——, ——, and W.R. Geijsbeek, Jr., 'Survey and Analysis of Capital Budgeting Methods,' *Journal of Finance* (March 1978), pp. 281–287.

Sundem, G.L., 'Evaluating Simplified Capital Budgeting Models Using a Time-State Preference Metric,' *The Accounting Review* (April 1974), pp. 306–320.

——, 'Evaluating Capital Budgeting Models in Simulated Environments,' *Journal of Finance* (September 1975), pp. 977–992.

Toyoda, T., 'Use of the Chow Test Under Heteroscedasticity,' *Econometrica* (May 1974), pp. 601–608.

Part Four

A Framework for Analysis

In *Accounting for Management Control*, we attempt to build a normative framework to describe certain design characteristics for the accounting information system (AIS) within the multidivisional firm. If the adoption of an organizational structure is a response to uncertainty, then we argue that divisional general management should actively participate in planning and setting performance targets; evaluation of managerial performance should not be solely based on achievement of these targets and instead an emphasis on longer-term criteria is necessary. By these means the AIS can help to promote learning and contribute to a management control system which highlights behaviour congruence, that is, does not provide incentives for the divisional management to 'play the system' and manipulate short-term performance indicators to show apparent improvements to further self-interest.

Other writers, particularly in more recent years, have also questioned the short-term emphasis on financial performance measures and how they are used. The fact that none of the readings selected here follow exactly the framework we have suggested reflects the variety and richness of design characteristics which the effective AIS is believed to encompass in order to enhance management control. However, all the writers address one or more of three basic questions to a greater or lesser extent, namely along what dimensions is it most appropriate or necessary to gauge success, what measures of performance are available to indicate success, and what incentives should be linked, if at all, to these performance measures?

PERFORMANCE INDICATORS

In his prize-winning article, Parker (1979) examines the range of alternative profit performance measures and lays bare their defects and limitations. The concept of goal congruence and the claim that a firm can somehow be assumed to develop goals divorced from actors comprising the firm is questioned. Central to the limitations argument is the potential control *versus* autonomy conflict, a concern mirrored in the transfer pricing literature (see Grabski (1985) in Part Three). Implicitly, the need for participation is recognized if the appropriate dimensions of performance are to be highlighted. By deductive reasoning, the need to develop several indicators of performance is proposed, not only along quantifiable but also along qualitative dimensions. This theme is extended to include external and environmental dimensions of performance in the seminal paper by Gordon and Miller (1976).

This work formed the first real attempt to construct a contingency framework for the design of AISs, identifying the environment, organizational attributes and managerial decision-making styles as influential variables. Several of the decision-style characteristics such as multiplexity, adaptiveness, proactivity, time horizon and consciousness or explicitness of strategies and objectives can be viewed as elaborations of the non-programmed and programmed distinction. To the authors' credit, the analysis is extended to archetypal organizations to discover the requisite qualities of the appropriate AIS in each of three situations. These are the running blind firm, the stagnant bureaucracy and the adaptive firm. The needs of the adaptive firm closely reflect our recommendations for the multidivisional enterprise.

THE USE OF PERFORMANCE INDICATORS

The challenges posed by the 'new' technology to the design of AISs is the theme of Kaplan's (1984) article. The need for flexibility and adaptability consistent with non-programmed decision-making is explicitly recognized, and the uniform and conventional use of measures like ROI to reward divisional managers is questioned. Taking a historical perspective, Kaplan provides sound reasons why incentive schemes strictly linked to short-term financial performance measures are inappropriate and possibly harmful as they may induce adverse or dysfunctional behaviour amongst managers taking non-programmed decisions. The conclusions call for a return to field-based research to discover the innovative practices of firms employing the new technology. This has been taken up in recent years, as witnessed by the number of case studies which are now being published. The Simons (1990) article, for example, is based on a two-year field study of two large US companies, and the findings suggest that viewing the AIS solely as a basis to reward managers is myopic.

Simons is concerned with the implementation of strategy and whether the management control system plays a role in the strategy formulation process. Top management may concentrate upon any one of several systems to convey changes in strategy or strategic uncertainties at any one point in time. The AIS is one of these and can be used interactively or diagnostically. Whilst the latter use accords with a conventional management by exception approach, the former use provides a means of evaluating the need for change, organizational learning and strategy revision. The interactive use of the AIS may trigger debate between different levels of management within the firm to uncover assumptions and critical success variables with a view to conveying necessary changes in strategy if, for example, financial performance measures are to be achieved. A model of the process is subsequently applied to a sample of 14 other companies and the distinction between interactive and diagnostic use appears to be upheld. This is a relatively recent development in the analysis of management control but the approach appears worthwhile as it focuses on the distinction between the short- and longer-term use of accounting information data.

SHORT- AND LONG-TERM PERSPECTIVES

The notion of non-programmed decision-making, especially for divisional managers of investment centres, requires the longer-term dimension to be incorporated in the AIS. This view is supported by Govindarajan and Gupta (1985). Based on data collected from 58 strategic business units of large diversified firms, several interesting findings are provided. In those divisions classified as 'build' or having growth potential, management are rewarded on long-run criteria which include qualitative and subjective dimensions. For 'harvest' or 'cash cow' divisions, management are rewarded on the basis of short-term criteria. Both approaches appear to be equally effective in achieving their own objectives. The degree of discretionary decision-making allowed by the strategy adopted seems to influence whether a longer or shorter time dimension is regarded as appropriate. Certainly the definitions of effectiveness and identification of strategy can be questioned, as the authors agree, but the conclusion that matching strategy and control systems is necessary to ensure managerial job satisfaction and involvement is difficult to ignore. This theme of developing personal-human control consistent with technical control is at the heart of Argyris's (1990) contribution.

Control as exercised through accounting follows primarily programmed assumptions and may thus establish targets which are embarrassing or threatening to management charged with their achievement. Defensive routines such as smoothing, biasing, gaming, filtering and 'illegal acts' may be engaged to protect the individual manager. These routines and others are essentially anti-learning but they do avoid embarrassment. Top management does not have to confront subordinates if performance is apparently being achieved. Perhaps, this is one reason Merchant and Manzoni (1989, in Part Three) found budgets which were very likely to be achieved on a regular basis. The task ahead as Argyris concludes is to acknowledge the defensive routines and to incorporate ways of intervening or questioning these routines as a part of the design of the control system. In the terminology we have used, the task is to design behaviour-congruent AISs which will contribute positively to managerial self-control.

CONCLUSION

In conclusion, it may be argued that the design characteristics of the AIS for the multidivisional enterprise outlined in *Accounting for Management Control* are partial, static and set in a limited time frame. The readings offered in this section testify to this. They are an indication of how far we have to progress in order to develop a comprehensive framework to design AISs which will ensure effective management control. The array of potentially influential perspectives from strategy to subjective performance measures and from personal-human control to incentive schemes is bewildering and requires the theorist to operate at more than one level of analysis simultaneously. The satisfying aspect is that these significant interrelationships are being addressed by field research and by induction. Uncertainty, whether it is within or outside the enterprise, is being considered rather than being assumed away. In the final analysis, we may never be able to design AISs which are completely behaviour-congruent across all perspectives at all points in time. A more attainable aim in the near future is to be able to recognize when the need to change the design arises in order to maintain the form of management control deemed appropriate. What comprises the dimensions along which performance should be gauged, what measures or indicators are regarded as appropriate and how they should be used are questions which will continually fuel the search for new answers. The need to incorporate flexibility and to view this as part of an ongoing process in the design of the AIS is therefore of paramount importance.

25

Divisional performance measurement: beyond an exclusive profit test

Lee D. Parker

The measurement of divisional performance in decentralized companies has come to be generally practised by means of a single index of divisional profitability. Accountants have traditionally been placed in the position of designing or adopting a measure of division performance which best 'represents top management objectives'.[1] This has been seen to be best represented by some form of divisional profit index in accordance with accountants' concentration upon the profit goal of the firm.[2] Divisional performance measurement literature has therefore concentrated upon the development and use of a single index of divisional success couched in terms of profit. Alternative indices of divisional profit which have become generally accepted include:

1. Division Net Profit
2. Division Controllable Profit
3. Division Contribution Margin
4. Return on Investment
5. Residual Income[3]

This approach to divisional performance measurement is based to a large degree upon accountants' acceptance of the concept of goal congruence which for instance Horngren[4] defines as achieved when a corporate accounting system specifies goals and subgoals to encourage behaviour such that individuals accept top management goals as their personal goals. This paper extends the argument against the validity of this goal congruence concept to argue that the current accounting approach to

[1] C.T. Horngren, *Cost Accounting: A Managerial Emphasis*, Prentice-Hall, 4th Edition, 1977, p. 709.
[2] G. Shillinglaw, *Managerial Cost Accounting*, Richard D. Irwin, 4th Edition, 1977, p. 777.
[3] C.L. Moore and R.K. Jaedicke, *Managerial Accounting*, South Western Publishing Company, 4th Edition, 1976, pp. 517–520.
[4] C.T. Horngren, *op. cit.*, p. 151.

Source: Parker, L.D. (1979) *Accounting and Business Research*, Autumn, pp. 309–19.

divisional performance measurement is biased, narrow and unrealistic in view of the range of objectives towards which any one division strives. This argument is further extended to consider the single divisional profit index as an instrument of top management control and the conflicts with divisional autonomy which that may involve. The alternative presented by this paper therefore is a return to the development of multiple measures of divisional success criteria of a quantitative and qualitative type.

GOAL CONGRUENCE QUESTIONED

The arguments against the efficacy of the goal congruence concept can be summarized as follows.[5] Accountants' belief in their responsibility for encouraging goal congruence among managers has its origins in part in their unitary view of the business enterprise. On the other hand many organization theorists hold a pluralist view of the business enterprise[6] in that it is comprised of a coalition of individuals and groups who cooperate to go some distance towards achieving their separate objectives. It can therefore be argued that a company is a coalition of which top management is only one part, where a whole range of aspirations are continually juggled and balanced.

The difference between the unitary and coalition views of the firm is largely attributable to the progression of concepts of the firm developed from the classical economic and management schools around 1900 to 1939 to the more behavioural perspective of the modern organization theorists around 1940 to 1970. The classical unitary view emanated from the works of such writers as Max Weber[7] and Frederick Taylor,[8] while the behavioural perspective can be assembled from the works of a considerable body of researchers such as Mayo, Merton, Selznick, Maslow, Gouldner, Simon and March, McGregor, Argyris, and Tannenbaum.[9] The classical economic/management theories of the firm are built upon the

---

[5] For a fuller discussion of this view refer to L.D. Parker, 'Goal Congruence: A Misguided Accounting Concept', *Abacus*, June 1976, pp. 3–13.
[6] Refer to A. Fox 'Industrial Relations: A Social Critique of Pluralist Ideology' in *Man and Organization*, J. Child (ed.), George Allen and Unwin, London, 1973, pp. 185–199.
[7] Refer for instance to M. Weber, 'Legitimate Authority and Bureaucracy', reprinted in *Organization Theory*, D.S. Pugh (ed.), Penguin 1971, pp. 15–29.
[8] F.W. Taylor, *The Principles of Scientific Management*, New York, 1913.
[9] Refer for instance to E. Mayo, *The Social Problems of an Industrial Civilization*, Harvard, Boston 1945; R.K. Merton, 'Bureaucratic Structure and Personality', in *A Sociological Reader on Complex Organizations*, A. Etzioni (ed.), Holt Rinehart and Winston, 1970, pp. 47–59; P. Selznick, 'Foundations of the Theory of Organizations', reprinted in *Systems Thinking*, F.E. Emery (ed.), Penguin Modern Management Readings, 1969, pp. 261–267; A.H. Maslow, *Motivation and Personality*, Harper, New York, 1954; A.W. Gouldner, *Patterns of Industrial Bureaucracy*, Free Press, Glencoe, Illinois, 1954; J.G. March and H.A. Simon, *Organizations*, Wiley, New York, 1958; D. McGregor, *The Human Side of Enterprise*, McGraw-Hill, New York, 1960; C. Argyris, *Integrating the Individual and the Organization*, Wiley, New

principles of division of labour, chain of command, line and staff structure and span of control.[10] The firm is viewed as an entrepreneur who seeks to maximize the firm's profit by rationally deciding upon courses of action with full knowledge of available alternatives.[11] This classical perspective is limited, however, by its concentration upon the formal structure of organization and by its neglect of individual personality, informal groups, intrafirm conflicts and decision processes.[12] The modern organization theory approach, however, focusing primarily on human organization and relying more upon empirical research data, investigates strategic parts of the organization's subsystems, their inter-relatedness, and their goals.[13] The frame of reference adopted is described as behavioural and it argues that:

1. The firm of itself does not act. Only its personnel act.
2. Behaviour is conditioned by personality as well as environmental factors.
3. Behavioural processes of organization members are a function of their cognitions, perceptions, beliefs and knowledge.
4. Rewards or goals are often complex.[14]

In seeking to promote goal congruence (rather than a looser form of coordination for instance) through divisional performance measurement, accountants are adhering to a predominantly classical view of organizations. (This will be demonstrated further in this paper with reference to the accounting literature on divisional performance measurement.) Their perspective of divisional performance measurement would be more amenable to modification if they incorporated more of the modern organization theory views into their thinking. In this way, the divisionalized firm could be considered in terms of the goals, motivations and decisions of its participants who form a bargaining, equilibrium-seeking, decision-making system.[15]

Organization and administrative theorists have further recognized that a single dominant enterprise goal is unlikely to be discovered and have argued for the simultaneous existence of a whole range of corporate goals

York, 1964; and A.S. Tannenbaum, *Social Psychology of the Work Organization*, Tavistock, London, 1966.
[10] W.G. Scott, 'Organization Theory: An Overview and an Appraisal', in *Organizations: Structure and Behavior*, Vol. 1, 2nd Edn, J.A. Litterer (ed.), Wiley, New York, pp. 16–17.
[11] J.W. McGuire, *Theories of Business Behaviour*, Prentice-Hall, Englewood Cliffs, NJ, 1964, pp. 19–20.
[12] W.G. Scott, *op. cit.*, pp. 16–17.
[13] *Ibid.*, pp. 21–25.
[14] J.W. McGuire, *op. cit.*, pp. 27–28.
[15] M. Schiff and A.Y. Lewin, *Behavioral Aspects of Accounting*, Prentice-Hall, Englewood Cliffs, NJ, 1974, pp. 4–5.

some of which may even conflict.[16] It is arguable, for instance, whether an organization can be conceived as having 'a goal'. An individual can be approached to determine his goals, but an organization cannot be approached in the same way.[17] Instead, the 'coalition' view of the organization allows the recognition of organizational goals which reflect the demands of an often conflicting coalition. Thus Schiff and Lewin[18] point out that these goals need not be internally consistent with each other, that they may vary in terms of prescription of action and measures of success and that they are the outcome of bargaining processes. This state of affairs reflects the fact that individuals provide the organization with goals and skills.[19] The composition of an organization's 'goal set' at any point of time will then reflect the bargaining power and position of its subcoalitions and the extent of consensus reached.[20] Empirical evidence for the existence of an organizational 'goal set' and some determinants of its components has been available as far back as 1959.[21]

The economic model of profit maximization which is usually utilized in accountants' treatment of goal congruence as the predominant goal of the firm has also been questioned from time to time.[22] Its assumption of the rational decision-maker is at odds with the perspectives adopted by psychologists, sociologists and anthropologists and its assumption of certainty about future outcomes has been criticized as being unrealistic. The observed tendency of individuals to adopt satisficing behaviour[23] provides further doubt as to the ability of companies to act as true profit maximizers. Huff and McGuire[24] point out that empirical studies as far back as 1939 have indicated that businessmen do not even know how to begin,

[16] Refer to C. Perrow, *Complex Organizations. A Critical Essay*, Scott Foresman, Glenview, Illinois, 1972, pp. 160–163 and R.L. Smith, *Management Through Accounting*, Prentice-Hall, Englewood Cliffs, NJ, 1962, pp. 228–229.

[17] D. Silverman, *The Theory of Organisations: A Sociological Framework*, Heinemann, London, 1970, p. 9.

[18] M. Schiff and A.Y. Lewin, *op. cit.*, pp. 5–7.

[19] R.D. Lansbury and P. Gilmour, *Organisations: An Australian Perspective*, Longman Cheshire, Melbourne, 1977, p. 83.

[20] M. Schiff and A.Y. Lewin, *op. cit.*, p. 7.

[21] Refer to a study conducted by J.K. Dent, 'Organizational Correlates of the Goals of Business Management', *Personnel Psychology*, 1959, pp. 365–393.

[22] Refer to J.W. McGuire, 'The Finalité of Business', in *Management and the Behavioral Sciences*, M.S. Wadia (ed.), Allyn and Bacon, Boston, 1968, p. 383 and M.F. Cantley, 'The Choice of Corporate Objectives', *Long Range Planning*, September 1970, pp. 36–42.

[23] C. Perrow, *op. cit.*, p. 149.

[24] D.L. Huff and J.W. McGuire, 'The Interdisciplinary Approach to the Study of Business', reprinted in *Management and Organizational Behavior Theories: An Interdisciplinary Approach*, W.T. Greenwood (ed.), South Western Publishing Co., Cincinnatti, Ohio, 1965, pp. 94–95. They cite the empirical studies of R.L. Hall and C.J. Hitch, 'Price Theory and Business Behavior', *Oxford Economic Papers*, May 1939 and R.A. Lester, 'Shortcomings of Marginal Analysis for Wage-Employment Problems', *American Economic Review*, March, 1946.

in the uncertain real world, to maximize profits. Indeed goals have even been likened to rationalizations of prior actions[25] which raises the question as to whether a goal is a means to an end rather than an end in itself.

An alternative view of corporate functioning therefore emerges. The company may be viewed as a coalition in which participants continually bargain for the composition of a set of corporate goals which continually change in response to the bargaining process and in response to personnel entering and leaving the company. That is to say, accountants must recognize that goal setting is essentially a human-political process. Top management's long term goals may not be shared by division managers. Goals are formulated by individual personnel, groups, departments, divisions etc., so that corporate goals may be at least in part formulated in response to pressures from all levels of the organizational hierarchy. This observation leads Leavitt *et al.*[26] to argue that organizational goals are set to a large extent through internal negotiation among organizational subunits. Corporate goals therefore become a set of short term stabilizers for expectations derived from a whole range of individual and group activities.[27] Should accountants come to recognize the 'goal set' as a realistic view of corporate goal structure, then they are still faced with the task of defining whether it includes policies, strategies, goals, forecasts and tactics. Even so, the 'goal set' has been implicitly recognized by many management writers in their descriptions of corporate objectives such as market standing, productivity, profitability, staff development, labour relations, public image, social responsibility, technical leadership etc.

Goal congruence as a concept for application in both centralized and divisionalized companies appears to be of doubtful relevance. Modern organization theory would appear to suggest that accountants' encouragement of congruence between divisional and corporate goals is both unnecessary and misdirected. This view would furthermore argue that only loosely coordinated divisional operations may be quite tolerable and indeed the best that can be hoped for in many decentralized organizations. Even when some operations are coordinated, the goals of different divisional groups may be far from reconciled or congruent. Instead, a divisionalized company is likely to accommodate a whole range of (sometimes inconsistent) goals, generated by a variety of individuals and groups, continually being modified, and being reviewed in terms of satisfactory rather than maximum performance. Nevertheless, accountants continue to pursue goal congruence in their construction of divisional performance measures. It is to the effects of this approach upon divisional performance measurement that this paper now turns.

[25] K.E. Weick, *The Social Psychology of Organizing*. Addison-Wesley, Reading, Mass, 1969, pp. 8, 37–38.
[26] H.J. Leavitt, W.R. Dill, H.B. Eyring, *The Organizational World*, Harcourt Brace Jovanovich, New York, 1973, pp. 23–25.
[27] Refer to C. Perrow, *op. cit.*, p. 162 and R.M. Cyert and J.G. March, *A Behavioral Theory of the Firm*, Prentice-Hall, Englewood Cliffs, NJ, 1963, pp. 4–43, 83–127.

GOALS IN TRADITIONAL DIVISIONAL PERFORMANCE MEASUREMENT

Classical management assumptions about corporate goals have been seriously questioned and yet traditional accounting thought has continued to subscribe to those assumptions. These appear to be largely unrealistic and yet they are still in evidence in accounting texts dealing with divisional performance measurements. Even so, accounting writers sometimes unwittingly make contradicting statements or indeed deliberately point out contradictions which have become evident to them. Horngren for instance makes two potentially contradictory claims on one page,

Keep in mind that an organization is a group of individuals seeking to achieve some common goals. . . .

Each member has objectives of his own, often not coinciding with those of the organization.[28]

The first statement merely expresses the classical management assumption while the second statement implies a coalition view of the company which appears to refute the assumption in the first statement. Solomons'[29] view of divisional and corporate goal-setting is similarly classical. He defines success in divisional performance merely as success in earning a profit and appears to base his complete examination of divisional performance upon this one premise.

Amey[30] has also taken a relatively classical view of the corporate objectives in his treatment of divisional performance. While considering profitability to be the key indicator of business success he does recognize the possibility of multiple objectives but still sees them only in the context of economic success and economic efficiency. Indeed quite early in his study, he recognizes the possibility of multiple corporate objectives other than profit and rate of return but chooses to ignore them in his economic efficiency calculations.

On the one hand Amey[31] advances convincing arguments for the probability that profit satisficing is an aim of companies rather than profit maximizing, since it reduces the risk of close substitutes appearing, reduces the risk of large established companies entering the industry and reduces the risk of governmental anti-monopoly legislation. On the other hand he suggests that whatever the company's overall objective is (and most organization researchers would claim that there is more than just

[28] C.T. Horngren, *Cost Accounting: A Managerial Emphasis*, Prentice-Hall, 1972, 3rd edition, p. 697.
[29] D. Solomons, *Divisional Performance: Measurement and Control*, Irwin, Homewood, Illinois, 1965, pp. 60, 238.
[30] L.R. Amey, *The Efficiency of Business Enterprise*, George Allen and Unwin, 1969, pp. 3–4, 15.
[31] *Ibid.*, pp. 152–154.

one), the first two elements for economic efficiency should be retained –
maximum physical productivity and minimum unit cost. Presumably
Amey has recognized the possible existence of the 'goal set' but has then
chosen to ignore it. For the purposes of fairly assessing divisional performance, it is difficult to see how it can be ignored. Furthermore given
the unlikely existence of the single, profit-maximizing corporate and
divisional goal, and given the suggested weaknesses in the concept of
goal congruence, these observations might cause accountants to wonder
whether the continued attempts to refine divisional profit measures are
really likely to be useful or relevant to the needs of the modern corporation.

THE MANAGER OR THE MEASURE

Horngren identifies one of the causes of dysfunctional decision making in
decentralized companies as being:

a lack of harmony or congruence between the overall organizational goals
and the individual goals of the decision makers.[32]

The accountant's task of persuading (by measurements or any other means)
managers to give up some of their personal objectives in favour of some
officially pronounced top management goals may be quite difficult and
misdirected in any case. ROI, for instance, may induce certain behavioural responses in managers but are hardly likely to cause them to alter
their desires, needs and philosophies. Top management goals, furthermore, may bear little resemblance to the real company goal set generated
from all levels of management, unions, interest groups and individual
employees.

The prime importance of divisional managers' own objectives is recognized by Moore and Jaedicke[33] when they support Dean's argument that
the selfish interests of division managers can be aligned more closely with
company (top management) goals by allowing transfer prices to be determined by negotiation and by allowing divisional managers recourse to
markets outside the company. Whether negotiation could fulfil such an
aim is debatable. Nevertheless the argument does recognize the direct
effects on company operations which divisional managers' objectives
can have. What the argument above also demonstrates about traditional
management accounting thinking is its preoccupation with refining measures for directing employee behaviour to suit top management ends. This
is even more amply demonstrated by Tomkins' statement that:

When examining operating decisions, it was generally assumed that delegation of the decision-making process to divisions was desirable provided

---

[32] C.T. Horngren, 3rd edition, *op. cit.*, p. 694.
[33] C.L. Moore and R.K. Jaedicke, *Managerial Accounting*, South Western Publishing,
1972, p. 556, supporting J. Dean, 'Decentralization and Intracompany Pricing,
Harvard Business Review, 1955.

that a suitable technical procedure was available for simultaneously achieving maximization of both corporate objectives and divisional objectives.[34]

Given the fickle nature of human behaviour and the range of ever changing corporate goals, that ultimately suitable technical procedure may in fact never be found. Tomkins[35] does concede the possibility of deliberate self-interest in division managers. The remedy, he suggests, lies in a 'good performance evaluation and reward procedure'. Given the questionable validity of the goal congruence concept, that procedure may be too narrowly based and largely misdirected. Furthermore, such an obvious 'carrot and stick' philosophy may cause division managers to ignore top management goals to an even greater extent.

It is therefore quite possible that accountants may have placed too much emphasis upon refining divisional profit measurement techniques for influencing manager behaviour rather than trying to serve managers with information which better relates to the real multiple corporate goals to which they themselves contribute. In his discussion of divisionalization of investment decisions, Tomkins[36] takes a small step in this direction when he wonders if there should be less emphasis placed upon the search for overall corporate models and divisional submodels and more time given to the investigation of the optimal degree of independence as suggested by some organizational theorists. This would seem to be a reasonable approach in view of the arguments against goal congruence and would seem to be closer to the spirit and intention of divisionalization. It should involve the discarding of the directive attitude of accounting measurement and the new concentration upon the autonomous behaviour and aims of the full spectrum of corporate personnel.

THE INADEQUATE DIVISIONAL PROFIT TEST

If accountants recognize that the performance of divisions can only be judged in relation to the whole corporate 'goal set' then they must be prepared to reject any divisional profit measure as the sole test of performance. Yet the profit test is still receiving major emphasis in the accounting literature. Horngren[37] sees Return on Investment or Residual Income as the quantitative measure best representing top management objectives. Shillinglaw[38] argues that profit-centre decentralization assumes that the performance of the profit-centre manager is gauged by his re-

---

[34] C. Tomkins, *Financial Planning in Divisionalised Companies*, Accountancy Age Books, Haymarket Publishing Co., 1973, p. 143.
[35] *Ibid.*, pp. 6–7.
[36] *Ibid.*, pp. 153–154.
[37] C.T. Horngren, 3rd Edition, *op. cit.*, pp. 698–699.
[38] G. Shillinglaw, 'Divisional Performance Review: An Extension of Budgetary Control', in *Contemporary Cost Accounting and Control*, G.J. Benston (ed.), Dickenson Publishing Co., Belmont, California, 1970, p. 305.

ported profit. Divisional accountability[39] is thus treated primarily in terms of the amount of income produced and top management's assessment is again based upon these questionable premises of the primacy of the company profit goal and its accompanying managerial goal congruence.

Solomons[40] claims that the term 'divisionalization' adds to the term 'decentralization' the concept of 'delegated profit responsibility' and continues to narrow the accounting perspective of divisional performance measurement in accordance with the classical management perspective:

Third, since the principal objective of divisional management is the long run maximization of the division's contribution to the profitability of the corporation as a whole, there is . . . a readily available measure of divisional success in the form of profit contribution.[41]

The mere availability of the profit contribution measure does not automatically imply that it is appropriate or sound yet Solomons advocates the restriction of divisional autonomy should the profit test prove difficult to apply. Any tendency for accountants to preserve measurement techniques that are inappropriate to company activities must risk the eventual bypassing of the accounting system by management altogether, in favour of a broader, possibly more qualitative means of divisional performance measurement.

Moore and Jaedicke[42] do realize that profit as an index of division performance may be inadequate. They feel that it does not account for a division manager's ability to build good customer relations, to secure employee loyalty etc. (even that list is narrow in perspective). Again, however, they return to traditional thinking in looking to the further refinement of profitability index measures. It hardly seems a logical step for accountants to further refine a measure which they consider to be unrepresentative of the total situation. In many firms, however, Caplan[43] argues that profitability is the only criterion that receives serious attention, whereas he suggests that business organizations should try to develop the best possible set of goals and criteria and that in evaluating performance against those criteria, they should remember that the process itself is imperfect. He cites the general empirical findings that single criterion indexes of performance over-emphasize that single factor (such as return on investment) to the exclusion of other important factors and that the more pressure that is related to return on investment, the more managers concentrate on that index instead of making decisions that benefit the whole organization.

---

[39] G. Shillinglaw, 'Toward a Theory of Divisional Income Measurement', in *Contemporary Issues in Cost Accounting*, H.R. Anton and P.A. Firmin (eds.), 2nd edition, Houghton, Mifflin & Co., Boston, 1972, pp. 463–464.
[40] D. Solomons, *op. cit.*, p. 3.
[41] D. Solomons, *op. cit.*, p. 9.
[42] C.L. Moore and R.K. Jaedicke, *op. cit.*, p. 544.
[43] E.H. Caplan, *Management Accounting and Behavioral Science*, Addison-Wesley, Reading, Mass., 1971, pp. 103–108.

The prospect for the further development of, say, return on investment, as a single criterion of divisional performance, should advisedly be considered by accountants as limited. Not only does an undue concentration upon it risk the difficulties outlined by Caplan, but as Hopwood argues, 'beyond some point the search for technical perfection is doomed to failure'.[44] The question of divisional performance measurement is both technical and behavioural. Important aspects may be ignored if accountants focus only upon technical issues.

TOP MANAGEMENT CONTROL

Why should accountants continue to subscribe to the goal congruence concept when its foundations have been subject to so much criticism? One possible reason might be their belief that it serves as a convenient vehicle for top management to exercise ultimate authority and control over all corporate personnel and operations. Indeed it could be argued that the accounting literature concerned with divisional performance measurement does assume the right and ability of top management to control total activity in the company.

Evidence for this underlying assumption in the accounting approach to divisional performance assessment appears fairly readily within the accounting literature. Arrow[45] claims that top management's enforcement rules should encourage the lower level manager to maximize top management goals after which he is rewarded and for this reason top management must have a way of measuring performance. Should accountants offer return on investment as the measure of divisional performance for Arrow's stated purpose, they may be merely acting as tools of, albeit thinly veiled, top management attempts to achieve overall corporate control. Organization theorists would claim that such complete control is not possible (and to the average accountant, the union presence might be the most immediately tangible evidence for that view).

Horngren, too, suggests that:

The optimal amount of decentralization is the amount that attains top management's overall objectives most efficiently and effectively.[46]

and that

The aim is to get a system that will point the managers toward the top management goals.... In addition, incentives must be provided that will spur managers towards those goals.[47]

In doing this, he opts for only one measure and then suggests that accountants concentrate upon defining the measure, measuring components,

---

[44] A.G. Hopwood, *Accounting and Human Behaviour*, Accountancy Age Books, London, 1974, p. 3.

[45] K.J. Arrow, 'Control in Large Organizations', *Management Science*, April 1964, p. 400.

[46] C.T. Horngren, 3rd Edition, *op. cit.*, p. 693.

[47] *Ibid.*, p. 697.

applying standards and timing feedbacks. Henderson and Dearden[48] argue for a divisional control system which carries out two functions:

1. Motivates division managers to make the same decisions that top management would have made if the company were not divisionalized.
2. Provides top management with a means of evaluating the effect of division managers' decisions upon the company.

In seeking to improve top management control over divisions, Solomons[49] claims that in the more 'successful' divisionalized companies, divisions are still allowed freedom in their daily operations but are strictly called to account for the results of their operations. This is a somewhat contradictory statement since any 'calling to account' must immediately increase top management control over divisions and therefore may reduce their autonomy.

Moore and Jaedicke[50] add to this view of divisional performance measurement as the means of perpetuating top management control by claiming that top management has no choice but must seek the most 'effective' control device. For this purpose they suggest that accounting measurements are most useful because they allow management by exception. Amey[51], too, demonstrates this bias when he claims that the decentralization of responsibility is controlled mostly by the use of accounting measurements which are highly centralized. Furthermore, he sees decentralization of authority and responsibility being related more to the control rather than the planning function of management. He cites one of the conditions laid down by the National Association of Cost Accountants of America for effective divisionalization of profit responsibility as being 'centrally established and administered policies to coordinate divisional operations in the interests of the company as a whole'.[52] This effective centralized control of divisions is more specifically supported by Amey[53] when he recognizes and approves the predominance of centralized asset control in divisionalized companies. This attitude is further demonstrated by Tomkins[54] when he suggests that top management may not be prepared to delegate decisions of 'great importance' (however defined). In general this accounting belief in top management control over divisions is best demonstrated by Shillinglaw[55] and Villers,[56] who treat measures such as 'return on investment' as simplified top management controls over

[48] B.D. Henderson and J. Dearden, 'New System for Divisional Control', in *Contemporary Cost Accounting and Control*, G.J. Benston (ed.), *op. cit.*, p. 337.
[49] D. Solomons, *op. cit.*, p. 15.
[50] C.L. Moore and R.K. Jaedicke, *op. cit.*, p. 565.
[51] L.R. Amey, *op. cit.*, pp. 116–120.
[52] *Ibid.*, p. 120.
[53] *Ibid.*, p. 129.
[54] C. Tomkins, *op. cit.*, pp. 143–144.
[55] G. Shillinglaw, 'Divisional Performance Review: An Extension of Budgetary Control', *op. cit.*, p. 305.
[56] R. Villers, 'Control and Freedom in a Decentralized Company', in *Topics in Managerial Accounting*, L.S. Rosen (ed.), McGraw-Hill, Toronto, 1970, p. 186.

profit-centre managers. They are the means by which answerability is exacted.

The systems view of organizational activity would offer an alternative approach to the emphasis upon accounting controls over divisions.[57] In this view, organizational events have multiple causes generated by long cause-effect chains and any one management action may have second and third level effects beyond any immediate consequence. A systems oriented manager would therefore allow organizational subsystems to adjust when disturbed rather than immediately intervening with a proliferation of controls. Accountants and management of divisionalized companies may have been too eager to adopt the latter course of action to date.

Further evidence of the tight control which top management has retained in divisionalized companies despite the apparent granting of autonomy is provided by a survey of UK companies conducted by Tomkins.[58] In the majority of cases examined, a heavy emphasis upon relatively detailed budgetary control over divisions was discovered (in 42 out of 51 cases, in fact). When asked how often divisions reported to head office, 46 respondents (out of 53) replied that they reported monthly or even more frequently (this involved assessment of divisional profit components). From this Tomkins concluded that divisional autonomy did not appear to be as great as he had at first assumed.

What can be concluded from all of these observations?

1. It appears probable that top management may often attempt to retain maximum control over company activities while overtly granting autonomy under the guise of divisionalization.
2. Accountants have assumed that this should be so and that really top management is the sole originator of overall corporate goals.
3. Accordingly accountants have concentrated upon developing divisional profit measures which have often been used to enhance top management command over corporate affairs.
4. The concept of goal congruence may have served as a convenient justification for this bias in accounting activity.

This state of affairs has left accountants with a seemingly insoluble problem in the shape of:

THE CONTROL-AUTONOMY CONFLICT

... it is clear that in the control of the typical organization, perfect decentralization is not possible because of the limitations on enforcement rules associated with uncertainty and risk aversion.[59]

---

[57] D.N. Duncan, 'Training Business Managers in General Systems Concepts', in *Man in Systems*, M.D. Rubin (ed.), Gordon and Breach Science Publishers, New York, 1971, pp. 300–303, 310–311.

[58] C. Tomkins, *op. cit.*, pp. 157–158, 166–167.

[59] K.J. Arrow, *op. cit.*, p. 407.

Top management and accountants might take this to mean that in any conflict between top management control and divisional autonomy, autonomy must be expensed to preserve control. Moore and Jaedicke[60] point to the conflict when naming the two main advantages of a decentralized company as being delegation of decision-making responsibility to levels lower than top management and motivation of managers in relation to the company's profit objectives. This action, they say, creates the problem of controlling and evaluating division management. There lies the conflict. Independence is apparently granted while control is actually retained, mostly via accounting measurement systems. Moore and Jaedicke further imply that when greater freedom has been granted to division managers, profit control is rendered necessary.

In his discussion of means of attaining optimal corporate effects from divisional decisions, Tomkins really highlights the conflict between control and autonomy:

If the reader is dissatisfied and feels that no ideal tool has been supplied for providing simultaneously both divisional autonomy and overall optimization of performance, perhaps he should be reminded that he is probably seeking something which cannot exist.[61]

From his examination of divisional transfer pricing models he concludes that most either allow divisional autonomy and thereby risk corporate non-optimality, or require full information to be transmitted to head office or require a lengthy calculation process which may emphasize 'the supervision and watchfulness of the head office'. Once again the emphasis tends to fall upon the accountant's view of the necessity of centralized control of divisions for the maximization of corporate profitability.

What might be concluded here is that accountants have probably recognized the conflict between control and autonomy in divisional performance measurement but have only considered it from one viewpoint. They appear to have seen the problem as being one of designing accounting measurements which retain maximum top management control of a company while still endeavouring to provide divisions with some feeling of autonomy. Possibly, in the conflict between divisional control and divisional autonomy, accountants have been only too eager to sacrifice the latter. 'Pseudo Participation' was a phrase coined by Argyris[62] denoting the apparent granting by management to employees an effective voice in decision-making while actually taking no notice of their views. This was found in cases to incur hostile and disruptive reactions from employees. Accountants might risk the same fate if divisional personnel perceive them to be encouraging pseudo-divisionalization.

[60] C.L. Moore and R.K. Jaedicke, *op. cit.*, pp. 542–543.
[61] C. Tomkins, *op. cit.*, p. 104.
[62] C. Argyris, *The Impact of Budgets on People*, Controllership Foundation, 1952.

As Hofstede[63] argues, since control and autonomy can either coexist or conflict, their simultaneous maximization is unlikely. Companies can at best hope to attain an optimal balance between the two. Decentralization therefore may be seen as one attempt to do this. Furthermore, it must be remembered that Tannenbaum[64] has demonstrated that the total amount of control in an organization does not have a rigid, finite limit. The total amount of control can be increased. Increases in the amount of autonomy allowed to divisions will not therefore automatically reduce total existing control. Contingency theory, with its roots in the systems perspective of organizations, is of further assistance here when it emphasizes that an organization should be designed to suit its environment. In this framework, Lawrence and Lorsch[65] argue that the more certain the environment, the more centralized an organization can be, while the more uncertain the environment, the less centralized an organization can be. In the former situation, coordination can be achieved through the organizational hierarchy while in the latter situation (an unstable environment) it must be carried out at lower organization levels where the required knowledge and information are available.

A REVISED VIEW OF DIVISIONAL PERFORMANCE MEASUREMENT

The arguments advanced in this paper have a range of implications for the assessment of divisional performance by accountants. Much of the divisional performance literature appears to be based upon a simplistic, unrealistic view of corporate and divisional goals and has often subscribed to the concept of goal congruence while conceding the power of corporate personnel's self-interest. Given the existing range of changing corporate and divisional goals, the divisional profit test taken by itself is inadequate as a measure of any division's progress towards the attainment of the corporate 'goal set'. Its perspective is far too narrow. If accountants wish to claim that they serve the creators of company goals, they should turn their attention to providing performance measures for divisional self-assessment since much of the corporate 'goal set' appears to be generated from the actions of divisional personnel as well as higher management. Furthermore, attempts by accountants to further refine divisional profit measures have been somewhat misdirected, given the need for additional measures of divisional performance.

An alternative approach to divisional performance measurement which accountants might adopt for the benefit of the decentralized company as a whole could be described as follows:

[63] C.H. Hofstede, *The Game of Budget Control*, Tavistock Publications, London, 1968, pp. 13–14.
[64] A.S. Tannenbaum, 'Control in Organization', in *Control in Organizations*, A.S. Tannenbaum (ed.), McGraw-Hill, 1968, pp. 3–23.
[65] P. Lawrence and J. Lorsch, *Organization and Environment: Managing Differentiation and Integration*, Harvard University Graduate School of Business Administration, Division of Research, Boston, 1967.

1. Discard the belief that accounting measures should be used to promote goal congruence among division managers.
2. Recognize the need to preserve some degree of autonomy in divisional operations.
3. Review the possible methods of assessing divisional performance with a view to accounting for the needs and objectives of all levels of management above and within each division.
4. Move beyond the single divisional profit-based index to provide an expanded number of measures of divisional performance which account for a broader range of success criteria.

Accordingly accountants ought to be able to bring their expertise to new areas of division performance and to further develop measures for these. Further attention could usefully be paid to the development of divisional productivity indices, projected monetary benefits of the maintenance of certain market positions, costs versus benefits of product development, division social accounts for social responsibility, and human resource accounting for aspects such as personnel development, employee turnover, accident frequency etc. Accounting has done much to facilitate the assessment of divisional profitability and has the resources to be of similar service for assessment of other aspects of divisional performance.

All of these proposals may require a considerable change in the basic attitudes of many accountants toward their role and towards the rights of corporate personnel. Goal congruence appears to have been used as a justification by accountants for their active promotion of maximum top management control over divisional affairs while ostensibly granting divisional autonomy. Accountants may have viewed divisional personnel as objects to be constrained by the use of accounting measures. This would appear to contravene directly their officially pronounced role of serving line departments. Rather, consideration should be given to re-designing the system to serve a broader spectrum of divisional personnel as well as higher management. In today's society many corporate activities have been the subject of public scrutiny and are being adjusted accordingly. Prime examples include employee participation in decision making, the reporting of financial information to employees, increased provisions for employee safety and welfare and the growth of various forms of social responsibility reporting. Accountants have always professed their prime aim as being that of serving information users. In present day society, the identity and needs of those users has expanded and it is in this context that this paper has advocated the redesign of the divisional performance measurement system to serve divisional as well as higher managements.

This proposal does not therefore hinge on any contention of the author's as to what he thinks the modern corporation should be like. It rests upon observations of what corporations have become and what society expects of them. Corporations have been recognized as a coalition of individuals and groups working towards a range of continuously changing goals which originate from their own desires rather than being handed down by some authority. In addition, these corporations now operate in a social and political climate which is causing them to offer lower level employees a more powerful role in daily operations, more rights and more access to corporate information, while at the same time providing the public with more information about the effects of their operations upon society at large and responding to social pressure for changes in policy when required. The expansion of accountants' service from top management to include lower levels of management at division level therefore represents a response to society's present view of what corporations ought to be like and to the observations of organization researchers as to what corporations are in fact like.

What of the divisional performance measurement system itself? Further investigation into the appropriate degree of divisional independence is required along with the development of measures for divisional self-assessment. Resulting benefits to the company may in fact outweigh the cost of non-optimal corporate decisions made at division level. Finally the diminishing influence of the goal congruence concept would seem to call for a reduction in accountants' emphasis upon the divisional profit test and its incorporation with other performance measures relating to other aspects of division operations. By way of suggestion, accounting researchers could begin to consider some specific performance criteria for different aspects of division operations as outlined below. As should become evident, considerable scope exists for the future development of the composite set of divisional performance indices.

In the first instance, the financial management of divisions might be reflected upon more fairly than by a single profitability index by such information as:

1. Stock and asset turnover statistics,
2. Gearing ratios,
3. Fixed asset statistics such as age of classes of equipment, depreciation policies, levels of maintenance expenditure etc., and
4. Major sources and applications of funds.

Productivity of a division is admittedly difficult to measure. A rough guide might be profit before interest and tax per employee although such a figure would have to be related to the capital intensiveness of the division's operations and other salient factors. Further refinement of productivity measures calls for further enlightened effort by accounting researchers.

A division's marketing strategy could usefully be assessed with reference to such measures as:

1. Its achieved volume of sales.
2. Its current share of the market.
3. Its estimated product mix related to average contribution margins attained.

4. Sales effort, efficiency and consumer response ratios such as sales/ visits, selling expenses/sales, visits/days, and sales/orders.[66]

Any divisional research and development might be scrutinized by measures such as expenditure percentage of sales, expenditure per employee, actual versus planned cost for progress actually achieved, actual versus planned progress, anticipated excess cost for complete projects, estimated project benefits achieved etc. No single one of these measures could be used in isolation as an accurate representation of a division's research and development effort but some combination could present a reasonable overall impression. A product-line matrix of total research and development effort (in £s or %s) could be designed for two groups of categories such as:

1. Cost reduction, product improvement, new product design.
2. General research, applied research, project development.[67]

Some elements of social responsibility accounting might be further developed and applied as divisional performance measures. This again would be a reflection of the variety of goals contained in the division/ company 'goal set'. Such measures might take one of the following forms:

1. Social responsibility budget.
2. Narrative social responsibility report.
3. Outlay cost social responsibility report.
4. Cost-benefit social responsibility report.[68]

Of course much more development work is required of accounting researchers in this area.

Employee related information could also be usefully included in this broadened scheme for divisional performance measurement. This would justify continued efforts by accounting researchers in developing means of accounting for company human resources. Accidents occurring in a division could be reflected by measures such as:

1. Number of accidents causing lost time.
2. Hours lost as a percentage of hours worked.
3. Injury costs (developed from tables of hospitalization costs, convalescence costs, worker compensation costs, and insurance premium increases).

[66] Refer for instance to G. Shillinglaw, *Managerial Cost Accounting*, 4th Edition, Richard D. Irwin, Homewood, Illinois, 1977, pp. 295–317.
[67] Refer for instance to G. Shillinglaw, *Managerial Cost Accounting*, 4th Edition, pp. 744–765. A. Matz and M.F. Usry, *Cost Accounting: Planning and Control*, South Western Publishing Co., Cincinnatti, Ohio, 1976, p. 502.
[68] Refer for instance to L.D. Parker, 'Accounting for Corporate Social Responsibility: The Task of Measurement', *Chartered Accountant in Australia*, October 1977, pp. 5–15.

The prevalence of industrial disputes within a division could be reflected by its number of working days lost in a year, hours lost as a percentage of hours planned, and lost contribution margins. Divisional human resource management might also be related to the average staff turnover rate for a period such as 6 months or a year. This could also be presented in monetary terms if average human resources of the division were valued in some way (e.g. on a basis of recruiting, acquisition, training, formal and informal development activities).

IN CONCLUSION

The above range of divisional performance measures is not an all-inclusive list and may not all be appropriate to each division. Nevertheless they demonstrate a range of possible goals, criteria and related activities which a single profit-based index fails to reflect. At any rate the adoption by a company of an expanded range of divisional performance measures may serve to identify potential long term operational problems in the short term before they actually eventuate so that *ex ante* corrective or preventative action can be taken. It must also be remembered that it is primarily the division which is being assessed by itself and higher management through these measures and that a division manager could control some components of these measures only to a certain degree. A division cannot be evaluated upon aspects of its operations which are beyond its control. Furthermore accountants should recognize the necessity of combining both qualitative and quantitative approaches to divisional performance measurement. A balanced view of divisional operations is unlikely to result from excessive reliance upon one particular approach only.

Finally some reference must be made to the potential problem of information overload which might result from the adoption of a range of divisional performance measures. Such a problem could most likely be averted by the presentation of the complete group of detailed measures to division managers for their own autonomous use in managing division operations and of a summarized group to higher management for their broader policy purposes. These difficulties in measurement and presentation however are essential aspects of a broadened scheme of divisional performance measurement which, formidable though they may seem, must be confronted by accountants if they are to render the measurement of divisional performance more realistic.

This paper therefore argues for the future development of a matrix of divisional performance measures both by area of operation (financial, market, employee, social etc.) and by degree of divisional controllability. A composite mix of quantitative and qualitative indices is required for balanced assessment of divisional performance. It is a critical problem which urgently awaits the attention of accounting researchers.

26

A contingency framework for the design of accounting information systems

Lawrence A. Gordon and Danny Miller
McGill University

ABSTRACT

Most of the research to date concerning the design of an accounting information system has taken a rather narrow and inflexible view of accounting information. The primary intent of this paper is to provide a broader and more adaptive framework for designing such systmes. A contingency approach, which takes into account the environment, organizational attributes, and managerial decision making styles, is advocated. In this context, several hypotheses are offered concerning the requisites of an accounting information system.

Problems of designing an accounting information system (A.I.S.) have long received the attention of management accountants. For the most part, the efforts to date have been directed at searching for the single most desirable method of generating financial data to promote effective decision making. On the other hand, little attention has been given to the need for considering environmental, organizational, and decision making style attributes in the design of an A.I.S. Also overlooked in much of the previous work is the contingent nature of most decision making. Accordingly, this paper represents the results of an effort to fill some of these gaps. Our objective is to provide a framework for designing accounting information systems which consider the *specific needs* of the organization. In order to accomplish this objective, we have drawn on the literature of organization theory, management policy, and accounting so as to isolate the environmental, organizational, and decision making variables which have been shown to be critical to organizational performance. We examine the impact of these variables upon the requisites of the

Source: Gordon, L.A. and Miller, D. (1976) *Accounting, Organizations and Society,*
1 (1), pp. 59–69.

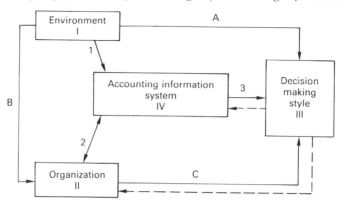

Fig. 26.1

accounting information system. The specific relationships considered are indicated by the solid lines in Fig. 26.1.[1]

The characteristics of the accounting information system, to which the environmental, organizational and decision making variables will be related are: information load, centralization of reporting, cost allocation methods (with reference to both amount and timing), frequency of reporting, method of reporting (e.g. statements, raw data, charts, pictures), time element of information (e.g. *ex ante* vs *ex post* data), performance evaluation, measurement of events (e.g. financial vs nonfinancial data and external vs internal data), and valuation methods (e.g. historical cost vs market value vs price level adjusted information).

We will also briefly discuss the relationships hypothesized in the literature among environmental, organizational, and decision style variables (links A, B, C in Fig. 26.1). Our discussion of these latter relationships will highlight the non-random nature of the required organization attributes and decision making styles, given the nature of the environment.

In the third section of the paper we discuss three 'archetypes' empirically derived by Miller (1975a) which characterize common clusterings of environmental, organizational and decision style traits. The thrust of this discussion is to relate these archetypes to the A.I.S. requisites which we hypothesize to be effective under each circumstance. The first archetype discussed is an 'adaptive' firm, while the second and third portray 'running blind' and 'stagnant bureaucracy' firms respectively. Implications are drawn about the required features of the A.I.S. under each circumstance. These archetypes are intended to illustrate that different information systems are required according to each situation and that these systems should be designed employing a total conception of the firm and

---

[1] The relationships indicated by the dashed lines will not be discussed in this paper. However, we do not believe that this restriction will mitigate the thrust of the paper. Further work by the authors, now underway, does include explicit consideration of these relationships.

its administrative tasks. However, it must be emphasized that we are attempting to provide a *framework for analyzing* the needs of the A.I.S., rather than prescribing a unique system. In fact, due to the contingent nature of a well designed A.I.S., we believe that no one prescribed system could ever be effective in all circumstances. On the other hand, we do offer several hypotheses on the A.I.S. characteristics which may be appropriate under certain conditions.

THE LINKS OF THE MODEL

A. The environment of the firm and the requisites of the accounting information system

The environment of an organization can be characterized by at least the following three key dimensions: (1) dynamism, (2) heterogeneity, and (3) hostility. A discussion of each of these dimensions and their relationships with the accounting system follows.

Environmental dynamism. Some organizations sell their products in environments where consumer tastes are stable and predictable, the technology required to produce goods or render services remains the same (or almost the same) as time passes, and competitors tend to behave in a predictable fashion in terms of their product-market orientations. Other firms face much more dynamic environments. In these settings, consumer tastes shift rapidly and unpredictably, new technologies and sources of supply often arise, and competitors introduce many radically new products. The same accounting information system cannot serve the needs of both these groups of firms equally well. Thus, we propose the following hypotheses: As environmental dynamism increases, the effective A.I.S.:

(a) begins to incorporate more nonfinancial data to provide managers with information on competitor actions, consumer tastes, and shifting demographic factors. Financial data alone will not provide information which is sufficiently precise to inform managers of important trends before they become crises.

(b) increases the frequency of reporting. Although Cook (1967) implies that an increase in the frequency of feedback will in general increase managerial performance, it is our contention that the relationship between frequency of feedback and performance becomes more crucial in a dynamic environment than in an unchanging environment.

(c) makes greater use of forecast information, again to inform managers of trends and important issues before they become difficult problems.

(d) is more conservative in the allocation of expenses; for example expense, rather than capitalize, costs for such things as R & D, so as to help inform managers of the additional risk associated with projects having a long-term payoff. Thus we would tend to concur with the FASB's recommendation (1974) to expense, rather than capitalize, R & D under these conditions. On the other hand, with a stable (unchanging) environment, the wisdom of their recommendation seems questionable.

Environmental heterogeneity. The environment of an organization might be homogeneous in terms of the required product-market orientations, consumer characteristics, production technologies, and raw materials markets. As pointed out by Lawrence and Lorsch (1967), Thompson (1967) and Khandwalla (1972a), for some organizations the environment may be extremely diverse in these respects. For example, a large conglomerate, such as I.T.T., deals in very different markets, with very different products and different required technologies – a heterogeneous environment. We hypothesize that, as the level of environmental heterogeneity increases, the effective A.I.S.:

(a) does more to tailor specific parts of the system to the sub-segments of the environment. In other words, there is greater need for more decentralized as opposed to centralized accounting systems. Some divisions of a firm may require an elaborate A.I.S. to cope with a dynamic setting, whereas others may cope with a simple system if they operate in a stable environment.

(b) compartmentalizes information so that it is possible for central management to assess the performance of the separate divisions and the personnel responsible for them. Cost, profit and investment centers are some of the compartmentalization techniques available by which to accumulate accounting information.

Environmental hostility. A dimension closely related to environmental dynamism is that of hostility (Hermann, 1969). Hostility results from threatening actions of competitors (e.g. cut-throat competition) or threatening shortages of scarce resources due to strikes, governmental regulations or credit squeezes. We hypothesize that, as hostility increases, the effective A.I.S.:

(a) provides more frequent reports to inform managers of impending dangers.

(b) provides substantial nonfinancial data to characterize the variables most sensitive to, and indicative of, threats in the environment. As pointed out by Mintzberg (1975) one of the existing impediments to managerial use of data gathered in formal information systems is that the information is too limited in scope. Presumably this recommendation would tend to offset this impediment.

(c) employs a fairly sophisticated cost accounting and control system. Khandwalla's study (1972b), where he points out that the sophistication of a firm's control system is highly correlated with the intensity of competition in that firm, clearly shows that many firms have already recognized this requisite of the A.I.S.

B. The organization and the requisites of the A.I.S.

The literature on organization theory is replete with findings on the types of organizational structures required given the conditions in the environment. Woodward (1965), Lawrence and Lorsch (1967), Burns and Stalker (1961), Thompson (1967), Perrow (1970), and a host of others, have pointed to the need for more 'sophisticated' organizational devices as the degree of environmental dynamism, heterogeneity, and hostility accelerate. Typical devices used by firms to cope with these more complex environments include uncertainty reduction mechanisms such as decentralization, divisionalization, differentiation of organizational sub-units, and integration of these diverse orientations via committees, rules and policies. We shall discuss five organizational attributes which derive from increased environmental dynamism, heterogeneity, and hostility, and focus upon the characteristics of the A.I.S. which are required for increasing levels of these organizational traits. The attributes, which are intended to be illustrative rather than exhaustive, are as follows: (1) decentralization, (2) differentiation, (3) integration, (4) bureaucratization, and (5) resources.

Decentralization. As the administrative task becomes more complex, subtasks and responsibilities must be delegated to lower levels of management to ease the burden of decision making. Thus increased environmental dynamism, heterogeneity and hostility must often be accompanied by decentralization of power and responsibilities. Such decentralization might take the form of divisionalization and/or departmentalization. Under these conditions, the A.I.S. may have to become more sensitive and sophisticated since the progress of divisions must be monitored at the top of the organization. There is an increased requirement for formal controls to replace informal controls. We hypothesize that under decentralization the effective A.I.S.:

(a) produces more explicit reports on the performance of organizational sub-units (i.e. the accounting system itself must become decentralized). As pointed out by Benston (1963), many have argued that this type of reporting system is not only the result of, but is in fact a prerequisite to, decentralization.

(b) develops substantial supporting information to enable sub-unit performance evaluation. For example, the development of a transfer pricing system will facilitate sub-unit profit evaluation. Other ways of facilitating performance evaluation, as pointed out by Abdel-Khalik & Lusk (1974), include analysis of costs and measurement of physical units of output.

(c) encompasses a sophisticated planning and control system. Decentralized firms must carefully consider how they will allocate and control their resources among divisions so that the maximum return is achieved without negating the potential motivational benefits to be derived from decentralization. In this regard, Godfrey (1971) has suggested a short run planning model for use in a decentralized firm, which recognizes the need for corporate allocation of scarce resources and also promotes divisional autonomy.

Differentiation. Some firms have sub-units which are quite similar to one another in terms of their modus operandi, time horizons, goal orientations, and the interpersonal habits of their staff. Others contain sub-units which are very different in these respects. The latter group of firms is referred to as being highly differentiated (Lawrence & Lorsch, 1967). Clearly the administrative control tasks and internal communication of the organization become much more difficult if managers with different orientations must come into contact with one another. Since they often perceive issues very differently (Lawrence & Lorsch, 1976), we hypothesize that the effective A.I.S. can help meet the challenge posed by these communication and control problems by:

(a) providing the different sub-units with an A.I.S. suited particularly to their needs. Accordingly the accounting system should be of a decentralized nature. For example, Watson & Baumler (1975) discuss the role the A.I.S. can play in facilitating the requisite degree of differentiation among organizational units via the appropriate transfer pricing system.

(b) gathering data from sub-units in a manner such that executives can assess the *relative* performance of each sub-unit. To the extent that units are very different, data collected for the top management must be chosen carefully so as not to mix 'apples with oranges'. Also, care must be taken so as to prevent information overload from occurring. As discussed by many in the accounting literature (e.g. Miller & Gordon, 1975; Driver & Mock, 1975; Revsine, 1970), more information is not necessarily better than less.

Integration. As the level of organizational differentiation increases, there is a greater need for more integrative devices to assure a consistent and coordinated strategic effort and avoid interdivisional conflict (Lawrence & Lorsch, 1967). Khandwalla (1972a) lists an array of integrative devices, such as: participative management, coordinative committees, explicit policies and group objectives. Thompson (1967) speaks of various modes of interdepartmental coordination, such as rules and reciprocal feedback mechanisms, which become required as the degree of environmental uncertainty (dynamism and hostility) increases. The A.I.S. can serve as a powerful coordinative device, particularly if the degree of organizational differentiation is quite high. We postulate that under these conditions the effective A.I.S.:

(a) incorporates plans and budgets which represent overall corporate targets to which each sub-unit must contribute. However, achieving goal congruency (Bierman & Dyckman, 1971) among sub-units is easier said than done and thus the difficulty of implementing this suggestion should not be underestimated.

(b) presents information to managers of sub-units on some vital matters or parameters concerning other units. Such information should help to encourage joint problem solving among the managers of separate units, which in turn can serve to foster invaluable inter-unit informal communication.

Bureaucratization. Bureaucratization refers to the extent to which organizational activities are structured, programmed, specialized, and narrowly prescribed. Formal rules abound and traditional modes of operation severely limit the individual discretion of lower level managers in highly bureaucratic settings.[2] Argyris (1964), Burns & Stalker (1961), Bennis (1966), among others, have indicated some dysfunctional side effects of bureaucratization, such as insensitivity to the need to change strategies and employee dissatisfaction. These are particularly severe in dynamic environments in which individual initiative at lower levels is very much required to prompt the organization to adjust to its external context. We hypothesize that some of the ill effects of bureaucratization can be countered by an effective A.I.S. as follows:

(a) the A.I.S. can provide upper level managers with financial and nonfinancial information on the external environment. This type of information may indicate important trends requiring more flexible and situational organizational responses. Specifically, the information presented can to some extent alert the executives and motivate them to eliminate some dysfunctional bureaucratic traditions or rules. The A.I.S. can act as a 'change agent'.

(b) the A.I.S. can provide price level adjusted and/or market value statements, as well as forecast statements, to inform managers of conditions which require the departure from traditional modes of operation. Unlike many proponents of market value accounting (see, e.g. Romano, 1975) and price level adjusted statements (e.g. AICPA, 1969) we believe that the virtues of these valuation methods depend on the specific organizational traits of the firm in question.

Resources. While some firms have an abundance of slack resources such as managerial expertise, technocratic skills, and financial and material resources, others may experience grave shortages. We hypothesize that the effective A.I.S. can help managers to cope with these shortages as follows:

(a) if managerial expertise is known to be deficient in any area, the accounting system can be used to provide data which could better inform managers about things they otherwise would not have been able to fully understand. For example, if a new manager is unfamiliar with the behaviour of his customers, the A.I.S. should be particularly thorough and informative in terms of the information which it provides to this manager about market characteristics and buyer purchasing patterns. Recent efforts in the area of human resource accounting (see, e.g. Flamholtz, 1974) may eventually go a long way in helping to isolate those areas where managerial expertise is, in fact, deficient.

(b) if technocratic expertise is lacking, then the A.I.S. could provide more detailed costing information such as quantity and cost variances, percentage of total costs due to scrap or poor quality, and number of units rejected because of production flaws. Such statistics would help to inform managers about the areas where production methods could be improved.

(c) scarcities in material and financial resources may also be reflected in the A.I.S. Such resources could be carefully monitored by the information system through sophisticated costing techniques, profit plans,

---

[2] Pugh *et al.* (1963) have denoted this situation as 'structuring' of activities.

resource allocation plans, resource utilization forecasts, and key indicators of the conditions prevailing in the financial markets.

C. The decision making style of executives and the requisites of the A.I.S.

The decision making style which an executive employs to adjust his organization's orientation to the needs of the environment is critical to the well being of the enterprise. For example, where the environment is dynamic, decision makers are sometimes required to be more proactive in their decision making (Ackoff, 1969). Perrow (1970) and Thompson (1967) claim that decision making must become more sensitive and adaptive to external requirements under these circumstances. Thompson & Tuden (1959) and Wheelright (1970) argue that a simpler, less analytical, more short run oriented type of decision making will tend to take place where environments are dynamic and heterogeneous. Organizational attributes also determine the types of decision styles needed. Normann (1971) and Allison (1971) indicate how structuring of activities reduces adaptiveness and innovativeness. Cyert & March (1963) indicate how decentralization might result in less integrated, more bargaining oriented, decision styles.

We shall focus on the ability of the A.I.S. to influence the following six dimensions of decision making styles: (1) analysis, (2) time horizons, (3) multiplexity, (4) adaptiveness, (5) proactivity, and (6) consciousness or explicitness of strategies and objectives. In other words, we shall examine the manner in which the A.I.S. may eventually *change* a manager's style of decision making behaviour (Hofstedt & Kinard, 1970).[3]

Analysis of decisions. The executives of some organizations spend a great deal of time and effort studying their environment and the problems and opportunities which confront the organization. Other managers tend to make 'seat of the pants' decisions on the basis of their intuition, scarcely regarding the objective characteristics of the situation. Although Mock *et al.* (1972) suggest that the payoffs from 'analytical' decision making will in general exceed those accruing to 'seat of the pants' executives, it is our contention that such payoffs will depend on a host of environmental and organizational variables. For example, under an extremely stable environment, the incremental costs associated with an analytical rather than 'seat of the pants' approach to decision making may well be more than the incremental benefits derived. On the other hand, where environmental dynamism and hostility are substantial, a more analytical approach to decision making may become necessary for survival (although difficult to implement). In the latter case, we hypothesize that the effective A.I.S.:

(a) provides substantial non financial data on key operating trends,

(b) provides a graphical presentation of information which compares actual with forecasted (budgeted) figures and clearly indicates historical

[3] Hopwood (1974) discusses a relationship of another direction – i.e., the manner in which leadership climate, another dimension of decision making style, influences the way managers use accounting information in performance evaluation.

trends. This type of presentation may stimulate managers to explore further key issues,

(c) stores adequately detailed financial information so that in-depth analysis can be performed where deemed appropriate.

Decision time horizons (futurity). Managers concerned only with day-to-day operating matters neglect to consider the long-term repercussions of their immediate decisions. It may be crucial to give serious attention to the long-term implications of decisions. Certain environmental and organizational conditions (e.g. a relatively stable environment, where certain key material resources are steadily being depleted) increase the feasibility and need for managers to take a long-term approach to decision making. Under such conditions, to provoke executives to look into the future, we hypothesize that the effective A.I.S.:

(a) presents trends, as well as data points,

(b) provides forecasts of expected events and financial variables which are critical to the operating performance of the firm. The recent (February, 1973) decision by the SEC in the U.S. to permit the filing of forecasted earnings statements should have interesting implications towards fostering the generation of this type of information,

(c) presents information on objective setting procedures which force managers to think more about goals, programs, and the future of the organization.

Multiplex decision making. Some corporate executives consider very few factors in making strategic decisions. For example, a manager may begin to introduce a new product on the basis of forecasted market demand, neglecting to examine such things as detailed estimates of product costs, production methods, and staff requirements. Other managers adopt a much more multiplex approach. In some environments, such as ones which are *extremely* heterogeneous and/or dynamic, a multiplex decision making orientation is probably not feasible. On the other hand, in a moderately dynamic and heterogeneous environment, multiplex decision orientation may be both feasible and desirable. Assuming the latter situation exists, the effective A.I.S. may be able to foster multiplexity by:

(a) providing both financial and nonfinancial data,

(b) supplying top level executives with information which pertains to a number of functions (e.g. marketing, finance, production) in the organization,

(c) allowing only the very crucial facts to appear on centralized reports, since, in order to prevent information overload, there is a need to sacrifice depth and detail for breadth,

(d) providing sub-unit heads with information, financial and non-financial, on the activities of other sub-units.

Adaptiveness. As dynamism increases, there is a greater need to track what competitors are doing and how consumers are behaving. Some corporate managers are quite adaptive to changes in the organization's environment, while others are not. The A.I.S. can be an extremely vital vehicle in promoting adaptiveness to external factors and internal needs. We hypothesize that, in promoting adaptiveness, an effective A.I.S. will:

(a) supply managers with information on what is going on in the external environment. Examples include information on the market share of the firm's various products, and reports of customer attitude surveys,

(b) increase the frequency of reporting so as to provide information or critical conditions before they become problems,

(c) highlight cost and budget variances and point to situations in which things are not going smoothly.

Proactivity. Proactivity is defined as the tendency to be ahead of competitors in taking certain actions. Its opposite is reactiveness in which decisions are only made upon provocation. Many managers tend to be overly conservative in their approach to decision making. They introduce new products or embark upon programs to execute technological innovations in the production process only when they have very clear evidence that they are in trouble. The absence of proactivity is especially serious in dynamic environments where it is extremely easy to fall behind the competition. To promote a proactive decision making style, we hypothesize that the effective A.I.S.:[4]

(a) includes information on the activities of competing firms. Information should be supplied on new product introductions and technological innovations being implemented in the industry. While this is hardly a standard sort of information for an A.I.S., it is likely to pay off handsomely in making managers more aware of the need for change,

(b) reports product demand forecasts (translated into forecasted revenues) and the long-run prospects for the costs of production. Such forecasts should help executives to think in terms of promising new markets and technologies which might be exploited before the old ones become uneconomical.

Consciousness of strategies. Lindblom (1968) describes a type of decision making which is disjointed. That is, organizational decisions are made more or less independently. It is difficult under this mode to ensure that the actions of organizational sub-units are congruent with overall organizational objectives. Executives tend to maximize short term objectives and parochial interests at the expense of strategic goals and long term plans. In an environment characterized by heterogeneity, an explicit and conscious conception of decision making is difficult to achieve but is most desirable. In an effort to facilitate such an orientation towards decision making, the effective A.I.S.:

---

[4] Although our discussion has been concerned with the impact that the A.I.S. can have on a given decision making style, it should be apparent that this relationship is like a two edged sword. For example, Sorter *et al.* (1964), have provided evidence showing how a corporation's conservative management can unfavourably affect that part of the accounting system related to depreciation policy.

(a) incorporates a system of targets and objectives which must be met by each department. Targets relating to costs and profits, quality control, customer satisfaction and market share are all potential candidates. The objective setting process may be a participative one, with information coming from all relevent departments,

(b) compares actual results with targeted or budgeted objectives so that the performance of organizational sub-units can be appraised in the light of overall organizational objectives.

ARCHETYPAL ORGANIZATIONS AND REQUISITE QUALITIES OF THE A.I.S.

By now it should be clear that an accounting information system should be designed in light of the contextual variables surrounding the specific organization. Our discussion thus far was intended to generate some conceptual anchor points and related hypotheses which might provide a basis for future research and which eventually designers might use as examples in the design of their own systems. We did not attempt to prescribe a panacea system. Instead, we have been trying to establish the point that a contingency approach must be taken in designing an organization's A.I.S.

In this section we discuss three 'archetypal' firms discovered by Miller (1975a) which represent typical agglomerations of environmental, organizational, and decision style traits. The three archetypes are (1) adaptive, (2) running blind, and (3) stagnant bureaucracy. We then relate these archetypes to the A.I.S. requisites which we hypothesize to be effective under each circumstance.

Based on Miller's analysis of the cases, *it seems that environmental, organizational, and decision style traits are not distributed randomly but actually cluster together to form commonly occurring configurations.* Thus, rather than having to worry about an unmanageable number of permutations of the variables discussed in the previous section, it appears that the designer of an A.I.S. may have only to focus on a few select variables from which a host of peripheral factors generally follow. Our emphasis here is not, however, on the derivation of the archetypes (since this is discussed at length in Miller, 1975); but rather with the generation of hypotheses concerning the requisites of the A.I.S. given the existence of such archetypes.

A. The adaptive firm

Several of the cases studied involved firms whose environments have been quite dynamic for a substantial length of time while heterogeneity is only moderate. In these firms, there exists substantial decentralization of authority, moderate to low differentiation and more than adequate integration. Managerial, technocratic, and financial resources are quite abundant. Decision making styles are characterized by great multiplexity, substantial analysis of strategic issues, an adaptive and responsive orientation to important trends in the environment, and an explicit and well defined strategy. Executives tend to be quite innovative and proactive, in that they seize upon opportunities in their environment rather than waiting until they are in trouble before they act. The performance level in these firms is high.[5] A large part of the apparent success of these 'adaptive' firms seems to be due to the type of information and intelligence systems which they employ.

Individuals designing accounting information systems for the above described firms have apparently done their jobs fairly well. The main information system characteristics which are hypothesized to be effective for such firms are:[6]

(a) a capacity for gathering information on the external environment. Environmental dynamism makes this a particularly important feature to incorporate into the A.I.S. in firms of this sort,

(b) the collection of nonfinancial, as well as financial, information (e.g. information on inflationary trends, new product ideas, technological ideas, and consumer taste trends). Again, environmental dynamism increases the importance of nonfinancial information in tracking the environment,

(c) a uniform accounting system from one sub-unit to another. Since differentiation is low in these firms, the same type of information system can be used across the firms' divisions. A centralized, rather than decentralized, A.I.S. seems more appropriate,

(d) the internal flow of information across departments (laterally) and levels of authority (vertically) should take place in an unimpeded, timely, and informative fashion. This is important due to environmental dynamism and is feasible because of moderate heterogeneity and lower differentiation,

(e) data analysis presented to top management should be of a *low* level of detail. Because decentralization has been operating successfully and resources are plentiful, top level executives need not be overly concerned with the minutia of lower level operating matters,

(f) the array of information provided to managers should be quite broad. This type of information can be effective since managers in these firms tend to be multiplex, adaptive, and analytically inclined. These sorts of executives will themselves seek more information (which the A.I.S. can store but not distribute) if and when they feel it is needed.

B. The running blind firm

Several of the cases studied involved firms in heterogeneous markets whose environments change markedly over a relatively short period of time. The tremendous dynamism and heterogeneity in some of these firms was created by the actions of competitors. In others, it came about

---

[5] Performance ratings were based on growth in revenues and profits, and return on invested capital.

[6] Accounting information system characteristics were not measured by Miller (1975) in his analysis of cases. We are hypothesizing these attributes in the light of the environmental, organizational, and strategy making attributes of the firm.

because executives have rapidly acquired new firms in very different types of markets. The organization structure of these companies is rather peculiar. Power is tightly centralized in the hands of a few top level executives. Organizational differentiation is, however, extremely high because of the manifest differences among departments, divisions, and subsidiaries. Furthermore, the various orientations are not easily reconciled through integrative devices. Separate and sometimes conflicting objectives seem to be pursued by the various organizational sub-units.

The decision making styles of the managers of these firms are characterized by low multiplexity, intuitive rather than analytical decision making, and an insensitivity to conditions in the environment. Perhaps most notably, managers in these firms are quite entrepreneurial – they are proactive and take substantial risks. For example, new product lines, which require a radically new or different type of technology are often introduced with little in-depth analysis. Also, large new subsidiaries are often acquired in businesses which are strange to the old entity.

Performance in these firms is low. The intelligence system seems to be inadequately suited to the emergent environmental conditions. The environment is scanned infrequently and only for a few select cues (e.g. acquisition candidates) by top level personnel. Controls which can inform managers of the performance of their divisions – old and new – are often lacking. Communication seems to run one way – from top level managers down to subordinates. Individual divisons in these firms are quite isolated from one another and top managers usually do not know what is happening in the divisions until crises arrive.

Designers of the A.I.S. can ostensibly go a long way in helping to reduce some of the problems in these firms. For instance:

(a) it is critical that facts be gathered about 'situations' out of control and be sent to top management in timely fashion,

(b) information on the new products and technological innovations of competitors should be provided to help facilitate an effective style of decision making,

(c) if a high degree of power centralization makes information overload a potential problem, the onus is on the information system to provide the top managers only with critical data which reveal a situation to be out of kilter. For example, only aggregated data for each division (e.g. total expenses) should be submitted to top managers, since he can quickly scan this information. If a problem is revealed, they can ask subordinates to investigate the situation in more detail.

(d) the large degree of environmental dynamism requires that the information system be oriented towards gathering data on external trends (e.g., changing national economic conditions, buying trends, and competitor moves) and forecasted financial variables,

(e) the high degree of organizational differentiation and the absence of effective integrative measures make necessary the employment of coordinative mechanisms in the A.I.S. For example, profit objectives and resource allocation plans may be set up on a company wide basis which should encourage 'goal congruency' within the organization. Such an effort should foster discussions between top and divisional managers, as well as between divisional managers themselves, thus leading to greater resolution of conflicts of interests among organizational sub-units,

(f) to enable assessment of divisional performance, adequate attention should be given to developing information on sub-unit costs, profits and physical output,

(g) to help eliminate the ill effects of pursuing divisional, rather than organizational, objectives a well designed cost accounting and control system should be set up.

C. The stagnant bureaucracy

Several of the cases studied involved firms which have been in an extremely stable and homogeneous environment. However, dynamism and heterogeneity have recently been increasing and, unfortunately, structural and decision-making styles are still geared to conditions of the past. Organizational differentiation is very low and integration is achieved by rigid rules and programs. Power is highly centralized in the hands of top managers. Managerial and technocratic expertise seems to be lacking. Decision-making styles are characterized by low multiplexity, poor analysis, unresponsiveness to external trends in the environment, and excessive conservatism. The performance level of these firms is low. The intelligence system of these organizations seems to be totally inadequate. The environment is rarely scanned for new problems or opportunities, controls are not sufficiently sensitive to highlight important trends before they become extremely troublesome, and internal communication is held to a minimum and is of an exclusively top-down nature.

The main role of the A.I.S. in these firms should be to make the enterprise more responsive to its changing environment. For example,

(a) there should be a move towards gathering information on external factors such as the conditions of the economy, new products, and trends in the market share of the firm. These factors are increasingly relevant under conditions of accelerating turbulence,

(b) reports should provide timely information on encroaching problematic trends with comparisons of future expectations to historical events,

(c) in an effort to invoke a performance orientation on the part of departments, and thus elicit pressure for change from below, a profit planning system could be established. Lower level managers will thus be motivated to change sub-optimal operating practices by putting pressure on a relatively complacent top management,

(d) price-level and/or market value statements may help provide some idea of the firm's growth potential,

(e) forecasted statements should also focus management's attention on upcoming changes in the organization's environment.

CONCLUSION

Most of the research to date concerning the design of an accounting information system (A.I.S.) has taken a rather narrow and inflexible view of accounting information. The primary intent of this paper has been to provide a broader and more adaptive framework for designing such systems. A contingency approach, which takes into account the environment, organizational attributes, and managerial decision making styles was advocated. In this context, several hypotheses were offered concerning the requisites of the A.I.S.

In the process of describing our framework, we have tried to integrate a small portion of the existing accounting and related literature. With respect to the accounting literature, one thing which became apparent is the fragmentary nature of the research to date. This point was also noted by Hofstedt & Kinard (1970, p. 45). Hopefully, this paper will help to provide an overall framework for integrating this literature and more importantly, for coordinating future research. Indeed one logical extension of our work is the further development and testing of the hypotheses suggested.

A secondary outgrowth of this paper has been our suggestions that in some circumstances the A.I.S. could act as an agent of change to facilitate organizational performance. In other words, it seems possible for a custom designed A.I.S. to improve poorly functioning organizations by providing information most relevant to the key organizational problems and opportunities.

Furthermore, we discussed three 'archetypal' firms which represent typical agglomerations of environmental, organizational, and decision style attributes and we hypothesized the requisites of the A.I.S. under several of these common conditions. These archetypes reinforced our point that a contingency approach must be taken in designing accounting information systems.

ACKNOWLEDGEMENTS

The authors wish to thank all the participants at the 1975 McGill Symposium entitled 'Behavioral Models and Processing Accounting Information', for their comments on a draft paper which contained some of the initial thoughts leading up to this manuscript. Subsequent comments on earlier versions of the paper by M. Bariff, J. Birnberg, H. Falk, W. Frank, D. Marshall and an anonymous referee are also greatly appreciated.

BIBLIOGRAPHY

Abdel-Khalik, R.A. & E.J. Lusk, Transfer Pricing: A Synthesis. *The Accounting Review* (January, 1974), pp. 8–23.

Ackoff, Russell, L., *A Concept of Corporate Planning* (New York: Wiley-Interscience, 1969).

Allison, G. *Essence of Decision* (Boston: Little Brown, 1971).

American Institute of Certified Public Accountants, *Statement of the Accounting Principles Board No. 3*, Financial Statements Restated for General Price-Level Changes, 1969.

Argyris, C. *Integrating the Individual and the Organization* (New York: J. Wiley & Sons, 1964).

Bennis, W. *Changing Organizations* (New York: McGraw-Hill, 1966).

Benston, G.J., The Role of the Firm's Accounting System for Motivation. *The Accounting Review* (April, 1963), pp. 347–354.

Bierman, Harold Jr. & Thomas R. Dyckman, *Managerial Cost Accounting* (New York: Macmillan Company, 1971).

Burns, T. & C. Stalker, *The Management of Innovation* (London: Tavistock, 1961).

Cook, Doris, The Effect of Frequency of Feedback on Attitudes and Performance. *Empirical Research in Accounting* (1967), pp. 213–224.

Cyert, R. & J. March, *A Behavioural Theory of the Firm* (Englewood Cliffs, N.J.: Prentice-Hall, 1963).

Driver, Michael J. & T.J. Mock, Human Information Processing, Decision Style Theory, and Accounting Information Systems. *The Accounting Review* (July, 1975), pp. 490–508.

Financial Accounting Standards Board Statement of Financial Accounting Standards No. 2, Accounting for Research and Development's Costs (October, 1974).

Flamholtz, Eric, *Human Resource Accounting* (Encino, California: Dicherson Publishing Co., Inc., 1974).

Godfrey, James T., Short-Run Planning in a Decentralized Firm. *The Accounting Review* (April, 1971), pp. 286–297.

Hermann, C. International Crisis as a Situational Variable, in J. Rosenau, *International Politics and Foreign Policy* (Free Press, 1969).

Hofstedt, Thomas R. & James C. Kinard, A Strategy for Behavioural Accounting Research. *The Accounting Review* (January, 1970), pp. 38–54.

Hopwood, Anthony G., Leadership Climate and the Use of Accounting Data in Performance Evaluation. *The Accounting Review* (July, 1974), pp. 485–495.

Khandwalla, Pradip, Environment and its Impact on the Organization. *International Studies of Management and Organization* (Fall, 1972a), pp. 297–313.

Khandwalla, Pradip, The Effect of Different Types of Competition on the Use of Management Controls. *Journal of Accounting Research* (Autumn, 1972b), pp. 276–285.

Lawrence, P. & J. Lorsch, *Organization and Environment* (Harvard University Press: 1967).

Lindblom, C., *The Policy Making Process* (Englewood Cliffs, N.J.: Prentice-Hall, 1968).

Miller, Danny, Towards a Contingency Theory of Strategy Formulation. *Academy of Management Proceedings* (1975), pp. 66–68.

Miller, Danny, Strategy Making in Context: Some Empirical Archetypes. *McGill University Working Paper* (1975a).

Miller, D. & L.A. Gordon, Conceptual Levels and The Design of Accounting Information Systems. *Decision Sciences* (April, 1975), pp. 259–269.

Mintzberg, Henry, *Impediments to the Use of Management Information* (New York: National Association of Accountants, 1975).

Mock, T.J., T. Estrin & M. Vasarhelyi, Learning Patterns, Decision Approach, and Value of Information. *Journal of Accounting Research* (Spring, 1972), pp. 129–153.

Normann, R. Organizational Innovativeness: Product Variation and Reorientation. *Administrative Science Quarterly* (Vol. 16, 1971), pp. 203–215.

Perrow, C., *Organizational Analysis: A Sociological View* (London: Tavistock, 1970).

Pugh, D., D. Hickson, C. Hinnings, K. Macdonald, C. Turner & T. Lupton, A Conceptual Scheme for Organizational Analysis. *Administrative Science Quarterly* (June, 1963), pp. 289–315.

Revsine, Lawrence, Data Expansion and Conceptual Structure. *The Accounting Review* (October, 1970), pp. 704–711.

Romano, M.B., Goodwill: A Dilemma, *Management Accounting* (July, 1975), pp. 39–44.

Sorter, G.H., S. Becker, T. Atchibald & W. Beaver, Corporate Personality as Reflected in Accounting Decisions: Some Preliminary Findings. *Journal of Accounting Research* (Autumn, 1964), pp. 183–192.

Thompson, J., *Organizations in Action.* (McGraw-Hill, N.Y., 1967).

Thompson, J. & A. Tuden, Strategies, Structures and Processes of Organizational Decision, *Readings in Managerial Psychology* (Chicago, 1969).

Watson, D.J. & J.V. Baumler, Transfer Pricing: A Behavioral Context. *The Accounting Review* (July, 1975), pp. 466–474.

Wheelright, S., An Experimental Analysis of Strategic Planning Procedures, *Research Paper #26*, INSEAD, 1970.

Woodward, J., *Industrial Organization: Theory and Practice* (London: Oxford University Press, 1965).

27

The evolution of
management accounting

Robert S. Kaplan

*Professor of Accounting at Carnegie-Mellon University and Arthur Lowes
Dickinson Professor of Accounting at the Harvard Business School*

ABSTRACT

This paper surveys the development of cost accounting and managerial control practices and assesses their relevance to the changing
nature of industrial competition in the 1980s. The paper starts with a
review of cost accounting developments from 1850 through 1915, including the demands imposed by the origin of the railroad and steel
enterprises and the subsequent activity from the scientific management movement. The DuPont Corporation (1903) and the reorganization of General Motors (1920) provided the opportunity for major
innovations in the management control of decentralized operations,
including the ROI criterion for evaluation of performance and formal
budgeting and incentive plans. More recent developments have included discounted cash flow analysis and the application of management science and multiperson decision theory models. The cost accounting and management control procedures developed more than
60 years ago for the mass production of standard products with high
direct labor content may no longer be appropriate for the planning
and control decisions of contemporary organizations. Also, problems
with using profits as the prime criterion for motivating and evaluating short-term performance are becoming apparent. This paper advocates a return to field-based research to discover the innovative
practices being introduced by organizations successfully adapting to
the new organization and technology of manufacturing.

The challenges of the competitive environment in the 1980s should cause
us to re-examine our traditional cost accounting and management control
systems. Virtually all of the practices employed by firms today and explicated in leading cost accounting textbooks had been developed by 1925.
Despite considerable change in the nature of organizations and the dimensions of competition during the past 60 years, there has been little innova-

Source: Kaplan, R.S. (1984) *The Accounting Review*, **LIX** (3), pp. 390–418.

tion in the design and implementation of cost accounting and management control systems. Therefore, it is not only appropriate but necessary that we understand the sources of today's practices, reflect on the new demands for planning and control information, and develop a research strategy to meet these new demands.

Section 1 traces the development of cost accounting practices from the early textile mills and railroads (circa 1850) through the formation of the great industrial enterprises in the U.S. and the emergence of the scientific management approach. This phase culminated about 1920. Section 2 describes the management control innovations of the DuPont Corporation (founded 1903) and the General Motors Corporation after its reorganization by Pierre du Pont and Alfred Sloan in 1920. The origins of decentralization through Return on Investment (ROI) control of both functional and multi-divisional organizations can be found in these two corporations. Section 3 surveys developments in cost accounting and managerial control from 1925 to the present. Section 4 poses challenges from the contemporary environment that may not be met by the cost accounting practices developed more than 60 years ago for a substantially different competitive situation. Section 5 concludes with an agenda for field-based research to document or develop innovative management control practices appropriate for the changing industrial environment.

1. A SUMMARY OF HISTORICAL DEVELOPMENTS IN COST ACCOUNTING

The development of cost accounting and management control practices in U.S. corporations has been well traced by Thomas Johnson (see Johnson [1972, 1975a, 1975b, 1978, 1980, 1981, and 1983]). This research builds upon the history of the development of U.S. corporations in Chandler [1962 and 1977], in which we learn of the great importance of cost and management control information to support the growth of large transportation, production, and distribution enterprises during the 1850–1925 period. Littleton [1933], Solomons [1968], and Garner [1954] provide additional historical perspectives on the evolution in cost accounting thought. I will briefly summarize these historical developments so that we can understand the sources of many of today's practices, though the interested reader should consult the above references for a more complete treatment.

The demand for information for internal planning and control apparently arose in the first half of the 19th century when firms, such as textile mills and railroads, had to devise internal administrative procedures to co-ordinate the multiple processes involved in the performance of the basic activity (the conversion of raw materials into finished goods by textile mills, the transportation of passengers and freight by the railroads).[1]

[1] The economic motivation for forming centralized firms to carry out the multiple processes for these basic activities, as opposed to allowing decentralized units to perform these functions by continuous contracts and transactions with other

Johnson [1972] describes the cost accounting system of Lyman Mills, a New England textile mill (established about 1855), that enabled the managers to monitor the efficiency of the mill's conversion of raw materials into a variety of finished goods. The system was based on the company's double-entry book of accounts and provided information on the cost of finished goods, on the productivity of workers, on the impact of changes in plant layout, and as a control on the receipt and use of raw cotton. Chandler [1977, pp. 109–120] provides evidence of how U.S. railroads, in the 1860s and 1870s, developed accounting procedures to aid them in their extensive planning and control procedures. Railroads handled a vastly greater number and dollar volume of transactions than had any previous business and, as a consequence, had to devise procedures to record and summarize an enormous number of cash transactions. These procedures also generated summary financial reports on the operations of the many sub-units within the large, geographically dispersed railroad companies. In addition to the financial summaries, the railroads developed a system of reporting operating statistics for evaluating and controlling the performance of their subunits. Statistics such as cost per ton-mile and the operating ratio (operating income divided by sales) were routinely reported for various sub-units and classes of service.

Later in the 1880s, the newly formed mass distribution [Chandler, 1977, Chapter 7] and mass production [Chandler, 1977, Chapter 8] enterprises adapted the internal accounting reporting systems of the railroads to their own organizations. The nationwide wholesale and retail distributors produced highly detailed data on sales turnover by department and by geographic area, generating performance reports very similar to those that would be used 100 years later to monitor the performance of revenue centers in the firm. Mass production enterprises formed in the 1880s for the manufacture of tobacco products, matches, detergents, photographic film, and flour. Most important was the emergence of the metal-making and fabricating industries. Andrew Carnegie's steel company was a particularly good example of the importance of cost accounting information for managing the enterprise.

Shinn's [the general manager's] major achievement was the development of statistical data needed for coordination and control. Shinn did this in part by introducing the voucher system of accounting which though it had long been used by railroads was not yet in general use in manufacturing concerns. By this method, each department listed the amount and cost of materials and labor used on each order as it passed through the sub-unit. Such information permitted Shinn to send Carnegie monthly statements and, in time, even daily ones providing data on the costs of ore, limestone, coal, coke, pig iron, spiegel, molds, refractories, repairs, fuel, and labor for each ton of rails produced. These cost sheets [were] called 'marvels of ingenuity and careful accounting.'

market-based units, has been developed by Coase [1937] and Williamson [1975 and 1981].

These cost sheets were Carnegie's primary instrument of control. Costs were Carnegie's obsession. . . . Carnegie concentrated . . . on the cost side of the operating ratio, comparing current costs of each operating unit with those of previous months, and where possible, with those of other enterprises. . . . These controls were effective. . . . 'The minutest details of cost of materials and labor in every department appeared from day to day and week to week in the accounts; and soon every man about the place was made to realize it. The men felt and often remarked that the eyes of the company were always on them through the books.'

In addition to using their cost sheets to evaluate the performance of department managers, foremen and men, Carnegie, Shinn and Jones relied on them to check the quality and mix of raw materials. They used them to evaluate improvements in process and in product and to make decisions on developing by-products. In pricing, particularly nonstandardized items like bridges, cost-sheets were invaluable. The company would not accept a contract until its costs were carefully estimated [Chandler, 1977, pp. 267–268].

Interestingly, the development of these elaborate cost reporting and estimation schemes by the 1880s focused exclusively on direct labor and materials, what we call today prime or direct costs; that is, little attention was paid to overhead and capital costs.

Carnegie's concern was almost wholly with prime costs. He and his associates appear to have paid almost no attention to overhead and depreciation. This too reflected on the railroad experience. As on the railroads, administrative overhead and sales expenses were comparatively small and estimated in a rough fashion. Likewise, Carnegie relied on replacement accounting by charging repair, maintenance, and renewals to operating costs. Carnegie had, therefore, no certain way of determining the capital invested in his plant and equipment. As on the railroads, he evaluated performance in terms of the operating ratio (the cost of operations as a percentage of sales) and profits in terms of a percentage of book value of stock issues [Chandler, 1977, p. 268].

Thus, cost accounting practice in the late 1800s did not include the allocation of fixed costs to products or to periods.[2]

Despite the enormous capital invested in these new manufacturing enterprises, there was apparently no systematic method for forecasting investments or coordinating and monitoring capital investment. Andrew Carnegie is reported to have undertaken almost any new investment that would reduce his prime operating costs:

---

[2] Richard Brief pointed out to me that late 19th-century texts and journals contained active discussions on both the allocation of fixed capital costs to periods and the allocation of fixed operating costs to products (see, for example, references in Edwards [1937]). Neither of these possibilities, however, was practiced by companies at that time.

Carnegie's operating strategy was to push his own direct cost below those of all competitors so that he could charge prices that would always ensure enough demand to keep his plant running at full capacity. . . . Secure in his knowledge that his costs were the lowest in the industry, Carnegie then engaged in merciless price-cutting during economic recessions. While competing firms went under, he still made profits [Johnson, 1981, p. 515].

Johnson [1980] proposes that because firms relied almost exclusively on internal sources of capital to finance new investments, and second, because firms were basically in only one line of business, the choice was only to invest more in this line of business or not to invest further in this business. For this decision, the effect of the new investment on reducing prime costs or in improving the operating ratio was deemed sufficient to guide the investment decision.[3]

The scientific management movement in American industry provided a major impetus to the further development of cost accounting practices [Chandler, 1977, pp. 272–283]. The major figures in this movement were engineers who, by detailed job analyses and time and motion studies, determined 'scientific' standards for the amount of labor and material required to produce a given unit of output. These standards were used to provide a basis for paying workers on a piece-work basis, and to determine bonuses for workers who were highly productive. The names associated with developing the scientific management approach include Frederick Taylor, Harrington Emerson, A. Hamilton Church, and Henry Towne.[4] This approach included not only the development of work standards but also a new form of organization, supplementing the traditional operating or line functions with staff function designed 'not to accomplish work, but to set up standards and ideals, so that the line may work more efficiently.'

The 'scientific management' advocates also started the practice of measuring and allocating overhead costs to products.

Innovations came primarily in determining indirect costs or what was termed the 'factory burden,' and in allocating both indirect and direct (or

---

[3] Habakkuk [1962, p. 59] argues that the relative scarcity of labor in the U.S. and the inadequacy of methods for estimating relevant capital costs explain why industrialists were willing to invest solely on the basis of increasing the productivity of labor.

The American manufacturer was averse to retaining old equipment when more labor-productive equipment was available because the old equipment made poor use of his scarce labor. So long as the saving of labour was vouched for, the capital-costs were less important, at least within a fairly wide range, and in the absence of clear ideas and relevant data about the proper components of capital-costs, manufacturers were probably disposed to underestimate rather than over-estimate them.

I am grateful to Richard Brief for this reference.
[4] Epstein [1978] documents the important influence on cost accounting practices of the 'scientific management' approach.

prime) costs to each of the different products produced by a plant or factory so as to develop still more accurate unit costs.... In a series of articles published in the *Engineering Magazine* in 1901, Alexander Church began to devise ways to account for a machine's 'idle time,' for money lost when machines were not in use. Henry Gantt and others then developed methods of obtaining standard costs based on standard volume of throughput by determining standard costs based on a standard volume of, say, 80 percent of capacity; these men defined the increased unit costs of running below standard volume as 'unabsorbed burden' and decreased unit costs over that volume as 'over-absorbed burden' [Chandler, 1977, pp. 278–279].

The practice of allocating fixed capital costs to products or to periods, however, had still not emerged.

...Nor did they concern themselves with the problem of depreciation in determining their capital account. The reason was that, until well into the twentieth century, nearly all large industrial firms continued to use replacement accounting, which their managers had borrowed from the railroads...they defined profits as the difference between earnings and expenses, and the latter included repairs and renewal [Chandler, 1977, p. 279].

The development of standard costs also came to fruition during this time. In a series of articles in 1908 and 1909, Harrington Emerson clearly describes the value of standard costing for timely planning and control. The literature of standard costing continued to evolve so that by 1918, G. Charter Harrison published a series of articles in *Industrial Management*, exhibiting

[a] sureness of touch and a comprehensiveness in their treatment which shows standard costing to have left the experimental stage and to have attained the status of established practice. In these articles, he produced the first set of formulas for the analysis of cost variances [Solomons, 1968, pp. 46–47].

In addition to these innovations by practicing managers and engineers, extensive discussions on cost accounting concepts appeared in textbooks, monographs and articles during this time (see Solomons [1952]). *Factory Accounting* by Garcke and Fells, first published in 1887, integrated cost accounts into the firm's double-entry financial accounting system and clearly identified a position that fixed overhead costs should not be allocated to production costs.

To distribute the charges over the articles manufactured would, therefore, have the effect of disproportionately reducing the cost of production with every increase, and the reverse with every diminution of business. Such a result is greatly to be deprecated, as tending neither to economy of management nor to accuracy in estimating for contracts. The principals of a business can always judge what percentage of gross profits upon cost is necessary to cover fixed establishment charges and interest on capital [Garcke and Fells, 1887, p. 74].

The use of breakeven charts to express the variation of cost with output could be found in writings in England and the United States in 1903 and 1904 [Solomons, 1968, p. 35].

Vangermeesch [1983] summarizes the extensive writings of A. Hamilton Church, an insightful observer of early twentieth-century cost accounting practices. Church disagreed with the practice of allocating all overhead based on direct labor cost:

We find that as against $100 direct wages on order, we have an indirect expenditure of $59, or in other terms, our shop establishment charges are 59 percent of direct wages in that shop for the period in question. This is, of course very simple. It is also as usually worked very inexact. It is true that as regards the output of the shop as a whole a fair idea is obtained of the general cost of the work. . . . And in the case of a shop with machines all of a size and kind, performing practically identical operations by means of a fairly average wages rate, it is not alarmingly incorrect.

If, however, we apply this method to a shop in which large and small machines, highly paid and cheap labor, heavy castings and small parts, are all in operation together, then the result, unless measures are taken to supplement it, is no longer trustworthy [Church, 1908, pp. 28–29].

In commenting on the importance of accounting for overhead costs directly rather than averaging them together and allocating them proportional to direct labor, Church observes:

These shop charges (overhead) frequently amount to 100 percent, 125 percent, and even much more of the direct wages. It is therefore often actually more important that they should be correct than that the actual wages cost should be correct [Church, 1908, p. 40].

Church's admonitions against loading all overhead costs onto direct labor, though, seem to have gone largely unheeded even in today's manufacturing environment where direct labor can represent less than ten or 20 percent of the value added to a product in the manufacturing process.[5]

J. Maurice Clark at the University of Chicago made one of the few academic contributions to the emerging cost accounting literature during this time. Clark [1923] provides an extensive discussion of the nature of overhead costs and their use in managerial decisions. Driven by a concern with the regulation of railroads and public utilities and with the broader

---

[5] See Schwartzbach and Vangermeersch [1983] for a proposal to implement Church's proposal by developing a separate costing rate for each important machine in a production process.

societal implications of cost measurement (including price discrimination, cut-throat competition, and labor compensation), Clark examines in depth the nature of overhead costs. Many cost concepts that are widely used today, such as escapable or avoidable overhead, sunk costs, incremental or differential costs, and the relevant time period for determining whether a cost is fixed or variable, can be found in Clark's book. An entire chapter is devoted to a discussion of 'Different Costs for Different Purposes,' a concept illustrated by considering the changing definition of cost in nine different decisions to be made about a plant and its output. The notion of opportunity cost is implied by the following statement:

... for certain purposes cost is not a mere present fact, but depends on the alternative offered [Clark, 1923, p. 483].

Also, Clark proposes that a statistical method be used to estimate cost behaviour. This would be an alternative to the accountant's somewhat arbitrary allocations, or subjective estimates, of fixed and variable components of total costs. He notes the possibility of both time-series and cross-sectional statistical analyses:

A concern may watch the monthly fluctuations of its expenses and compare them with the fluctuations of output, in order to learn what the differential cost of added output is. Or it may be possible to compare the costs of different establishments some of which are integrated and others of which are not (for example, sugar factories which buy their beets and factories which raise their own)... [Clark, 1923, p. 217].

and the advantages of statistical over judgmental analysis:

The statistical method has a further advantage in that it catches everything which expert judgment might overlook, and corrects automatically any possible fallacies due to the semi-intuitive methods of arriving at conclusions [Clark, 1923, pp. 223–224].

An excellent discussion of the dangers and limitations of statistical analyses is also presented [pp. 224–227], a discussion that could well be incorporated in many of today's cost accounting texts.[6]

Finally, Clark understood the importance of keeping the cost accounting information separate from the financial accounting system.

Undoubtedly, the ultimate solution lies in the development of systems of cost analysis which shall be separate from the formal books of account, though based on the same data [Clark, 1923, p. 68].

---

[6] Of particular concern to Clark is the existence of confounding factors that distort the statistical relationship between output and cost. Today, we would recognize the role of multiple regression to control for these additional explanatory factors.

Thus, by 1925 sophisticated cost accounting theories and practices had been developed.[7] Many of these innovations were being used to improve the efficiencies of enterprises actively engaged in the mass production of standard products with relatively high direct labor content. Unlike the situation today, the cost accounting, capital accounting, and financial accounting systems were kept separately, with the cost accounting system typically designed for and operated by the manufacturing departments. Cost information was used to assess operating efficiencies, to aid in pricing decisions, and to control and motivate worker performance. The emphasis was on job and factory efficiency, not on the commercial success of the overall corporation.[8] The demand for a management accounting system to facilitate the control and coordination of a firm's diverse activities did not occur until the appearance of vertically integrated, multi-activity firms (see Johnson [1975b]). The emergence of these firms in the early 1900s probably marked the start of modern managerial control practices.

2. HISTORICAL DEVELOPMENT OF MANAGERIAL CONTROL

Both Chandler [1977] and Johnson [1975a, 1975b, 1980] look to the DuPont Company as the innovator in developing modern managerial control systems:

In 1903, three Du Pont cousins consolidated their small enterprises with many other small single-unit family firms. They then completely reorganized the American explosives industry and installed an organizational structure that incorporated the 'best practice' of the day. The highly rational managers at DuPont continued to perfect these techniques, so that by 1910 that company was employing nearly all the basic methods that are currently used in managing big business [Chandler, 1977, p. 417].

The DuPont Powder Company became a centrally managed enterprise coordinating through its own departments most of the manufacturing and selling activities formerly mediated through the market by scores of specialized firms. A centralized accounting system was indispensable to the DuPont Powder Company's elaborate department structure.

Information provided by the Powder Company's centralized accounting system enabled top management to carry out two basic activities that comprised the task of planning: the allocation of new investment among competing economic activities (including the maintenance of working capital) and the financing of new capital requirements [Johnson, 1975a, pp. 186–187].

---

[7] See Carner [1954] for a summary of the state-of-the-art of cost accounting practices and literature as of 1925.

[8] Church's writings (see Vangermeersch [1983] and Wells [1977; p. 53]) seem to be an exception to this observation.

The development of vertically integrated, multi-activity organizations for mass production and mass distribution provided the potential for dramatic breakthroughs in efficiency. The complexity and diversity of these enterprises, however, could have caused the firms to fail due to lack of coordination, planning, and control, had not new organizational forms evolved to allow senior managers to guide their operations.

One innovation was to develop the functional or unitary form of organization that is still characteristic of many contemporary firms. Firms were decentralized into separate departments – manufacturing, sales, finance, and purchasing. The managers of each department became specialists in that area and could pursue strategies that maximized the performance of their departments and the entire firm. The senior managers, freed from day-to-day operating responsibility, could focus more on coordinating the firm's diverse activities and developing its long-term strategies (including capital allocation and financing).

The decentralized, functional organization required a performance measurement system to motivate and evaluate departmental performance and to guide overall firm strategy. The DuPont Company devised an accounting measure, Return on Investment (ROI), to serve both as an indicator of the efficiency of its diverse operating departments and as a measure of financial performance of the company as a whole. Pierre du Pont rejected the (then) widely-used measure of profits or earnings as a percentage of sales or costs, because it failed to indicate the rate of return on capital invested.

A commodity requiring an inexpensive plant might, when sold only ten percent above its cost, show a higher rate of return on the investment than another commodity sold at double its cost, but manufactured in an expensive plant. The true test of whether the profit is too great or too small is the rate of return on the money invested in the business and not the percent of profit on the cost [A DuPont executive writing in 1911 as quoted by Johnson, [1975, p. 88].

The ROI measure was used to evaluate new proposals for building manufacturing facilities and thereby facilitated the allocation of funds among competing product lines; capital was allocated to those products and mills that were earning the highest returns. Apparently, depreciation was used both to compute net income and as a deduction from gross assets to determine investment (see Johnson [1975a, fn. 12, pp. 187–188]), but how depreciation was computed is not indicated.

The ROI approach was extended in about 1912 by one of DuPont's financial officers, Donaldson Brown, when he decomposed the ROI calculation into the product of the sales turnover ratio (sales divided by total investment) and the operating ratio of earnings to sales. These two ratios were decomposed into their component parts many times further so that each of DuPont's departments knew how its performance affected either the sales turnover or the operating ratio, and hence the company's overall return on investment. As a further benefit, the disaggregation of the ROI measure enabled management to explain the reasons why actual ROI would have differed from budgeted ROI in any given period.

Pierre du Pont also established a formal capital appropriation procedure and a systematic process for formulating and approving both operating and capital budgets. The treasurer's office prepared short- and long-term financial forecasts. All these procedures were in place by 1910 [Johnson, 1975a; Chandler, 1977, pp. 448–449].

The functionally departmentalized DuPont system is the first example of applying local profit measures to evaluate the performance of operating departments. It was successful in coordinating and rationalizing the operations of the large industrial corporations that formed in the early 1900s. The basic functional organization is still used in many worldwide corporations today, more than 70 years after its introduction. The development of the ROI criterion, applied at a departmental level, seems to be the origin of the profit and investment center concept used in most modern corporations. It is remarkable to note these lasting legacies of Pierre du Pont and Donaldson Brown on modern industrial enterprises.

Nevertheless, there were still problems in organizing the large industrial corporations in the World War I era. The allocation of responsibility between the top managers in the centralized office and the middle managers in the operating departments was not clearly delineated. Senior managers intervened excessively in day-to-day operations, frequently neglecting their responsibilities for long-range planning and assessing the impact of trends in the external environment on their company's operations [Chandler, 1977, pp. 453–454].

The recession following the end of World War I dramatically revealed the shortcomings of the planning and control systems of most industrial enterprises. From these difficulties, General Motors and DuPont developed a new form of organizational structure, the multi-divisional firm. The two companies are linked because the DuPont Corporation became a leading GM stockholder, and Pierre du Pont became president of General Motors after GM's financial difficulties in 1920, when many other senior DuPont executives also transferred to General Motors. Pierre du Pont promoted Alfred P. Sloan to work with him in rehabilitating GM's organizational structure. (The details of this story are described in Sloan [1963], Chandler [1977, pp. 456–463], and Johnson [1978].) Johnson [1978] provides an excellent description of the innovative managerial accounting system established by Pierre du Pont, Donaldson Brown, and Alfred Sloan at General Motors in the early 1920s. The following summary indicates the scope and impact of the system.

GM's management accounting system did three things to help management accomplish 'centralized control with decentralized responsibility.' First, it provided an annual operating forecast that compared each division's *ex ante* operating goals with top management's financial goals. This forecast made it possible for top management to coordinate each division's expected performance with company-wide financial policy. Second, the management accounting system provided sales reports and flexible budgets that indicated promptly if actual results were deviating from planned results. They specified, furthermore, the adjustments to current operations that division managers should make to achieve their expected perform- ance goals. The sales reports and the advanced flexible budget system provided, then, for control of each division's actual performance. Third, the management accounting system allowed top management to allocate both resources and managerial compensation among divisions on the basis of uniform performance criteria. This simultaneously encouraged a high degree of automatic compliance with company-wide financial goals and greatly increased the division manager's decentralized autonomy [Johnson, 1978, pp. 493–494].

From this summary (and the supporting details in Sloan [1963] and Johnson [1978]), it is clear that the organizational form and reporting and evaluation system for virtually all modern enterprises had evolved in General Motors by 1923–60 years ago.

A few highlights of the GM system are worth noting. First, the goal of General Motors was to earn an average satisfactory Return on Investment over an entire business cycle, not to achieve annual increases in earnings. There was ample recognition that a below-average ROI would be earned in a year when car demand was slack, to be offset by an above-average ROI in an exceptionally strong sales year.

Second, Donaldson Brown devised an ingenious pricing formula [John- son, 1978, pp. 498–500, 505–507] to determine a target price that would yield the desired ROI when production and sales were at a 'standard' or 'normal' volume, defined to be 80 percent of capacity. This formula recog- nized not only the investment in fixed plant and equipment but also the investment in working capital, especially accounts receivable and inven- tory, which Brown assumed to vary with the level of production and sales activity. Donaldson Brown's formula, devised in the early 1920s, is as good an approach to a target, cost-based pricing scheme as any that can be found today. Johnson notes that the Brown pricing formula was not fol- lowed blindly:

GM did not use standard price data to determine the actual prices to be charged during any given model year.... Top management professed the position that the proposed price for any particular year was determined in the competitive marketplace.... If the proposed price for any model fell below the dollar equivalent of the standard price ratio, and if the gap between these two prices could not be attributed to short-run competitive pressures, then top management requested a division manager to reduce his proposed operating cost [Johnson, 1978, p. 500].

Thus, the pricing formula provided a powerful link between a division's short-term operating plan and the top management's financial strategy.

An additional feature of the Brown pricing formula is that depreciation is included as a fixed expense. Just when this allocation became part of the overall management control scheme is not clear from reading the secondary sources available. Perhaps the institution of the U.S. federal income tax before and during World War I made this accounting treatment more important and visible to senior U.S. managers than it had been prior to 1910.

The third highlight of the GM system is an explicit incentive and profit-sharing plan for the senior managers of the corporation.[9] The practice of a formula-based incentive plan, widespread in today's U.S. corporations (and also heavily criticized), can be traced back to the innovative organization designed by Pierre du Pont and Alfred Sloan:

Before we had the Bonus Plan in operation throughout the corporation, one of the obstacles to integrating the various decentralized divisions was the fact that key executives had little incentive to think in terms of welfare of the whole corporation.... Under the incentive system in operation before 1918, a small number of division managers had contracts providing them with a stated share of profits of their own divisions, irrespective of how much the corporation as a whole earned. Inevitably, this system exaggerated the self-interest of each division at the expense of the interest of the corporation itself. It was even possible for a division manager to act contrary to the interests of the corporation in his effort to maximize his own division's profits.

The Bonus Plan established the concept of corporate profit in place of divisional profits.... At first total bonus awards were limited to 10 percent of the net earnings after taxes and after a 6 percent return (on net capital employed) [Sloan, 1963, p. 409].

The GM bonus plan was administered through an elaborate process designed to provide rewards to those employees and managers who had made substantial contributions to the company's performance. While guided by accounting measures, such as divisional return on invested capital, the system involved a systematic review of each individual's performance and also considered special circumstances in a division [Sloan, 1963, pp. 422–428].

Fourth, a sophisticated market-based transfer pricing system was established among General Motors' many operating divisions. The pricing of interdivisional transfers arose initially in the functional organization of DuPont. For Dupont, at about 1905, we learn that:

Each of the company's mills manufactured many of the intermediate products, such as acids, that were used to make explosives. An important question, therefore, was whether money could be saved by purchasing these intermediate products from outside firms instead of making them in the Powder Company's mills. The Powder Company's cost figures for intermediate products could not be compared with outside market prices,

---

[9] In an unpublished interview with Professor Alfred D. Chandler, Donaldson Brown reported that the GM bonus plan was actually modeled after one established at the DuPont Corporation in 1903.

however, because mill overhead and general administrative charges were allocated only to finished goods and not to intermediate products. This accounting policy caused an understatement of the cost of company-made intermediate products [Johnson, 1975a, p. 195].

Alfred Sloan, ten years later, had already worked out the market-based solution to this problem. As president and chief operating officer of United Motors, Sloan reports:

My divisions in the United Motors Corporation had sold both to outside customers and to their allied divisions at the market price.

When the United Motors group was brought into the General Motors Corporation in late 1918, I found that if I followed the prevailing practice, I would no longer be able to determine the rate of return on investment for these accessory divisions individually, or as a group. . . .

At that time, material within General Motors was passing from one operating division to another at cost plus some predetermined percentage [Sloan, 1963, p. 48].

Sloan recommended to Durant, then president of GM:

For exclusively interdepartmental transactions . . . the starting point should be cost plus some predetermined rate of return, but only as a guide. To avoid the possibility of protecting a supplying division which might be a high-cost producer, I recommend a number of steps involving analysis of the operation and comparison with outside competitive production where possible [Sloan, 1963, pp. 49–50].

While Sloan does not relate what transfer price practice he implemented upon becoming chief executive at General Motors, Donaldson Brown provided a forceful description of GM's policy:

The question of pricing product from one division to another is of great importance. Unless a true competitive situation is preserved, as to prices, there is no basis upon which the performance of the divisions can be measured. No division is required absolutely to purchase products from another division. In their interrelation they are encouraged to deal just as they would with outsiders. The independent purchaser buying products from any of our divisions is assured that prices to it are exactly in line with prices charged our own car divisions. Where there are no substantial sales outside, such as would establish a competitive picture – at times partial requirements are actually purchased from outside sources so as to perfect the competitive situation [Brown, 1927, p. 8].

In summary, by 1925 DuPont and General Motors had developed many of today's managerial control practices: decentralization via a functional or multi-divisional organization, the ROI performance measure, formal capital appropriation procedures, budgeting and planning cycles, flexible budgets, target ROI pricing based on standard volume, incentive and profit-sharing plans, and a market-based transfer price policy.

3. DEVELOPMENTS SINCE 1925 IN COST ACCOUNTING AND MANAGERIAL CONTROL

The preceding sections document that the growth of the modern corporation, between 1880 and 1925, provided the stimulus for the development of innovative management accounting practices. These practices were devised by engineers and industrialists, working in actual organizations, rather than by academic researchers. This probably explains the rapid adoption of these innovative practices by other organizations.

The period since 1925 has not been devoid of interesting developments in cost accounting and management. For example, many aspects of cost behaviour have been developed, embellished, and imbedded in the literature.[10] But these developments have been primarily by academics and, with few exceptions, have had relatively little impact on practice. Unlike the situation described in the preceding two sections, there have been virtually no major innovations by practicing managers or management accountants during the most recent 60 years to affect contemporary management accounting thought.[11]

One innovation has been the emergence, in the past 30 years, of the modern treatment of capital budgeting.[12] Shillinglaw [1980, p. 6] reports:

When I started my professional career in the early 1950s, the consulting firm I worked with played a missionary role in the introduction of discounted cash-flow analysis in industry ... the older systems, based on pay back period or on some undiscounted form of the return-on-investment ratio, were designed by financial managers, most of them accountants. The engineers had been tinkering with cash-flow discounting for years, but they were not very influential.

Joel Dean is often acknowledged for introducing modern capital budgeting procedures to firms. His book [Dean, 1951] is an excellent summary of

[10] Economists and accountants at the London School of Economics wrote extensively on the nature of costs and the importance of opportunity costs in economic decisions (see Buchanan and Thirlby [1973]). Today's cost accounting texts contain extensive discussions on various cost behaviour concepts such as fixed vs. variable, incremental, escapable, opportunity, traceable, controllable, relevant, etc. These concepts are generally illustrated in simplified production settings.

[11] Kaplan [1981] describes a rather depressing exercise, attempting to glean innovative management accounting practices from reading through recent volumes of a practitioner-oriented journal.

[12] Parker [1968] summarizes the pre-1950 development of discounted cash flow in the actuarial, engineering economy, and political economy literature. He notes that there is little evidence that firms used this technique before the 1950s.

the practices of leading corporations in the post-World War II era but, surprisingly, does not advocate the discounting of future cash flows. He describes the discounting of the stream of earnings, not the cash flows, from a project and concludes that for many investments, discounting 'frequently may not be worth the cost.' By the mid-1950s, however, Dean was advocating the discounted cash flow (DCF) approach [Dean, 1954] over the previously used payback and ROI methods, and this recommendation also appeared in the accounting literature [Christenson, 1955]. The publication of the first edition of Bierman and Smidt in 1960 provides additional support for the acceptance of DCF analysis (at least among academic scholars), and numerous surveys during the past 20 years have indicated the widespread adoption of this analytic technique by U.S. firms. Whether the procedure is being used wisely is currently being questioned (see, for example, Pinches [1982] and Myers [1984]), but the criticisms are about how DCF is implemented in firms rather than about the merits of discounting cash flows versus the previously used, nondiscounted measures such as ROI or payback.

The Residual Income (RI) extension to the Return on Investment criteria also emerged in the post-World War II period. It is generally attributed to the General Electric Corporation, though its antecedents can be traced to writings earlier in this century (see Scovell [1924], Church [1917, pp. 393–394] and Clark [1923]). The earliest references to residual income in the management accounting literature are quite recent [Solomons, 1965 and Anthony, 1965]. The Residual Income concept overcame one of the dysfunctional aspects of the ROI measure in which managers had an incentive to decline investments that yielded returns in excess of the firm's (or division's) cost of capital, but below the average ROI for their division. The RI approach has not been widely adopted (see Reece and Cool [1978]). Even General Electric has apparently discarded RI and returned to ROI as its basic financial measure for investment center performance (see General Electric [1981]).

The transfer price problem remained a thorny issue for vertically integrated or multi-divisional firms, though there are very few references to this subject until the most recent 30 years. In the mid-1950s, three articles [Cook, 1955, Dean, 1955, and Stone, 1956] were published on transfer pricing that described the full range of available practices (full cost, standard cost, market price, and negotiated or bargained price) and advocated one or the other as being preferable. Not a single reference was made in these three articles to any prior literature on the subject. Hirschleifer [1956, 1957], in two classic articles, developed the micro-economic foundations of the transfer pricing problem and demonstrated, in a limited setting, the optimality of using the opportunity cost of the selling division as the appropriate transfer price. This rule includes the market price as a special case when the intermediate product is sold in a perfectly competitive market, but the rule reverts to the selling division's marginal cost when there is no market or an imperfectly competitive market for the intermediate product.

Examples of firms using the marginal cost rule in practice are quite rare (see Umapathy [1978]), suggesting that the deterministic, cooperative, full-information setting assumed in the Hirschleifer analysis is not realized very often. In fact, the existence of private information by division managers, and the gains from strategic behaviour within the firm (see Williamson [1975] and Waterhouse and Tiessen [1978]), require that the transfer pricing problem be solved in an environment that clearly permits noncooperative bargaining in an uncertain environment with informational asymmetries among division managers and central management.[13] Thus, the transfer price issue remains an open problem to this day, though researchers are much more aware of the analytic complexity of this problem than they were thirty years ago. In the meantime, it is probable that the distribution of transfer-pricing practices among firms in 1983 would be indistinguishable from that of thirty years ago, when the transfer pricing problem first attracted the attention of academics.

About 1960 a major stream of management accounting literature started on the application of quantitative models to a variety of planning and control problems. This literature, stimulated by the development of operations research as an academic discipline in the post-World War II era, described how analytic techniques, including regression analysis, linear and nonlinear programming, probability theory, hypothesis testing, and decision theory, could be applied to cost accounting problems (see Kaplan [1977 and 1982]).

The introduction of quantitative analysis has not extended the domain of management accounting. It simply provides analytic tools for aiding the planning and control decisions that firms have been making for the past century, e.g., determining fixed and variable costs, assessing product profitability and determining improved product mixes, aiding the make vs. buy decision, deciding whether to discontinue an existing product or launch a new one, allocating costs to products, and analyzing the sources of deviation between actual and budgeted performance. Quantitative analysis therefore appears to be a descendant of the scientific management era of cost accounting (1895–1915), with the renewed interest in this approach occurring, after a half-century gap, because of newly developed techniques. Had these techniques been available to the engineers who developed the scientific management approach, it seems likely that many of the recommendations of the past two decades would have been considered and tested for their usefulness in the 1895–1925 era.

The most recent 15-year period has been characterized by the application of information economics and agency theory to management accounting problems. The first phase of this research, the information economics approach, viewed the management accountant as choosing an information system in an uncertain environment to aid decision-making in the firm. The information system was useful if it provided signals about an unknown, random state of nature that could influence the actions of an optimizing decision-maker with a known preference (or utility) function

[13] The discussion in Dearden [1964] provides a vivid illustration of the difficulties in implementing transfer pricing schemes in actual organizations.

for monetary rewards. In theory, the values of alternative information (management accounting) systems could be measured by their effects on the decision-maker's expected utility. The academic literature of this genre had a relatively brief duration, starting with an introduction to the problem in 1968 [Feltham, 1968] and basically culminating, less than a decade later, with a monograph [Demski and Feltham, 1976]. The approach is also well summarized in Demski [1980].

The single-person information economics approach was supplanted by principal/agent, or agency theory, research. In this model, accounting information is viewed as the basis of contracting between economic agents who have different ownership rights, different information, perhaps different prior beliefs, and different preferences for outcomes. Thus, rather than viewing the firm as a single organizational entity, agency theory models the diverse interests, information, and beliefs of economics agents contracting with the firm. The information, or management accounting, system serves to inform the principal (owner, shareholder, central manager) and agent (management, division, or department head) about the actual outcome, to supply signals to the agent and, in some cases, to inform the principal about the likelihood of various state occurrences. It can also provide information to the principal about the agent's effort and actions. The sharing of the outcome between the principal and agent depends critically on the particular information available to both parties (see, for example, Demski and Feltham [1978] as an example of agency theory applied to a budgeting problem). Baiman [1982] provides an excellent survey of the rapidly developing research that has occurred in this field since 1975.

Information economics and agency theory research offers the potential for a rigorous, analytic theory of management accounting, rooted in the utility and profit-maximizing behaviour of neo-classical economics, as well as in the more recent analytic tools of statistical decision theory and noncooperative multiperson game theory. But this potential, if ever realized, will be many years in the future. Despite the technical virtuosity of the agency theory researchers, the complexity and difficulty of computing equilibrium solutions in mutiperson noncooperative game settings with private information has limited the analysis to only extremely simple organizational settings. In fact, none of the models considers an organization any more complex than the Lyman Mills Textile Co., in which the owners hired workers and needed to devise employment contracts, performance monitors, and incentive payments for the workers.

Basically, agency theory is a theory of contracting with production workers, not with managers. A critical assumption is that agents need to be motivated to take actions or exert effort for which they have disutility. In other words, the theory assumes that agents prefer not to exert effort or take desired actions and, as a consequence, need to be compensated financially to induce them to take actions that will benefit the firm. This assumption may be useful for modeling the behaviour of agricultural and production workers, but its extension to a theory of managerial behaviour is rather strained. In practice, managers do not seem to have much effort aversion; frequently the problem is the reverse – they work too long and too hard at their jobs, not too little. Also, the decisions or actions required to benefit the overall firm do not seem to be obviously more distasteful or more arduous to these managers than making decisions that are harmful to the firm.

About the only 'managerial' story that gets told via agency theory requires a liberal interpretation of effort aversion as a surrogate for conflicts of interest between managers (the agents) and shareholders (the principals). With this interpretation, contracting is required to insure that managers do not consume too many nonpecuniary benefits from which managers receive utility but that reduce the principals' wealth (and utility). The overconsumption of nonpecuniary benefits may be an interesting topic for a few researchers to explore. But certainly, developing a theory of the firm, or a theory of managerial behaviour, that focuses on limiting expensive carpeting and art objects in executives' offices is not likely to address central managerial issues.

Omitted from agency theory/contracting models is the role of knowledge and innovation to create value in the firm.[14] Agency theory assumes a static technology. It misses the options for entrepreneurial managers to make major changes in their environment through product and process improvements. Also missing is the role for managers to increase value through enhanced marketing activities, training and motivating their employees, and improved quality and maintenance policies. Management accounting procedures are means by which senior managers communicate the goals and strategies of the firm to their division and local managers and thereby guide the managers in their day-to-day operating and resource allocation decisions. Focusing entirely on an effort-aversion or conflict of interest story will be overly restrictive as we study the role of management accounting practices in actual organizations.

Agency theory should be viewed as a very exploratory investigation to develop a formal theory of the demand for information within the firm. But its limitations should be well recognized and should not supplant other efforts to improve management accounting systems in contemporary managerial and production settings.

Related to agency theory, and developing in parallel with it, is a theory of the firm based on transaction costs.[15] Transaction cost economics comes from the same intellectual roots as agency theory research, emphasizing the limits of market transactions due to private information among economic agents, and the nature of opportunistic, individual maximizing behaviour by these agents. It differs from agency theory research by not attempting to analyze all transactions via formal contracts. The trans-

---

[14] Similar criticisms of the 'received wisdom' from contemporary economic theory appear in Teece and Winter [1984].

[15] This literature has been explicated by Williamson [1975 and 1981], building on the seminal work of Coase [1937]. The transaction cost model has been introduced into the accounting literature by Waterhouse and Tiessen [1978], Johnson [1980 and 1983], Spicer and Ballew [1983], and Tiessen and Waterhouse [1983].

actions cost model attempts to explain why bounded rationality in the presence of environmental complexity, uncertainty, and opportunistic behaviour limits market-based behaviour. According to this theory, firms arise and organize hierarchically to form a cooperative organization that can adapt sequentially to cope with a complex, uncertain environment. Transactions that might otherwise be handled in the market at considerable cost or loss of efficiency are performed internally and governed by administrative processes.

While many authors have written about the transactions cost model, little progress has been made in analyzing actual organizations and gaining insight about which 'administrative processes' would be most effective and efficient in organizing the firm's internal transactions. In part, this stems from a lack of precise definition of the transactions cost environment.[16]

A second reason for the lack of impact of this literature is that it has been tested in only a limited way on actual organizations. Armour and Teece [1978], in a study of 28 petroleum firms during 1955–1973, found a positive relationship between profitability (measured by the accounting rate of return on stockholders' equity) and the adoption by a firm of a divisionalized structure from a functionally organized one. Steer and Cable [1978] detected higher returns on sales and equity, among 82 large British companies, for 'optimally organized' firms. The multidivisional form was considered 'optimal' for large firms with diversified activities, whereas the traditional functional organization was considered appropriate for smaller firms or for firms in process-oriented (single product) industries such as steel. No study, however, has yet to address the central managerial accounting issue of the properties of alternative performance measures for decentralized operating units. Armour and Teece acknowledge in a footnote:

First, there must be an explicit definition of an objective function, usually in terms of a profit or rate of return measure. Second, there must exist machinery within the firm that induces division managers to maximize with respect to the specified objective function.... The existence of these control systems serves the purpose of attenuating the internal control loss encountered by the management of a functionally organized firm as it expands [Armour and Teece, 1978, fn. 4, p. 107].

We still have no systematic evidence on the efficacy or dysfunctionality of alternative objective functions, or even whether a single objective function is sufficient to minimize the control loss in decentralized organizations.

Thus, the transaction cost literature has given us a vocabulary, some intuition, and a conceptual framework for understanding the development of a firm's organizational structure. But its implications for devising

---

[16] Baiman [1982, p. 155] acknowledges agency theory's debt to the transactions cost literature but criticizes the approach because 'most of its results are based on casual, rather than rigorous, analysis.'

administrative processes or performance and control measures in firms have not been developed.

In thinking about the lack of innovation in contemporary firms' management accounting systems, I am impressed by the difference between innovations that occur in businesses and innovations that occur in academic institutions. The developments in cost accumulation and cost control in the railroads, in the steel industry, and later in vertically integrated and multidivisional firms, such as DuPont and General Motors, spread rapidly to other organizations. Managers in these innovating organizations could see how well the new procedures worked in practice and this likely provided a credible basis for disseminating the successful innovations to other organizations. Individuals such as Frederick Taylor, Pierre du Pont, and Donaldson Brown were able to apply techniques that worked well in one organization to other organizations that subsequently employed them. Wells [1977], in a review of early cost accounting developments, notes the extensive communication among the U.S. mechanical engineers who were developing the new managerial technology:

A shop culture developed which had all the hallmarks of a 'gentlemen's club.' Within the club, information was freely shared. The result was 'a vast, mutually owned store of knowledge and experience closely akin to a body of scientific knowledge' [Wells, 1977, p. 51, with quotes from Calvert, 1967, p. 7 and p. 111].

Papers dealing with costing invariably described a system actually in use.... They provided intimate detail of the systems installed in well-known machine shops [Wells 1977, p. 52].

In contrast, the recent academic management accounting literature is devoid of references to actual organizations.[17] Today's researchers do not learn about cost accounting and management control from studying IBM, Texas Instruments, Procter & Gamble, 3-M, Johnson & Johnson, or McDonald's. Rather, the references in today's management accounting literature are to economists such as Arrow, Jensen, Meckling, Hirschleifer, Marschak, Radner, Ross, Simon, Williamson, and Wilson. That is, contemporary researchers' knowledge of managers' behaviour is based not on studying decisions and procedures of actual firms, but on the stylized models of managerial and firm behaviour that have been articulated by economic theorists who, themselves, have limited first-hand knowledge of the behaviour they have modeled. These models have not been developed for or tested on actual enterprises.[18] Certainly, the roles of knowledge,

[17] A few academics, mostly current or former faculty of the Harvard Business School (e.g., Anthony, Dearden, Vancil, Shank, Barrett, and Bruns), observe and write about the management accounting and control systems of individual firms. The output of these efforts is contained in many interesting teaching cases.

[18] Recently, Wolfson [1982 and 1983] has provided actual applications of agency theory models for shared-equity mortgages and for limited partnerships for oil and gas drilling. These articles, however, describe contracting with agents external to

technology, and innovation, so critical for the survival of contemporary firms, have yet to be examined by any contemporary theorists from economics or managerial accounting.

4. NEW CHALLENGES FOR COST AND MANAGERIAL ACCOUNTING RESEARCH

There are some obvious new directions to extend cost accounting research. First, the traditional cost accounting model, developed for the mass production of a few standardized products, can be updated to accommodate the realities of the manufacturing environment of the 1980s (see Kaplan [1983]). Companies are now making fundamental changes in their organization of manufacturing operations. These include Just-in-Time scheduling, zero defect and zero inventory production systems, and cooperative and flexible work-force management policies. The cost accounting implications of these more advanced production control systems have barely been investigated and, as a result, our cost accounting textbooks continue to describe production processes using extremely simplified models, such as the single product, deterministic EOQ formula. It is unlikely that our current accounting graduates will have any understanding of the complex production environment in which cost accounting must be applied today. Future manufacturing processes will be even more unfamiliar to them as firms invest in computer-controlled machinery, including Flexible Manufacturing Systems, CAD/CAM, and robots, for their production processes. This trend to computer-integrated manufacturing facilities, permitting efficient production of small batches of customized products, introduces a new setting for cost estimation, planning, and control.

Investigating the cost accounting implications of the major changes in the organization and technology of manufacturing operations represents a new path for management accounting research. In retrospect, the field in 1970 could have gone in either of two directions. At the time, accounting researchers were being trained in quantitative techniques from operations research, probability and statistics, and economic theory. This provided researchers with a broad array of analytic tools to investigate an expanded role for management accounting information in complex settings. As described previously, the path actually followed froze the production setting (in fact, for many cases, it simplified the production setting back to the primitive production processes of the mid-nineteenth century) in order to investigate complex information production, risk-sharing, incentive, and contracting issues. This agency theory research stream has now attracted the attention of virtually all analytic management accounting researchers. The alternative (not mutually exclusive) path, of investigating the role of accounting information in the more complex production and assembly operations of contemporary manufacturing settings, has hardly been pursued by any researcher. Certainly there should be a place both for

the economic unit rather than within an organization or hierarchy – the situation we wish to study in managerial accounting.

researchers investigating complex information and contracting problems in simplified production settings and for researchers dealing with the managerial demand for information in realistic and rich production settings. I am not able to conclude that our present allocation of effort between these two alternative research directions is desirable.

5. NEW DIRECTIONS FOR MANAGEMENT CONTROL RESEARCH

Research to remedy current problems with the traditional profit center form of organization provides an opportunity for new thought in management control systems. As described earlier, the profit center concept evolved in the DuPont and General Motors Corporations. It has been viewed as the key step in permitting the efficient and effective administration of large, multidivisional enterprises.

By an ingenious use of return on investment, the DuPont organization used conventional measures of financial performance corresponding to each of the company's separate activities, and yet avoided the narrow 'shop floor' view of top management's role that often pervaded single-activity enterprises before 1900.

In their internal accounting systems, multidivisional companies such as DuPont and General Motors especially emphasized return on investment. This emphasis suggests that the founders of those organizations attached great importance to how their new hierarchical structure might achieve economies by overcoming imperfections in existing capital markets.

The firm's executives believed that the primary responsibility of top management was to insure that the company earned the required market return on invested capital [Johnson, 1980].

While ROI control and the profit center organization have contributed greatly to the success of large corporations during the past 60 years, problems have begun to emerge with the excessive focus on short-term financial performance.[19] These problems arise because managers, being clever, resourceful people, have learned that there are a variety of ways to meet profit and ROI goals. Initially, and perhaps for many years after

---

[19] Many articles have accused U.S. executives of focusing too narrowly on short-term performance at the expense of long-term profitability. Perhaps the most convincing of these criticisms comes from the executives themselves:

Dun's Business Month queried the 230 chief executives who are members of its President's Panel. . . . A thumping majority of the panelists agrees that management in the U.S., unlike its counterpart in Japan, is excessively concerned with the short-term, at the expense of longer-range considerations that may be far more important. . . . Most of the executives differ among themselves only on how much the shortcoming results from outside pressure for quarter-to-quarter performance, particularly from Wall Street.

Among the comments of these most senior U.S. executives are:

profit centers and ROI centers were introduced, managers attempted to achieve good performance by making operating and investment decisions to develop new and better products, to increase sales, and to reduce operating costs. Over time, however, it probably occurred to some managers that during difficult times, when sales were decreasing and operating costs were increasing, profits could be 'earned' not just by selling more or producing for less, but by engaging in a variety of nonproductive and typically nonvalue-creating activities. We will briefly summarize three types of short-run behaviour: exploiting accounting conventions, engaging in financial entrepreneurship, and reducing discretionary expenditures.

Accounting conventions

The historical cost accounting model and generally accepted accounting principles (GAAP) provide ample opportunities for firms to manage their income measurement. For example, managers can time the recognition of some income and expense items so as to exhibit steady earnings growth or to meet budgeted goals for the current period.[20] Managers can also choose among accounting methods permitted by GAAP.

A more subtle effect of the overemphasis on achieving current earnings goals has occurred because the internal management accounting function has now become subservient to the external financial reporting function in U.S. firms. Recall that the cost accounting and management control practices that developed in U.S. corporations between 1850 and 1925 evolved from the demands of senior executives to help them understand their internal operations, to make new product and investment decisions, and to motivate and evaluate the performance of their employees. Contemporary U.S. practice, in contrast, is characterized by the internal use of accounting conventions that have been developed and mandated by external reporting authorities. Thus if the Financial Accounting Standards Board (FASB) says that, for external financial statements, all R&D

It behoves U.S. management to look beyond the immediate future. The Japanese, West Germany, and Switzerland have taught us the need to address long-term results.

The current trend towards high compensation rewards based on the immediate year's performance rather than long-range growth is a serious disincentive to management objectivity.

Amid today's takeover scramble, short-term performance is needed for survival.

The financial community's stress on very, very short range performance often can be ignored only at a company's peril, especially if it is contemplating equity or debt financing.

It would be a very healthy change if quarterly reports were to longer required.
['What's Wrong with Management,' 1982.]

I am grateful to Kenneth Merchant for this reference.

[20] Occasionally, managers meet budgeted earnings goals by extending the conventions of the historic cost accounting model; see the recent examples described in 'Cooking the Books' [1983].

expenditures must be expensed, then these expenditures are generally expensed on the internal books too. If the FASB requires that certain types of leases must be capitalized for external reporting, then these same leases, and only these leases, are generally capitalized for internal evaluation too. An extreme version of this dominance of the external reporting mentality has companies using a modified form of residual income but charging divisions not a risk-adjusted cost a capital on all assets under the control of a division manager, but rather a pro-rata share of the company's actual interest expense for the year. Thus, the capital charge could be as low as two to three percent annually, if the company has a low debt-equity ratio, even though the opportunity cost of additional funds tied up in working capital could be ten percentage points higher.

The profit center concept has seemingly become distorted into treating each division as a mini-company, attempting to allocate all corporate expenses, common and traceable, to divisions (frequently on an arbitrary basis that confuses the underlying microeconomics and cost structure of the divisions).[21] Firms use accounting conventions for internal planning and control, not because they support the corporate strategy, but because they have been chosen via an external political process by regulators at the FASB and the Securities and Exchange Commission (SEC). With management accounting practices now driven by an external reporting mentality, we can start to understand why there has been so little innovation recently in management accounting thought and practice.[22]

Financial entrepreneurship

The second area for misleading profit center measurements arises from the financial entrepreneurship of senior managers. Instead of attempting to generate earnings in the factory, in the product laboratory, and in the sales offices, many U.S. executives have attempted to generate earnings by financial transactions. These actions, such as mergers and acquisitions, divestitures and spinoffs, leveraged buy-outs, debt swaps and debt repurchases, and periodic sales of assets can increase short-term earnings without necessarily creating long-term value to the firm. These actions are more available to senior managers than to division managers, but opportunities for financial gamesmanship are still available to profit center

---

[21] Again, contemporary managers could benefit from the wisdom of Donaldson Brown:

I may state that we do not distribute against the production of the individual divisions any of the expense of the General Motors central office. This is considered a charge against the operating earnings of the divisions. . . . All net earnings of the divisions are brought together on a statement total, from which is taken the expense of the General Motors Corporation [Brown, 1927, p. 21].

[22] Two decades ago, Davidson [1963] also urged that the internal informational needs for managing the organization not be made subservient to the external reporting system. I appreciate Roman Weil's suggestion for this reference.

managers. These opportunities include the sale of low book-value assets and off-balance-sheet leasing.

Short-run opportunistic behaviour

Perhaps the most damaging dysfunctional behaviour induced by a pre-occupation with short-term profit center performance is the incentive created for division managers to reduce expenditures on discretionary and intangible investments. When profit targets become hard to achieve because sales are not increasing as fast as expected, or variable and operating costs are rising faster than expected, managers may try to minimize the adverse impact on short-term earnings by reducing expenditures on product and process development, promotion, distribution, quality improvement, applications engineering, human resources, customer relations, and other such intangibles. The immediate effect of such expenditure reductions is to improve the reported profitability of the division, but this is achieved by risking the long-term competitive position of the enterprise.

The ability of the firm and the division to increase reported profits while sacrificing the long-term economic health of the firm is a fundamental weakness in the accounting model. At one level, we can criticize the firm for following, for internal purposes, the same accounting practices used for the external reporting of expenditures on intangibles; that is, immediate expensing of all these expenditures. A few firms, such as General Electric, do segregate these discretionary, programmatic expenses on the divisional income statement so that it becomes apparent which divisions are achieving their profit goals by risking their future competitive positions.

But at a deeper level, the opportunity to increase reported income by foregoing both tangible and intangible investments, yielding long-term economic benefits to the division, illustrates a flaw in the basic goal of using short-term profit as an indicator of improvement in the economic wealth of the firm. Beaver and Demski [1979] demonstrate that when some of the assets of the firm cannot be traded in organized markets, it may be impossible to agree on an income measure for the firm. While they developed this impossibility result with financial reporting in mind, it is equally compelling for demonstrating the great difficulty of measuring periodic income for profit centers within the firm. Certainly, if we had market prices for the stock of new products and improved processes from R&D expenditures, for the level of employee talents and morale, for flexible and high-quality manufacturing operations, for customer loyalty and product awareness, for reliable and high-quality suppliers, and for an efficient distribution network, then we could achieve a more valid and reliable periodic divisional income measure. But the failure to have market prices for the outcomes of investments in intangibles makes the short-term divisional income measure highly manipulable and reduces the correlation between this measure and the increases in the economic value of the division.

One might reasonably ask: Why did these problems with profit center measures not emerge earlier? Why do we not read about Alfred Sloan or Pierre du Pont being concerned with their divisional managers foregoing profitable tangible and intangible investments in order to increase their annual divisional profit or ROI measure? At this time, I can only speculate on possible reasons for the relatively recent decline in the ability of profit center measures to motivate behaviour to increase the economic value of the firm. This issue can and should be studied more systematically.

Nevertheless, casual empiricism suggests that the following menu of explanations be considered. *First*, there was apparently less pressure for short-term financial performance in the 1920s and 1930s than exists in the 1970s and 1980s. For example, we can read in Sloan [1963] and in the description of Donaldson Brown's GM pricing formula that General Motors' goal was not to show steady year-to-year earnings increases. Rather, it was recognized that, for a cyclical business, an appropriate goal needed to be defined as an average over the entire business cycle. Years of slack demand were recognized as 'normal' and not the signal to contract expenditures on new product development, marketing, or other intangibles.

A *second* factor to investigate would be the mean time between managers' promotions in 1924 vs. 1984. Many of the difficulties in profit center evaluations arise from attempting to measure performance over a brief period, when the long-term adverse consequences from short-term optimizing actions have not yet become apparent. If division managers expected to remain in their jobs for at least five to seven years, there would be less incentive to curtail beneficial investments with potential long-term payoffs.

Third, the difference in size of organizations between 1924 and 1984 may play an important role. Perhaps the smaller organizations that existed earlier in this century would have made decisions by division managers to sacrifice long-term competitive position for short-term profits more obvious to the senior and central management. Today's much larger organizations, especially those that take pride in running their company 'by the numbers,' are more vulnerable to short-term optimizing actions by profit center managers. In transactions cost terms, the increased size of organizations, without corresponding changes in the control system or objective function, provided increased latitude for managers' opportunistic behaviour.

Fourth, there may have been a shift in hiring practices during the past 60 years. Formerly, employees, especially those destined to become divisional and senior managers, tended to spend their entire careers with the same firm. Thus there would be less incentive for them to take actions that would not be in the best long-run interests of the firm. As a professional managerial class developed in the U.S. during the middle part of the 20th century, certainly abetted by the rapid increase of MBAs whose managerial skills were more transferable across different firms, turnover probably increased, thereby reducing the incentives for these managers to avoid actions that would compromise the long-term viability of their current firm.

An often made (though still unsubstantiated) criticism of MBAs in significant managerial positions in U.S. corporations is that in contrast to the situation 50 and more years ago, firms today are being run by managers who are untrained in, and unfamiliar with, the technology of the firm's products and processes. As a consequence, they are less knowledgeable about how to create value through improved products and processes and therefore rely more on attempting to create value through finance and accounting activities labeled 'paper entrepreneurship' by critics such as Reich [1983].

A *fifth* reason for the decline in usefulness of divisional profit measures may be attributed to the widespread use of executive bonus plans based on accounting measures. While we saw that GM had an accounting-based bonus more than 60 years ago, it has only been recently that accounting-based performance plans became prevalent in U.S. corporations. Problems with these plans are well documented (see Rappaport [1978 and 1981] and Meadows [1981]), but the plans are still used extensively. Senior executives whose annual and deferred compensation are strongly influenced by reported annual income are surely able to communicate the importance they place on achieving annual profit goals to divisional managers. Once alerted to senior managers' interest in achieving certain income targets, resourceful division managers will find many ways to meet their obligations to contribute to overall corporate profits (see fn. 20).

Sixth, the environment of the 1980s is probably sufficiently different from that of the 1920s so that any management control system that served well in earlier times is likely to be inadequate today. Contemporary factors that differ from the circumstances earlier in this century are much more vigorous global competition, the rapid worldwide movement of technology and capital, an increased pace of technological change, more intervention in the private marketplace by governments through higher taxes and increased regulation, and generally higher inflation rates. Whatever the differences, it would indeed be surprising if the managerial control systems devised for the environment of 60 years ago would still be useful and relevant in the very different circumstances of the 1980s. How then can we embark on a research path in management control to develop improved performance measures for decentralized operating units?

Financial measures, such as operating cash flows, will undoubtedly continue to be among the measures used to evaluate the performance of decentralized units. But we should acknowledge the difficulties associated with attempting to measure economic profits in periods as short as a year. Even granting that the objective of a division should be to maximize long-term profits, this does not imply that an annual profit is the best short-term indicator of how well the division is proceeding along a long-term profit-maximizing path. Other measures, such as product innovation, product leadership, employee skills and morale, or customer loyalty, may be much better indicators of future profitability than annual profits. It is unlikely (I would say impossible) that any single measure can both summarize the economic events affecting a firm or division during a period and serve as a basis for motivating and evaluating managers. Therefore, multiple performance indicators may improve the motivation and evaluation of divisional performance.[23] Some of these indicators will be financial; others will not be. There seems no particular reason why financial measures should be primary in determining short-term divisional goals, even if the long-term goal is to maximize the long-term cash flow of the firm. Peters and Waterman [1982] provide a highly provocative conjecture on the importance of nonfinancial goals (what they call 'basic beliefs' or 'overriding values') and the limited value of focusing on financial goals.

Virtually all of the better performing companies we looked at ... had a well-defined set of guiding beliefs. The less well-performing institutions, on the other hand, were marked by one of two characteristics. Many had no set of coherent beliefs. The others had distinctive and widely discussed objectives, but the only ones that they got animated about were the ones that could be quantified – the financial objectives, such as earnings per share and growth measures. Ironically, the companies that seemed the most focused – those with the most quantified statements of mission, with the most precise financial targets – had done *less* well financially than those with broader, less precise, more qualitative statements of corporate purpose [Peters and Waterman, 1982, p. 281].

Also,

We find among the excellent companies a few common attributes that unify them despite their very different values. First ... these values are almost always stated in qualitative, rather than quantitative, terms. When financial objectives are mentioned, they are almost always ambitious but never precise. Furthermore, financial and strategic objectives are never stated alone. They are always discussed in the context of the other things the company expects to do well. The idea that profit is a natural by-product of doing something well, not an end in itself, is also almost universal [Peters and Waterman, 1982, p. 284].

Management accounting must serve the strategic objectives of the firm. It cannot exist as a separate discipline, developing its own set of procedures and measurement systems and applying these universally to all firms without regard to the underlying values, goals, and strategies of particular firms. For example, some firms, such as Andrew Carnegie's steel company, will have cost control and cost reduction as their primary strategic goal. For these firms, the management accounting system will then need to collect elaborate information on relevant costs to support the corporate goal. For other firms, product innovation, service, quality, or employee morale may be the most important goal. If a management accounting system is to serve division and senior managers, it must support these overriding corporate goals and not focus narrowly on an earnings

---

[23] Ridgway [1956] described the limitations of single measures of performance, indeed of any system relying solely on quantitative measures.

measure because that measure was helpful to DuPont, General Motors, and General Electric when these companies formed earlier in this century.

The inertia from 60 years of concentration on financial performance measures will not be easy to overcome. The Management Accounting Practices Committee of the National Association of Accountants restricts the domain of management accounting to:

the process of identification, measurement, accumulation, analysis, preparation, interpretation, and communication of *financial* information used by management to plan, evaluate, and control within an organization. . . . [Statement on Management Accounting No. 1A, 'Definition of Management Accounting,' 1981 (emphasis added)].

Presumably, if a firm's managers felt that measurements of product quality, productivity, product innovation, employee morale, or customer satisfaction were relevant for their planning and control decisions, then these measurements would need to be supplied by persons other than management accountants. Thus, a fundamental choice does need to be made. Management accountants may feel that their own area of comparative advantage is to measure, collect, aggregate, and communicate *financial* information. This will remain a valuable mission. But it is not likely a goal that will be decisive to the success of their own organizations, and if senior managers place too much emphasis on managing by the financial numbers, the organization's long-term viability may become threatened.

The option to include nonfinancial measures in the firm's planning and control system will be more unfamiliar, more uncertain, and, consequently, less comfortable for managerial accountants. It will require them to understand those factors that are most critical to the company's long-term success. Financial goals will be among these but they will not be the only critical success factors, and probably will not be the most important short-term indicators of long-term success. It will not be easy to develop nonfinancial performance measures to support long-term corporate objectives. After research and experimentation, we may discover that the benefits of producing nonfinancial measures are too low, relative to the costs. Perhaps division and senior managers will rely on informal communication, including MBWA (Management By Walking About; see Peters and Waterman [1982, pp. 288–291]) to determine whether local managers' actions are consistent with long-term corporate goals. Financial measures would continue to be collected and reported, but would not necessarily be the primary measure by which managers and divisions are evaluated.

In summary, financial performance measures, such as divisional profit, give an illusion of objectivity and precision. But these measures are relatively easy to manipulate in ways that do not enhance the long-term competitive position of the firm, and they become the focus of opportunistic behaviour by divisional managers. By de-emphasizing financial performance measures and relying more on multiple measures of performance, including subjective evaluation based on personal communication and observation by superiors, division managers will not have as clear a target for short-run optimizing behaviour. Thus, there is probably a need for more ambiguous, less precise performance evaluation systems. It is not that nonfinancial performance measures are any less vulnerable to this opportunistic behaviour; but by adopting a system of multiple measures, subjectively aggregated, the gains a manager sees from short-run opportunistic behaviour become more uncertain and hence, such behaviour may be inhibited. In any case, this does provide an opportunity for new research.

My final comments relate to how this research can be performed. I suspect that researchers will not learn about the production and organization problems of contemporary industrial corporations by reading economics and management science journals. Researchers will need to leave their offices and study the practices of innovating organizations. Companies are responding to changes in their environment by introducing new organizational arrangements and new technology for producing their outputs. They may even be introducing new measurement systems in their organization. The challenge for academic researchers is to discover the Pierre du Ponts, Donaldson Browns, Alfred Sloans, and Frederick Taylors of the 1980s; to describe and document the innovative practices that seem to work for successful companies. The research will be more inductive than deductive, but likely productive, both for the individual researcher and for the management accounting discipline.

One of the leading academic practitioners of field-based, inductive research has been Henry Mintzberg, who has produced influential studies on managerial behaviour and organizational design (see Mintzberg [1973, 1981, and 1983]). Mintzberg [1979] has described his philosophy and strategy of small-sample, field-based research. Seven themes in his research are noted, but I would like to close by quoting from just one of them. It captures the fun and excitement that have been missing from our managerial accounting research because of our reluctance to get involved in actual organizations and to muck around with messy data and relationships.

The research, in its intensive nature, has ensured that systematic data are supported by anecdotal data. More and more we feel the need to be on site, and to be there long enough to be able to understand what is going on. (We began with a week and are now spending months and even years.) For while systematic data create the foundation for our theories, it is the anecdotal data that enable us to do the building. Theory building seems to require rich description, the richness that comes from anecdote. We uncover all kinds of relationships in our 'hard' data, but it is only through the use of this 'soft' data that we are able to 'explain' them, and explanation is, of course, the purpose of research. I believe that the researcher who never goes near the water, who collects quantitative data from a distance, without anecdote to support them, will always have difficulty explaining interesting relationships (although he may uncover them). Those creative leaps seem to come from our subconscious mental processes, our intuition. And intuition apparently requires the 'sense' of things – how they feel, smell, 'seem.' We need to be 'in touch.' Increasingly in our research, we are impressed by the importance of phenomena that cannot be measured – by the impact of an organization's history and its ideology on its current strategy, by the role that personality and intuition play in decision-making. To miss this in research is to miss the very life-blood of the organization. And missed it is in research that, by its very design, precludes the collection of anecdotal information [Mintzberg, 1979, pp. 587–588].

If managerial accounting research is to progress, we will need to start collecting our anecdotes from 1980s corporations.

ACKNOWLEDGEMENTS

I greatly appreciated conversations with and articles and references provided by Professor H. Thomas Johnson of the University of Puget Sound. An earlier version of the paper benefited from the comments and suggestions of participants at the Stanford University Summer Accounting Workshop, especially Joel Demski, and many of my colleagues at Carnegie-Mellon and Harvard. Richard Brief, Gordon Shillinglaw, Germain Boer, and a reviewer provided valuable suggestions to improve the final draft. The usual disclaimer, that the views, interpretations, and errors remain solely the responsibility of the author, is particularly relevant for this paper.

Editor's Note: This paper served as the basis for a plenary address given at the 1983 Annual Meeting of the American Accounting Association. It was subsequently submitted and reviewed for publication.

Manuscript received September 1983.
Accepted February 1984.

REFERENCES

Anthony, R.N., 'Accounting for Capital Costs,' in R.N. Anthony, J. Dearden, and R.F. Vancil, Eds., *Management Control Systems: Cases and Readings* (Richard D. Irwin, 1965).

Armour, H.O. and D.J. Teece, 'Organizational Structure and Economic Performance: A Test of the Multidivisional Hypothesis,' *Bell Journal of Economics* (Spring 1978), pp. 106–122.

Baiman, S., 'Agency Research in Managerial Accounting: A Survey,' *Journal of Accounting Literature* (Spring 1982), pp. 154–213.

Beaver, W. and J. Demski, 'The Nature of Income Measurement,' *The Accounting Review* (January 1979), pp. 38–46.

Bierman, H. and S. Smidt, *The Capital Budgeting Decision* (MacMillan, 1960).

Brown, D., 'Centralized Control with Decentralized Responsibilities,' American Management Association Annual Convention Series: No. 57 (1927), reprinted in H.T. Johnson, Ed., *Systems and Profits: Early Management Accounting at DuPont and General Motors* (Arno Press, 1980).

Buchanan, J.M. and G.F. Thirlby, Eds., *L.S.E. Essays on Cost* (London School of Economics and Political Science, 1973).

Calvert, M.A., *The Mechanical Engineer in America 1830–1910: Professional Cultures in Conflict* (Johns-Hopkins Press, 1967).

Chandler, A.D., *Strategy and Structure: Chapters on the History of the Industrial Enterprise* (M.I.T. Press, 1962).

——, *The Visible Hand: The Managerial Revolution in American Business* (Harvard University Press, 1977).

Christenson, C., 'Construction of Present Value Tables for Use in Evaluating Capital Investment Opportunities,' *The Accounting Review* (October 1955), pp. 666–672.

Church, A.H., *The Proper Distribution of Expense Burden* (London: The Engineering Magazine, 1908) (Works Management Library).

——, *Manufacturing Costs and Accounts* (McGraw-Hill, 1917).

Clark, J.M., *Studies in the Economics of Overhead Cost* (University of Chicago Press, 1923).

Coase, R., 'The Nature of the Firm,' *Economica* (November 1937), pp. 386–405.

Cook, P.W., 'Decentralization and the Transfer-Price Problem,' *Journal of Business* (April 1955), pp. 87–94.

'Cooking the Books,' *Dun's Business Month* (January 1983), pp. 40–47.

Davidson, S., 'The Day of Reckoning: Accounting Theory and Management Analysis,' *Journal of Accounting Research* (Autumn 1963), pp. 117–126.

Dean, J., *Capital Budgeting; Top-Management Policy on Plant, Equipment, and Product Development* (Columbia University Press, 1951).

——, 'Measuring the Productivity of Capital,' *Harvard Business Review* (January/February 1954), pp. 120–130.

——, 'Decentralization and Intra-company Pricing,' *Harvard Business Review* (July/August 1955), pp. 65–74.

Dearden, J., 'The Case of the Disputing Divisions,' *Harvard Business Review* (May/June 1964), pp. 159–178.

Demski, J., *Information Analysis*, Second Edition (Addison-Wesley, 1980).

—— and G. Feltham, *Cost Determination: A Conceptual Approach* (Iowa State University Press, 1976).

—— and ——, 'Economic Incentives in Budgetary Control Systems,' *The Accounting Review* (April 1978), pp. 336–359.

Edwards, R.S., 'Some Notes on the Early Literature and Development of Cost Accounting in Great Britain – V and VI,' *The Accountant* (September 4, 1937), pp. 313–316; (September 11, 1937), pp. 343–344.

Epstein, M.J., *The Effect of Scientific Management on the Development of the Standard Cost System* (Arno Press, 1978).

Feltham, G.A., 'The Value of Information,' *The Accounting Review* (October 1968), pp. 684–696.

Garke, E. and J.M. Fells, *Factory Accounts* (New York: McGraw-Hill, 1887).

Garner, S.P., *Evolution of Cost Accounting to 1925* (University of Alabama Press, 1954).

'General Electric Company, Background Note on Management Systems: 1981,' HBS Case 9–181–111 (Boston: Harvard Business School).

Habakkuk, H.J., *American and British Technology in the Nineteenth Century: The Search for Labour-Saving Inventions* (Cambridge University Press, 1962).

Hirschleifer, J., 'On the Economics of Transfer Pricing,' *Journal of Business* (July 1956), pp. 172–184.

——, 'Economics of the Divisionalized Firm,' *Journal of Business* (April 1957), pp. 96–108.

Johnson, H.T., 'Early Cost Accounting for Internal Management Control: Lyman Mills in the 1850s,' *Business History Review* (Winter 1972), pp. 466–474.

——, 'Management Accounting in Early Integrated Industrial: E.I. duPont de Nemours Powder Company, 1903–1912,' *Business History Review* (Summer 1975a), pp. 184–204.

——, 'The Role of Accounting History in the Study of Modern Business Enterprise,' THE ACCOUNTING REVIEW (July 1975b), pp. 444–450.

——, 'Management Accounting in an Early Multidivisional Organization: General Motors in the 1920s,' *Business History Review* (Winter 1978), pp. 490–517.

——, 'Markets, Hierarchies, and the History of Management Accounting,' Third International Congress of Accounting Historians, London, England (August 1980).

——, 'Toward a New Understanding of Nineteenth-Century Cost Accounting,' THE ACCOUNTING REVIEW (July 1981), pp. 510–518.

——, 'The Search for Gain in Markets and Firms: A Review of the Historical Emergence of Management Accounting Systems,' *Accounting, Organizations and Society* (No. 2/3, 1983), pp. 139–146.

Kaplan, R.S., 'Application of Quantitative Models in Managerial Accounting: A State of the Art Survey,' in *Management Accounting-State-of-the-Art*, Beyer Lecture Series (University of Wisconsin, Madison, 1977).

——, 'The Impact of Management Accounting Research on Policy and Practice,' in J.W. Buckley, Ed., *The Impact of Accounting Research on Policy and Practice* (Arthur Young Professors Round-table, 1981), pp. 57–76.

——, *Advanced Management Accounting* (Prentice-Hall, 1982).

——, 'Measuring Manufacturing Performance: A Challenge for Management Accounting Research,' *The Accounting Review* (October 1983), pp. 686–705.

Littleton, A.C., *Accounting Evolution to 1900* (American Institute Publishing Co., 1933).

Meadows, D., 'New Targeting for Executive Pay,' *Fortune* (May 4, 1981), pp. 176–184.

Mintzberg, H., *The Nature of Managerial Work* (Harper & Row, 1973).

——, 'An Emerging Strategy of "Direct" Research,' *Administrative Science Quarterly* (December 1979), pp. 582–589.

——, 'Organization Design: Fashion or Fit,' *Harvard Business Review* (January/February 1981), pp. 103–115.

——, *Designing Effective Organizations* (Prentice-Hall, 1983).

Myers, S., 'Finance Theory and Financial Strategy,' *Interfaces* (January–February 1984), pp. 126–137.

Parker, R.H., 'Discounted Cash Flow in Historical Perspective.' *Journal of Accounting Research* (Spring 1968), pp. 58–71.

Peters, T.J. and R.H. Waterman, *In Search of Excellence: Lessons from America's Best-Run Companies* (Harper & Row, 1982).

Pinches, G.E., 'Myopia, Capital Budgeting and Decision-Making,' *Financial Management* (Autumn 1982), pp. 6–19.

Rappaport, A., 'Executive Incentives vs. Corporate Growth,' *Harvard Business Review* (July/August 1978), pp. 81–88.

——, 'Selecting Strategies that Create Shareholder Value,' *Harvard Business Review* (May/June 1981), pp. 139–149.

Reece, J.S., and W.R. Cool, 'Measuring Investment Center Performance,' *Harvard Business Review* (May/June 1978), pp. 28–46 and 174–176.

Reich, R., *The Next American Frontier* (Time Books, 1983).

Ridgway, V.F., 'Dysfunctional Consequences of Performance Measurement,' *Administrative Science Quarterly* (September 1956), pp. 240–247.

Schwarzbach, H.R. and R.C. Vangermeersch, 'Why We Should Account for the 4th Cost of Manufacturing,' *Management Accounting* (July 1983), pp. 24–28.

Scovell, C.H., *Interest as a Cost* (Ronald Press, 1924).

Shillinglaw, G., 'Old Horizons and New Frontiers: The Future of Managerial Accounting,' in H.P. Holzer, Ed., *Management Accounting 1980* (Department of Accounting, University of Illinois, 1980).

Sloan, A.P., *My Years with General Motors* (Doubleday, 1963).

Solomons, D., 'Evaluating Divisional Performance by Return on Investment and Residual Income,' in *Divisional Performance: Measurement and Control* (Financial Executives Research Foundation, New York, 1965), pp. 123–159.

——, 'The Historical Development of Costing,' in D. Solomons, Ed., *Studies in Cost Analysis*, Second Edition (Richard D. Irwin, 1968), pp. 3–49.

Spicer, B.H. and V. Ballew, 'Management Accounting Systems and the Economics of Internal Organization,' *Accounting, Organizations and Society* (March 1983), pp. 73–96.

Steer, P. and J. Cable, 'Internal Organization and Profit: An Empirical Analysis of Large U.K. Companies,' *Journal of Industrial Economics* (September 1978), pp. 13–30.

Stone, W., 'Intracompany Pricing,' *The Accounting Review* (October 1956), pp. 625–627.

Teece, D.J. and S.G. Winter, 'The Limits of Neoclassical Theory in Management Education,' *American Economic Review* (May 1984).

Tiessen, P. and J.H. Waterhouse, 'Towards a Descriptive Theory of Management Accounting,' *Accounting, Organizations and Society* (No. 2/3, 1983), pp. 251–267.

Umapathy, S., 'Transfers Between Profit Centers,' in R.F. Vancil, Ed., *Decentralization: Managerial Ambiguity By Design* (Dow Jones-Irwin, 1978), pp. 167–183.

Vangermeersch, R., 'The Wisdom of A. Hamilton Church' (University of Rhode Island, August 1983).

Waterhouse, J.H. and P. Tiessen, 'A Contingency Framework for Management Accounting Systems Research,' *Accounting, Organizations and Society* (August 1978), pp. 65–76.

Wells, M.C., 'Some Influences on the Development of Cost Accounting,' *The Accounting Historians Journal* (Fall 1977), pp. 47–61.

'What's Wrong with Management,' *Dun's Business Month* (April 1982), pp. 48–52.

Williamson, O.E., *Markets and Hierarchies: Analysis and Antitrust Implications* (Free Press, 1975).

——, 'The Modern Corporation: Origins, Evolution, Attributes,' *Journal of Economic Literature* (December 1981), pp. 1537–1568.

Wolfson, M.A., 'Tax, Incentive, and Risk-Sharing Considerations in the Design of Shared Real Estate Ownership Contracts' (Graduate School of Business, Stanford University, September 1982).
——, 'Empirical Evidence of Incentive Problems and their Mitigation in Oil and Gas Tax Shelter Programs' (Graduate School of Business, Stanford University, June 1983).

28

The role of management control systems in creating competitive advantage: new perspectives

Robert Simons
Harvard University Graduate School of Business Administration

ABSTRACT

For the last two decades, management control systems have been conceputalized in terms of implementing a firm's strategy. This view fails to recognize, however, the power of management control systems in the strategy formulation process. Based on a 2 year field study, a new model is presented to show how interactive management control systems focus organizational attention on strategic uncertainties. This process is examined in two competing firms to illustrate how top managers use formal systems to guide the emergence of new strategies and ensure continuing competitive advantage.

We know surprisingly little about the effects of strategy on management control systems or, alternatively, about how these systems affect strategy. How do top managers actually use planning and control systems to assist in the achievement of organizational goals? What formal processes are emphasized at top management levels where responsibility rests for strategy formulation and implementation? Does the strategy of the firm affect the administrative systems used to set competitive policies?

Most writing on this subject has been normative and not based on analysis of organizational practices; as a result, the function of management control described in accounting literature has changed little since Anthony (1965) defined management control in terms of assuring that organizational objectives are achieved. During the 1960s and 1970s, researchers built on Anthony's work and that of others by attempting to develop the best way to design and use formal systems to help organizations implement their strategies and objectives.

Meanwhile, new directions were emerging in the strategy field. While early normative research had focused on the processes used by managers to develop successful strategies, descriptive research in the 1970s and

Source: Simons, R. (1990) *Accounting, Organizations and Society*, **15** (1/2), pp. 127–43.

early 1980s began to identify patterns and commonalities in the ways that firms compete in different industries (e.g. Mintzberg, 1973a; Utterback & Abernathy, 1975; Miles & Snow, 1978; Porter, 1980). The identification of patterns in strategic activity posed a new question for management control researchers: what is the relationship, if any, between the way a firm competes and the way that it organizes and uses its management control systems?

The few recent studies that have addressed this question indicate that there are systematic differences in management control systems among firms that compete in different ways (e.g. Miller & Friesen, 1982; Govindarajan & Gupta, 1985; Simons, 1987a). But these large sample, cross-sectional studies reveal little about the process of management control in these firms. The studies begin to provide answers to 'how' management control systems differ among firms, but not to 'why' they differ.

As part of a broader research program (Simons, 1987b,c), the present study seeks to address this question directly by focusing on management *process* as it relates to management control and strategy. The familiar normative approach to management control describes a feedback process of planning, objective setting, monitoring, feedback and corrective action to ensure that outcomes are in accordance with plans. Two attempts have been made in the past to link this framework with strategy. The first is Anthony's (1965, 1988) – strategies are taken as given and management control systems motivate, monitor and report on their implementation. Another attempt to couple strategy and management control can be seen in the concept of strategic control. Strategic control has been described as a system to assess the relevance of the organization's strategy to its goals, and when discrepancies exist, to highlight areas needing attention (Lorange & Scott Morton, 1986, p. 10). Although strategic control has been identified as an important topic of strategic management (Schendel & Hofer, 1979, p. 18), the area has yet to generate a vigorous research program (Shrivastava, 1987). This failure is due in part to a lack of understanding of the relationship between management control systems and strategy.

The view of management control presented in this paper differs from the traditional framework. My research indicates that management control systems are not only important for strategy implementation, but also for strategy formation. I define management control systems, therefore, to recognize that these systems are more than devices of constraint and monitoring: management control systems are the formalized procedures and systems that use information to maintain or alter patterns in organizational activity. Using this definition, these systems broadly include formalized procedures for such things as planning, budgeting, environmental scanning, competitor analyses, performance reporting and evaluation, resource allocation and employee rewards (Simons, 1987a).

Although most strategy theorists correctly recognize that strategy formulation and strategy implementation are interrelated (Andrews, 1980, p. 24), researchers still tend to conceptually separate strategy implementation from strategy formation. This split has contributed to a lack of understanding of the nature of management control. Separating strategy formulation and implementation results in an artificial dichotomy that equates strategic planning with formulation and management control with implementation. The findings from the current study underscore the shortcomings of this approach by demonstrating the power of management control systems in empowering organizational learning and interactively influencing strategy.

I have three objectives in the discussion to follow. The first is to review the limited cross-sectional studies that have uncovered systematic relationships between management control systems and a firm's strategy. This literature suggests that the identification of these patterns remains an important agenda for management control research. Second, based on extensive field research, a dynamic process model is introduced to describe the use of management control systems at the top level of the firm. In this model, systems are used by top managers to set agendas for the discussion of uncertainties that arise as the firm attempts to create competitive advantage. Management control systems are used not only to monitor that outcomes are in accordance with plans, but also to motivate the organization to be fully informed concerning the current and expected state of strategic uncertainties. This general model may provide insight in explaining the fragmented relationships noted in previous empirical studies. Finally, a research agenda is outlined that may provide further knowledge about the relationship between management control systems and strategy. This leads to a discussion of some of the methodological issues that have to be addressed in future research.

STRATEGY, COMPETITIVE ADVANTAGE AND MANAGEMENT CONTROL

Before attempting to discuss the relationship between management control and strategy, we must first differentiate among a number of inter-related concepts in the strategy literature: strategy as process, strategy as competitive position, strategy at the business level and corporate strategy.

Strategic process describes the managerial activity inherent in shaping expectations and goals and facilitating the work of the organization in achieving these goals. Many influential writers from Barnard (1938) through Andrews (1980) have considered how business leaders should manage organizational processes to gain competitive advantage.

A firm's strategic position, by contrast, refers to how the firm competes in its markets, i.e. the product and market characteristics chosen by the firm to differentiate itself from its competitors and gain competitive advantage. Unlike the process analysis, the positional approach examines the strategic choices made by firms independent of the management process by which those choices were made; patterns in business unit strategic action are the unit of analysis.

Patterns in strategic actions have been identified at both the business level and the corporate level of the firm. Business strategy refers to how a company competes in a given business and positions itself among its competitors (Andrews, 1980, p. 18). Defining strategy as patterns of action (Mintzberg, 1978; Mintzberg & Waters, 1985), this vein of research has de-emphasized the link between observed strategies and prior, explicit managerial intentions. Research has concentrated instead on uncovering recurring patterns in the way that firms deliver value to customers.

These recurring patterns have been identified empirically and clustered into strategic archetypes (Table 28.1 provides a summary of four illustrative studies that identify and describe strategic archetypes).[1] Strategic archetypes demonstrate that firms can compete successfully in a variety of ways: for example, superior value can be offered to customers through new product features, high service levels, outstanding quality or low cost (Porter, 1985).

Other research has investigated patterns in strategic activities at the corporate level of diversified firms. Corporate strategy is concerned with determining what business(es) the organization chooses to compete in and the most effective way of allocating scarce resources among business units (Schendel & Hofer, 1979, p. 12). Patterns have been identified using typologies that describe the operating and financial characteristics of the divisions in diversified firms. These typologies are exemplified by the portfolio approach to corporate strategy popularized by U.S. consulting firms in the 1970s and reviewed in Hamermesh (1986, pp. 9–17).

The research discussed in this paper focuses on the relationship between business strategy (i.e. how a firm achieves competitive advantage) and the firm's use of management control systems. The analysis considers the importance of both strategic process and strategic position in understanding the role of formal systems. The relationship between control and corporate strategy, while not a focus of this research, is addressed briefly in the conclusion of the paper.

Previous studies of strategy and management control

If firms compete in identifiable but different ways, e.g. low cost or product uniqueness, what are the opportunities to design management control systems in accordance with the strategy of the firm? Three strategy researchers, Miles & Snow (1978) and Porter (1980), for example, agree that overall cost leadership and Defender strategies require sophisticated cost controls. Other than this simple observation, the strategy studies that have identified strategic archetypes offer little insight into how management control systems might be designed in different strategic situations.

Studies in other areas, however, are beginning to illustrate how these systems may differ among firms following different strategies. Khandwalla (1972, 1973), in the first study of its kind, focused on the relationship between formal accounting-based control systems and the type of

---

[1] Other studies that have attempted to identify strategic archetypes include Miller & Friesen (1978), Wissema *et al.* (1980), Galbraith & Schendel (1983) and Herbert & Deresky (1987).

Table 28.1 Illustrative studies of strategic archetypes

Study	Idenfied archetypes	Features
Mintzberg (1973a)	Entrepreneurial	Opportunity seeking, founding CEO, bold decisions, growth-oriented, high uncertainty.
	Adaptive	Reactive, incremental goal-setting, relative certainty in decision-making.
	Planning mode	Analysis dominates decisions, integrated strategies, placid environment.
Utterback & Abernathy (1975)	Performance-maximizing	Uncertain environment, offers unique products, searches for new opportunities
	Sales-maximizing	Standardized products, more stable environment, high level of competition, some product differentiation.
	Cost-minimizing	Standard product, extreme price competition, high efficiency, low innovation, sophisticated control techniques.
Miles & Snow (1978)	Defender	Stable environment, limited product range, competes through low cost or high quality, efficiency paramount, centralized structure.
	Prospector	Always seeking new product and market opportunities, uncertain environment, flexible structure.
	Analyzer	Hybrid. Core of traditional products, enters new market after viability established, matrix structure.
	Reactor	Lacks coherent strategy, structure inappropriate to purpose, misses opportunities, unsuccessful.
Porter (1980)	Overall cost leadership	Low price, high market share focus. Standardized product, economies of scale, tight cost control.
	Differentiation	Product uniqueness brings brand loyalty, emphasis on marketing and research.
	Focus	Focus on defined buyer group, product line or geographic market. Niche strategy.

competition in an industry. He concluded that increased competition leads to increased use of management control procedures. This relationship was strongest for product competition, moderate for marketing competition and weakest for price competition. This study, like others focusing on the relationship between formal control systems and external environments of the firm (e.g. Gordon & Narayanan, 1984; Ewusi-Mensah, 1981; Hedberg & Jönsson, 1978), did not consider the strategies of the firm, but did suggest that control system design was sensitive to the way that the firm competes.

Miller & Friesen (1982) studied the relationship between two strategic archetypes, which they labelled 'entrepreneurial' and 'conservative', and the use of control systems.[2] The firms in their sample were split into two strategic groups based on ratings of innovation and risk taking. The conservative subsample possessed many of the attributes of Miles & Snow's (1978) 'Defenders' and Mintzberg's (1973a) 'Adapters': low differentiation, homogeneous markets and stable environments. The second subsample was the entrepreneurial firm, similar to Miles & Snow's 'Prospector' and Mintzberg's 'Entrepreneurial' firms. These firms experienced more hostile environments and competed through product differentiation.

Miller & Friesen's analysis indicates that the strategy of the firm affects the way that management controls are used to either encourage or discourage innovation. Control was positively correlated with innovation for conservative firms and negatively correlated with innovation for entrepreneurial firms. The authors speculated that conservative firms use formal control systems to signal market opportunities and/or declining results; as a result, innovation increases. For entrepreneurial firms, however, control systems flag innovative excess and result in less innovation.

Govindarajan & Gupta (1985) studied the relationship between corporate strategy and one aspect of management control – bonus remuneration. The research focused on corporate-level, portfolio strategies in diversified firms (e.g. build market share, maximize cash flow, prepare to liquidate business). Govindarajan & Gupta concluded that long run evaluation criteria and subjective, non-formula bonus calculations are effective for businesses following a 'build' strategy, but detrimental to business units pursuing a 'harvest' strategy.

Building on the Miles & Snow (1978) typology, Simons (1987a) studied firms classified as either Prospectors or Defenders to determine whether management control systems differ between the two groups. Using concepts derived from the management control literature, factor analysis was

---

[2] In the Miller & Friesen (1982) study, 'controls' was a single variable among a set of 13 variables. The 13 variables measured organizational attributes such as environment, information processing, structure, and decision making. The 'controls' variable was calculated by averaging the scores of six Likert-type scales that related to the comprehensiveness of controls, and the use of cost and profit centers, statistical quality control practices, variance analysis and formal personnel appraisals.

used to reduce questionnaire scales to ten dimensions of management control.[3]

Statistical analysis and interview data indicated that control systems differ systematically between Prospector and Defender firms. Successful Prospectors use a high degree of forecast data in control reports, set tight budget goals and monitor outputs carefully. Cost control is reduced. Moreover, large Prospectors emphasize frequent reporting and use uniform control systems that are modified frequently. These results led to speculation that Prospectors use their management control systems intensively to monitor uncertain and changing environments. Defenders, by contrast, use management control systems less actively. Negative correlations were calculated between profit performance and attributes such as tight budget goals and the monitoring of outputs. Defenders, operating in stable environments, emphasize bonus remuneration based on achieving budget targets and report little change in their control systems over time.

A CLOSER LOOK AT STRATEGY AND MANAGEMENT CONTROL SYSTEMS

The studies cited in the preceding section suggest that there is a link between the way that firms achieve competitive advantage and the design and use of their management control systems. Little is known, however, about how this association should be conceptualized to increase our knowledge and improve our predictive ability.

The research which provides the basis for the present analysis, conducted over a 2 year period, focuses on the use of management control systems by top management – those responsible for ensuring that strategies are formulated and implemented. (In some organizations, top management refers to one individual; in large complex organizations, top management commonly refers to an operating committee, comprising heads of businesses or sectors, chaired by a CEO.) The concepts and model presented in the paper were developed during a series of field studies in a single U.S. industry. The first stage of the project involved in-depth interviewing and document review in three competing companies in this industry. The concepts reported in this paper were developed from this work and were then tested by expanding the sample to include an additional 13 firms in the industry. In all, over 70 interviews (augmented by reviews of relevant documentation and, in some cases, observations of company meetings) with top managers, each of approximately 2 hours duration, were conducted in the sixteen firms that agreed to participate in the study.

The subsequent analysis focuses on how two competing firms in this

---

[3] The ten factors developed and used in the Simons (1987a) study were tightness of budget goals, extent of external scanning, monitoring of results, use of cost control, use of forecast data, extent to which goals relate to output measures, reporting frequency, use of formula-based remuneration, extent to which control systems are tailored and the degree of changeability of control systems.

industry organize their management control systems at top management levels. The strategy of each firm is described followed by a brief overview of selected aspects of their management control systems. The control system aspects described are those identified by top managers of these firms as important to the way they manage their business. If a particular aspect of management control was identified as important by the managers in one firm, then a description is also provided of how the competing firm uses this aspect of management control. After this brief description, a conceptual model is presented to explain the differences in control system configuration between the two firms.

Company A and company B compete in the same industry; each company employs over 30,000 people and both companies are successful. Over the last 10 years, both companies have recorded compound growth rates of approximately 10% in sales and earnings and each has outperformed industry averages in terms of growth in sales, earnings, and cash flow. The shares of both company A and company B are rated by market analysts as high quality investments. Each company, however, follows a distinctly different strategy.

Company A competes in its various markets through cost leadership and customer service. Its products are a diverse group of well-known, mature products concentrated in high volume, low price categories. The company specializes in offering products that heighten efficiency and cut costs for the customer. Some of its intermediate products are licensed from competitors. Compared to competitors, the company has done historically little R&D (approximately 4% of sales in 1986) and is ranked as the lowest R&D spender in the industry.

'We are now definitely the low-cost producer in the markets we serve,' observes the CEO of company A. 'However, once in a while, by serendipity, we come across something promising. We have a habit of seizing on products the pack has scored'. Company A rarely introduces revolutionary new products, although existing product features evolve over time to take advantage of new technology and perceived customer needs. In terms of the strategic archetypes described in Table 28.1, company A might be described as a 'Defender' (Miles & Snow, 1978), an 'Adaptive firm' (Mintzberg, 1973), an 'Overall Cost Leader' (Porter, 1980), or as a 'Cost-Minimizing' firm (Utterback & Abernathy, 1975).

The company is organized into approximately 100 divisions which are grouped into four major sectors. *Business Week* magazine reports that company A is 'considered to be one of the best-managed firms in the industry.'

In contrast, company B competes through product inovation and marketing. Its products are premium priced and have advanced features. Products are developed internally and the features of most products are updated and improved on a regular basis. Marketing is intensive, using both media and sales representatives. The company has been successful in developing new markets through research-based product development. The company is widely regarded within the industry as an innovation leader. Most of the company's R&D effort is concentrated on product development; in 1986 company B spent approximately 10% of sales on R&D, making it the largest spender on R&D in its industry.

Company B differentiates its products on quality and innovativeness. The company attempts to achieve market leadership by aggressively marketing new products and enhancing its leadership image. Since it is often developing new markets, it competes in rapidly changing environments. Its Statement of Strategic Direction states, in part, 'We are dedicated to profitable high growth. To achieve this, we must be well positioned in growth markets. Each management must be aggressively innovative, willing to take risks, and strive to grow faster than the markets in which it competes'. This company could be described as a 'Prospector' (Miles & Snow, 1978), a 'Differentiation firm' (Porter, 1980), 'Performance-maximizing' (Utterback & Abernathy, 1975), or 'Entrepreneurial' (Mintzberg, 1973).

The company is decentralized. It is structured into three sectors with over 100 operating companies worldwide that manufacture and sell over 20 basic product categories. *Fortune* magazine's annual survey recently rated this company as one of the most admired companies in America.

Management control systems in the two companies

Given that these two highly-regarded competitors follow different strategies, what are the differences in the way they organize their management control systems? Companies of this size and complexity are bound to have many differences; the analysis is limited, therefore, to the use of management control systems at top management levels, since it is this group of individuals that has ultimate responsibility for strategy making and implementation. At this level, the differences in management control systems between the two firms (highlighted in Table 28.2) are striking.

Company A. Company A has a 5-year strategic plan that has not been revised for over 2 years. The plan is prepared by operating managers with the assistance and coordination of head office staff groups and presented to the top managers who comprise the Office of the Chief Executive (OCE). These managers report that the plan is for informational purposes and is not used actively in running the business.

Based on prior operating performance and market expectations, profit goals are established each year by the CEO and President of company A and communicated to division heads. Each division then prepares an annual budget to meet these goals. After the finance department verifies that the consolidated budget will meet corporate profit goals, the completed budgets are submitted to top management for approval. Annual budget presentations to top management are characterized by the CEO as 'show and tell'; problems and issues have been identified and worked out in person with the CEO and President prior to the meetings. Once approved, budgets are never changed.

Budget reviews by top management during the year are limited to

Table 28.2 Comparison of competitive characteristics and top-level management control systems used at two companies

	Company A	Company B
Competitive characteristics		
Miles & Snow (1978)	Defender	Prospector
Mintzberg (1973a)	Adaptive	Entrepreneurial
Porter (1980)	Overall cost leader	Differentiation
Management control systems at top management levels		
1. Strategic planning review	Sporadic. Last update 2 years ago. Does not motivate a lot of discussion in the company.	Intensive annual process. Business managers prepare strategic plans for debate by top management committee.
2. Financial goals	Set by top management and communicated down through organization.	Established by each business unit and rolled up after a series of review and challenge meetings.
3. Budget preparation and review	Budgets prepared to meet financial goals. Budgets coordinated by Finance Dept and presented to top management when assured that goals will be met.	Market segment prepares budgets with focus on strategy and tactics. Intensive debate at presentations to top management committee.
4. Budget revisions and updates	Not revised during budget year.	Business units rebudget from lowest expense levels three times during year with action plans to deal with changes.
5. Program reviews	Intensive monitoring of product- and process-related programs. Programs cut across organizational boundaries and affect all layers of company.	Programs limited to R&D which is delegated to local operating companies.
6. Evaluation and reward	2/3 of bonus based on contribution to generating profit in excess of plan. 1/3 based on personal goals (usually quantified).	Bonus based on subjective evaluation of effort. MBO system used throughout organization.

monthly reports to the OCE of sales, gross margin percentages, total operating expenses, tax rates and earnings per share.

Top management pays extremely close attention to a series of ongoing programs: these programs are established for the review of new product technologies, changes in existing product features and a variety of 'value improvement' efforts. Since programs are designed to explore new ways of doing things, they often cut across organizational boundaries and involve many people at different levels of the company.

Each program is reviewed regularly (at least once every 6 weeks and often more frequently) using formal reports and presentations to the highest level of management. Goals are established for all individuals working with each program and achievement against goals is measured on a regular basis. The ongoing review process generates product and process ideas throughout the organization that are tested and ultimately implemented. New programs are often established from ideas generated during existing program review.

Bonuses at company A are received by a relatively small group of middle and senior managers (the management group eligible for bonuses is 2.5% of total employees). Bonuses range from 15% to 50% of salary and are allocated to employees based on corporate performance against budget (⅓), operating unit performance against budget (⅓) and individual objectives that are negotiated with superiors (⅓).

Company B. Company B invests heavily in long range planning. All planning, however, is done by operating managers; there are no planning staff groups. Long range plans are based on 5 and 10 year forecasts and are updated each year by comparison with the plan prepared the year before. All changes in estimates require proposed tactics to deal with the changed environments. Included in the plans for each operating company are forecasts of competitive environments, *pro forma* income statements by product category for each major competitor, as well as an analysis of each competitor's perceived strategy.

Long range plans are debated heavily in the organization and must ultimately be sent, in summary form, to the CEO. The final debate and approval of long range plans takes place annually in an Executive Committee meeting which comprises the CEO, President and key sector heads and company group chairmen.

In company B, budgets, as well as a second-year forecast, are prepared annually by operating managers throughout the organization. Budgets are formally revised three times during the year; each revision requires a full re-estimation of all budget items and programs. Budgets are the focus of a great deal of debate among operating managers and are used, not as purely financial documents, but rather as agendas to discuss tactics, new marketing ideas, and product development plans throughout the organization and ultimately at the top management level. To focus the debate on strategies rather than financials, the plans and budgets are reduced at the top management level to four numbers only (estimated unit sales, revenues, net income and ROI) and to the tactics that will be used to achieve these numbers.

Profit goals are established on a bottom-up basis as managers throughout the organization set personal and business unit goals based on perceived corporate needs. These goals are challenged rigorously at all levels in the organization during a series of profit planning meetings held at various times during the year. Once the review process at lower levels is complete, top management rarely makes a formal request to operating managers to reconsider their budget to deliver more profit.

Unlike company A, the use of programs is generally limited to the R&D area, which is decentralized to operating companies. Programs are therefore managed at the local level and are not typically an agenda for top corporate management.

Bonuses at company B are entirely subjective and are based on effort and innovation rather than performance against predetermined targets. Managers throughout the organization spend a great deal of time each year discussing and reviewing suggestions concerning appropriate bonus levels for subordinates. Bonus recommendations for all managers with salaries in excess of $95,000 are reviewed by the Executive Committee. Below the executive committee level, all managers are eligible for annual bonuses, the amount of which is determined subjectively by operating company presidents. After bonuses have been awarded, the Executive Committee also uses a 'post audit' to review the reasons for unusually high or low bonus awards throughout the organization. Through a special bonus plan for entrepreneurial accomplishment, the company distributes additional bonuses in excess of $1 million annually; recommendations for these special bonuses, which typically represents 10–15% of an individual's salary, are reviewed and acted upon by the Executive Committee.

A PROCESS MODEL

Casual observation suggests that all large, complex organizations have similar types of management control systems. Short and long range plans, financial budgets, capital budgets, variance analyses and project reporting systems are commonplace tools in virtually every large, professionally managed corporation. But the illustrative example presented above shows that there are distinct differences in the way that management control systems are used at top management levels in different firms. How can we explain the differences in management control systems between company A and company B? How do these differences relate to their strategies?

The answer lies in how and why top managers choose to personally monitor certain management control systems and to delegate other aspects to subordinates. Four concepts are used to develop the model: limited attention of managers; strategic uncertainties; interactive management control; and organizational learning.

Limited attention

Interviews conducted during this research reveal that managers have neither the time nor the capacity to process all the information available to them. Two concepts, well established in the literature, support this observation. First, managers are rational only within cognitive boundaries (Simon, 1957). Mind is a scarce resource (Williamson, 1986, p. 5) and must be viewed as a constraint on the information processing capabilities of managers. Second, top managers must engage in many concurrent activities. Mintzberg (1973b) argues that top managers have ten working roles including that of figurehead, leader, liaison, monitor, disseminator, spokesman, entrepreneur, disturbance handler, resource allocator and negotiator. Decision-related activities represent only a subset of the activities of top managers; interpersonal and informational roles are equally important.

The concept of limited attention has important implications for management control. A multitude of activities demand attention – appearing at outside functions, speeches to employees, reading reports, making and ratifying decisions, evaluating employees, planning for succession – and daily choices must be made. Thus, only limited subsets of the organization's formal management control process can have the attention of top management; most areas of management control are delegated, by necessity, to subordinates.

Strategic uncertainties

Because of these attention constraints, top managers report that they implicitly rank the set of activities they monitor from most critical to least critical: this ranking allows top managers to attend to strategic uncertainties – uncertainties that top managers believe they must monitor personally to ensure that the goals of the firm are achieved.[4]

Although firms competing in the same industry face the same set of potential uncertainties (changes in government regulation, intensity of competition, advance of new technologies, nature of customers and suppliers, product life cycles and diversity in product lines), the strategy of the firm strongly influences which uncertainties are critical to the achievement of chosen objectives.[5] For example, managers in company A believe that they can only sustain their low cost position if their products evolve to offer superior efficiency to users. The strategic uncertainties that top managers in company A monitor personally, therefore, relate to potential changes in product technology that yield superior cost-in-use benefits to customers.

Although company B faces the same set of potential uncertainties as

[4] Strategic uncertainties are different than the concept of critical success factors that was popularized by business consultants in the 1960s and is taught in business schools today (Daniel, 1966). Critical success factors are the distinctive competencies that the firm must possess to sustain current competitive advantage (e.g. manufacturing efficiency for a strategy of overall cost leadership; research and development productivity for a strategy of new product introduction).

[5] A critical uncertainty for all firms is the ability to internally generate profit to provide resources to fund business strategies (Donaldson, 1984, p. 12). Thus, top managers always monitor personally the profit-generating ability of the firm.

company A, its strategy has resulted in different strategic uncertainties. Top managers in this firm monitor the choice of appropriate competitive responses for its various operating companies that compete through aggressive marketing tactics and new product introductions.

Interactive management control

Top managers must decide which aspects of management control systems to use interactively and which aspects to program (Simons, 1987b). Management controls become interactive when business managers use planning and control procedures to actively monitor and intervene in ongoing decision activities of subordinates. Since this intervention provides an opportunity for top management to debate and challenge underlying data, assumptions and action plans, interactive management controls demand regular attention from operating subordinates at all levels of the company. Programmed controls, by contrast, rely heavily on staff specialists in preparing and interpreting information. Data are transmitted through formal reporting procedures and operating managers are involved infrequently and on an exception basis.

Modern companies have many different types of management control systems. How do top managers decide which systems to make interactive and which to program? Top managers will choose to make a management control system interactive if the system collects information about strategic uncertainties. The selected interactive system can then be used by top managers for three functions: signalling, surveillance and decision ratification.

Signalling is the use of information to reveal preferences (Spence, 1974; Meyer, 1979). Signalling is necessary since top managers cannot always know when or where the impetus for important policy decisions will originate, how or why a decision will be made, or by whom. The decision process is diffuse with inputs from multiple actors over a protracted time period (Pinfield, 1986; Leifer & White, 1986; Burgelman, 1983; Mintzberg *et al.*, 1976; Cohen *et al.*, 1972). For this reason, top managers do not know *ex ante*, and often not even *ex post*, who in the organization initiates and fosters important policy decisions. By using interactive management controls to monitor strategic uncertainties, top managers reveal their values and preferences to the many individuals in the organization who have input in decision processes.

Surveillance is the search for surprises; interactive management controls provide guidance to organizational members as to where to look for surprises and what types of intelligence information to gather. Feldman & March (1981) describe this function:

Organizations, as well as individuals, ... gather information that has no apparent immediate decision consequences. As a result, the information seems substantially worthless within a decision-theory perspective. The perspective is misleading. Instead of seeing an organization as seeking information in order to choose among given alternatives in terms of prior preferences, we can see an organization as monitoring its environment for surprises (or for reassurances that there are none). The surprises may be new alternatives, new possible preferences, or new significant changes in the world (p. 176).

Finally, decision ratification by top managers (as distinct from decision making) is necessary when any strategic policy decision commits the organization and its resources (Mintzberg 1973b, p. 87; Bower, 1986, pp. 64). Interactive management controls allow top managers to be fully informed about such decisions throughout the organization.

Organization learning

The final concept needed to complete the analysis is organizational learning. Organizational learning describes the ways that organizations adjust defensively to reality and use knowledge to improve the fit between the organization and its environment (Hedberg, 1981, p. 3). Comprehensive reviews of the concept of organizational learning are found in Argyris & Schön (1978) and Fiol & Lyles (1985).

I have argued that the personal involvement of top managers, the defining characteristic of interactive control, influences strongly the incentives to produce and share information. Moreover, this focusing of organizational attention and the interactive exchange of information stimulates learning throughout the organization about the strategic uncertainties that are perceived by top management. By focusing attention throughout the organization, top managers use interactive management control to influence and guide the learning process – understanding that individual ideas and initiatives will emerge over time in unsystematic ways. By emphasizing select management controls and making them interactive (and programming and delegating others) top managers ensure that the organization is responsive to the opportunities and threats that the firm's strategic uncertainties present.

The four concepts presented above can now be summarized and integrated: the intended business strategy of a firm creates strategic uncertainties that top managers monitor. While all large companies have similar management control systems, top managers make selected control systems interactive to personally monitor the strategic uncertainties that they believe to be critical to achieving the organization's goals. The choice by top managers to make certain control systems interactive (and program others) provides signals to organizational participants about what should be monitored and where new ideas should be proposed and tested. This signal activates organizational learning and, through the debate and dialogue that surrounds the interactive management control process, new strategies and tactics emerge over time.

The recursive nature of the model (Fig. 28.1) illustrates why management control systems should be considered as an important input to strategy formation. We know that strategies can be both intended and emergent (Mintzberg, 1978). This model illustrates, moreover, that emerg-

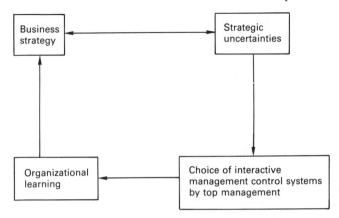

Fig. 28.1 Process model of relationship between business strategy and management control systems.

ent strategies can be influenced and managed – serendipity can be guided by top managers who use formal process to focus organizational attention and thereby generate new ideas, tactics and strategies. Management control processes, which have been characterized solely as tools for implementing goals, can be instrumental in allowing the organization to learn and adapt over time.

Applying the model

Since company A and company B compete in the same industry, each firm faces the same set of potential uncertainties (Fig. 28.2). From this set of potential uncertainties, top managers of each firm have identified

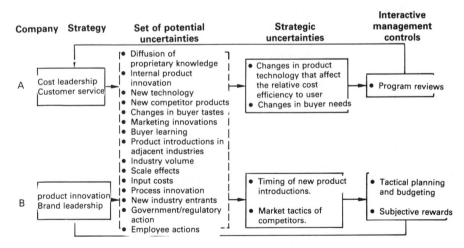

Fig. 28.2 Summary of interactive process model in two firms.

strategic uncertainties that relate to their company's individual strategy. From interviews at company A, it is clear that top managers believe that the major strategic uncertainty facing the firm is new product technologies or attributes that could shift existing low cost advantage. They recognize that company A's success derives from continually providing customers with products that offer low end-use cost: new, more efficient product technologies of competitors and changes in buyer needs are potential threats.

To manage these strategic uncertainties, top management has made a limited subset of management controls interactive and programmed other controls. The program review system, which operates from the lowest organizational level to the CEO's office, is an example of an interactive management control system that is a major information source for both top management and all operating managers in the company. Programs focus on ways to improve value for customers ('cost improvement with equal or better quality'), new technologies that build on existing product lines and product enhancements to help customers be more efficient. Programs typically have the potential of affecting a wide range of the company's products and therefore cut across formal organizational boundaries.

Managers in company A know, by the emphasis that top management puts on the review of selected programs, which aspects of the business are considered critical to long term organizational success. For each program, information is continually gathered throughout the organization, agendas are set to review progress and new information, and changes and surprises are rapidly communicated. The organizational learning engendered through the interactive management control system is a powerful influence on strategy making.

The CEO of company A described how new strategies emerge from the process, 'I really work those programs. Everyone understands how important they are. New initiatives are not decided as part of the planning process, but as part of the program review process. The Capital Expenditure Committee is not doing strategic thinking about programs – they just say "yes" when a proposal is developed out of a program review and someone comes to them asking for money. In fact, many of our new programs arise out of the review process. As we sit and discuss these things, someone will have a bright idea for product enhancement or a new way of doing something. This often leads to new programs which can eventually take us into new technologies or open up a whole new group of products.'

Top management at company A pays little day-to-day attention to aspects of the firm's management control systems that do not relate to strategic uncertainties. Long range planning is programmed and is not an agenda item for top management: strategies throughout the firm are clear and consistent. Profit planning and budgeting, an annual event orchestrated by staff departments, are not interactive because the environment is relatively stable and well understood; top managers do not need to rely on these systems to motivate the organization to constantly scan changes in the market. The rewards system is also programmed since bonuses are determined largely by reference to quantitative targets and require minimal attention from top management. Even aspects of management control systems that are associated with the success of current strategies, i.e. so-called 'critical success factors', are programmed and delegated to staff specialists.

The programming of critical success factors is apparent in the way that top management at company A deal with manufacturing and logistical operations – clearly critical success factors for this low cost producer. Every Wednesday at 10:00 a.m., a 20 minute meeting is held with 15 key managers, chaired by a member of the top management group. Conversation focuses on one sheet of paper that reviews twelve product categories in terms of unit sales, inventory levels, backorders, service levels and quality control release times – all against target. The chairman described the meetings, 'we run the day-to-day operations by focusing on things off track. If there is a problem, the individual had better have the answer before he walks in. In this way, we can review the entire business in twenty minutes each week. We have become very good at understanding what we were looking at so we can just do it.'

Because company B follows a different strategy, its top managers focus on different strategic uncertainties. By competing through product innovation rather than price and efficiency, top managers want their organization to focus on marketing tactics that can exploit new product development and thereby build market share or open new markets. Top managers perceive strategic uncertainties that relate to the timing of new product introductions and the defensive actions of competitors. Accordingly, the top management of company B has chosen to make planning and budgeting highly interactive and tactical.

The development and discussion of 5 and 10 year plans, for example, is an important agenda for top management and, by implication, for all operating managers in company B. Each year, plans for each operating unit are revised with reference to the previous year's plan; product life cycles are carefully monitored. All anticipated changes are coupled with action plans that focus on marketing tactics and the timing of new product introductions – both strategic uncertainties for company B. These plans, which are based on environment, competitor and technology assessments, are prepared, challenged and debated over a period of several months each year by successive levels of operating managers until they are debated at the Executive Committee level. Staff units play no role in this process. The highly interactive nature of long range planning results in intense organizational learning about changes in the competitive product markets and ideas on how to react offensively to these threats and opportunities. From these discussions, new strategies emerge.

Top management has also made profit planning and budgeting interactive at company B by focusing attention, almost continuously during the year, on budget changes and action plans to deal with changed conditions. Managers use this bottom-up process not as a financial exercise, but rather to set agendas to debate current and future product/market strategies in the company's changing markets. Budget discussions throughout the year revolve around unanticipated changes in the competitive environment, marketing tactics to preempt competitor actions, and the type and timing of new product developments. Managers point out that they are planning and budgeting so frequently and with so much discussion about appropriate tactics and targets that it is unnecessary to formally issue corporate goals. One top manager elaborated, 'the feeling that we are forever planning is due to the fact that you never have the luxury of putting the plan on a shelf – it forces you to continually look at your mistakes and learn how to do better next time.'

The reward system at company B has been made interactive and thus also demands a great deal of attention from managers throughout the organization. Managers cannot rely on a formula, but must rather attempt to subjectively assess each individual's contribution in rapidly changing market environments. Rewarding effort rather than results requires evaluators to understand competive business environments, potential opportunities and constraints, and the range of action alternatives available to subordinate managers. This information gathering process generates learning about strategic uncertainties and about possible new tactics and strategies.

Like company A, the top managers at company B are not normally involved in controls that do not focus on strategic uncertainties. The review of detailed cost information is programmed and is not an agenda for top management. Efficiency programs are typically overseen by staff groups. As a top manager stated, 'I leave the analysis of variances, etc., to the financial people. I let them bring any problems to me. I don't check it or get involved in it myself.' Even programs for new product development, a critical success factor, are managed at the local operating company without regular attention from top management; given limited attention, top management chooses to focus instead on the strategic uncertainties that arise from the actions of competitors.

Managers in each of these firms have made certain management controls interactive and programmed others. This phenomenon is not limited to these two companies, but was observed also in the other 14 companies in the sample. One CEO captured the spirit of the phenomenon, 'we can have all the formal processes in the world and some of these, frankly, I don't give a damn about and others I do. And everyone understands the difference.'

DISCUSSION AND CONCLUSION

The model presented in this paper departs from the traditional analysis of 'fit' between formal systems and critical success factors. Instead, new concepts are introduced to link management control systems with competitive advantage. The research underscores the importance of the dynamic relationship between formal process and strategy: competitive strategic positioning, management control and the process of strategy-making play one upon the other as the firm evolves and adapts over time. The analysis shows that interactive management control processes can be used to manage emergent strategy: rather than focusing on what the organization already understands and does well, these systems direct organizational attention to emerging threats and opportunities.

Theories of information provide additional perspective to the ideas presented in this paper. Language theorists differentiate between rules that constrain and those that open up new realms of activity (Campbell, 1982, p. 128). The latter type of rule is capable of generating variety, novelty, and surprise. This distinction is analogous to that between pro-grammed and interactive controls. Campbell (1982) illustrates the power of fixed rules in producing unpredictable amounts of complexity as in-formation and meaning is generated. The necessity of structure to produce meaning, a concept fundamental to theories of information and language, is echoed in the way that managers use structured, formal process inter-actively to motivate organizational learning. 'Structure and freedom,' summarizes Campbell, 'like entropy and redundancy, are not warring opposites, but complementary forces' (p. 264).

Top managers use formal process to gain maximum advantage from these forces. These managers know that decisions and actions affecting current strategies will emerge from all corners of the organization; their primary job is to provide guidance, resources and incentives to motivate the organization to gather and interpret new information so that the organization can respond and adapt. Energy is channelled and directed by the interactive process; formal management control systems provide a common language. The organization is energized: momentum is created to exploit existing strategies and to anticipate strategic uncertainties. Information is shared and interpreted. Action plans are tested. New strategies emerge.

Our analysis suggests that caution is necessary in interpreting previous studies that have focused on strategy and control. Cross-sectional studies such as Khandwalla (1972, 1973) and Miller & Friesen (1982) were con-ducted using a single measure for control that was computed as the simple average of the importance of various aspects of a firm's administrative controls system. Thus, scores to represent the use of cost control and variance analysis, formal appraisal of personnel, capital budgeting tech-niques and flexible budgeting were averaged to produce one summary index. The process model developed here, however, suggests that it is not the mean value that is importance, but rather the distribution of man-agement attention among the various control subsystems.

Studies that have decomposed control systems into constituent elements support the process model presented in this paper. Govindarajan & Gupta (1985) noted that subjective bonus systems were beneficial for emerging businesses following 'build' strategies, but detrimental to businesses in a 'harvest' mode. Interactive reward systems based on subjective evaluation of effort are appropriate for firms that need to motivate organizational learning in rapidly changing environments and where rewarding team effort is important – typical conditions of firms in a growth phase. This approach is costly, however, and generally uneconomic for businesses in slow decline.

Simons (1987a) found that Prospectors generally use a lot of forecast data, set tight budget goals, monitor outputs carefully and emphasize frequent reporting with uniform control systems. Like company B, the prototypical Prospector faces strategic uncertainties owing to rapidly changing product or market conditions; interactive management control systems such as planning and budgeting are used to set agendas to debate strategy and action plans in these rapidly changing conditions. Defenders, by contrast, use planning and budgeting less intensively. Like company A, which operates in a relatively stable environment, many aspects of the business that are important in terms of current competitive advantage are highly controllable and managers need only focus on strategic uncertainties – often related to product or technological changes that could undermine current low cost positions.

Further research must also be sensitive to the unit of analysis. This study has focused on business strategy. But what are the process relationships between management control systems and corporate strategy? Recently, the portfolio management approach that has been the cornerstone of corporate strategy has been strongly criticized (Porter, 1987). The ability of diversified firms to add value through portfolio techniques is argued to be increasingly limited in today's efficient capital markets. In terms of the process model presented here, a strategic uncertainty for the diversified firm is the appropriate allocation of resources among diverse business units. Given the scarce attention of top management, focusing attention on portfolio allocations may limit the attention that can be accorded to business-related aspects of management control to the detriment of organizational learning and effective strategy making.

This research offers a new perspective for understanding how and why firms make the design choices that we observe in practice. But there are many other questions to be answered. How do managers identify strategic uncertainties? What types of interactive management controls are used by managers in different organizations? Do patterns exist among firms following similar strategies? Are strategic uncertainties unique to each firm or do patterns exist across firms? Research to answer these questions is ongoing and some further results are reported in Simons (1987c).

Management theorists must strive to understand better the dynamic relationship between strategy and management control processes. This means not only recognizing that strategy formation and implementation are intertwined, but also opening up the meaning of management control to a broader notion that builds upon guidance rather than coercion, and on learning as well as constraint. We need, in fact, a better language to describe management control processes. Control systems are used for multiple purposes: monitoring, learning, signalling, constraint, surveillance, motivation and others. Yet, we use a single descriptor – management control systems – to describe these distinctly different processes. Eskimos use precise words to describe different types of snow and sailors have specialized words for ropes that perform different functions. Management control theorists also need a precise vocabulary to develop and communicate the concepts necessary to describe complex organizational phenomena.

ACKNOWLEDGEMENTS

For comments on an earlier draft of this paper, I wish to thank my colleagues Robert Anthony, Chris Argyris, Joseph Bower, C. Roland Christiansen, Robert Eccles and Howard Stevenson. I also thank the participants of the Harvard Business School Control Workshop, especially Charles Christenson, Rajib Doogar, Julie Hertenstein, Robert Kaplan, Jean-François Manzoni, Kenneth Merchant and Richard Vancil. Last, but not least, I thank Anthony Hopwood for encouragement and suggestions.

BIBLIOGRAPHY

Andrews, K.R., *The Concept of Corporate Strategy* (Homewood, IL: Irwin, 1980).

Anthony, R.N., *Planning and Control Systems: a Framework for Analysis* (Boston, MA: Graduate School of Business Administration, Harvard University, 1965).

Anthony, R.M., *The Management Control Function* (Boston: Harvard Business School Press, 1988).

Argyris, C. & Schön, D.A., *Organizational Learning* (Reading, MA: Addison-Wesley, 1978).

Barnard, C.I., *The Functions of the Executive* (Cambridge, MA: Harvard University Press, 1968; originally published 1938).

Bower, J.L. *Managing the Resource Allocation Process: a Study of Corporate Planning and Investment*, 2nd Edn (Boston, MA: Harvard Business School Press, 1986).

Burgelman, R.A., Corporate Entrepreneurship and Strategic Management: Insights from a Process Study, *Management Science* (1983) pp. 1349–1364.

Campbell, J., *Grammatical Man: Information, Entropy, Language, and Life* (New York: Simon & Schuster, 1982).

Cohen, M.D., March, J.D. & Olsen, J.P., A Garbage Can Model of Organizational Choice, *Administrative Science Quarterly* (1972) pp. 1–25.

Daniel, R., Reorganizing for Results. *Harvard Business Review* (November–December, 1966) pp. 96–104.

Donaldson, G., *Managing Corporate Wealth* (New York: Praeger, 1984).

Ewusi-Mensah, K., The External Organizational Environment and Its Impact of Management Information Systems, *Accounting Organizations and Society* (1981) pp. 301–316.

Feldman, M.S. & March, J.G., Information in Organizations as Signal and Symbol, *Administrative Science Quarterly* (1981) pp. 171–186.

Fiol, C.M. & Lyles, M.A., Organizational Learning, *Academy of Management Review* (1985) pp. 803–813.

Galbriath, C. & Schendel, D., An Emprical Analysis of Strategy Types, *Strategic Management Journal* (1983) pp. 153–173.

Gordon, L.A. & Narayanan, V.K., Management Accounting Systems, Perceived Environmental Uncertainty and Organization Structure: an Empirical Investigation, *Accounting Organizations and Society* (1984) pp. 33–47.

Govindarajan, V. & Gupta, A.K., Linking Control Systems to Business Unit Strategy: Impact on Performance, *Accounting, Organizations and Society* (1985) pp. 51–66.

Hamermesh, R.G., *Making Strategy Work: How Senior Managers Produce Results* (New York: John Wiley, 1986).

Hedberg, B., How Organizations Learn and Unlearn, in Starbuck, W.H. and Nystrom, P.C. (eds) *Handbook of Organizational Design* pp. 3–27 (New York: Oxford University Press, 1981).

Hedberg, B. and Jönsson, S., Designing Semi-Confusing Information Systems for Organizations in Changing Environments, *Accounting, Organizations and Society* (1978) pp. 47–64.

Herbert, T.T. & Dereksy, H., Generic Strategies: an Empirical Investigation of Typology Validity and Strategy Content, *Strategic Management Journal* (1987) pp. 135–147.

Khandwalla, P.N., The Effect of Different Types of Competition on the Use of Management Controls, *Journal of Accounting Research* (Autumn 1972) pp. 275–285.

Khandwalla, P.M., Effect of Competition on the Structure of Top Management Control, *Academy of Management Journal* (1973) pp. 285–295.

Leifer, E.M. & White, H.C., Wheeling and Annealing: Federal and Multidivisional Control, in Short, J.F. (ed.) *The Social Fabric* (New York: Sage, 1986).

Lorange, P., Scott Morton, M.F. & Ghoshal, S., *Strategic Control Systems* (St Paul, MN: West, 1986).

Meyer, M.W., Organizational Structure as Signalling, *Pacific Sociological Review* (1979) pp. 481–500.

Miles, R.E. & Snow, C.C., *Organizational Strategy, Structure, and Process* (New York: McGraw-Hill, 1978).

Miller, D. & Friesen, P.H., Archetypes of Strategy Formulation, *Management Science* (1978) pp. 921–933.

Miller, D. & Friesen, P.H., Innovation in Conservative and Entrepreneurial Firms, *Strategic Management Journal* (1982) pp. 1–27.

Mintzberg, H., Strategy Making in Three Modes, *California Management Review* (Winter 1973a) pp. 44–53.

Mintzberg, H., *The Nature of Managerial Work* (New York: Harper & Row, 1973b).

Mintzberg, H., Patterns in Strategy Formation, *Management Science* (May 1978) pp. 934–948.

Mintzberg, H., Raisinghani, D. & Théorêt, A., The Structure of "Unstructured" Decision Process, *Administrative Science Quarterly* (June 1976) pp. 246–275.

Mintzberg, H. & Waters, J.A., Of Strategies, Deliberate and Emergent, *Strategic Management Journal* (1985) 257–272.

Pinfield, L.T., A Field Evaluation of Perspective on Organizational Decision Making, *Administrative Science Quarterly* (September 1986) pp. 365–388.

Porter, M.E., *Competitive Strategy* (New York: The Free Press, 1980).

Porter, M.E., *Competitive Advantage* (New York: The Free Press, 1985).

Porter, M.E., From Competitive Advantage to Corporate Strategy, *Harvard Business Review* (May–June, 1987) pp. 43–59.

Schendel, D.E. & Hofer, C.W. (eds), *Strategic Management* (Boston, MA: Little, Brown, 1979).

Shrivastava, P., Rigor and Practical Usefulness of Research in Strategic Management, *Strategic Management Journal* (January–February 1987) pp. 77–92.

Simon, H., *Models of Man* (New York: John Wiley, 1957).

Simons, R., Accounting Control Systems and Business Strategy: an Empirical Analysis, *Accounting, Organizations and Society* (1987a) pp. 357–374.

Simons, R., Planning, Control, and Uncertainty: a Process View, in Bruns, W.J. Jr and Kaplan, R.S. (eds), *Accounting and Management: Field Study Perspectives*, (Boston, MA: Harvard Business School Press, 1987b) pp. 339–362.

Simons, R., Implementing Strategy: Configurations in Management Control Systems. Paper presented at the 1987 annual meeting of the Strategic Management Society held in Boston, 14–17 October (1987c).

Spence, M., *Market Signalling* (Cambridge, MA: Harvard University Press, 1974).

Utterback, J.M. & Abernathy, W.J., A Dynamic Model of Product and Process Innovation, *Omega* (1975) pp. 639–656.

Williamson, O.E., Economics and Sociology: Promoting a Dialogue, Yale School of Organization and Management, Working Paper Series D no. 25, August 1986.

Wissema, J.G., Van der Pol, H.W. & Messer, H.M. Strategic Management Archetypes, *Strategic Management Journal* (1980) pp. 37–47.

29

Linking control systems to business unit strategy: impact on performance

V. Govindarajan
The Ohio State University

and

Anil K. Gupta
Boston University

ABSTRACT

Rooted in contingency theory, this paper examines linkages between strategy, incentive bonus system and effectiveness at the strategic busines unit (SBU) level within diversified firms. Data from 58 SBUs reveal (1) that greater reliance on long-run criteria as well as sub-jective (non-formula) approaches for determining the SBU general managers' bonus contributes to effectiveness in the case of 'build' SBUs but hampers it in the case of 'harvest' SBUs, and (2) that the relationship between extent of reliance on short-run criteria and effectiveness is virtually independent of SBU strategy.

Recent studies in accounting and control have tended to utilize 'contingency' rather than 'one best way' perspectives. Mirroring earlier research in organization theory (e.g., Burns & Stalker, 1961; Woodward, 1965; Lawrence & Lorsch, 1967), these studies have sought to uncover the impact of *size* (Merchant, 1981), *technology* (Daft & McIntosh, 1981), *environment* (Hayes, 1977; Govindarajan, 1983) and organizational *structure* (Bruns & Waterhouse, 1975; Merchant, 1981) on the design of budgets and other organizational control mechanisms. Given this relevance of developments in organization theory for research on organizational control, it is noteworthy that while the broader field of organization theory has, in recent years, come to view organizational *strategy* as yet another and perhaps the pre-eminent source of contingencies for the design of organizations (e.g., Chandler, 1962; Fouraker & Stopford, 1968; Child, 1972; Rumelt, 1974; Miles & Snow, 1978; Galbraith & Nathanson, 1978; Snow & Hrebiniak, 1980; Hambrick, 1981; Gupta & Govindarajan, 1984), concep-

Source: Govindarajan, V. and Gupta, A.K. (1985) *Accounting, Organizations and Society*, **10** (1), pp. 51–66.

tual as well as empirical investigations on linkages between strategy and control systems have tended to be very sparse.

Further, the few studies that have focused explicitly on the relationship between strategy and control systems have tended to operationalize strategy only in terms of the degree and nature of the organization's product and geographic diversification (Salter, 1973; Lorsch & Allen, 1973; Dermer, 1977; Vancil, 1980; Otley, 1980; Pitts, 1980). Given the increasing trend towards diversification in most industrialized countries (Scott, 1973), this focus on corporate diversification strategy seems highly relevant. However, strategy formulation and implementation take place not just at the level of the diversified firm as a whole but also at the level of the diversions/strategic business units (or SBUs) comprising the firm (Hofer, 1975; Hambrick, 1980). In such a context, the near absence of empirical studies on the role played by control systems in implementing business unit level strategies presents a significant research opportunity.

This paper presents the results of an empirical study of the effects of linking the SBU general manager's incentive compensation (an important organizational mechanism for controlling managerial behaviour) to SBU strategy on SBU performance. SBU strategy is operationalized in terms of the strategic mission. The components of incentive compensation system studied are: (1) the relative importance given to long- and short-run criteria in assessing the general manager's performance for the purposes of bonus determination, and (2) for any given level of performance, the degree of reliance on quantitative formulas vs subjective discretion in determining the amount of bonus to be paid to the manager.

THEORETICAL BACKGROUND AND PROPOSITIONS

Business unit strategy

Strategic mission/portfolio strategy (Henderson, 1970; Hofer & Schendel, 1978), competitive posture (Porter, 1980), and the extent and nature of linkages with other SBUs within the same corporation (Rumelt, 1974; Vancil, 1980) constitute some of the most critical strategic issues at the level of SBUs within diversified firms. While all of these strategic dimensions have the potential to influence the choice of control mechanisms, this study focuses only on the implications of variations in strategic mission.

By definition, strategic mission (or portfolio strategy) signifies the nature of the SBU's intended trade-offs between market share growth and short-term earnings/cash flow maximization (Abell & Hammond, 1979; Henderson, 1970). Similar to Larreche & Shrinivasan (1982), this study views alternative strategic missions as spanning a *continuous* spectrum. At one end of the spectrum are SBUs whose mission is to increase market share (usually resulting in low short-term profitability and low or negative short-term cash flow); these SBUs typically have 'low relative market share' in 'high growth industries.' At the other end are SBUs whose mission is the maximization of short-term earnings and cash flow (usually resulting in a slippage in market share); these SBUs typically have 'high relative market share' in 'low growth or declining industries.' While most strategy researchers (e.g., Buzzell & Wiersema, 1981; Hofer & Schendel, 1978; MacMillan, 1982; Rothschild, 1976) have tended to operationalize strategic mission as a nominal variable, a closer examination of the typologies developed indicates that these nominal approaches are essentially consistent with the continuous approach being taken in this study. For instance, the six categories of Hofer & Schendel (1978) – share increasing strategies, growth strategies, profit strategies, market concentration and asset reduction strategies, turnaround strategies and liquidation or divestiture strategies – and the eight categories of MacMillan (1982) – aggressive build, gradual build, selective build, aggressive maintain, selective maintain, competitive harasser, prove viability and divest – both reflect a more or less steady transition from a 'pure build' strategy at one end to a 'pure harvest' or 'divest' strategy at the other. Since this study focuses on strategy implementation for *ongoing* businesses only, its focus is only on the continuum from 'pure build' to 'pure harvest' and it does not deal with the implications of a 'divest' strategy.

Importance of bonus criteria

Three groups of literature provide support to expectations of linkages between importance of bonus criteria, SBU strategy, and SBU effectiveness.

The first set of studies has dealt with the implications of *corporate* (rather than SBU) level strategy for the design of incentive compensation systems for SBU level general managers. For instance, in comparing financial conglomerates to relate diversified firms, Berg (1965) reported that, unlike the latter, the former reward their managers solely on the basis of divisional financial results. He argued that the financial conglomerates' strategy of unrelated diversification resulted in very little interdependency among the divisions; hence the logic for an incentive system based on the divisional 'bottomline'. Similarly, in comparing diversified with vertically integrated firms, Lorsch & Allen (1973) reported that while the former made bonus decisions for their division managers almost exclusively on the basis of the divisions' profit performance, the latter did not link division managers' incentive compensation solely to divisional profits thereby relying also on top management's discretion; the researchers explained the differences in the incentive systems of these two types of companies in terms of the degree of interdependence among divisions created by their respective corporate strategies. Consistent with these empirical findings, Salter (1973) has also argued that there is no single 'best' incentive compensation system for all companies and that such systems should 'fit' the requirements of corporate strategy. While the focus of all of these studies has been on strategy at the corporate rather than the SBU level, it might be noted that, at least on a prima-facie basis, the rationale for linking the SBU general manager's incentive compensation to SBU-level strategy would be even stronger than that for linking it to corporate-level strategy; as such, the above studies lend support to the research being presented here.

The second set of studies has dealt with the behavioural effects of incentive mechanisms on individual motivation and task performance. The common conclusions of these studies has been that when an individual's rewards are tied to performance along certain criteria, his/her behaviour would be guided by the desire to optimize performance with respect to those criteria. For instance, Spitzer (1964) reported a significant positive correlation between employees' actual contribution to cost reduction and their perceptions regarding the degree to which contribution to cost reduction would be helpful in attaining more pay. Similarly, Schuster, *et al.* (1971) found that the more an employee believed that performance influenced pay, the harder he worked to improve his performance. Based on data collected from questionnaires filled in by managers in both private industry and government, Porter & Lawler (1968) also found a definite tendency for managers who believe that their performance on the job would have a significant impact on their pay to be assessed by their superiors as more effective than managers who believed that performance had relatively insignificant impact on their pay. Similar linkages between financial incentives and task performance have also been observed in a series of related laboratory studies by Locke *et al.* (1968), Pritchard & Curts (1973) and Terborg & Miller (1978). The general conclusion of these behavioural studies are also consistent with the normative implications of 'agency theory' (e.g., Holmstrom, 1979).

The third set of studies has focused on the dysfunctional – rather than the functional – consequences of incentive compensation systems. In a study of the responses of government administrators to evaluation on the basis of statistical performance indices, Blau (1955) found that the administrators behaved so as to increase their performance in terms of these indices even if the overall result was dysfunctional for the organization. Dearden (1961) has also reported many situations where the incentive system led division managers to optimize their divisions' performance while, at the same time, suboptimizing corporate performance. Similarly, citing several examples of poor performance on the part of subordinates, Kerr (1975) has put the blame on incentive systems that tended to reward behaviours the superior was trying to discourage while the desired behaviours were not being rewarded at all. While these studies help emphasize that incentive systems can indeed have dysfunctional consequences, the implication is not that such systems should be done away with. Rather, in pointing out that incentive systems can have powerful behavioural consequences, they imply that such systems must be linked very carefully to the desired rather than the nondesired behaviours/outcomes.

Extrapolating from the studies reviewed above, it seems valid to hypothesize that business unit objectives are more likely to be achieved if the incentive compensation system is tied to the strategy being pursued by the focal SBU rather than to a uniform set of performance criteria (such as return on investment) across *all* SBUs. Taking note of the fact that, by definition, a build strategy demands attention to tasks which have long-term implications whereas a harvest strategy demands attention to tasks with short-term payoffs, it follows that:

P1: Greater reliance on long-run criteria (specifically: sales growth, market share, new product development, market development, R&D, personal development, and political/public affairs) in the determination of the incentive bonus for SBU general managers will have a stronger positive impact on effectiveness in the case of SBUs at the 'build' end of the strategy spectrum than in the case of SBUs at the 'harvest' end.

P2: Greater reliance on short-run criteria (specifically: cost control, operating profits, profit margins, cash flow, and return on investment) in the determination of the incentive bonus for SBU general managers will have a stronger positive impact on effectiveness in the case of SBUs at the 'harvest' end of the strategy spectrum than in the case of SBUs at the 'build' end.

Reliance on formula vs subjective (non-formula) approaches towards the determination of incentive bonus

For any SBU, in addition to varying the importance of different bonus criteria, given a specific level of performance, superiors must also decide as to what approach to take in determining a specific bonus amount: at one exteme, the bonus amount may be derived strictly from a formula where numerical measures of performance on one or more criteria constitute the independent variable(s); at the other extreme, the superior may rely totally on his/her subjective judgment in determining the SBU general manager's bonus; alternatively, part of the bonus may be formula-based and part may be subjective.

This study hypothesizes that, in terms of impact on effectiveness, the utility of determining the bonus in a subjective rather than formula-based manner will be greater for build than for harvest managers. Two reasons are offered in support of this expectation: (1) Unlike the case for a harvest manager, more aspects of a build manager's job – such as market development, new product development, R&D, and personnel development – are not quantifiable and, therefore, objective performance measures for such tasks are not available; and (2) Managers in charge of build units face greater environmental uncertainty than do managers in charge of harvest units and that strategy implementation under conditions of greater uncertainty requires a more subjective approach towards the determination of the incentive bonus.

At the SBU level, performance along most long-term criteria (product development, market development, personnel development, political/public affairs, etc.) is *clearly* less amendable to objective measurement than is performance along most short-term criteria (cash flow, return on investment, profits, profit margins, etc.). Since build managers – in contrast to harvest managers – need to focus more on the long rather than short-run, it follows that build managers should be evaluated more subjectively than harvest managers. Salter (1973) used very similar logic to argue that the greater the need to optimize an SBU's performance over the long rather than short-run, the greater should be the extent of reliance on subjective as opposed to formula-based approaches to determine the SBU manager's incentive bonus. As might be expected, his argument has been that performance along many long-run criteria cannot usually be measured in objective, quantitative terms.

Further support to the prediction that subjective bonus determination approaches will be more beneficial for build than for harvest units is provided by the expectation that build units face greater environmental uncertainty than do harvest units. Such an expectation is based upon the following reasons: (1) As Hofer (1975), Hofer & Schendel (1978, pp. 102–104) and Hambrick *et al.* (1982) have argued, build strategies are typically undertaken in the growth stage of the product life cycle (PLC) whereas harvest strategies are typically undertaken in the mature/decline stage of the PLC; and that factors such as technology, product design, process design, market demand, number of competitors and competitive structure change more rapidly and are more upredictable in the growth rather than the mature/decline stage of the PLC; (2) Since the total market share of all firms in an industry would always be 100%, a build mission, signifying a desire to increase market share pits an SBU into greater 'conflict' with its competitors than does a harvest mission. Further, to increase market share, it is not sufficient to merely increase the demand for one's products; one must also increase the volume of production and, thus, the input resources (raw materials, labor, capital, etc.) by corresponding amounts. Thus, on both the output and the input sides, a build manager faces greater 'dependencies' than does a harvest manager. As Pfeffer & Salancik (1978, p. 68) and Thompson (1967) have argued, the greater the external conflict and dependencies facing an organization, the greater would be the uncertainty confronted by it; and (3) Since build SBUs are typically in new and evolving industries as compared to harvest SBUs, build managers' experience in their industries is likely to be less; this would again contribute to the greater uncertainty faced by build managers in dealing with external constituencies. As Keely (1977) has argued, the more uncertain the environment, the less reliable predictions about future performance are likely to be thus requiring a greater reliance on subjective bonus determination approaches.

The two sets of arguments advanced above yield the following proposition regarding linkages between SBU strategy, formula vs subjective approaches towards bonus determination, and SBU effectiveness:

P3: Greater reliance on subjective (non-formula) approaches towards the determination of the SBU general manager's incentive bonus will have a stronger positive impact on effectiveness in the case of SBUs at the 'build' end of the strategy spectrum than in the case of SBUs at the 'harvest' end.

METHOD

Sample

Data were collected from general managers of SBUs in diversified firms. Previous studies (e.g., Rumelt, 1974) have indicated that more than 80% of the largest 500 industrial firms in the United States (i.e., the Fortune 500) are diversified into more than one business and have adopted a profit center structure for the management of their numerous businesses. Thus, eight Fortune 500 diversified firms with headquarters in Massachusetts, Connecticut and New York were selected. The need to obtain access and constraints of time and funding prevented the use of a random sample either from the entire Fortune 500 or from the entire subset of firms headquartered in the Northeast. Given, however, their size range (in 1980 sales, from about $500 million to about $10 billion) and the diversity in industries in which they operate (consumer products, industrial machinery, chemicals, electronic components, electronic equipment, etc.), there is no prima facie reason to expect any systematic bias in the findings from SBUs within these firms.

Within each firm, the senior-most corporate executive in charge of strategic planning (usually the Vice President for Planning) and one or more senior line executives (usually a Group Vice President) were interviewed. During the interviews, agreement was obtained from the planning executive that he would send a questionnaire instrument to four or more SBU general managers within his firm making sure that a mix of businesses along the spectrum from 'pure build' to 'pure harvest' would be covered so as to provide the needed strategic diversity. The cover letter to the questionnaire guaranteed that individual responses would not be communicated to anybody within or outside the firm, and that only summary data from the total responses from several business unit heads would be published. A preaddressed stamped envelope was also enclosed with each questionnaire to enable the respondents to mail these directly back to the researchers without any risk of perusal by others in their firms. Our primary contacts – the corporate-level executives – distributed these questionnaires to the general managers of 70 SBUs. A total of 58 usable responses were received. Because of the high response (82%), no tests for non-response bias were considered necessary.

The 58 respondents were also asked to indicate the extent of maximum bonus (as a percentage of basic salary) that they were eligible to receive. Since linkages between strategy, incentive bonus system, and effectiveness would not be very meaningful in those situations where the maximum earnable bonus was relatively small (see, e.g., Pritchard & Curts, 1973), for the purpose of this study, it was decided to focus only on those 46 SBUs where the maximum earnable bonus was greater than 20% of basic salary. For these 46 SBUs, the maximum earnable bonus (as a percentage of basic salary) averaged 39.3%.

Variables measured

Business unit strategy (X_1). Preliminary interviews with four SBU managers in one firm had revealed – as expected – that although the terms build, hold, harvest and divest can be applied to the business unit as a whole, each SBU usually consists of several products which together form one or more closely related product lines, thus constituting a single business. As such, strategy for the SBU as a whole needed to be regarded as an aggregate of the strategies of its products. Based on this logic, the following question was posed to the SBU manager:

Given below are descriptions of several alternative strategies. Depending upon the context, each of these descriptions may represent the strategy for all or only a fraction or none of a business unit's prducts. Please indicate below what percentage of your business unit's current total sales is accounted for by products represented by each of these strategy descriptions. Your answers should total 100%.

Increase sales and market share, be willing to accept low returns on
    investment in the short-to-medium term, if necessary   ____%
Maintain market share and obtain reasonable return on investment ____%
Maximize profitability and cash flow in the short-to-medium term, be
    willing to sacrifice market share if necessary   ____%
Prepare for sale or liquidation   ____%
None of the above (please specify)   ____%
                                                            Total   100%

In descending order, the strategy descriptions given in this question were intended to signify the following strategies: build, hold, harvest, divest, and other. All respondents entered 0% under 'none of the above'. Only 12 out of the 58 respondents entered anything other than zero for the divest strategy – even here, the percentage ranged from 2% to 13%. Thus, at the level of the SBU *as a whole*, all 58 SBUs have strategies that can be characterized as falling somewhere along the continuum from 'pure build' to 'pure harvest'.

The strategy measure was derived as follows A value of +1 was attached to a build strategy, a 0 to a hold strategy, a −1 to a harvest strategy and a −2 to a divest strategy. The percentage breakdown provided by the SBU manager was then used to arrive at a weighted average strategy index for the SBU. Summary data on this measure are included in Exhibit 29.1.

The construct validity of this strategy index was assessed by asking each respondent to provide data on the *current* market share of the SBU's principal products, a 'factual' rather than 'perceptual' item of information. It was anticipated that, in general, the probability of an SBU wanting to increase market share further (i.e., a 'build' mission) would be greater when its current market share is low as compared to when it is high; thus, if the strategy index is valid, one should expect a negative correlation between strategy and current market share. The negative correlation (Pearson $r = -0.23$, $p < 0.05$) between the two variables bears out these expectations.

To test for response consistency (a surrogate for internal reliability), each respondent was also asked to indicate whether (s)he *expected* the market share of the SBU's principal products to decline rapidly (=1), decline slowly (=2), remain at the current level (=3), increase slowly (=4), or increase rapidly (=5). As anticipated, the strategy index correlates

Exhibit 29.1 Summary statistics on all variables under study ($n = 46$ SBUs)

Variable	Minimum	Maximum	Mean	Standard Deviation	Median
Effectiveness (Y)	1.463	4.800	3.241	0.699	3.280
Strategy (X_1)	−1.000	1.000	0.018	0.478	0.000
Extent of the incentive system's reliance on:					
Long-run oriented criteria (X_2)	7.000	20.000	9.951	2.985	9.017
Short-run oriented criteria (X_3)	5.000	15.000	9.696	2.547	9.125
Subjective (as opposed to formula-based) approaches (X_4)	0.000	100.000	29.876	34.708	20.500

positively with expectations of an increase in market share (Pearson r = 0.49, $p < 0.001$).

Effectiveness (Y). This study chose *not* to use objective measures of performance since many performance dimensions critical to the success of a 'build' strategy (for instance: new product development, market development, R&D, and personnel development) are not amendable to objective, quantitative measurement. Thus, the use of objective measures (such as operating profits, cash flows, and return on investment) to evaluate the performance of *every* SBU disregarding its strategic mission would have violated one of the fundamental axioms underlying this research. In utilizing a subjective approach, it was also decided (1) to undertake performance assessment along a multiplicity of dimensions rather than on any single dimension, and (2) to weight the various performance dimensions in terms of their relative importance for the SBU. In addition to the general arguments advanced by Steers (1975), such a multivariate approach with criterion weights was seen as particularly appropriate in a context where, by definition, different strategic missions imply quite *different* sets of priorities. Finally, given this study's focus on *implementation*, it was deemed essential to control for the effects of the chosen strategy itself on SBU performance (Porter, 1980; Lenz, 1981). Thus, effectiveness was measured in the form of a *comparison* between actual performance and *a-priori* expectations rather than on an *absolute* scale. Since managers' *a-priori* expectations of business unit performance are likely to take into account the anticipated impact of the strategy itself, it was anticipated that such an approach would indirectly control for the effects of strategic choice on performance.

Each respondent was asked to rate each of twelve performance dimensions on a 5-point Likert type scale (ranging from 'of little importance' to 'extremely important') indicating the degree of importance attached by superiors to the SBU's performance on that dimension. The twelve dimensions include financial as well as nonfinancial criteria: sales growth rate, market share, operating profits, profit to sales ratio, cash flow from operations, return on investment, new product development, market development, R&D, cost reduction programs, personnel development and political/public affairs. Each respondent was also asked to rate on each of the twelve performance dimensions SBU's performance as compared with his/her assessment of superiors' expectations from the SBU along that dimension. Again a 5-point Likert type scale (ranging from 'not at all satisfactory' to 'outstanding') was used. Using the data on dimensional importance obtained in the first question as weights, a weighted average performance index was obtained for each SBU. Summary data on this effectiveness measure are given in Exhibit 29.2. As this exhibit indicates, the effectiveness index does not correlate with strategy – either for the overall strategy index ($r = 0.01$, n.s.) or for each of the 12 performance dimensions examined separately – an indication that the impact of strategy on SBU effectiveness has been adequately controlled.

Given the exclusive reliance on self-assessment to measure effectiveness, the reader is urged to regard this measure with some caution.

Exhibit 29.2 Response structure: effectiveness along various performance criteria ($n = 46$ SBUs)

Performance criteria	Effectiveness along performance criteria				Pearson product-moment correlations	
	Range		Mean	Standard deviation	Strategy vs effectiveness along criterion	Impact of performance criterion on the SBU general manager's incentive bonus vs effectiveness along criterion
	Minimum	Maximum				
Sales growth rate	2	5	3.356	0.933	0.23	0.05
Market share	2	5	3.419	0.932	0.08	0.15
Operating profits	1	5	3.220	1.255	-0.09	0.19
Profit margins	1	5	3.318	1.177	-0.04	-0.04
Cash flow	1	5	3.152	1.121	-0.03	-0.04
Return on investment	1	5	3.455	1.130	0.05	0.00
New product development	1	5	3.163	0.974	-0.06	0.09
Market development	1	5	3.098	0.831	-0.06	0.19
Research & development	1	4	2.833	0.986	-0.22	0.19
Cost reduction programs	1	5	3.024	0.975	0.18	0.21
Personnel development	1	5	3.238	1.031	-0.04	0.17
Political public affairs	1	5	3.222	0.929	0.13	0.34*
'Aggregate' effectiveness (a weighted average of effectiveness response with criterion importance serving as weights)	1.463	4.800	3.241	0.699	0.01	

* One-tail $p < 0.05$

Notwithstanding this caveat, however, the following evidence/arguments might be noted in support of this measure's validity: (1) as Exhibit 29.2 indicates, on virtually all performance dimensions, responses pertaining to effectiveness ranged from 'not at all satisfactory' to 'outstanding'; looking also at the data on means and standard deviations, the respondents, as a class, cannot be characterized as having been lenient in assessing the performance of their own SBUs; (2) the questionnaire was pretested with four SBUs – two in each of two divisions in one firm; each superior was asked to indicate which of the two SBUs under him was more effective at implementing its strategic mission; in both divisions, the self-ratings were consistent with superior assessments of the more and less effective SBUs; while a test with just four SBUs clearly constitutes insufficient evidence in support for the validity of the effectiveness measure, taken along with other evidence/arguments, it might contribute to an increased confidence in it; and, (3) in an earlier empirical study, Heneman (1974) had reported a very high correlation between superior and self-ratings in situations where the subordinate is guaranteed anonymity and understands that the objective of data collection is scientific research and not his personal evaluation from the organization's perspective; Heneman's conditions were met fully in this study.

Relative importance of performance criteria for bonus determination (X_2, X_3). Each respondent was asked to rate on a 3-point Likert-type scale (1 = 'little or no impact'; 2 = 'high impact'; 3 = 'greater impact') the degree of impact that superiors' evaluation of the SBU's performance along each of twelve dimensions has on decisions regarding his/her incentive bonus. The twelve dimensions were the same as those used earlier to measure effectiveness. The sum of the responses to seven of these performance criteria – sales growth rate, market share, new prouduct development, market development, R&D, personnel development and political/public affairs – was interpreted as 'extent of the incentive system's reliance on *long-run* oriented criteria for bonus determination' (X_2). The inter-item reliability estimate for this measure is: Coefficient $\propto$ = 0.82. Similarly, the sum of the responses on the remaining five performance criteria – operating profits, profit to sales ratio, cash flow from operations, return on investment, and cost reduction programs – was interpreted as 'extent of the incentive system's reliance on *short-run* oriented criteria for bonus determination' (X_3). The inter-item reliability estimate for this measure is: Coefficient $\propto$ = 0.74. Summary data on the variables X_2 and X_3 are given in Exhibit 29.1.

As a check for reliability, for each performance criterion, correlation was computed between importance of the criterion for bonus purposes and general managers' responses on criterion importance obtained earlier to generate criterion weights for developing the effectiveness measure. It was anticipated that correlations between these two variables would be positive and significant since SBU managers would tend to place higher importance on those criteria that their superiors rely more heavily on for bonus determination. As expected, 11 out of these 12 correlations are positive and significant at $p < 0.05$.

Since the 12 items used for assessing the relative importance of bonus criteria and those used for computing the effectiveness measure are the same, it was deemed necessary to also test for the existence of 'circularity,' i.e., to see if SBU managers tended to rate their effectiveness higher on those criteria that they perceived as more important for bonus determination. As can be seen from Exhibit 29.2, correlations between the importance of performance criterion for bonus determination and effectiveness ratings on that criterion are positive and significant for only 1 out of the 12 criteria. Thus, the data can be regarded as relatively free from problems of 'circularity.'

Reliance on formula vs subjective (non-formula) approaches towards the determination of incentive bonus (X_4). Each respondent was asked to indicate whether, in determining his/her bonus, superiors relied totally on a formula-based approach, or totally on a subjective (non-formula) approach, or partly on a formula-based approach and partly on a subjective (non-formula) approach indicating, in the last case, the percentage breakdown for the two approaches. Summary data on this variable are given in Exhibit 29.1.

RESULTS

Test of propositions

Data analysis technique. All three propositions to be tested in this study are of the following form: the positive impact of S_1 on Y will be stronger when S_2 is high (low) as compared to when S_2 is low (high). Following the arguments of Allison (1977) and Southwood (1978) and similar to the approaches taken by Argote (1982), Brownell (1982) and Schoonhoven (1981), the most appropriate analytical method to test such a hypothesis is to run the two regression equations given below:

$$Y = c_1 + a_1 S_1 + a_2 S_2 + \varepsilon_1 \tag{1}$$

$$Y = c_2 + b_1 S_1 + b_2 S_2 + b_3 S_1 S_2 + \varepsilon_2 \tag{2}$$

If the unstandardized regression coefficient b_3 is *positive and significant*, one can conclude that the positive impact of S_1 on Y is indeed stronger for higher as compared to lower values of S_2. Alternatively, a *negative and significant* b_3 would lead to the conclusion that the positive impact of S_1 on Y is stronger for lower rather than higher values of S_2. Finally, if b_3 is *not significantly different from zero*, one would conclude that S_2 does not have any contingency effect on the relationship between S_1 and Y.

Southwood's (1978) mathematical analysis also points out a few other important characteristics of equation (2) – all of which have been computationally crosschecked and confirmed to be true by the present authors. If S_1 and S_2 are interval (but not ratio) scale variables, then their points of origin are totally arbitrary. As Southwood illustrates, if these origin points are changed (i.e., if S_1 and S_2 are replaced by $S_1 + k_1$ and $S_2 + k_2$ respectively), then in equation (2) the following also change: the unstandardized regression coefficients b_1 and b_2, their standard errors, their levels of significance, even the standardized counterparts (β_1 and β_2) of these regression coefficients, and, of course, the constant c_2. While the standardized regression coefficient (β_3) of the crossproduct term also changes, what remain invariant are the following: the unstandardized regression coefficient b_3, its standard error, its level of significance and the R^2 and F-ratio for the whole equation itself. In fact, with a suitable choice of origin points for S_1 and S_2, the coefficients b_1 and b_2 can be reduced to zero leaving only the crossproduct term with its unchanged coefficient b_3 in the equation. The net conclusion is that the only utility of equation (2) is to learn about the significance and nature of the impact of interaction between S_1 and S_2 on Y and *not* about the nature of their main effects. If one is interested in learning about the main effects of S_1 and/or S_2 on Y, it is equation (1) that can be of some value.

Three pairs of regression equations were developed for the purposes of testing Propositions 1, 2, and 3. The results of these equations are presented in Exhibit 29.3.

The results – see regression equations (3), (5) and (7) in Exhibit 29.3 – indicate that none of the independent variables – X_1, X_2, X_3 or X_4 – have any statistically significant *direct* impact on effectiveness. Attention was, therefore, turned to an examination of Propositions 1, 2 and 3 which predicted the existence of contingency relationships between SBU strategy, incentive bonus system and SBU effectiveness.

Test of propositions. The results of regression equation (4) provide clear and strong support to Proposition 1. The unstandardized regression coefficient of the crossproduct term (X_1X_2) is positive and significant ($p < 0.05$).

An examination of the results of the regression equation (6) reveals that the unstandardized coefficient for the crossproduct terem (X_1X_3) is negative, as hypothesized but not statistically significant. Thus, the expectation of Proposition 2 that the reliance on short-run oriented criteria for bonus determination would make a greater contribution to SBU effectiveness in the case of harvest rather than build SBUs is not supported by the data. In other words, an emphasis on short-run oriented criteria seems to be *equally* relevant for *all* SBUs irrespective of differences in their strategies. One explanation for such a finding might be that whereas an emphasis on short-run objectives may not always imply an emphasis also on long-run objectives, an emphasis on long-run objectives may always imply an emphasis on short-run objectives also. Conceivably, therefore, managers at the build end of the strategy spectrum face a greater multiplicity of objectives than do managers at the harvest end of the strategy spectrum.

From the results of the regression equation (8), it can be seen that the unstandardized coefficient for the cross product term (X_1X_4) is positive and significant ($p < 0.01$). Proposition 3 is, therefore, strongly supported by the data.

Tests for the presence or absence of monotonicity

While equation (2) is a sufficient test of the hypothesized contingency impact of S_2 on the relationship between S_1 and Y, in its current form, it

Exhibit 29.3 Results of multiple regression analyses with 'effectiveness' (= Y) as the dependent variable

Equation No.	Constant	Main effects only Unstandardized regression coefficients (standard errors)				F-ratio (DOF = 2,43)	R^2
		X_1	X_2	X_3	X_4		
(3)	3.070	-0.033 (0.252)	0.017 (0.041)			0.09	0.004
(5)	3.528	0.016 (0.222)		-0.030 (0.042)		0.26	0.012
7	3.194	0.105 (0.244)			0.002 (0.003)	0.47	0.024

Exhibit 29.3 (Contd.)

Equation No.	Constant	Main and interaction effects Unstandardized Regression Coefficients (standard errors)							F-Ratio‡ (DOF = 3,42)	$R^{2\ddagger}$
		X_1^*	X_2^*	X_3^*	X_4^*	$X_1X_2^\dagger$	$X_1X_3^\dagger$	$X_1X_4^\dagger$		
4	3.536	-1.174§ (0.679)	-0.038 (0.050)			0.122§ (0.068)			1.15	0.078
6	3.523	0.123 (0.804)		-0.029 (0.042)			-0.011 (0.080)		0.17	0.013
8	3.185	-0.388 (0.288)			0.000 (0.003)			0.016$_{\amalg}$ (0.006)	2.90§	0.190

NB: (1) Variables were coded as follows: X_1 = Strategy; X_2 = Importance of long-run oriented criteria for bonus determination; X_3 = Importance of short-run oriented criteria for bonus determination; X_4 = Subjective (Non-formula) approaches towards bonus determination; Y = Effectiveness.

(2) Results in the *circled cells* represent the exact tests for each of the three propositions advanced in this study.

* All of the results (including the significance levels) given in these four columns vary with changes in the points of origin of the main variables (X_1, X_2, X_3 and X_4). Hence, all information in these four columns should be regarded as essentially meaningless. For details, see Southwood (1978) as well as the results section of this paper.

† For the crossproduct terms, the values of the *unstandardized* regression coefficient, their standard errors, and their levels of significance are *independent* of the points of origin of the main variables (X_1, X_2, X_3 and X_4). Hence, the data in these columns do have information content.

‡ The F-Ratio and R^2 for the equation are also independent of the points of origin of the variables X_1, X_2, X_3 and X_4.

§ One-tail $p < 0.05$.

$_\amalg$ One-tail $p < 0.01$.

provides no information on whether the latter relationship is monotonic or nonmonotonic. As demonstrated by Schoonhoven (1981), Southwood (1978) and Kerlinger & Pedhazur (1973), such information can be obtained by examining the partial derivative of this equation over S_1, as indicated below:

$$\partial Y/\partial S_1 = b_1 + b_3 S_2. \tag{9}$$

A graphical plot with $\partial Y/\partial S_1$ on the vertical axis and S_2 on the horizontal axis drawn over the entire observed range of S_2 can indicate whether the relationship between Y and S_1 is monotonic or nonmonotonic. If the value of $\partial Y/\partial S_1$ is always positive or always negative over the entire range of S_2, then the relationship between Y and S_1 would be regarded as monotonic. Alternatively, if $\partial Y/\partial S_1$ crosses the horizontal axis at any point, then the relationship would be regarded as nonmonotonic. For each of the propositions supported by the data – i.e., Propositions 1 and 3 but not Proposition 2 – the analysis was, therefore, pushed to a second stage in order to yield information on the presence or absence of monotonicity in the impact of the contingency relationships on SBU effectiveness.

The partial derivative of the original regression equation (4) from Exhibit 29.3 yields the following:

$$\partial(Y)/\partial(X_3) = -0.038 + 0.122X_1 \tag{10}$$

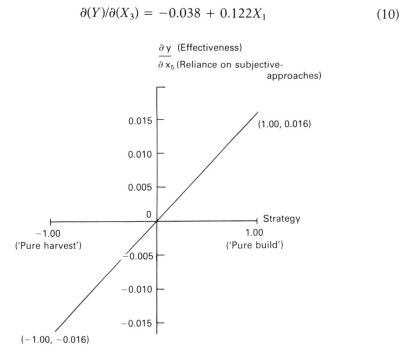

Fig. 29.1 The effect of strategy on the relationship between the incentive system's reliance on long-run oriented criteria and effectiveness.

Figure 29.1 plots the above partial derivative over the entire range of SBU strategy (X_1). From the plotted line, it can be seen that the effect of X_2 on effectiveness is positive in the strategy range above 0.311 and negative in its range below the value of 0.311. Thus Figure 29.1 reveals the following *nonmonotic* relationships:

For SBUs at the build end of the strategy spectrum, greater reliance on long-run criteria for bonus determination has a positive influence on effectiveness.

For SBUs at the harvest end of the strategy spectrum, greater reliance on long-run criteria for bonus determination has a negative influence on effectiveness.

The partial derivative of the original regression equation (8) from Exhibit 29.3 yields the following:

$$\partial(Y)/\partial(X_5) db 0.000 + 0.016X_1 \tag{11}$$

Figure 29.2 plots the above partial derivative over the entire range of SBU strategy (X_1). As can be seen from Fig. 29.2, the impact of X_4 on effectiveness is also *nonmonotonic* over the range of strategy, with the

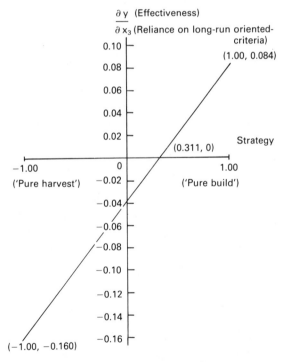

Fig. 29.1 The effect of strategy on the relationship between the incentive system's reliance on subjective (as opposed to formula-based) approaches and effectiveness.

inflection point of the slope falling exactly at strategy = 0. Thus, greater reliance on subjective (non-formula) approaches for determining the bonus contributes to effectiveness in the case of build SBUs *but* hampers it in the case of harvest SBUs.

DISCUSSION

There is now increasing recognition in the accounting literature of the need to utilize contingency approaches towards the design of planning and control systems in organizations (e.g., Dermer, 1977; Ansari, 1977, 1979; Gordon *et al.*, 1978; Waterhouse & Tiessen, 1978; Otley, 1980; Ewusi-Mensah, 1981). While previous empirical studies (e.g., Bruns & Waterhouse, 1975; Hayes, 1977; Merchant, 1981) had examined contingency relationships between organizational control mechanisms and variables such as environment, size, and technology, this study has explored the utility of relating control systems to strategy. In particular, it has provided empirical support for the idea that, in terms of SBU effectiveness, the utility of any particular incentive bonus system employed in an attempt to influence the SBU general manager's behaviour is *contingent upon* the strategy of the focal SBU. The results of this study can be summarized as follows: (1) greater reliance on long-run criteria as well as greater reliance on subjective (non-formula) approaches for determining the SBU general managers' bonus contributes to effectiveness in the case of build SBUs but hampers it in the case of harvest SBUs, and (2) the relationship between the extent of bonus system's reliance on short-run criteria and SBU effectivness is virtually independent of SBU strategy.

At the level of practice, these findings hold the greatest relevance for those executives responsible for the design and implementation of control systems in diversified corporations, especially in terms of helping them differentiate the incentive systems according to variations in SBU strategy. On the other hand, at the level of theory, the primary relevance of this study lies in its demonstration of *strategy* as a source of contingency for the design of control systems as well as in its extension of the contingency theory of organization from the *inter*firm to the *intra*firm context. Thus, future contingency research on a variety of SBU-level strategic and organizational variables (including but not limited to incentive bonus systems) not examined in this study can be expected to yield fruitful results. The design of future research in this area might also benefit from the following examination of the key limitations in the present study.

An obvious limitation of this study has been its exclusive reliance on self-report measures particularly for the two kep variables – 'strategy' and 'effectiveness'. While the authors believe that the results of validity and reliability tests carried out and discussed in the 'method' section argue for sufficient confidence in these measures, a similar study with multimethod, multirater measurements should undoubtedly yield more powerful results.

A second limitation of this study has to do with the establishment of causality. Although all hypotheses were stated in associational terms, the logic behind them implies that interaction between strategy and incentive bonus systems is not just associated with but causes greater effectiveness. The cross-sectional and snapshot nature of the data in this study has prevented any tests for such causality. Nonetheless, on an *a-priori* basis, the results of this study do lend promise to the fruitfulness of longitudinal studies undertaken specifically for the examination of casual linkages.

Arguably the most significant limitation of this study has been its focus on only a few variables pertaining to both strategy and control systems. Strategies of business units within diversified firms differ not just in terms of the 'strategic mission' but also in terms of the 'competitive posture' (e.g., cost leadership vs differentiation) adopted by a business unit relative to other firms in its industry (Porter, 1980). For instance, both Texas Instruments and Hewlett-Packard are diversified firms with a business unit in each firm competing in the personal computer industry. However, the competitive posture of the Texas Instruments SBU appears to be 'low price' whereas that adopted by the Hewlett-Packard SBU appears to be 'product features and performance rather than low price'. It is not inconceivable that an SBU trying to achieve a low cost position might require different control systems as compared to an SBU whose primary concern is upgrading of product features/performance rather than cost reduction. Other dimensions along which SBU strategies can be differentiated might also exist – for instance, the degree of 'interconnectedness' between the focal SBU and other SBUs within the same corporation (Rumelt, 1974).

Similarly, matching incentive bonus systems to strategy is only one – albeit a significant one – of the control mechanisms used by corporate level executives to ensure effective implementation of SBU strategies. Other important control mechanisms whose relationship to SBU strategy might be worthy of investigation include: use of administrative control vs interpersonal control (Bruns & Waterhouse, 1975), degree of decentralization with regard to the preparation of long-range plans as well as annual budgets, linkages between long-range plans and budgets, hurdle rates used in capital investment analysis, nature of data included in internal reports (e.g., financial vs non-financial data, historical vs inflation adjusted data, internal vs external environmental data), etc.

Finally, it is worth noting that the focus of the present study as well as of virtually all previous literature dealing with linkages between strategy and control systems has been on the implications of matching strategy and control systems for only an 'organizational' outcome viz., effectiveness. Given the normally high degree of interaction between personal and organizational outcomes, research on the implications of matching strategy and control systems for managerial job involvement and job satisfaction would seem to be of at least equal significance.

ACKNOWLEDGEMENTS

Both authors contributed equally. The sequence of names, as presented here, was arrived at randomly. The authors wish to acknowledge the useful comments provided by Professors Robert N. Anthony, W.W. Cooper, J.F. Dillard, Jim Kinard, Ken Merchant, John K. Shank, Gordon Shillinglaw,

Ray Stephens, Richard F. Vancil, participants at The Ohio State University Accounting Research Colloquium, and two anonymous reviewers. Funding support for research on which this paper is based was provided by the Graduate School, Boston University, Graduate School of Business Administration, Harvard University and College of Administrative Science, The Ohio State University.

BIBLIOGRAPHY

Abell, D.F. & Hammond J.S., *Strategic Market Planning* (Englewood Cliffs, NJ: Prentice Hall, 1979).

Allison, P.D., Testing for Interaction in Multiple Regression, *American Journal of Sociology* (1977) pp. 144–153.

Ansari, S., An Integrated Approach to Control Systems Design, *Accounting Organizations and Society* (1977) pp. 101–112.

Ansari, S., Towards an Open Systems Approach to Budgeting, *Accounting, Organizations and Society* (1979) pp. 149–161.

Argote, L., Input Uncertainty and Organizational Co-ordination in Hospital Emergency Units, *Administrative Science Quarterly* (1982) pp. 420–434.

Berg, N.A., Strategic Planning in Conglomerate Companies, *Harvard Business Review* (1965) pp. 79–92.

Blau, P.M., *The Dynamics of Bureaucracy* (University of Chicago Press, 1955).

Brownell, P., The Role of Accounting Data in Performance Evaluation, Budgetary Participation and Organizational Effectiveness, *Journal of Accounting Research* (1982) pp. 12–27.

Bruns, W.J. & Waterhouse, J.H., Budgetary Control and Organization Structure, *Journal of Accounting Research* (Autumn 1975) pp. 177–203.

Bruns, T. & G.M. Stalker, *The Management of Innovation* (London: Tavistock, 1961).

Buzzell, R.D. & Wiersema, F.D., Modeling Changes in Market Share: A Cross-Sectional Analysis, *Strategic Management Journal* (1981) pp. 27–42.

Chandler, A.D., *Strategy and Structure* (Cambridge, MA: The MIT Press, 1962).

Child, J., Organization Structure, Environment and Performance: The Role of Strategic Choice, *Sociology* (1972) pp. 1–22.

Daft, R.L. & MacIntosh, N.B., A Tentative Exploration into the Amount and Equivocality of Information Processing in Organizational Work Units, *Administrative Science Quarterly* (1981) pp. 207–224.

Dearden, J., Problems in Decentralized Financial Control, *Harvard Business Review* (1961) pp. 72–80.

Dermer J., *Management Planning and Control Systems* (Irwin, 1977).

Ewusi-Mensah, K., The External Organizational Environment and Its Impact on Management Information Systems, *Accounting, Organizational and Society* (1981) pp. 302–316.

Fouraker, L.E. & Stopford, J.M., Organization Structure and Multinational Strategy, *Administrative Science Quarterly* (1968) pp. 57–70.

Galbraith, J.R. & Nathanson, D.A., *Strategy Implementation: The Role of Structure and Process* (St. Paul MN: West Publishing, 1978).

Gordon, L.A., Larcker, D.F. & Tuggle, F.D., Strategic Decision Processes and the Design of Accounting Information Systems: Conceputal Linkages, *Accounting, Organizations and Society* (1978) pp. 203–213.

Govindarajan, V., Appropriateness of Accounting Data in Performance Evaluation: Environmental Uncertainty as an Intervening Variable, *Accounting, Organizations and Society* (1983) pp. 000–000.

Gupta, A.K. & Govindarajan, V., Business Unit Strategy, Managerial Characteristics and Business Unit Effectiveness at Strategy Implementation, *Academy of Management Journal* (March 1984, Forthcoming).

Hambrick, D.C., Operationalizing the Concept of Business-Level Strategy in Research, Academy of Management Review (1980) pp. 567–575.

Hambrick, D.C., Environment, Strategy, and Power Within Top Management Teams, *Administrative Science Quarterly*, (1981) pp. 253–276.

Hambrick, D.C., MacMillan, I.C. & Day, D.L., Strategic Attributes and Performance in the Four Cells of the BCG-matrix: A PIMS-based Analysis of Industrial-Product Business, *Academy of Management Journal* (1982) pp. 510–31.

Hayes, D.C., The Contingency Theory of Managerial Accounting, *The Accounting Review* (January 1977).

Henderson, B.D., *Perspectives on the Product Portfolio* (Boston, MA: Boston Consulting Group, 1970).

Heneman, H.G., Comparisons of Self and Superior Ratings of Managerial Performance, *Journal of Applied Psychology* (October 1974) pp. 638–642.

Hofer, C.W., Towards a Contingency Theory of Business Strategy, *Academy of Management Journal* (1975) pp. 784–810.

Hofer, C.W. & Schendel, D.E., *Strategy Formulation: Analytical Concepts* (St. Paul, MN: West Publishing, 1978).

Holmstrom, B., Moral Hazard and Observability, *Bell Journal of Economics* (Spring 1979).

Keely, M., Subjective Performance Evaluation and Person-Role Conflict Under Conditions of Uncertainty, *Academy of Management Journal* (1977) pp. 301–314.

Kerlinger, F.N. & Pedhazur, E.J., *Multiple Regression in Behavioral Research* (New York: Holt, Rinehart & Winston, 1973).

Kerr, Steven, On the Folly of Rewarding A, While Hoping for B, *Academy of Management Journal* (1975) pp. 769–783.

Larreche, J. & Srinivasan, F., Stratport: A Model for the Evaluation and Formulation of Business Portfolio Strategies, *Management Science* (1982) pp. 979–1001.

Lawrence, P.R. & Lorsch, J.W., *Organization and Environment* (Boston, MA: Division of Research, Harvard Business School, 1967).

Lenz, R.T., 'Determinants' of Organizational Performance: An Interdisciplinary View, *Strategic Management Journal* (1981) pp. 131–154.

Locke, Edward A., Bryan, J.F. & Kendall, L.M., Goals and Intentions as Mediators of the Effects of Monetary Incentives on Behavior, *Journal of Applied Psychology* (1968) pp. 104–121.

Lorsch, J.W. & Allen, S., *Managing Diversity and Interdependence* (Boston, MA: Division of Research, Harvard Business School, 1973).

MacMillan, I.C., Seizing Competitive Initiative, *The Journal of Business Strategy* (Spring 1982) pp. 43–57.

Merchant, K.A., The Design of the Corporate Budgeting System: Influences on Managerial Behavior and Performance, *The Accounting Review* (October 1981) pp. 813–829.

Miles, R.E. & Snow, C.C., *Organizational Strategy, Structure, and Process* (New York: McGraw-Hill, 1978).

Otley, D.T., The Contingency Theory of Management Accounting: Achievement and Prognosis, *Accounting, Organizations and Society* (1980) pp. 413–428.

Pfeffer, J. & Salancik, G.R., *The External Control of Organizations* (New York: Harper & Row, 1978).

Pitts, R.A., Toward a Contingency Theory of Multibusiness Organization Design, *Academy of Management Review* (1980) pp. 203–210.

Porter, L.W. & Lawler, E.E., *Managerial Attitudes and Performance* (Homewood, IL: Richard D. Irwin, 1968).

Porter, M.E., *Competitive Strategy* (New York: The Free Press, 1980).

Pritchard, R.D. & Curts, M.I., The Influence of Goal Setting and Financial Incentives on Task Performance, *Organizational Behavior and Human Performance* (1973) pp. 175–183.

Rothschild, W.E., *Putting It All Together: A Guilde to Strategic Thinking* (New York: AMACOM, 1976).

Rumelt, R.P., *Strategy, Structure, and Economic Performance* (Boston, MA: Division of Research, Harvard Business School, 1974).

Salter, M., Tailor Incentive Compensation to Strategy, *Harvard Business Review* (1973) pp. 94–102.

Schoonoven, C.B., Problems with Contingency Theory: Testing Assumptions Hidden within the Language of Contingency Theory, *Administrative Science Quarterly* (1981) pp. 349–377.

Schuster, J.R., Clark, B. & Rogers, M., Testing Portions of the Porter and Lawler Model Regarding the Motivational Role of Pay, *Journal of Applied Psychology* (1971) pp. 187–195.

Scott, B.R., The Industrial State: Old Myths and New Realities, *Harvard Business Review* (March–April 1973) pp. 133–148.

Snow, C.C. & Hrebiniak, L.G., Strategy, Distinctive Competence, and Organizational Performance, *Administrative Science Quarterly* (1980), pp. 307–335.

Southwood, K.E., Substantive Theory and Statistical Interaction: Five Models, *American Journal of Sociology* (1978) pp. 1154–1203.

Spitzer, M.E., *Goal Attainment, Job Satisfaction and Behavior* (Doctoral Dissertation, New York University, Ann Arbor, Michigan, University Microfilms, No. 64–110–048, 1964).

Steers, R.M., Problems in the Measurement of Organizational Effectiveness, *Administrative Science Quarterly* (1975) pp. 546–558.

Terborg, J.R. & Miller, H.E., Motivation, Behavior and Performance: A Closer Examination of Goal Setting and Monetary Incentives, *Journal of Applied Psychology* (1978) pp. 29–39.

Thompson, J.D., *Organizations in Action* (New York: McGraw-Hill, 1967).

Vancil, R.F. *Decentralization: Managerial Ambiguity by Design* (New York: Financial Executive Research Foundation, 1980).

Waterhouse, J.H. & Tiessen, P., A Contingency Framework for Management Accounting Systems Research, *Accounting, Organizations, and Society* (1978) pp. 65–76.

Woodward, J., *Industrial Organization: Theory and Practice* (London: Oxford University Press, 1965).

30

The dilemma of implementing controls: the case of managerial accounting

Chris Argyris

Schools of Business and Education, Harvard University

ABSTRACT

Managerial accounting contains a technical theory of control. Whenever this technical theory of control is correctly implemented to deal with issues that are embarrassing or threatening, the players activate their personal-human theory of control in order to remain 'in control'. The correct implementation of the personal-human theory of control necessary inhibits the effective implementation of the technical theory and vice versa.

The purpose of managerial functional disciplines, of which accounting is one, is to help managers govern. Each functional discipline represents a theory about how to govern in order to master events over which managers are responsible. Each theory may be described as a theory of control.

All theories of control have two features. One is the theory as it is espoused. Espoused theories of control are usually idealized visions that are rarely achieved. They represent an aspiration to be approximated.

The espoused theory of accounting recommends the use of concepts, usually coordinated to numbers, that are intended to be objective. The use of the concepts are dictated by a set of rules that are defined by the professionals as rigorously as they can make them. Once formulated, the rules are intended to apply to all cases in which they are considered relevant. (Ijiri, 1975; Solomons, 1986; Sterling, 1979; Yu, 1976.)

Productive reasoning is at the heart of the espoused theory of accounting. Productive reasoning includes defining premises as clearly as possible and making inferences explicit. Conclusions should be tested (testable) with the toughest tests that are available to the profession at that time.

If we observe the practice of accounting, we find that these ideals are rarely fully achieved. There are, at least, two reasons for the gap between theory and practice. First it is unlikely that any theory of control can be

Source: Argyris, C. (1990) *Accounting, Organizations and Society*, **15** (6), pp. 503–11.

formulated that is usable in practice that, ahead of time, is able to account for the full complexity and uniqueness of a given context. Given the present degree of sophistication of the discipline there will always be a requirement for gap-filling.

Second, accounting is often sold and defended as being objective and rigorous. Since this claim is likely to fall short in practice, a tension frequently develops between those who use the claim to defend accounting and those who use accounting but do not believe the claim. Often this results in conflicts whose discussion could lead the players to feel embarrassment or threat.

As we shall see below, most human beings activate a human theory of control to deal with embarrassment or threat. The dilemma is that this human theory of control is counterproductive to objectivity, rigor, tough testing of conclusions, that is, to productive reasoning. Practitioners often react by defining defensive routines to protect their practice. But the routines themselves may escalate the defensiveness. For example, in trying to deal with the espoused requirements of objectivity and the realities of conflict, practitioners may define rules that are 'precisely imprecise' and 'clearly vague' while at the same time denying not only the inherent ambiguity but, the fact that the ambiguity is designed. This may be an explanation for Hopwood's observation that accounting practice is positively invested in ambiguity and lacks the scientific, objective features in its espoused theory (Hopwood, forthcoming).

In this paper, I want to examine several dilemmas of implementing accounting. They are dilemmas because, I suggest, that the correct use of accounting ideas can lead to productive, *and at the same time*, counterproductive consequences.

EFFECTIVE IMPLEMENTATION

If productive reasoning is produced by implementing accounting principles then, not surprisingly, the first step in implementation is to teach the accounting principles that are relevant to problems at hand.

Implementation therefore often begins with a theory of instruction which assumes if human beings learn the principles of accounting; if they understand them fully; if they wish to use them; and *if* they are permitted to use them, then they will go ahead and use them. As long as they use the ideas consistently with sound accounting principles, the consequences promised by accounting will result.

There are two consequences that follow from the enthusiastic application of this theory of instruction. The accountants can come to believe that effective implementation is largely implementing the theory of instruction just described. This belief assumes an organization relatively dedicated to following the accounting ideas, especially if it can be shown that they do solve the problems at hand. The assumption is probably valid as long as the effective use of accounting knowledge is not embarrassing or threatening. But, sound accounting knowledge can be embarrassing and threatening precisely when it is most needed that is, when the organization is in real trouble.

The second consequence of the theory of implementation described above, is that the accountants are held responsible for producing and advocating sound concepts and principles. As a result accountants understandably turn much of their attention inward into their discipline in order to make sure that their discipline is correct. This inward orientation, in turn, may also become an orientation for defense against the outsider.

Non-accountants see this self referential defense as signs that accountants are acting like techies. A techie is one who uses the technical ideas at his or her command to attempt to influence and control others. Techies sense of competence, confidence, and self esteem are wrapped up in accounting ideas and rules. The stronger the techie orientation the less likely is the individual going to deal competently with user disbelieve because the techie deals with disbelief by upping the level of accounting evidence and proof which may have triggered off the disbelief in the first place.

A strong techie orientation can make it difficult for accountants to 'bend' their ideas without losing their validity in order to communicate to non-accountants. For example, metaphors may be useful to explain quantitative analyses. It takes a lot of skill and experience to take a precise quantitative analysis and communicate it in ways that users who may be threatenend by quantitative precision will listen.

Accountants, indeed most professionals, do not look forward to encounters where they are disbelieved or resisted. Such conditions lead to conflict with the potential for embarrassment or threat. As noted above, a techie response will tend to escalate the embarrassment and threat.

THE IMPLEMENTATION DILEMMA

We now come to the heart of the dilemma. Individuals have human theories of how to remain in control when embarrassment and threat occur. To our surprise, this *theory* of control is the same across cultures, and regardless of age, sex, education, or wealth. The behaviour that they use to implement the theory may vary. For example, all human beings that we have studied use the same theory of face saving. However, the actual behaviour may vary widely (Argyris & Schon, 1974; Argyris, 1982, 1985).

Some features that do not vary are:

1. The theory of control is primarily unilateral.
2. The action strategies depend on 'selling', 'persuading', 'fighting' designed to win and not to lose one's point.
3. This results in the creation of a behavioural environment characterized by defensiveness, error escalation, self fulfilling prophecies, and self sealing thinking.
4. Defensive reasoning predominates (i.e. premises are tacit, inferences are not made explicit, and, conclusions are not falsifiable).
5. Threat or embarrassment are dealt with by striving to bypass them and by covering up the bypass. Social virtues of concern and caring are often defined to be consistent with being 'diplomatic', 'easing-in', and similar bypass actions.

There is a paradox in using a human theory of control that has these features. If I use a theory of control that is unilaterally controlling because I believe it is effective then the player at the other end must act in a dependent submissive mode if my unilateral dominant mode is to be implemented. The paradox is: in order for me to act effectively, I require others to use a theory of action that I consider ineffective.

These consequences make it more likely that the information produced will be distorted; that the players will be unaware of their personal responsibility for the distortion; while clearly aware of the other's responsibility. In short, human beings' theories-in-use (not the ones that they espouse) when dealing with embarrassment or threat, are anti-learning and over protective.

The reasoning embedded in the human theory of control described above may be called, defensive. The rules of defensive reasoning are, keep premises tacit, make inferences with covert logic, and subject conclusions to a private test; the test should be consistent with the logic used by the person reaching the conclusion. Such reasoning is contrary to productive reasoning. Yet both the accountant and the line manager will tend to use it. Ironically, defensive reasoning will be activated when it is least likely to be effective and most likely to inhibit problem solving.

Organizational defensive routines

Defensive reasoning is not formally sanctioned by organizations. As a result, human beings create organizational defensive routines that are consistent with their individual defensive routines. The defensive reasoning individuals use to defend themselves now becomes acceptable, if not required, by organizational practices and policies (Argyris, 1985).

Organizational defensive routines are any routine policies or actions that are intended to circumvent the experience of embarrassment or threat by bypassing the situations that may trigger these responses. Organizational defensive routines make it unlikely that the organization will address the factors that caused the embarrassment or threat in the first place. Organizational defensive routines are anti-learning and overprotective.

Organizational defensive routines differ from individual defensive routines in that they exist even though (1) individuals move in and out of the organization, (2) psychologically different individuals use them in the same ways, (3) the source of learning them is socialization, and (4) the trigger to use them is concern and being realistic rather than a personal anxiety (Argyris, 1985).

Mixed messages: a dominant organizational defensive routine

An example of a prominent defensive routine is mixed messages. Mixed messages contain meanings that are simultaneously ambiguous and clear, imprecise and precise.

Anyone who deals with mixed messages experiences the dilemmas that are embedded in them. The designers know that designing a message to be clearly ambiguous requires skill and knowledge about the receiver. They know that to be both vague and clear is inconsistent. Furthermore, to be clearly vague is not only inconsistent, but is designed inconsistency. Because of the construction, the designer is vulnerable – unless, of course, the receiver does not question the inconsistency.

There are therefore four rules about designing and implementing mixed messages. They are:

1. Design a message that is inconsistent.
2. Act as if the message is not inconsistent.
3. Make the inconsistency in the message and the act that there is no inconsistency undiscussable.
4. Make the undiscussability of the undiscussable also undiscussable.

The strategies embedded in this logic are: when dealing with organizational defensive routines, be inconsistent, yet act as if you are not being inconsistent. Make the issues undiscussable and uninfluenceable, and act as if this is not the case. Thus the undiscussability and uninfluenceability become undiscussable.

Organizational defensive routines can lead people to feel helpless and cynical about changing them. This leads people to distance themselves from trying to enage the defensive routines in order to reduce them. As a result, organizational defensive routines not only become unmanageable (it is difficult to manage what is undiscussable), but they become the source of much distorted information. The distortion of the information is taken for granted because it is seen as necessary for the survival of the players as well as for the organization.

Adapting: organizational defensive routines

How does managerial accounting as a system of control ever work under the conditions described above? First, these counterproductive consequences occur primarily when the players are experiencing potential or actual embarrassment or threat. There is a large domain in managerial accounting practice where there is little disagreement and feelings of disempowerment. Second, where there are difficulties, individuals often strive to work out their differences, especially through upward delegation: take it to the boss and let him decide. If subordinates lose the fight they can maintain that they did their best and the superior is responsible.

Neither of these two strategies deals effectively with the double binds that actors experience when the accounting systems are used in accordance with best current practice yet they produce for the players varying degrees of embarrassment or threat. Under these conditions, organizational and individual defensive routines are activated by the players to protect themselves (Lawler & Rhode, 1976). Birnberg *et al.* (1983) identified six methods used by subordinaters to distort accounting information. They are smoothing, biasing, focusing, gaming, filtering, and 'illegal acts'.

What is common about all these activities is that they bypass the causes of the threat and that they cover-up the bypass while it is being produced. These are the properties of organizational defensive routines. Hence, to deal with defensive behaviour norms in the system, the players adapt by producing further defensive behaviour. In doing so, the players subject themselves to further potential embarrassment or threat that arises if they are caught. After all, such actions violate formal organizational politics and espoused managerial stewardship. Defensive routines beget defensive routines.

To the extent they are undiscussable and their undiscussability is undiscussable, the defensive routines will be difficult to manage. Under these conditions not only subordinates but superiors may feel a sense of helplessness and cynicism about reducing them.

Adapting: reducing the potential embarrassment or threat

As I interpret the recent research by Merchant (1989) and Merchant & Manzoni (1988) it suggests that some superiors may be dealing with the problem by trying to reduce the likelihood of embarrassment and threat arising in the first place. The choice of strategy is partially influenced by the superiors' fundamental assumptions about their relationships with their subordinates and with the budgeting process. They seemed to behave as if (1) they had great difficulty in evaluating (profit center) manager's performance, (2) they believed that managers cannot be trusted to give fair evaluation of their performance, and (3) they felt ill-equipped to openly confront threatening issues (p. 2) (Manzoni, 1988). All these conditions are normally not discussable as they are occurring.

One way to bypass these problems is to design budgets that the players agree are 'very likely to be achieved'. In a study of 54 profit centers from 12 corporations the subordinates and superiors agreed that the budgets were designed to be achievable (e.g. subjective probability of 80 or 90% given that the management team exerts a high level of effort) (Merchant & Manzoni, 1988). Under these conditions the potential for embarrassment or threat is minimized.

However, there may be an unintended consequence leading to another dilemma. The dilemma is that success under these conditions may be self limiting. It is possible, for example, that setting goals is a bargaining process where the superior is ultimately in control. This is not surprising given the personal theory of control described above. The subordinates therefore participate within the limits (personal and organizational) set by the superior.

To the extent the superior is in control then the ownership or responsibility for setting the goals and the paths is ultimately the superior's. To the extent that the performance goals do not stretch old abilities or do not require new skills, successful performance is predictable as long as the subordinate works hard and there are no unforseen externalities. Under these conditions, subordinates may also feel very good about achieving the easily achievable performance targets and a great relief from pressure. But the success will not strengthen the individual's self-esteem and confidence in learning new abilities, taking risks, producing and successfully dealing with surprises. (Lewin *et al.*, 1944).

Bandura's theory of perceived self efficacy (Bandura 1986), leads to similar conclusions in the world of organizational management (Bandura, 1988; Wood & Bandura, 1989). Briefly, perceived self efficacy is the belief in one's capabilities to exercise control over events and to accomplish goals. Human beings with strong beliefs of self efficacy are often in, or seek situations, in which they focus on mastering tasks that are challenging, that are central to their needs, and that they have some non-trivial responsibility to figure out how to achieve. They are not depressed by error; they see it as an opportunity for learning. They persevere and are resilient in the face of difficulties.

As I interpreted the research on setting predictably achievable goals, the profit center managers are not likely to strengthen their belief in their self efficacy. Indeed, if these conditions become routine the individuals' self efficacy beliefs may be eroded or limited to aspirations that are easily achievable. Under these conditions individuals will tend to shy away from difficult tasks, seek goals with a level of aspiration that is similar to previous ones, be committed as long as there are rewards, give up quickly, and come to blame themselves or the environment for failure.

What difference does it make as long as the targets are achieved?

Individuals who succeed in achieving easily achievable budgets in the defensive world described above should report that they feel safe, secure, and in control. They should be observed to be dependent on and grateful toward their supervisor, to seek a world that is programmable so that it is easily manageable, to except that competence is equated with easily achievable, that a just world is one where objectives are easily achievable, where no surprises is a sign of credibility and trust. The same individuals should express concern and fear about developing objectives that stretch their minds (not their energy) that requires risk taking, that produce uncertainty.

What may be happening is this. In order for superiors to feel confident that (1) earnings can be predicted correctly, (2) overconsumption of resources will be reduced, (3) meddling into the players' space will be reduced, (4) harmful earnings management practice will be reduced, and (5) the probability of ensuring a competitive compensation package will be increased (Merchant & Manzoni, pp. 16–22), they use strategies (like early achievable goals) that may simultaneously produce in subordinates feelings of fear of risk taking and stretching their capacities, fear of questioning the status quo.

Simons (1987) describes a different form of adaption in Johnson & Johnson. Compensation is separated from absolute output performance. Hence the managers are shielded from the variability in outcome due to uncertain environment. This encourages subordinates to make their efforts visible which, in turn, requires more knowledge by superiors than that required by simply rewarding performance on the bases of output. Simons' description suggests that Johnson & Johnson uses information as much, if not more so, for the purpose of learning than for control. Or, to put it another way, Johnson & Johnson see control as an on-going iterative process and hence require learning to go on continuously. This practice leads to a reduction of embarrassment and threat. It would be interesting to study if embarrassment or threat does occur and how they are handled by the players.

An incorrect theory of motivation

The argument embedded in the strategy of achievable budgets, fundamentally assumes that implementation will be more effective if individual goals and organizational goals are congruent. By defining budgets that, within reason, assure success then both the organization and the individual are well served. This theory of implementation stems from expectency theory: a theory of motivation popular in the psychological literature a decade ago (Lawler, 1973). The theory states that human beings will expand effort in a particular direction when they believe their actions will result in outcomes that they desire. This has led accountants to recommend goal congruence as the basis for motivating individuals to act consistently with the requirements of managerial central systems (Anthony, pp. 94–96).

Unfortunately the theory never included nor, to my knowledge was there any empirical research conducted, to explore the conditions that are at the heart of this analysis: actions that are simultaneously congruent *and* incongruent with organizational and individual needs.

For example, Jaworski & Young (1988) hypothesize that in governing behaviour, the actors choose actions that achieve their 'most favorable personal outcome regardless of the actions that the firms prefers' (p. 6). But our research suggests that choosing gaming behaviour is often experienced as 'most' *and* 'least' favorable. 'Most' refers to protecting one's self, 'least' refers to having to do so and to cover it up. The choice is made because individuals believe they have no other choice (Argyris, 1985). The goal congruence theory, is not very helpful in advising management how to design congruence between individual and organizational goals where due to the layers of double binds, inner contradictions exist in each and between both.

There is a second feature of the current ideas on motivation that appears misleading. Accountants are aware that managerial accounting systems can be threatening because they evaluate managers' performance. (Horngren & Foster, p. 10.) The authors often counsel patience and education, persuasion, and intelligent interpretation (p. 159). These three activities should be put in the service of convincing subordinates that budgets are positive devices.

As I read such advice it contains the following logic:

(i)   If accountants describe reality accurately.
(ii) If the description is objective (quantifiable) and testable.

(iii) If accountants communicate their descriptions accurately.

(iv) Then accountants have fulfilled a key feature of their stewardship.

But fulfilling this feature is not enough as long as line management finds accounting information threatening. How should accountants deal with this problem? As far as I can tell the primary advice is to repeat the logic above with the line manager. The accountant sits down with the line and persuades and convinces the line managers that the accounting information is good for them.

Unfortunately, the accounting text books do no describe in concrete detail what accountants should actually say and do. According to our research, it is highly likely that accountants will use a theory-in-use that is unilateral and coercive, and they will be unaware that this is the case. Line managers will react by using a similar theory-in-use. The result will be escalating misunderstanding usually in the name of honesty and integrity (Argyris & Schon, 1988). The only transcript that I was able to locate of a dialogue illustrates our prediction. According to the footnote by the authors, versions of the dialogue have been printed many times (Horngren & Foster, pp. 473–475).

In one of the more comprehensive text books on accounting (Horngren & Foster 1987) one may read:

(a) Budgeting systems change human behaviour in ways sought by top management (p. 139).

(b) Budgets compel managers to look ahead. This forced planning is by far the greatest contribution of budgeting to management (p. 141).

(c) Budgets force executives to think (p. 148).

(d) Budgets (help) to remove unconscious bias (p. 142).

(e) Budgets (help) to search out weaknesses (p. 142).

Budgets change, compel, force, remove and search out. Strictly speaking budgets do not do these things. It is individuals who implement these actions. If the authors mean that accountants should use budgets to compel, force, etc. line management then they are recommending a strategy of implementation that will probably backfire. Such unilateral and coercive activity will activate, as we have seen, individual and organization defensive routines that are over-protective and anti-learning.

Human beings are capable of looking ahead, of planning, of searching for this biases, weaknesses and blindness. They are not likely to do so when the fundamental assumption is that they have to be forced or coerced to do so. The dilemma is how to implement accounting practice in ways that change, look ahead, think, remove unrecognized biases that are produced through internal commitment rather than the external commitment implicit in the statements above.

IMPLICATIONS FOR CORRECTIVE ACTION

The idea that implementation is enhanced by creating goal congruence; and that, in turn, by using appropriate monetary rewards is not likely to be relevant where the implementation of managerial controls is embarrassing or threatening to the players. The challenge under these conditions is less one of motivating individuals. It is more one of dealing with their automatic reactions to use skilfully a theory of action whose consequence is to produce defensive reactions, bypass a cover-up. It is also one of engaging organizational defensive routines that protect and exacerbate the individual defensive but highly skilled behaviour.

In order to accomplish these consequences individuals will have to be taught a new theory-in-use, one that, at present, few have although many espouse.

Such a theory-in-use exists. It can be taught as a general theory of learning (individual and organizational) (Argyris & Schon, 1974, 1976; Argyris, 1982). Moreover, it appears that the most powerful way to teach the new theory-in-use is in conjunction with a technical (functional) discipline such as managerial accounting, strategy, or a human resources activity such as evaluating human performance in ways that lead to genuine pay for performance. The reason this is true, is that this behavioural theory, like all theories that underly the management disciplines, is a normative theory of how to achieve intended consequences. Most theories of human behaviour are descriptive; their objective is to understand. They espouse that applicability is important. The theory-in-use however leaves much to be desired (Argyris, 1989).

This theory-in-use is pro-learning and against over protection. The new theory-in-use solves other dilemmas, namely being tought yet inquiry oriented; making compelling arguments yet subjecting them to test, evaluating performance yet being confrontable. With these skills individuals can begin to deal with challenges such as accounting as a score keeping and evaluating function as well as instrument of coercion of managerial attention. To advise that it is possible to act as an interpreter of the technical features of the accounting system 'and not be seen by line as an evaluator or as encroaching on line manager's decision making process' (Horngren & Foster, p. 10) is to suggest something that, in my opinion, is not possible. It will place accountants in a defensive position of denying something which they and line often experience as true. The skills and competencies that line and staff should be taught is how to deal openly with being evaluative and with encroaching on line management space.

Another example, is the predisposition of many accountants to see line management's predisposition to ignore valid feedback as a weakness on their part. A different interpretation is that this behaviour, given the organizational defensive routines, is a sign of strength and skill that indeed does prevent features of the organization from blowing apart.

Focusing on organizational defenses

Organizational defensive routines are created by actions that bypass embarrassment or threat and cover-up that this is the case. The emphasis on bypass and cover-up has a distinct influence on what is considered to constitute a successful dealing with the problems that they create. For example, if gaming activity becomes public, management usually stops the gaming and sets new rules to reduce the likelihood that the gaming will continue. The rules could be to increase the rewards and punishments or, as in the examples described above, they could lead to a lowering of budget objectives so that they are easily achievable.

In none of the accounting literature cited above, is it recommended that the players should engage rather than bypass the causes of defensive routines themselves. For example, what causes the general managers to mistrust profit center managers? If budgets are made easily achievable because general managers seek to reduce the likelihood that profit center managers will act in ways that are detrimental to the company's interest, why not explore what leads the profit center managers to act in these counterproductive manners in the first place? Otherwise, the strategy of designing easily achievable objectives is itself a bypass and cover-up of a more fundamental problem.

Otley (1988) describes how information is systematically distorted as it goes to headquarters. He then writes, '. . . it seems surprising that better formal methods of dealing with (uncertainty) in budgetary control systems have not yet made' (p. 25). I asked Professor Otley what the likelihood is that representatives of headquarters and the relevant subordinates would explore face to face what leads the latter to distort the information and cover-up that they are doing so. He replied that the likelihood was very low indeed. Such a strategy would be rare.

The time has come, I suggest, that we go beyond describing the gaming, distorting, etc. and beyond trying to find ways to bypass the causes of the necessity for such behaviour. It is time that practitioners attempt to engage the organizational defensive routines. It is time that researchers and practitioners join to design interventions to accomplish the engagement of organizational defensive routines.

ACKNOWLEDGEMENTS

I should like to express my thanks to Professors Robert Anthony, Kenneth Merchant, and Robert Simons for their helpful comments.

BIBLIOGRAPHY

Anthony, N., *The Management Control Function* (Boston, MA: The Harvard Business School Press, 1988).

Argyris, C., *Reasoning, Learning and Action* (San Francisco, CA: Jossey-Bass, 1982).

Argyris, C., *Strategy, Change and Defensive Routines* (Cambridge, MA: Ballinger, 1985).

Argyris, C. & Schon, D., *Theory in Practice* (San Francisco, CA: Jossey-Bass, 1974).

Argyris, C. & Schon, D., *Organizational Learning* (Reading, MA: Addison Wesley, 1976).

Argyris, C. & Schon, D., Reciprocal Integrity: Creating Conditions That

Encourage Personal and Organizational Integrity, in Suresh Srivastva and Associates (ed.), *Executive Integrity* (San Francisco, CA: Jossey-Bass, 1988) pp. 197–222.

Argyris, C. & Schon, D., Conceptions of Causality in Social Theory and Research: Normal Sciences and, Action Science Compared (in preparation, 1989).

Bandura, A., *Social Foundations of Thought and Action: A Social Cognitive Theory* (Englewood Cliffs, NJ: Prentice-Hall, 1986).

Bandura, A., Organizational Applications of Social Cognitive Theory, *Australian Journal of Management* (December 1988) pp. 275–301.

Birnberg, G., Turopolec, L. & Young, S.M., The Organizational Context of Accounting, *Accounting Organizations, and Society* (1983) pp. 111–129.

Hopwood, A.G., Ambiguity, Knowledge and Territorial Claims: Some Observations on the Doctrine of Substance Over Forms, *British Accounting Review* (forthcoming).

Horngren, C.T. & Foster, G., *Cost Accounting A Managerial Emphasis*, 6th edn (Englewood Cliffs, NJ: Prentice-Hall, 1987).

Irji, Y., *Studies in Accounting Research #10, Theory of Accounting Measurement* (American Accounting Association, 1975).

Jaworski, J. & Young, S.M., Goal Congruence, Information Asymmetry, and Dysfunctional Behavior: An Empirical Study (mimeographed). University of Arizona and University of Colorado at Boulder.

Lawler, E., *Motivation in Organization* (Monterey, CA: Brooke/Cole, 1973).

Lawler, E. & Rhode, J.G., *Information and Control in Organizations* (Pacific Palisades, CA: Goodyear, 1976).

Lewin, K., Tamard, D., Festinger, L. & Snedden-Sears, P., Level of Aspiration, in Hunt J.M.V. (ed.), *Personality and Behavior Disorder* (New York: Ronald Press, 1944).

Manzoni, J.-F., Control Systems and Double-loop Learning, Unpublished paper: Harvard Business School, 1988.

Merchant, K.A., *Rewarding Results: Designing and Managing Contracts to Motivate Profit Center Managers* (Boston, MA: Harvard Business School, 1989).

Merchant, K.A. & Manzoni, J.-F., The Achievability of Budget Targets in Profit Centers: A Field Study, working paper, Boston, MA: Division of Research, Harvard Business School (1988).

Otley, D., Issues in Accountability and Control: Some Observations from a Study of Colliery Accountability in the British Coal Corporation, (mimeographed). University of Lancaster (1988).

Simons, R., Planning, Control, and Uncertainty: A Process View, Bruno, W.J. Jr and Kaplan, R.S., (eds), *Accounting and Management: Field Study Perspectives* (Cambridge, MA: Harvard Business School Press, 1987) pp. 339–362.

Solomons, D., *Making Accounting Policy* (New York: Oxford University Press, 1986).

Sterling, R., *Toward a Science of Accounting* (Houston, TX: Scholars Book Co., 1979).

Wood, R. & Bandura, A., Social Cognitive Theory of Organizational Management, *Academy of Management Review* (1989) pp. 361–384.

Yu, S.C., *The Structure of Accounting Theory* (Gainesville, FL: Presses of the University of Florida, 1976).